Estate and Retirement Planning Answer Book

Second Edition

William D. Mitchell, Esq.

THE PANEL ANSWER BOOK SERIES

A PANEL PUBLICATION
ASPEN PUBLISHERS, INC.

This publication is designed to provide accurate and authoritative information in regard to the subject matter covered. It is sold with the understanding that the publisher is not engaged in rendering legal, accounting, or other professional services. If legal advice or other professional assistance is required, the services of a competent professional person should be sought.

—From a Declaration of Principles jointly adopted by a Committee of the American Bar Association and a Committee of Publishers and Associations.

Copyright © 1997

by
PANEL PUBLISHERS
A division of Aspen Publishers, Inc.
A Wolters Kluwer Company

1185 Avenue of the Americas
New York, NY 10036
(212) 597-0200

All rights reserved. No part of this book may be reproduced in any form or by any means without permission in writing from the publisher.

ISBN 1-56706-321-7

Printed in the United States of America

About Panel Publishers

Panel Publishers derives its name from a panel of business professionals who organized in 1964 to publish authoritative, timely books, information services, and journals written by specialists to assist business professionals and owners of small to medium-sized businesses in the areas of human resources administration, compensation and benefits management, and pension planning and compliance. Our mission is to provide practical, solution-based "how-to" information to business professionals.

Also available from Panel Publishers:

The Pension Answer Book*
401(k) Answer Book*
Pension Investment Handbook
Employee Benefits Answer Book
ERISA Fiduciary Answer Book
Nonqualified Deferred Compensation Answer Book*
Individual Retirement Account Answer Book*
Flexible Benefits Answer Book
The Employment Law Answer Book*
Executive Compensation Answer Book
S Corporation Answer Book

*A companion volume of forms and worksheets is also available.

PANEL PUBLISHERS
A division of Aspen Publishers, Inc.
Practical Solutions for Business Professionals

SUBSCRIPTION NOTICE

This Panel product is updated on a periodic basis with supplements to reflect important changes in the subject matter. If you purchased this product directly from Panel Publishers, we have already recorded your subscription for this update service.

If, however, you purchased this product from a bookstore and wish to receive future updates and revised or related volumes billed separately with a 30-day examination review, please contact our Customer Service Department at 1-800-901-9074, or send your name, company name (if applicable), address, and the title of the product to:

PANEL PUBLISHERS
A division of Aspen Publishers, Inc.
7201 McKinney Circle
Frederick, MD 21701

About the Author

William D. Mitchell, President of Mitchell & Rogers, P.A., is a frequent lecturer on the subject of employee benefits. A co-author of several books and articles in the benefits field, Mr. Mitchell received a B.A. in Economics from the University of Washington, an M.A. in Economics from the University of California at Berkeley, a J.D. from the University of California at Berkeley, and an M.A. in Taxation from Georgetown University.

Introduction

Estate and Retirement Planning Answer Book, Second Edition, provides expanded coverage of financial and estate planning strategies for implementing individualized solutions for the special problems associated with retaining accumulated wealth for retirement and estate planning purposes. With its comprehensive two-part approach to the complex issues that link retirement planning and estate planning, *Estate and Retirement Planning Answer Book, Second Edition,* includes new coverage of such topics as asset protection trusts and other methods of limiting creditor liability; using grantor retained income trusts, grantor retained annuity trusts, and grantor retained unitrusts; general characteristics, benefits, and administration of family limited partnerships; taxability of property transfers in marital settlements; use of qualified domestic relations orders to assign plan benefits; and coverage of the innocent spouse rules.

Highlights of *Estate and Retirement Planning Answer Book, Second Edition,* include the following:

- All new chapter on the use of trusts that carry both tax saving and estate planning characteristics: grantor retained income trusts, grantor retained annuity trusts, and grantor retained unitrusts (see chapter 12)
- Comparison of traditional methods for limiting liability (the protection provided by a business entity) with domestic and offshore asset protection trusts (see chapter 13)
- All new chapter on tax and estate planning issues related to marital settlements, including alimony and separate mainte-

nance payments; the relationship of these payments to child support payments; the taxability of property transfers in connection with a marital settlement; sale of the marital home; and the assignment of an interest in an employee's benefit plan under a qualified domestic relations order (see chapter 14)
- All new chapter covering the estate planning advantages, benefits, and controllability of family limited partnerships (see chapter 31)
- An all-new index

Replete with scores of new examples that illustrate and analyze the estate planning strategies and their effects, *Estate and Retirement Planning Answer Book, Second Edition,* brings insight and expertise to the realm of estate and retirement planning by focusing on the tax-free transfer of wealth by the small business owner and by providing an insider's view of the various retirement benefits available to the corporate executive under both qualified and nonqualified retirement plans.

How to Use This Book

The *Estate and Retirement Planning Answer Book, Second Edition,* is designed specifically for professional advisors and business executives who need quick and authoritative answers to help them decide how to integrate the receipt of retirement plan distributions with their estate plans, how to choose and design the type of retirement plan that best suits their needs, and how to comply with the growing number of federal requirements and tax rules that apply to these plans.

This book uses simple, straightforward language and avoids technical jargon wherever possible. The question-and-answer format, with its breadth of coverage and plain-language explanations, effectively conveys the complex and essential subject matter of flexible benefits plans. In addition, the book provides numerous examples that illustrate specific applications and situations as well as practice pointers that highlight recent interpretations of IRS regulations and provide cautions concerning common pitfalls.

Citations to authority are provided as research aids to those who need to pursue particular items in greater detail. To provide additional assistance in locating related topics, the *Estate and Retirement Planning Answer Book, Second Edition,* makes use of an extensive system of cross-referencing.

List of Questions. The detailed List of Questions is designed to help the reader locate specific areas of immediate interest. Questions are grouped and organized by topic within each chapter.

Index. This index collates current references as a further aid to locating specific information. References in the index are to question numbers.

Contents

List of Questions xv

Part I.   Family Estate Planning

    Chapter 1
The Accumulation and Preservation of Wealth 1-1

    Chapter 2
Wills, Revocable Trusts, and Other Alternatives 2-1

    Chapter 3
Overview of Tax Principles 3-1

    Chapter 4
The Marital Deduction 4-1

    Chapter 5
Bypass Trusts 5-1

Chapter 6
Gifts 6-1

Chapter 7
Life Insurance 7-1

Chapter 8
Annuities 8-1

Chapter 9
Valuation of Business Interests and Other Property .. 9-1

Chapter 10
Charitable Contributions 10-1

Chapter 11
Funding for Liquidity 11-1

Chapter 12
Using Trusts in Estate Planning 12-1

Chapter 13
Asset Protection Trusts 13-1

Chapter 14
Tax and Estate Planning in Marital Settlements ... 14-1

Chapter 15
Post-Death Estate Planning 15-1

Table of Contents

Part II. Benefit Plans and Other Sources of Retirement Assets

CHAPTER 16
Benefit Plans 16-1

CHAPTER 17
Tax-Qualified Retirement Plans 17-1

CHAPTER 18
Employee Stock Ownership Plans 18-1

CHAPTER 19
Nonqualified Retirement Plans 19-1

CHAPTER 20
Personal Investing 20-1

CHAPTER 21
Business Transfers 21-1

CHAPTER 22
IRAs and Simplified Employee Pensions 22-1

CHAPTER 23
Distributions from Tax-Qualified Retirement Plans 23-1

CHAPTER 24
Distributions from Nonqualified Plans 24-1

CHAPTER 25
Protection of Retirement Income 25-1

CHAPTER 26
Incapacity and Other Retirement Issues 26-1

CHAPTER 27
Estate Planning for Qualified Retirement Plan Benefits 27-1

CHAPTER 28
Estate Planning for Nonqualified Retirement Plans ... 28-1

CHAPTER 29
IRA Distributions 29-1

CHAPTER 30
IRS Audits 30-1

CHAPTER 31
Family Limited Partnerships 31-1

INDEX I-1

List of Questions

Part I Family Estate Planning

Chapter 1 The Accumulation and Preservation of Wealth

Chapter 2 Wills, Revocable Trusts, and Other Alternatives

Overview

Q 2:1	Why should an individual plan for the transfer of his or her assets in anticipation of death?	2-1

Probate

Q 2:2	What is probate?	2-2
Q 2:3	What is the difference between dying testate and intestate?	2-2
Q 2:4	How do the federal estate tax provisions affect the estate of the testate versus the intestate individual?	2-3
Q 2:5	Should probate be used in every case where a decedent leaves a will?	2-3
Q 2:6	What significance is attached to the domicile of an individual?	2-4
Q 2:7	What is the customary procedure involved in probating a will and administering the estate of a decedent?	2-5
Q 2:8	If an individual's ownership of property is entirely by means of structures such as joint tenancies, revocable trusts, insurance, and other kinds of lifetime transfers not subject to probate, does it make any sense to have a will?	2-6

Estate and Retirement Planning Answer Book

Q 2:9	Are there simplified and less costly probate procedures for smaller estates?	2-6
Q 2:10	Which assets are subject to probate?	2-6
Q 2:11	Are assets that are not subject to probate also excluded from the taxable estate?	2-7
Q 2:12	Are contract proceeds subject to probate?	2-8
Q 2:13	What duties apply to fiduciaries?	2-8
Q 2:14	What is a fiduciary's duty with respect to acts of co-fiduciaries?	2-9
Q 2:15	Is a fiduciary responsible for the actions taken by his or her co-fiduciaries?	2-9
Q 2:16	Can a fiduciary be liable for spending estate money?	2-9
Q 2:17	Is a fiduciary entitled to compensation?	2-10
Q 2:18	What are the disadvantages of probate?	2-10
Q 2:19	What costs are associated with probate?	2-10
Q 2:20	What are the delays that may sometimes occur during the probate process?	2-11
Q 2:21	What is a will contest?	2-11
Q 2:22	Why is publicity a disadvantage of probate?	2-12
Q 2:23	How are creditor's claims treated when an estate is probated in contrast to when it is not probated?	2-12
Q 2:24	What methods exist for avoiding probate?	2-12

Joint Tenancies

Q 2:25	What does *joint ownership* of property mean?	2-12
Q 2:26	When is joint ownership of property advisable?	2-13
Q 2:27	What gift taxes are associated with a joint tenancy?	2-14
Q 2:28	Can an individual who is a party to a joint tenancy sell his or her interest in the joint tenancy?	2-14
Q 2:29	What happens with a joint tenancy upon the simultaneous death of both owners where the owners are not husband and wife?	2-15
Q 2:30	How is a joint tenancy created?	2-15
Q 2:31	How are joint tenants treated on the taxable income produced by the joint tenancy property?	2-15
Q 2:32	How is joint tenancy property taxed for federal estate tax purposes?	2-15
Q 2:33	How is a joint tenancy that is established by a husband and wife taxed?	2-16

List of Questions

Q 2:34	What income tax basis does the surviving joint tenant have in joint tenancy property?	2-17
Q 2:35	What is the basis of the survivor's interest in the joint tenancy property?	2-18
Q 2:36	Is a joint bank account a joint tenancy?	2-18
Q 2:37	What is the tax effect of converting from a joint tenancy with right of survivorship to a tenancy in common which eliminates the survivorship feature?	2-18
Q 2:38	Is the interest of a husband and wife in a cooperative apartment considered an interest in real property?	2-19
Q 2:39	How may an individual prove that he or she contributed all of the proceeds into the account or the survivorship feature of the account?	2-19
Q 2:40	Does naming an individual as a joint owner of a safety deposit box give that individual joint ownership of the contents inside?	2-19
Q 2:41	May securities such as stocks and bonds be held as joint tenancies?	2-19
Q 2:42	What disadvantages exist in relying on joint tenancies to dispose of assets?	2-20
Q 2:43	What gift tax consequences occur if a joint tenancy is dissolved?	2-20

Totten Trusts

| Q 2:44 | What is a Totten trust? | 2-21 |

Funded Revocable Living Trusts

Q 2:45	What is a funded revocable living trust?	2-21
Q 2:46	How does a funded revocable living trust work?	2-21
Q 2:47	Why is a funded revocable living trust used?	2-22
Q 2:48	What are the disadvantages of using a funded revocable living trust?	2-23
Q 2:49	What problems exist in transferring assets to a funded revocable living trust?	2-23
Q 2:50	How is income earned by the funded revocable living trust taxed?	2-24
Q 2:51	Must income earned by a funded revocable living trust be reported?	2-24
Q 2:52	Does a transfer of an installment obligation to a revocable living trust constitute a disposition of the obligation?	2-24

Estate and Retirement Planning Answer Book

Q 2:53	Can assets from a funded revocable living trust be given as gifts?	2-24
Q 2:54	What are the income tax advantages of probate as opposed to those of a funded revocable living trust?	2-25
Q 2:55	Can the use of a funded revocable living trust adversely affect the estate tax treatment of the qualified plan death benefits?	2-26
Q 2:56	Does the use of a funded revocable living trust adversely affect the estate tax deduction for administrative expenses?	2-27
Q 2:57	How does the use of a revocable living trust affect the tax deduction for the decedent's debts?	2-27
Q 2:58	If the estate contains out-of-state real property, does the use of a funded revocable living trust affect the amount of inheritance taxes payable on such property?	2-27
Q 2:59	How does the use of a funded revocable living trust work with respect to stock in an S corporation?	2-28
Q 2:60	How is the taxation of a distribution of a fixed sum affected by the choice of a funded revocable living trust?	2-29
Q 2:61	Is the personal liability of the fiduciary affected by the choice of a funded revocable living trust?	2-29
Q 2:62	What are the advantages of a funded revocable living trust and a durable power of attorney?	2-29

Unfunded Revocable Trusts

Q 2:63	What are the advantages of not funding revocable trusts?	2-30
Q 2:64	When should an unfunded revocable living trust be used in preference to a testamentary trust?	2-30

Chapter 3 Overview of Tax Principles

Overview

Q 3:1	What is estate planning?	3-2
Q 3:2	Why is it important to establish a domicile in one state?	3-2
Q 3:3	What is ancillary probate?	3-3

The Gross Estate

Q 3:4	What are the requirements for filing a federal estate tax return?	3-3
Q 3:5	What are the requirements for filing a federal gift tax return?	3-3

List of Questions

Q 3:6	What is the gross estate?	3-4
Q 3:7	What assets are includible in a decedent's gross estate?	3-4
Q 3:8	Are accrued interest and rents includible in the gross estate?	3-5
Q 3:9	Is community property includible in the gross estate?	3-5
Q 3:10	How is property transferred at death in community property states?	3-5
Q 3:11	Is joint tenancy property includible in the gross estate?	3-5
Q 3:12	Is tenancy in common property includible in the gross estate?	3-6
Q 3:13	Is property that is subject to a power of appointment includible in the gross estate?	3-7
Q 3:14	Are life insurance proceeds includible in the gross estate?	3-7
Q 3:15	Are annuities includible in the gross estate?	3-8
Q 3:16	Are gifts made within three years of death includible in the gross estate?	3-8
Q 3:17	Is gift tax paid on gifts made during the decedent's lifetime includible in the gross estate?	3-9
Q 3:18	Are transfers that take effect at death includible in the gross estate?	3-9
Q 3:19	Are gifts with possession or enjoyment retained includible in the gross estate?	3-10
Q 3:20	Are transfers with a retained power to alter, amend, revoke, or terminate includible in the decedent's gross estate?	3-10

Valuation of Estate Property

Q 3:21	When property is includible in the gross estate, how is it valued?	3-11

Deductions from Gross Estate

Q 3:22	Can administrative expenses be deducted from the gross estate?	3-12
Q 3:23	Are mortgages deductible from the gross estate?	3-13
Q 3:24	Is an estate tax deduction available for charitable contributions?	3-13

Credits Against Estate Tax

Q 3:25	What is the unified credit against estate tax?	3-14
Q 3:26	What is the exemption equivalent?	3-14
Q 3:27	What credits other than the unified credit can offset estate taxes?	3-15

| Q 3:28 | Is there a credit against estate tax if the same property is included in the gross estates of two decedents who died within a short time of each other? | 3-15 |

Determination and Payment of Estate Tax

Q 3:29	How is the federal estate tax determined?	3-16
Q 3:30	How is the estate tax paid?	3-16
Q 3:31	Who is responsible for paying estate taxes that are owed by the estate?	3-17

Income Taxes on Estates

| Q 3:32 | What income tax rates apply to trusts and estates? | 3-18 |

Gift Taxes

Q 3:33	What transfers are subject to the gift tax?	3-19
Q 3:34	How is the federal gift tax computed?	3-20
Q 3:35	What is the unified gift credit?	3-21
Q 3:36	What is the annual exclusion that applies to gifts?	3-22
Q 3:37	How is the marital deduction determined for gift tax purposes?	3-22
Q 3:38	Who is responsible for paying gift tax?	3-22
Q 3:39	Does the recipient of a gift have any liability for gift tax?	3-22
Q 3:40	When are gift tax returns due?	3-23

Basis of Property Acquired from Decedents

Q 3:41	What is the basis of property acquired from a decedent?	3-23
Q 3:42	What planning considerations apply to a spousal residence?	3-24
Q 3:43	What is the basis in community property upon the death of one of the spouses?	3-26
Q 3:44	How is income in respect to a decedent treated?	3-27
Q 3:45	What is the basis of property acquired by gift?	3-27
Q 3:46	What effect does federal gift tax have on the basis of gift property?	3-28
Q 3:47	What basis applies if one spouse sells or exchanges an asset with his or her spouse?	3-28
Q 3:48	What are the holding periods for capital gains purposes for gift assets and for inherited assets?	3-28

List of Questions

Nontax Considerations

Q 3:49	How great a role should nontax considerations play in estate planning?	3-28
Q 3:50	Can the surviving spouse be given access to trust principal without having to make a request for principal from the trustee?	3-29
Q 3:51	What actions can be taken if trust investments become extremely successful?	3-29
Q 3:52	When setting up trusts for children, what factors dictate the use of a single trust as opposed to separate trusts?	3-29
Q 3:53	What is an advantage of giving trustees for children's trusts broad discretion to distribute trust principal?	3-30
Q 3:54	What considerations apply in selecting trustees?	3-30
Q 3:55	If a bank is chosen as trustee, should an individual also be selected?	3-31
Q 3:56	Should children be chosen as trustees for their siblings?	3-31
Q 3:57	Should a child be appointed trustee of his or her own trust?	3-32
Q 3:58	Should a trust contain a provision for removal of the trustee?	3-32
Q 3:59	What provisions can be made for successor trustees?	3-32
Q 3:60	What kinds of conflicts can arise between beneficiaries who are currently entitled to trust income and beneficiaries who will receive trust principal at future dates?	3-33
Q 3:61	How can a trust be designed to reflect a desire to favor current beneficiaries over future beneficiaries?	3-33

Chapter 4 The Marital Deduction

Overview

Q 4:1	What is the marital deduction?	4-2
Q 4:2	What are the property interests that qualify for the marital deduction?	4-2
Q 4:3	Why must an interest in property *pass* from the decedent to the surviving spouse in order to qualify for the marital deduction?	4-3

Q 4:4	If an estate has administrative expenses that it elects or is required to allocate between the property received on the decedent's death and the income earned on the property subsequent to death, does the entire amount of administrative expenses paid by the estate reduce the amount available for the marital deduction?	4-4

Eligible Property

Q 4:5	Can the marital deduction be made available if the surviving spouse is not a U.S. citizen?	4-4
Q 4:6	What is the terminable interest rule?	4-5
Q 4:7	How can the marital deduction be obtained?	4-6
Q 4:8	What is contained in a probate estate?	4-6
Q 4:9	Can a bequest that is conditioned on the surviving spouse's outliving the decedent for six months or less qualify for the marital deduction?	4-6

Considerations in Using the Marital Deduction

Q 4:10	What is the $600,000 exemption equivalent?	4-7
Q 4:11	What is the optimal way to use the marital deduction?	4-7
Q 4:12	Why should the estate of a husband and wife be equalized?	4-10
Q 4:13	When should the maximum marital deduction not be taken?	4-11
Q 4:14	Can a control premium be used to increase the size of the marital deduction?	4-11
Q 4:15	How should the marital deduction be used in a large estate?	4-12

Using a Trust with the Marital Deduction

Q 4:16	What is a trust?	4-13
Q 4:17	What factors determine the circumstances under which a trust should be created to hold assets given to the surviving spouse?	4-13
Q 4:18	What is a qualified terminable interest property trust?	4-14
Q 4:19	Can a surviving spouse be given a power of disposition at death over qualified terminable interest property trust assets?	4-15
Q 4:20	Must an election be made to obtain the marital deduction for assets placed in a qualified terminable interest property trust?	4-16

List of Questions

Q 4:21	Is the marital deduction available if under an estate plan the executor can determine what property is to be placed into a qualified terminable interest property trust after the decedent's death?	4-16
Q 4:22	Who is responsible for paying the estate taxes on the assets in a qualified terminable interest property trust when the surviving spouse dies?	4-17
Q 4:23	What is a power of appointment trust?	4-17
Q 4:24	Aside from the differences described above between a QTIP trust and a trust providing the surviving spouse with a general power of appointment, is their tax effect the same?	4-18
Q 4:25	How are capital gains from the sale of trust assets treated in a power of appointment trust?	4-19
Q 4:26	What is an estate trust?	4-19
Q 4:27	What considerations apply in deciding whether to establish a power of appointment trust or a QTIP trust?	4-19
Q 4:28	Is it ever desirable to have trust income attributed to the grantor under a grantor trust?	4-20
Q 4:29	Can the surviving spouse for a power of appointment or QTIP trust be given access to the trust principal?	4-21

Spousal Bequests

Q 4:30	What is a formula clause?	4-21
Q 4:31	What types of formula clauses exist?	4-22
Q 4:32	What is a pecuniary clause?	4-22
Q 4:33	What are the income tax effects of a pecuniary clause?	4-22
Q 4:34	What factors should be considered in using a pecuniary clause?	4-23
Q 4:35	How does a fractional share clause work?	4-24
Q 4:36	What factors should be considered in using a fractional clause?	4-24
Q 4:37	What is an estate tax value pecuniary clause?	4-25
Q 4:38	What considerations apply in using an estate tax value pecuniary clause?	4-25

Chapter 5   Bypass Trusts

Overview

Q 5:1	What is a bypass trust?	5-2

Q 5:2	How does a bypass trust reduce the surviving spouse's estate taxes?	5-2

Combining a Bypass Trust with a Marital Deduction Trust (A-B Trust Plan)

Q 5:3	What is an A-B trust plan?	5-3
Q 5:4	How should the A-B trust plan be structured to give the surviving spouse maximum power and control over trust assets?	5-4
Q 5:5	Can the A-B trust be structured to limit the right of the surviving spouse to withdraw principal during his or her lifetime and to appoint assets at death?	5-4
Q 5:6	How much access to marital trust assets should a surviving spouse be given without having to make a request for principal from the trustee?	5-5
Q 5:7	How is the B trust taxed?	5-5
Q 5:8	Can a disclaimer be used in connection with an A-B trust plan?	5-6

Powers Under a Bypass Trust

Q 5:9	If the intention is to give the surviving spouse as much control as possible over the assets in the bypass trust, what powers may be given to the spouse?	5-7
Q 5:10	How is a power to invade trust assets under an ascertainable standard used with a bypass trust?	5-7
Q 5:11	How is a $5,000 or 5 percent power used with a bypass trust?	5-8
Q 5:12	How is a special power of appointment used with a bypass trust?	5-8

Discretionary Trusts

Q 5:13	What is a discretionary trust?	5-9
Q 5:14	What are the advantages of discretionary trusts?	5-9
Q 5:15	Should the surviving spouse who is a beneficiary of a bypass trust be the sole trustee if the discretionary trust contains a sprinkling power?	5-10
Q 5:16	If a spousal beneficiary is given the power to remove a trustee of a discretionary trust and substitute an independent corporate trustee, what are the estate tax consequences?	5-10

List of Questions

Income Tax Consequences

Q 5:17	What are the income tax consequences if a bypass trust is established?	5-11

Generation Skipping Transfer Tax

Q 5:18	What is the generation skipping transfer tax?	5-11
Q 5:19	What is a generation skipping transfer?	5-12
Q 5:20	What is the amount of the generation skipping transfer tax?	5-13
Q 5:21	What is the rate of the generation skipping transfer tax?	5-13
Q 5:22	Under what circumstances is the generation skipping transfer tax imposed?	5-13
Q 5:23	What is a direct skip?	5-14
Q 5:24	When is the generation skipping transfer tax imposed on transfers that are direct skips?	5-14
Q 5:25	What is a taxable distribution for generation skipping transfer tax purposes?	5-14
Q 5:26	What is a taxable termination for generation skipping transfer tax purposes?	5-15
Q 5:27	Which exemptions and exclusions apply in computing the generation skipping transfer tax?	5-16
Q 5:28	Are any trusts protected from the generation skipping transfer tax?	5-16
Q 5:29	What provisions must a trust contain to avoid the generation skipping transfer tax?	5-16
Q 5:30	What is the maximum generation skipping exemption that married couples have?	5-17
Q 5:31	How can the $1 million lifetime exemption be used in connection with a generation skipping trust?	5-17
Q 5:32	What planning can be done to minimize generation skipping transfer taxes?	5-17
Q 5:33	What requirements must a trust meet to ensure that gifts to the trust are nontaxable gifts for generation skipping transfer tax purposes?	5-19
Q 5:34	Does the beneficiary of a generation skipping transfer have to be a relative of the deceased in order to take advantage of the $1 million exemption?	5-19
Q 5:35	Do payments from trusts escape the generation skipping transfer tax if they are made for tuition or medical expenses?	5-19
Q 5:36	How can insurance be used to minimize the effect of the tax on generation skipping transfers?	5-20

Chapter 6 Gifts

Overview

Q 6:1	How does a program for transferring property provide a donor with meaningful tax savings both during the life of the donor and on his or her death?	6-1

Gifts

Q 6:2	How may gifts be made?	6-2

The Gift Tax

Q 6:3	What amount of assets can be the subject of a gift so as to avoid both gift and estate tax on the transferred property?	6-3
Q 6:4	Can a spouse refuse to consent to a gift that his or her spouse wishes to make for purposes of the $10,000 gift tax exclusion?	6-3
Q 6:5	What is the tax consequence if a donor makes a gift of property having a value in excess of $10,000?	6-3
Q 6:6	Should a donor consider giving an amount in excess of the $10,000 annual exclusion?	6-4
Q 6:7	How long does the IRS have to examine a gift tax return?	6-4
Q 6:8	Can the IRS revalue, as part of an estate tax valuation, prior taxable gifts made by a decedent after the statute of limitations has passed for examining a gift tax return?	6-5
Q 6:9	What gifts qualify for the gift tax exclusion?	6-6
Q 6:10	Does a gift made in trust qualify as a gift of a present interest?	6-6
Q 6:11	Does gift tax arise when income is given in order to discharge a legal obligation?	6-7
Q 6:12	Are payments to educational institutions or health care providers for medical services a taxable gift?	6-7
Q 6:13	What is a net gift?	6-7

Financial Effects of Making Gifts

Q 6:14	What events require the filing of a gift tax return?	6-8
Q 6:15	When is a gift tax return due?	6-8

Also at top of page:

Q 5:37	How can trusts be used to minimize the generation skipping transfer tax?	5-20

List of Questions

Q 6:16	Is it better to use the $192,800 unified credit during the donor's lifetime rather than saving it until death?	6-8
Q 6:17	Is the money used to pay gift tax during the decedent's lifetime includible in the gross estate?	6-9
Q 6:18	Are gifts includible in the gross estate?	6-10
Q 6:19	If a gift is made within three years of death, is the gift tax paid on it includible in the gross estate?	6-11
Q 6:20	What income tax advantages result from making gifts?	6-12
Q 6:21	What legal requirements must be satisfied in order for a gift to be valid for estate tax purposes?	6-12
Q 6:22	What are the tax consequences of making gifts to spouses?	6-13
Q 6:23	What are the tax consequences of making gifts to a non-U.S. citizen spouse?	6-13
Q 6:24	What estate tax advantages result from making gifts to spouses?	6-13
Q 6:25	What income tax advantages result from making interspousal gifts?	6-14

Designing a Gift Giving Program

Q 6:26	What guidelines apply in giving assets?	6-14
Q 6:27	What factors other than tax factors should be considered in estate planning for children?	6-16
Q 6:28	What pitfalls exist if appreciated assets are given to a donee who is expected to predecease the donor?	6-16

Gifts in Trust

Q 6:29	How are gifts made under the Uniform Transfers to Minors Act?	6-17
Q 6:30	What considerations apply in making a gift in trust?	6-18
Q 6:31	What steps must be taken to obtain the $10,000 annual gift tax exclusion in making gifts to a trust?	6-18
Q 6:32	What is a Crummey trust?	6-19
Q 6:33	What happens if a beneficiary fails to withdraw assets pursuant to a Crummey power?	6-19
Q 6:34	Can the hanging power be combined with the five-and-five withdrawal power?	6-20
Q 6:35	What is a minor's trust?	6-21
Q 6:36	What is the chief disadvantage of a minor's trust?	6-21
Q 6:37	Can any action be taken if it appears that the donee of a minor's trust is likely to dissipate trust assets?	6-22

Q 6:38	How does the minor's trust differ from a custodianship under the Uniform Transfers to Minors Act?	6-22
Q 6:39	Is it desirable to retain income in a trust because of the compressed income tax rates under which trusts operate? (The top income tax bracket for trusts, 39.6 percent, is reached at $7,500.)	6-22
Q 6:40	What are the tax consequences if assets given to an irrevocable trust are included in the estate of the donor?	6-23
Q 6:41	What causes irrevocable trust assets to be included in the gross estate of the donor?	6-23
Q 6:42	Can the donor be given administrative powers or control over trust investments without having trust assets included in his or her gross estate?	6-24

Charitable Gifts

Q 6:43	Can a beneficiary be the sole trustee?	6-24
Q 6:44	How may principal be removed from the trust without causing the entire trust to be taxed when the beneficiary dies?	6-24
Q 6:45	Should children be chosen as trustees for their siblings?	6-25
Q 6:46	Should a child be appointed trustee of his or her own trust?	6-25
Q 6:47	Should a trust contain a provision for removal of the trustee?	6-26
Q 6:48	What provisions can be made for successor trustees?	6-26
Q 6:49	Who pays income tax on trust income that is reinvested?	6-27
Q 6:50	Who pays the tax on trust capital gains that go to principal?	6-27
Q 6:51	Is it preferable to make lifetime charitable gifts rather than testamentary charitable gifts?	6-27

Anatomical Gifts

Q 6:52	What rules apply to giving anatomical gifts?	6-28
Q 6:53	How can gifts of organs be made under the UAGA?	6-28
Q 6:54	Can a donation of organs be made if the decedent's wishes are unknown?	6-28
Q 6:55	What are the requirements for an anatomical gift?	6-29
Q 6:56	Should a document making gifts of organs be included in a person's will?	6-29

List of Questions

Chapter 7 Life Insurance

Overview

Q 7:1	How can life insurance be a useful tool in estate planning?	7-1
Q 7:2	What are the basic types of life insurance policies?	7-2
Q 7:3	What precautions must be taken when buying life insurance for estate planning purposes?	7-3
Q 7:4	How is life insurance sold?	7-3
Q 7:5	What factors should be considered when choosing a life insurance company?	7-4
Q 7:6	When choosing an insurance policy, what features are most important?	7-5

Premiums

Q 7:7	What restrictions exist on the amount of premiums that can be required for life insurance?	7-6

Policy Proceeds

Q 7:8	How are life insurance proceeds that are payable upon the death of the insured treated for estate tax purposes? ..	7-6
Q 7:9	If the insured has any incident of ownership, does it matter whether the insured exercises it alone?	7-8
Q 7:10	Are gifts (i.e., assignments) of insurance policies includible in the insured's gross estate?	7-8
Q 7:11	Can the rule requiring the inclusion of insurance proceeds in the gross estate be avoided if the insured transfers the premium payments to a trust and has the trust buy the insurance?	7-9
Q 7:12	What is includible in the insured's estate if the insured pays the premiums on a life insurance policy transferred more than three years before the insured's death?	7-10
Q 7:13	What are the tax consequence to the estate of the noninsured owner of a life insurance policy who predeceases the insured?	7-10
Q 7:14	When does the transfer of a life insurance policy result in a taxable gift?	7-11
Q 7:15	When does the annual gift tax exclusion apply?	7-11
Q 7:16	Are life insurance proceeds payable upon the death of the insured taxable to the recipient?	7-11
Q 7:17	What is split-dollar insurance?	7-12

Q 7:18	What is the transfer for value rule?	7-12

Policy Loans

Q 7:19	What are the reasons for taking loans from an insurance policy?	7-13
Q 7:20	Is interest on a policy loan deductible?	7-13

Estate Planning

Q 7:21	From an estate planning perspective, who should be the owner of a life insurance policy?	7-14
Q 7:22	From an estate planning perspective, who should be designated the beneficiary of life insurance?	7-15
Q 7:23	From an estate planning perspective, who should be the contingent beneficiaries of a life insurance policy?	7-16
Q 7:24	What are settlement options?	7-16
Q 7:25	When should insurance settlement options be used? . . .	7-17
Q 7:26	What actions should be taken to exclude life insurance proceeds from the gross estate?	7-17
Q 7:27	What policies should be transferred to an irrevocable trust?	7-17
Q 7:28	What actions need to be taken in order to transfer an insurance policy?	7-18
Q 7:29	For estate planning purposes, who should be the beneficiary of a policy owned by someone other than the insured? .	7-18
Q 7:30	For estate planning purposes, who should be the owner of a life insurance policy?	7-18
Q 7:31	Should one spouse be both the owner and the beneficiary of a policy on the life of the other spouse?	7-19
Q 7:32	What is a *second-to-die* life insurance policy?	7-19
Q 7:33	What is a first-to-die life insurance policy?	7-20
Q 7:34	What is an irrevocable insurance trust?	7-21
Q 7:35	What are the gift tax consequences of creating an irrevocable insurance trust?	7-21
Q 7:36	What are the income tax consequences of creating an irrevocable insurance trust?	7-22
Q 7:37	Should the grantor's spouse be a beneficiary of an irrevocable life insurance trust?	7-22
Q 7:38	Should the surviving spouse act as trustee of an irrevocable life insurance trust?	7-23
Q 7:39	Can life insurance be used in a buy/sell agreement as an estate planning device?	7-23

List of Questions

Q 7:40	Are the optional settlement provisions in insurance agreements adequate substitutes for trusts?	7-24
Q 7:41	What are the disadvantages of making insurance payable to the insured's estate?	7-24
Q 7:42	How can a trust be designed so that insurance proceeds can be paid into it and used to buy estate assets without the risk of incurring estate taxes?	7-24
Q 7:43	May insurance be disqualified and therefore treated as taxable income?	7-25
Q 7:44	What is income for purposes of inclusion under Code Section 7702?	7-25
Q 7:45	What is the cost of the insurance provided?	7-25
Q 7:46	What is the effect of a disqualification of the policy under Code Section 7702?	7-25
Q 7:47	How should one evaluate which type of insurance policy to invest in?	7-26
Q 7:48	What is the taxable effect for a policy owner if he or she dies before the insured?	7-26
Q 7:49	How is the value of the unmatured policy determined?	7-26
Q 7:50	What recommendations can be made when naming a beneficiary?	7-26
Q 7:51	How much insurance should be taken out on an individual?	7-26
Q 7:52	Should an insured replace an old policy if he or she determines that the selected policy does not meet the insured's objectives?	7-27
Q 7:53	What factors should be taken into consideration when transferring an insurance policy for value?	7-27
Q 7:54	Is a transfer for valuable consideration recommended as an investment?	7-28
Q 7:55	What are the advantages to a settlement option as opposed to a trust?	7-28
Q 7:56	What are the advantages of a trust as opposed to a settlement option?	7-28
Q 7:57	Can there be a tax-free exchange of insurance policies?	7-28

Chapter 8 Annuities

Overview

Q 8:1	What is an annuity?	8-1

Estate and Retirement Planning Answer Book

Q 8:2	How are annuities invested?	8-2
Q 8:3	How does a variable annuity work?	8-2
Q 8:4	What different types of annuity payment options are available?	8-3

Purchasing an Annuity

Q 8:5	How are annuities purchased?	8-4
Q 8:6	What are the advantages of purchasing an annuity? . . .	8-4
Q 8:7	What are some of the disadvantages of purchasing an annuity?	8-5
Q 8:8	Are there any other costs or expenses involved in purchasing an annuity other than the annuity premium payment? . .	8-5

Tax Treatment of Annuities

Q 8:9	What is the tax treatment of annuities and annuity payments?	8-6
Q 8:10	Are there any penalties for making withdrawals from annuities?	8-6

Private Annuities

Q 8:11	What are private annuities?	8-7
Q 8:12	What are the advantages of private annuities?	8-7
Q 8:13	What risks are associated with private annuities?	8-8
Q 8:14	Are the payments that are received from a private annuity ever includible in the decedent's gross estate?	8-9
Q 8:15	Can the yearly payments from a private annuity be given by the grantor in an amount not exceeding the annual gift tax exclusion, thereby avoiding gift tax or payments?	8-9
Q 8:16	What is the income tax treatment for a grantor of a private annuity where property is involved?	8-9
Q 8:17	What is the income tax treatment for a grantee of a private annuity where property is involved?	8-9
Q 8:18	What factors should be considered when considering establishing a private annuity?	8-10
Q 8:19	What is a deferred annuity?	8-10
Q 8:20	What happens to a deferred annuity if the taxpayer dies before he or she begins to receive payments?	8-10
Q 8:21	What is a wrap-around annuity?	8-10
Q 8:22	What is the tax treatment of a wrap-around annuity? . . .	8-10

List of Questions

Q 8:23	May an annuitant deduct unrecovered annuity investments on his or her tax return?	8-11
Q 8:24	When may a beneficiary deduct unrecovered annuity investments on his or her tax return?	8-11
Q 8:25	When will an insurance contract under a qualified plan be treated as an annuity?	8-11
Q 8:26	What is a single annuity contract, and why is it an important consideration?	8-11
Q 8:27	Can a person purchase an annuity for another individual?	8-12
Q 8:28	Are annuities includible in a decedent's gross estate for tax purposes?	8-12
Q 8:29	Is the entire amount of the fair market value of the survivor's interest included in the estate even if the payments go directly to a beneficiary after the death of the annuitant?	8-12
Q 8:30	May an annuitant make a withdrawal prior to the starting date of the annuity without paying income taxes on the funds?	8-12
Q 8:31	What is the disadvantage of annuities with regard to estate taxes?	8-13
Q 8:32	Are members of the armed forces allowed to exclude annuity payments received on account of personal injuries or sickness resulting from active service in the military?	8-13
Q 8:33	Must a certain type of injury have occurred in order for Code Section 104 to apply?	8-13
Q 8:34	If a taxpayer who is a member of the armed forces falls ill while on active duty and is paid for his or her leave time, will this be excludable?	8-13
Q 8:35	How much disability pay is excludable under Code Section 104?	8-14
Q 8:36	What is the maximum number of years over which an employee may receive installment payments from a tax-qualified plan?	8-14
Q 8:37	How is the initial year in which installment payments must be made determined for the taxpayer?	8-16
Q 8:38	Must the maximum defined injury benefit rules also meet the tests under a defined benefit plan?	8-16
Q 8:39	May the maximum defined injury benefit rules apply to a joint and survivor annuity?	8-16
Q 8:40	If there is more than one beneficiary, how is the difference in age determined for maximum defined injury benefit purposes?	8-16

Estate and Retirement Planning Answer Book

Q 8:41	Under Proposed Treasury Regulations Section 1.401(a)(9)-2, what is the effect on the maximum defined injury benefit percentage requirement of adding a new, younger beneficiary?	8-16
Q 8:42	How do the requirements of Proposed Treasury Regulations Section 1.401(a)(9)-2 change when the beneficiary is the annuitant's spouse?	8-17
Q 8:43	What if the annuitant and the annuitant's spouse are divorced and the court orders that a portion of the employee's annuity payments be paid to the spouse under a qualified domestic relations order?	8-17
Q 8:44	What is the expected return of an annuity?	8-17
Q 8:45	Can an annuitant deduct a percentage of his or her return of capital from each payment and therefore exclude this percentage from income?	8-17
Q 8:46	Are there any circumstances under which the percentage deductible may continue after the total amount invested has been excluded from income?	8-17
Q 8:47	Was there a time when the exclusion ratio did not apply to annuity payments?	8-18
Q 8:48	What type of payments are considered annuities?	8-18
Q 8:49	How much of an employer's contribution must be included in an annuitant's income?	8-18
Q 8:50	If an employee is given an option to receive a lump-sum payment or an annuity, how much is includible in the employee's income for the year in which the offer is made?	8-18
Q 8:51	Is there an exception to Code Section 72's harsh inclusion requirement?	8-19
Q 8:52	How long must the option be irrevocable for the exception to Code Section 72 to apply?	8-19

Simplified Safe Harbor Exclusion

Q 8:53	What is the simplified safe harbor exclusion ratio?	8-19
Q 8:54	Will the simplified safe harbor exclusion ratio comply with Code Section 72?	8-19
Q 8:55	Who qualifies for the simplified safe harbor exclusion ratio?	8-19
Q 8:56	What qualifications must a taxpayer meet in order to use the simplified safe harbor exclusion ratio?	8-20
Q 8:57	How is the simplified safe harbor exclusion ratio determined?	8-20
Q 8:58	Is the simplified safe harbor exclusion ratio modified for changes in the annuity payments such as cost-of-living increases?	8-20

List of Questions

Q 8:59	What if the amount determined to be excluded under the simplified safe harbor method is greater than the annuity payment received?.................	8-20
Q 8:60	How is the excludable portion determined under the simplified safe harbor exclusion ratio where there is more than one beneficiary to an annuity?.............	8-21
Q 8:61	How is the investment in the contract determined under the simplified safe harbor exclusion method?.......	8-21
Q 8:62	Can the investment in the contract be increased by any method other than payments to the annuity?.......	8-21
Q 8:63	How does a taxpayer elect to use the simplified method?.	8-21
Q 8:64	How is the total number of monthly expected payments determined?............................	8-21
Q 8:65	Once the election to use the simplified method is made, can the taxpayer later decide to use the actual calculation of the exclusion ratio or vice versa?..............	8-22
Q 8:66	How does a taxpayer change from using the simplified exclusion method to the actual exclusion?........	8-22
Q 8:67	How is the value of the taxpayer's annuity determined?..	8-22
Q 8:68	May a taxpayer be required to include loans on annuities in gross taxable income in the year the loan is made?...	8-22
Q 8:69	Even if an exclusion applies, may a taxpayer later be required to treat the loan as a distribution?............	8-23
Q 8:70	Are payments contributed to an annuity by an employer on behalf of a self-employed individual excludable by the self-employed individual?.................	8-23
Q 8:71	Is it true that the early withdrawals tax does not apply to some employee distributions made after separation from service if the employee has attained age 55?...........	8-23
Q 8:72	Does the Section 72(t) exception apply even if the employee later returns to employment with the same employer?..	8-23

Chapter 9 Valuation of Business Interests and Other Property

Overview

Q 9:1	Why is valuation of business interests and other property an important aspect of estate planning?...........	9-2
Q 9:2	What are the basic valuation rules?..............	9-2
Q 9:3	Is it always better to have property valued low?.......	9-2
Q 9:4	What is the market approach to valuation?..........	9-3

Estate and Retirement Planning Answer Book

Q 9:5	What is the income approach to value?	9-3
Q 9:6	What is the cost approach to value?	9-3

Mortgages and Notes

Q 9:7	How are mortgages and notes valued?	9-3

Closely Held Securities

Q 9:8	What is the basic approach used in valuing closely held securities?	9-4
Q 9:9	Can developments subsequent to the valuation date be used in determining fair market value?	9-4
Q 9:10	What market should be used for valuation purposes if no market exists for the shares of a closely held corporation?	9-4
Q 9:11	What is the book value approach to valuating closely held securities?	9-5
Q 9:12	What is the earnings approach to valuing closely held securities?	9-5
Q 9:13	What is the market approach to valuing closely held securities?	9-6
Q 9:14	What factors does the IRS consider fundamental in valuing closely held corporations?	9-6
Q 9:15	What factors does the federal Tax Court consider in determining the value of closely held corporations?	9-9

The Estate Tax Freeze

Q 9:16	What is an estate tax freeze?	9-10
Q 9:17	How are estate freezes taxed?	9-10
Q 9:18	When do the special valuation rules of Code Section 2701 apply?	9-10
Q 9:19	How are gifts subject to Code Section 2701 valued?	9-12
Q 9:20	What happens if a qualified payment is not made?	9-14
Q 9:21	Does the lapse of rights result in a taxable transfer?	9-15
Q 9:22	Does the lapse of a restriction on liquidation result in transfer tax?	9-15

Restrictive Stock Agreements

Q 9:23	What are the primary types of restrictive stock agreements?	9-15
Q 9:24	What is the approach of the IRS to restrictive agreements?	9-16

List of Questions

Q 9:25	What threshold requirements must a buy/sell agreement meet to fix values for estate tax purposes?	9-16
Q 9:26	Can restrictive agreements also fix the value of stock for gift tax purposes?	9-17

Minority Interests

Q 9:27	What is a minority interest discount?	9-17
Q 9:28	What happens if a noncontrol block is given away by the controlling stockholder with no one thereafter holding a majority of shares?	9-18
Q 9:29	What is a control premium?	9-18
Q 9:30	Is stock owned by a minority shareholder whose family owns a majority of the corporation's stock valued to include a control premium?	9-19
Q 9:31	Under what circumstances does a taxpayer want to assert the existence of a control premium?	9-19
Q 9:32	What is the lack of marketability discount?	9-19
Q 9:33	What discounts have been allowed by the courts for minority interests and lack of marketability?	9-19

Real Estate

Q 9:34	Why is the valuation of real estate important in estate planning?	9-20
Q 9:35	What happens if there is a dispute over real estate valuation between the IRS and the taxpayer?	9-20
Q 9:36	What is the definition of fair market value for real estate valuation purposes?	9-21
Q 9:37	Can local appraised values be used in determining fair market value of real estate?	9-21
Q 9:38	Do any special valuation methods apply to real estate or closely held business property?	9-21
Q 9:39	What are the qualification requirements for using the Section 2032A special valuation for real estate?	9-22
Q 9:40	Who are qualified heirs for purposes of the special valuation tests?	9-22
Q 9:41	Does the special valuation apply to indirect ownership interests?	9-23
Q 9:42	Are tax benefits under Code Section 2032A(c)(1) subject to recapture?	9-23

Penalties for Improper Valuation

Q 9:43 What penalties apply if a valuation is improper? 9-24

Chapter 10 Charitable Contributions

Income Tax Deduction for Charitable Contributions

Q 10:1 Is there an income tax deduction for charitable gift giving? 10-1
Q 10:2 What are the elements of a deductible charitable contribution? 10-2
Q 10:3 Must the transfer consist of a present interest in money or property? 10-2
Q 10:4 Does transfer of a partial interest in property qualify for a charitable deduction? 10-2
Q 10:5 Does a donation of the taxpayer's services qualify for a charitable contribution deduction? 10-3
Q 10:6 Can the donor restrict the charitable contribution to a certain class of beneficiaries? 10-3
Q 10:7 Can a donor retain control to determine which individuals will receive the benefits from the donor's contribution? . . . 10-4
Q 10:8 Are tuition payments to tax-exempt private or parochial schools charitable contributions? 10-4
Q 10:9 For purposes of tax-deductible contributions, how does the Code define *charitable organizations*? 10-4
Q 10:10 What is the income tax deduction for gifts to private foundations? 10-5
Q 10:11 What limits apply if an individual makes contributions to both a public charity and a private foundation? 10-5
Q 10:12 What happens if contributions to charity exceed the 50 percent limit? 10-5
Q 10:13 What deduction is available for gifts of noncash property? 10-6
Q 10:14 Does the donor recognize gain if appreciated property is contributed to a charity? 10-6
Q 10:15 What deduction is available for gifts of encumbered property? 10-7
Q 10:16 What substantiation requirements are necessary to obtain the deduction? 10-8
Q 10:17 When may penalties be assessed against a donor? 10-8

List of Questions

Charitable Organizations

Q 10:18	Which charities qualify for the 50 percent deduction? . . .	10-9
Q 10:19	What is a private operating foundation?	10-9
Q 10:20	What is a private distributing foundation?	10-9
Q 10:21	What is the tax advantage of giving long-term capital gain property to a public charity?	10-10
Q 10:22	What are the tax effects if an individual sells his long-term capital gain property to a charity at less than fair market value?	10-10
Q 10:23	May an individual contribute a life insurance policy to a public charity?	10-11

Estate and Gift Tax Deductions

Gifts

Q 10:24	What are the gift tax ramifications for contributions to a public charity?	10-11
Q 10:25	What is the advantage of donating assets to a charity during the individual's lifetime as opposed to devising them to a charity in a will?	10-11

Bequests

Q 10:26	For purposes of determining the estate tax imposed by Code Section 2001, are charitable devises subtracted from the value of the gross estate?	10-11
Q 10:27	Are transfers to charities resulting from disclaimers deductible?	10-12
Q 10:28	Can the amount of charitable deductions exceed the value of the property included in the gross estate?	10-12
Q 10:29	Can estate taxes imposed by Code Section 2001 be paid out of charitable bequests?	10-12
Q 10:30	Are devises to a trustee or trustees or a fraternal order deductible from the gross estate when determining the value of the taxable estate subject to the estate tax of Code Section 2001?	10-12
Q 10:31	Are charitable deductions from estate taxes disallowed for certain transfers?	10-13

Charitable Trusts

Q 10:32	Why do charitable trusts figure so prominently in estate planning?	10-13

Q 10:33	How do tax-saving strategies interact in a charitable trust?	10-14
Q 10:34	What is a charitable trust?	10-14
Q 10:35	How does a charitable trust differ from a charitable foundation?	10-15
Q 10:36	What are the rules for determining the nature and extent of a charitable contribution deduction for income, gift, and estate tax purposes?	10-15
Q 10:37	If contributions made to a charitable lead trust or charitable remainder trust are not made directly to the charity, how is the charitable contribution calculated?	10-16
Q 10:38	What is a charitable remainder trust?	10-17
Q 10:39	What forms of charitable remainder trusts are recognized under the Internal Revenue Code?	10-17
Q 10:40	What is the difference between a charitable remainder annuity trust and a charitable remainder unitrust?	10-17
Q 10:41	How does a donor benefit from creating a charitable remainder trust?	10-18
Q 10:42	Is a charitable remainder trust exempt from federal income tax?	10-19
Q 10:43	What are the factors to consider in choosing between a charitable remainder annuity trust and a charitable remainder unitrust?	10-19
Q 10:44	What types of assets should be used in funding a charitable remainder annuity trust or charitable remainder unitrust?	10-20
Q 10:45	What are the tax consequences to a grantor in creating a charitable remainder annuity trust or charitable remainder unitrust?	10-20
Q 10:46	What are the income tax consequences to the beneficiary of a charitable remainder trust?	10-21
Q 10:47	How does a charitable remainder trust work?	10-21
Q 10:48	What is a charitable lead trust and how does it differ from a charitable remainder trust?	10-22
Q 10:49	How may a charitable lead trust be used for accomplishing any of the purposes described above?	10-23
Q 10:50	What is a pooled income fund?	10-24
Q 10:51	What are the advantages to a potential donor of a pooled income fund over a charitable remainder trust?	10-25
Q 10:52	What are the disadvantages of a pooled income fund? . .	10-25
Q 10:53	What is a tax-exempt charitable foundation?	10-26
Q 10:54	What are the tax benefits that may be derived from qualifying as a charitable foundation?	10-26

List of Questions

Q 10:55	What is a private charitable foundation?	10-26
Q 10:56	Are there any restrictions in being classified as a private foundation?	10-27
Q 10:57	Is a private foundation automatically tax-exempt and eligible to receive tax-deductible contributions if it complies with the provisions of the Internal Revenue Code?	10-27

Chapter 11 Funding for Liquidity

Tax-Free Exchange Under Code Section 303

Q 11:1	What help does Code Section 303 offer for resolving an estate's liquidity needs?	11-2
Q 11:2	What requirements must be met for Code Section 303 to apply?	11-2
Q 11:3	Can asset distributions besides cash satisfy Code Section 303?	11-3
Q 11:4	What if the estate is paid with a promissory note of the corporation that is payable in five years?	11-3
Q 11:5	Do the proceeds of the stock redemption have to be used to pay federal and state death taxes and funeral and administrative expenses?	11-3

Life Insurance

Q 11:6	How can life insurance be used to provide liquidity for an estate?	11-3
Q 11:7	What is survivorship insurance?	11-4
Q 11:8	How is survivorship insurance used in estate planning?	11-4

Deferral of Payments

Q 11:9	What extensions for paying estate taxes are available?	11-4
Q 11:10	Can the personal representative of an estate elect to defer the payment of estate taxes if a substantial portion of estate assets consist of a closely held business or a farm?	11-5
Q 11:11	Does the business interest have to be included in the probate estate to qualify for the 15-year extension?	11-5
Q 11:12	What requirements must be met to take advantage of the election to defer estate taxes?	11-6
Q 11:13	Does the conduct of a rent producing activity constitute a trade or business for purposes of the 15-year deferral of taxes?	11-6

Sale of Business

Q 11:14	When is the sale of a business a realistic option for solving estate liquidity options?	11-7

Chapter 12 Using Trusts in Estate Planning

Overview

Q 12:1	In the context of estate planning, are trusts feasible only for affluent taxpayers?	12-1
Q 12:2	What benefit does a trust provide that a direct gift does not?	12-2
Q 12:3	What is a trust, and why is one generally used?	12-2
Q 12:4	How does the Internal Revenue Service view trusts that are established for the benefit of a pet?	12-3
Q 12:5	Do the legal and other professional fees incurred in creating a trust warrant the tax savings to be generated?	12-4
Q 12:6	When does a trust begin its life?	12-4
Q 12:7	What is a *grantor* trust?	12-4
Q 12:8	Once a trust is established upon reliance of competent professional advice, can the grantor be assured that the IRS and the local taxing jurisdiction will not challenge the tax results expected to be derived from the trust?	12-5
Q 12:9	How can a taxpayer be certain that his or her personal, emotional, and business needs are being properly attended to when he or she is caught up in the urgency of trying to save on taxes?	12-5
Q 12:10	What are the different kinds of trusts currently being considered by estate planning practitioners in the framing of an estate plan?	12-6

Estate Planning Trusts

Grantor Retained Income Trust

Q 12:11	What is a grantor retained income trust?	12-6
Q 12:12	How is a personal residence defined for GRIT purposes?	12-6
Q 12:13	Why would one transfer a personal residence merely to save on taxes?	12-7
Q 12:14	What other reasons are there for creating a GRIT?	12-7

List of Questions

Q 12:15	If a married person owns a residence jointly with right of survivorship to a spouse or owns it solely but provides that the residence be devised to the surviving spouse, the marital deduction will effectively keep the residence from being subject to an estate tax. Why then should a GRIT be considered?	12-7
Q 12:16	Practically speaking, how does a GRIT work?	12-8
Q 12:17	What if the term of a GRIT is for a period longer than the grantor's life expectancy?	12-11
Q 12:18	How would a GRIT be employed for a married couple as compared to a single person?	12-11
Q 12:19	Does any part of the gift of the remainder interest qualify for the $10,000 annual gift tax exclusion?	12-12
Q 12:20	How can a grantor use the $10,000 annual gift tax exclusion and still maximize the prospective benefit of a qualified personal residence trust?	12-12
Q 12:21	What is a personal residence trust?	12-12
Q 12:22	What is the difference between a personal residence trust and a qualified personal residence trust?	12-13
Q 12:23	Inasmuch as a personal residence trust is precluded from holding cash, what is the effect of such a trust receiving cash as a result of destruction of the residence by fire or its condemnation by local government?	12-13
Q 12:24	Qualified personal residence trusts are not described in Code Section 2702 or under any other provisions of the Code. What authority is there to provide the tax benefit expected from the creation of such a trust?	12-14
Q 12:25	Why is a grantor entitled to the advantages of Code Sections 1034 and 1033, and the over 55 years of age exemption under Code Section 121, if the taxpayer does not own the residence during the years it is held in trust?	12-15
Q 12:26	What does it signify that commutation of the grantor's interest is prohibited under a QPRT and a PRT?	12-16
Q 12:27	Can a residence encumbered by a mortgage be transferred to either a PRT or QPRT?	12-16
Q 12:28	Does a QPRT lose its special status if the residence held by it ceases to be the grantor's residence for any reason (e.g., sale, destruction, or condemnation, or change in use)?	12-16
Q 12:29	Will using a portion of the residence on a regular basis exclusively for business purposes preclude transferring the residence to a PRT or a QPRT?	12-17
Q 12:30	Can anyone other than the grantor occupy the residence during the trust term?	12-17

Q 12:31	What is the effect on either a personal residence trust or a qualified personal residence trust arrangement if the grantor is required to move to a nursing home during the trust term?	12-18
Q 12:32	Can a grantor establish more than one trust for each residence he or she owns?	12-18
Q 12:33	Can the grantor be the trustee of his or her own personal residence or qualified personal residence trust?	12-18
Q 12:34	What are the gift and estate tax advantages of a qualified personal residence trust?	12-18
Q 12:35	How is the amount of the gift determined?	12-19
Q 12:36	What is the grantor's retained reversionary interest?	12-19
Q 12:37	Are there changed circumstances where a married couple owns a residence jointly as tenants by the entirety?	12-19
Q 12:38	What are the benefits of such undivided interest?	12-20
Q 12:39	Are there any situations when only one of the spouses should create the trust?	12-20
Q 12:40	Can a married couple owning a residence in joint name create a QPRT jointly, and, if so, what are the pitfalls?	12-20
Q 12:41	Are any discounts available for these gifts?	12-21
Q 12:42	What are the income tax consequences of the QPRT?	12-21
Q 12:43	May a grantor create more than one QPRT?	12-21
Q 12:44	Is there a tax strategy that can be employed to obtain a step-up in basis while the residence is owned by a qualified personal residence trust?	12-22
Q 12:45	Can the grantor continue living in the residence if he or she survives the trust term?	12-22
Q 12:46	What are the disadvantages in establishing a qualified personal residence trust?	12-22
Q 12:47	What are the tax effects to the donee who receives the personal residence at the end of the trust term?	12-23
Q 12:48	Should a qualified personal residence trust or a personal residence trust be considered if a gross estate, including a personal residence, does not exceed $600,000?	12-23

Grantor Retained Annuity Trusts and Grantor Retained Unitrusts

Q 12:49	What are grantor retained annuity trusts and grantor retained unitrusts?	12-24

List of Questions

Q 12:50	Would it not be easier for the grantor to keep the property otherwise placed in the GRAT or GRUT, enjoy its economic benefits for a period equaling the trust term, and then make a direct gift to the intended beneficiaries?	12-25
Q 12:51	Why should a taxpayer consider using a GRAT or GRUT in his or her estate planning?	12-25
Q 12:52	What did Congress have in mind when it enacted Code Section 2702 permitting the use of GRATs and GRUTs?	12-26
Q 12:53	How does a GRAT work?	12-27
Q 12:54	What are the requirements that must be met by a GRUT?	12-28
Q 12:55	Are there any other additional rules pertaining to a GRAT or a GRUT?	12-28
Q 12:56	How is a gift zeroed out in the case of an annuity trust?	12-29

Chapter 13 Asset Protection Trusts

Overview

Q 13:1	What does estate planning have to do with protecting an individual from his or her creditors?	13-1

Traditional Methods for Limiting Liability

Q 13:2	How do individuals generally protect their personal assets from creditors?	13-2
Q 13:3	Are there other forms under which business may be conducted that will also protect individuals from liabilities created by the businesses they have organized?	13-2
Q 13:4	Why have LLCs and LLPs become increasingly popular?	13-3

Using Trusts as Protection from Creditors

Q 13:5	Why should a trust be used for protection from creditors instead of a corporation, limited partnership, LLC, or LLP, all of which are intended to accomplish the same purpose?	13-3
Q 13:6	Is there any method currently being used to thwart personal liability claims?	13-4
Q 13:7	What is an OAPT?	13-4
Q 13:8	Why use an OAPT?	13-4

Estate and Retirement Planning Answer Book

Domestic Trusts Used as Protection from Creditors

Q 13:9	Why not use a domestic trust instead of an OAPT to protect assets from creditors?	13-5
Q 13:10	What is a spendthrift trust?	13-5
Q 13:11	Can a spendthrift trust also be used by the person who created it (the grantor) to ward off creditor claims?	13-5
Q 13:12	What is a forfeiture clause in a trust?	13-6
Q 13:13	What is a support trust?	13-6
Q 13:14	What is a discretionary trust?	13-6
Q 13:15	Are spendthrift and forfeiture provisions also contained in discretionary trusts?	13-7
Q 13:16	Are there circumstances under which a creditor can reach the interest of a beneficiary in a trust despite its being discretionary or containing spendthrift or forfeiture provisions?	13-7
Q 13:17	What effect, if any, does the bankruptcy of a beneficiary have on the status of a spendthrift provision contained in a trust in which he or she is the beneficiary?	13-8
Q 13:18	Can a fraudulent conveyance be protected in a trust with a spendthrift provision?	13-8
Q 13:19	How does one distinguish under UFTA between a fraudulent conveyance affecting present creditors and one affecting future potential creditors?	13-8
Q 13:20	Can a grantor of an OAPT reserve a reversionary interest so that, at the termination of the OAPT, its property reverts to the grantor?	13-9
Q 13:21	How can an individual avoid fraudulent conveyance laws when making a transfer from his or her name?	13-10
Q 13:22	What is the distinction between protection from creditors through use of an OAPT and protection through use of domestic trusts, which include spendthrift provisions and forfeiture provisions?	13-10
Q 13:23	How does an OAPT protect a grantor from his or her creditors?	13-10
Q 13:24	How long does a creditor usually have to press his or her domestic judgment in a foreign jurisdiction that serves as a haven for OAPTs?	13-11
Q 13:25	Has the IRS taken a position on OAPTs?	13-11
Q 13:26	What is a protector of an OAPT?	13-12

List of Questions

| Q 13:27 | What are some of the risks and expenses in the creation and operation of OAPTs? | 13-12 |
| Q 13:28 | What are the ethical and policy considerations that a professional person should entertain before being linked to an OAPT? | 13-13 |

Chapter 14   Tax and Estate Planning in Marital Settlements

Overview

Alimony and Separate Maintenance Payments

Q 14:1	In structuring a separation agreement or legal instrument for incorporation into a divorce decree, do the laws of the state in which the separation or divorce takes place determine the tax effects governing the provisions of the agreement?	14-3
Q 14:2	How are alimony or separate maintenance payments treated for federal income tax purposes?	14-3
Q 14:3	What is an alimony or separate maintenance payment?	14-3
Q 14:4	Are there any exceptions to the recapture rule?	14-5
Q 14:5	What is the *divorce or separation instrument,* required under Code Section 71, under which an alimony payment must qualify in order to be deductible?	14-6
Q 14:6	If the divorce decree or written separation agreement providing for a continuation of the alimony payments after remarriage conflicts with a state law that precludes such payments from constituting alimony, are the alimony payments nondeductible for federal income tax purposes?	14-7
Q 14:7	In order to be treated as alimony or separate maintenance payments, must the payments be *periodic*, as that term was defined prior to enactment of the Tax Reform Act of 1984, and be made in discharge of a legal obligation of the payor to support the payee arising out of a marital or family relationship?	14-7
Q 14:8	May alimony or separate maintenance payments be made in a form other than cash?	14-7
Q 14:9	May payments of cash to a third party on behalf of a spouse qualify as alimony or separate maintenance payments if the payments are made to the third party at the written request of the payee spouse?	14-8

xlvii

Estate and Retirement Planning Answer Book

Q 14:10	How may spouses designate that payments otherwise qualifying as alimony or separate maintenance payments shall be excludable from the gross income of the payee and nondeductible by the payor?	14-8
Q 14:11	What are the consequences if, at the time a payment is made, the payor and payee spouses are members of the same household?	14-9
Q 14:12	Assuming all other requirements relating to the qualification of certain payments as alimony or separate maintenance payments are met, what are the consequences if the payor spouse is required to continue to make the payments after the death of the payee spouse?	14-9
Q 14:13	What are the consequences if the divorce or separation instrument fails to state that there is no liability for any period after the death of the payee spouse to continue to make any payments that would otherwise qualify as alimony or separate maintenance payments?	14-10
Q 14:14	Will a divorce or separation instrument be treated as stating that there is no liability to make payments after the death of the payee spouse if the liability to make such payments terminates pursuant to applicable local law or oral agreement?	14-10
Q 14:15	What are the consequences if the payor spouse is required to make one or more payments (in cash or property) after the death of the payee spouse as a substitute for the continuation of pre-death payments that would otherwise qualify as alimony or separate maintenance payments?	14-11
Q 14:16	Under what circumstances will one or more payments (in cash or property) that are to occur after the death of the payee spouse be treated as a substitute for the continuation of payments that would otherwise qualify as alimony or separate maintenance payments?	14-11

Child Support

Q 14:17	What are the consequences of a payment which the terms of the divorce or separation instrument fix as payable for the support of a child of the payor spouse?	14-12
Q 14:18	When is a payment fixed (or treated as fixed) as payable for the support of a child of the payor spouse?	14-12
Q 14:19	When does a contingency relate to a child of the payor?	14-13
Q 14:20	When will a payment be treated as to be reduced at a time which can clearly be associated with the happening of a contingency relating to a child of the payor?	14-13

List of Questions

Taxability of Property Transfers

Q 14:21	What are the tax consequences of property transfers between spouses in a marital separation?	14-15
Q 14:22	Is the above rule of the *Davis* case still in effect?	14-15
Q 14:23	Does the rule of nontaxability of transfers of property between spouses apply only to those spouses involved in the divorce process?	14-16
Q 14:24	Does the nontaxability of property between divorcing spouses also apply where one of the spouses assigns income to which he or she is entitled?	14-16
Q 14:25	Will the nontaxability rules also apply where one spouse transfers U. S. Savings Bonds with accrued but unrecognized interest to the other spouse?	14-16
Q 14:26	Who and what is excepted from the nontaxability rules of transfers between spouses?	14-16
Q 14:27	What is the effect of a transfer of property after the divorce?	14-17

Alimony Trusts

Q 14:28	What is an alimony trust?	14-17
Q 14:29	When does Code Section 682 apply to an alimony trust to keep the paying spouse from being taxed on the trust income and cause said trust income to be taxed to the payee spouse?	14-18
Q 14:30	What purpose does an alimony trust serve?	14-18
Q 14:31	It appears that Code Sections 71 and 682 cover the same situations by providing the payor spouse a deduction for alimony [IRC § 71] that is essentially the same as avoiding tax on the trust income received by the payee spouse [IRC § 682]. Do these two Code sections cover the same situations?	14-19
Q 14:32	What is the effect to the payee spouse where the income from the alimony trust is derived exclusively from tax-exempt municipal bond interest?	14-19

Employee Retirement Benefits

Q 14:33	Why are retirement plans an integral part of the property division process?	14-19
Q 14:34	What is a qualified domestic relations order?	14-20
Q 14:35	Are there any proscriptions by which the qualified domestic relations order is limited?	14-21

Annulments and Sham Divorces

Q 14:36	What are the income tax consequences of an annulment?	14-21
Q 14:37	Can a married couple achieve tax savings by divorcing before the end of the year to file separate returns as single taxpayers—with the expectation of tax benefit from such filing—and subsequently remarry early in the next year?	14-22

Filing Status

Q 14:38	Can a married couple file a joint return if they are legally separated?	14-22
Q 14:39	Can a married person qualify for head of household status?	14-22
Q 14:40	In connection with the filing status of the separated or divorced parties, who is entitled to claim the child dependency exemption?	14-23

Selling the Marital Home

Q 14:41	What must a divorcing couple consider when selling their marital residence in connection with or as a result of their divorce?	14-23

Deductibility of Legal and Accounting Fees

Q 14:42	Can a separated or divorced couple deduct the legal and accounting fees incurred in connection with their marital split?	14-24

The Innocent Spouse Rules

Q 14:43	How is a spouse who innocently signs a joint return protected from tax liability, interest, and potential penalties as a result of income omissions or fictitious or exaggerated deductions claimed by the other spouse on the joint return?	14-25
Q 14:44	How does one qualify for innocent spouse relief?	14-25
Q 14:45	What is a *grossly erroneous item* for purposes of the innocent spouse provisions?	14-26

Estate Tax Considerations

Q 14:46	Can the estate of a deceased payor-spouse claim a deduction, for federal estate tax purposes, for the deceased individual's obligation to make future alimony or support payments to his or her former spouse, pursuant to a divorce decree?	14-26

List of Questions

Chapter 15 Post-Death Estate Planning

Overview

Q 15:1	What is post-death estate planning?	15-2

Required Tax Returns

Q 15:2	Which federal tax returns must be filed by the executor? .	15-2
Q 15:3	What requirements apply to the filing of the decedent's final income tax return?	15-2
Q 15:4	When must the estate fiduciary tax return be filed?	15-2
Q 15:5	When must the federal estate tax return be filed?	15-3
Q 15:6	What time period is covered by the decedent's final income tax return?	15-3
Q 15:7	Can the executor, on behalf of the decedent, file a joint income tax return with the surviving spouse?	15-3
Q 15:8	What kinds of taxable years can be used for the estate's tax reporting purposes?	15-3

Deductions

Q 15:9	What is the medical deduction election?	15-4
Q 15:10	What deductions are available for administrative expenses and casualty losses?	15-5
Q 15:11	How are deductions taken on the estate's income tax return?	15-5
Q 15:12	Is a double deduction against the estate tax and estate income tax ever available?	15-5
Q 15:13	When must the election to waive the estate tax deduction be made?	15-5
Q 15:14	What factors should be taken into account when deciding on which return to deduct administrative expenses?	15-6
Q 15:15	If the estate tax deduction is waived, must the tax savings be allocated to beneficiaries?	15-8

Valuation of Assets

Q 15:16	What factors should be considered when selecting a valuation date for estate assets?	15-8
Q 15:17	Is there a penalty for overvaluing assets to obtain a higher income tax basis?	15-9

li

Elections

Q 15:18	What special elections can an executor make?	15-10
Q 15:19	When should the executor elect to waive his or her fees?	15-11
Q 15:20	What post-death partnership elections should be considered?	15-11
Q 15:21	How is the Section 754 election made?	15-12
Q 15:22	How is income collected by an estate taxed?	15-12

Distribution Income Planning

Q 15:23	What is distribution income planning?	15-13
Q 15:24	How can deductions from estate income be maximized?	15-13
Q 15:25	How can additional taxpayers be created by the use of a trust?	15-14
Q 15:26	How should installment obligations arising after death be treated?	15-14

Disclaimers

Q 15:27	What is a disclaimer?	15-15
Q 15:28	When should a disclaimer be used?	15-15
Q 15:29	What are the requirements for a qualified disclaimer?	15-16
Q 15:30	How are joint tenancies treated for disclaimer purposes?	15-16
Q 15:31	Can a power of appointment be disclaimed?	15-17
Q 15:32	Are there any exceptions to the rule that a disclaimed interest must pass to a person other than the disclaiming party?	15-17
Q 15:33	What other factors should be considered in making a disclaimer?	15-17
Q 15:34	Can a disclaimer be made in favor of a charity?	15-18

PART II Benefit Plans and Other Sources of Retirement Assets

Chapter 16 Benefit Plans

Overview

Q 16:1	What are the crucial retirement planning issues for small business owners and executives?	16-2
Q 16:2	What are the basic types of retirement plans?	16-2

List of Questions

Q 16:3	What are the advantages of tax-qualified retirement plans?	16-3
Q 16:4	What are the advantages of nonqualified retirement plans?	16-3

Labor Law Requirements

Q 16:5	What labor laws play a significant role in the administration of employee benefit plans?	16-3

ERISA

Q 16:6	What is the Employee Retirement Income Security Act of 1974?	16-4
Q 16:7	What is the Pension Benefit Guaranty Corporation, and what retirement plans does it insure?	16-5
Q 16:8	What benefits are guaranteed by the Pension Benefit Guaranty Corporation?	16-6
Q 16:9	What rights does ERISA give plan participants and beneficiaries?	16-6
Q 16:10	Under ERISA, is the prevailing party entitled to an award of attorneys' fees?	16-7

Fiduciary Responsibility

Q 16:11	What is a fiduciary?	16-8
Q 16:12	What are the duties of ERISA fiduciaries?	16-8
Q 16:13	What legal responsibilities and requirements pertain to ERISA fiduciaries of retirement plans?	16-9
Q 16:14	To which assets do the fiduciary responsibility rules apply?	16-10
Q 16:15	Do assets in a tax-qualified plan have to be held in trust? .	16-10
Q 16:16	Does ERISA permit retirement plans to hold employer securities and property as plan assets?	16-10
Q 16:17	How may a plan limit the liability of plan fiduciaries and trustees?	16-11
Q 16:18	What general requirements must plans that offer individually directed accounts satisfy to avoid fiduciary liability? . . .	16-12
Q 16:19	How can a plan fiduciary determine whether it is providing plan participants and beneficiaries with sufficient exercise of control to satisfy the ERISA requirements?	16-13
Q 16:20	How can a plan determine whether it is providing plan participants and beneficiaries with sufficient opportunity to receive information to satisfy ERISA's requirements regarding informed decision making?	16-13

Estate and Retirement Planning Answer Book

Q 16:21	What opportunities for giving investment instructions must be available to plan participants to satisfy the requirements of ERISA and the Code?	16-15
Q 16:22	What opportunities for a broad, diversified range of investment alternatives must be made available to the plan participants to satisfy the requirements of ERISA?	16-16
Q 16:23	How are plan fiduciaries shielded if the participant direction regulations are complied with?	16-16
Q 16:24	What are prohibited transactions?	16-17
Q 16:25	Do any exceptions exist to the prohibited transaction rules?	16-19
Q 16:26	What penalties apply if a prohibited transaction occurs?	16-19
Q 16:27	Who are parties in interest and disqualified persons for prohibited transaction purposes?	16-20
Q 16:28	What reporting and disclosure rules apply to ERISA plans?	16-21

Age and Sex Discrimination

Q 16:29	What sex discrimination laws apply to retirement plans?	16-22
Q 16:30	What age discrimination laws apply to retirement plans?	16-23
Q 16:31	What protections does the ADEA give participants in retirement plans?	16-23

Veterans' Rights

Q 16:32	What impact do the labor laws that apply to veterans have on retirement plans?	16-24

WARN

Q 16:33	How does WARN affect retirement plans?	16-25

Taft-Hartley Act

Q 16:34	What retirement plans are governed by the Taft-Hartley Act?	16-25
Q 16:35	What concerns does an employer have with respect to plans governed by the Taft-Hartley Act?	16-26

Multiemployer Plans

Q 16:36	What are multiemployer plans?	16-26
Q 16:37	Does ERISA specifically address multiemployer plans?	16-26
Q 16:38	Should an employer be concerned about the withdrawal liability that applies to multiemployer plans?	16-26

List of Questions

Collective Bargaining

Q 16:39	Must an employer bargain with a union over retirement benefits?	16-27
Q 16:40	What effect does ERISA have on collective bargaining?	16-27
Q 16:41	Does the NLRA limit coverage of retirement plans?	16-28
Q 16:42	Can an employer subject to a collective bargaining agreement unilaterally amend a retirement plan?	16-28
Q 16:43	Does an employer have an obligation to continue to provide retirement benefits after the collective bargaining agreement expires?	16-28
Q 16:44	Can an employer discontinue accrued benefits during a strike?	16-29

Chapter 17 Tax-Qualified Retirement Plans

Overview

Q 17:1	How do tax-qualified retirement plans generate retirement income?	17-2
Q 17:2	What favorable tax treatment exists for payments from tax-qualified retirement plans?	17-3
Q 17:3	What is an insured tax-qualified retirement plan?	17-3
Q 17:4	When should a plan have insurance as a plan asset?	17-3
Q 17:5	What are master and prototype retirement plans?	17-4
Q 17:6	Can a nonstandardized plan be converted into a standardized plan?	17-5

Design Considerations

Q 17:7	How does a retirement plan achieve tax-qualified status?	17-5
Q 17:8	What happens if a plan is disqualified?	17-6
Q 17:9	What alternatives exist to plan disqualification if a tax-qualified plan violates the requirements for tax-qualified status?	17-7
Q 17:10	What are the vesting requirements for tax-qualified plans?	17-8
Q 17:11	Must a tax-qualified retirement plan include all employees?	17-8
Q 17:12	What are the most common eligibility requirements for participation in a tax-qualified retirement plan?	17-9
Q 17:13	Can a tax-qualified plan give credit for an employee's service in years prior to the adoption of the plan?	17-9
Q 17:14	Which nondiscrimination rules apply to tax-qualified plans?	17-10

… Estate and Retirement Planning Answer Book …

Q 17:15	May a tax-qualified plan discriminate against rank-and-file employees on the basis of benefits, rights, and features?	17-10
Q 17:16	What kind of benefits can be provided under a tax-qualified retirement plan?	17-11
Q 17:17	May a tax-qualified plan provide for plan loans for participants?	17-12
Q 17:18	Can an employer provide different tax-qualified plan benefits for participants in different lines of business?	17-12
Q 17:19	May a tax-qualified retirement plan provide health insurance?	17-13
Q 17:20	Can a company take Social Security benefits into consideration in designing its tax-qualified retirement plan?	17-13
Q 17:21	What is adequate consideration for the sale of stock held by tax-qualified plans?	17-14

Defined Contribution Plans

Q 17:22	What is a defined contribution plan?	17-14
Q 17:23	Are benefits in a defined contribution plan guaranteed?	17-15
Q 17:24	What is a money purchase pension plan?	17-15
Q 17:25	What is a target benefit plan?	17-16
Q 17:26	What is a profit sharing plan?	17-17
Q 17:27	What is an age-weighted profit sharing plan?	17-18
Q 17:28	What is a thrift plan?	17-18
Q 17:29	What is a 401(k) plan?	17-18
Q 17:30	What practical problems can an employer expect if it establishes a 401(k) plan?	17-19
Q 17:31	Is it a good idea to allow multiple investment options?	17-20
Q 17:32	What is a stock bonus plan?	17-20
Q 17:33	What is an employee stock ownership plan?	17-21
Q 17:34	How may an ESOP or stock bonus plan benefit a corporation or its shareholders?	17-21

Defined Benefit Plans

Q 17:35	What is a defined benefit plan?	17-21
Q 17:36	What is a flat benefit plan?	17-22
Q 17:37	What is a unit benefit plan?	17-22
Q 17:38	Are benefits in a defined benefit plan guaranteed?	17-23
Q 17:39	What are the advantages of defined benefit plans?	17-23
Q 17:40	Does a plan sponsor of a defined benefit pension plan have to be concerned about overfunding?	17-24

List of Questions

Q 17:41	What actions should a plan sponsor take if a defined benefit pension plan is overfunded?	17-24
Q 17:42	What are the advantages of a defined benefit plan with regard to service?	17-25
Q 17:43	What is the wear away method of calculating benefits? . .	17-25
Q 17:44	How are benefits calculated without the wear away method?	17-26
Q 17:45	What is annuity value?	17-27

Actuarial Factors

Q 17:46	What is the importance of actuarial assumptions to defined benefit pension plan participants?	17-27
Q 17:47	What are the common mortality tables used to administer defined benefit pension plans?	17-27
Q 17:48	Can a table containing data exclusively on males be used to approximate a unisex table?	17-29
Q 17:49	Does the choice of mortality tables affect the amount of money that must be paid into a defined benefit pension plan to fund it?	17-29
Q 17:50	Can a tax-qualified plan use an actuarial table containing data on males to compute benefits for males and an actuarial table containing data on females to compute benefits for females?	17-30
Q 17:51	What actuarial assumptions are used to determine the amounts of plan distributions?	17-30
Q 17:52	How are defined benefit pension plans funded?	17-30
Q 17:53	How are the funding calculations made for defined benefit pension plans that own life insurance?	17-31
Q 17:54	How are the funding calculations made if the envelope funding method is used?	17-31
Q 17:55	What is the effect of using envelope funding instead of traditional funding methods?	17-32
Q 17:56	What are the individual aggregate method and group methods of funding?	17-33
Q 17:57	What is the relation of the normal retirement benefit to plan funding?	17-33
Q 17:58	How are the sums paid by defined benefit pension plans prior to normal retirement age determined?	17-34
Q 17:59	What postretirement interest rate should be used?	17-35
Q 17:60	Are there limits on the interest rates that can be used for single-sum payments?	17-37

lvii

Estate and Retirement Planning Answer Book

Q 17:61	What effect do Section 415 limits have on single-sum distributions from defined benefit pension plans?	17-38
Q 17:62	What actuarial factors apply if a participant elects one type of annuity instead of another?	17-39
Q 17:63	What interest rates should be used in plan administration?	17-39
Q 17:64	What is the effect of using the unit credit method of funding?	17-40
Q 17:65	How must service after retirement affect the accrued benefit under a tax-qualified plan?	17-41
Q 17:66	What is the significance of the method of accrual used in determining benefits?	17-41
Q 17:67	Should career average compensation be used to determine benefits in a defined benefit plan?	17-42

Keogh Plans
| Q 17:68 | What are Keogh plans? | 17-42 |

General Considerations
Q 17:69	What type of plan should a new business consider adopting?	17-43
Q 17:70	What should be done with a benefit if the plan participant cannot be located and the participant's plan terminates?	17-43
Q 17:71	What is the plan year?	17-44
Q 17:72	Can the plan year be changed?	17-44

Chapter 18 Employee Stock Ownership Plans

Overview
Q 18:1	What is an employee stock ownership plan?	18-2
Q 18:2	Why would an employer want to establish an employee stock ownership plan?	18-2
Q 18:3	Why would an employer not want to establish an employee stock ownership plan?	18-3
Q 18:4	How is an employee stock ownership plan different from a stock bonus plan?	18-3
Q 18:5	What are the basic types of employee stock ownership plans?	18-3
Q 18:6	What is a nonleveraged employee stock ownership plan?	18-3
Q 18:7	What is a leveraged employee stock ownership plan?	18-4

List of Questions

Q 18:8	Can employee stock ownership plans be used by publicly traded companies to defend against unwanted takeovers?	18-4
Q 18:9	Can an S corporation establish an employee stock ownership plan?	18-4

Establishing an Employee Stock Ownership Plan: Funding Requirements

Q 18:10	What are employer securities?	18-5
Q 18:11	How much may an employer contribute to an employee stock ownership plan each year on a tax-deductible basis?	18-6
Q 18:12	Can a company obtain a tax deduction for stock contributions to its employee stock ownership plan?	18-6
Q 18:13	What tax incentives are provided to encourage commercial lenders to make loans to employee stock ownership plans or to employers sponsoring employee stock ownership plans?	18-6
Q 18:14	What is a securities acquisition loan?	18-8
Q 18:15	What is a mirror loan?	18-9
Q 18:16	Do employer loans or guarantees of loans to employee stock ownership plans violate the Code's prohibited transaction provisions?	18-9
Q 18:17	Is a loan from a shareholder to an employee stock ownership plan a prohibited transaction under ERISA?	18-10
Q 18:18	How can an employee stock ownership plan be used to finance a business?	18-10
Q 18:19	What actions can be taken to prevent a depletion of employee stock ownership plan assets as a result of market conditions?	18-11
Q 18:20	How can an employee stock ownership plan be used to facilitate a buyout of shareholders in a closely held corporation?	18-11
Q 18:21	How can an employee stock ownership plan be used to provide a market for the stock of controlling shareholders in a closely held corporation?	18-12
Q 18:22	How do ERISA and the Code regulate employee stock ownership plans?	18-13

Plan Design Parameters

Q 18:23	How much can be added to an employee stock ownership plan participant's account each year?	18-14

Q 18:24	Are employee stock ownership plan participants entitled to the voting rights of the employer securities allocated to their individual accounts under the plan?	18-15
Q 18:25	Are employee stock ownership plan participants entitled to be involved in decisions to tender plan stock in response to a tender offer?	18-15
Q 18:26	What are the fiduciary obligations of an employee stock ownership plan trustee with regard to unallocated stock?	18-16
Q 18:27	Must an employee stock ownership plan allow participants to diversify the investment of any portion of their individual accounts?	18-16
Q 18:28	If an employee stock ownership plan participant elects to diversify a portion of his or her plan account, what special rules apply to the amounts so diversified?	18-17
Q 18:29	Is the entire amount allocated to the participant's individual account under the employee stock ownership plan subject to diversification?	18-17
Q 18:30	How does the employee stock ownership plan determine which employer securities allocated to the participant's account are counted for purposes of the participant's diversification election rights?	18-18
Q 18:31	May an employee stock ownership plan permit a qualified participant to elect diversification of amounts in excess of that required by statute?	18-20
Q 18:32	Can benefits payable under an employee stock ownership plan be integrated with Social Security?	18-20
Q 18:33	Can a profit sharing plan be converted to an employee stock ownership plan?	18-21
Q 18:34	Is a bankrupt participant's interest in an employee stock ownership plan exempt from a creditor's claims?	18-21

Dividends

Q 18:35	Is the company permitted to deduct dividends paid on employer securities held by an employee stock ownership plan?	18-21
Q 18:36	Are dividends paid to participants deductible by the company even if participants can elect whether to receive them in a current cash payment?	18-22
Q 18:37	How are dividends paid to employee stock ownership plan participants taxed?	18-22

List of Questions

Distributions

Q 18:38	Must distributions under an employee stock ownership plan commence by specified dates?	18-23
Q 18:39	Must distributions under an employee stock ownership plan be made at certain intervals?	18-23
Q 18:40	What can be distributed?	18-24
Q 18:41	When can an employee stock ownership plan participant exercise his or her put option?	18-24
Q 18:42	What steps should be taken to ensure an employee stock ownership plan has sufficient cash to pay for required distributions?	18-25
Q 18:43	How are distributions from an employee stock ownership plan taxed?	18-25
Q 18:44	When must employee stock ownership plan assets be valued?	18-26
Q 18:45	What factors are used to appraise employer securities that are not readily tradable?	18-26

Sale of Employer Securities

Q 18:46	May gains on the sale of securities to an employee stock ownership plan be deferred?	18-27
Q 18:47	How does the selling shareholder elect to defer recognition of gain on the sale of employee stock ownership plan stock?	18-28
Q 18:48	What is the basis of qualified replacement property?	18-29
Q 18:49	What happens if the taxpayer who elects nonrecognition treatment later disposes of the qualified replacement property?	18-30
Q 18:50	Do all dispositions of qualified replacement property result in the recapture of gain?	18-30
Q 18:51	What is the statute of limitations when a selling shareholder elects nonrecognition of the gain on the sale of qualified securities?	18-31
Q 18:52	What happens if an employee stock ownership plan disposes of qualified securities within three years of their acquisition?	18-31
Q 18:53	What is the amount of excise tax on the disposition of qualified securities?	18-32

Estate and Retirement Planning Answer Book

Q 18:54	Are there any restrictions on the allocation of employer securities acquired by the employee stock ownership plan in a transaction in which the seller elected nonrecognition of gain?	18-33

Estate Planning Implications

Q 18:55	How can an employee stock ownership plan be used as an estate planning tool for the owner of a closely held corporation?	18-33
Q 18:56	Is there an estate tax deduction for sales of employer securities to an employee stock ownership plan?	18-34
Q 18:57	Can an employee stock ownership plan enter into an agreement obligating itself to purchase stock when a shareholder dies?	18-35
Q 18:58	Is it a good idea to require that an employee's stock be sold to an employee stock ownership plan when the employee terminates employment?	18-35

Chapter 19 Nonqualified Retirement Plans

Overview

Q 19:1	What are nonqualified deferred compensation plans?	19-2
Q 19:2	Why do organizations establish nonqualified deferred compensation arrangements?	19-2

Applicable Tax Principles

Q 19:3	When is an employer entitled to a deduction for contributions to a nonqualified deferred compensation arrangement?	19-4
Q 19:4	Are amounts deferred in a nonqualified deferred compensation arrangement subject to Social Security and Medicare tax?	19-4
Q 19:5	When is an employee subject to income tax on benefits received under a nonqualified deferred compensation arrangement?	19-4
Q 19:6	What is the constructive receipt doctrine?	19-5
Q 19:7	Will the Internal Revenue Service provide a favorable private letter ruling that an unfunded nonqualified deferred compensation arrangement will defer compensation without running afoul of the constructive receipt doctrine?	19-5

List of Questions

Q 19:8	What is the economic benefit doctrine?	19-7
Q 19:9	Does the making of a promise to make a future payment result in taxation under the economic benefit doctrine? . .	19-7
Q 19:10	How does Code Section 83 affect nonqualified deferred compensation arrangements?	19-7
Q 19:11	Is an employer's promise to make a future payment a taxable event under Code Section 83?	19-7
Q 19:12	How are employees taxed under Code Section 402(b)? . .	19-8
Q 19:13	Can a favorable private letter ruling be obtained for a nonqualified deferred compensation arrangement that provides for the payment of benefits if an unforeseen emergency occurs?	19-8
Q 19:14	Will the IRS issue favorable private letter rulings for nonqualified deferred compensation arrangements for controlling shareholders?	19-9
Q 19:15	Can a participant in a nonqualified deferred compensation arrangement make the decision to defer compensation after the services have been performed?	19-9
Q 19:16	Will an employee be subject to current taxation if he or she has the right to decide whether to accept nonqualified deferred compensation payments in a single sum rather than in installments?	19-9

Supplemental Executive Retirement Plans

Q 19:17	What are supplemental executive retirement plans?	19-10
Q 19:18	What are excess benefits plans?	19-10
Q 19:19	What are the reasons for establishing a supplemental executive retirement plan?	19-10

Rabbi Trusts

Q 19:20	What is a rabbi trust?	19-11
Q 19:21	Will the IRS issue private letter rulings for rabbi trusts? . .	19-12
Q 19:22	Is a rabbi trust subject to the vesting requirements of Title I of ERISA?	19-12
Q 19:23	What are the tax effects of using the model rabbi trust? . .	19-12
Q 19:24	What are the requirements for using the model rabbi trust?	19-12

Surety Bonds

Q 19:25	How are surety bonds used in connection with nonqualified deferred compensation arrangements?	19-13

Estate and Retirement Planning Answer Book

Secular Trusts

Q 19:26	What is a secular trust?	19-13
Q 19:27	Why is a secular trust used?	19-14
Q 19:28	What is the tax treatment of a secular trust?	19-14
Q 19:29	When does the employer receive a deduction for amounts contributed to a secular trust?	19-15
Q 19:30	Who is taxed on income generated by secular trust assets?	19-16
Q 19:31	How are distributions from a secular trust taxed?	19-16

ERISA Implications

Q 19:32	How does Title I of ERISA apply to nonqualified deferred compensation arrangements?	19-17
Q 19:33	Does Title I of ERISA apply to excess benefit plans?	19-18
Q 19:34	Does ERISA apply to top-hat plans?	19-18
Q 19:35	What are the ERISA vesting requirements?	19-18

Chapter 20 Personal Investing

Overview

| Q 20:1 | How does personal investing relate to estate planning? | 20-1 |

Capital Gains and Losses

Q 20:2	Why is the tax rate for capital gains important to consider when planning for retirement?	20-2
Q 20:3	What are capital gains and losses?	20-2
Q 20:4	What are capital assets?	20-2
Q 20:5	What are long-term and short-term capital gains and losses?	20-3
Q 20:6	How are capital gains and losses treated for income tax purposes?	20-4
Q 20:7	What capital losses cannot be deducted from ordinary income?	20-5
Q 20:8	Can gains from the sale of small business stock be excluded from income?	20-5
Q 20:9	If capital assets are held for personal use, what is the income tax treatment when they are sold or exchanged?	20-5
Q 20:10	What kinds of transactions are accorded special treatment for capital gains purposes?	20-5

List of Questions

Investment Principles

Q 20:11	What are some basic investment principles?	20-7

Investment Terms and Concepts

Q 20:12	What is an investment time horizon?	20-8
Q 20:13	What are investable assets?	20-9
Q 20:14	What is a portfolio?	20-10
Q 20:15	What is risk tolerance?	20-10
Q 20:16	How is risk tolerance measured?	20-10
Q 20:17	What is tax-free investing?	20-10
Q 20:18	What is an investment policy statement?	20-11
Q 20:19	What is compounding?	20-11
Q 20:20	What are compounded annualized returns?	20-11
Q 20:21	What is the difference between a broker and an investment manager?	20-13
Q 20:22	What is discretion?	20-13
Q 20:23	What is the difference between equity and fixed income? .	20-13
Q 20:24	What is the difference between Treasury bills, Treasury bonds, and Treasury notes?	20-14
Q 20:25	What are asset classes?	20-14
Q 20:26	What is a commission?	20-14
Q 20:27	What is an investment advisory fee, and how is it different from a broker's commission?	20-15
Q 20:28	What is bundling?	20-15
Q 20:29	What is a wrap fee?	20-15

Tax-Qualified Retirement Plans

Q 20:30	Should employees be given the opportunity to direct their investments?	20-16
Q 20:31	What resources should an investment advisor have? . . .	20-17
Q 20:32	What are the different types of accounts (portfolios) an investor should have?	20-17
Q 20:33	Under what circumstances should an investor have an equity account, fixed-income account, or balanced account? .	20-17
Q 20:34	When should a mutual fund (an open-ended investment company) be used in place of an individual stock/bond portfolio?	20-18

Choosing an Investment Advisor

Q 20:35	What are the different investment manager styles?	20-19
Q 20:36	How is the performance of an investment manager or mutual fund reviewed?	20-21
Q 20:37	How does an investor evaluate the costs of an investment manager or a mutual fund in view of the performance of the portfolio?	20-22
Q 20:38	What factors should be considered in deciding whether to hire an investment manager or use mutual funds?	20-22
Q 20:39	Why not use certificates of deposit or other investments provided by banks?	20-24
Q 20:40	What is the harm in earning less than the inflation rate if the money is safe?	20-24
Q 20:41	What is the difference between mutual funds purchased from a broker and those purchased directly from the fund company?	20-25
Q 20:42	Why would a broker recommend an investment manager?	20-25
Q 20:43	Why pay a wrap fee?	20-26
Q 20:44	Are bonds purchased commission-free?	20-26
Q 20:45	When should investors pick individual stocks for a portfolio?	20-27
Q 20:46	How can a portfolio be diversified?	20-27
Q 20:47	What is the advantage of using pretax dollars for investing purposes?	20-28
Q 20:48	How does a financial planner differ from a stockbroker?	20-29
Q 20:49	How would an insurance agent assist with investments?	20-30
Q 20:50	What is the difference between a stockbroker who is also a consultant and other stockbrokers or individual consultants?	20-30
Q 20:51	Who can be a trustee?	20-31
Q 20:52	What is the advantage of having fees unbundled?	20-31
Q 20:53	Should a broker be granted discretion on an account?	20-32
Q 20:54	What are soft-dollar fees?	20-32
Q 20:55	What are sectors, and where are they found?	20-33

List of Questions

Chapter 21 Business Transfers

Overview

Q 21:1 Why are business transfers important to retirement and estate planning? ... 21-2
Q 21:2 What is basis? ... 21-2

ESOPs

Q 21:3 How can an ESOP be used in succession planning? ... 21-2

Sales to Outsiders

Q 21:4 How can a transfer of the business to an outside party be structured? ... 21-5
Q 21:5 Is a stock sale preferable to an asset sale? ... 21-5
Q 21:6 How is a sale of stock taxed? ... 21-6
Q 21:7 Is an exchange of stock preferable to an asset or stock sale? ... 21-7
Q 21:8 Can a buyer obtain an increased basis with a stock sale? ... 21-7
Q 21:9 What can be done with unwanted assets in a business? ... 21-8
Q 21:10 What other items need to be considered in selling a family business? ... 21-9
Q 21:11 When selling a business, what are the advantages of creating a family limited partnership? ... 21-9

Buyouts

Q 21:12 What constitutes an inside group? ... 21-9
Q 21:13 How is a buyout used to sell the business to insiders? ... 21-10
Q 21:14 What kinds of devices can be used to pay the departing owner? ... 21-10
Q 21:15 How is a noncompete agreement used in an insider buyout? ... 21-10
Q 21:16 How is a nonqualified deferred compensation arrangement used in an insider buyout? ... 21-11
Q 21:17 How can employment agreements and consulting agreements be used in an insider buyout? ... 21-11
Q 21:18 How can a rabbi trust be used in an insider buyout? ... 21-11

Stock Redemptions and Direct Sales of Stock

Q 21:19 What are the tax effects of a stock redemption? ... 21-12

lxvii

Estate and Retirement Planning Answer Book

Q 21:20	What are the advantages of a stock redemption?	21-12
Q 21:21	What is family attribution?	21-13

Stock Sales

Q 21:22	What is a direct sale of stock?	21-13
Q 21:23	What advantages does a direct sale of stock have over a stock redemption?	21-13
Q 21:24	What arrangements should be made for the stock of a key employee if the key employee dies, becomes disabled, or terminates employment?	21-13

Sales of Assets

Q 21:25	Should all assets be sold in an asset sale?	21-14
Q 21:26	How is an asset purchase financed?	21-14
Q 21:27	How is goodwill treated in an asset sale?	21-14
Q 21:28	What happens if assets are sold that were depreciated under an accelerated method?	21-15
Q 21:29	What are the advantages of an asset sale?	21-15
Q 21:30	How can a tax-qualified retirement plan be used with an asset sale?	21-15
Q 21:31	What are the income tax consequences if a sale of corporate assets is followed by a liquidation of the selling corporation?	21-16
Q 21:32	What alternatives to liquidation exist if a C corporation sells its assets?	21-17
Q 21:33	Should a C corporation be converted to an S corporation if it is contemplated that the C corporation will sell its assets?	21-17

Stock Split-Offs and Spin-Offs

Q 21:34	What is a stock split-off?	21-19
Q 21:35	How can a split-off help in succession planning?	21-20
Q 21:36	What is a stock spin-off?	21-20
Q 21:37	How can spin-offs be used to reduce estate taxes?	21-21

List of Questions

Chapter 22 Individual Retirement Accounts and Simplified Employee Pensions

Individual Retirement Accounts

Q 22:1	What are individual retirement accounts?	22-1
Q 22:2	What requirements must a plan meet to qualify as an individual retirement account?	22-2
Q 22:3	Who is eligible to establish an individual retirement account?	22-2
Q 22:4	When may someone establish an individual retirement account?	22-3
Q 22:5	What limits apply to contributions to an individual retirement account?	22-3
Q: 22:6	Does an individual retirement account have to be standardized?	22-4
Q 22:7	What is the annual individual retirement account deduction limit?	22-4
Q 22:8	What are the advantages of making tax-deductible individual retirement account contributions?	22-6
Q 22:9	Is an individual retirement account available for a nonworking spouse?	22-7
Q 22:10	How are excess individual retirement account contributions treated?	22-7
Q 22:11	How are individual retirement accounts funded?	22-8
Q 22:12	How may individual retirement account funds be invested?	22-9
Q 22:13	When must distributions from an individual retirement account begin?	22-9
Q 22:14	How are distributions from an individual retirement account taxed?	22-10
Q 22:15	Does a penalty apply to early withdrawals from an individual retirement account?	22-10
Q 22:16	Are there any exceptions to the 10 percent penalty for early withdrawals from an individual retirement account?	22-11
Q 22:17	What is an individual retirement account rollover?	22-12
Q 22:18	What are the tax effects if part of an individual's individual retirement account balance is transferred to his or her spouse as a result of divorce?	22-13
Q 22:19	Can an irrevocable trust be a designated individual retirement account beneficiary without causing gift tax?	22-13

Estate and Retirement Planning Answer Book

Simplified Employee Pensions

Q 22:20	What is a simplified employee pension?	22-13
Q 22:21	Which employees must be covered by a simplified employee pension?	22-14
Q 22:22	Must a simplified employee pension cover employees other than those of the sponsoring employer?	22-15
Q 22:23	What contributions can be made to a simplified employee pension?	22-15
Q 22:24	What is a salary-reduction simplified employee pension? .	22-15
Q 22:25	Can employees who participate in a simplified employee pension also contribute to an individual retirement account?	22-16
Q 22:26	How are distributions from a simplified employee pension made?	22-16
Q 22:27	Can a simplified employee pension provide a lump-sum distribution?	22-16
Q 22:28	Can an employee roll over funds from a simplified employee pension to another individual retirement account?	22-16

Chapter 23 Distributions from Tax-Qualified Retirement Plans

Overview

Q 23:1	Are distributions from tax-qualified plans treated more favorably than distributions from other plans?	23-2
Q 23:2	Can an employee withdraw benefits from his or her vested account at any time without being subject to a penalty? .	23-2
Q 23:3	Does the exception for distributions to employees who separate from service after age 55 apply even if the employee later returns to employment with the same employer? . .	23-4

Distributions at Termination of Employment

Q 23:4	How are distributions at retirement or earlier termination of employment taxed?	23-4
Q 23:5	How are distributions taxed under Code Section 72? . . .	23-5
Q 23:6	Is the exclusion ratio ever redetermined?	23-6
Q 23:7	Was there a time when the exclusion ratio did not apply to annuity payments?	23-7
Q 23:8	What type of payments are considered annuities?	23-7

lxx

List of Questions

Q 23:9	When must an employer's contribution be included in an annuitant's income?	23-7
Q 23:10	If an employee is given an option to receive a lump-sum payment or an annuity, how much is includible in the employee's income for the year in which the offer is made?	23-7
Q 23:11	Are there any exceptions to the harsh inclusion requirements referred to above?	23-8
Q 23:12	How long must the option to take payments as an annuity be irrevocable for this exception to apply?	23-8
Q 23:13	What is the simplified safe harbor exclusion ratio?	23-8
Q 23:14	Will the simplified safe harbor exclusion ratio comply with Code Section 72?	23-8
Q 23:15	Who qualifies for the simplified safe harbor exclusion ratio?	23-8
Q 23:16	What qualifications must a taxpayer meet in order to use the simplified safe harbor exclusion ratio?	23-9
Q 23:17	How is the simplified safe harbor exclusion ratio determined?	23-9
Q 23:18	Is the simplified safe harbor exclusion ratio modified for changes in the annuity payments such as cost-of-living increases?	23-9
Q 23:19	What if the amount determined to be excluded under the simplified safe harbor method is greater than the annuity payment received?	23-9
Q 23:20	How is the excludable portion determined under the simplified safe harbor exclusion ratio when an annuity has more than one beneficiary?	23-10
Q 23:21	How is the investment in the contract determined under the simplified safe harbor exclusion method?	23-10
Q 23:22	May the investment in the contract be increased by any method other than payments to the annuity?	23-10
Q 23:23	How does a taxpayer elect to use the simplified method?	23-10
Q 23:24	How is the total number of monthly expected payments determined?	23-11
Q 23:25	Once the election to use the simplified method is made, may the taxpayer later decide to use the actual calculation of the exclusion ratio or vice versa?	23-11
Q 23:26	How does a taxpayer change from using the simplified exclusion method to the actual exclusion method?	23-11
Q 23:27	How is the value of the taxpayer's annuity determined?	23-11
Q 23:28	Do payments contributed to an annuity by an employer on behalf of a self-employed individual count as investments in the contract?	23-11

Estate and Retirement Planning Answer Book

Q 23:29	How is investment under the contract allocated when a portion of plan benefits is paid out pursuant to a QDRO?	23-12
Q 23:30	How are amounts received before the annuity starting date taxed?	23-12
Q 23:31	How are non-annuity payments received after the annuity starting date treated for tax purposes?	23-13
Q 23:32	How are increases in annuity payments from tax-qualifed trusts after the annuity starting date taxed?	23-13

Lump-Sum Distributions

Q 23:33	What is a lump-sum distribution for purposes of income averaging?	23-13
Q 23:34	What interest rates are used to calculate lump sums?	23-14
Q 23:35	What is the effect on pension plans of the rules using the 30-year Treasury bond rate in determining the amount to be paid out in a single-sum distribution?	23-14
Q 23:36	What is five-year forward income averaging, and when can a forward averaging election be made?	23-15

Rollover Distributions

Q 23:37	Is a distribution from an eligible retirement plan always taxed in the year it is distributed?	23-15
Q 23:38	What is a rollover?	23-16
Q 23:39	What is the definition of an eligible rollover distribution?	23-16
Q 23:40	What is an eligible retirement plan?	23-17
Q 23:41	What is the maximum amount a recipient may roll over?	23-17
Q 23:42	What is the time limit for making a rollover?	23-18
Q 23:43	If a deceased employee's spouse receives a distribution after the employee's death, is the distribution eligible for rollover treatment?	23-18
Q 23:44	Must a participant actually receive a distribution and roll it over to obtain rollover treatment?	23-18
Q 23:45	What are the advantages of a direct transfer from a tax-qualified plan compared to those of a rollover?	23-19

Required Distributions

Q 23:46	What rules govern the timing of plan distributions?	23-19
Q 23:47	When must a participant's distributions begin?	23-20
Q 23:48	What is the time frame for making distributions from a tax-qualified plan?	23-20

List of Questions

Q 23:49 What is the required beginning date for plan distributions? **23-21**

Designation of Beneficiaries

Q 23:50 What factors should be considered in naming beneficiaries for tax-qualified plans? **23-21**

Q 23:51 Who can be a designated beneficiary? **23-21**

Q 23:52 Can a plan provide for discretionary payments among multiple beneficiaries? **23-22**

Q 23:53 When must separate accounts for each beneficiary be established? **23-23**

Q 23:54 Does an employee have an absolute right to designate a beneficiary? **23-23**

Q 23:55 What is the applicable date for determining a designated beneficiary? **23-23**

Q 23:56 May designated beneficiaries be changed after the required beginning date? **23-24**

Q 23:57 Can plans provide each beneficiary with an election regarding the period of distribution? **23-24**

Applicable Life Expectancies

Q 23:58 What life expectancy is used to determine the distribution period if a spouse, the designated beneficiary, dies on or after the applicable date for determining the distribution period? **23-25**

Q 23:59 How is the time frame for installment payments determined for the taxpayer? **23-25**

Payments Following Death

Q 23:60 What happens if a participant dies after his or her benefits commence? **23-25**

Q 23:61 When are benefits deemed to commence? **23-27**

Q 23:62 What if an employee dies before his or her benefit payments under a tax-qualified retirement plan commence? **23-28**

Q 23:63 How is the five-year rule applied when there are designated beneficiaries and charitable beneficiaries? **23-29**

Q 23:64 Is a participant constructively receiving income because of a plan's provision specifying that a discretionary power that allows a plan to provide that between a participant's *normal retirement date* and the April 1 of the calendar year following the participant's age 70½, a participant can request and receive ad hoc payments? **23-30**

lxxiii

Estate and Retirement Planning Answer Book

Recalculation of Life Expectancy

Q 23:65 Can a participant's or spouse's life expectancy be recalculated? **23-31**

Q 23:66 Why would one want to recaluate life expectancies? ... **23-31**

Q 23:67 Can the life expectancy of a non-spouse designated beneficiary be recalculated? **23-31**

Q 23:68 How is the life expectancy of the designated beneficiary determined when the designated beneficiary is not the participant's spouse? **23-31**

Q 23:69 If recalculation is elected, what effect does the participant's or spouse's death have on distribution? **23-31**

Q 23:70 What is the result of the death of both the participant and the spouse on recalculating life expectancies? **23-32**

Minimum Distribution Individual Benefit Requirement

Q 23:71 Is there any restriction limiting a qualified plan's payment of nonretirement benefits such as life, accident, or health benefits? **23-32**

Q 23:72 What does the preretirement incidental benefit requirement do? **23-32**

Q 23:73 What does the minimum distribution individual benefit requirement do? **23-32**

Q 23:74 How does the minimum distribution individual benefit requirement work? **23-33**

Q 23:75 If there is more than one beneficiary, how is the difference in age determined for purposes of the minimum distribution individual benefit requirement? **23-34**

Q 23:76 Under Proposed Treasury Regulations Section 1.401(a)(9)-2, what is the effect on the minimum distribution individual benefit percentage requirement of adding a new, younger beneficiary? **23-34**

Q 23:77 What if the annuitant and the annuitant's spouse are divorced and the court orders that a portion of the employee's annuity payments are to be paid to the spouse under a qualified domestic relations order? **23-34**

Excise Tax

Q 23:78 What tax penalites are imposed for failure to adhere to the minimum distribution requirements? **23-34**

List of Questions

Special Cases

Q 23:79	What tax rules apply to the distribution of employer securities from a qualified plan?	23-35
Q 23:80	How are distributions of life insurance proceeds taxed?	23-35
Q 23:81	May a plan participant obtain a loan from a tax-qualified plan?	23-35
Q 23:82	Are loans made to participants from a tax-qualified plan under Code Section 401(a) treated as distributions?	23-36
Q 23:83	Is it true that even if an exclusion applies, a taxpayer may later be required to treat the loan as a distribution?	23-37

Witholding and Notices

Q 23:84	What is a designated distribution for purposes of the income tax withholding provisions of Code Section 3405(c)(1)?	23-37
Q 23:85	Is a participant's consent needed before a tax-qualified plan may pay out benefits?	23-38
Q 23:86	Are distributions from tax-qualified retirement plans subject to the withholding provisions of Code Section 3405(c)?	23-39
Q 23:87	What notice requirements apply to plan distributions?	23-39
Q 23:88	What must this notice include?	23-40
Q 23:89	May a participant waive the 30-day or 90-day notice requirements associated with plan distributions?	23-40

Survivor Annuity Requirements

Q 23:90	What is the purpose of the survivor annuity requirements?	23-41
Q 23:91	What types of plans are subject the rules of the Retirement Equity Act of 1984?	23-41
Q 23:92	May distribution deviate from a statutory QPSA?	23-41
Q 23:93	When must the QJSA benefit be available?	23-42
Q 23:94	In a QJSA, when must the participant's waiver and the spouse's consent be made to be effective?	23-42
Q 23:95	Are alternatives to the QJSA available that allow the flexibility to change beneficiaries and the form of payment after the annuity starting date?	23-42
Q 23:96	Are payments made during the life of the participant subject to QJSA rules?	23-42
Q 23:97	Are there any special considerations for defined contribution plans subject to the REA statutory annuity rules?	23-43
Q 23:98	May a spouse choose the form of distribution under a deferred contribution plan subject to the REA rules?	23-43

Estate and Retirement Planning Answer Book

Q 23:99	Is spousal consent to the QPSA or QJSA waiver revocable or irrevocable?	23-43
Q 23:100	Is it necessary in a qualified joint and survivor annuity for a waiver/consent form to specify the optional form of benefit?	23-43
Q 23:101	Is a waiver/consent required to specify an optional form of benefit in a QPSA?	23-43
Q 23:102	What is a general consent?	23-44
Q 23:103	Can a general consent be limited?	23-44
Q 23:104	Is a general consent available when the designated beneficiary is a trust?	23-44
Q 23:105	Is spousal consent necessary for direct rollover to another qualified plan to an IRA?	23-44
Q 23:106	Do rollover contributions subject the transferee plan to the survivor annuity requirements?	23-45
Q 23:107	Are profit sharing plans subject to the REA, QPSA, and QJSA rules?	23-45
Q 23:108	Is spousal consent necessary for the profit sharing plans that are not subject to the QPSA and QJSA rules to make distributions to a participant or to make plan loans? . . .	23-45
Q 23:109	When can the death benefit under profit sharing plan that is not subject to the QPSA and QJSA rules be waived? . .	23-45
Q 23:110	What must the waiver/consent under a nonsubject profit sharing plan that is not subject to the QPSA and QJSA rules state?	23-46
Q 23:111	Does naming a trust as a beneficiary satisfy the specificity requirement of Treasury Regulations Section 1.401(a)-20 Q&A-33(b)?	23-46
Q 23:112	Is there a notice requirement with regard to the spousal consent for a waiver for a profit sharing plan that is not subject to the QPSA and QJSA rules?	23-46

Estate Planning

Q 23:113	Does the gross estate of an employee include the value of distributions (other than life insurance proceeds) from a tax-qualified plan made to a beneficiary?	23-46
Q 23:114	Are life insurance proceeds payable under a policy on a qualified participant's life includible in such participant's gross estate?	23-47

List of Questions

Chapter 24 Distributions from Nonqualified Plans

Overview

Q 24:1	How are distributions from nonqualified deferred compensation arrangements taxed?	24-1

Contractual Right to Future Payments

Q 24:2	How is a participant taxed under a deferred compensation arrangement consisting only of a contractual right to future payments?	24-2
Q 24:3	If an employee participates in a deferred compensation arrangement consisting only of contractual rights to future payments, can he or she elect to defer a portion of salary prior to the beginning of the taxable year?	24-2
Q 24:4	When is an employee in constructive receipt of income?	24-2

Trust Payments

Q 24:5	Is an employee taxed on employer contributions made to a nonqualified trust?	24-3
Q 24:6	How is an employee taxed when he or she receives distributions from a nonqualified trust?	24-3

Chapter 25 Protection of Retirement Income

Qualified Retirement Plan Assets

Q 25:1	Can qualified retirement plan assets be reached by judgment creditors?	25-2
Q 25:2	What is asset protection?	25-2
Q 25:3	What is a fraudulent transfer?	25-2
Q 25:4	What are the most common methods used to protect assets?	25-3
Q 25:5	How effective is a gift as a means of protecting an asset?	25-3
Q 25:6	How does a gift in trust protect assets?	25-4
Q 25:7	How do co-tenancies protect assets?	25-4
Q 25:8	How does the homestead exemption protect assets?	25-4
Q 25:9	How does an annuity protect assets?	25-5
Q 25:10	Can qualified retirement plan assets be reached by judgment creditors?	25-5
Q 25:11	Can qualified retirement plan assets be reached if a participant is bankrupt?	25-5

lxxvii

Estate and Retirement Planning Answer Book

Q 25:12 Can the qualified retirement plan benefits of the sole owner of a business be reached in bankruptcy proceedings? . . 25-6

IRA Assets

Q 25:13 Are IRA assets protected from creditors? 25-6
Q 25:14 What is the effect of a judgment creditor reaching IRA assets or qualified plan benefits? 25-6
Q 25:15 How does life insurance protect assets? 25-7
Q 25:16 How can a limited liability company be used to protect assets? 25-7
Q 25:17 Can qualified retirement plan assets be reached by a bankruptcy trustee? 25-7
Q 25:18 Operating under its escheat laws, may a state take the unclaimed account balance of a plan participant? 25-7
Q 25:19 What exceptions exist to the rule that plan assets may not be attached? 25-8
Q 25:20 What requirements must a domestic relations order meet to qualify as an exception to the rule that plan assets may not be attached? 25-8
Q 25:21 Who determines whether a domestic relations order is a qualified domestic relations order? 25-9
Q 25:22 Which plans are subject to the laws concerning qualified domestic relations orders? 25-10
Q 25:23 What does a qualified domestic relations order do? 25-10
Q 25:24 Who can be an alternate payee? 25-10
Q 25:25 When does a qualified domestic relations order make payments? 25-10
Q 25:26 May a qualified domestic relations order require payment of the participant's entire plan account? 25-10
Q 25:27 Who pays the income taxes due on qualified domestic relations order distributions? 25-11
Q 25:28 Are qualified domestic relations order payments exempt from the 10 percent premature distribution penalties? 25-11
Q 25:29 Can qualified domestic relations order payments be rolled over? 25-11
Q 25:30 Do the mandatory income tax withholding rules apply to qualified domestic relations order distributions? 25-11
Q 25:31 What happens to qualified domestic relations order payments pledged to prior payees if a second divorce occurs? 25-12
Q 25:32 May a participant be charged for the administrative costs of a qualified domestic relations order? 25-12

List of Questions

Q 25:33	If the retirement plan participant dies, should the participant's former spouse be treated as the participant's surviving spouse for joint and survivor and preretirement survivor annuity purposes?	25-12
Q 25:34	What actions should the plan administrator take if a domestic relations order is received by the plan?	25-13
Q 25:35	What procedures must be established to handle domestic relations orders?	25-13
Q 25:36	What fiduciary duties apply with respect to the processing of domestic relations orders?	25-14

Life Insurance Proceeds

Q 25:37	Are life insurance proceeds exempt from creditors?	25-14

Fraudulent Conveyances

Q 25:38	What are fraudulent conveyance laws?	25-14
Q 25:39	How can an intent to defraud be established?	25-15
Q 25:40	How are subsequent creditors protected?	25-15

Chapter 26 Incapacity and Other Retirement Issues

Overview

Q 26:1	Why is the possibility of incapacity an important issue in retirement planning?	26-1
Q 26:2	What is the cost of long-term health care?	26-2
Q 26:3	What kind of estate planning can be done to prepare for a person entering a nursing home?	26-2
Q 26:4	What estate planning can be done to mitigate the financial impact of catastrophic illness or accident?	26-2

Living Wills

Q 26:5	What is a living will?	26-3

Durable Powers of Attorney

Q 26:6	What is a durable power of attorney?	26-3
Q 26:7	What can durable powers of attorney be used for?	26-4
Q 26:8	What are medical durable powers of attorney?	26-4

Estate and Retirement Planning Answer Book

Q 26:9	What requirements must a durable power of attorney meet to be valid?	26-4
Q 26:10	Are there limits on the scope of durable powers of attorney?	26-4
Q 26:11	Can durable powers of attorney result in the imposition of gift or estate tax on the agent?	26-4
Q 26:12	Must any special steps be taken if the durable power of attorney covers life insurance?	26-5
Q 26:13	What are the disadvantages of durable powers of attorney?	26-5
Q 26:14	What are the reasons for creating a living trust?	26-5

Revocable Trusts

Q 26:15	Do revocable trusts have advantages in meeting the needs of individuals in nursing homes?	26-6
Q 26:16	Do revocable trusts have to be funded immediately?	26-6
Q 26:17	What is the income tax treatment of a revocable trust?	26-6
Q 26:18	What is the estate and gift tax treatment of a revocable trust?	26-7
Q 26:19	How should a revocable trust be funded for a person who may go into a nursing home?	26-7
Q 26:20	Who should be the trustee for a living trust?	26-7
Q 26:21	Should a co-trustee be named for a revocable trust?	26-8

Long-Term Health Care Insurance

Q 26:22	What is long-term health care insurance?	26-8
Q 26:23	What issues should be examined when considering long-term health care insurance?	26-8

Medicaid Planning for Institutionalization

Q 26:24	What is Medicaid planning?	26-9
Q 26:25	How do Medicare and Medicaid differ?	26-9
Q 26:26	Is Medicare limited, or does it pay for all of an individual's nursing home expenses?	26-10
Q 26:27	What conditions must an individual meet to qualify for Medicare coverage?	26-10
Q 26:28	How is Medicaid administered?	26-11
Q 26:29	Who is covered by Medicaid?	26-11
Q 26:30	What benefits are provided under Medicaid?	26-11
Q 26:31	What resources are excluded in determining whether a person is entitled to Medicaid?	26-12
Q 26:32	What are 1634 states for Medicaid purposes?	26-13

List of Questions

Q 26:33	What is the lookback rule?	26-13
Q 26:34	How do transfers of property affect Medicaid eligibility?	26-14
Q 26:35	How is the number of months of Medicaid ineligibility determined?	26-14
Q 26:36	What is the starting date of the lookback period?	26-15
Q 26:37	Are any transfers excluded from affecting Medicaid eligibility?	26-15
Q 26:38	Are the assets of both spouses considered in determining whether the institutionalized spouse satisfies the resource limitation?	26-16
Q 26:39	What can be done to protect the noninstitutionalized spouse from impoverishment?	26-17
Q 26:40	What rules apply in determining whether the assets of a trust will be treated as a resource of the beneficiary?	26-17
Q 26:41	What are Medicaid qualifying trusts?	26-18
Q 26:42	What makes a fund available for Medicaid purposes?	26-18
Q 26:43	What effect does an individual retirement account or Keogh plan have on Medicaid eligibility?	26-18
Q 26:44	Are tax-qualified plans treated differently than individual retirement accounts for purposes of Medicaid eligibility?	26-19
Q 26:45	Is a testamentary trust a Medicaid qualifying trust?	26-19
Q 26:46	What must be done to make an individual eligible for Medicaid?	26-19
Q 26:47	How is a person's Medicaid eligibility determined?	26-20
Q 26:48	What planning should be done to obtain Medicaid eligibility?	26-20
Q 26:49	What reasons exist for not transferring assets to become eligible for Medicaid?	26-20
Q 26:50	What asset planning can be done prior to institutionalization?	26-21
Q 26:51	What techniques can be used to transfer assets if institutionalization is expected?	26-21
Q 26:52	What gift tax consequences may occur in connection with property transfers?	26-23
Q 26:53	What are Medicaid estate recovery programs?	26-23

Estate Planning for Institutionalization

Q 26:54	If a spouse is expected to be institutionalized, what are the estate planning considerations?	26-23

Estate and Retirement Planning Answer Book

Chapter 27 Estate Planning for Qualified Retirement Plan Benefits

Overview

Q 27:1	What are the key estate planning considerations for qualified retirement plan benefits?	27-2
Q 27:2	What is the basic tax treatment of benefits payable on death from tax-qualified retirement plans?	27-2
Q 27:3	Are any benefits from tax-qualified plans and individual retirement accounts exempt from estate tax?	27-3
Q 27:4	How should income tax on the plan benefits be handled?	27-4

Estate Planning Before Retirement

Q 27:5	What estate planning should occur before retirement for qualified retirement plan benefits?	27-4
Q 27:6	What is a qualified preretirement survivor annuity?	27-5

Qualified Joint and Survivor Annuity

Q 27:7	What is a qualified joint and survivor annuity?	27-6
Q 27:8	What exemptions are available from the qualified preretirement survivor annuity and qualified joint and survivor annuity requirements of the REA?	27-7
Q 27:9	What is the annuity starting date, and what does it mean with respect to the frequency of waivers?	27-8
Q 27:10	What is the effect of a divorce on benefit elections made by a participant and on the qualified joint and survivor annuity protections?	27-8
Q 27:11	When must a waiver be signed?	27-8
Q 27:12	Can a spousal consent to a waiver of benefits be irrevocable?	27-9
Q 27:13	What constitutes a valid spousal consent?	27-10
Q 27:14	Is spousal consent necessary if the spouse cannot be located?	27-10
Q 27:15	What happens if the non-spouse beneficiary is a trust?	27-10
Q 27:16	What is a general consent?	27-11
Q 27:17	What is a limited general consent?	27-11
Q 27:18	Does a spousal consent to a waiver of REA rights constitute a taxable gift?	27-11

List of Questions

Q 27:19	What prenuptial planning can be done with respect to the qualified joint and survivor annuity and the qualified preretirement survivor annuity?	**27-12**
Q 27:20	What are the advantages of having the spouse as the death beneficiary of a tax-qualified retirement plan?	**27-12**
Q 27:21	Under what circumstances is the marital deduction available?	**27-13**
Q 27:22	Can a qualified retirement plan meet the requirements for a qualified terminable interest property or other marital deduction trust?	**27-14**
Q 27:23	Is the 15 percent estate tax on excess retirement accumulations deductible from the decedent's taxable estate?	**27-15**
Q 27:24	How can a surviving spouse avoid the excise tax on excess retirement plan accumulations or excess distributions relating to the decedent spouse?	**27-15**
Q 27:25	Should a marital trust be the named beneficiary?	**27-16**
Q 27:26	Should a credit shelter trust be named as primary beneficiary of a qualified retirement plan?	**27-17**
Q 27:27	Can a spouse be named as primary beneficiary and a credit shelter trust be named as contingent beneficiary so the spouse can disclaim whatever amounts are needed to fund the credit shelter trust?	**27-17**
Q 27:28	When must a disclaimer be made?	**27-17**
Q 27:29	Can qualified plan assets be paid to an irrevocable trust?	**27-18**
Q 27:30	What income tax concerns exist if a retirement plan death benefit is paid in installments to a marital deduction trust?	**27-18**
Q 27:31	Why make a child or grandchild the beneficiary of a tax-qualified retirement plan?	**27-18**
Q 27:32	Should a charitable organization be the beneficiary of a qualified retirement plan?	**27-19**
Q 27:33	Is it advantageous to name a charity in the plan participant's will as a beneficiary?	**27-19**
Q 27:34	Can a charitable organization be named a beneficiary of a portion of the plan benefits and individuals be named as beneficiaries of the remaining benefits?	**27-19**
Q 27:35	Can plan assets be paid to a charitable remainder trust?	**27-20**

Estate Planning Considerations at Retirement

Q 27:36	What estate planning should be done at retirement?	27-21

lxxxiii

Estate and Retirement Planning Answer Book

Q 27:37	What is the maximum permissible payout period for retirement plan benefits?	27-21
Q 27:38	What is the maximum payout period for retirement plan benefits if the spouse is the beneficiary?	27-22
Q 27:39	What are the advantages of electing not to recompute either spouse's life expectancy?	27-22
Q 27:40	What happens if the participant's life expectancy is recomputed and the spouse's life expectancy is not recomputed?	27-22
Q 27:41	What life expectancy applies if a trust is the beneficiary for qualified retirement plan benefits?	27-23
Q 27:42	Why is a child or grandchild named as beneficiary of a tax-qualified retirement plan?	27-24

Estate Planning Considerations at Death

Q 27:43	What estate planning actions should be taken upon the participant's death?	27-24
Q 27:44	Are any special estate taxes imposed on tax-qualified retirement plan distributions?	27-25

Chapter 28 Estate Planning for Nonqualified Retirement Plans

Overview

Q 28:1	What is the basic tax treatment of benefits payable on death in nonqualified plans?	28-1

Treatment of Specific Benefits

Q 28:2	How is a straight life annuity treated for estate tax purposes?	28-2
Q 28:3	How is a participant's receipt of straight life annuity payments taxed?	28-2
Q 28:4	How are refund annuities, term annuities, and joint and survivor annuities treated for estate tax purposes?	28-2
Q 28:5	What happens if an employee dies before all deferred payments have been made under a deferred compensation arrangement?	28-3
Q 28:6	What estate tax treatment occurs under a contract that permits no deferred payments to be payable to the employee during his or her lifetime and permits only a death benefit to be payable to a named beneficiary?	28-3

List of Questions

Q 28:7	What are the tax effects where the insurance that funds a nonqualified plan is owned by the employer when the employee dies and the death benefits are paid to the employer?	28-4
Q 28:8	What are the tax effects where a nonqualified plan is funded by insurance, the insurance is owned by the employer when the employee dies, and the insurer pays the death benefits directly to the beneficiary?	28-5
Q 28:9	What should an employer do to help ensure that death benefits will not be taxable in an employee's estate?	28-5
Q 28:10	Does the fact that an employee owns stock in the employer corporation affect the taxability of death benefits?	28-6
Q 28:11	Does a contract that provides only a death benefit create a gift?	28-6
Q 28:12	When is a life estate includible in a decedent's gross estate?	28-7

Chapter 29 IRA Distributions

Taxation and Timing of Distributions

Q 29:1	Does the constructive receipt doctrine apply to IRAs?	29-1
Q 29:2	Are IRA distributions eligible for income averaging or capital gains treatment?	29-1
Q 29:3	Are IRA distributions fully includible in gross income?	29-2
Q 29:4	Are IRA distributions subject to an early-distribution excise tax?	29-2
Q 29:5	Are there any exceptions to the 10 percent additional tax on early distributions?	29-2
Q 29:6	Must an IRA owner receive distributions?	29-3
Q 29:7	What happens if an IRA owner fails to withdraw the minimum amount required by law?	29-3
Q 29:8	When must required distributions be made?	29-3
Q 29:9	What happens if a designated IRA beneficiary exists at the required beginning date?	29-4
Q 29:10	What are the minimum distribution requirements if no designated beneficiary exists at the required beginning date?	29-4
Q 29:11	How is the minimum distribution calculated for IRAs?	29-5
Q 29:12	Can life expectancies be recalculated?	29-5
Q 29:13	What happens if a beneficiary is added or substituted after the required beginning date?	29-5

Estate and Retirement Planning Answer Book

Q 29:14	How often must required minimum distributions be made?	29-5
Q 29:15	Can the required minimum distribution amount be rolled over into another IRA?	29-6
Q 29:16	Is the owner of several IRAs required to make minimum distributions from each IRA?	29-6
Q 29:17	Are withdrawals of excess IRA contributions subject to excise tax?	29-6
Q 29:18	Can excess contributions to IRAs be withdrawn after the date of the tax return?	29-7
Q 29:19	If the IRA owner dies, how are distributions made?	29-7
Q 29:20	Are distributions to IRA beneficiaries on account of death taxable?	29-7
Q 29:21	Must distributions to a death beneficiary be made at required times?	29-7
Q 29:22	Can an IRA lose its tax-exempt status for failing to make regular distributions?	29-8
Q 29:23	Are excess retirement accumulations in an IRA subject to excise tax?	29-9
Q 29:24	Can IRA beneficiaries disclaim their interest in an IRA?	29-9
Q 29:25	Can a transfer be made to an IRA owner's ex-spouse upon divorce without incurring federal income tax?	29-9
Q 29:26	Under what circumstances is an IRA owner treated as if a distribution is received even though no funds are paid?	29-9

Transfers and Rollovers

Q 29:27	What is a transfer between IRAs?	29-10
Q 29:28	What are the advantages of IRA-to-IRA transfers over rollovers?	29-10
Q 29:29	Are IRA-to-IRA transfers subject to the $2,000 annual contribution limit?	29-11
Q 29:30	Can funds be moved directly from a tax-qualified retirement plan to an IRA?	29-11
Q 29:31	Can distributions from tax-qualified retirement plans be rolled over to IRAs?	29-11
Q 29:32	What are the tax consequences if an eligible rollover distribution is not rolled over?	29-12
Q 29:33	What basic rules apply to IRA rollovers?	29-12
Q 29:34	Can rollovers from a tax-qualified retirement plan be made to several IRAs?	29-12
Q 29:35	Can IRA distributions be rolled over to other IRAs?	29-13

List of Questions

Q 29:36	Can distributions from an IRA be rolled over into a tax-qualified retirement plan, Section 403(a) annuity plan, or Section 403(b) tax-sheltered annuity?	29-13
Q 29:37	If property is sold in the 60-day period following distribution, can the proceeds of the sale be rolled over if the distribution is from an IRA?	29-13
Q 29:38	What is an inherited IRA?	29-13
Q 29:39	Can distributions from an inherited IRA be rolled over into another IRA or to a tax-qualified retirement plan?	29-14
Q 29:40	Can rollovers be made from a tax-qualified retirement plan into an IRA?	29-14
Q 29:41	When is the determination made as to whether a series of payments is a series of substantially equal payments?	29-15
Q 29:42	What happens if a payment is significantly larger than other payments in a series?	29-15
Q 29:43	What happens if a rollover fails to meet the legal requirements for rollovers?	29-16
Q 29:44	How are distributions made from a simplified employee pension taxed?	29-16
Q 29:45	How are rollovers from SEPs treated?	29-16

Savings Incentive Match Plans for Small Employers

Q 29:46	What is a savings incentive match plan?	29-16

Chapter 30 IRS Audits

Overview

Q 30:1	What is an IRS audit?	30-1
Q 30:2	Which estate tax returns are selected for audit?	30-2

Taxpayer's Response

Q 30:3	What rights do taxpayers have when audited?	30-2
Q 30:4	What is a taxpayer assistance order?	30-4
Q 30:5	How is a taxpayer assistance order obtained?	30-4
Q 30:6	Can a taxpayer obtain damages for unauthorized IRS actions?	30-4
Q 30:7	When should a taxpayer seek help if he or she is audited?	30-5

Estate and Retirement Planning Answer Book

Q 30:8	How should taxpayers approach an audit?	30-5

Contesting Additional Assessments

Q 30:9	How does an appeal within the IRS work?	30-5
Q 30:10	When must an appeal be filed with the IRS?	30-5
Q 30:11	What happens if the audit of an estate is settled?	30-6
Q 30:12	What factors does the IRS consider on appeal?	30-6
Q 30:13	Can the IRS reopen settled issues on appeal?	30-6
Q 30:14	Can the IRS raise a new issue on appeal?	30-6
Q 30:15	What is an offer in compromise?	30-7
Q 30:16	What courts handle federal tax disputes?	30-7
Q 30:17	What is the advantage of litigating in Tax Court?	30-7
Q 30:18	Does the Tax Court have a small tax case procedure? . . .	30-8
Q 30:19	Can a taxpayer represent himself or herself in Tax Court? .	30-8

Tax Returns

Q 30:20	If a return is being prepared that involves a gray area of taxation law, is there any way to know in advance whether the IRS will accept a particular position under specific facts?	30-8
Q 30:21	How is a copy of an individual's tax return or the information contained thereon for any given year obtained from the IRS?	30-9
Q 30:22	What should a taxpayer do to discover the total liability, penalties, interest, or payments made for any previous year?	30-9
Q 30:23	What should a taxpayer do if the taxpayer cannot locate tax information necessary to complete his or her tax return?	30-9
Q 30:24	What is the difference between an office examination and a field examination?	30-9
Q 30:25	How long after a return is filed may the IRS flag it for audit?	30-10
Q 30:26	How may a taxpayer prove that his or her return was filed by the yearly filing due date?	30-10

Tax Liability

Q 30:27	If a taxpayer agrees that he or she owes the taxes assessed by the IRS but is unable to pay the full amount, what are the options?	30-10
Q 30:28	Once a taxpayer establishes an installment payment agreement with the IRS, is the IRS bound by the agreement? .	30-11

List of Questions

Q 30:29	Once an installment agreement is defaulted on by the IRS, may it be reinstated?	30-11
Q 30:30	What is an IRS tax lien?	30-11
Q 30:31	When must a lien be released by the IRS?	30-11
Q 30:32	When may a taxpayer's assets be seized immediately without the usual administrative remedies?	30-12
Q 30:33	What is the advantage to filing a married filing separate return over a married filing joint return?	30-12
Q 30:34	When one spouse is responsible for income tax liability, can the other avoid liability?	30-12
Q 30:35	When a return has not been signed by one or both of the taxpayers, is the return considered filed?	30-12
Q 30:36	Will Chapter 7 bankruptcy remove a taxpayer's federal income tax liability?	30-12
Q 30:37	If the IRS prepares a return for a taxpayer based on informational returns it receives at year-end, may a taxpayer then file his or her own return?	30-13
Q 30:38	When a taxpayer is visited by a representative of the IRS who advises the taxpayer of his or her *Miranda* rights, should the taxpayer seek counsel?	30-13
Q 30:39	What is the Criminal Investigations Division of the IRS?	30-13
Q 30:40	What is an IRS levy?	30-13
Q 30:41	How is a release of a levy obtained?	30-13
Q 30:42	When a taxpayer dies leaving an estate and the beneficiaries are ready to close the estate but for the fact that the taxpayer did not file all of his or her returns, what options do the beneficiaries have in order to ensure that the IRS will not audit the returns after the estate is closed?	30-14
Q 30:43	What is the benefit of filing a return and paying the total liability due on its due date?	30-14
Q 30:44	If a taxpayer files a return under the guidance of his or her tax professional, who turns out to have advised the client incorrectly, does the taxpayer have any recourse?	30-14
Q 30:45	If a taxpayer receives a check from the IRS that he or she is not entitled to, what should the taxpayer do to avoid later liability?	30-14
Q 30:46	If a taxpayer filed an income tax return in one district, but later moved, does the taxpayer have to go to the area where the return was filed to be audited?	30-15
Q 30:47	May a taxpayer receive a tax refund for the current year even though he or she has an outstanding balance for an earlier year?	30-15

Q 30:48	If a taxpayer marries someone who owed a liability to the IRS from a year prior to the marriage, is the taxpayer liable, too?	30-15
Q 30:49	How long may the IRS pursue a taxpayer for the liability due?	30-15
Q 30:50	If a taxpayer submits a Form 433-A or Form 433-B, which is generally required for an installment agreement or offer in compromise, what risks does the taxpayer take?	30-15
Q 30:51	What benefit is served by Form 433-A or Form 433-B? . .	30-16
Q 30:52	If the taxpayer is about to reach the tenth year that the liability is due and the IRS levies the taxpayer's wages and demands an extension of the statute of limitations in order for the taxpayer to obtain a release, what should the taxpayer do?	30-16
Q 30:53	The Automatic Collections Service has a tendency to send the monthly installment payment vouchers too late for the taxpayer to make monthly payments on time. What can a taxpayer do to avoid a default?	30-16
Q 30:54	If a taxpayer is in the middle of an audit, does he or she have the right to request time to obtain counsel and a later appointment?	30-17
Q 30:55	If the taxpayer terminates an appointment with the IRS to obtain representation, does the taxpayer have to appear or may his or her representatives appear at the next appointment?	30-17
Q 30:56	If a taxpayer's liability is determined to be uncollectible, does this mean that the taxpayer will not be liable for the debt?	30-17
Q 30:57	What criteria does the IRS use in determining when it will abate a penalty?	30-17
Q 30:58	If the IRS refuses to abate a penalty, what options does a taxpayer have?	30-18
Q 30:59	What is the difference between an offer in compromise based on doubt as to liability and an offer in compromise based on doubt as to collectibility?	30-18
Q 30:60	What are the chances that an offer in compromise will be accepted by the IRS?	30-18
Q 30:61	How is the amount to be submitted with an offer in compromise determined?	30-18
Q 30:62	How are pension plans valued for purposes of an offer in compromise?	30-19
Q 30:63	How does the IRS value property owned as tenants by the entirety with a spouse who is not liable for the debt in determining the asset value for an offer in compromise?	30-19
Q 30:64	May an offer in compromise be rejected by the IRS after it is accepted?	30-19

List of Questions

Q 30:65	When can the IRS seize assets from a taxpayer's home?	30-19
Q 30:66	During the pendency of consideration of an offer in compromise, will collection activity such as levies and liens continue against the taxpayer?	30-20
Q 30:67	What safeguards should a taxpayer use when preparing for an audit by the IRS?	30-20
Q 30:68	May the IRS also tape-record the interview with the taxpayer?	30-20
Q 30:69	Where might a taxpayer obtain tax forms?	30-20
Q 30:70	If a taxpayer takes his or her case to the Tax Court, can the taxpayer recover costs such as attorneys' fees and litigation costs?	30-20
Q 30:71	How is a tax return selected for an audit?	30-21
Q 30:72	How may a taxpayer check on the status of his or her tax return?	30-21
Q 30:73	How may a taxpayer learn of the different types of penalties that may be assessed against him or her and the penalty rates that would apply?	30-21
Q 30:74	Is it true that the IRS takes factors such as level of education into account when determining whether reasonable cause exists in abating taxation penalties?	30-21
Q 30:75	How is the interest rate used by the IRS determined?	30-22
Q 30:76	What is the difference between simple and compound interest, and which does the IRS use?	30-22
Q 30:77	If a taxpayer timely files an extension, will interest accumulate on the liability that is eventually determined, even if good cause existed for not being able to file the return timely?	30-22
Q 30:78	If interest is compounded daily, does the running of interest stop on the date the payment of liability is sent or the date the payment is received?	30-22
Q 30:79	If a taxpayer is a non-filer, what are the benefits of voluntarily filing his or her returns with respect to installment payments?	30-22
Q 30:80	Is there an exception to the tax civil penalites for circumstances beyond the taxpayer's control?	30-23
Q 30:81	Can the IRS partially waive a penalty for failure to show reasonable cause?	30-23
Q 30:82	What standards apply to the reasonable cause exception?	30-23
Q 30:83	When and how should the taxpayer request abatement of the penalty?	30-23
Q 30:84	What is the reasonable cause standard?	30-24
Q 30:85	What are common reasons given as reasonable cause?	30-25

Chapter 31 Family Limited Partnerships

General Characteristics and Benefits

Q 31:1	What is a family limited partnership?	31-1
Q 31:2	What are the intended benefits of a family limited partnership?	31-2
Q 31:3	How does a family limited partnership achieve income shifting?	31-2
Q 31:4	What are the estate planning advantages of a family limited partnership?	31-3
Q 31:5	How does a family limited partnership facilitate a valuation discount?	31-3
Q 31:6	How vulnerable are partnerships to the attacks of creditors?	31-4
Q 31:7	How many partners may a family limited partnership have?	31-4

Exercising Control

Q 31:8	Who generally controls family limited partnerships?	31-4
Q 31:9	How much control in a family limited partnership can be retained by the donor?	31-5
Q 31:10	What do the Treasury regulations mean by *significant controls*?	31-5
Q 31:11	Can a minor be a member of a family limited partnership?	31-5
Q 31:12	Are there any restrictions on the types of property that can be transferred to a family limited partnership?	31-5
Q 31:13	Can a family limited partnership own life insurance?	31-6
Q 31:14	What is the difference between a general partner's liability and a limited partner's liability?	31-6

Transferability of Interests

Q 31:15	Is there free transferability of interests in a family limited partnership?	31-6
Q 31:16	How does the Internal Revenue Service determine whether a family limited partnership has more corporate than partnership characteristics?	31-7
Q 31:17	What is a capital interest in a partnership?	31-8
Q 31:18	How does the Internal Revenue Service view a partnership?	31-8
Q 31:19	How are family limited partnerships treated by the Internal Revenue Service?	31-8

List of Questions

Q 31:20	Can a partner in a family limited partnership simply assign the income for services or from income-producing property to another taxpayer?	31-9

Administrative Matters

Q 31:21	When does the Internal Revenue Service treat a partner as if he or she has received a distribution?	31-9
Q 31:22	What determines the taxable year of a partnership?	31-9
Q 31:23	What determines a family limited partnership's method of accounting?	31-10
Q 31:24	Does a partnership file a tax return?	31-10
Q 31:25	Does the Internal Revenue Service provide any other rules affecting FLPs other than those found in Code Section 702?	31-10
Q 31:26	How is the requirement that capital be a material income-producing factor satisfied?	31-11
Q 31:27	Is the determination of partnership status by the Internal Revenue Service binding on all members of the partnership?	31-11
Q 31:28	How does a gift transaction satisfy the complete transfer requirement for donees?	31-11
Q 31:29	How is ownership determined?	31-11
Q 31:30	Is the motive of the transfer determinative of ownership?	31-12
Q 31:31	What conduct on the part of the donee shows the donee's real ownership?	31-12
Q 31:32	What is a limited liability company?	31-12
Q 31:33	Can an limited liability company be used in the same way as an family limited partnership to create the same estate planning opportunities for discount valuations on transfers of minority interests?	31-12
Q 31:34	What effect, if any, do the anti-abuse rules announced by the IRS have on family limited partnerships?	31-13

Part I

Family Estate Planning

Chapter 1

The Accumulation and Preservation of Wealth

This book takes as its subject the accumulation and preservation of wealth, activities that are usually of special interest to both the executives of large corporations and the owners of small businesses. Despite the interest that these topics generally provoke, most people, including executives, do not begin to plan their estates until after they have begun to accumulate substantial assets. *Estate and Retirement Planning* contains financial and estate planning strategies that can provide individualized solutions to the special problems of accumulating and retaining sufficient assets for retirement and estate planning purposes.

Part I—Family Estate Planning discusses family estate planning in conjunction with pertinent principles of taxation: what the probate process consists of, the use of wills and trusts to bypass or reduce taxation, the reduction of the taxable estate of the donor through judicious lifetime gift giving to beneficiaries, how to take full advantage of the marital deduction by transferring estate assets to the surviving spouse, as well as the use of life insurance and annuity contracts. In short, **Part I—Family Estate Planning** provides a basic outline of the means available to individuals to defend their resources against the erosion of taxation. Among the many solutions provided in this section are the following:

- A wealthy individual can save up to $330,000 in estate taxes by giving $600,000 to his or her children (thus fully using the unified estate and gift tax exemption) and the remainder to his or her spouse, whose marital deduction permits the transfer of an unlimited amount of property.

- By removing assets from the estate before the death of the donor, the donor's taxable estate can be reduced, thus decreasing estate taxes at death. A donor may give up to $10,000 per year to any number of individuals who would otherwise be beneficiaries under the donor's will at death, thus reducing the taxable estate in his or her lifetime.

- Another important estate planning device involves the use of the marital deduction, which permits the transfer of an unlimited amount of property from one spouse to the other. If, however, a large amount of assets is transferred to the surviving spouse when the first spouse dies, high estate taxes may result when the second spouse dies. A bypass trust can be used to shield the estate of the second spouse from taxation.

- Whether the probate process should be circumvented by using alternatives such as life insurance, joint property interests, or revocable trusts is an important issue for most people. Probate is widely criticized because of its costs (legal fees and executor's commissions) and the risk of lengthy court proceedings; however, it may be the most workable option for some individuals. One alternative to probate is the purchase of life insurance by an irrevocable trust. Two other methods for distributing property and assets at death are revocable trusts and joint tenancies. The advantages and disadvantages of revocable trusts, one of the most frequently used devices for avoiding probate, are presented in detail.

This section closes with an examination of the many important estate planning decisions that must be made after death by the executor of the estate regarding the timing of tax returns and possible elections concerning them. In addition, the executor can reduce or minimize the tax burden on the estate and on the beneficiaries by a careful distribution of the assets.

Part II—Benefit Plans and Other Sources of Retirement Assets focuses on the various strategies that can be initiated as individuals accumulate wealth to help them preserve it. Included in this section are chapters discussing the different types of retirement plans: qualified, nonqualified, IRAs, SEPs, ESOPs, and

The Accumulation and Preservation of Wealth

other sources of retirement income. Many different aspects of estate and retirement planning are addressed, including the receipt of distributions by individuals under the full array of these plans. Situations that commonly arise for small business owners and/or executives include the following:

- Business owners and executives may need to choose between establishing tax-qualified or nonqualified retirement plans for themselves and their employees; tax-qualified plans offer an impressive array of potential tax advantages for both employers and employees, but can be expensive to set up. Nonqualified plans lack these tax advantages but are less expensive to establish and are extremely useful in retaining key employees.

- Small business owners may find it advantageous to establish employee stock ownership plans (ESOPs), a special type of tax-qualified plan that enables employees to invest in the business and provides a tax-free mechanism for transferring ownership. Special stock redemption provisions permit an estate to generate cash to cover estate taxes and administrative expenses without forcing the sale or liquidation of the business.

- Business owners may wish to use the sale or transfer of business ownership to generate retirement income; in fact, given the limits on benefits that may be provided by retirement plans, income from the sale of a business may be the primary source of an individual's retirement benefits.

Finally, **Part II—Benefit Plans and Other Sources of Retirement Assets** addresses the protection of accumulated wealth through the difficult situations associated with incapacity or medical emergency. Medical directives and durable powers of attorney allow individuals to designate the persons who will make important health-related decisions for them in the event of incapacity. These chapters contain explanations of the complex eligibility rules for qualifying for Medicaid, as well as financial and estate planning strategies to help keep an individual's entire resources from being spent on nursing home care. The section closes with discussion of a variety of issues that both executives and business owners need to be aware of: a special chapter highlights distributions from IRAs and actions to take in the event of an IRS audit.

Chapter 2

Wills, Revocable Trusts, and Other Alternatives

This chapter discusses the probate process: what it consists of, which property is subject to probate, and the advantages and disadvantages of having an estate pass through probate. It then describes various techniques for avoiding probate, including the use of joint tenancies and living trusts.

Overview	2-1
Probate	2-2
Joint Tenancies	2-12
Totten Trusts	2-21
Funded Revocable Living Trusts	2-21
Unfunded Revocable Trusts	2-30

Overview

Q 2:1 Why should an individual plan for the transfer of his or her assets in anticipation of death?

Many individuals are fearful of confronting their own mortality and therefore are reluctant to consider planning for the transfer of their assets after their deaths. As a result, such individuals leave no wills, make no lifetime transfers either to save currently on their income taxes or on the taxes ultimately to be paid by their estates, and generally do not concern themselves with how those they love will carry on after their deaths. Those individuals who die without a will permit the laws of the state of their domiciles to take over for the distribution of their assets.

Allowing a state to determine the distribution of one's assets is generally a careless and uneconomical method of seeing to an estate; however, it must be admitted that distributing assets is not an easy task. The process of planning for the disposition of one's estate—the drawing up of a last will and having it undergo the probate process or relying on alternative means of disposing of assets on death, such as living trusts or joint tenancies—often raises complex questions. Attention must be paid to the benefits as well as to the pitfalls of making an estate planning decision. Joint tenancies and revocable trusts, though often advantageous, both have disadvantages. The questions and answers that follow will explore all the opportunities that attach to the determination of ownership and ultimate transfer of property.

Probate

Q 2:2 What is probate?

Probate is the process by which a court (generally called a *surrogate's court*) validates the will of a deceased person by determining that the decedent was mentally competent and was under no duress at the time that he or she signed it and that the will was properly executed under the laws of the state in which the decedent was domiciled. Once these conditions have been satisfactorily proven (i.e., the will has been *probated*), the surrogate's court issues *letters testamentary* to the person or organization (such as a bank or trust company) that was named as the executor in the decedent's will. The letters testamentary provide notice to third parties dealing with the estate that the parties named therein are authorized to represent the decedent's estate in the conduct of its affairs.

Q 2:3 What is the difference between dying testate and intestate?

When an individual dies leaving a will, such individual is deemed to have died *testate,* thereby obligating the executors named in the will, after probate, to dispose of the decedent's estate as the decedent has directed in the provisions of the will.

When an individual dies without leaving a will, the individual is deemed to have died *intestate,* and an administrator is appointed by the surrogate's court to dispose of the decedent's property in accordance with the laws of distribution enacted by the state in which the decedent was domiciled. When an individual dies intestate, state laws control the disposition of his or her property, and whatever intentions the decedent may have entertained prior to death regarding the disposition of assets are of no relevance. Dying without leaving a will is undesirable because it allows the state, rather than the decedent, to determine how his or her assets should be conveyed. Furthermore, harsh tax consequences may arise for both the decedent's estate and the intended beneficiaries of the estate because no steps were taken prior to death to sidestep the imposition of estate taxes that the provisions in a will could have anticipated.

Q 2:4 How do the federal estate tax provisions affect the estate of the testate versus the intestate individual?

The federal estate tax provisions do not distinguish between a testate or an intestate estate; they are applied to an estate as it exists. The estate tax provisions determine which assets are includible in the gross estate of a decedent and the validity of the deductions that are available in ascertaining a taxable estate. It should be clear, therefore, that a carefully conceived estate plan, tailored to remove or reduce the value of assets from the gross estate and enlarge the available deductions, will permit the intended beneficiaries of a decedent's estate to enjoy more of the estate's assets unencumbered, wherever possible, by estate taxes.

Q 2:5 Should probate be used in every case where a decedent leaves a will?

No, not necessarily. In many cases, an individual dies owning only assets in joint name with right of ownership to the surviving joint tenant, insurance policies on his or her life made payable to designated persons or organizations (but not to the estate), retirement plan benefits payable to designated individuals, and contracts entered into during his or her life providing continuing benefits to designated beneficiaries in the event of death. None of the foregoing items is includible in a probate estate. Therefore, it would only cause an unnecessary expenditure of money to undergo probate when there would be no assets to probate. Sometimes, however, the family of the decedent is unaware, at the time of death, of assets that the decedent owned in his or her name and that only become known some time after death. The argument presented is that steps should be taken to anticipate this possibility by probating the will as soon as possible after death, while witnesses are alive (although probate procedures in all states do allow probate to proceed where deceased witnesses' signatures are properly corroborated) and the interested family members are actively involved. Probate expense under such circumstances is not necessarily prohibitive.

Q 2:6 What significance is attached to the domicile of an individual?

A *domicile* is generally defined as the place that an individual considers a permanent home and to which he or she intends to return whenever absent. Once established, a domicile continues until such person moves to a new location with the bona fide intention of making his or her fixed and permanent home there. The significance of a decedent's domicile lies in the fact that the state laws of his or her domicile control the administration of the estate and determine the validity of the provisions contained in the decendent's will. Dying intestate permits the state of the decedent's domicile to control the disposition of his or her assets. Other states can also enter the picture if assets, such as real estate, are located outside the domiciliary state. A process known as *ancillary* administration of the estate is then required in the other state. Domicile is also important in lifetime planning because the state of domicile generally is entitled to tax all the income of a taxpayer, wherever earned, allowing generally only a credit for taxes paid to other states on income earned there.

The following steps can be taken to establish domicile:

1. Register to vote in the desired state.
2. Apply for a certificate of domicile if the state issues one.

3. Transfer all bank accounts to the desired state of domicile.
4. Purchase all securities in the desired state of domicile and have them located in the broker's local office or in a safe deposit box in that state.
5. Address credit cards and correspondence to the appropriate office in the desired state of domicile.
6. Obtain a driver's license in the desired state of domicile.
7. Have Social Security checks mailed to a residential address in the desired state of domicile.

Q 2:7 What is the customary procedure involved in probating a will and administering the estate of a decedent?

The probate process varies from state to state and according to the size of an estate. Typically, a family member or an executor named in the will commences the process soon after the death of an individual by submitting to the surrogate's court a petition to probate (with the decedent's will attached). When the surrogate's court satisfies itself as to the validity of the will and its proper execution, it authorizes the executor named in the will to proceed with his or her (or its) duties as set forth in the will.

The executor gathers all of the decedent's assets and arranges for the payment of the debts of the decedent and the expenses of administering the estate. The executor usually retains a lawyer and an accountant, who perform the duties of probate, file the appropriate federal and state income and estate tax returns (and conduct a tax audit where that becomes necessary), and advise generally as to the proper management of the estate. When all liabilities of the estate are discharged, the executor may then make distributions of the remaining assets of the estate in the amounts and to the persons indicated in the decedent's will. Often, a formal accounting is filed in the surrogate's court that, when approved, will allow for the executor to be discharged from further responsibility in the management of the estate. It is at this time that the executor makes final distribution of the assets to the estate beneficiaries.

A less time-consuming and more economical approach used by many executors and estate beneficiaries is an informal accounting, which does not require the intrusion of the surrogate's court. In an informal accounting, the estate beneficiaries are given an accounting by the executor of the financial activities of the estate, and the estate beneficiaries, if satisfied with the accounting details, then execute releases to the executor relieving him or her from any liability to them or the estate. The executor, in turn, then arranges for the final distribution to the beneficiaries of the estate's net assets.

Q 2:8 If an individual's ownership of property is entirely by means of structures such as joint tenancies, revocable trusts, insurance, and other kinds of lifetime transfers not subject to probate, does it make any sense to have a will?

Yes. A last will should be drawn by every responsible person as a cover-all strategy to provide for the transfer of property that may be overlooked or forgotten in the estate planning process. Moreover, there is always the possibility that individuals owning property in joint name may die in a common disaster with no will available to control the ultimate disposition of the then jointly owned property. In retrospect, the drawing of a will may prove to have been unnecessary; however, careful planning requires that a property overlooked or forgotten have its future determined by a provision in the decedent's will and not by an intestacy provision.

Q 2:9 Are there simplified and less costly probate procedures for smaller estates?

Many states provide simple procedures requiring no lawyers, where the gross assets of the estate are less than $25,000. To cover these situations, the surrogate's court issues its own forms, written in lay language. Furthermore, the filing fees for probating the will are generally nominal.

Q 2:10 Which assets are subject to probate?

Assets in which the decedent has sole title are subject to probate. For example, if the decedent is the sole owner of certain stock certificates, the value of the stock certificates will be included in the decedent's probate estate. The following assets do not pass via probate:

1. Assets held in joint tenancy with right of survivorship;
2. Assets in a funded living trust, even though revocable; and
3. Assets disposed of by contracts, such as the proceeds of life insurance contracts.

Q 2:11 Are assets that are not subject to probate also excluded from the taxable estate?

No, not necessarily. An asset can be excluded from the decedent's probate estate (that is, the portion of a decedent's property and assets that passes via a court proceeding) but still may be included in the decedent's estate for estate tax purposes. For example, a decedent's joint tenancy interest in land (see Qs 2:27, 2:28, 2:40) will be excludable from the probate estate but will be includible in the taxable estate.

Actions taken to avoid probate do not necessarily result in a reduction of estate tax liability. This disparity occurs because the underlying purposes of probate and the estate tax system are different. The goal of the probate process is to distribute property that was held solely by the decedent. Because other laws provide, for example, for the distribution of joint tenancy property, probate does not concern itself with that type of asset.

The federal estate tax system, however, attempts to tax the estate of a decedent on all of the property in which he or she had any interest at death. For estate tax purposes, it makes no difference who will receive the property under the decedent's will. In order to determine what is to be included in the decedent's gross estate, the estate tax system examines the decedent's ownership interests immediately prior to death. As a result, the value of the decedent's interest in joint tenancy property is included in his or her gross estate even though, upon the decedent's death, it passed by operation of property law to the remaining joint tenants.

Q 2:12 Are contract proceeds subject to probate?

Contract proceeds (e.g., payments from a nonqualified deferred compensation arrangement) that are payable to a named beneficiary are not subject to probate. In contrast, contract proceeds that are payable to the estate are subject to probate.

The reason for this discrepancy in treatment can be found by studying the purpose of the probate system (see Q 2:11). Contract proceeds that are payable to a beneficiary who is named in the contract will automatically be distributed to that beneficiary through the operation of contract law. Those proceeds do not need to go through the probate process, because another applicable law determines their distribution.

In contrast, contract proceeds that are payable to the estate must go through the probate process because no other law governs the distribution of these proceeds. As a result, they are subject to probate and will be distributed according to the decedent's will (if he or she had a valid will) or according to state laws of intestacy.

Q 2:13 What duties apply to fiduciaries?

A *fiduciary* is the generic title given to individuals and organizations who are authorized to manage assets owned by another. In this context, a fiduciary includes an executor, administrator, trustee, personal representative, and a custodian. The following duties generally apply to fiduciaries:

1. *Exercise loyalty in making decisions concerning the estate.* Trustees and personal representatives must act for the benefit of the estate's beneficiaries. Confidentiality is implied in this duty.

2. *Exercise care, diligence, and prudence in handling the estate's property generally.* This duty requires the fiduciary to act with the skill and care that a prudent man or woman would exercise in administering his or her own affairs. Corporate and professional fiduciaries are often deemed to have special skills and are held to a correspondingly higher standard than personal representatives and trustees who are not professionals.

3. *Preserve and protect estate assets.* Conservation includes providing adequate security for coin, stamp, art, and other types of collections. Conservation also includes a duty to protect capital and to make investment assets (e.g., stocks or bonds) productive. In fulfilling this duty, the fiduciary must consider both inflation and the risk of the investment under consideration. In general, it is the fiduciary's conduct, rather than actual results, that is reviewed.

Q 2:14   What is a fiduciary's duty with respect to acts of co-fiduciaries?

The fiduciary that approves a breach of fiduciary duty on the part of another fiduciary is responsible as if he or she had committed the breach. For instance, if a predecessor trustee or executor commits a breach of duty and the successor trustee or executor does not take appropriate action on behalf of the beneficiaries, the successor may be liable. Accordingly, in accepting the appointment of another fiduciary, it is important to review all of the acts of the previous fiduciary before taking action.

Q 2:15   Is a fiduciary responsible for the actions taken by his or her co-fiduciaries?

When several co-executors or co-trustees are appointed to administer an estate, each one is responsible for using reasonable care to prevent the other co-executors from breaching their fiduciary responsibilities. A fiduciary (i.e., an executor or trustee) who approves a breach of fiduciary duty on the part of another executor or trustee is as responsible for the action as if he or she had committed the breach.

Q 2:16   Can a fiduciary be liable for spending estate money?

In some circumstances, a court may consider a fiduciary's unnecessary expenditure of an estate's funds or undue delay in selling an estate's assets to be evidence of negligence.

Q 2:17 Is a fiduciary entitled to compensation?

State statutes generally provide that a fiduciary is entitled to compensation for his or her services. Various approaches have been used to calculate fees. For example, some states have based the compensation payable on the amount of estate assets and have approved the award of extra compensation for extraordinary services. [See Fla Stat § 733.617.] Other states determine compensation using a multifactor test, which evaluates such items as the difficulty of the questions involved, the time and labor required to administer the estate, and the fee customarily charged for these services.

Q 2:18 What are the disadvantages of probate?

Three commonly perceived disadvantages of probate are excessive costs (Q 2:19), excessive delays (Q 2:20), and the publicity associated with court proceedings (Q 2:22).

Q 2:19 What costs are associated with probate?

Probate costs include attorneys' fees for appearing in probate court and court costs. These fees are deductible either against income or against the estate tax. [IRC § 2503] To some extent, these costs are reduced by the availability of summary probate procedures (that is, shortened procedures for small and/or uncomplicated estates) in many states. In Florida, for example, if the value of an estate does not exceed $25,000, or if the decedent has been dead for more than two years, summary administration is available. [Fla Stat § 735.201(2)]

In determining whether avoiding probate will save money, it is important to keep in mind that some fees are going to be incurred in connection with the death in any event; for example, the fees associated with tax planning and the tax filings necessitated by the death. Another consideration is that there are costs associated with avoiding probate. A common device used to avoid probate is the funded revocable trust, also referred to as a *living trust*. If this trust is created, attorneys' fees will be incurred in creating the trust, and fees will be incurred in transferring assets to the trust.

Q 2:20 What are the delays that may sometimes occur during the probate process?

As indicated, the probate process starts with the filing of a petition to probate and ends with the appointment of an executor. During the course of this process time may be consumed in tracking down witnesses to the will; in determining all of the decedent's distributees (those persons who would have inherited had the decedent died intestate); and in dealing with the typically busy court calendars of many of the surrogate's courts, particularly in the larger urban communities. Typically, an uncomplicated probate procedure generally is completed within two to twelve weeks subsequent to the filing of a petition to probate with a surrogate's court.

Q 2:21 What is a will contest?

A will contest generally occurs when an individual or organization believes that the decedent was not mentally competent or was unduly influenced when making his or her will. Will contests are usually initiated by those who were omitted from the decedent's will or when a bequest in the will is less than was allegedly promised by the decedent to the person or organization commencing the action. Will contests can be costly and time-consuming. Moreover, distributions from estates are postponed pending their outcomes. Many good-faith will contests are ultimately settled between the parties as a means of saving time and money. Still, there are will contests engineered by their proponents for the nuisance value they engender in the hope that a settlement will be reached allowing the proponent to obtain funds from the decedent's estate not otherwise obtainable.

An Arizona court recently added *lack of knowledge* as an additional basis to the usual grounds (i.e., lack of mental capacity, undue influence, and fraud) for contesting admission of a will to probate by holding that a will was invalid because the testatrix "lacked any understanding of its contents and indeed was misled as to its true nature." In the case, the son of the testatrix was found to have misled his mother on her deathbed as to the true nature of the instrument she was signing. [Estate of Gillespie, 903 P 2d 590 (Arizona 1995)] Fraud and undue influence no doubt also played a part in the court's decision.

Q 2:22 Why is publicity a disadvantage of probate?

Probate is a court proceeding; thus the documents filed in court are public records available to newspapers and television. In contrast, a trust document is not a public document, although the trust document may have to be produced in order to transfer assets. Consequently, although an individual might have to show the trust document to the court or a bank, newspaper and television reporters would not have access to it.

Q 2:23 How are creditor's claims treated when an estate is probated in contrast to when it is not probated?

If an estate is probated, creditors have a set period of time in which to file their claims. If the claims are not filed within that time period, they are barred forever. Of course, these time periods vary from state to state. Some forms of ownership, such as joint tenancy, are generally not subject to the claims of the deceased's creditors at all. Instead, the property passes to the surviving joint tenant without regard to the creditors' claims (assuming that the joint tenant has not assumed personal liability for the joint tenancy asset).

Q 2:24 What methods exist for avoiding probate?

Probate can be avoided in a number of ways. Four basic methods of avoiding probate are as follows:

1. Creating joint tenancies (see Q 2:25);
2. Using trusts (see Qs 2:36–2:38, chapter 5);
3. Creating a tenancy by the entireties (see Q 2:1); or
4. Establishing a funded revocable living trust (see Qs 2:36–2:38).

Joint Tenancies

Q 2:25 What does *joint ownership* of property mean?

Joint ownership occurs when two or more persons own interests, of one kind or another, in the same property. These kinds of joint ownership fall into the following categories: (1) ownership in which the property passes to the survivor on the death of his or her joint tenant (if property is owned jointly by husband and wife it is generally characterized as a *tenancy by the entirety* or if not, as a *joint tenancy with a right of survivorship*); or (2) a *tenancy in common* in which each of the co-owners owns an individuate interest in the property that, upon the death of a co-owner, rather than passing to the surviving joint tenant, passes to whomever the deceased tenant in common designates in his or her will or, where there is no will, passes according to the laws of intestacy.

Q 2:26 When is joint ownership of property advisable?

Joint ownership, particularly with right of survivorship, allows for ease of transfer by operation of law upon death. When one of the co-tenants dies, the surviving co-tenant automatically becomes sole owner without the need for probate. It also allows for the sharing of income and loss from rental property without the need of a formal partnership arrangement and the filing of additional tax returns. When a bank account is held in joint names, the sole or principal contributor can hold the bankbook and continue controlling the bank account (and thereby have the entire interest on the account includible on his or her income tax return) until his or her death. Joint ownership can also be helpful if a person wishes to leave funds to another without having others aware of its creation or existence until death. Where the filing of an estate tax return is required, the joint ownership must be reported, and then disclosure of the joint account is made known. At that point, however, it is obviously of no relevance to the decedent, and, in the absence of fraud or any other legal ground, it would be difficult to undo the transfer made by the deceased joint tenant during his or her lifetime to the surviving co-tenant.

> **Example 2-1:** After the death of her husband, a wealthy businesswoman develops a close relationship with a man who is fifteen years younger than herself. The woman's son and daughter are unaware of their mother's relationship, which evolved while they were attending college. The woman wishes to make a gift to the young man without divulging the existence of the relationship to her children. She creates a $200,000 joint bank account in her own

name and in that of the young man. Upon her death, the young man will have access to the full $200,000. This amount also will be included in the businesswoman's gross estate for estate tax purposes, so her children will eventually learn about the existence of their mother's relationship but will be unable to voice their opinions to her. The deceased mother's estate will be charged with the estate tax attributable to the value of the joint account includible in her estate, thus causing her children not only to lose what they believe is their rightful share of their mother's estate but also to have what they do receive reduced by the estate tax paid on the inclusion of the joint account in the taxable estate.

Q 2:27 What gift taxes are associated with a joint tenancy?

No taxable gift occurs if each joint tenant contributes equally to the creation of the joint tenancy. If one joint tenant contributes a larger share than the other joint tenants, a taxable gift is deemed to have been made by the joint tenant contributing the greater share. [Treas Reg § 25.2511-1(e)] For example, if a father contributes $100,000 to a 50 percent joint tenancy and his son contributes $40,000 to the joint tenancy, the father is deemed to have made a gift to the son of $30,000 (i.e., 50 percent of the total value of $140,000 ($70,000) is assigned to the son, who contributed only $40,000—this implies a $30,000 gift to the son). After the application of the $10,000 exclusion, the father still owes gift tax on a $20,000 gift which, under the current rate structure, would equal $3,800. [IRC § 2001(c)] Similarly, if the father purchased property worth $140,000 for himself and his son as joint tenants, the father is deemed to have made a taxable gift to his son of one half of the property. In this situation, the father is taxed on $60,000 ($70,000 minus the $10,000 annual exclusion) which, under the current rate structure, would result in $13,000 of gift tax liability. This is not the case, however, if the joint tenants are husband and wife, because there is an unlimited marital deduction for all gifts between husbands and wives (see chapter 4).

Q 2:28 Can an individual who is a party to a joint tenancy sell his or her interest in the joint tenancy?

A person who has an interest in a joint tenancy may sell that interest. Such a sale in effect destroys the joint tenancy with respect to that interest and turns that interest into a tenancy in common. Furthermore, the market value of the interest is usually significantly less than a divided interest in the property because the other owners may use the entire property and are entitled to proceeds from income from the property.

Q 2:29 What happens with a joint tenancy upon the simultaneous death of both owners where the owners are not husband and wife?

Generally, one half of the value of the property is included in both individuals' estate. Where one individual contributed the entire proceeds for the property, however, that individual includes the full value in his or her estate, and the other individual includes one half of the value in his or her estate. [IRC § 2040]

Q 2:30 How is a joint tenancy created?

Generally, a joint tenancy is created when an individual deeds property to two or more individuals as joint tenants. The language used for this intention is very specific. Although the creation of a joint tenancy may be done orally, in some jurisdictions a written instrument is required.

Q 2:31 How are joint tenants treated on the taxable income produced by the joint tenancy property?

If the joint tenancy property generates taxable income, each joint tenant must report a share of the taxable income that is proportional to the share of proceeds that each joint tenant is entitled to receive. If, however, the joint tenancy is in the nature of an arrangement for convenience only, the contributor is taxable on the entire amount of taxable income.

Q 2:32 How is joint tenancy property taxed for federal estate tax purposes?

When a joint tenant dies, the entire value of the joint tenancy asset is includible in the decedent's estate for death tax purposes, except to the extent the surviving joint tenant can prove contributions to its purchase from the survivor's own funds. For this purpose, gifts from the decedent are not considered to be part of the survivor's own funds. [IRC § 2040] If the survivor's contribution can be proved, the percentage of the purchase price that the survivor contributed is excluded from the joint tenant's gross estate at his or her death.

Example 2-2: A brother and sister establish a joint tenancy in a parcel of land. The brother contributes $3,000 (60 percent of the purchase price), and the sister contributes $2,000 (40 percent of the purchase price). On the brother's death, the land is worth $10,000. Forty percent of the value of the land ($4,000) will be excluded from the brother's estate, and sixty percent of the value of the land ($6,000) will be included in the brother's gross estate.

If a taxable gift results from the creation of a joint tenancy and if because of the rule of contribution the joint tenancy property is included in the taxable estate of the donor, a gift tax credit will be allowed in computing the estate tax. [IRC § 2012] This credit will not be allowed, however, if the gift was made after December 31, 1976. [IRC § 2012(e)]

Q 2:33 How is a joint tenancy that is established by a husband and wife taxed?

The general rule of contributions is not applicable to assets owned by husbands and wives as tenants by the entirety or as joint tenants with a right of survivorship. In general, when the decedent spouse dies, only one half of the value of the property will be included in the spouse's estate regardless of which spouse furnished the consideration (that is, paid for it). [IRC § 2040(b)] However, decedents who were married before 1976 may be able to receive a step-up in basis in the full amount of the property if the property was acquired before 1976. [Gallenstein v United States, 92-2 USTC ¶ 60.114 (6th Cir 1992)] For instance, in 1978 a husband purchases an asset for $100,000 out of his separate funds and makes the wife a joint tenant with him. On the death of the first spouse, the asset is worth $150,000. One half of the value ($75,000) is includible in the decedent spouse's estate. The one half that is included will not be taxed, however, because it will be deductible under the unlimited estate tax marital deduction.

Exception for non-U.S. citizens. If, however, the joint tenancy is between a husband and wife, one of whom is not a citizen of the United States, the general rule of contribution applies instead.

Q 2:34 What income tax basis does the surviving joint tenant have in joint tenancy property?

The surviving joint tenant receives a step-up in basis (see Q 18:2) equal to the fair market value of the property on the date of death of the deceased joint tenant for the portion of the joint tenancy property that is includible in the deceased joint tenant's gross estate. The surviving joint tenant retains his or her existing cost basis in the portion of the joint tenancy property that is not includible in the deceased joint tenant's gross estate.

> **Example 2-3:** A mother and her son establish a joint tenancy. The mother contributes $900 and the son contributes $300 to purchase 20 shares of stock priced at $60 per share. At the mother's death, the fair market value of the stock is $100 per share. The son receives a step-up in basis for the portion of the stock that is includible in the mother's gross estate. The mother's gross estate must include the value of 75 percent of the total shares of stock, or $1,500 (15 shares = 75 percent of 20 total shares; 15 shares × $100/share = $1,500), because she paid for 75 percent of the stock initially purchased. The son now holds 15 shares of stock with a basis of $100, and 5 shares of stock with a basis of $60. If he immediately sells all of the stock for fair market value (20 shares × $100/share = $2,000), he would have $200 of taxable gain ([5 shares × $100 = $500] − [5 shares × $60 = $300] = $200). If he had received his mother's interest in the joint tenancy property without the step-up in basis, his taxable gain upon selling all of the shares would be $800.

If the joint tenancy is created by husband and wife, only one half of the joint tenancy property is includible in the decedent's estate regardless of the amount of the contribution. Accordingly, unless special circumstances exist, the surviving spouse will obtain a stepped-up basis in one half of the joint tenancy property and will retain the original basis in the other half of the property (*see* Q 2:35).

Q 2:35 Estate and Retirement Planning Answer Book

Q 2:35 What is the basis of the survivor's interest in the joint tenancy property?

According to Internal Revenue Code Section 1014, the survivor will receive a stepped-up basis equal to the fair market value as listed in the decedent's estate. The remainder of the property not listed in the decedent's estate will retain the survivor's adjusted basis.

Example 2-4: Husband and wife purchased their residence as tenants by the entirety for $200,000 in 1970. The husband dies in 1996 when the residence has a fair market value of $500,000. The wife, as surviving joint tenant, has a new cost basis equal to $350,000, derived as follows: one half of the fair market value of the husband's joint interest ($\frac{1}{2}$ of $500,000 = $250,000) plus one half of the wife's share of the original cost of the residence ($\frac{1}{2}$ of $200,000 = $100,000). This example assumes no additions or subtractions from the original cost of the residence to the date of the husband's death.

Q 2:36 Is a joint bank account a joint tenancy?

Generally, joint bank accounts may be one of the following three types of joint accounts:

1. *Immediate vesting.* Each individual becomes the owner of his or her interest in the account and may not withdraw more than that percentage of ownership.
2. *Convenience.* The person who deposited the funds is the sole owner of the account during that individual's lifetime, and the other may withdraw funds only as an agent for that individual.
3. *Revocable.* Both have full access to all of the proceeds from the account.

Q 2:37 What is the tax effect of converting from a joint tenancy with right of survivorship to a tenancy in common which eliminates the survivorship feature?

The IRS has ruled that such a conversion in the case of stock in a corporation is a nontaxable transaction because it is not considered a sale or exchange. [Rev Rul 56-347, 1956-2 CB 507]

Q 2:38 Is the interest of a husband and wife in a cooperative apartment considered an interest in real property?

Not according to the IRS. In a ruling interpreting Code Section 2215, which was repealed in 1986, the IRS took the position that an interest in cooperative stock is personal property. [Rev Rul 66-40, 1996-1 CB 227] Code Section 2040(b) provides, however, that a *qualified joint interest* in any property held by spouses jointly with right of survivorship qualifies, so that only one half of the value of the stock in a cooperative apartment would be includible in the gross estate of the first of the spouses to die.

Q 2:39 How may an individual prove that he or she contributed all of the proceeds into the account or the survivorship feature of the account?

Maintaining adequate records, such as passbooks, ledgers, and other documents reflecting the amount of deposits and withdrawals and who made each will be invaluable in assisting the taxpayer or estate in this area.

Q 2:40 Does naming an individual as a joint owner of a safety deposit box give that individual joint ownership of the contents inside?

As a general rule, local laws must be consulted to respond to this question; however, all that the individual usually gets is joint access to the contents of the box. If a transfer of the contents is intended, it should be done in the form of a written document that leaves no room for doubt as to the intention of the owner.

Q 2:41 May securities such as stocks and bonds be held as joint tenancies?

Yes. The disadvantage is that the stockbroker must deal with both individuals when making an investment decision. It is possible to open a joint brokerage account but list only one individual as the registered owner of the stock. This enables stockbrokers to deal with either one of the individuals as opposed to both when making investment decisions.

Q 2:42 What disadvantages exist in relying on joint tenancies to dispose of assets?

An equal joint tenancy exists between husband and wife regardless of who furnished the consideration for the joint tenancy property. Accordingly, unless special circumstances exist, at the death of the first spouse, the surviving spouse gets a stepped-up basis in one half of the joint tenancy property. This is disadvantageous if only one of the spouses contributed to the purchase of the property and the contributing spouse dies first. If, instead, the decedent spouse had retained ownership of the entire property, the surviving spouse would have received a stepped-up basis in the entire property.

Furthermore, joint tenancy works as a probate avoidance device only at the time of the death of the first joint tenant. Once that death occurs, the entire property is owned by the second joint tenant and will be includible in his or her probate estate.

> **Example 2-5:** A stockbroker owns 1,000 shares of stock valued at $60 per share with a basis of $20 per share. If he continues to hold the shares and passes them to his wife at death, she will have a basis of $60 per share in the stock. On the other hand, if he creates a joint tenancy with his wife, at death she will have a basis of $60 in 500 of the shares and a basis of $20 per share in the remaining 500 shares. She will receive a stepped-up basis only for the 500 shares included in her husband's estate.

Q 2:43 What gift tax consequences occur if a joint tenancy is dissolved?

If the original creation of the joint tenancy resulted in a taxable gift and the original transaction is reversed, a second taxable gift will result when the property is transferred back to the original owner. If there was no taxable gift on the creation of the joint tenancy, there will be no gift tax when the asset is returned to the original owner. If the asset is not returned to the original owner, gift tax will exist to the extent that a noncontributing party receives an interest in the property. Owing to the unlimited gift tax marital deduction, there is no gift tax payable on the dissolution of a husband-and-wife joint tenancy.

Totten Trusts

Q 2:44 What is a Totten trust?

This kind of trust owes its name to a landmark court decision involving a woman named Fannie Totten. She created a bank account in her name for the benefit of another person (i.e., "Fannie Totten in trust for Anita Totten"). The bank account was revocable because Fannie held the bankbook, and its proceeds (to the extent Fannie did not use them during her life) were to be paid to the beneficiary named in the bank account upon Fannie's death. The court ruled that the bank account was similar to a revocable trust and therefore was not subject to probate. Totten trust accounts are subject to inclusion in the decedent's gross estate for federal estate purposes; most states impose similar treatment. [IRC § 2033]

Funded Revocable Living Trusts

Q 2:45 What is a funded revocable living trust?

A funded revocable living trust is a trust that has been created by the transfer to it of property owned by the trust's grantor, although others may contribute property to the trust during the course of its existence. Upon transfer to the trust, the property becomes trust property, owned by the trust and subject to the provisions of the trust; third parties dealing with the trust are then put on notice or require authentication validating the proper ownership.

Q 2:46 How does a funded revocable living trust work?

A funded revocable living trust is a trust created during the asset owner's lifetime that gives the asset owner both (1) beneficial rights in the trust and (2) the right to revoke the trust. Once the trust is created, the asset owner (and sometimes others) transfers assets to the trust, thereby funding it. When he or she dies, the trust becomes irrevocable, and the trust assets are administered and distributed in accordance with the trust instrument. Because trust assets are owned by the trustee, the assets transferred to the trust are not subject to probate. These trust assets are, however, part of the trust creator's gross estate for estate tax purposes.

Q 2:47 Why is a funded revocable living trust used?

Funded revocable living trusts are used for the following reasons:

1. *To avoid probate.* In comparison with other methods of avoiding probate, the funded revocable living trust is relatively flexible. Further, the trust can provide that when the transferor dies, the trust will be divided into a marital (or A) trust and a bypass (or B) trust. Sufficient assets can be channeled to the B trust to obtain the maximum estate tax savings, and the remaining assets can go to the A trust (see chapters 4 and 5 for discussion of the marital deduction and bypass trusts). By way of contrast, under a joint tenancy, the surviving spouse is the sole owner of the assets, and the $600,000 exemption equivalent (see Qs 3:20, 3:21) is not taken advantage of.

2. *To obtain professional advice.* These trusts permit an individual to obtain professional management of trust assets while still retaining the power to revoke the trust.

3. *To manage assets.* Funded revocable living trusts provide a means for managing assets in the event the asset owner becomes incapacitated, thereby also saving the cost of creating a guardianship or conservatorship. If state law recognizes a durable power of attorney (i.e., powers of attorney that survive the incapacity of the grantor), the durable power of attorney may serve as an alternative. There is an important consideration, however: sometimes durable powers of attorney, although legal, are not accepted by those asked to transfer assets, such as stock brokerage firms and banks. (See chapter 23 for durable powers of attorney.)

4. *To protect Assets.* Living trusts may provide protection against creditors after death occurs and assets are transferred to irrevo-

cable trusts. This protection will not be available if assets are transferred to the trust while a lawsuit is pending.

Q 2:48 What are the disadvantages of using a funded revocable living trust?

The disadvantages of using a funded revocable living trust include the legal costs incurred in setting up the living trust, the cost of recordkeeping, and other expenses incident to administering the trust.

The title to assets held in a funded revocable living trust must be held in the name of the trustee. Sometimes transfer agents and other individuals and entities have difficulty in dealing with someone acting in a trustee capacity and will require documentary evidence of the trust. This can make the ordinary dealings of the trustee, such as making investments, more burdensome.

Q 2:49 What problems exist in transferring assets to a funded revocable living trust?

Several problems need to be addressed when transferring assets to a funded revocable living trust, as follows:

1. If partnership interests are transferred to a living trust, it may be necessary under the partnership agreement to obtain the consent of the other partners; otherwise, the partnership agreement may be violated.

2. Similarly, a buy-sell agreement for corporate stock may prohibit the transfer of the stock to a trust.

3. Assets in a professional corporation may not be transferable to a trust.

4. If real property is transferred to the revocable trust, lenders on the property should be consulted to determine whether, under the lender's agreement with the borrower, the transfer will cause an acceleration of the loan.

Q 2:50   **Estate and Retirement Planning Answer Book**

Q 2:50   How is income earned by the funded revocable living trust taxed?

In most instances, the grantor is treated as the owner of the assets transferred to the funded revocable living trust. Accordingly, during the grantor's lifetime, he or she must pay taxes on the income earned by the trust. [IRC § 676] At death, trust assets are includible in the grantor's gross estate. [IRC §§ 2036, 2038]

Q 2:51   Must income earned by a funded revocable living trust be reported?

During the period that the trust is revocable, the grantor includes any income earned by the trust on his or her individual (or joint) Form 1040. This rule does not apply, however, if any of the trust assets are located outside of the United States or if the trust was created before January 1, 1981. [Treas Reg §§ 1.671-4(b)(4), 1.671-4(c)] If the grantor or the grantor's spouse is a trustee or co-trustee, a trust income tax return need not be filed and an employer identification number need not be obtained until the trust becomes irrevocable (see Q 2:37). [Treas Reg §§ 1.671-4(b), 301.6109-1(a)(2)]

Q 2:52   Does a transfer of an installment obligation to a revocable living trust constitute a disposition of the obligation?

The general rule is that a disposition of an installment obligation by a seller will cause immediate tax on the difference between the fair market value of the installment obligation and its cost basis to the seller. [IRC § 453B] The Internal Revenue Service (IRS) has ruled, however, that a transfer of an installment obligation to a revocable living trust is not a disposition of an installment obligation. [Rev Rul 74-613, 1974-2 CB 153] Accordingly, the transfer of ownership of the installment obligation by the grantor to his or her revocable trust does not result in the grantor's incurring income tax.

Q 2:53   Can assets from a funded revocable living trust be given as gifts?

Yes, they can, but the IRS asserted in a letter ruling that gifts made from a revocable trust to third persons within three years before the grantor's death are includible in the grantor's gross estate under Code

Sections 2035(d)(2) and 2038. [Ltr Rul 8609005 (Nov 26, 1985)] The IRS's reasoning in this ruling was somewhat complicated. First, the IRS noted that one aspect of a revocable trust is the fact that the grantor retains the right to replace the trustee at any time. As a result of this power, the grantor is deemed to have the powers of a trustee. [Treas Reg § 20.2038-1(a)(3)] The IRS then determined that when gifts were made from the trust, the trustee's control over the assets comprising the gifts was relinquished. Correspondingly, the grantor was viewed as having relinquished control over the particular trust assets, bringing the transaction under Code Section 2038(a). Alternatively, the IRS noted that even if the gift resulted in a termination of the grantor's power over the assets, rather than a relinquishment, the gifts would still be covered by Code Section 2035(d)(2) as transfers includible in the gross estate under Code Section 2038. (Code Section 2038 addresses interests subject to a power to alter, amend, revoke, or terminate.) [IRC § 2035(d)(2)]

In contrast, had the grantor transferred the gift directly within three years of death, the gift property would not be includible in his or her gross estate. This is because the three-year rule of Code Section 2035(a) has been repealed, except with respect to certain transfers. [IRC §§ 2035(d)(1), 2036, 2037, 2038, 2042] Furthermore, if the gifts discussed in Private Letter Ruling 8609005 had been made more than three years before the grantor's death, they would not have been included in the grantor's gross estate. To summarize, assets can be transferred as gifts from a revocable living trust, but only with an increased risk that they will be includible in the grantor's gross estate.

Q 2:54 What are the income tax advantages of probate as opposed to those of a funded revocable living trust?

Probate offers a number of advantages that a living trust does not. A probate estate can accumulate income without risk of the income being subject to the throwback rule; however, a funded revocable living trust that accumulates income is subject to the throwback rule. Under the throwback rule, if trust income is accumulated rather than distributed, the taxpayer's applicable income tax bracket is deemed to be the applicable bracket for the year in which the accumulated income was earned, not the bracket for the year the accumulated income is actually distributed. Application of the throwback rule discourages the taxpayer from requesting that a trustee not distribute trust income until the taxpayer is in a low tax bracket. [IRC § 665(a)(b)]

> **Example 2-6:** In 1983, the income beneficiary of a trust occupied the 33 percent income tax bracket. The trust was in the 19 percent bracket. The beneficiary encouraged the trustee to accumulate $7,500 of the $10,000 in income the trust might have distributed and to distribute only $2,500 to the beneficiary. The trust incurred tax on the accumulated $7,500 of $1,200, leaving undistributed income of $6,300. In 1993, the beneficiary occupied the 15 percent tax bracket and requested that the $6,300 in accumulated income be distributed to him. The tax on the $6,300 accumulation distribution was levied in 1993 and imposed at the 33 percent rate; the income tax on the $6,300 distribution was $2,100.

Because the probate estate is not subject to the throwback rule, income earned by probate estate assets can be accumulated over a period of time and paid out subsequently. The probate period for administration for tax purposes can continue for whatever period is in fact required by the executor to perform the ordinary duties of administration. [Treas Reg § 1.641(b)(3)]

The administrative requirements that pertain to trusts are quite different from those that pertain to probate estates. Trusts are required to select a calendar year and do not have the additional option, available to probate estates, of selecting an alternate fiscal year. [IRC § 625] In addition, trusts must make quarterly estimated payments of income tax; estates need not do so during the first two taxable years of their existence. [IRC § 6654(1)]

Q 2:55 Can the use of a funded revocable living trust adversely affect the estate tax treatment of the qualified plan death benefits?

No. By way of providing background, the full exclusion from estate tax is permitted for death benefits payable from a qualified plan to deceased employees who retired prior to January 1, 1983, and $100,000 exclusion is allowed for employees who retire during 1983 or 1984. An exclusion is available only if the death benefits from a retirement plan are not payable to the employee's estate and the recipient elects to forego ten-year averaging and capital gain treatment for income tax purposes. Furthermore, death benefits payable under a retirement plan are not subject to probate except to the extent they are payable to the employee's estate. Payment to a funded revocable living trust created to avoid probate will qualify for the federal estate tax exemption, provided the trustee is not required to use the funds for the benefit of the decedent's estate. The trustee can be given discretionary authority to loan money or purchase assets from the probate estate. [Rev Rul 77-157, 1977-1 CB 279]

Q 2:56 Does the use of a funded revocable living trust adversely affect the estate tax deduction for administrative expenses?

To obtain the deduction for administrative expenses on the federal estate tax return, a trust must pay the expenses before the expiration of the statute of limitations (generally three years, with some exceptions) for the assessment of estate tax. [IRC § 2053(b)]

Q 2:57 How does the use of a revocable living trust affect the tax deduction for the decedent's debts?

Debts on the federal estate tax return of a trust must be paid prior to the filing of the federal estate tax return. [IRC § 2053(c)] This is not true for a probate estate. Similarly, a decedent's debts cannot be deducted on the decedent's federal estate tax return unless they are paid before the federal estate tax return is filed. In contrast, for probate, all that is required is that the debt be in effect at the time of the decedent's death even if it is unpaid when the federal estate tax return is filed.

Q 2:58 If the estate contains out-of-state real property, does the use of a funded revocable living trust affect the amount of inheritance taxes payable on such property?

A general probate rule is that real property is subject to inheritance tax in the state in which the property is located. Inheritance tax rates vary among states; therefore, the property's location can have a significant tax effect. If the real property is held by a trust, it may be treated as personal property and thus be treated as located (and subject to inheritance tax) in the state in which the decedent is domiciled (even if that is different from the state in which the real property is physically located). Because of this variance among states in the applicable inheritance tax rates, the successful use of an irrevocable trust can significantly lower the amount of inheritance taxes payable on such real property.

Q 2:59 How does the use of a funded revocable living trust work with respect to stock in an S corporation?

A funded revocable living trust can be the owner of stock in an S corporation. If, upon the grantor's death, the revocable trust becomes irrevocable and the entire amount of the principal and income is included in the grantor's estate, the trust may continue to own the stock of the S corporation for two years without terminating S corporation status. [IRC § 1361(c)(2)(A)(ii)] If the trust holding the S corporation stock after the grantor's death is a qualified subchapter S trust, the subchapter S election can continue indefinitely. For this to occur, the following requirements must be met:

1. All trust income must be distributed to a citizen or resident of the United States;

2. At any given time, there can be only one income beneficiary, who during his or her lifetime is the exclusive beneficiary of both income and principal distributions;

3. The trust must provide for the termination of the income interest on the earlier of either the death of a beneficiary or the termination of the trust. It must require that on termination of the trust during the beneficiary's life, all assets of the trust be distributed to such beneficiary; and

4. The beneficiary must make an irrevocable election to be treated as the owner of the trust for tax purposes. [IRC § 1361(d)]

Unlike a trust, a probate estate may own stock in an S corporation during the entire period of administration, and the ownership of the stock may be continued by a trust to which the estate is distributed under the terms of the will for an additional 60 days after distribution. [IRC § 1361(c)(3)(A)(iii)]

Q 2:60 How is the taxation of a distribution of a fixed sum affected by the choice of a funded revocable living trust?

If an asset is distributed to satisfy a requirement that a will or trust distributes a fixed sum to a beneficiary, the probate estate will recognize a loss on the distribution of the asset, whereas the irrevocable trust cannot. [IRC § 267(b)(6)] (Both the estate and the trust will recognize any gain on such distributions, however.)

Q 2:61 Is the personal liability of the fiduciary affected by the choice of a funded revocable living trust?

Perhaps. Both an executor and a trustee of a funded revocable living trust are personally liable if they make distributions to beneficiaries before federal income taxes are paid. [IRC § 6324(a)(2)] Usually, probate procedures prevent an executor from having to make distributions until tax liability is satisfied. If the terms of the trust require the immediate distribution of assets, however, the trustee would be forced to make distributions with the risk of personal liability if the remaining assets in the estate are insufficient to satisfy all applicable taxes.

Q 2:62 What are the advantages of a funded revocable living trust and a durable power of attorney?

Funded revocable living trusts are more widely accepted than durable powers of attorney and can be used as means of property management in general, which is why individuals often establish and fund them. The use of a funded revocable living trust requires the grantor to re-title the assets placed into the trust. The costliness associated with the re-titling of assets often discourages individuals from placing all of the intended assets into the trust. To address this practical consideration, a revocable trust is often accompanied by a durable power of attorney, which can be used subsequently to take care of any assets not included in the living trust.

A durable power of attorney may be less expensive to draft than a funded revocable living trust and, unlike a funded revocable living trust, it does not require the re-titling of assets. Furthermore, the holder of a durable power of attorney can execute a disclaimer to prevent the inclusion in his or her gross estate of assets subject to a power of appointment that could be exercised in favor of the holder of the power of appointment.

Unfunded Revocable Trusts

Q 2:63 What are the advantages of not funding revocable trusts?

Every trust must have a grantor, a trustee, a beneficiary, and property contributed to it. An unfunded revocable trust is generally formed by the grantor acting as trustee and funding the trust with a nominal amount of property (generally cash) to justify the trust's legal existence.

Using an unfunded revocable trust eliminates the cost of maintaining a trust during the grantor's lifetime. At death, these trusts can become irrevocable funded trusts, and assets may be paid into them and held in trust. If the grantor of the trust wishes to manage the estate personally during his or her lifetime but wants a corporate trustee to become successor trustee on his or her death, it may be preferable to use an unfunded rather than a funded revocable living trust. Problems may arise, however. A corporate fiduciary may be reluctant to accept a successor trusteeship because of its duty to investigate the acts of the prior trustee and obtain redress for prior breaches of trust.

Q 2:64 When should an unfunded revocable living trust be used in preference to a testamentary trust?

An unfunded revocable living trust established prior to death does not avoid probate because the assets used subsequent to death in funding it generally are derived from funds or property owned by the decedent in his own name prior to death. Nonetheless, there may still be some advantages in using it as opposed to a testamentary trust (that is, a trust established by will). These advantages are as follows:

1. A testamentary trust, unlike an unfunded irrevocable living trust, is subject to continuing jurisdiction of probate in many states. As a result, the fees associated with maintaining the

testamentary trust may be higher than those of an unfunded revocable living trust.
2. A testamentary trust is in the public record; an unfunded trust is not.
3. A testamentary trust cannot be made the beneficiary of life insurance proceeds on the life of the testator (that is, the individual who provides for the establishment of the trust) when the policy is owned by a third party. This is because the testator always has the authority to revoke or alter his or her will and thus has an incident of ownership in any proceeds that are payable to the testamentary trust. In contrast, a revocable unfunded living trust can be drafted to allow future receipt of the life insurance proceeds and to provide that the grantor cannot affect the distribution of life insurance proceeds. This will keep the life insurance proceeds out of the testator's estate.

Chapter 3

Overview of Tax Principles

This chapter introduces the principles of estate planning. It discusses the goal of preservation of income and assets and treats the kinds of taxes that can reduce accumulated income and assets at death: estate, income, and gift taxes. Subsequent chapters will explore each of these taxes in more detail and set forth special planning techniques designed to minimize or avoid their effects. It also discusses key nontax considerations that apply in estate planning.

Overview	3-2
The Gross Estate	3-3
Valuation of Estate Property	3-11
Deductions from Gross Estate	3-12
Credits Against Estate Tax	3-14
Determination and Payment of Estate Tax	3-16
Income Taxes on Estates	3-18
Gift Taxes	3-19
Basis of Property Acquired from Decedents	3-23
Nontax Considerations	3-28

Overview

Q 3:1 What is estate planning?

Estate planning is the process in which thoughtful consideration is given to accumulating and allocating income and assets for the purpose of creating a better quality of life for oneself and one's loved ones during life and after death. In order to achieve the goals sought by estate planning, the accumulation and retention of income and assets must be accomplished by avoiding, through every legal means, the severe impact of income, estate, and gift taxes. The income tax rates range from 15 percent at the lowest level to 39.6 percent at the highest level. Estate and gift taxes are integrated so that taxable gifts reduce the available overall exemption of $600,000 (equal to a $192,800 credit against the aggregate total of both taxes). After the $600,000 exemption is exceeded, estate and gift tax rates begin at a 37 percent tax rate, which can grow to a 55 percent tax rate at the highest taxable estate tax levels. State estate and inheritance taxes are also significant in depleting an estate, although not nearly as high as federal estate taxes. Some states also impose gift taxes.

Learning the techniques for dealing with the federal and local tax systems so as to enjoy the benefits of one's labor and investments, without being unnecessarily burdened by those systems, is the goal of estate planning.

Q 3:2 Why is it important to establish a domicile in one state?

A person who occupies residences in more than one state in the course of the year (e.g., a summer home in Maine, a winter home in Florida) should establish a state of domicile so that in the event of the person's death, the estate will not be burdened with the payment of death taxes to more than one state. The following steps can be taken to establish domicile:

1. Register to vote in the desired state.
2. Apply for a certificate of domicile if the state issues one.
3. Transfer all bank accounts to the desired state of domicile.

Overview of Tax Principles   Q 3:5

4. Purchase all securities in the desired state of domicile and have them located in the broker's local office or in a safe deposit box in that state.
5. Address credit cards and correspondence to the appropriate office in the desired state of domicile.
6. Obtain a driver's license in the desired state of domicile.
7. Have Social Security checks mailed to the residence in the desired state of domicile.

Q 3:3 What is ancillary probate?

This occurs when an individual who is a domiciliary in one state dies while owning property—generally real estate—in another state. It then becomes necessary to undergo a special probate proceeding in the state in which the property is located to clear title to the property and allow for its disposition as provided in an individual's will. Under such circumstances, the will should contain a provision for the appointment of an ancillary executor who is qualified to act in that capacity in the state in which the property is located.

The Gross Estate

Q 3:4 What are the requirements for filing a federal estate tax return?

Federal estate tax returns are due within nine months after the date of a decedent's death. For U.S. citizens and residents, a federal estate tax return must be filed if the gross estate exceeds $600,000. For estates of nonresidents not citizens of the United States, an estate tax return must be filed of that part of the gross estate located in the United States exceeds $60,000. (The gross estate of a nonresident alien consists only of assets located in the United States.) [IRC § 2103]

Q 3:5 What are the requirements for filing a federal gift tax return?

For gifts made after 1981, gift tax returns are to be filed, and any owing gift tax is to be paid, on an annual basis. The gift tax return, like the income tax return, is due by April 15 following the calendar year in which the gift was made. Where a donor dies during the calendar year in which the gift was made, the gift tax return must be filed no later than the due date for the donor's estate tax return, including extensions.

A gift tax return must be filed if the donor (1) made gifts to any donee other than the donor's spouse that are not fully excludable under one or a combination of the annual educational or medical exclusions, (2) made gifts of terminal interests (other than a life estate with a general power of appointment) to a spouse, or (3) made gifts of any amount that are split with a spouse.

Q 3:6 What is the gross estate?

The gross estate of a decedent who was a citizen or resident of the United States at the time of his or her death is the value of all property in which the decedent had an interest at the time of his or her death, to the extent of the interest. [IRC § 2033; Treas Reg § 20.2033-1]

Q 3:7 What assets are includible in a decedent's gross estate?

Property owned by the decedent during his or her lifetime is includible in the gross estate if the decedent (1) beneficially owned it at death or (2) transferred property within three years of the date of death while retaining certain testamentary-like rights in that transferred property. Life insurance proceeds, if the decedent or his or her estate had any interest in the proceeds at the time of death, are includible in the gross estate. Real property (e.g., land, buildings), and personal property, both tangible and intangible (e.g., stocks, copyrights), are includible in the gross estate. [Treas Reg § 20.2033-1] The Internal Revenue Service (IRS) recently ruled that the present value of the right to receive lottery payments at the time of a lottery winner's death is includible in the winner's estate and must be determined under the IRS valuation tables. [Ltr Rul 9616004]

Some Social Security payments to widows and widowers are excluded from the gross estate, however. [Rev Rul 67-277, 1967-2 CB 322]

Nonresident aliens. The gross estate of a nonresident alien consists only of assets located in the United States. [IRC § 2103]

Q 3:8 Are accrued interest and rents includible in the gross estate?

Yes, interests and rents accrued at the date of the decedent's death are part of the gross estate. [Treas Reg § 20.2033-1(b)]

Q 3:9 Is community property includible in the gross estate?

Community property is property acquired during marriage by either spouse while permanently residing in a community property state. All such property is treated as being owned jointly by the spouses regardless of which spouse paid for or worked for such property. Because each spouse has a vested interest in one half of the community property, only one half of the community property will be includible in that spouse's gross estate. Community property generally does not include property received by one of the spouses by inheritance or gift.

The community property states are as follows: Arizona, California, Idaho, Louisiana, Nevada, New Mexico, Texas, and Washington. Wisconsin adopted the Uniform Marital Property Act in 1983 and thus became, for all practical purposes, a community property state.

Q 3:10 How is property transferred at death in community property states?

In community property states, each spouse owns one half of the community property. This means that each spouse can bequeath his or her half of the community property as well as any separate property that he or she owns. Separate property is property acquired by one of the spouses prior to the marriage or by gift or inheritance during the marriage.

Q 3:11 Is joint tenancy property includible in the gross estate?

Joint tenancy property is property owned by two or more individuals (the joint tenants). In the case of a tenancy by the entirety or joint ownership with a right of survivorship, on the death of one joint tenant, the surviving joint tenant(s) becomes the sole owner(s) of the decedent's share by operation of law; the transfer of property is not governed by the terms of a will. The value of property held in joint tenancy is generally included in the decedent's gross estate, except to the extent that the surviving joint tenant can show that he or she contributed to its acquisition cost. [IRC § 2040] The percentage contribution by the surviving joint tenant to the acquisition cost will be the percentage of the joint tenancy asset that is excludable from the estate of the deceased joint tenant.

Example 3-1: The surviving joint tenant (not the surviving spouse of the decedent) contributed one quarter of the $100,000 purchase price for land that has increased in value to $300,000 as of the date of the death of the other joint tenant. The decedent contributed three quarters of the purchase price. One quarter of the value of the asset ($75,000) is excluded from the decedent's gross estate, and three quarters ($225,000) is included in the decedent's gross estate. The surviving co-tenant then obtains a cost basis for income tax purposes of $300,000 determined by the value at date of death of the deceased co-tenant's includible estate tax joint interest equal to $225,000 plus the original cost of the property of $75,000 contributed by the surviving co-tenant.

The survivor's contribution does not include funds originally given to the survivor by the decedent.

Special rule for spouses. If the joint tenants are husband and wife, on the death of the first spouse to die only one half of the value of the asset is included in the deceased spouse's gross estate, regardless of which spouse furnished the consideration (that is, paid for the property). Decedents who were married before 1976 may be able to receive a step-up in basis in the full amount of the property if the property was acquired before 1976. [Gallenstein v United States, 92-2 TC ¶ 60,114 (1992)]

Q 3:12 Is tenancy in common property includible in the gross estate?

Tenancy in common property is jointly owned property; however, if one co-owner dies, the surviving co-owners do not automatically receive the decedent's interest (as would be the case if the property was held in joint tenancy). Instead, the decedent's interest passes by will or the laws of intestacy (state-mandated rules for dispensing property if no valid will exists). The value of tenancy in common property is includible in the gross estate to the extent that the decedent had an interest in the property. For example, if the decedent had a one-third tenancy in common interest in a parcel of land worth $300,000, $100,000 would be includible in the decedent's gross estate.

Q 3:13 Is property that is subject to a power of appointment includible in the gross estate?

Includibility in the gross estate of property that is subject to a power of appointment depends on the nature of the particular power of appointment. A general power of appointment allows the holder to appoint the property to the holder, the holder's estate, or the holder's creditors. A special power of appointment is exercisable only in favor of someone other than the holder or the holder's estate or creditors. A power to invade principal or interest for oneself under an ascertainable standard relating to health, support, and education is a type of special power of appointment.

The value of property subject to a general power of appointment at the time of death is includible in the decedent's gross estate because the holder of a general power of appointment could technically use that power to grant himself or herself a beneficial interest in the property. It is this possibility that Congress is taxing by including general powers of appointment in a decedent's gross estate. [IRC § 2041]

In contrast, property subject to a special power of appointment is not includible in the decedent's gross estate because, for the most part, a special power of appointment cannot be exercised in favor of the decedent, the decedent's estate, or the decedent's creditors. As a result, the decedent does not have a sufficient beneficial interest to justify subjecting the property covered by the special power of appointment to estate taxes as part of the decedent's gross estate.

Q 3:14 Are life insurance proceeds includible in the gross estate?

Proceeds of an insurance policy owned by the decedent or payable to the decedent's estate are includible in the decedent's gross estate. If the policy proceeds are not payable to the estate and if the decedent retained no incidents of ownership in the policy, the proceeds are not included in the gross estate. [IRC § 2042] A decedent retains an incident of ownership in an insurance policy if the decedent had the right to borrow on the policy, cash the policy in, or change a beneficiary, or if the decedent retained a reversionary interest in the policy that was valued at more than 5 percent of the value of the policy immediately before the decedent's death. The U.S. Supreme Court, in a now-famous opinion, held that flight insurance proceeds must be included in a decedent's gross estate where, under the terms of the policy, the decedent had the right to change the beneficiary, even though practically speaking he or she could not do so during the flight. [Commr v Estate of Noel, 380 US 678 (1965)]

Q 3:15   Are annuities includible in the gross estate?

An annuity is an agreement to pay a person a fixed sum over two or more calendar years. Straight life annuities, which cease on the annuitant's death, are not includible in the gross estate. Annuities that have value after death are includible in the decedent's gross estate, however, at least to the extent the decedent contributed to the value of the annuity still to be paid after his or her death. [IRC § 2039] Such annuities include annuities that provide a refund if a person dies before the annuity is paid, annuities with a term certain (e.g., a guaranteed payment period of ten years), and joint and survivor annuities (which make payments over the lives of two designated individuals, such as spouses).

Q 3:16   Are gifts made within three years of death includible in the gross estate?

Only gifts of property made within three years of death and in which the transferor retains certain interests are includible in the gross estate. [IRC § 2035(d)(2)] Those interests are includible in the gross estate under Section 2036 (life estates), Section 2037 (transfers effective at death), Section 2038 (powers to alter or revoke transfers), or Section 2039 (annuities and life insurance policies) of the Internal Revenue Code (Code). The gifts and transfers are includible in the gross estate even if they do not exceed the $10,000 annual gift tax exclusion. [IRC § 2035(b)(2)]

Prior rule. Prior to 1982, all gifts made within three years of the donor's death except those qualifying for the $10,000 annual gift tax exclusion were includible in the gross estate. [IRC § 2035]

Example 3-2: A rancher retains a life estate in a parcel of land. In 1993, he transfers his life estate interest to his son. Two years later he dies. The life estate he gave is includible in his gross estate.

The value of the transferred property is determined on the date of death (or alternate valuation date). Any improvements made to the property by the transferee are not included in the gross estate. [Treas Reg § 20.2035-1(e)]

Q 3:17 Is gift tax paid on gifts made during the decedent's lifetime includible in the gross estate?

The amount of any gift tax payable on any gift made within three years of death is includible in the gross estate. [IRC § 2025(c)] This rule applies to gift tax paid on all gifts, not merely those that are includible in the gross estate. The purpose of this rule is to prevent an individual who knows that death is imminent from making a taxable gift of property so as to eliminate the amount of gift tax from the gross estate, thereby causing a lower estate tax.

Example 3-3: A businessman with cancer who expects to die within six months makes a taxable gift of $100,000 to his oldest daughter and pays a gift tax of $18,200 on the gift. If the gift was not made, the businessman's taxable estate would be increased by $118,200 and he would pay estate tax on both the $100,000 and $18,200. The three-year rule prevents this last-minute attempt to avoid estate taxes by imposing estate tax on the $18,200.

Q 3:18 Are transfers that take effect at death includible in the gross estate?

Transfers that take effect at death will be includible in the gross estate if, as a condition of the transfer, the donee (the recipient) must survive the donor (in this case, the deceased) for the transfer to occur and if the donor retains a reversionary interest that immediately before the donor's death exceeds 5 percent of the value of the property. [IRC § 2037] In other words, completed, no-strings-attached taxable gifts will not be included in the gross estate. They will, however, factor into the estate tax computation as *adjusted taxable gifts* (unless full consideration is paid). If the value of a retained reversionary interest is less than 5 percent of the value of the property, only the value of the reversionary interest will be included in the donor's estate.

Example 3-4: A manufacturer transfers $300,000 in trust. The trust provides that the income from the $300,000 is payable to his wife and that the $300,000 will be returned to him if his wife predeceases him. The trust also provides that his son will obtain the $300,000 if the manufacturer predeceases his wife. The value of the manufacturer's right to the $300,000 if his wife dies exceeds 5 percent of the $300,000 sum transferred. Because his son cannot obtain possession of the $300,000 unless the manufacturer dies, the $300,000 is includible in the manufacturer's gross estate.

Q 3:19 Are gifts with possession or enjoyment retained includible in the gross estate?

If the donor of property retained the right to income for life or for any period that does not terminate prior to the donor's death, the entire value of that property will be includible in the donor's gross estate. [IRC § 2036]

Example 3-5: A businessman executes a deed that lets him retain a life interest in a ten-acre parcel of land but lets him transfer full ownership of the parcel to his son at death. The value of the parcel is included in the businessman's estate.

Example 3-6: A physician creates a trust in which trust income is to be paid to the physician for 15 years and then trust assets are to be paid to the physician's son. The physician dies at the end of 12 years. The trust assets are included in the physician's estate because the 15-year period had not terminated prior to his death.

Q 3:20 Are transfers with a retained power to alter, amend, revoke, or terminate includible in the decedent's gross estate?

Yes, the value of donated property is includible in a deceased donor's gross estate to the extent the donor retains the right to alter, amend, revoke, or terminate the transfer. [IRC § 2038] This is so even if the donor's power is not exercisable in favor of himself or herself. For example, assets would be included in the gross estate if the donor reserves the right to substitute the beneficiaries of a trust.

The exercise of a retained power governed by an ascertainable standard does not cause inclusion in the gross estate under Code Section 2038, however. An example of an ascertainable standard is a power to distribute trust property for the health, education, or support of a named beneficiary. If, for instance, a donor established a trust with income to go to his minor children for life, his retention of a power to dip into trust principal for his children's health, education, or support would not cause the trust assets to be includible in his gross estate.

Valuation of Estate Property

Q 3:21 When property is includible in the gross estate, how is it valued?

Property includible in the gross estate is generally valued at fair market value at the date of death. Fair market value is generally defined as the price at which a willing seller will sell and a willing buyer who has knowledge of the facts will purchase, neither being under any compulsion to buy or sell. [Treas Reg § 20.2031-1(b)] The Tax Court recently concluded that the value of restricted stock must be included and its fair market value determined at the moment of death because death caused the restrictions (such as SEC restrictions as to unregistered stock) to lapse. [Estate of McClatchy, 106 TC No 9 (1966)]

Alternate valuation date. If both the value of the gross estate and the estate tax would be reduced as a result of using the alternate valuation date, an estate representative may elect instead to value the property included in the gross estate as of six months after the date of death. [IRC § 2032] If the alternate valuation date is elected, however, any estate property sold, distributed, exchanged, or otherwise disposed of during the six-month period following the date of death is valued as of the date of disposition rather than as of the date of death.

Example 3-7: A businessman dies on October 10, 1995. Most of the value of his gross estate resides in a stock portfolio containing many shares of stock from a variety of companies. On the date of his death, the normal valuation date for estate taxes, the fair market value of this portfolio is $2.5 million. The remainder of the assets in the businessman's gross estate are worth $500,000. On October 18, 1995, the stock market crashes. The businessman's stock portfolio is now valued at $500,000. Under normal estate tax valuation rules, estate tax liability is based on the value of the gross estate on the date of death. In this case, the estate tax liability, $1,290,800, would exceed the total value of assets in the estate at the time the tax was due ($1.1 million). Fortunately, Code Section 2032 allows an estate representative to elect an alternate valuation date six months after the decedent's death. On the alternate valuation date, April 10, 1988, the value of the gross estate is $1,100,000. The corresponding estate tax liability is also lower: $386,800.

Special valuation rules. Special rules can apply to the valuation of real property devoted to farming or used by closely held businesses (see Q 9:38). [IRC § 2032A]

Penalties for understatement of tax liability. Penalties can be imposed for the substantial understatement of estate and gift taxes resulting from the undervaluation of property (see Q 9:43). [IRC § 6662(a)(5)]

Deductions from Gross Estate

Q 3:22 Can administrative expenses be deducted from the gross estate?

Yes, administrative expenses such as executors' commissions, attorneys' fees, accountants' and appraisers' fees, and other expenses incurred in preserving and distributing the estate can be deducted from the gross estate to the extent they are not claimed as deductions on the estate's *income tax* return. The deduction is limited to expenses actually and necessarily incurred in the administration of the estate and does not include expenditures for the individual benefit of heirs, legatees, or devisees. [Treas Reg § 20.2053-3]

In order to ensure that a deduction for administrative expenses will not be claimed on both the federal estate tax and fiduciary income tax return, the executor or administrator of an estate is required under Code Section 642(g) to attach a statement to the Form 1041 (fiduciary income tax return) waiving the specific deductions claimed on the Form 1041, such as fiduciary fees, attorney and accountant fees, and, selling expenses, from also being claimed on the estate tax return.

Q 3:23 Are mortgages deductible from the gross estate?

The treatment of mortgaged property included in the estate depends on the type of mortgage. If only a specific property can be used to satisfy the debt, only the net value of the property is includible in the gross estate (that is, the value of the property less the unpaid amount of the mortgage and minus mortgage interest accrued to the date of death). For example, only the net value of property subject to a nonrecourse mortgage (i.e., a mortgage that can only be satisfied by a particular property) is includible in the gross estate. Thus, an unpaid nonrecourse residential mortgage would effectively be excluded from the estate. If, on the other hand, the entire estate is liable for the mortgage, the full value of the property is includible in the gross estate and a deduction is allowed in the amount of the mortgage. [Treas Reg § 20.2053-7] The deduction is allowed for the unpaid amount of a mortgage or other indebtedness, including interest accrued to date of death on any property in the gross estate.

Q 3:24 Is an estate tax deduction available for charitable contributions?

If the will or trust specifically permits the contribution, an unlimited estate tax deduction is available for the value of property included in the decedent's gross estate that is transferred at death to qualifying governmental, charitable, or religious organizations. [IRC § 2055] The availability of the estate and gift tax charitable deduction differs from the charitable deduction available for income taxes, in that bequests and gifts to foreign organizations are allowed for estate and gift tax purposes (but not for income tax purposes); furthermore, the charitable deduction is unlimited for estate and gift tax purposes but is subject to percentage of gross income limitations for income tax purposes. [IRC §§ 2055, 2522]

Credits Against Estate Tax

Q 3:25   What is the unified credit against estate tax?

Since January 1, 1977, a unified estate and gift tax (also referred to as the unified transfer tax) has been imposed on the value of property transferred by gift or as a result of death. This means that the same tax rates apply regardless of whether the property is given during the decedent's lifetime or whether the value of the property is included in the decedent's gross estate. The unified credit against estate tax is $192,800 for decedents dying as of December 31, 1986, and later (until such time as this limit is amended again by Congress). [IRC § 2010] This $192,800 credit is equivalent to a $600,000 exemption in that the tentative tax on a taxable estate of $600,000 is $192,800. At death, the portion of the unified credit that the decedent used during his or her lifetime in computing gift tax is restored (so that the full credit is available on death), and the tax base used in computing the estate tax is increased by the value of the taxable gifts (that is, the value at the date of gift and not at date of death) associated with the portion of the credit previously used.

Q 3:26   What is the exemption equivalent?

The exemption equivalent is the portion of the transfer that will pass free of gift or estate tax because of the unified tax credit. Each individual has a $192,800 credit that can be used to offset estate or gift taxes incurred by that person as a result of gifts or bequests. The current unified tax credit of $192,800 permits the transfer of $600,000 without gift or estate tax being incurred under the existing tax rates. The exemption equivalent is thus $600,000. [IRC § 2010]

> **Example 3-8:** In 1994, a landowner makes a taxable gift of land worth $600,000 to his son. He has made no prior taxable gifts. Under the existing gift tax schedules, the associated gift tax on a $600,000 transfer is $192,800, which just equals the unified credit. The landowner therefore owes no gift tax due to the unified credit.

Q 3:27 What credits other than the unified credit can offset estate taxes?

In addition to the unified credit (see Q 3:25), the following credits also can reduce estate taxes:

1. Credit for state death taxes. [IRC § 2011] This credit is limited by an IRS table that generally provides a credit of a lesser amount than the actual state estate and inheritance tax paid by the estate.
2. Credit for gift taxes paid on gifts made before January 1, 1977, if any portion of the gifts is included in the decedent's gross estate. [IRC § 2012]
3. Credit for foreign death taxes paid. [IRC § 2014]

Q 3:28 Is there a credit against estate tax if the same property is included in the gross estates of two decedents who died within a short time of each other?

A credit is available if the same property is included in the gross estates of two decedents who died shortly after one another only if estate tax was payable in both estates. [IRC § 2013] This estate tax credit is subject to maximum limits. If the second decedent died within two years after the first decedent, the gross estate of the second decedent is allowed full credit. If the first decedent predeceased the second decedent by more than two years, the credit is gradually reduced depending on the time period between the two deaths (up to a maximum of ten years between the two deaths). [IRC § 2013(a)]

Example 3-9: An investment advisor has a general power of appointment over the assets of a trust established by her brother. She exercises this power to provide a portion of the trust assets to her son. When the investment advisor dies, the assets are taxable as part of her gross estate through the operation of Code Section 2038. The son dies 18 months after his mother. The assets are also includible in the son's estate under Code Section 2033. Because both decedents paid estate taxes on the property and they died within two years of each other, Code Section 2013 allows an estate tax credit to the son's estate.

Determination and Payment of Estate Tax

Q 3:29 How is the federal estate tax determined?

The federal estate tax can generally be determined as follows:

1. List the values of property included in the gross estate.
2. Subtract all allowable deductions from the gross estate.
3. Add taxable gifts made after December 31, 1976, except for gifts that are already included in the gross estate.
4. Compute the tentative tax using the unified rate schedule.
5. Subtract unified transfer tax on taxable gifts made after 1976.
6. Subtract the unified estate tax credit.
7. Subtract other applicable credits.

Example 3-10: A woman dies in 1993, leaving an estate of $2 million. Estate debts and the cost of administration total $300,000. In 1982, the decedent made taxable gifts of $300,000 and paid $25,000 in gift tax. Under these circumstances the estate tax is determined as follows:

Gross estate	$2,000,000
Less deductions	$ 300,000
Taxable estate	$1,700,000
Add post-1976 gifts	$ 300,000
Tax base	$2,000,000
Tentative tax	$ 780,800
Gift tax paid on post-1976 gifts	$ 25,000
Tentative tax less gift tax paid	$ 755,800
Less unified credit	$ 192,800
Estate tax payable	$ 563,000

Q 3:30 How is the estate tax paid?

A federal estate tax return (Form 706) must be filed if the gross estate exceeds $600,000 at date of death.

Example 3-11: A farmer who died in 1993 was the owner of farmland worth $1 million but subject to a $700,000 recourse mortgage. A federal estate tax return must be filed on behalf of the farmer's estate because the gross estate exceeds $600,000 despite a taxable estate of $300,000.

The return is due within nine months of the estate owner's death, but a six-month extension is available for reasonable cause. Reasonable cause can include such things as estate assets being located in several jurisdictions, estate assets being involved in litigation, and a large portion of the estate assets involving the right to receive money in the future (e.g., annuities, royalties). [IRC § 6081] Any estate tax owed is payable within nine months of death, but an extension of time (not exceeding ten years) for payment is available for reasonable cause. [IRC § 6161(a)] If the time for payment of tax is extended, interest will be charged on the unpaid tax liability. [IRC § 6601]. Also, under Code Section 6166, if more than 35 percent of the adjusted gross estate is an interest in a farm or other closely held business, an executor may elect to defer payments of tax attributable to the interest for five years (paying interest only) and thereafter pay the tax plus interest on the unpaid balance in equal installments over the next ten years. For purposes of this 35 percent rule, the adjusted gross estate consists of the gross estate less debts, expenses, claims and losses deductible under Code Sections 2053 and 2054.

Q 3:31 Who is responsible for paying estate taxes that are owed by the estate?

Federal tax law imposes the responsibility for payment of federal estate taxes on the executor. The taxes themselves are paid out of estate assets. A will, when properly drafted, will contain a tax allocation clause, directing where to place the burden for paying estate taxes. Sometimes the burden is placed on everyone who receives an asset from the estate, sometimes the burden is placed on only some of the beneficiaries. This is an important issue because the burden of taxation can significantly the amount that an estate beneficiary would otherwise receive. Where an executor was chargeable with knowledge of the decedent's income tax liabilities at the time of death but nevertheless chose to pay state income taxes and general creditors, the executor became personally liable to the IRS for those delinquent income taxes. [Rev Rul 79-310, 1979-2 CB 404]

Example 3-12: The owner of a perfume business dies leaving an estate of $2 million. She bequeaths $1 million to her son and the remainder of her estate to her daughter. She specifies that the estate taxes are to be paid out of the portion of the estate going to her daughter. Those taxes ($563,000 when the full unified credit is used) reduce the daughter's portion of the estate to $437,000.

Income Taxes on Estates

Q 3:32 What income tax rates apply to trusts and estates?

Trusts and estates are subject to tax on the income they receive. The top rate for trusts and estates for 1996 is 39.6 percent. This top rate is the same as the top income tax rate for individuals. The top rates for trust and estates, however, are applicable to much lower levels of income and, consequently, take a bigger bite out of trust and estate incomes than do income taxes applicable in nondeath situations. The income tax rate schedule for estates and trusts for 1995 is as follows:

If Taxable Income Is:	The Tax Is:
Not over $1,550	15% of the taxable income
Over $1,550 but not over $3,700	$232.50 plus 28% of the excess over $1,550
Over $3,700 but not over $5,600	$834.50 plus 31% of the excess over $3,700
Over $5,600 but not over $7,650	$1,423.50 plus 36% of the excess of $5,600
Over $7,650	$2,161.50 plus 39.6% of the excess over $7,650

[IRC § 1(e)]

In contrast, the top income tax rate of 39.6 percent for individuals is generally only effective when an individual's taxable income exceeds $256,500.

Gift Taxes

Q 3:33 What transfers are subject to the gift tax?

Irrevocable transfers, whether made outright or in trust, are subject to gift tax, even when the property is transferred for less than adequate and full consideration. This does not mean that a bad bargain automatically results in gift tax consequences; in fact, gift tax does not apply to a sale or exchange for less than adequate and full consideration if it occurs in the ordinary course of business. *Ordinary course of business* is defined as a bona fide transaction free from donative intent that is made by parties who are dealing at arm's length. [Treas Reg § 25.2512-8] Generally, gift tax liability also arises when the holder of a general power of appointment exercises a power in favor of someone other than the holder or the holder's creditors. [IRC § 2514(b)]

> **Example 3-13:** A father sells his son a plot of land worth $100,000 for $60,000. Part of the sale consists of a gift of $40,000 to the son because the land was transferred for less than adequate and full consideration.

Net gifts. A net gift occurs when the donor conditions receipt of the gift upon the donee's paying the gift tax on the gift. Accordingly, the value of the gift is reduced by the amount of gift tax payable by the donee. If the gift tax paid by the donee is greater than the donor's adjusted basis in the property that was the subject of the gift, the excess is treated as taxable gain to the donor.

Split gifts. A gift made by a spouse to a third person may be treated as if half of the gift was given by each spouse. Such gifts are known as split gifts. Both spouses must consent to treat all gifts made to third parties during the calendar year as split gifts. [IRC § 2513(a)] Split gifts are advantageous because each spouse's $10,000 exclusion (see Q 3:36) can be applied to the gift and because the joint tax bracket is lowered. The unified credit (see Q 3:25) is also doubled if a split gift is made.

> **Example 3-14:** A husband and wife embark on a gift-giving program for their children and elect to make split gifts. The husband may give each child $20,000 without incurring gift tax.

Educational or medical expenses. An unlimited exclusion from gift tax is available for amounts paid on behalf of an individual for medical payments or for tuition paid to an educational institution eligible for a charitable deduction (but not for other educational or support expenses). The payments excluded must be paid by the donor directly to the medical care provider or educational institution. [IRC § 2503(e)]

Charitable contributions. Like the estate tax, an unlimited deduction is allowed for gifts to qualifying charitable, religious, or governmental organizations. [IRC § 2522]

Q 3:34 How is the federal gift tax computed?

The federal gift tax is computed as follows:

1. Total the value of all gifts made by the donor during the donor's lifetime through the current calendar year, making the following adjustments:
   a. Exclude the portion of any gift that qualifies for the $10,000 annual exclusion or the exclusion for educational and medical expenses.
   b. Subtract all gift tax deductions (e.g., marital deduction, charitable deduction).
   c. For gifts made before 1977, subtract that portion of the then applicable $30,000 lifetime exemption that the donor elected to use.
2. Compute the tentative gift tax on the aggregate total adjusted gifts for all years through the current calendar year using the current gift tax rate schedule.
3. Compute the tentative gift tax on the aggregate total adjusted gifts for all prior years, using the current gift tax rate schedule.
4. Subtract item 3 from item 2 to determine the tentative tax for the current year.
5. Subtract the unused portion of the unified credit against the tentative gift tax for the current year.

The effect of this computation approach is to bring the higher gift tax brackets into play as additional gifts are made.

Example 3-15: In 1993, a landowner gave land worth $300,000 to his son. Prior to 1977, the landowner gave land worth $130,000 to his son (after taking into account the $10,000 annual exclusion). In 1987, the landowner gave property to his son worth $400,000 (after taking into account the $10,000 annual exclusion). The total gift tax payable is computed as follows:

Pre-1977 gifts (adjusted for annual exclusion)	$130,000
Less: Pre-1977 lifetime exemption	$ 30,000
Net taxable pre-1977 gifts	$100,000
1987 gifts (adjusted for annual exclusion)	$400,000
1993 gifts (adjusted for annual exclusion)	$300,000
Total Gifts:	$800,000
Tentative tax on total gifts	$267,800
Less tentative tax on prior-year gifts	$155,800
Tentative tax on 1993 gifts	$112,000
Less unified credit	$192,800
Less unified credit used for 1987 gifts	$121,800
Available credit	$ 71,000
Gift tax payable in 1993	$ 41,000

Q 3:35 What is the unified gift credit?

The unified gift credit consists of $192,800 of credit against gift tax. [IRC § 2505] This dollar amount is reduced by the amount of credit used up by previous gifts. If, for example, $50,000 of credit was used because a donor made gifts in excess of the $10,000 annual exclusion, the remaining gift tax credit available at death is $142,800. The unified credit is restored at death and becomes a credit against estate tax (see Q 3:25).

Q 3:36 What is the annual exclusion that applies to gifts?

The first $10,000 per year of gifts that a donor gives to each beneficiary is excluded in computing the gift tax. [IRC § 2503(b)] There is no restriction on the number of beneficiaries. The $10,000 exclusion is allowable only for gifts of a present interest and is not available for gifts of a future interest. For an interest to be a present interest, an unrestricted right to the immediate use possession or enjoyment of the asset must be given. [Treas Reg § 25.2503-3(b)] If a gift is made to a trust, care must be taken to ensure that a present interest is given.

> **Example 3-16:** A physician makes a gift to a trust that provides that income is to be paid currently to the income beneficiary and that the payment of principal is deferred until the income beneficiary dies. The income interest is a present interest, but the gift of principal is a gift of a future interest. The $10,000 exclusion is not available for the value of the principal.

Q 3:37 How is the marital deduction determined for gift tax purposes?

Subsequent to 1981, a donor is allowed an unlimited marital deduction for lifetime gifts of property to his or her spouse. [IRC § 2523(a)] The deduction is not allowable for gifts of life estates or other terminable interests, except in the case of a qualifying terminable interest election under Code Section 2523(f).

Q 3:38 Who is responsible for paying gift tax?

The donor is responsible for paying the gift tax. [IRC § 2501] The donor can, however, require the donee to pay the gift tax as a condition of making the gift. These gifts are known as net gifts (see Q 3:33).

Q 3:39 Does the recipient of a gift have any liability for gift tax?

Yes. If the donor does not pay the gift tax owed, the donee is personally liable for the tax to the extent of the value of the gift received. Furthermore, even if the gift received by a particular donee was tax free, that donee can be held liable to the extent of the value of the gift for the tax owed on all other gifts made by the donor during that year. [Baur v Commr, 145 F 2d 338 (3d Cir 1944)]

Example 3-17: A father gives his son property worth $8,000 in 1993. The gift is not subject to gift tax because it is less than the $10,000 annual exclusion. The father, however, owes gift taxes totaling $30,000 for gifts he made to his daughters. The son is subject to gift tax of up to $8,000 if his father does not pay the gift tax of $30,000 that he owes for 1993.

Q 3:40 When are gift tax returns due?

Except for the calendar year in which the donor dies, gift tax returns are due annually on or before April 15 following the year the taxable gift is made. Gift tax returns for the calendar year in which the donor dies must be filed no later than the due date for filing the donor's estate tax return, including extensions (see Q 3:30). Gift tax returns are filed using Form 709.

Basis of Property Acquired from Decedents

Q 3:41 What is the basis of property acquired from a decedent?

Income tax basis is the cost allowed to a taxpayer that is used in determining gain or loss, for income tax purposes, on the sale, disposition, or abandonment of an asset or, in the case of depreciable property, as a measure for determining the annual depreciation on such property. The income tax basis for property acquired from a decedent is equal to the fair market value of the property on the date of the decedent's death or, if the alternate valuation date is used (see Q 3:21), its value on the alternate valuation date. [IRC § 1014(a)] Similarly, assets transferred by a decedent during the decedent's lifetime but includible in the estate for estate tax purposes receive a new basis in the hands of the recipient. [IRC § 1014(b)] Only that portion of a joint tenancy asset (see Qs 2:25–2:41, 3:11) that is includible in the gross estate receives a new basis; the excludable portion retains the survivor's basis. Assets that are included in a marital deduction bequest (see chapter 4) also receive a new basis even though these bequests are not subject to estate tax. Assets subject to generation skipping transfer taxes (see chapter 5) generally receive a new tax basis equal to the fair market value of the assets at the time the generation skipping transfer tax is imposed. In a recent decision, the Tax Court held that a surviving spouse had to use as her cost basis in property, the value of said property to which her husband had previously agreed in an estate tax proceeding involving the death of her mother-in-law. This is commonly referred to as the duty of consistency doctrine. [Kristine Cluck, 105 TC No 21 (1966)]

Q 3:42 What planning considerations apply to a spousal residence?

If the spousal residence is held as a tenancy in common, a tenancy by the entirety, or a joint tenancy with rights of survivorship, an increase in basis on one half of the value of property will occur upon the death of one of the spouses. [IRC § 1014(b)] If the surviving spouse stays in the residence until death, the tax basis is not a consideration. If the surviving spouse sells the residence, however, there may be taxable gain. [IRC § 1001(a)] Two opportunities for tax relief exist in this situation, and both opportunities depend on the home being the surviving spouse's principal residence. Because of these relief provisions, a sale of a house by a surviving spouse may not be too harmful even if a full basis step-up is not obtained.

One opportunity for tax relief arises if all of the proceeds from the sale of the principal residence are reinvested in another principal residence within two years of the sale. [IRC § 1034(a)] As long as the price of the new residence is at least equal to the sales price of the former residence, no gain will be recognized on the sale of the old residence. [Treas Reg § 1.1034-1(a)] This permits potential gain to be deferred or suspended. The gain is merely deferred and not completely avoided because it must be subtracted from the taxpayer's basis in the new residence. [IRC § 1034(e)] If the new principal residence costs the taxpayer less than the sales price of the old residence, the taxpayer must recognize gain to the extent of the difference between the sales price of the old residence and the cost of the new residence. [Treas Reg § 1.1034-1(a)]

Example 3-18: A husband and wife purchase a house in 1970 for $75,000 that they use as their principal residence. The husband dies in 1992. His widow sells the principal residence for $200,000 on May 10, 1995. One year later, she purchases a new principal residence for $300,000. Because the cost of the new residence is higher than the sales price of the old residence, no portion of the $125,000 gain on the sale of the first residence is taxable.

Example 3-19: The same facts apply as in Example 3-18, except that the purchase price of the new principal residence is $150,000. In this situation, gain will be recognized to the extent of the difference between the sales price of the old residence and the cost of the new residence. The surviving spouse will recognize gain of $50,000 on the transaction. This gain is subject to federal income tax.

Example 3-20: The same facts apply as in Example 3-18, except that the surviving spouse acquires the new principal residence three years after selling the old residence. In this case, Code Section 1034 does not apply; the regular rules for recognizing gain apply. [IRC § 1001(a)] The sales price of the old residence, $200,000, minus its original cost, $75,000, equals the gain, $125,000. The entire $125,000 of gain must be recognized. [IRC § 1001(c)] It is clearly to the taxpayer's advantage to structure the purchase and sale of a principal residence to fit the parameters of Code Section 1034 whenever possible.

The other relief provision can be used only once in a lifetime. [IRC § 121(b)(2)] It is available only if the seller is 55 years old or older and the house has been the seller's principal residence for three of the last five years. [IRC § 121(a)] If these requirements are met and the taxpayer elects to be subject to Code Section 121, up to $125,000 in gain is exempted from taxation. This is an especially attractive provision because it completely excludes realized gain as opposed to merely deferring it as in transactions involving exchanges of property under Code Section 1034.

The IRS takes the position that, for purposes of the two-year rule and the exclusion rule where one of the spouses is 55 years of age or over, interests in a cooperative apartment or condominium apartment and outright ownership in a residence are to be treated the same. [Rev Rul 60-36, 1960-1 CB 296; Rev Rul 85-132, 1985-2 CB 182]

Example 3-21: A husband and wife purchase a house in 1970 for $75,000, which they use as their principal residence. The husband dies in 1992. The surviving spouse reaches age 55 in 1994. In 1995, she sells the house for $200,000. Because the surviving spouse is over the age of 55 and has owned the house and used it as her principal residence for at least three of the past five years, she makes a Section 121 election. She is allowed to exclude up to $125,000 of gain on the sale of the house. [IRC § 121(b)(1)] The total gain realized on the sale is $125,000 ($200,000 − $75,000 = $125,000). [IRC § 1001(a)] Consequently, the surviving spouse has no recognized gain from the sale of the house.

Q 3:43 What is the basis in community property upon the death of one of the spouses?

Each spouse may generally dispose of his or her share of community property at death as that person wishes. At death, only half of the community property is included in the deceased spouse's gross estate for estate tax purposes. Because of the marital deduction, there is no estate tax if the surviving spouse inherits the decedent's share of the property. [IRC § 2056(a)] The entire community property asset does, however, receive a step-up in basis to the fair market value of the property at the date of the decedent's death. [IRC § 1014(b)(6)] This basis change is not limited to the half of the property that went through the deceased spouse's estate, but applies to the entire property.

Example 3-22: The owner of a computer distribution company who resides in a community property state dies. He and his wife own $1 million in stock as community property. Their basis in the stock is $200,000. The decedent bequeaths his $500,000 in stock to his spouse. The wife's basis in all of the stock is $1 million.

Example 3-23: The same facts apply as in Example 3-22 except that the stock is not community property but is owned by the businessman and his wife as joint tenants. The wife's basis in all of the stock is $600,000. She receives an increase in basis to $500,000 for one half of the property while retaining a $100,000 basis in the remaining half of the property.

Q 3:44 How is income in respect to a decedent treated?

Income in respect of a decedent results when an income item is earned at the date of death but is received by the estate or estate beneficiary thereafter. If income in respect of a decedent results from a sale made prior to the decedent's death, the gain is includible in the gross estate. In order to minimize the effect of double taxation on an item, the estate tax attributable to the inclusion of the income is deductible for income tax purposes. This does not truly eliminate a double tax because the estate tax is not a credit against income tax, but is rather a deduction in computing the taxable income of an estate. [IRC § 691(c)(4)]

> **Example 3-24:** Prior to his death, a businessman agrees to sell land with a basis of $100,000 for $200,000. The proceeds of the sale are not paid until two months after the businessman's death. The estate tax on the businessman's estate is increased by $30,000 as a result of the extra income. The $100,000 gain is income with respect to a decedent, but is reduced by the $30,000 of estate taxes attributable to the property sold.

Q 3:45 What is the basis of property acquired by gift?

For income tax purposes, the basis of property acquired by gift is the same as the donor's basis. [IRC § 1015(a)] If the donor acquired the property by gift, the basis is the same as that of the last preceding owner who did not acquire the property by gift. If the basis of property when the gift is made exceeds the fair market value of the property, however, the basis used to determine loss is fair market value.

> **Example 3-25:** A real estate broker gives her daughter land with a basis of $50,000. The land has just been declared a protected wetlands area, so the fair market value at the time of the gift is $20,000. The daughter sells the land the next day for $15,000. Her loss on the sale is $5,000 ($20,000 fair market value – $15,000 amount received). If the mother had kept the property and sold it herself, she would have had a $35,000 loss on the sale ($50,000 basis – $15,000 amount received).

Q 3:46 What effect does federal gift tax have on the basis of gift property?

The basis of gift property is increased when federal gift tax is paid on the transfer. [IRC § 1015] The increase in basis for gifts made after December 3, 1976, is limited to the portion of the gift tax paid on the amount by which the fair market value of the gift property exceeds the donor's adjusted basis in the gift property immediately before the gift is made.

Q 3:47 What basis applies if one spouse sells or exchanges an asset with his or her spouse?

If one spouse sells or exchanges an asset with his or her spouse, the transaction is not treated as a sale or exchange but as if the transferee received the property by gift. [IRC § 1041(b)] As a result, the transferee has the same basis in the property as did the transferor. [IRC § 1015]

Q 3:48 What are the holding periods for capital gains purposes for gift assets and for inherited assets?

For capital gains purposes, the holding period of a gift asset includes the holding period of the decedent or donor. [IRC § 1223(2)] In contrast, for capital gains purposes, the holding period of an inherited asset commences with the date of death. Recipients are, however, automatically entitled to long-term capital gains treatment on inherited assets regardless of the actual length of the holding period. [IRC § 1223(11)(a)]

Nontax Considerations

Q 3:49 How great a role should nontax considerations play in estate planning?

Although tax planning principles are important in estate planning because they can make a significant difference to the estate, nontax principles often overshadow the tax issues. A donor must balance the desirability of implementing a gift program against the desirability of having a comfortable retirement. In many cases, nontax considerations such as these will outweigh the tax considerations.

Q 3:50 Can the surviving spouse be given access to trust principal without having to make a request for principal from the trustee?

Yes, the surviving spouse can be authorized to make withdrawals of principal from the trust. If the power is entirely unrestricted, however, the beneficiary spouse could use up all of the assets. One approach is to put a ceiling on the amount that the spouse can withdraw from the trust. There could be, for example, an annual maximum of $10,000 or a lifetime maximum of $75,000.

Q 3:51 What actions can be taken if trust investments become extremely successful?

If the trust fund becomes so large that it seems unwise to turn it over to a young adult (even though the beneficiary is mature), one solution may be to spend some of the trust assets on the beneficiary. For example, trust assets might be used to pay for computer school, ballet lessons, vacations, summer camp, tennis lessons, or skiing instruction.

Q 3:52 When setting up trusts for children, what factors dictate the use of a single trust as opposed to separate trusts?

A single trust may make more sense if trust assets are limited because assets can be directed to the child with the greatest need. A single trust may also be appropriate if the children have widely different circumstances.

Example 3-26: A family consists of three children, a daughter who is 25 years old and two sons who are 10 and 11 years old. Family assets are modest. The daughter is half way through graduate school. The younger son has a learning disability and receives therapy regularly. Under these circumstances, it may be advisable to set up a single trust so that more than one third of the family assets, if necessary, are available to take care of the younger son, and so that the daughter can receive less than one third of the family assets if additional assets are needed to take care of the younger son.

On the other hand, separate trusts may make more sense if assets are substantial enough so that each trust fund can be adequately funded to meet the particular needs of each child. By funding separate trusts, parents may be able to prevent some children from feeling that other children are favored.

Q 3:53 What is an advantage of giving trustees for children's trusts broad discretion to distribute trust principal?

An important advantage of broad discretion is that the trustees can react to unexpected events that may arise during the children's lifetimes. By providing the trustees with broad discretion, the creator of the trust prevents the trustees from being unduly hampered in dealing with the needs of the children.

Example 3-27: A child who is the beneficiary of a trust suddenly and unexpectedly loses his job and is faced with the possibility of personal bankruptcy if he does not immediately make payments to creditors. A trustee with broad discretion could distribute trust principal to that child to help him through this difficult financial situation.

Q 3:54 What considerations apply in selecting trustees?

First, one should consider whether to select more than one trustee. One reason for doing this is that different people have different skills. One person may know about investing, whereas another may be sensitive to the needs of the beneficiaries. Different tasks can be assigned to different trustees; if one person has great empathy for people but limited investment skills, that person's role as trustee can be limited to determining how trust assets will be distributed. Other trustees can determine how to invest trust assets. It is probably unwise to appoint more trustees than are needed to do the job. Trusteeship can be a demanding job and should not be regarded as a political plum.

Recent volatility in both the stock and bond markets emphasizes the importance of selecting a capable trustee and giving that trustee a good deal of flexibility in choosing investments. The value of bonds can fluctuate greatly, and inflation rates also may vary. A trustee whose investment skills are limited may still prove to be a good choice if he or she is given the flexibility to hire a financial advisor. Indeed, many states permit trustees to delegate their investment function to an advisor who makes investment decisions. If the trustee picks the investment advisor with care, the trustee is not responsible for mediocre investment results.

Because they offer permanence, banks are often used as trustees. Banks can also provide all the services needed, including investment services, physical custody of the assets, preparation of trust tax returns, and recordkeeping services. As many banks are acquired by other banks and shift their personnel around, however, there is no assurance that a particularly competent bank official will be available in the future. If a bank is not used, the necessary services must be provided by another entity. In determining whether to appoint a bank as trustee, it is important to compare the bank's charges to the fees of the administrative specialists who will otherwise be needed to administer the trust.

Q 3:55 If a bank is chosen as trustee, should an individual also be selected?

If a bank is chosen as trustee, the creator of the trust may also want an individual to serve as co-trustee. This individual trustee will be chosen for the personal and more familiar knowledge that he or she has of the needs of the beneficiaries (e.g., spouse, children) named in the trust.

Q 3:56 Should children be chosen as trustees for their siblings?

It is usually a bad idea for children to serve as trustees for each other. If one sibling is involved in the financial affairs of the other, misunderstandings, jealousies, and rivalries may result.

Q 3:57 Should a child be appointed trustee of his or her own trust?

It can be a good idea to permit a child to be a co-trustee of his or her own trust. If the child can work well with others, serving as co-trustee can be a learning experience for the child. Presumably, it would also give the child a sense of participation in his or her financial future.

Q 3:58 Should a trust contain a provision for removal of the trustee?

One argument against including these kinds of provisions is that they may limit the independence of the trustee. This may make the trustee too susceptible to outside influences. In some cases, however, this may be consistent with the creator's intent. For instance, if the creator set up a trust primarily for tax purposes, he or she may not be too concerned if the beneficiaries have a power of removal over the trustee, even though the effect of such power may be to limit the trustee's independence. This would be especially true if the creator has great confidence in his or her beneficiaries.

Another concern in creating authority to remove a trustee is that there could be significant expenses associated with such an act. If a trustee is removed, he or she is likely to insist on an accounting. This means that all trust transactions will be reviewed. The accounting process can be prolonged and expensive.

Q 3:59 What provisions can be made for successor trustees?

The initial trustee can be authorized to select his or her successor. Alternatively, the grantor can provide a successor trustee in the trust document itself. It may not be a bad idea to permit a trustee to name his or her own successor. If the trust creator has sufficient confidence in the initial trustee to name him or her as trustee, the trust creator is likely to believe that the trustee is capable of doing a good job in choosing a successor. The advantage of permitting the trustee to select his or her successor is that the responsibilities of trusteeship will be met should circumstances change so that the successor trustee appointed in the trust document is unable to serve.

Example 3-28: An attorney, aged 73, is appointed as successor trustee for a trust. Because the trust is likely to continue for another

20 years, the attorney chooses a 35-year-old successor trustee. Ten years later, the attorney dies, and the successor trustee assumes responsibility.

Q 3:60　What kinds of conflicts can arise between beneficiaries who are currently entitled to trust income and beneficiaries who will receive trust principal at future dates?

Many trusts are designed in such a way that one group of beneficiaries receives the income held by the trust while the actual assets contributed to the trust (the trust principal) are held for the benefit of a different group of people.

Example 3-29: An entrepreneur sets up a trust and transfers $1 million to it. He provides in the trust document that his wife will have all income generated by the $1 million during her life and that on her death the $1 million principal amount will be paid to his children.

Several types of conflicts can arise under this type of trust. One possible conflict arises if the trust provides for the possible payment of principal to the income beneficiary. For instance, the trust described in Example 3-28 could provide that principal could be withdrawn for the benefit of the wife under certain circumstances. If the wife were a second wife and the children were the children of a first marriage, such a provision could lead to a strong conflict.

Another potential source of conflict could be the investment policy of the trustees. The income beneficiary might prefer that the trust be invested in risky yet potentially high income investments while the principal beneficiaries might prefer that the trust be invested in more conservative investments to ensure that there will be trust principal left when it comes time to pay them.

Q 3:61　How can a trust be designed to reflect a desire to favor current beneficiaries over future beneficiaries?

This can be accomplished by including a trust provision directing that the interests of principal beneficiaries be subordinate to the interest of the current income beneficiary. Moreover, trust investments that favor the current income beneficiary—such as investments in high income securities—can be included.

Chapter 4

The Marital Deduction

The federal income, estate, and gift tax systems are structured to favor married taxpayers. In the case of income taxes, married couples are allowed to file joint income tax returns that usually provide greater tax savings than if the couple were to file as married filing separately. In the case of estate and gift taxes, transfers between spouses are permitted an unlimited deduction (the marital deduction) resulting in no tax with respect to the transfer. For estate planners, the marital deduction is the major focus for generating overall estate and gift tax savings for the family unit. It allows property eligible for the marital deduction to completely escape estate tax in the estate of the first of the spouses to die. Often, when combined with the $600,000 exemption, which is available to all estates, estate tax can also be eliminated upon the subsequent death of the surviving spouse. Where estates exceed $1.2 million, estate tax although not necessarily capable of being wholly avoided, is nevertheless capable of being substantially reduced. This chapter explains the marital deduction, the kinds of property that can be transferred using the marital deduction, and how the marital deduction can be used in conjunction with a trust.

Overview	4-2
Eligible Property	4-4
Considerations in Using the Marital Deduction	4-7
Using a Trust with the Marital Deduction	4-13
Spousal Bequests	4-21

Overview

Q 4:1 What is the marital deduction?

It is the unlimited estate and gift tax deduction for transfers made during life or on death to a spouse. Accordingly, if an individual were to die with an estate of $10 million which, under his or her will, conveys the entire estate to a surviving spouse, the decedent's estate would incur no estate tax liability. As explained below, this transfer could prove to be a costly mistake, because it would leave a major tax burden on the estate of the surviving spouse, who may not have remarried by the time he or she dies. The significance of this fact is that without remarriage, the surviving spouse would have no marital deduction. The marital deduction is, in effect, a deferral of the estate tax to the date of the second death. This deferral can present a great opportunity to accumulate funds and to create estate planning opportunities for the surviving spouse. It allows for the time and use of funds for the duration of his or her life and provides opportunities for saving estate taxes. On the other hand, if the surviving spouse does not remarry by the time of his or her death, the estate tax can be significant because there is no marital deduction available to shield the estate from it.

The marital deduction is not optional, except in the case of QTIP property (see Q 4:18), and it works very simply. The marital deduction is allowed (1) for property that is a deductible property interest; (2) for property that is included in the decedent's gross estate; (3) for property that passes from the decedent to the surviving spouse; and (4) to a surviving spouse who is a U.S. citizen.

Q 4:2 What are the property interests that qualify for the marital deduction?

Code Section 2056(c) provides that property interests that pass from the decedent to a surviving spouse include property that:

1. Passes to the surviving spouse under the will of the deceased spouse as a bequest or devise, or pursuant to the laws of intestacy of the decedent's domicile;

2. Passes to a surviving spouse as the surviving tenant by the entirety or as the surviving joint tenant;
3. Passes to the surviving spouse where the decedent has exercised a power of appointment. A power of appointment authorizes the person who holds it to designate who will receive the property that is subject to the power of appointment.
4. Passes to the surviving spouse as the beneficiary of life insurance, an employee benefit plan, IRA or other benefit for which the decedent had made a beneficiary designation naming his or her spouse;
5. Passes to the surviving spouse because of dower or curtesy interest, an elective share against the deceased spouse's will or the lump sum amount distributed to the surviving spouse as part of an arm's length estate settlement. Dower is an interest in property to which a wife becomes entitled upon the death of her husband. The corresponding right for a surviving husband is called curtesy. Most states have replaced dower and curtesy with the statutory elective share. Under such statutes, a surviving spouse can generally opt for an elective share, which allows him or her to receive a percentage of the decedent spouse's estate despite contrary provision in the decedent's will.
6. Passes to the surviving spouse as the beneficiary of an annuity or pension benefit; and,
7. Passes to the surviving spouse under the laws of intestacy or under the will of the decedent, as a result of a disclaimer of an interest which would have otherwise passed to another.

Q 4:3 Why must an interest in property *pass* from the decedent to the surviving spouse in order to qualify for the marital deduction?

The concept of passing can best be understood in the following context. A husband dies and his will provides a trust for his wife eligible for the marital deduction and another trust that is ineligible. His surviving spouse and children, acting with the consent of the surrogate's court, enter into an agreement that allows the entire estate to pass outright to the surviving spouse under the laws of intestacy. The IRS disallows the marital deduction holding that the assignment or surrender to a surviving spouse of a property interest must be as a result of a controversy involving a bequest or devise contained in a decedent's will. [Treas Regs § 20.2056(c)-2(d)(2)] According to the IRS, the surviving spouse had no legally enforceable claim and her agreement with the children was voluntary and not at arm's length; therefore, no controversy. Thus, the IRS holds that "the interest in property passes to" the surviving spouse "by virtue of the agreement (between her and the children) and the petition granted by the local court, not from the decedent." [Ltr Rul 9610004]

Q 4:4 If an estate has administrative expenses that it elects or is required to allocate between the property received on the decedent's death and the income earned on the property subsequent to death, does the entire amount of administrative expenses paid by the estate reduce the amount available for the marital deduction?

The U.S. Supreme Court is taking up this question as a result of a conflict in approach by various federal circuit courts of appeal. [Hubert v Comm (11th Cir 1995) *aff'g* 101 TC 314] The *Hubert* decision holds that because allocation of administrative expenses to estate income was permitted by state law (Georgia), the marital deduction was not required to be reduced by such allocation. Estate planners should be alerted to the outcome of this case when decided by the U.S. Supreme Court.

Eligible Property

Q 4:5 Can the marital deduction be made available if the surviving spouse is not a U.S. citizen?

Yes, provided a qualified domestic trust (QDOT) is used to hold the assets so that they are not given directly to the surviving spouse. [IRC § 2056(d)(2)] A QDOT is a trust that has at least one trustee who is a U.S. citizen or U.S. corporation who is responsible for seeing that the estate tax due from the trust is paid. [IRC § 2056A(a)]

Congress was concerned when it enacted the Technical and Miscellaneous Revenue Act of 1988 that the principal purpose of allowing the marital deduction—deductibility in the estate of the first-to-die spouse and subsequent includibility in the estate of the second-to-die spouse—would be contravened in the case of a non-citizen surviving spouse. The non-citizen spouse could return to his or her country of citizenship and the transferred marital deduction property would escape tax on his or her death. The QDOT is intended to remedy this potential tax avoidance situation.

Q 4:6 What is the terminable interest rule?

To qualify for a marital deduction, the property passing from the decedent to the surviving spouse must avoid the terminable interest rule. This rule states that the marital deduction is disallowed if the interest passing from the decedent to the surviving spouse terminates or fails because of a lapse of time, the occurrence of a specified event, or the failure of a specified event to occur.

Example 4-1: A surviving spouse's interest in an estate terminates unless she establishes a memorial park for her deceased husband. The requirement that she establish the park or else lose her interest in the estate makes that interest a terminable interest. As a result, her interest in the estate would not qualify for the marital deduction.

Example 4-2: A casino owner puts a bequest in his will to his surviving spouse providing that the bequest will terminate on her death or remarriage. This bequest is a terminable interest. A limited survivorship requirement for up to six months after the decedent's death is permitted.

The policy behind the terminable interest rule is to ensure that property that avoids estate tax on the death of the decedent spouse will eventually be subject to tax on the death of the surviving spouse. Therefore, if the property interest that passes from the decedent to a surviving spouse will terminate or fail because of a lapse of time or the failure of an event to occur and then will pass on to some third person without being taxed at the surviving spouse's death, no marital deduction will be allowed. The terminable interest rule ensures that a property interest that avoids taxation on the death of the first spouse to die will be taxed when the surviving spouse dies.

Q 4:7 How can the marital deduction be obtained?

The most direct way to obtain the marital deduction is for the individual (the donor) to simply bequeath property directly to his or her spouse so that the spouse becomes the owner of the property when the individual dies. Sometimes, however, the donor wishes to keep the property out of the surviving spouse's probate (as opposed to taxable) estate, or place restrictions on the bequest, or have the property managed by a professional manager. In these cases, certain kinds of trusts such as QTIP trusts and power of appointment trusts can be used.

Q 4:8 What is contained in a probate estate?

A decedent's probate estate is composed of the property interests that he or she owns at death. This is different from the decedent's taxable estate, which is used to determine estate taxes and includes the property in the probate estate and certain other interests such as joint tenancy property and property held in revocable trusts. [IRC § 2033]

> **Example 4-3:** A race-car driver dies, leaving, among other assets, stock in his name worth $100,000 and a joint tenancy in a race car with his son. The son contributed one half of the cost of the race car. The stock is part of both the probate estate and the taxable estate; the race car is not in the probate estate, but one half of the value of the race car is included in the taxable estate.

Q 4:9 Can a bequest that is conditioned on the surviving spouse's outliving the decedent for six months or less qualify for the marital deduction?

Bequests conditioned on the surviving spouse's outliving the decedent for a period of time generally are nondeductible terminable interests; however, a bequest conditioned solely on a spouse's surviving for a period not exceeding six months after the decedent's death will qualify for the marital deduction as a nonterminable deduction, provided that the spouse does survive for the designated period. [IRC § 2056(b)(3)] If the surviving spouse dies within six months (or within a shorter designated period), however, the bequest is considered a terminable interest because the surviving spouse's interest actually terminated.

Considerations in Using the Marital Deduction

Q 4:10 What is the $600,000 exemption equivalent?

The $600,000 exemption equivalent is determined with respect to the unified credit. [IRC § 2010] The unified credit allows the estate of every decedent to subtract $192,800 from its estate tax bill. This $192,800 figure is equivalent to the amount of tax that would be due if the decedent had a taxable estate worth $600,000. So, as long as the decedent's taxable estate consists of $600,000 or less, no estate tax will be owed to the IRS. Furthermore, if the taxable estate is greater than $600,000, the first $600,000 will not be considered when calculating estate taxes.

Q 4:11 What is the optimal way to use the marital deduction?

Consider husband and wife as one economic unit and estate taxes as a major cost to the unit that must be reduced on an overall basis. Accordingly, the estates of both spouses must be considered. By using the unlimited marital deduction, an individual avoids taxation of the estate of the first spouse to die. It is important to realize, however, that the consequence of using the unlimited marital deduction is that the taxable estate of the second spouse may be greatly increased. Planning the marital deduction thus requires comparing the marginal estate tax brackets expected to apply when the first spouse dies with those expected to apply when the surviving spouse dies. If the marginal tax rate will be higher upon the death of the second spouse, it must be decided whether to (1) defer the estate tax on the death of the first spouse to die by fully using the marital deduction, or (2) have part of the property included in the estate of the first spouse and pay some estate tax on the first spouse's death, to reduce the marginal tax rate on the second spouse's death. The decision to fully use the marital deduction upon the death of the first spouse depends on various factors, described below. The following guidelines should be considered in deciding on the marital deduction. They assume that the surviving spouse has no individually owned assets.

1. If an individual's taxable estate is likely to be less than $600,000, it may be sensible to give the entire amount to the surviving spouse and take advantage of the marital deduction; no estate taxes are saved by bequeathing property to someone else. The $600,000 figure is significant because this is the amount of assets exemption that is equivalent to the unified credit of $192,800, thus permitting an individual to bequeath this amount without incurring estate tax.

2. If the individual's projected taxable estate is more than $600,000 but less than $1.2 million, it may be sensible to give $600,000 to his or her surviving spouse and the remainder to other persons. This permits the use of unified credits for both estates.

Example 4-4: A consultant has a projected taxable estate of $1 million. His wife's expected taxable estate is negligible. He decides on an estate plan that gives his spouse $600,000 in the event of his death and his children $400,000. Two years later, the consultant dies. No estate tax is payable on the consultant's death because of the marital deduction and because the estate can use the $192,800 unified credit to shelter up to $600,000 from estate tax. Because the bequest to the children is only $400,000, no estate tax is due. Two years later the consultant's wife dies. Because she was able to live on the income generated by the $600,000 bequest, she has $600,000 to bequeath to the children. Her estate can use her $192,800 unified credit to shelter the $600,000 bequest from estate taxes.

3. If the individual's projected taxable estate is between $1.2 million and $1,350,000, it may be sensible to limit the amounts bequeathed to persons other than the surviving spouse to $600,000 and to give the surviving spouse the remainder, rather than to split the estate equally between the surviving spouse and other persons. This is because the total estate tax is the

same under both approaches, but the time in which tax is paid is likely to be delayed if the surviving spouse receives all but $600,000.

Example 4-5: A businessman's projected taxable estate is $1,350,000. His wife's projected taxable estate is negligible. Because the 39 percent estate tax bracket begins at $500,000 and ends at $750,000, the businessman decides to bequeath $600,000 to his children and $750,000 to his spouse. By doing this he takes advantage of the $192,800 unified credit to shelter $600,000 of assets. If his spouse dies after he does and she does not deplete the $750,000 he bequeaths to her, he can expect that $600,000 will be sheltered from estate tax by the $192,800 unified credit. The remaining $150,000 will be taxed at a rate of 37 percent. Had the businessman given $650,000 to his children and $700,000 to his wife, $50,000 would have been subject to the 37 percent rate when he died and $100,000 would be taxed at 37 percent when his wife died. Although the total amount of estate tax is the same under both scenarios, under the second approach, part of the tax bite occurs earlier.

4. If the individual's projected taxable estate is between $1,350,000 and $6 million, the dollar amount of estate taxes generally can be reduced by splitting the estate equally between the surviving spouse and others; however, because the payment of tax will be delayed on amounts given to the surviving spouse, it may still be better to give the bulk of the estate to the surviving spouse and limit bequests to others to no more than the $600,000 exemption equivalent.

The following factors favor giving the surviving spouse the bulk of the estate and perhaps limiting others to the $600,000 exemption equivalent:

1. The surviving spouse will have the use of the assets during his or her lifetime.
2. The surviving spouse can reduce his or her estate through consumption or through a program of annual giving of amounts that are less than the $10,000 annual exclusion contained in Code Section 2503(b).

3. When the surviving spouse dies, the assets will receive a step-up in basis for income tax purposes. To the extent the assets have appreciated, they will obtain a higher basis. [IRC § 1014(b)]

Example 4-6: As part of her estate distribution, a surviving spouse receives a parcel of land with a fair market value of $200,000. At her death three years later, the property is worth $1 million. Her heirs will have a tax basis of $1 million in the property for income tax purposes. The heirs immediately sell the property. No income tax is due on the sale of the property.

Q 4:12 Why should the estate of a husband and wife be equalized?

The following factors favor planning the respective estates of a married couple so that one half of their property is subject to estate taxation upon the death of the first spouse and one half is subject to estate taxation at the death of the second spouse (this is known as *equalizing the estates*):

1. The additional appreciation of assets after the death of the first spouse can be kept out of the surviving spouse's estate.

Example 4-7: A $2 million estate is divided equally between the surviving spouse and the decedent's children. Upon the death of the first spouse, $1 million is subject to estate taxation. By the time the second spouse dies, the $1 million that passed to the surviving spouse using the marital deduction has appreciated in value 100 percent. The surviving spouse's taxable estate is $2 million. In contrast, if the surviving spouse receives $1.4 million under the marital deduction and only the $600,000 exemption equivalent goes to other persons, the surviving spouse's taxable estate (again assuming a 100 percent appreciation) is $2.8 million.

It is important to consider the circumstances of the persons who become beneficiaries rather than those of the surviving spouse. If they predecease the surviving spouse or if they are in a higher estate tax bracket than the surviving spouse, the tax savings will be negated.

2. The surviving spouse may not need the income from all of the decedent spouse's assets. If the estates are equalized, more income can go to other beneficiaries, when the first spouse dies.
3. If both spouses are expected to die within a short period of time, equalizing the estates can result in a lower overall estate tax if the estate is between $1,350,000 and $6 million. Normally the tax advantage of equalizing the estates is offset by the possibility of deferred estate tax on appreciated assets if most assets are given to the surviving spouse. However, if both spouses are expected to die soon, this deferral advantage does not exist, and it may be better to equalize the projected estates of the spouses.

Q 4:13 When should the maximum marital deduction not be taken?

The difficulty with taking the maximum marital deduction is that it may leave insufficient funds for children or other nonspousal beneficiaries. The marital deduction for assets is effective only if the assets provide no benefits for the children during the life of the surviving spouse. This effect can be alleviated by using the exemption equivalent to direct $600,000 to the children; however, if the surviving spouse is a step-parent who receives several million dollars through the marital deduction, the children may still be unhappy with the result. Even if the surviving spouse is a natural parent, the children may be unhappy if the surviving spouse marries someone else and lives lavishly on his or her inheritance with his or her new spouse. Because of these consequences, it may be preferable to make provision for the reasonable needs of the surviving spouse and to leave the children or grandchildren more than the exemption equivalent of $600,000.

Q 4:14 Can a control premium be used to increase the size of the marital deduction?

A control premium is often associated with a majority stock ownership. For example, a person who owns 51 percent of the stock of a company may be allocated 70 percent of the value of that stock because of his or her ability to control the activities of the corporation. Usually the IRS asserts that a control premium applies to estate assets; however, if a majority interest in a business is given to a surviving spouse, the estate may want to increase the size of the marital deduction by asserting a control premium. [See Estate of Chenoweth, 88 TC 1577(1987)]

> **Example 4-8:** A brewery owner dies, leaving 55 percent of the stock in the brewery to his wife. The brewery is worth $2 million. The estate asserts that the 55 percent interest in the brewery is worth $1.4 million when the control premium is considered and takes a deduction in that amount. The estate asserts that the remaining $600,000 of stock, which goes to the owner's children, is protected from estate tax by the unified credit. By taking this stance, the estate can pass 45 percent of the stock in the brewery to the decedent's children.

Q 4:15 How should the marital deduction be used in a large estate?

If an individual's taxable estate is $6 million or more, estate taxes may be reduced by giving the surviving spouse at least $3 million and other persons at least $3 million. The reduction occurs because the highest marginal tax bracket begins at $3 million. [IRC § 2001] After at least $3 million has been given to the surviving spouse and $3 million has been given to other beneficiaries, it is advantageous to give estate assets in excess of $6 million to the surviving spouse in order to delay the imposition of estate tax on these assets (even though the marginal rates are the same). Considerations such as the needs of family members and their life expectancies should also be used to determine the allocation of estate assets between the surviving spouse and others.

A number of different factors determine the extent to which the marital deduction should be used (see Q 4:14). Because it is often a difficult decision to make, the Internal Revenue Code allows this choice to be made after the death of the first spouse. For example, a wife could leave a marital deduction bequest to her husband with the provision in her will that if her husband should disclaim any or a portion of the bequest within eight months of her death, the portion disclaimed could pass into another trust for their children. The husband could choose to disclaim the bequest in order to reduce the marital deduction bequest and minimize the estate tax that eventually would be payable on his death.

Using a Trust with the Marital Deduction

Q 4:16 What is a trust?

A trust is a means of owning property in which the beneficiary (the person who will eventually receive the trust income or property) has an equitable interest and the trustee (the person who manages the trust) has legal title. Control of trust assets is determined by the terms contained in the trust agreement; however, the trustee is generally responsible for managing these assets.

Q 4:17 What factors determine the circumstances under which a trust should be created to hold assets given to the surviving spouse?

Some of the factors to be considered are:

1. Is the surviving spouse well enough to manage an inheritance? If not, a trust is a sensible solution.

2. Does the surviving spouse have sufficient analytical and managerial skills, and is he or she conversant with financial matters? Many a spouse does not share matters of family finances with the other spouse. As a result, death is not only an emotional trauma for the surviving spouse, but also sets the stage for an unsophisticated spouse, who is unprepared to deal with finances, to make errors of judgment and selection in determining who to rely on for financial guidance. Not all individuals can make a competent review of investments, which is an important part of asset management. Moreover, the surviving spouse may not be comfortable with the risk associated with certain investments, such as stock. Special considerations may have influenced the decedent to retain certain assets during life that no longer apply after death. For example, the sale of stock acquired at a very low price and retained as its value skyrocketed, would result in hefty capital gains taxes; however, because of the step-up in basis that occurs at death, this consideration may no longer be significant, and selling the stock may make

sense. This type of decision requires knowledge of the tax law that a surviving spouse may not have.

3. If the surviving spouse is not the parent of the decedent's children, a QTIP trust may be advisable (see Qs 4:16, 4:18).
4. Is the prospect of the surviving spouse's remarrying bothersome, or is the surviving spouse vulnerable to requests for money from indigent relatives? If either of these concerns applies, it may be desirable to establish a trust to protect the assets.

It is also possible and sensible in many cases to bequeath some property outright so as to provide liquidity to the surviving spouse that may not be immediately available from other sources, (e.g., insurance or a pension benefit). The remainder of the decedent's estate can then be considered for inclusion in a trust.

Example 4-9: A cellular-phone entrepreneur has liquid assets of $2 million and an art collection worth $700,000. Her husband knows little about investing but is a very shrewd art collector and is especially adept at buying and selling watercolors. The entrepreneur designs an estate plan that directs the liquid assets into a trust for the benefit of the spouse and leaves the art collection directly to him.

Q 4:18 What is a qualified terminable interest property trust?

Prior to 1982, an interest provided to a surviving spouse that was terminable was not eligible for the marital deduction. Congress then decided that the decedent should be able to control the destination of a trust created under his or her will after the death of the surviving spouse. Accordingly, the qualified terminable interest property (QTIP) trust was authorized to qualify for the marital deduction as long as the only person who could benefit from the QTIP trust during its life was the surviving spouse; however, the decedent could determine under the trust who would be the ultimate beneficiaries of the QTIP trust property upon the death of the surviving spouse.

Example 4-10: A stockbroker who has two children by his first marriage is concerned that his second wife will not adequately provide for his children from his prior marriage, and he also wants to provide for his existing wife. To meet these goals, the stockbroker funds a QTIP trust with stock worth $2.3 million. The trust provides his wife with the income from the trust for her life, and (when his wife dies) his children with equal shares in the stock used to fund the trust.

The following requirements must be met to qualify for QTIP trust status:

1. The surviving spouse must be entitled to receive all the income from the entire interest or all the income from a specific portion of the entire interest for life, payable at least annually in the year earned. [IRC §§ 2056(b)(7)(B)(ii), 2056(b)(7)(B)(iv)]

2. The accumulated or accrued income at the surviving spouse's death must either be paid to the estate of the surviving spouse or be subject to the surviving spouse's testamentary general power of appointment; otherwise the trust will not qualify as a QTIP trust. [Estate of Rose Howard, 91 TC 329 (1988)]

3. No person, including the surviving spouse, can have any power to appoint (i.e., direct the transfer of) trust property to a third person during the surviving spouse's life. [IRC § 2056(b)(7)(B)(ii)] This means, for example, that the surviving spouse cannot make decisions regarding the use of trust property nor may the surviving spouse assign his or her interest in trust property. However, the surviving spouse may assign his or her income interest in the trust to other persons during his or her lifetime. QTIP status is elected by the executor of the decedent's estate and, once elected, is irrevocable. [IRC § 2056(b)(7)(B)(v)]

4. The remaindermen of a QTIP trust (i.e., those individuals who obtain the property upon the death of the surviving spouse) are as determined by the decedent who created the QTIP in his or her last will.

Q 4:19 Can a surviving spouse be given a power of disposition at death over qualified terminable interest property trust assets?

Yes. A QTIP trust can be designed so that the surviving spouse has the power of disposition at death over the QTIP trust assets. This power can be limited in scope so that, for example, it can only be exercised in favor of the children and other descendants of the spouse who created the trust. This option introduces flexibility into a trust.

Example 4-11: An entrepreneur has two sons whose ages are 20 and 18, and a daughter age 16. The entrepreneur's will creates a QTIP trust for his spouse because he is concerned about protecting the assets that he is leaving to her. The entrepreneur also wants money to pass to his children when his wife dies. Because he does not know what his children's financial circumstances will be at that time, the entrepreneur provides in the QTIP trust that his wife may bequeath the trust assets available upon her death to their children in any manner she sees fit. Two years later the entrepreneur dies. Twenty years later his spouse dies. At the time of the widow's death, the oldest son appears to have become a career student, so his inheritance is held in trust. The second son is a successful singer and has ample income. He is given a small amount as a token of affection. The remainder of the trust is passed on to the daughter, who seems financially responsible but is a teacher with limited financial prospects.

Q 4:20 Must an election be made to obtain the marital deduction for assets placed in a qualified terminable interest property trust?

Yes. For a QTIP to qualify for the marital deduction, the executor (i.e., the person legally responsible for estate administration) for the decedent spouse must elect to take the marital deduction. This must be done on the federal estate tax return (Form 706) filed for the estate. As a result of the executor's election, the assets in the QTIP trust eventually will be includible in the surviving spouse's estate. [IRC § 2044] Once made, the marital deduction election is irrevocable.

Q 4:21 Is the marital deduction available if under an estate plan the executor can determine what property is to be placed into a qualified terminable interest property trust after the decedent's death?

The Sixth Circuit and two other federal appeals courts have held that an executor can designate after death the amount of property that is to be placed in a QTIP trust. [Estate of J. Spencer v Comm, 6th Cir (1995)] The Sixth Circuit reasoned that property is not QTIP property until the QTIP designation is made. Therefore, permitting an after-death designation of QTIP property did not violate prohibitions under Code Section 2056(b)(7)(B)(ii)(II) against appointing QTIP property away from the surviving spouse.

> **Example 4-12:** A manufacturer gave his wife, as executrix of his estate, the right to determine the amount of property to be placed in her QTIP trust. Six months after his death, his wife appoints $1.5 million to her QTIP trust. The remaining $600,000 in his estate goes to their children. According to the Sixth Circuit decision in Spencer, the estate is entitled to a marital deduction for the amounts placed in the QTIP trust.

Q 4:22 Who is responsible for paying the estate taxes on the assets in a qualified terminable interest property trust when the surviving spouse dies?

Unless the surviving spouse's will directs otherwise, the estate taxes attributable to assets in the QTIP trust can be recovered from the QTIP trust by the surviving spouse's executor. [IRC § 2207(A)] In many cases, the surviving spouse will want to be sure that his or her will does not contain a provision saying that all estate taxes will be paid out of his or her estate. If the will contains this provision, the surviving spouse's beneficiaries, not the QTIP beneficiaries, will bear the tax burden of the QTIP assets.

> **Example 4-13:** A surviving spouse's QTIP trust contains assets worth $2 million. The QTIP trust assets are to go to her deceased husband's children by a prior marriage. The surviving spouse, who also has two children by a prior marriage, has assets in her name worth $1 million that she wishes to give to them. The estate taxes attributable to the QTIP trust are $780,000. If these taxes are paid out of the $1 million targeted for the wife's children, their inheritance will be substantially depleted. To avoid this result, the wife's will specifies that the estate taxes associated with the QTIP trust are not to be paid by her estate.

Q 4:23 What is a power of appointment trust?

A power of appointment trust is another kind of trust that is exempt from the terminable interest rule. It gives the surviving spouse a general power of appointment over trust assets (i.e., the principal) and the right to receive all the income from the trust for life. At a minimum, trust income must be payable annually. In contrast to a QTIP trust, a power of appointment trust gives the surviving spouse control over trust assets. [IRC § 2056(b)(5)]

The power of appointment trust provides the surviving spouse with a general power of appointment that allows the surviving spouse to take the property of the trust for himself or herself or to give the trust property to his or her estate. This right to appoint to themselves or to their estates must be unconditional. The surviving spouse can also be given power to appoint (or give) the trust property to others.

To qualify for a marital deduction, the power of appointment must be exercisable by the surviving spouse alone and under all circumstances. [Treas Reg § 20.2056(b)-5(a)(4)] The decedent spouse may, however, include a provision in his or her will that names the beneficiaries of the trust to whom the trust assets or the power of appointment will go in case the surviving spouse fails to exercise the power of appointment. The reason for including this provision in the will is to ensure that the trust continues for the decedent spouse's children should the surviving spouse not exercise the power of appointment.

The surviving spouse may exercise the power of appointment while he or she is living or by putting a provision in his or her will. In practice, these trusts are often drafted so that the surviving spouse may exercise the right of disposition by means of his or her will only. Because making a will is a ceremonial and solemn event, the widow or widower may be more circumspect in directing disposition of trust assets after the death of the spouse.

Q 4:24 Aside from the differences described above between a QTIP trust and a trust providing the surviving spouse with a general power of appointment, is their tax effect the same?

Yes and no. A marital deduction is available to both trusts if they are drafted properly to meet the requirements of the Code provisions which authorize their use. However, a general power of appointment trust, so qualifying, is a required marital deduction; whereas the

QTIP trust is eligible for the marital deduction only if elected by the executor of the decedent's estate.

Q 4:25 How are capital gains from the sale of trust assets treated in a power of appointment trust?

Gains from the sales of trust assets do not go to the surviving spouse. Consequently, although capital gains from such sales are taxed like other capital gains, they are not taxed to the surviving spouse. This is because assets of the trust and gains or losses relating to those assets are considered principal and are not part of the surviving spouse's entitlement unless treated differently by the provisions of the trust. The tax on capital gains is thus paid from the trust principal by the trustee.

Q 4:26 What is an estate trust?

An estate trust requires that trust principal and accumulated income be distributed to the probate estate of the surviving spouse when the surviving spouse dies. The terminable interest rule can also be avoided if a decedent transfers property to an estate trust. Unlike the power of appointment trust, the estate trust is not subject to a requirement that income from the trust be paid at least annually, so the income in an estate trust can be accumulated for the surviving spouse. The main advantage of using an estate trust instead of a power of appointment trust is that an estate trust does not require the surviving spouse to receive all of the income from the trust property during his or her lifetime. In this way the spouse will not be forced to attempt to manage excess or unneeded funds. This situation can also be a disadvantage, however, because the maximum tax rate of 39.6 percent commences when the taxable income of the estate exceeds only $7,650; whereas, an individual's taxable income must exceed $256,500 before being subject to a maximum rate of 39.6 percent.

Q 4:27 What considerations apply in deciding whether to establish a power of appointment trust or a QTIP trust?

The QTIP trust is generally favored by estate planners over the power of appointment trust because the decedent retains control over the disposition of the QTIP trust assets upon the death of the surviving spouse. Another advantage of a QTIP trust is that an election to utilize a marital deduction for a QTIP trust can be made for only a portion of the trust even if the entire trust would qualify for the election. Therefore, it is possible for the executor to elect to qualify only a portion of the QTIP trust for the marital deduction after the decedent's death. This provides for greater flexibility in planning. Another significant feature of the QTIP trust is that it allows the executor of the decedent's estate a second look at the circumstances between the date of death of the decedent and the date of election (at the time of the filing of the estate tax return) to measure the age and health of the surviving spouse and the likelihood of any significant deferral of tax in the decedent's estate versus the additional prospective cost in estate tax (as a result of the inclusion of the QTIP trust property) upon the death of the surviving spouse.

A power of appointment trust is, of course, used in some circumstances. It is particularly attractive to those who want to utilize a trust to provide stability in the management of trust property—a feature that may be attractive for those persons who want to convey ownership of the property to their surviving spouses but who are concerned about the surviving spouse's ability to manage the property effectively without assistance. If a power of appointment trust is used, a bank or other institutional trustee can be appointed, and that trust can manage trust assets. The power of appointment trust can also be designed so that the surviving spouse can make lifetime gifts from the trust. This cannot be done under a QTIP trust. Under a power of appointment trust, the spouse's ability to give can be circumscribed so that only a favored group, such as the trust creator's descendants, can receive gifts.

Q 4:28 Is it ever desirable to have trust income attributed to the grantor under a grantor trust?

This can be a very desirable approach because the grantor's tax bracket may be lower than that of the trust. Moreover, this approach permits the tax-free compounding of income by the trust. This means that additional amounts are available for trust beneficiaries. The grantor pays the income tax, but doing so reduces the grantor's estate, which can also be a desirable result.

Example 4-14: A 45-year-old attorney creates a grantor trust in favor of his children and funds it with $100,000. The trust earns 15 percent each year. Because the attorney pays the income tax on trust earnings, the trust grows at a rate of 15 percent a year. Had the trust incurred the taxes, the growth rate would have been slower. Also, as indicated above, maximum income tax rates are imposed on a much lower level of income to a trust or estate than to an individual.

Q 4:29 Can the surviving spouse for a power of appointment or QTIP trust be given access to the trust principal?

Yes. The trustees can be empowered to dip into the principal on behalf of the surviving spouse. They cannot, however, be authorized to use principal for anyone other than the surviving spouse because that action would reduce trust assets and thereby decrease the income available to the surviving spouse.

The trustee's power to pay out principal can be narrow or broad. For example, a narrow power could permit the trustees to use trust principal to pay the medical and nursing expenses of the surviving spouse. Similarly, a narrow power could be authorized to allow the trustees to pay principal in any year that the surviving spouse's income from the trust is less than $50,000. On the other hand, the power to pay out principal can be made broad enough to permit the trustees to pay principal to the surviving spouse for any reason or purpose. In all situations, though, the trustees and not the spouse must hold the power.

Spousal Bequests

Q 4:30 What is a formula clause?

A formula clause leaves to the surviving spouse an amount determined by a specified formula. For example, the clause might provide the surviving spouse with an amount equal to the maximum marital deduction (see Q 4:1) reduced by all other assets that have passed to the surviving spouse through other means (for example, property passing by joint tenancy (see Qs 2:25–2:43)). Formula clauses are used to avoid revising wills or trusts whenever the value of the estate changes.

Q 4:31 What types of formula clauses exist?

The three basic types of formula clauses are as follows: pecuniary clauses, fractional share clauses, and estate tax value clauses. Each of these types is discussed in the following questions.

Q 4:32 What is a pecuniary clause?

Pecuniary clauses bequeath amounts that can be reduced to fixed dollar amounts (called pecuniary bequests). Pecuniary clauses can take a number of forms. For example, the clause might provide that "the sum of $100,000 is to be paid to my wife." The clause also might provide, however, that "the amount allocated to the marital trust shall equal the maximum marital deduction allowable in my estate for federal estate tax purposes, but in no event shall such amount exceed an amount that is greater than is necessary to eliminate the federal estate tax on my estate." This second example, though more complex than the first example, also results in a fixed numerical amount. Thus, for example, if a businessman has a taxable estate of $2 million and if the exemption equivalent is $600,000, then this second sample clause would imply that an amount equal to $1.4 million would be payable to the marital trust. This is because the federal estate tax is eliminated at the point that $600,000 is payable to persons other than the surviving spouse. Pecuniary bequests do not share in the income earned by the estate during administration.

Q 4:33 What are the income tax effects of a pecuniary clause?

The value of property transferred pursuant to a pecuniary clause is its value on the date the transfer occurs (i.e., date of death, not the date of distribution). This means that if assets are distributed to pay the pecuniary bequest in kind, the estate realizes gain equal to the fair market value of the assets less the basis of the assets. In most but not all cases, the relevant basis of the asset will be the fair market value of the asset as of the estate valuation date. Under these circumstances, the taxable gain will be the post-death appreciation in the asset.

Example 4-15: Property with a fair market value of $100,000 at the date of death is distributed from an estate six months later to satisfy a pecuniary bequest. On the date of distribution, the property is worth $150,000. The taxable gain to the estate is $33,333. The property has appreciated 50 percent, which means that property with a basis of $66,666 and a value of $100,000 can satisfy the $100,000 bequest. This results in taxable gain of $33,333.

Q 4:34 What factors should be considered in using a pecuniary clause?

If the pecuniary clause provides that the values to be considered in satisfying the marital bequest are date of death values, post-death appreciation in assets will not benefit the surviving spouse.

Example 4-16: A businesswoman with an anticipated taxable estate of $2 million makes a marital bequest to her husband using a pecuniary clause specifying that the marital bequest will be just large enough to eliminate estate taxes on the businesswoman's death, provided, however, that date of death values are used in making this determination. If there is no appreciation or depreciation in the trust assets, the husband will receive $1.4 million, and the other beneficiaries will receive $600,000. If the value of the businesswoman's estate increases to $2.5 million between the date of death and the date of distribution, the husband will still receive $1.4 million, and the other beneficiaries will receive $1.1 million instead of $600,000.

Example 4-17: The facts remain the same as they were in Example 4-16, except that the value of the estate falls to $1.6 million by the date of distribution. The husband still receives a distribution of $1.4 million; the other beneficiaries receive $200,000 instead of $600,000.

If the pecuniary clause provides the executor with the authority to select the assets to be used in satisfying the pecuniary bequest, opportunities for tax planning may arise. For example, if the surviving spouse is in a high tax bracket, it may be desirable to bequeath him or her tax-exempt bonds.

Q 4:35 How does a fractional share clause work?

The fractional share clause bequeaths a fraction of the estate rather than a fixed dollar amount.

> **Example 4-18:** A businessman dies leaving a taxable estate of $2 million. His will contains a fractional share clause that allocates 14/20 (70 percent) of all estate assets to his wife. His wife receives assets worth $1.4 million and his other beneficiaries receive assets worth $600,000. If the estate appreciates to $2.5 million, the fractional share clause causes the wife to receive $1.75 million. The marital estate receives an interest in each asset that is allocated under this clause. No gain or loss for income tax purposes arises as the result of the use of this clause.

Q 4:36 What factors should be considered in using a fractional clause?

The following factors should be considered:

1. If the fractional clause is used the marital estate will automatically increase or decrease if the estate assets either appreciate or depreciate after the valuation date. If the value of the estate assets declines drastically, the surviving spouse's share will be reduced, resulting in a less comfortable lifestyle than planned for.

2. The fractional clause requires the distribution of undivided interests in each asset making up the residue, which can create potential problems. For example, a surviving spouse would be given a proportionate share of the decedent's business, which might not be desirable. These problems may be eliminated by appropriate drafting, but they must be recognized and addressed.

3. The standard fractional clause does not allocate assets with significant potential appreciation to a particular trust. This may or may not be desirable. For example, an individual may want to allocate assets that are expected to appreciate to his or her

children, rather than to the surviving spouse, in an effort to reduce estate taxes when the surviving spouse dies. The standard clause can be modified to give the estate administrator the authority to allocate assets. This flexibility can be used to prevent the estate from recognizing disproportionate gain on the distribution of the assets. [Rev Rul 55-117, 1955-1 CB 233]

Q 4:37 What is an estate tax value pecuniary clause?

The estate tax value pecuniary clause requires the executor to satisfy the bequest with assets that are valued for distribution purposes as of the date of the estate valuation (i.e., their value on the date of death or on the alternate valuation date) rather than as of their date of distribution. This permits the executor to allocate some of the appreciation (or depreciation) in the estate to the marital portion. If the marital bequest is $900,000 and the estate appreciates from $1.5 million to $2 million between the date of death and the date of distribution, the marital bequest is satisfied with assets that have an estate tax value of $900,000. Thus, for example, stocks with a collective value of $900,000 as of the date of estate valuation can be used to satisfy the bequest even though their value as of the date of distribution has increased to $1,200,000. Similarly, the bequest could be satisfied by stocks whose collective worth has declined to $700,000 on the date of distribution if their value on the estate valuation date was $900,000.

Q 4:38 What considerations apply in using an estate tax value pecuniary clause?

Because the marital bequest is satisfied by assets equal to the estate value, no gain exists if the bequest is satisfied with assets that have appreciated after the date of death. For example, if the bequest is satisfied by stock that appreciates from $25,000 to $50,000 after the decedent's death, no gain is recognized by the estate on the transfer of stock. The distributee's basis in the stock would be $25,000.

Chapter 5

Bypass Trusts

A bypass trust (also referred to as a credit shelter trust) is a special kind of trust that shields assets from being taxed in the estate of the second spouse to die. It is called a *bypass* trust because it bypasses inclusion in the surviving spouse's taxable estate. It is also called a *credit shelter* trust because it is sheltered from tax in the estate of the first spouse to die by being covered by the tax credit of $192,000 (equivalent to the exemption of $600,000 from the taxable estate). The combination of credit shelter in the estate of the first spouse to die with the bypass of includibility in the estate of the surviving spouse allows $1.2 million of assets to avoid estate tax otherwise payable by the overall family unit.

This chapter discusses how bypass trusts work, how they can be combined with the marital deduction to shield a married couple's assets from estate taxation, and how much power the surviving spouse can exercise over the principal and income of the bypass trust without losing the benefit of the bypass of estate taxation. This chapter also discusses the generation skipping transfer tax, which often comes into play when a bypass trust is used.

Overview	5-2
Combining a Bypass Trust with a Marital Deduction Trust (A-B Trust Plan)	5-3
Powers Under a Bypass Trust	5-7
Discretionary Trusts	5-9

Q 5:1   Estate and Retirement Planning Answer Book

Income Tax Consequences 5-11
Generation Skipping Transfer Tax 5-11

Overview

Q 5:1   What is a bypass trust?

The virtue of a bypass trust is that assets equivalent in value to the $600,000 exemption are able to escape taxation in the estates of both spouses. The amount of $600,000 deductible from the estate of the first spouse to die can appreciate with time and good investment so that it has a greater value at the time of the surviving spouse's death, but nevertheless is not includible in his or her estate.

Q 5:2   How does a bypass trust reduce the surviving spouse's estate taxes?

Bypass trusts can reduce estate taxes if the surviving spouse is likely to have assets at death that exceed the $600,000 exemption equivalent (see Qs 3:25, 3:26).

Example 5-1: A physician anticipates a taxable estate of $2 million and her husband has an additional $1 million of his own property. Because the husband is a conservative spender, it is entirely possible that he can live off the income on his own assets and that any assets bequeathed to him will not be depleted. Under these circumstances, if the husband receives $2 million from his wife at her death, he may have a taxable estate of $3 million when he dies. Assuming the husband makes no taxable gifts, the amount of his estate tax would be $1,098,000. (The tentative tax on his taxable estate of $3 million is $1,290,800. This is reduced by the unified credit of $192,800 to give a total estate tax of $1,098,000.) This leaves $1,902,000 to be given to children or others.

By using a bypass trust, the physician and her husband can retain funds that would otherwise be paid out in estate taxes. The physician could will $600,000 to the bypass trust at death. Income from the bypass trust could be made available to the husband during his lifetime, and the $600,000 principal paid into the bypass trust would be reserved for the children. No estate tax would be payable on the wife's death and the husband would have a taxable estate of $2,400,000. The estate tax would be $784,000. (The tentative tax on the husband's taxable estate of $2.4 million is $976,800. This is reduced by the unified credit of $192,800, resulting in an estate tax of $784,000.) Thus, by creating a bypass trust, the physician reduces total estate taxes by $314,000.

Bypass trusts are often established so that a surviving spouse receives the trust income on a regular basis during his or her lifetime. The trust also provides the trustees with power to invade principal for the benefit of the surviving spouse. Upon the death of the surviving spouse, the trust generally provides that the trust balance be transferred to the children of the marriage or other favored beneficiaries. The power of the trustees to invade trust principal should be based on an *ascertainable standard* relating to the health, education, support or maintenance needs of the surviving spouse. [Treas Reg § 20.2041-1(c)(2)] Where the surviving spouse is a co-trustee of the bypass trust, extreme care should be taken in the drafting of such standards (see Q 5:10). For example, the IRS included the trust property in the estate of a decedent who was a co-trustee of a trust established by his mother. The trust gave him the power to invade trust corpus as "required for [his] continued comfort, support, maintenance or education." The Tax Court, agreeing with the IRS, held that the use of the phrase "continued comfort" prevented this power from being limited by an ascertainable standard and included the trust principal in the decedent's estate, because it was equivalent to a general power of appointment. [Estate of Vissering, 96 TC 749 (1991)]

Combining a Bypass Trust with a Marital Deduction Trust (A-B Trust Plan)

Q 5:3 What is an A-B trust plan?

The A-B trust plan uses one trust (the A trust) as a marital deduction trust and a second trust (the B trust) as a bypass trust. The A trust contains the assets that are subject to the marital deduction. The B trust is intended to take advantage of the $192,800 unified

Q 5:4 **Estate and Retirement Planning Answer Book**

credit against estate taxes. This credit permits the decedent to place up to $600,000 of assets in the B trust without incurring estate tax. In one common type of A-B trust plan, $600,000 of assets is allocated to the B trust and the remaining assets are allocated to the A trust. Under that setup, the surviving spouse has the right to withdraw assets from the A trust and to receive A trust income, plus the right to allocate A trust assets at death. The surviving spouse also has the right to receive the income and assets of the B trust if such assets are needed for his or her support.

Q 5:4 How should the A-B trust plan be structured to give the surviving spouse maximum power and control over trust assets?

If it is desirable for the surviving spouse to have as much power and control as possible, the A trust (that is, the trust subject to the marital deduction) can provide that the surviving spouse will receive all of the net income, have an unlimited right to withdraw principal during his or her life, and have a general testamentary power of appointment which, if not exercised, will result in the remainder going to the B trust. The part of the total estate that goes to the A trust will not be taxable on the death of the first spouse to die, because this portion of the estate will qualify for the marital deduction. The assets remaining in the A trust at the surviving spouse's death will be included in his or her estate for estate tax purposes because the surviving spouse has a general power of appointment over these assets at the time of his or her death. [IRC § 2041(A)(2)]

A corporate trustee can be appointed to the B trust and can be given discretionary authority to distribute trust income to the surviving spouse. (If the surviving spouse becomes trustee of the B trust, the spouse can distribute assets from the B trust to himself or herself only under limited conditions (see Q 5:9).)

Q 5:5 Can the A-B trust be structured to limit the right of the surviving spouse to withdraw principal during his or her lifetime and to appoint assets at death?

Yes, if either spouse is concerned about giving the survivor a right to withdraw principal during his or her lifetime or giving the surviving spouse a testamentary general power of appointment on death, the A trust (that is, the trust subject to the marital deduction) can be structured as a QTIP trust. These trusts can limit the surviving spouse to receiving income only; or can give the surviving spouse or a third-party trustee limited rights to invade the principal for the benefit of the surviving spouse; or can give the surviving spouse or a third-party trustee the right to dispose of the principal on the surviving spouse's death.

A recent case in which the decedent received annual income from both trusts demonstrates that invasion powers involving A-B trusts should be carefully drafted. The decedent was also entitled to as much principal from the A trust as she wanted by notifying the A trustee in writing. She could also withdraw 5 percent from the B trust annually if the A was exhausted. The IRS argued that the decedent had a general power of appointment over 5 percent of the B trust and therefore 5 percent of the value of the B trust was includible in her estate. The estate argued that the withdrawal power over the B trust was subject to a contingency that had not occurred (i.e., exhaustion of the A trust). The court, in upholding the IRS, determined that the decedent exercised economic dominion over all the funds withdrawn at any given moment, so that the decedent, until her death, could have withdrawn all the A trust property and 5 percent of the B trust property by notifying the trustee of her right to do so. [Estate of Kurtz (7th Cir 1995)]

Q 5:6 How much access to marital trust assets should a surviving spouse be given without having to make a request for principal from the trustee?

If the surviving spouse's right to withdraw trust assets is entirely unrestricted, the beneficiary spouse could use up all of the assets. One approach is to put a ceiling on the amount that the spouse can withdraw from the trust. For example, there could be an annual maximum of $10,000 or a lifetime maximum of $75,000.

Q 5:7 How is the B trust taxed?

The portion of the estate going into the B trust (that is, the bypass trust) will be subject to estate tax on the death of the first spouse to die (of course, if the marital deduction is taken advantage of and if the amount put into the B trust is less than or equal to the exemption equivalent, no estate tax will be payable). However, when the B trust qualifies as a bypass trust, the assets in that trust will not be taxed again on the surviving spouse's death. They will pass free of death taxes to children or other persons who become entitled to trust assets (i.e., remainder beneficiaries) once the surviving spouse dies.

Q 5:8 Can a disclaimer be used in connection with an A-B trust plan?

Yes, it can be. A disclaimer is a voluntary repudiation of an individual's right to some interest. Each spouse can arrange for his or her estate to go outright to the surviving spouse, but specify that to the extent the surviving spouse disclaims the estate of the first spouse to die, the disclaimed portion will go into the A and B trusts. When the first spouse dies, the surviving spouse can decide whether to take outright ownership of the assets or to disclaim them and allow them to go into an A-B trust. The advantage of this approach is that the decision about estate asset allocation is made on the basis of conditions in effect at the time of the deceased spouse's death rather than on the basis of conditions as perceived at the time the will of the deceased spouse was drawn up. The disclaimer must be a *qualified* disclaimer to prevent the surviving spouse from being treated for estate and gift tax purposes as having received and then transferred the disclaimed property. A qualified disclaimer is a written disclaimer made within a certain period, under which the person disclaiming the interest has not accepted the interest or any of its benefits. The person making the qualified disclaimer cannot dictate who the recipient of the interest shall be. [IRC § 2518] If the disclaimer is not qualified, the surviving spouse will be deemed to have received the assets in question and then transferred such disclaimed assets to the A trust and B trust. The rights and benefits of the surviving spouse in these trusts (i.e., a life estate or power of appointment) often will cause the disclaimed assets to be included in the surviving spouse's estate. [IRC §§ 2036, 2041]

In a recent court case, a father bequeathed his estate to his son who, in turn, disclaimed his interest in the estate, intending a transfer to the surviving spouse so as to allow the estate to claim an unlimited marital deduction. The son had two illegitimate children and the IRS argued that since disclaimed property passes as if the son predeceased his father, the son's illegitimate children, not the surviving spouse, are the recipients legally entitled to the disclaimed property. The court held under the laws of the state involved (New Mexico) that the son's illegitimate children were not his heirs, and upheld the marital deduction for the transfer to the surviving spouse. [DePaoli v Commr (10th Cir 1995)] The decision, although based on unique facts, makes clear that the legal effects of a disclaimer should be carefully analyzed before a disclaimer is effected.

Powers Under a Bypass Trust

Q 5:9 If the intention is to give the surviving spouse as much control as possible over the assets in the bypass trust, what powers may be given to the spouse?

The surviving spouse cannot be given a general power of appointment over the assets of the bypass trust, or else the assets in the bypass trust would be includible in the surviving spouse's estate and the bypass would fail, thereby defeating the whole purpose for creating the bypass trust. The surviving spouse can, however, be given the following powers:

1. A power to invade trust assets (i.e., both income and principal) under an ascertainable standard (see Q 5:10);
2. A $5,000 or 5 percent power (see Q 5:11); or
3. A special power to appoint to third parties (see Q 5:12).

[IRC § 2041(b)(2)]

Q 5:10 How is a power to invade trust assets under an ascertainable standard used with a bypass trust?

A power to invade trust assets under an ascertainable standard permits the surviving spouse to use the bypass trust assets, provided that a standard related to education, support, maintenance, or health is met. Because such power is not a general power of appointment, its existence does not cause property to be includible in the gross estate under Code Section 2041.

The formula that is used to describe the standard is important. The regulations require that the holder's (that is, the surviving spouse's) discretion be limited by a standard that is reasonably measurable in terms of his or her needs for health, education, or support (or any combination of them). It is acceptable to give the surviving spouse the right to use trust assets for health, education, support, and maintenance in the surviving spouse's accustomed manner of living. It is not acceptable to give the surviving spouse the right to use trust assets for the surviving spouse's comfort, welfare, or happiness. [Treas Reg § 20.2041-1(c)(2)] If the surviving spouse's power to use trust assets is limited by an ascertainable standard, the surviving spouse can be the sole trustee. [Rev Rul 78-398, 1978-2 CB 237] (See Qs 5:15, 5:16 below, however, for when that might not be a good idea.)

Q 5:11 How is a $5,000 or 5 percent power used with a bypass trust?

A surviving spouse can be given the right to invade the bypass trust principal for any purpose (without causing the bypass trust assets to be included in his or her estate) if the right is limited to the greater of $5,000 or 5 percent of the principal in each calendar year. [IRC § 2041(b)(2)]

A failure to exercise the $5,000 or 5 percent power will not cause bypass trust assets to be includible in the surviving spouse's estate, regardless of the benefits and powers the surviving spouse has in the bypass trust. The failure to exercise the $5,000 or 5 percent power also is not treated as a taxable gift. [IRC §§ 2514(b), 2514(c)(1), 2514(e)]

Q 5:12 How is a special power of appointment used with a bypass trust?

A special power of appointment can be given to the surviving spouse to permit the surviving spouse to dispose of bypass trust assets during life or at death. The assets that are subject to the special power of appointment are not includible in the surviving spouse's estate. A special power of appointment exists so long as the surviving spouse can direct trust income to anyone other than the surviving spouse, the surviving spouse's creditors, the surviving spouse's estate, or creditors of the surviving spouse's estate; however, the surviving spouse may direct trust income to his or her children. [IRC § 2041(b)(1)] An important feature of this power is its flexibility. When the power is created, future circumstances will not be known. For example, ten years after the power is created, one child could have a dire need for assets. A special power of appointment gives the surviving spouse an opportunity to react to this circumstance by diverting assets to that child from the bypass trust.

Discretionary Trusts

Q 5:13 What is a discretionary trust?

A discretionary trust is a type of bypass trust that gives the trustee the discretion to accumulate income during the surviving spouse's lifetime or distribute trust income and principal to the surviving spouse and/or any of the decedent's children. These trusts are useful if the decedent wished to have estate assets managed for the benefit of the surviving spouse.

Q 5:14 What are the advantages of discretionary trusts?

Discretionary trusts can have a flexible distribution pattern. Income can be distributed to trust beneficiaries when they need it. Aggregate income taxes can be reduced because trust income can be distributed to persons in low tax brackets. If the surviving spouse is not given a general power of appointment, a discretionary trust can result in estate tax savings when the surviving spouse dies. This occurs because a failure to distribute income from this trust will cause the surviving spouse to consume his or her other assets, thus minimizing the estate tax on that spouse's death.

Q 5:15 Should the surviving spouse who is a beneficiary of a bypass trust be the sole trustee if the discretionary trust contains a sprinkling power?

No, the surviving spouse generally should not be the sole trustee of a bypass trust that gives the trustee a *sprinkling power* and that benefits the surviving spouse. A sprinkling power is the power to decide which beneficiaries are to get asset distributions (i.e., the power to decide how and when to sprinkle or spread out the assets among various potential beneficiaries).

Sole trustee. The surviving spouse will be taxable on trust income if he or she has the sole power to vest income or principal in himself or herself. [IRC § 678(a)] Accordingly, unless the sprinkling power to distribute trust assets is limited by an ascertainable standard (see Q 5:10) the surviving spouse will be taxable on all trust income. Even if an ascertainable standard exists, if the surviving spouse actually distributes trust assets to persons whom the surviving spouse must support, any amounts that are actually paid to those persons are taxable to the surviving spouse. The rationale is that the surviving spouse is in effect using trust assets for his or her own benefit.

Co-trustee. Even if the surviving spouse is only a co-trustee, trust assets will be includible in the surviving spouse's estate if the surviving spouse can exercise the power for his or her own benefit, unless the trustee's discretionary powers to distribute income and principal are limited by an ascertainable standard (see Q 5:10). [IRC § 2041(b)(1)(C)]

Gift tax consequences. If the surviving spouse who is a trustee of a bypass trust uses the sprinkling power that is a general power of appointment to distribute income or principal to third persons whom the spouse is not obligated to support, a taxable gift of the amount distributed results. [IRC § 2514(b)]

Q 5:16 If a spousal beneficiary is given the power to remove a trustee of a discretionary trust and substitute an independent corporate trustee, what are the estate tax consequences?

If a spouse who is a trust beneficiary can remove an existing trustee of a discretionary trust and appoint an independent corporate successor trustee, the IRS has concluded that a general power of appointment exists. [Rev Rul 79-353, 1979-2 CB 325] The existence of such a power causes trust assets to be includible in the estate of the surviving spouse.

Income Tax Consequences

Q 5:17 What are the income tax consequences if a bypass trust is established?

If a bypass trust is established and the surviving spouse has an unrestricted power to invade trust principal or income, he or she will be taxable on the income earned by the trust. This is true regardless of whether the surviving spouse ever exercises such power. Also, an unrestricted power to invade trust principal prevents the trust from qualifying as a bypass trust, since such an unrestricted power to invade trust principal is tantamount to the surviving spouse having a general power of appointment. If, on the other hand, the spouse's authority to invade principal and income is limited by an ascertainable standard (see Q 5:10), the spouse is not taxable on trust income unless the spouse uses the power. [Townsend v Comm, 5 TC 1380 (1945)] If such power is actually used and assets are removed from the trust, the withdrawn amount is included in the spouse's income to the extent that the trust has distributable net income. [IRC § 662]

Generation Skipping Transfer Tax

Q 5:18 What is the generation skipping transfer tax?

The generation skipping transfer (GST) tax is neither a gift tax nor an estate tax. It is intended to impose a tax where property passes outright, or through a trust to someone two generations or more younger than the person giving the property. The tax is further intended to impose itself where transfers result in one or more generations escaping the estate and gift tax as the beneficial use passes to them. The GST tax therefore does not apply where the transferred property is taxed in the estate of a member of the intervening (skip) generation. The GST tax is an addition to any gift or estate tax payable by the transferor and is based on the amount received by the transferee. [IRC § 2623]

> **Example 5-2:** A grandchild receives $100,000 after the payment of estate tax on the grandparent's estate. The generation skipping transfer tax on this transfer will be $55,000. The grandparent's estate is liable for this tax, not the transferee (the grandchild). Thus, the grandchild will receive the full $100,000 and the estate must pay an additional $55,000 in transfer taxes.

The generation skipping transfer tax is generally applicable to all generation skipping lifetime transfers made after September 25, 1985. The tax is applicable to all generation skipping transfers made by a decedent dying on or after October 22, 1986. [Pub L No 99-514 (1986), § 1433]

The generation skipping transfer tax is imposed whenever a transfer is made to a person more than one generation below the transferor's generation. For example, if a businesswoman creates a trust and gives a lifetime income interest (i.e., life estate) in trust assets to her children and gives the trust principal to her grandchildren, the portion going to the grandchildren is potentially subject to the generation skipping transfer tax. The generation skipping transfer tax is a flat rate tax equal to the maximum estate tax rate (55 percent). [IRC §§ 2001, 2641(a)]

Q 5:19 What is a generation skipping transfer?

A generation skipping transfer is a transfer to or for the benefit of a *skip person*. A skip person is a person who is more than one generation removed from the transferor. [IRC § 2613] The transferor, his or her spouse, and the transferor's brothers and sisters are one generation. Children of this group are the first younger generation, the grandchildren are the second younger generation. [IRC § 2651(b)] Husbands and wives of family members are assigned the same generation as their spouses. [IRC § 2651(c)] However, a grandchild whose deceased parent was the child of the transferor or the transferor's spouse is not a skip person; instead, the grandchild is deemed to belong to his or her parent's generation. [IRC § 2612(c)(2)]

If the generation skipping occurs outside of the family, generations are determined on the basis of the transferor's age. Individuals not more than 12½ years younger than the transferor are treated as members of the transferor's generation. Individuals more than 12½ years younger than the transferor, but less than 37½ years younger are considered members of the transferor's children's generation. [IRC § 2651(d)]

Q 5:20 What is the amount of the generation skipping transfer tax?

The generation skipping transfer tax imposed is an addition to any gift tax or estate tax payable by the transferor and is based on the amount received by the transferee. [IRC § 2623]

Example 5-3: A grandchild receives $100,000 after the payment of estate tax on the grandparent's estate. The generation skipping transfer tax on this transfer will be $55,000. The grandparent's estate is liable for this tax, not the transferee (the grandchild). Thus, the grandchild will receive the full $100,000 and the estate must pay an additional $55,000 in transfer taxes.

The generation skipping transfer tax is generally applicable to all generation skipping lifetime transfers made after September 25, 1985. The tax does not apply if the lifetime transfer is made from a trust that was irrevocable on that date, except to the extent that an addition was made to the trust after such date. The tax is applicable to all generation skipping transfers made by a decedent dying on or after October 22, 1986. [Pub L No 99-514 (1986), § 1433]

Q 5:21 What is the rate of the generation skipping transfer tax?

The generation skipping transfer tax is a flat tax, imposed at a rate of 55 percent on all generation skipping transfers, regardless of the amount transferred.

Q 5:22 Under what circumstances is the generation skipping transfer tax imposed?

The generation skipping transfer tax is imposed if:

1. A direct skip occurs (Qs 5:23, 5:24);
2. A taxable distribution occurs (Q 5:25); or
3. A taxable termination occurs (Q 5:26).

[IRC § 2611(a)]

Q 5:23 What is a direct skip?

A direct skip is a transfer of a property interest subject to estate or gift tax to a skip person (see Q 5:19). The most common example of a direct skip is an outright gift to a grandchild.

If the transfer is made to a trust, all of the current beneficiaries of the trust must be skip persons for a direct skip to occur. [IRC § 2612(c)] For example, a direct skip occurs if all the income beneficiaries of a trust are the transferor's grandchildren. This is true even if the remainder interest goes to the grantor's children. If the trust provides that the grandchildren and the children of the transferor are to receive trust income, the transfer is not a direct skip.

Q 5:24 When is the generation skipping transfer tax imposed on transfers that are direct skips?

If the transfer of the property interest is a direct skip, the generation skipping transfer tax is imposed at the time of transfer. If the direct skip is a lifetime gift, the generation skipping tax is imposed during life. [IRC § 2515] If the direct skip is a death transfer, the tax is imposed at death. [IRC § 2033] The tax is payable by the transferor or the transferor's estate. [IRC § 2603(a)(3)]

Q 5:25 What is a taxable distribution for generation skipping transfer tax purposes?

A taxable distribution is any distribution from a trust to a skip person that is not a direct skip (see Q 5:23) or a taxable termination (see Q 5:26). [IRC § 2612(b)] For example, if a trust that is currently paying income to a child makes a distribution to a grandchild, that distribution is a taxable distribution.

If a taxable distribution occurs, the taxable amount is the value of the property received by the transferee less expenses incurred by the transferee in connection with the determination, collection, or refund of the generation skipping transfer tax imposed by the distribution. [IRC § 2621] The tax is imposed at the time of distribution and is payable by the transferee. Thus, for example, if $100,000 is payable to a skip person in a taxable distribution, the transferee will actually receive $45,000. [IRC § 2603(a)(1)] If the generation skipping transfer tax is paid out of trust assets, the tax paid is treated as an additional taxable distribution and a generation skipping transfer tax is imposed on that amount as well. [IRC § 2621(b)]

Q 5:26 What is a taxable termination for generation skipping transfer tax purposes?

The termination of an interest in trust property as a result of death, lapse of time, release of power, or otherwise is a taxable termination unless either:

1. Immediately after the termination a nonskip person has an interest in the property; or
2. At no time after such termination may a distribution be made from the trust to a skip person. [IRC § 2612(a)(1)]

Example 5-4: A scientist creates a trust that provides that trust income is to go to his child and upon the child's death, the principal goes to his grandchildren. There is a taxable termination on the child's death. However, if the trust provided that the income would go to a nonskip person after the child's death, a taxable termination would occur only after both the child and the nonskip person died.

If a taxable termination occurs, the generation skipping transfer tax is computed on the value of the property to be transferred less the associated expenses and debts. [IRC § 2622] The tax is paid by the trustee out of the assets to be transferred. Thus, the beneficiary of $100,000 transferred in a terminable distribution gets $45,000 and $55,000 goes toward taxes.

Q 5:27 Which exemptions and exclusions apply in computing the generation skipping transfer tax?

These exemptions apply in computing the generation skipping transfer tax:

1. Each transferor is entitled to a $1 million exemption. [IRC § 2631(a)] Married couples who make lifetime gifts and elect gift splitting (i.e., making gifts jointly to take advantage of both $10,000 annual exclusions) will be deemed to have each made one-half of the gift, and each will be entitled to a $1 million exemption. [IRC § 2652(a)(2)] The $1 million exemption can be allocated among several transfers any time prior to the due date for filing the transferor's estate tax return. [IRC §§ 2631, 2632]
2. There is a special exclusion applicable to aggregate transfers to each grandchild for direct skips made before January 1990. [Pub L No 99-514 (1986), § 1433(b)(3)]

Q 5:28 Are any trusts protected from the generation skipping transfer tax?

Trusts that were created before September 25, 1985, and that cannot be changed or revoked after that date by the creator are protected from the generation skipping transfer tax. Additional property or cash cannot be put into such trusts if they are to retain their protected status. [Pub L No 99-514 (1986), § 1433]

Q 5:29 What provisions must a trust contain to avoid the generation skipping transfer tax?

The generation skipping transfer tax can be avoided only if the trust contains the following special provisions: The trust may have only one beneficiary, that beneficiary must take over all trust assets when the trust terminates (regardless of the beneficiary's age), and if the beneficiary dies prematurely, the trust assets must be part of his or her estate for estate tax purposes.

Q 5:30 What is the maximum generation skipping exemption that married couples have?

Each person receives a $1 million exemption from the generation skipping transfer tax (see Q 5:27). Accordingly, a married couple receives a total of $2 million in exemptions; however, this is their total exemption and must be spread among all potential beneficiaries.

Q 5:31 How can the $1 million lifetime exemption be used in connection with a generation skipping trust?

A generation skipping trust can be created during an individual's lifetime that will benefit his or her children and grandchildren. The trust assets can increase through accumulation of income and capital appreciation. If trust investments are successful, a large amount of money can pass to grandchildren and other younger beneficiaries without being subject to the generation skipping transfer tax.

Example 5-5: A 40-year-old entrepreneur creates a generation skipping trust. He and his wife give $2 million to the trust. He lives to age 65. During that 25-year period the trust fund grows from $2 million to $15 million. Because of the $1 million lifetime exemption for each spouse, totalling $2 million, a generation skipping transfer tax is not owed.

Furthermore, if the entrepreneur designs the trust so that he is responsible for paying the income tax that is attributable to the trust investments, after 25 years the trust will be worth $24 million.

Q 5:32 What planning can be done to minimize generation skipping transfer taxes?

The following planning steps can be taken to minimize generation skipping transfer taxes:

1. Lifetime gifts that are less than the $10,000 gift tax exemption authorized by Code Section 2503(b) can be made to grandchildren and other persons. Such gifts are exempt from the genera-

tion skipping transfer tax and they do not use up the transferor's $1 million exemption.

2. If sufficient assets are available, each spouse can be allocated $1 million in taxable assets. Transfers can be made from the richer spouse to the poorer spouse while they are both still living, if necessary, to permit each spouse to take advantage of the $1 million generation skipping transfer tax exemption to which each transferor is entitled.

3. If the transfer to the generation skipping trust exceeds the amount of available tax exemptions and exclusions, the trustee should be authorized or directed to divide the trust into an exempt part and a nonexempt part. Appreciation in the assets allocated to the exempt part of the trust (the portion of the trust protected by the $1 million exclusion) is not taxed; however, appreciation in assets allocated to the nonexempt part of the trust is taxed. Accordingly, the assets that do not appreciate should be allocated to the part of the trust subject to the generation skipping transfer tax, and the assets that appreciate should be allocated to the part of the trust that is exempt from the generation skipping transfer tax to reduce the amount of generation skipping transfer tax.

4. The estate owner should consider giving a child a general power of appointment over a trust that is likely not to be exempt from the generation skipping transfer tax. The result will be that the trust assets will be subject to estate tax in the child's estate but will not be subject to the generation skipping tax. This result is advantageous if the child's taxable estate is less than $3 million, because the child's marginal tax bracket will be less than 55 percent. (In contrast, the generation skipping tax rate is 55 percent.)

5. Often, distributions from a trust directly to grandchildren should be avoided. Such distributions will be subject to the generation skipping transfer tax because they involve a direct skip (see Q 5:23). It is often preferable for the distribution to be made to children rather than to grandchildren because the generation skipping tax is avoided if distributions are made to children. The children can then give the distribution to the grandchildren.

Q 5:33 What requirements must a trust meet to ensure that gifts to the trust are nontaxable gifts for generation skipping transfer tax purposes?

Gifts that avoid the generation skipping transfer tax can be made to trusts for the benefit of grandchildren and other persons in a lower generation. However, the exemption is available only if the trust has one current beneficiary. Also, if the trust is to terminate at a certain time (for example, when a beneficiary reaches age 30), the trust assets must go to the beneficiary. If the beneficiary dies before the planned trust termination date (at age 30), the beneficiary's rights must be such that trust assets would be included in his or her gross estate for estate tax purposes. A trust that satisfies these requirements will be eligible for the $10,000 annual exclusion.

Q 5:34 Does the beneficiary of a generation skipping transfer have to be a relative of the deceased in order to take advantage of the $1 million exemption?

No, the exemption is available whether the beneficiary is the donor's grandchild, his or her spouse's grandchild through another marriage, or an unrelated person who is young enough to be a grandchild had the donor and that person been related.

Example 5-6: A businessman gives $300,000 to the 23-year-old college roommate of his son. The businessman also makes one other small gift to his daughter. The gift to the college roommate is exempt from the generation skipping transfer tax.

Q 5:35 Do payments from trusts escape the generation skipping transfer tax if they are made for tuition or medical expenses?

A trust that pays tuition that is covered by the tax-free tuition statute [IRC § 2503(e)] or a trust that pays medical expenses that are covered by the medical expenses exemption [IRC § 2503(e)] escapes the generation skipping transfer tax.

Q 5:36 How can insurance be used to minimize the effect of the tax on generation skipping transfers?

Insurance policies can be used to benefit grandchildren. Because the amount of the gift in such cases is the amount of the premium and not the face amount, it is likely that only a relatively small portion of the $1 million exemption from the generation skipping transfer tax would be used.

Example 5-7: A physician takes out a $1 million insurance policy on his life in favor of his grandchild. The annual premium on the policy is $40,000 per year. This premium can be paid for 25 years before the $1 million generation skipping transfer tax exemption is used up. If the physician is 55 years old when he makes the gift, it is unlikely that he will exceed the $1 million exemption as a result of paying the insurance premiums.

Q 5:37 How can trusts be used to minimize the generation skipping transfer tax?

One planning idea is to use a trust to take advantage of the $600,000 exemption against estate taxes. This trust is funded with $600,000 in assets and designed so that its assets will eventually be paid to the grandchildren. However, it can also be designed to provide benefits exclusively for the lifetime benefit of the surviving spouse.

The remaining $400,000 of the $1 million generation skipping tax exemption can be utilized by creating a QTIP trust in the amount of $400,000. The surviving spouse is the lifetime beneficiary of the QTIP trust but does not have control of trust principal. At death, the designation of the trust principal is controlled by the trust creator's will. This trust will be part of the surviving spouse's estate in determining the amount of estate tax on his or her death; however, because it is less than the exemption equivalent estate tax can be avoided.

Example 5-8: An artist wishes to give $1 million to his sole grandchild. He creates a family trust with $600,000 that gives the trustee the discretion to pay trust income to his wife while she is alive. When his grandchild attains age 21, one third of the trust principal is paid to him, and when he attains age 30, the remainder of trust principal is paid to him. The artist also creates a QTIP trust in favor of his spouse. That trust is funded with a $400,000 contribution and provides that the trust income will be paid to the spouse annually. On her death, the trust principal is held in trust until the artist's grandson attains age 30, when it is paid to him.

Chapter 6

Gifts

Gifts are a valuable estate planning tool for lifetime transfers by an individual because, when properly arranged, they can provide significant savings on overall income, estate, and gift taxes. This chapter discusses various types of gifts, when making gifts may be advisable, how the gift tax is applied, and the beneficial financial consequence of gifts as part of an estate plan.

Overview	6-1
Gifts	6-2
The Gift Tax	6-3
Financial Effects of Making Gifts	6-8
Designing a Gift Giving Program	6-14
Gifts in Trust	6-17
Charitable Gifts	6-24
Anatomical Gifts	6-28

Overview

Q 6:1 How does a program for transferring property provide a donor with meaningful tax savings both during the life of the donor and on his or her death?

A gift program can minimize a donor's overall estate and gift taxes and maximize the overall after-tax income available to a family unit during the donor's lifetime. The most common tax-avoidance vehicle used by experienced estate planners is the $10,000 per donee annual exclusion allowed for gifts of a present interest of money or other property. This exclusion is increased to $20,000 per donee when combined with marital gift splitting.

Employing the annual exclusion allows a donor to transfer the maximum amount possible, free of estate and gift taxes (without eroding the overall estate and gift tax exemption of $600,000) to children and other beneficiaries.

Gifts of property during a donor's lifetime can produce surprising tax-saving results because the fair market value of property that is given in appropriate cases can be discounted and because the post-gift appreciation in the property from estate tax is removed. If this property was held by the donor until death, its full fair market value at death would be subject to an estate tax. Making a charitable gift in trust can also produce significant overall tax savings. Another reason for making gifts within a family unit, generally to children, is that giving increases the availability of the donor's after-tax income within the family unit, because the parent is typically in a higher tax bracket than the child.

> **Example 6-1:** A stockbroker owns a large piece of land just outside of Missoula, Montana, with a fair market value in 1994 of $50,000. She gives the land to her son that year, incurring a gift tax liability of $8,200 (taking into account the $10,000 per donee exclusion). [IRC §§ 2001(c)(1), 2502(a)] In 1995, an entertainment company announces that it plans to build a new amusement park ten miles from Missoula. The stockbroker dies in 2005. The stockbroker's gross estate is negligible; there is no estate tax liability. At the time of her death, the property is valued at $2.5 million. Had she not given the land away, the entire value would have been included in the stockbroker's gross estate, resulting in estate taxes of $833,000. [IRC § 2001(c)(1)]

Gifts

Q 6:2 How may gifts be made?

Gifts can be made outright, in trust, or, if the donee is a minor, pursuant to the Uniform Transfers to Minors Act or the state law equivalent.

The Gift Tax

Q 6:3 What amount of assets can be the subject of a gift so as to avoid both gift and estate tax on the transferred property?

During a calendar year, a donor can give $10,000 to each intended donee without paying any gift tax. This donated property escapes estate tax. [IRC § 2503] If the donor's spouse joins in the gift, the married couple can give each donee $20,000 each year without incurring gift tax. [IRC § 2513] If the donee's spouse is the recipient, an unlimited amount can be given to the spouse without incurring gift tax. [IRC § 2523] Similarly, if a qualified charity is the recipient, an unlimited amount can be given to the charity without incurring gift tax.

Q 6:4 Can a spouse refuse to consent to a gift that his or her spouse wishes to make for purposes of the $10,000 gift tax exclusion?

Yes. However, if an individual wishes to take advantage of the $20,000 exclusion for joint gifts, he or she must consent to all gifts made by the spouse. The consenting spouse does not have to provide the funds with which the gift is made in order for the $20,000 exclusion to apply.

Example 6-2: An attorney wishes to make a $20,000 joint gift with his wife to their son and a $20,000 joint gift to his daughter by a previous marriage. His wife consents to the $20,000 gift to their son, but is less enthusiastic about making a $20,000 gift to the daughter from the previous marriage. If the wife wants to take advantage of the $20,000 exclusion for her son, she must also consent to the $20,000 gift to her husband's daughter. Alternatively, the husband can fund the $20,000 gift to his daughter out of his own property.

Q 6:5 What is the tax consequence if a donor makes a gift of property having a value in excess of $10,000?

If a donor wishes to give more than $10,000 in a single calendar year, two methods are possible. First, the donor could pay gift tax on any amount over $10,000. Second, the donor could use some of his or her $192,800 unified credit (equivalent to the $600,000 exemption) against estate and gift tax. [IRC § 2010]

Q 6:6 Should a donor consider giving an amount in excess of the $10,000 annual exclusion?

Some specialists recommend giving more than $10,000 and paying some gift tax on the transaction in order to build a valuation history. By filing gift tax returns and paying modest gift taxes, the donor establishes a record of appraisal values based on valuation methods that the IRS found appropriate at the time the gifts were given. This record may preclude an IRS challenge at a later date. (See Q 6:8 for an alternative approach the IRS uses on an estate tax examination for revaluing lifetime gifts made by donor decedents.)

For instance, a father who owns a closely held business might want to give stock in that business to his children each year. It would be a good idea for him to give stock worth more than $10,000 in order to establish a valuation history. If, for example, he gave his daughter stock worth $12,000 in one year, he would only have to pay $360 in gift taxes. This might be a good idea because later, when the father dies with a large amount of company stock in his gross estate, the estate will be able to show the IRS the previously accepted valuation method and to argue that it should still apply. Even if this does not reduce estate taxes overall, it increases certainty as to the amount of estate tax that will be due, which, in turn, allows for more informed estate planning.

Q 6:7 How long does the IRS have to examine a gift tax return?

Ordinarily, the IRS has three years from the April 15 filing date. [IRC § 6501] If the taxpayer receives an extension of time to file the return, the three-year period runs from the extension date. If a gift tax return is examined by the IRS during the three-year period and the IRS needs more time to determine the correctness of the donor's valuation, it will request that the donor consent, on a Form 872, to the extension of the statute of limitations for an additional period (generally a year). If the donor refuses to consent to an extension of the statute of limitations, then the IRS typically issues a statutory notice of deficiency, which gives the donor 90 days within which to file a petition in the U.S. Tax Court; and if the donor fails to file the petition, the IRS can assess a gift tax against the donor based upon its determination of the correct valuation for the gift.

Q 6:8 Can the IRS revalue, as part of an estate tax valuation, prior taxable gifts made by a decedent after the statute of limitations has passed for examining a gift tax return?

Yes. The Tax Court has upheld the IRS's position on this issue. [Estate of Smith, 94 TC 872 (1990)] The basis for the IRS's position is that the statute of limitations for gift tax purposes is not applicable for estate tax purposes. In computing the estate tax, *adjusted taxable gifts* as required in the estate tax computation must be taken into account so that the IRS may reexamine and adjust prior taxable gifts to reflect their value as of the date of donation. [IRC § 2001(b)(1)(B)]

The Tax Court also held in *Smith* that in computing the credit for gift taxes against the estate tax payable, the gift tax credit should be computed on the basis of the gift tax that would have been payable on the gifts revalued by the IRS for purposes of computing the estate tax and not on the gift tax actually paid by the decedent. [IRC § 2001(b)]

Example 6-3: Grace Smith made a gift six years before her death which was valued at $1 million on her gift tax return, and the gift tax was reported and paid in the amount of $550,000 (assume that she was subject to a 55 percent gift tax rate). The statute of limitations for the IRS to examine the gift tax return passed without any audit of the gift tax return; however, the IRS subsequently examined the estate tax return filed by the estate of Grace Smith and determined that the correct value of the gift, when made, should have been $1.5 million. Because of the IRS's change in valuing the adjusted taxable gift on the estate tax return, the estate is allowed a credit for gift taxes previously payable of $825,000 (assuming a 55 percent tax rate) rather than the $550,000 of gift tax actually paid when the gift tax return was filed. While this result seems incongruous and without logic, a majority of the judges on the Tax Court found that a strict reading of the Code provisions involved demanded this result.

Q 6:9 What gifts qualify for the gift tax exclusion?

The gift tax exclusion is available only for gifts of a present interest. The exclusion does not apply to gifts of a future interest. For this purpose, a future interest is any vested or contingent interest, the use, enjoyment, or possession of which does not commence until a future time. [Treas Reg § 25.2503-3(a)] A remainder interest, for instance, is a future interest; so, if a business person gave money to a trust, stipulating that the income is to be paid currently to his or her children and upon termination of the trust the principal is to be transferred to his or her grandchildren, the value of the remainder interest to the grandchildren would not be eligible for the $10,000 gift tax exclusion.

Example 6-4: A stockbroker pays the premiums on an insurance policy on his life that is owned by his son. This payment of premiums is a gift of a present interest.

Example 6-5: A stockbroker transfers an insurance policy to a trust for the benefit of her son. When the stockbroker dies, the insurance proceeds will be invested and the son will be entitled to the income from the investments. The son has a future interest in the insurance policy.

Q 6:10 Does a gift made in trust qualify as a gift of a present interest?

A gift made in trust will be a gift of a present interest if, under the trust, the beneficiary has the power to demand immediate possession of the transferred property.

Example 6-6: The owner of a roofing business creates a trust to acquire life insurance so that the funds will be available to pay estate taxes at his death. The trust permits beneficiaries to request payment of the cash contributed to the trust to buy insurance. Because the beneficiaries can request payment to themselves, the gifts of cash made to the trust to purchase insurance will be gifts of a present interest.

Q 6:11   Does gift tax arise when income is given in order to discharge a legal obligation?

No. For example, if income is used by a parent for the support of a minor child, no gift tax applies because the expenditure is in discharge of the parent's legal obligation.

Q 6:12   Are payments to educational institutions or health care providers for medical services a taxable gift?

No, a payment on behalf of a donee directly to an educational institution or to a health care provider for medical services is not a taxable gift. [IRC § 2503(e)] Some estate planners recommend these exclusions as an effective means for eliminating gift and estate tax otherwise payable. For example, if a donor in deteriorating health has a child entering college, consideration should be given to prepaying the child's entire four-year college tuition. By so doing, the amount of tuition, which in today's educational climate can be substantial, will not be subject to either gift tax or estate tax on the donor's death. There is no requirement that the donee be related to the donor for this gift tax exemption to be available.

Q 6:13   What is a net gift?

A net gift is a gift in which the donor, as a condition of the gift, requires the donee to pay the gift tax. The value of the gift is reduced by the amount of the gift tax payable by the donee, which reduces the total gift tax payable on the gift. [Rev Rul 75-72, 1975-1 CB 310] If the gift tax paid by the donee exceeds the donor's adjusted basis in the gift, the excess gift tax is treated as taxable gain to the donor. For example, if a businessman gives stock with an income tax basis of $40,000 to his son and the gift tax on the stock is $200,000, the businessman will have a taxable gain of $160,000. However, if the stock has an income tax basis of $200,000 or more, the businessman will incur no taxable gain.

Financial Effects of Making Gifts

Q 6:14 What events require the filing of a gift tax return?

A gift tax return (Form 709) must be filed for gifts of present interests exceeding $10,000 in value to a donee for the calendar year and for gifts of future interests, regardless of the amount. A gift tax return need not be filed for any transfer to a spouse that qualifies for the unlimited marital deduction, or for any medical or educational related transfer that is exempt from gift tax. A short-form gift tax return (Form 709-A) may be filed instead of the regular form for most common types of gifts that do not exceed $20,000 per donee, if gift splitting is elected for all gifts made during the year. If gift tax is not payable because the donor and the donor's spouse take advantage of the $20,000 joint exclusion, a gift tax return that shows the consent of the consenting spouse must be filed and signed by both spouses. [IRC § 2513]

Q 6:15 When is a gift tax return due?

A gift tax return is due on April 15 of the year following the year in which the gift was made, and an automatic extension to file the return by August 15 can be obtained by checking the appropriate box on IRS Form 4868. An extension of time to pay the gift tax may also be requested [IRC § 6081]; however, if the tax is not paid by the date on which the return is due, interest is due from the due date of the return to the date on which the gift tax is paid. [IRC § 6601] If a donor dies during the calendar year the gift is made, the gift tax return is due when the estate tax return is due. [IRC § 6075]

Q 6:16 Is it better to use the $192,800 unified credit during the donor's lifetime rather than saving it until death?

Each individual is entitled to a $192,800 unified credit against estate and gift taxes. This credit may be used either against gift taxes while the individual is alive, or against estate taxes at death. This credit is sufficient to offset the estate or gift tax associated with the transfer of $600,000 in assets.

There are two reasons for using the $192,800 unified credit against estate and gift taxes while the donor is alive. First, the credit permits the transfer of $600,000 in assets without gift tax; however, the present value of this credit decreases with the passage of time, because gifts made now are more valuable than gifts made in the future. Second, removing a $600,000 asset from the estate earlier rather than later can be beneficial because the donor removes the post-gift appreciation in the property that was the subject of the gift from the estate.

Example 6-7: A physician gives stocks to his son worth $600,000 that over a 20-year period are expected to appreciate to $1.8 million (i.e., less than 10 percent per year). By making this gift immediately, the physician keeps $1.2 million in future value from being subject to estate tax.

Q 6:17 Is the money used to pay gift tax during the decedent's lifetime includible in the gross estate?

No, generally not. An advantage of making lifetime gifts is that the amount used to pay gift tax ordinarily will not be taxed as part of the donor's estate. The reason for the difference is that the gift tax is imposed only on the actual amount received by the donee; the estate tax, in contrast, will be imposed on the total amount of the death transfer, including both the part that would otherwise have been given to the donee while the decedent was alive and the part that would have been paid to the IRS as gift tax.

Example 6-8: An entrepreneur whose estate is likely to be taxed at the 55 percent marginal bracket rate intends to transfer $1 million to his children. His estate plan contemplates that the transfer will occur when he dies. To accomplish this, the entrepreneur actually must leave $2,222,222 to the children because an estate tax of $1,222,222 (55 percent of the total) must be paid out of the estate first, to give the children a net amount of $1 million.

Example 6-9: The entrepreneur gives $1 million to his children during his lifetime. A total of $1,550,000 will be required to make the transfer if the entrepreneur is in the 55 percent bracket ($1 million for the children and $550,000 for gift tax applicable to the amount that exceeds the annual gift tax exclusion). The $1 million that the entrepreneur gives will be added back to his estate, but the gift tax of $555,000 will be credited against the estate tax, resulting in no additional transfer tax at the time of death. If the entrepreneur lives at least three years after making the gift, the amount of the gift taxes paid will be kept out of the estate.

To some extent, the advantage of a large lifetime gift is offset by the lost earnings on the amounts used to pay gift tax, because money used to pay gift tax can alternatively be retained and used to generate earnings; however, to the extent these earnings are retained at death, they will be reduced by the 55 percent estate tax rate.

Example 6-10: Both the entrepreneur and his children can double $550,000 in seven years after income taxes are paid. The entrepreneur, rather than giving any money, retains the $1,550,000 (i.e., the $1 million gift and $550,000 gift tax payment) for seven years and then dies. As a result of this action his estate is increased by $3,110,000. After the estate tax is paid on this amount, $1,395,000 is left for the children.

Example 6-11: The entrepreneur pays a gift tax of $550,000 and gives $1 million to his children. He dies seven years later. In that seven-year period the $1 million given to his children grows to $2 million. The children are better off than the children in the previous example, because they receive an additional $605,000. If the entrepreneur dies within three years after making the gift, the net advantage of the gift will be reduced (but not eliminated) because the gift tax will be added back to his estate, increasing the gift tax on his remaining assets. Assuming the estate is in the 55 percent bracket, the resulting increase in tax is $302,500. Even under these circumstances the children receive an additional $302,500 ($605,000 − $302,500 = $302,500).

Q 6:18 Are gifts includible in the gross estate?

The answer depends on when the gift is made. For decedents dying prior to January 1, 1982, the gross estate included all gifts made within three years of death. For decedents dying on or after January 1, 1982, this three-year rule applies to gifts of life insurance and other transfers where the gift property would be included in the gross estate under Code Section 2036 (transfers with retained life estates), Code Section 2037 (transfers taking effect at death), Code Section 2038 (revocable transfers), or Code Section 2042 (life insurance proceeds) had the interest been retained by the decedent. These gifts are includible in the gross estate even if the gift otherwise qualified for the annual $10,000 exclusion. Gifts includible in the gross estate under this rule are valued for estate tax purposes as of the date of death (or the alternative valuation date, if elected by the executor) rather than as of the date of gift. Any appreciation after the date of gift is subject to estate tax. However, the gift tax paid on these transfers is excluded from the donor's estate.

Example 6-12: An heiress gives a life insurance policy worth $5,000 to her nephew two years prior to her death. When the heiress dies, the policy has a face value of $100,000, which is includible in her gross estate because she did not live at least three years after making the gift.

Q 6:19 If a gift is made within three years of death, is the gift tax paid on it includible in the gross estate?

The amount used to pay gift tax on all gifts made within three years of death is includible in the gross estate. [IRC § 2025(c)] The gift tax paid by a decedent's spouse on gifts made by such spouse when the gift was split with the decedent is not includible in the decedent's estate.

Example 6-13: A chemist who has a terminal illness makes a $100,000 gift to his son. He pays gift tax of $23,800 on the gift. Two years later he dies. The $23,800 he paid in gift tax is includible in his gross estate.

Example 6-14: Apply the same facts as in Example 6-13, except that the chemist and his wife make a joint gift of $100,000. The wife pays the gift tax on the gift. Two years later, the chemist dies. The gift tax that was paid by the chemist's spouse is not included in his gross estate because it was the chemist's surviving spouse who paid the gift tax.

Q 6:20 What income tax advantages result from making gifts?

An important reason for making a gift of income-producing property is to eliminate the income tax payable by the donor on the property. For instance, if the donor is in the 39.6 percent income tax bracket and the donee is in the 15 percent income tax bracket, substantial tax savings within the family unit can result if the income-producing property is given to the donee. However, if the donee is a child under age 14, a "kiddie tax" is imposed on the net unearned income of the child which is computed on the parent's rather than the child's usually lower marginal tax rate. To arrive at the net unearned income taxed to the parent, there is subtracted from unearned income received by the child the greater of $1,300 or $650 plus certain itemized deductions. Making gifts also will prevent the donor's estate from being increased by income (after taxes) from the gift assets, thereby reducing the estate tax on the donor's estate.

Q 6:21 What legal requirements must be satisfied in order for a gift to be valid for estate tax purposes?

If a valid gift has been made, the amount of the gift will not be added back into the decedent's estate for estate tax purposes. If the gift is not valid for gift and estate tax purposes, the relevant assets are not excluded from the donor's gross estate. Any transfer of property for less than adequate and full consideration is deemed a gift for estate and gift tax purposes. A voluntary act of transfer must occur, however. This means that the transferor must do some act with the intent of transferring the property. For example, in a case before the U.S. Tax Court, the decedent had been part of an employees' benefit plan adopted by his employer. He had no power over the plan except that he could terminate it by quitting his job. Upon his death, the plan paid benefits to his wife. The IRS then attempted to tax these benefits as a gift. The court, however, held that no taxable gift had occurred since the decedent had not acted or intended to make a gift. [DiMarco Estate v Commr, 87 TC 653 (1986), *acq in result*, 1990-2 CB 1]

Donative intent is required. Transfers in the ordinary course of business are not treated as gifts. Otherwise, any bad bargain would be taxed as a gift. [See generally, Commr v Wemyss, 324 US 303 (1945)]

Q 6:22 What are the tax consequences of making gifts to spouses?

After 1981, either spouse may give property to the other spouse, and such property (1) will not be subject to gift tax, and (2) will not be added back into the estate tax base. [IRC §§ 2523(a), 2001(b)] There is no limit on the amounts that may be given to a spouse during the donor spouse's lifetime. If the donor spouse does not want to make an outright gift to the donee spouse, the donor may give a qualifying terminable interest property (QTIP) to a QTIP trust. A QTIP trust must require that the donee spouse be entitled to receive all the income from the property at least annually and that no person, including the spouse, be able to appoint property during the spouse's lifetime to anyone other than the spouse (see Q 4:18). The donor can elect to avoid gift tax at the time the transfer to the QTIP trust is made. If the donor makes this election, however, the property is subject to gift tax or estate tax when the donee spouse either dies or disposes of the QTIP property during his or her lifetime. [IRC §§ 2044, 2519, 2523(f)]

Q 6:23 What are the tax consequences of making gifts to a non-U.S. citizen spouse?

If the recipient spouse is not a U.S. citizen, the amount of tax-free gifts is limited to an aggregate value of $100,000 annually. [IRC § 2523(i)] If the donor spouse is not a U.S. citizen, but the donee spouse is, the usual rule allowing unlimited tax-free gifts applies.

Q 6:24 What estate tax advantages result from making gifts to spouses?

Interspousal gifts can create significant estate tax savings. If one spouse has no estate or a much smaller estate than the other spouse, interspousal gifts to the poorer spouse should be considered. If the poorer spouse dies first, these gifts can prevent the loss of the unified credit against the estate and gift tax. The marital deduction is available only if the donee spouse is a U.S. citizen [IRC § 2523(i)(1)]; however, the annual gift tax exclusion for gifts of a present interest to a donee noncitizen spouse is $100,000. [IRC § 2523(i)(2)]

Example 6-15: A manufacturer and his wife jointly own property worth $5 million. The manufacturer has separate property worth $1 million. They have two children and have been married for 25 years. The marriage is stable. The wife has no separate property. The manufacturer gives $600,000 of jointly owned property to his wife with the understanding that she will bequeath it to their children. This action might save a significant amount of estate taxes. If the manufacturer's wife dies first, the wife's unified credit will permit her to pass $600,000 to their children without incurring estate tax. Further, $600,000 is removed from the manufacturer's estate. In contrast, if this is not done and if the manufacturer's estate is in the 55 percent estate tax bracket (which seems likely), the $600,000 would be subject to $330,000 in estate taxes.

Q 6:25 What income tax advantages result from making interspousal gifts?

Interspousal gifts can create income tax advantages if one spouse owns an appreciated asset and it seems likely that the other spouse will die first. If the spouse who owns the appreciated asset gives it to the spouse who is likely to die first, the asset will receive a stepped-up basis (see Q 3:47) on the death of the donee/recipient spouse. [IRC §§ 1014(a), 1014(b)] This step-up in basis does not occur if the donee spouse dies within one year of the gift and the gift property is returned to the donor. [IRC § 1014(e)]

Designing a Gift Giving Program

Q 6:26 What guidelines apply in giving assets?

The following guidelines should be considered when designing a gift program:

1. Consider giving assets that yield higher amounts of income as opposed to assets that yield lower amounts of income. This will prevent a buildup of income in the estate that would be taxed at the donor's estate tax rate.

2. If the donee is in a lower income tax bracket than the donor, give assets that produce as much taxable income as possible. Assets that do not produce taxable income, such as municipal bonds, should be retained if the donor is in a higher tax bracket than the donee.

3. Give growth as opposed to nongrowth assets. This will prevent the post-gift appreciation from being taxed in the donor's gross estate.

4. Give high-basis assets as opposed to low-basis assets. Any asset that is given has the same basis for a donee as a donor. On the other hand, an asset that is held at death receives a step-up in basis equal to its fair market value on the date of the decedent's death. Generally, a capital asset included in a taxable estate is subject to an initial 37 percent estate tax rate after the $600,000 exemption is exhausted and an increasingly higher tax rate based on the size of the taxable estate. On the other hand, a donee receiving a gift during the decedent's lifetime, although required to retain the donor's tax basis, pays a 28 percent maximum capital gains tax only on the income recognized. Therefore, it is wise to weigh an estate tax based on the fair market value of the property against an income tax measured only on the income realized on the sale of the property so as to determine which provides the most beneficial after-tax result to an intended beneficiary.

5. Assets whose value is less than their basis should not be either given or retained until death; they should be sold. Selling these assets results in the recognition of the owner's loss. If these assets are retained, the basis for determining loss is lost:

   a. If these assets are given during the owner's life, the donee's basis for determining loss is equal to the fair market value of the assets (rather than the donee's basis) at the time the gift is made; and

   b. If the estate owner dies holding the assets, the basis is the fair market value of the assets.

6. Installment obligations should not be given. A gift or other disposition of an installment obligation will cause the entire untaxed profit to be recognized and taxed to the donor at the time of transfer. [IRC § 453B]

7. Stock in an S corporation should not be given to a trust unless it is determined that the gift will not cause a loss of S corporation status. This generally means that the trust must be a *qualified subchapter S trust*. These trusts have the following characteristics:
   a. All trust income must be distributed to one individual who is a citizen or resident of the United States;
   b. A trust beneficiary must make an irrevocable election to have the trust treated as a qualified subchapter S trust; and
   c. The trust instrument contains terms requiring that:
      - The trust can have only one income beneficiary during the life of the current income beneficiary;
      - The income interest of the beneficiary must terminate on the earlier of the beneficiary's death or the termination of the trust; and
      - All assets of the trust must be distributed to the income beneficiary if the trust terminates during the current income beneficiary's life. [IRC § 1361(d)(3)]

As this book goes to press, Congress is considering adding to the categories of trusts that can qualify as subchapter S stockholders.

Q 6:27 What factors other than tax factors should be considered in estate planning for children?

One important consideration is the maturity of the children. It may be inadvisable to give large sums of money to children who do not have the maturity or experience to manage money. In such cases, it is prudent to create a trust. The trust can be designed so that as the child matures, the trustee has the flexibility to make distributions to the child. Other factors, such as discouraging the child from growing dependent on trust funds and becoming self-sufficient instead, also play a role.

Q 6:28 What pitfalls exist if appreciated assets are given to a donee who is expected to predecease the donor?

Sometimes it is desirable to give appreciated property to a donee who is expected to predecease the donor because the property will get a basis increase on the donee's death; however, if property is given during the one-year period preceding the donee's death and the property subsequently passes back to the donor, this strategy does not work because no step-up in basis will occur.

Gifts in Trust

Q 6:29 How are gifts made under the Uniform Transfers to Minors Act?

Under the Uniform Transfers to Minors Act (UTMA) or the state equivalent, gifts are made by the donor placing the asset in the name of a custodian, who then holds the property for the benefit of the minor. [Uniform Transfers to Minors Act, 8A ULA 153-85 (Supp 1987)] The minor has legal title to the gift property, but the custodian has the right to hold and manage the property consistent with the provisions of the statute. Technically, although the transfer is not considered a trust (since the minor has legal title), the custodian is given trustee-like powers to manage the custodianship for the benefit of the minor.

During the minority of the minor, the custodian is required to pay for the benefit of the minor as much of the income derived from the property, and the property itself, as the custodian deems advisable for the support, maintenance, education, or benefit of the minor. When the minor attains the age of majority, which in most states is 18, but under the UTMA is 21, the custodianship terminates and the assets are owned outright by the minor.

Income earned on assets given under the custodian statutes is generally taxable to the minor; however, the IRS has contended that, to the extent income from a custodian account is used for the minor's support, the income is taxable to the person who is legally obligated to support the minor. [Rev Rul 56-484, 1956-2 CB 23]

Gifts made under the Uniform Transfers to Minors Act qualify for the $10,000 annual gift tax exclusion; however, if the donor is the custodian and dies while serving in that capacity, the custodianship assets are includible in the donor's estate. [Rev Rul 59-357, 1959-2 CB 212] This is because the custodian has the power to transfer all custodial assets to the minor before the minor reaches the age when the custodianship automatically terminates, and this power to terminate the custodianship makes the transfer taxable under Code Section 2038. For this reason, the donor should name a third party as custodian.

Q 6:30 What considerations apply in making a gift in trust?

Trusts are extremely flexible devices for holding assets. Unlike gifts made under the Uniform Transfers to Minors Act, trusts do not have to distribute assets at any given time. Trustees can be given a wide range of powers. Giving through trusts is important for the following reasons:

1. To use the annual gift tax exclusion;
2. To prevent assets from being included in the donor's estate; and
3. To prevent income from the trust from being taxable to the donor.

Q 6:31 What steps must be taken to obtain the $10,000 annual gift tax exclusion in making gifts to a trust?

To obtain the $10,000 gift tax exclusion, the gift must be of a present interest (see Q 6:9). [IRC § 2503(b)] If a gift is made in trust, the principal is often not a gift of a present interest because the trust beneficiaries do not have the unrestricted right to its immediate use, possession, or enjoyment. [Treas Reg § 25.2503-3(b)]

If the trust provides that income is to be paid currently to an income beneficiary, the value of the income interest is a present interest and qualifies for the $10,000 annual gift tax exclusion; however, some income interests may not be present interests, and the exclusion is not available for them. For instance, an income interest is not a present interest if the trust requires gains and losses to be credited to or charged against income. [Rev Rul 77-358, 1992-CB 342] If the trust requires that income be accumulated or if the trustee is given discretionary powers over the payment of income, there is no gift of a present interest unless the trust qualifies as a Crummey trust or a minor's trust.

Q 6:32 What is a Crummey trust?

A Crummey trust, named after a court decision giving rise to its use [Crummey v Commr, 397 F 2d 82 (9th Cir 1968)], provides that the beneficiary is allowed to withdraw, during each calendar year, the lesser of the amount of the annual gift tax exclusion or the value of assets transferred to the trust during that year. The beneficiary's withdrawal right may be extended to the next calendar year without destroying the validity of the Crummey power. [Rev Rul 83-108, 1983-2, CB 167] The exclusion is available even if the beneficiary is a minor and/or has no legal guardian. The IRS asserts that any adult beneficiary must be informed of his or her right to withdraw assets and must be given a reasonable time in which to make the withdrawal. [Rev Rul 81-7, 1981-1 CB 474]

Q 6:33 What happens if a beneficiary fails to withdraw assets pursuant to a Crummey power?

If a beneficiary has been given the right to withdraw annually more than the greater of $5,000 or 5 percent of the value of principal but fails to exercise this right, the failure will be considered a lapse for gift and estate tax purposes. The consequence of this lapse is that the Crummey power beneficiary will be treated as having made a taxable gift to the trust's remainder beneficiary and also as having made a transfer that may cause the assets that the Crummey power beneficiary could have withdrawn to be included in his or her gross estate.

This problem can be eliminated through the use of the so-called five-and-five power. By definition, if the five-and-five power is not exercised, there is no lapse. This power limits the Crummey power beneficiary's right to withdraw assets to the lesser of (1) the amount of the annual gift tax exclusion or (2) the greater of $5,000 or 5 percent of the principal of the trust. If the beneficiary holds several $5,000 or 5 percent powers (either in the same trust or in different trusts), he or she is not entitled to more than one exemption in any calendar year. [Rev Rul 85-88, 1985-2 CB 201]

If the amount of the potential lapse exceeds the five-and-five power, the trust can be drafted to give the beneficiary a so-called hanging power. A hanging power is a power that, unless otherwise limited, does not lapse if it is not exercised but continues into future years until such time as it is exercised. (See Q 6:34 for a discussion of how this hanging power can be coupled with a five-and-five power to permit the hanging power to lapse without incurring gift tax.)

The income attributable to the amount that the holder of a Crummey power may have withdrawn in any year is taxable to the holder in that year regardless of whether he or she actually withdraws that income.

Q 6:34 Can the hanging power be combined with the five-and-five withdrawal power?

Yes, and this may be an effective estate planning device. The hanging power is combined with a provision to the effect that any portion of the hanging power that is still in existence that is less than or equal to the five-and-five withdrawal power (i.e., less than or equal to the greater of $5,000 or 5 percent of trust assets) lapses. This modified hanging power allows the beneficiary the right to withdraw the remaining amounts of principal in subsequent years if no additional gift is made. The five-and-five provision permits a limited lapse of the hanging power and prevents the imposition of gift tax if no withdrawal is made in a year in which no additional gift is made. Upon the beneficiary's death, any trust assets subject to an unexercised and nonlapsed power of withdrawal will be taxable in his or her estate.

Example 6-16: A physician transfers $100,000 to a trust for his son. The son is given the right to withdraw $10,000, (i.e., the lesser of $10,000 or the amount of the gift ($100,000)) from the trust. This right of withdrawal is a hanging power limited by a five-and-five power (i.e., the trust provides that the portion of the withdrawal power that is not used will lapse to a limited extent). The amount of the lapse is limited to an amount that is less than or equal to 5 percent of trust assets. In the year in which the $100,000 is placed in trust, the son declines to use his withdrawal right; however, a portion of the withdrawal right still lapses (i.e., an amount equal to $5,000 (the lesser of 5 percent of trust assets or $5,000)). The remaining portion of the withdrawal right, $5,000, carries over to the next year. If no gift is made in the next year, the son still has the right to withdraw $5,000. If he chooses not to withdraw that amount, the right lapses. There is no gift tax arising from the lapse because the amount of the lapse is less than the greater of $5,000 or 5 percent of the trust assets. The $10,000 gift tax exclusion is available because the son was given the right to withdraw the lesser of the $100,000 or the $10,000 gift tax exclusion.

Q 6:35 What is a minor's trust?

A minor's trust provides that trust property and income may be expended for the benefit of the donee before the donee attains age 21. To the extent the income and property are not expended for this purpose, they must pass to the donee when the donee attains age 21. If the donee dies before attaining age 21, trust income and principal must be payable to the donee's estate or as the donee directs under a power of appointment. [IRC § 2503(c)] The advantage of a minor's trust is that the $10,000 annual gift tax exclusion is available to the donor even though the transfer is to a discretionary trust.

The courts and the IRS have held that the income interest alone may qualify for the annual gift tax exclusion. [Rev Rul 68-670, 1968-2 CB 413] This means that the minor's trust may provide that net income alone must either be paid or be accumulated at the trustee's discretion until the beneficiary reaches age 21, at which time all undistributed income will be distributed to the beneficiary or to his or her estate. The value of the income interest will then qualify for the annual gift tax exclusion. If the income exceeds $10,000, the entire annual exclusion will be used.

Q 6:36 What is the chief disadvantage of a minor's trust?

The main disadvantage of a minor's trust is that it lacks flexibility because it must distribute trust assets when the donee reaches the age of majority (i.e., age 21). If, for instance, the donee has a drug problem or cannot manage his or her financial affairs, the trust will make a distribution to him or her on attaining the age of majority even though the likely result of the distribution is that the donee will dissipate the assets.

Q 6:37   Estate and Retirement Planning Answer Book

Q 6:37 Can any action be taken if it appears that the donee of a minor's trust is likely to dissipate trust assets?

One possible solution is that once the beneficiary reaches the age of majority (18 in many states), he or she can agree in writing that at age 21 the assets in the trust are to be rolled over to another trust that will hold the assets for his or her benefit. Of course, this is a rather uncertain solution, because the donee may not agree to such a proposal. Another alternative is to design the trust so that it continues past age 21 but gives the beneficiary the right for a brief time at age 21 to terminate the trust and remove the assets. For example, the trust can be designed so that it will continue unless the beneficiary acts to terminate the trust within a period of 60 days after attaining age 21. The advantage of this course is that the trust continues unless the beneficiary takes adverse action.

Q 6:38 How does the minor's trust differ from a custodianship under the Uniform Transfers to Minors Act?

The minor's trust differs from a custodianship under the Uniform Transfers to Minors Act because, under the act, income is taxable to the minor whether or not it is distributed. In contrast, under a minor's trust, income is taxable to the minor if it is distributed and it is taxable to the trustee if it is accumulated. Accordingly, aggregate income taxes on the minor and the trust can be minimized selectively by accumulating or distributing all or a portion of trust income.

Q 6:39 Is it desirable to retain income in a trust because of the compressed income tax rates under which trusts operate? (The top income tax bracket for trusts, 39.6 percent, is reached at $7,500.)

No, it is generally not advisable to retain income in a trust unless it is undesirable to have a child receive the income. If neither of the child's parents is living, the kiddie tax does not apply—normal income tax rules apply even for children under 14 years of age. [IRC § 1(g)] Under these rules the maximum income tax bracket is not reached until the child has taxable income in excess of $250,000. [IRC § 1(c)]

Q 6:40 What are the tax consequences if assets given to an irrevocable trust are included in the estate of the donor?

If assets given to an irrevocable trust are included in the donor's estate, the $10,000 annual gift tax exclusion previously taken by the donor will be lost and the value of the asset at the time of death rather than at the time of the gift transfer will be includible in the donor's estate. Any appreciation after the gift is made also will be subject to the estate tax.

Q 6:41 What causes irrevocable trust assets to be included in the gross estate of the donor?

The donor's retention of benefits, rights, and powers causes trust assets to be included in the donor's estate. The persons given benefits, rights, or powers over trust assets by the donor do not have trust assets included in each of their gross estates, unless the benefits, rights, or powers constitute a general power of appointment.

Two kinds of transfers result in the inclusion of trust assets in the donor's gross estate. The first kind is the donor's retention of a beneficial interest in the given assets, such as a reversionary interest, a life estate, or a power to revoke. The second kind is the retention by the owner of a power to change the beneficial interests given to others. [IRC §§ 2036(a)(2), 2038] Congress reasoned that these transfers in trust should be included in the estate of the decedent, because the decedent reserved testamentary-like powers in these transfers that provided full enjoyment to the beneficiaries only on the death of the decedent.

Trust assets are also includible in the gross estate when the donor has the right at death to designate the person who shall possess or enjoy trust property or income. [IRC § 2036(a)(2)] In addition, the donor's retention until his or her death (or during the three-year period preceding the donor's death) of a power to alter, amend, revoke, or terminate a trust also results in the inclusion of trust assets in the donor's estate, even if these powers are held by the donor only in his or her capacity as a trustee or co-trustee. [IRC § 2038]

In addition, two other powers should be avoided if the goal is to keep trust assets out of the donor's gross estate: (1) allocating to the

Q 6:42   Estate and Retirement Planning Answer Book

donor the power, either alone or with anyone else, to make trust distributions without regard to an ascertainable standard, and (2) retained powers to terminate a trust prior to the termination date specified in the trust agreement. [IRC §§ 2041, 2038]

Q 6:42   Can the donor be given administrative powers or control over trust investments without having trust assets included in his or her gross estate?

The donor's retention of administrative powers or control over trust investments, without more, generally does not result in the inclusion of trust assets in the donor's gross estate. [Royal Trust Company v United States, 423 F 2d 601 (1st Cir 1970)] For example, the donor may be given the power to allocate receipts and expenses between principal and income pursuant to a fiduciary standard, but the trust document must provide that all discretionary distribution powers are allocated solely to another trustee.

Charitable Gifts

Q 6:43   Can a beneficiary be the sole trustee?

The tax concern in having a beneficiary of a trust be the sole trustee is that in many instances trust assets will be includible in the beneficiary's estate. This may occur even though the estate lacks sufficient funds with which to pay the estate taxes. In addition, if a trustee is an income beneficiary and also has discretionary powers to invade corpus based on certain standards, the remaindermen of the trust may seek to remove the trustee, citing the inherent conflict of interest of the trustee-beneficiary.

Q 6:44   How may principal be removed from the trust without causing the entire trust to be taxed when the beneficiary dies?

If the beneficiary is the sole trustee, there are two means of taking principal out of the trust without causing the entire trust to be taxed on the beneficiary's death. One is to authorize the beneficiary or trustee to withdraw from principal each year either $5,000 or an amount equal to 5 percent of the current value of the principal, whichever is greater. The second way is to empower the beneficiary or trustee to withdraw principal for his own support, maintenance, education, and health.

> **Example 6-17:** A 23-year-old woman is the sole trustee of a trust that permits her to distribute trust assets to herself if she wants to. The trust contains $2 million in assets. The woman dies shortly after attaining age 23 without having distributed trust assets to herself. At death she has no other significant assets. Nonetheless, the $2 million in trust assets is includible in her estate and the estate incurs estate tax of $780,800.

If it is desirable to have the beneficiary or trustee withdraw principal for reasons other than support, maintenance, education, or health, a co-trustee can be named. The co-trustee could then be given the power to withdraw trust principal for those other reasons. The trust could also be designed so that the trust investments were controlled exclusively by the beneficiary.

> **Example 6-18:** A businessman creates a trust for his son that names his son as trustee and gives him the authority to withdraw trust principal for his own support, maintenance, education, and health. The businessman's attorney is appointed as co-trustee with the authority to order the payment of trust assets to the son if an attractive business opportunity is presented to the son. The son, rather than the attorney, is authorized to determine how trust assets are to be invested.

Q 6:45 Should children be chosen as trustees for their siblings?

It generally is not a good idea to have children serve as trustees for each other. If one sibling is involved in the financial affairs of the other, misunderstandings, jealousies, and rivalries may result.

Q 6:46 Should a child be appointed trustee of his or her own trust?

No, generally a parent creates a trust for his or her child to protect the child due to inexperience, immaturity, or other impediment. Appointing a child to be the trustee of his or her own trust would generally contravene this intention of the parent for creating the trust. Having the child serve as co-trustee could also cause a strain between the child and a co-trustee because of the lack of objectivity of the child in dealing with the standards contained in the trust that affect him or her.

Q 6:47 Should a trust contain a provision for removal of the trustee?

These kinds of provisions may limit the independence of the trustee. In some cases, this may be consistent with the creator's intent. For instance, if the creator set up a trust primarily for tax reasons, he or she may not be too concerned if the beneficiaries have a power of removal over the trustee. The effect of such power, to limit somewhat the trustee's independence, might be consistent with the creator's intent.

Another concern is that there are potentially significant expenses associated with removing a trustee. If a trustee is removed, he or she is likely to insist on an accounting—a review of all trust transactions. Accountings can be prolonged and expensive; however, sometimes these provisions are desirable. If the trustee is an institutional trustee such as a bank, and if the trust creator is concerned about a future decline in the level of services, a provision permitting an independent third party such as an attorney or accountant to remove the trustee may be desirable.

Q 6:48 What provisions can be made for successor trustees?

The initial trustee can be authorized to select his or her successor. Alternatively, the grantor can provide for a successor trustee in the trust document itself. It may not be a bad idea to permit a trustee to name his or her own successor. If the trust creator has sufficient confidence in the initial trustee to name him or her as trustee, the trust creator is likely to believe that the trustee is capable of doing a good job in picking a successor. The advantage of permitting the trustee to pick his or her successor is that it allows for the possibility that the successor trustee appointed by the trust document may become unable to serve.

Example 6-19: An attorney is appointed as trustee for a trust. The trust provides that the attorney can name the successor trustee. The trust becomes much larger than expected, and, shortly before his death, the attorney exercises his power to appoint a successor trustee. He appoints an experienced certified financial planner and a certified public accountant as successor trustees. At the time of the attorney's death, the trust is likely to continue for another 20 years.

Q 6:49 Who pays income tax on trust income that is reinvested?

The trust; however, if the trust is a grantor trust under Code Sections 671–679 (i.e., a trust whose creator retains certain powers, such as the right to dispose of trust income), this income is taxable to the trust creator.

Q 6:50 Who pays the tax on trust capital gains that go to principal?

The trust pays these taxes out of principal unless the person establishing the trust specifically elects to have that burden shifted to him or her.

Q 6:51 Is it preferable to make lifetime charitable gifts rather than testamentary charitable gifts?

It is generally preferable to make lifetime charitable transfers (rather than testamentary charitable transfers) because the donor is able to obtain an income tax deduction. Such donations also avoid gift tax and are not includible in the gross estate. In contrast, a donation that is willed to a charity is includible in the gross estate (although an unlimited charitable deduction is allowed for estate tax purposes).

The charitable deduction is not available unless the recipient organization meets the requirements of Code Section 2055. The status of the organization on the date of death rather than the date the will was executed controls. [IRC §§ 2001, 2055] Accordingly, if an organization becomes disqualified before the date of death, the charitable deduction will be lost.

Anatomical Gifts

Q 6:52 What rules apply to giving anatomical gifts?

The Uniform Anatomical Gifts Act (UAGA) generally applies to gifts of organ donations. It provides that any person over the age of 18 may donate his or her entire body or any one or more of its parts to any hospital, surgeon, physician, medical or dental school, or various organ banks or storage facilities. These gifts can be made for purposes of education, research, therapy, or transplant. The UAGA provides that no body or organ gift can be made if an express objection to the gift is registered, either by will or some other document.

Q 6:53 How can gifts of organs be made under the UAGA?

Gifts may be made directly by the decedent's will, by designating a specific individual as a gift recipient. Alternatively, the decedent may grant other persons the power to make a gift. For example, a businessman might provide that his wife can donate his body or organs to a local hospital. If an anatomical gift is made by will, it is important for the decedent, during his or her lifetime, to inform his executor or family of this bequest so that the donated organs can be made immediately available on death.

Q 6:54 Can a donation of organs be made if the decedent's wishes are unknown?

If there is no evidence that the decedent did not want to make an anatomical gift, one of four classes of people can make a donation: spouses, adult children, parents, or siblings, in that order. Gifts can be made unless there is actual knowledge that the decedent did not want to make an anatomical gift or that someone in the same or a higher class opposes the gift.

Q 6:55 What are the requirements for an anatomical gift?

The UAGA requires that gifts be made in writing and attested to by at least two witnesses. Additionally, the donor must be of sound mind at the time of the writing.

Q 6:56 Should a document making gifts of organs be included in a person's will?

Documents making gifts under the UAGA should be prepared separately and apart from the will. A codicil to the will can state the maker's intentions regarding anatomical gifts, so that the other provisions of the will are not disclosed.

Chapter 7

Life Insurance

This chapter discusses how life insurance can be an important factor in estate planning. It reviews the basic types of life insurance, taxation of policy loans and proceeds payable upon the death of the insured, and various methods for keeping the proceeds out of an individual's estate.

Overview	7-1
Premiums	7-6
Policy Proceeds	7-6
Policy Loans	7-13
Estate Planning	7-14

Overview

Q 7:1 How can life insurance be a useful tool in estate planning?

Life insurance can play a significant role in the planning of an estate. It is a useful tool as an investment vehicle, as a means for the purchase of a business interest, as security to provide liquidity for one's family on the death of the family's principal breadwinner, and as a repository for paying estate and inheritance taxes. Life insurance allows assets that have been accumulated through resourceful estate planning (e.g., a family residence, a family business, nonliquid and liquid investments) to be transferred, intact, to estate beneficiaries unaffected by estate taxes.

Q 7:2 What are the basic types of life insurance policies?

The basic types of life insurance policies are as follows:

1. *Term insurance.* Term insurance is insurance against the risk of dying during a specified period. If the term expires and the insurance is not renewed, the policy does not have any value. Over a period of time, as the insured ages, the cost of term insurance will increase. Term insurance is pure insurance in the sense that the premium paid by the insured has no investment feature, nor does it create a cash value in the policy. Rather, it can be compared to a wager in which the insured bets the life insurance company that he or she will die during the term of purchase and the life insurance company takes the wager believing (based on its experience and mortality tables) that death will not occur. Most insurance companies do not make term insurance available beyond age 70.

2. *Whole life insurance.* Whole life insurance provides life insurance for an insured's entire life. Typically, a level premium is paid for this kind of policy throughout the insured's life. In the early years of payment, a reserve accumulates, and the earnings earned by this reserve help fund the age-related increases in premium in later years (so that the insured continues to pay a level amount of premium). The reserve provides a cash value so that if the insured surrenders the policy during his or her lifetime, the remaining insurance protection is canceled and the insured receives a portion of the reserve as a cash payment.

3. *Endowment insurance.* Endowment insurance provides life insurance for a specified period and a guaranteed payment to the insured if he or she is still living at the end of such period. Premiums for endowment insurance are paid for a specific period. At the expiration of the premium payment period, the cash value of the policy equals the face value of the policy. If the insured is living at the endowment date, the policy matures and the face value of the policy is paid to the insured.

4. *Universal life insurance.* Universal life policies are designed to offer relatively high rates of return and to permit the policyholder to vary the amount and frequency of premium payments. Essentially, universal life policies provide an investment program and a term insurance contract, and so generally build up a cash surrender value as well as provide death benefits. The amount of those benefits depends on the amount and frequency of the premium payments that are taken out of the cash value account. The death benefit is equal to the term insurance purchased plus the amount in the cash value account.

Q 7:3 What precautions must be taken when buying life insurance for estate planning purposes?

The computer projections used to describe the potential financial effects of insurance transactions are not guarantees of results. Although the projections may show that after a certain period no premium will need to be paid, if the assumptions on which the policy is based are not met, the policy may very well require that premiums be paid to keep the policy in force.

Example 7-1: A insurance projection of premiums is based on an estimated return of 8.5 percent. The projection is made while interest rates are high. Using this projection, the agent calculates that no premium will need to be paid after ten years have elapsed. Interest rates drop after two years. As a result of the drop, premium payments must be continued for an estimated fifteen years.

Projections could be inaccurate if the insurance company's expenses increased significantly because of bad loans or because of changes in mortality experience. If the insurance company's earnings fall off for some reason, it is possible that the policy's assumptions will not be met and that additional funds will be required to keep the policy in force.

Q 7:4 How is life insurance sold?

There is no single inflexible answer to this question. Historically, life insurance was sold under a commission system in which an agent sometimes received substantial commissions (often 50 percent of the premium), particularly during the first year of the policy. Recently, commission levels have started to drop, and noncommission insurance products have become available. Noncommission policies are typically less expensive than commission policies, but the number of companies that offer noncommission policies is limited. If personal service is important, a commission product may be preferable to a noncommission product.

Stock brokerage firms are beginning to enter the insurance market by offering low-load insurance, which expends very little of the insurance premium for the payment of sales commissions or administrative expenses for acquiring the policy. Most people who purchase life insurance do not realize that usually 55 percent to 100 percent of the first year's premium on a whole life ordinary insurance policy is not directed towards creating cash value in the policy but is instead directed toward paying loading costs.

Q 7:5 What factors should be considered when choosing a life insurance company?

Three factors to consider when choosing a life insurance company are as follows:

1. Premium payments,
2. Expected levels of return, and
3. The stability of the insurance company.

Premium payments. Premium payments for equivalent insurance from equivalent companies do vary substantially. It may be possible to reduce a premium by purchasing insurance from a company that offers a noncommissioned insurance product (see Q 7:4).

Rate of return. Insurance agents typically make proposals that contain projected rates of return. In evaluating those rates of return, it is important to remember that they are only projections and not guarantees.

Stability of the insurance company. There are a number of publicly available services that rate insurance companies, and specialists can be hired to evaluate insurance companies. This is advisable if the policy amount is large. There is no one way to find information about evaluating insurance. The rating services have been criticized for being too positive about insurance companies (and, in at least one case, too negative). Furthermore, the services do not have complete information about the insurance companies. An approach that sometimes works is to obtain the recommendation of a specialist such as an attorney or accountant. No approach is infallible, however.

Q 7:6 When choosing an insurance policy, what features are most important?

The following features are important when choosing an insurance policy:

1. The ability of an insured to make an assignment to others, such as loan companies. The insured needs to be aware of the insurance company's policy regarding assignments and how they are to be made.
2. Often, insurance companies allow the insured to borrow money on the policy at substantially lower rates than market loan rates. When selecting an insurance policy, the insured will want to check into this feature and the ability of the insurance company to use the proceeds from the insurance to pay the loan payments to keep the policy from defaulting.
3. The insured will want to be extremely careful about whom he or she can name as the beneficiary. The insured may not wish to possess any incidents of ownership. Therefore, naming the beneficiary is vital.
4. Insurance contracts often have a cash surrender value. The insured will want to verify whether this feature is part of the contract when determining which policy to buy.
5. Insurance contracts may also provide yearly dividends. If the insured wishes to see yearly return on his or her investment, the insured may wish to purchase a contract with this feature.
6. Recently, policies have come into existence that allow insured individuals who are suffering from terminal illnesses to draw amounts in excess of his or her policy limits. These are usually described as living benefits or accelerated death benefit pay-

ments. The insurance companies are protected by charging interest on these policy draws and making certain that the death benefits are sufficient to enable them to earn a profit.

Premiums

Q 7:7 What restrictions exist on the amount of premiums that can be required for life insurance?

With the development of various new forms of insurance products that contain an investment element as well as an insurance element, concern developed that some of the more aggressive new products were really not insurance. To prevent what was regarded as an excessive buildup of cash surrender value in life insurance policies, Congress enacted legislation aimed at limiting the amount of premiums that can be paid into life insurance policies. It is important that the product be structured to adhere to these limits. A failure to follow these limits can result in the insurance policy's death proceeds being taxable and the loss of the income tax exemption on the increase in cash value in the policy.

Briefly, this legislation limits the amount of premiums that can be paid and requires that the death benefits must exceed the cash value by specified amounts. [IRC § 7702] Further, if the premium payments are accelerated (that is, payable up front over the first few years of the policy) so that certain statutory tests are not met, the policy will be deemed to have modified endowment contract (MEC) status. [IRC § 7702A] If MEC status is assigned, distributions from the policy (including any policy loans) are subject to immediate income taxation plus a 10 percent penalty tax. [IRC § 72(v)] Insurance policies sold today typically contain information regarding the maximum amounts that can be paid without violating these statutory limits.

Policy Proceeds

Q 7:8 How are life insurance proceeds that are payable upon the death of the insured treated for estate tax purposes?

Life insurance proceeds are includible in the insured's estate for estate tax purposes unless (1) the insured possesses none of the incidents of ownership at the time of death, and (2) the policy proceeds are not payable directly to or for the benefit of the estate. [IRC § 2042] A policy is payable for the benefit of the insured's estate if the beneficiary is required to use the proceeds to pay the decedent's taxes or other obligations of the estate. [Treas Reg § 20.2042-1(b)(1)] This result can be avoided by having the insurance proceeds paid to a trusted individual, such as the decedent's spouse, and then requesting, but not requiring, him or her to pay the estate taxes with those proceeds. Because such proceeds are paid directly to the surviving spouse, the marital deduction prevents the insurance from being subject to an estate tax.

Incidents of ownership. An incident of ownership is any right of the insured or his or her estate to obtain or channel the economic benefits of an insurance policy. It includes the power to change the beneficiary, to surrender or cancel the policy, to assign the policy, to revoke an assignment, to pledge the policy for a loan, or to borrow the case surrender value. [Treas Reg § 20.2042-1(c)(2)] More than a 5 percent reversionary interest is an incident of ownership. [IRC § 2042(2)] The reversionary interest includes a possibility that the policy or its proceeds may return to the insured or become subject to a power of disposition by the insured.

An illustration of a reversionary interest is an insurance policy that provides that proceeds are to be paid to the insured's wife, if she survives him, if not, to his daughter, if alive, and finally, to the insured's estate, if none of the previous beneficiaries is alive at the insured's death. If the value of this reversionary interest at the time of the decedent's death is more than 5 percent of the value of the policy at that time, the entire value of the life insurance proceeds will be included in the decedent's gross estate.

Mandatory inclusion of death proceeds in estate. If a decedent assigns or gives away all rights in the policy within three years of death, the insurance proceeds are includible in the decedent's gross estate. [IRC § 2035(d)(2)] Thus, even if the decedent retains no incidents of ownership at his or her death, if the decedent gave away all of the rights in the policy within three years of his or her death, the entire policy value (as of the date of his death) will be included in the decedent's gross estate.

Q 7:9 If the insured has any incident of ownership, does it matter whether the insured exercises it alone?

If the insured had any incident of ownership (see Q 7:8), it is immaterial whether the insured could have exercised it alone or whether the consent of another person was required to exercise it. In either case, the death benefit proceeds of the life insurance policy are includible in the gross estate. [IRC § 2042(2)]

The Internal Revenue Service (IRS) recently issued a private letter ruling bearing on the question of incidents of ownership. The facts involved a father who created an irrevocable trust for his daughter, who was precluded from serving as a trustee. Under the terms of the trust, the trustees were required to distribute trust income to the daughter periodically and were also given discretion to distribute trust principal to her. The daughter was given a special power to appoint trust principal (meaning she could distribute to others but not to herself, her creditors, her estate or the creditors of her estate). This special power was not effective, however, if the trust held any insurance on the daughter's life. The IRS ruled that the daughter had no incidents of ownership in the life insurance because her control over the life insurance was nonexistent due to the ineffectiveness of the special power of appointment. [Ltr Rul 9602010]

Q 7:10 Are gifts (i.e., assignments) of insurance policies includible in the insured's gross estate?

Gifts of life insurance policies are typically made by assigning the policy to another. Gifts of life insurance policies within three years of the death of the insured are includible in the decedent's gross estate. [IRC § 2035] The full amount of the death proceeds is includible in the gross estate, and the annual $10,000 exclusion is not available. [IRC § 2503(b)]

Example 7-2: A physician gave a $1 million life insurance policy with a cash surrender value of $10,000 to his daughter. Two years later, the physician died. One million dollars in death proceeds were includible in the physician's estate because the three-year requirement of Section 2035 of the Internal Revenue Code (Code) was not satisfied.

Example 7-3: An executive received employer-paid life insurance equal to two-times compensation. Her salary was $80,000, so the amount of coverage was $160,000. The executive designated her husband as the beneficiary and then assigned all rights in the policy to her husband. Four years later, she died and the $160,000 life insurance proceeds were paid to her husband. Because the three-year requirement was satisfied, the proceeds were not includible in the executive's estate.

Q 7:11 Can the rule requiring the inclusion of insurance proceeds in the gross estate be avoided if the insured transfers the premium payments to a trust and has the trust buy the insurance?

Yes, provided the insured does not retain any incidents of ownership in the trust. [Estate of Leder, 90 TC 235 (1987), *aff'd*, 893 F 2d 237 (10th Cir 1989)] In *Leder*, an individual created a trust and gave insurance premiums to it. The trustee then used the premiums to purchase life insurance on the grantor. The Tax Court held and the Tenth Circuit affirmed that the proceeds of the insurance policy purchased using such an arrangement were not includible in the insured's estate, even though the insured gave the premiums to the trustee within three years of death. This decision suggests that the donor should first establish a trust, then give the insurance premiums to the trustee and have the trustee subsequently apply for the life insurance and pay for it with the gift premiums. The decedent cannot retain any incidents of ownership in the trust. The IRS has ruled that a grantor-decedent's reservation of an unqualified power to remove a trustee and appoint an individual or corporate successor trustee that is not related or subordinate to the grantor (as defined under Code Section § 672(c)) is not considered a reservation of the trustee's discretionary powers of distribution over the property transferred by the decedent-grantor to the trust.[Rev Rul 95-58, 1995-36 IRB 16] Accordingly, it follows that such a reservation of power to remove and replace a trustee does not constitute an incident of ownership in the policy.

Q 7:12 What is includible in the insured's estate if the insured pays the premiums on a life insurance policy transferred more than three years before the insured's death?

The amount of each yearly premium paid since 1976 in excess of the $10,000 annual gift tax exclusion is a taxable gift. At one time the IRS asserted that if the insured paid the policy premiums, a proportionate part of the policy proceeds would be included in the insured's gross estate. The IRS has largely abandoned this position, except for the payment of premiums on accidental death policies or on one-year term policies. [Rev Rul 71-497, 1971-2 CB 329]

> **Example 7-4:** A physician transfers a life insurance policy to an irrevocable trust for the benefit of his son and continues to pay the yearly $15,000 premium on the policy. He makes no other gifts to his son. The $5,000 difference between the insurance premium and the yearly exclusion is a taxable gift.

Q 7:13 What are the tax consequence to the estate of the noninsured owner of a life insurance policy who predeceases the insured?

If the owner of a life insurance policy is not the insured and he or she dies before the insured, the cash value—not the face value—of the insurance policy is includible in the owner's estate. If the policy is paid up, the cash value is established using the sale of comparable contracts by the insurance company. [Treas Reg § 20.2031-8(a)(1)] If the policy is one on which further premiums are to be paid, the value can be approximated by adding to the interpolated terminal reserve value (that is, the approximate cash surrender value) at the owner's death the unused portion of the premiums paid prior to the owner's death. [Treas Reg § 20.2031-8(a)(2)] It is important in anticipating this eventuality that the policy owner provide a successor owner in the life insurance contract itself or designate a successor-owner in his or her will.

> **Example 7-5:** A retired plumbing contractor takes out an insurance policy on his son's life and designates himself as the owner of the policy on the insurance application. The contractor predeceases his son while premiums are still being paid. The unused portion of the premiums paid thus far is $500 while the interpolated

reserve value is $10,000. The face value of the policy is $50,000. The amount of $10,500 is includible in the contractor's gross estate.

Q 7:14 When does the transfer of a life insurance policy result in a taxable gift?

The assignment or transfer of all the ownership rights in a life insurance policy results in a gift that is taxable to the transferor. If the donor (the transferor) continues to pay the premiums on the policy after he or she has given it away, the amount of premiums paid will also be a gift to the new owner. The $10,000 annual gift tax exclusion applies, however. [IRC § 2503(b)]

Q 7:15 When does the annual gift tax exclusion apply?

To obtain the exclusion, gifts of a present interest must be made. [IRC § 2503(b)] The gift to one person of outright ownership of a life insurance policy is a gift of a present interest; however, the gift of a policy to more than one person where no single owner is empowered to exercise all ownership rights without the consent of the other owners does not constitute a gift of a present interest. The IRS has concluded that the gift of a policy to a trust under circumstances such that the trustee has the authority to retain the policy until the insured's death is not a gift of a present interest because no beneficiary will receive the proceeds until a future date. [Rev Rul 69-344, 1969-1 CB 225]

Q 7:16 Are life insurance proceeds payable upon the death of the insured taxable to the recipient?

Generally not. The proceeds of life insurance policies that are paid because of the insured's death are generally excludable from the gross income of the recipient. [IRC § 101(a)] If, however, the owner acquired the policy in a transfer for valuable consideration (see Q 7:18), the proceeds may be subject to income tax. If life insurance is used to fund a deferred compensation agreement and the proceeds are payable to the employer, the employer's receipt of the proceeds as the policy beneficiary does not result in the employer's incurring income tax; however, the employer might be subject to alternative minimum tax. Moreover, the payment by the employer of an amount equal to the death proceeds to the beneficiary of the employee's estate is taxable income to the payee because it is a payment of deferred compensation (the obligation of which was secured by life insurance purchased by and paid to the employer) to the employee's designated beneficiary under the deferred compensation arrangement and does not constitute life insurance to the employee.

Q 7:17 What is split-dollar insurance?

Split-dollar insurance involves a sharing arrangement between two parties, typically an employer and a key employee, who agree to share the premium payments and the insurance proceeds. Generally, the employer contributes annually a portion of the premium equal to the annual increase in the cash surrender value, and the employee pays the difference. These plans are popular because they provide key employees an inexpensive opportunity to purchase substantial amounts of insurance. The IRS taxes the employee on the economic benefit derived from the employer's sharing of the annual premium payment with the employee that is determined under the IRS's P.S. 58 table or, where lower, the current published premium rate charged by a commercial insurer for one-year term insurance available for standard risks. [Rev Rul 55-747, 1995-2 CB 228; Rev Rul 66-110, 1966-1 CB 12] Accordingly, the employee's cost of this insurance is limited to the tax he or she pays on the inclusion by the IRS of the economic benefit. The employer loses nothing by this arrangement because its contribution towards the purchase of the insurance is secured by the employer's being a collateral beneficiary under the life insurance policy, meaning that it recovers its investment in the policy by being paid the cash surrender value of the policy at the employee's death, with the balance of the death benefit payable to the employee's designated beneficiaries.

Q 7:18 What is the transfer for value rule?

This rule states that if a transferee of a life insurance policy gives something of value for the policy, the insurance death proceeds are subject to income tax. [IRC § 101(a)(2)]

Example 7-6: A businessman sells a life insurance policy on his life with a face amount of $10,000 to a pawnbroker. The transfer for value rule applies.

The amount includible in the gross income of the individual or entity that receives the death proceeds is the amount received less the amount of consideration paid by the transferee and the premiums paid by the transferee. The transfer for value rule does not apply when the transferee obtains the policy by gift or through any transaction in which he or she keeps the same income tax basis as the transferor had in the policy. [IRC § 101(a)(2)(A)] The rule also does not apply if the transferee is the insured, a partner of the insured, a partnership in which the insured is a partner, or a corporation in which the insured is a shareholder or officer. [IRC § 101(a)(2)(B)]

Policy Loans

Q 7:19 What are the reasons for taking loans from an insurance policy?

Loans are commonly taken from an insurance policy to reduce the value of the policy before making a gift of the policy so that gift taxes will be less. If the policy loan is less than the actual value of the policy at the time of transfer, the policy will have the same basis in whole or in part in the donee's hands as it had in the donor's hands. [Rev Rul 68-197 1961-1 CB 45] (See Qs 3:41–3:48, 21:2.)

Example 7-7: A businessman gives a policy with a cash surrender value of $45,000 to his son. If the cash surrender value is retained in the policy, the amount of the gift (disregarding the $10,000 annual gift exclusion) is $45,000. If a policy loan in the amount of $45,000 is taken out, however, the amount of the gift is zero.

Q 7:20 Is interest on a policy loan deductible?

Individuals can no longer deduct interest on policy loans. [IRC § 163(h)] Interest on policy loans is also not deductible if it is paid or accrued on indebtedness incurred to purchase or continue in effect a single premium life insurance policy. [IRC § 264(a)(2)] For this purpose, a single premium life insurance policy is defined as a policy in which substantially all the premiums are paid within four years from the date of purchase or in which an amount is deposited with the insurance company for the payment of a substantial number of future premiums. [IRC § 264(b)] Finally, with four exceptions, interest on policy loans is not deductible if made pursuant to a plan of purchase that contemplates the systematic borrowing of all or part of the increase in the policy's cash value. [IRC § 264(c)] These exceptions are as follows:

1. If no part of the annual premiums due during the seven years commencing with the date of payment of the first premium is paid with funds borrowed in connection with such plan, the interest deduction will not be denied.
2. Interest is deductible if the total amount of the deduction otherwise disallowable is $100 or less—and the number of policies or plans maintained by the taxpayer is not relevant.
3. The interest deduction will not be lost if the taxpayer borrows because of an "unforeseen substantial loss of income or unforeseen substantial increase in his or her financial obligations"—and it does not matter if the borrowed funds are actually used to pay the premiums.
4. The interest deduction is available if an indebtedness is incurred in connection with a taxpayer's trade or business.

Estate Planning

Q 7:21 From an estate planning perspective, who should be the owner of a life insurance policy?

If the insured's projected estate is less than $600,000, the insured typically is designated the owner of the insurance policy. This is because there is no significant tax saving concern that would indicate naming another owner. What many overlook, however, is that those states having an estate and inheritance tax do not provide the same $600,000 federal exemption. As a result, there could be a state estate tax where an individual retains an incident of ownership in his or her life insurance policy. Of course, where the life insurance proceeds are payable to the surviving spouse, the insurance would not be taxed because of the marital deduction. In large estates, irrevocable trusts are often set up to own life insurance policies. The intention is to keep the insurance proceeds outside of the insured's taxable estate and, in most cases, also outside of the estate of the surviving spouse.

Example 7-8: An unmarried physician with a net worth of $4 million establishes an irrevocable trust. The trustee purchases a life insurance policy with a face value of $1 million on the physician. Because the trust is the owner of the policy, the insurance proceeds will be payable to the trust and will not be included in the physician's gross estate. The trust can then distribute the proceeds to the physician's intended beneficiaries. These insurance proceeds will make up for some or all of the losses the physician's beneficiaries will incur as a result of estate taxes. If the physician were married, it might be desirable to establish an irrevocable life insurance trust that was funded with insurance that is payable when both the physician and his or her spouse die. Such trust could replace funds lost to estate taxes when the second spouse dies.

Q 7:22 From an estate planning perspective, who should be designated the beneficiary of life insurance?

It is usually not desirable to make the insurance policy payable to the estate of the insured because this will subject the insurance proceeds to probate and the expenses (legal fees and executors' commissions) normally associated with probate. Also, the insurance proceeds, being part of the probate estate, would be subject to the claims of creditors. Unless the marital deduction applies, the insurance proceeds are subject to estate tax.

In contrast, if the insurance proceeds are payable to someone other than the decedent, they will not be subject to probate, and, if the decedent has no incidents of ownership in the policy, the proceeds will not be subject to estate tax. In a small estate (less than $200,000), the spouse probably should be made the primary beneficiary of the insurance policy. A trust could be made the primary beneficiary of the insurance policy, but a corporate trustee's fees will usually be expensive in relation to the size of the estate.

Q 7:23 From an estate planning perspective, who should be the contingent beneficiaries of a life insurance policy?

Contingent beneficiaries are beneficiaries who receive the proceeds of a life insurance policy if the primary beneficiary dies before the insured (and thus cannot be paid the proceeds). Ideally, the contingent beneficiary is an adult. Children who are minors present a special problem. If the policy is made payable directly to the children, a guardian must be appointed for them, which can be an expensive and cumbersome process. Another option is to make the insurance proceeds payable to a trust for the benefit of the insured's minor children. A third option is to have the proceeds made payable to a custodian for the children under the Uniform Transfers to Minors Act.

Q 7:24 What are settlement options?

Settlement options are methods (other than a single lump-sum cash payment) that payments may be made from an insurance policy. The common types of settlement options are as follows:

1. *Interest option.* Under this option, the death proceeds of the insurance policy are left with the insurance company, and interest on the proceeds is paid periodically to the beneficiary. The proceeds can be withdrawn by the beneficiary at a future date.

2. *Fixed-period option.* Under this option, the proceeds of the insurance policy, plus earnings on such proceeds, are payable to the beneficiary in equal installments over a fixed period of time with a guaranteed rate of interest.

3. *Installments for life.* Under this option, the proceeds of the insurance policy plus the earnings on the proceeds are payable in installments over the life of the beneficiary.

4. *Fixed-income option.* In contrast to the fixed-period option, the amount of each installment payable is fixed, rather than the time period.

The interest portion of the amounts payable under each of the settlement options is taxable income to the beneficiary. [IRC § 101(d)]

Q 7:25 When should insurance settlement options be used?

It may be sensible to elect a settlement option if the beneficiary of a small estate is an adult who cannot manage finances. Alternatively, a trust can be created to hold the insurance proceeds. A trust may not be practical for a small estate, however, because the cost of trust administration may be excessive in relation to the size of the estate. Sometimes settlement options may be used in large estates. If this is done, it is important to select a settlement option that will preserve the marital deduction by ensuring that the surviving spouse does not have a terminable interest. For instance, payments could be permitted to be made over the spouse's lifetime and the spouse given a general power of appointment over unpaid amounts. [IRC § 2056(b)(6)]

Q 7:26 What actions should be taken to exclude life insurance proceeds from the gross estate?

The steps that should be taken to exclude life insurance proceeds from the gross estate depend upon whether the policy has already been purchased or a purchase is being contemplated.

Existing policies. Existing life insurance policies can be transferred to other indviduals or to an irrevocable trust. If the insured possesses no incidents of ownership (see Q 7:8) in the transferred policy and if the insured lives three years after the date of the transfer policy, the proceeds will be excluded from the insured's gross estate. [IRC §§ 2035(d)(2), 2042]

New policies. If the purchase of a new policy is contemplated, an irrevocable trust usually should be created and the insurance policy should be purchased by the trustee. If this is done, and the insured has no incidents of ownership in the trust, the proceeds will be excluded from the insured's gross estate, even if the insured dies within three years. [Estate of Leder, 90 TC 235 (1987), *aff'd* 893 F 2d 237 (10th Cir 1989)]

Q 7:27 What policies should be transferred to an irrevocable trust?

If the insured has a choice of policies, it is usually advisable to transfer the policies with the lowest gift tax value in relation to face value. It may be possible to reduce the gift tax value of the policy transferred by taking out a policy loan. This may be desirable even if the interest deduction is not available for interest paid on the loan. In either case, the objective is to try to keep the gift tax value of the transferred policies under the $10,000 annual exclusion.

Q 7:28 What actions need to be taken in order to transfer an insurance policy?

To transfer a life insurance policy, all ownership rights should be assigned. To avoid taxation of the insurance proceeds under the transfer for value rule (see Q 7:18), the assignment should be gratuitous. Unless the policy is an accidental death policy or a one-year term policy, the insurance proceeds will not be included in the gross estate if the insured pays the premiums, even if the premiums are paid within three years of death. [Rev Rul 71-797, 1971-2 CB 329] Each time the insured pays a premium, however, a taxable gift is made.

Q 7:29 For estate planning purposes, who should be the beneficiary of a policy owned by someone other than the insured?

In general, the owner should be the beneficiary of the policy. This will prevent the IRS from asserting when the insured dies that the beneficiary received a gift from the owner equal to the amount of the insurance proceeds. [Goodman v Commr, 156 F 2d 218 (2nd Cir 1946)]

Q 7:30 For estate planning purposes, who should be the owner of a life insurance policy?

In large estates, it is often advisable to make the children or an irrevocable trust both the owners and beneficiaries of life insurance policies. This will permit the exclusion of the insurance proceeds from the estates of both the husband and wife.

Q 7:31 Should one spouse be both the owner and the beneficiary of a policy on the life of the other spouse?

Yes, if one spouse owns an insurance policy on the other spouse's life. It is generally preferable that the uninsured spouse be the beneficiary of the insurance policy. This will prevent the IRS from asserting that the uninsured spouse made a gift on the death of the insured spouse.

Q 7:32 What is a *second-to-die* life insurance policy?

Many estate plans are geared to providing the surviving spouse with the entire estate of the deceased spouse, which results in the estate of the deceased spouse having no estate tax because of the unlimited marital deduction. The purpose of a well-thought-out estate plan, however, is to consider the effect of estate taxes on the overall family unit, and, under this arrangement, without more, the surviving spouse's estate could have a substantial estate tax to pay because it has no marital deduction to shield it from tax.

A second-to-die life insurance policy is the antidote intended to protect the surviving spouse's estate from this tax calamity. It works as follows: An irrevocable life insurance trust is created that purchases a life insurance policy that becomes payable to the trust on the death of the second-to-die of the spouses. Because the insurance trust owns and is the beneficiary of the life insurance policy, the policy proceeds are not subject to estate tax upon the death of either spouse. Upon the death of the surviving spouse, the estate taxes of his or her estate are paid with the proceeds of the tax-free life insurance, and the assets of the surviving spouse's estate remain intact for distribution to the estate beneficiaries.

> **Example 7-9:** A married physician whose assets are valued at $5 million adopts an estate plan in which $600,000 is given in trust to his children on his death and the remainder is given to his spouse. A second-to-die policy was purchased by an irrevocable life insurance trust, created as part of the estate plan adopted by the spouses. The face amount of the policy is $2 million. When both the physician and his wife die, significant estate taxes will be due if the physician's net worth has not been depleted. The proceeds from the second-to-die policy will not be includible in

either the physician's or his spouse's gross estate, however. Those estate tax-free proceeds will be used to pay the estate taxes of the surviving spouse's estate and permit the assets accumulated both during the marriage and prior to the death of the surviving spouse to be distributed whole to family members.

Q 7:33   What is a first-to-die life insurance policy?

This kind of life insurance is not currently as marketable as second-to-die life insurance, but it can be equally as beneficial in savings to an estate plan. It is a life insurance policy insuring two individuals with benefits payable at the first death. One of the significant attractions of this kind of policy is its cost savings. When the primary need is for guaranteed cash when the first person dies, this type of life insurance offers a savings in insurance premiums ranging from approximately 25 percent to 35 percent, depending on the jointly equivalent age of the insureds, compared with separate policies for the insured

Although this policy has not achieved the degree of attention paid to second-to-die life insurance, it is capable of serving valuable estate planning purposes. It works as follows: An insurance policy is acquired insuring two individuals with death benefits payable at the first death. This policy can offer a savings in premium payments from approximately 25 percent to 35 percent, depending on the joint equivalent ages of the insureds, compared with purchasing separate policies for each insured. It also eliminates the impact of further premium payments after the death of the first to die, and in the case of married persons allows the surviving spouse to accumulate, through the time and use of money in an irrevocable life insurance trust (so as to prevent estate tax on the proceeds), sufficient funds to provide the means for paying estate taxes on death.

A first-to-die policy can also be used where one of the spouses is a resident alien and the spouses do not want to create a QDOT with all of its restrictions. If the citizen spouse is the first to die and the first-to-die policy is in an irrevocable life insurance trust, the proceeds can be used to pay estate taxes rather than to comply with the QDOT restrictions; this will free assets for distribution to the noncitizen surviving spouse.

In a business setting, a first-to-die policy becomes payable to a surviving shareholder in a two-shareholder corporation, who then pays the estate or designated beneficiary of the deceased shareholder with the insurance proceeds. The result is a one-premium cost for the policy rather than having the shareholders purchase two separate insurance policies.

Q 7:34 What is an irrevocable insurance trust?

An irrevocable insurance trust is created to hold and own life insurance policies in order to keep the policy proceeds out of the estate of the insured and that of his or her spouse. These trusts cannot be amended even if family or personal circumstances change. One way to maintain some flexibility in using these trusts is to transfer term insurance policies rather than whole life insurance policies to them. If that is done and the insured later decides that it is no longer advisable to fund the trust, payments to the trust can be stopped and the term insurance will expire. In contrast, if whole life insurance is used, the policy will have a cash surrender value, and the trust will continue to remain in existence, even if the insured stops paying premiums.

Q 7:35 What are the gift tax consequences of creating an irrevocable insurance trust?

The transfer of life insurance policies to a trust may constitute a taxable gift. Because the gift is considered to be a gift of future interest, the $10,000 annual gift tax exclusion usually is not available; however, gift tax can be avoided by taking out policy loans and thereby reducing the cash surrender value of the transferred policy to zero. Typically, the donor will make payments to the trust to pay the insurance premiums. To assure that such payments qualify for the $10,000 annual exclusion, the trust can (1) provide that insurance proceeds are to be paid out directly to the trust beneficiaries or their estates [Rev Rul 76-490, 1976-2 CB 300] or (2) give the trust beneficiaries Crummey powers (i.e., powers that generally permit the beneficiaries to withdraw each year the lesser of the $10,000 gift tax

Q 7:36 Estate and Retirement Planning Answer Book

annual exclusion or the value of assets transferred to the trust during that year).

Q 7:36 What are the income tax consequences of creating an irrevocable insurance trust?

If the income of the trust is or may be used to pay premiums on a life insurance policy on the life of the grantor or the grantor's spouse, the grantor is taxable on the premium payments. [IRC § 677] If a policy that has a policy loan is transferred to an irrevocable unfunded life insurance trust, the owner of the policy loses the interest deduction to the extent it is otherwise allowable because only the owner of an insurance policy can claim the interest deduction for policy loans; however, this deduction has been phased out for individuals anyway, so this result is of limited interest.

Q 7:37 Should the grantor's spouse be a beneficiary of an irrevocable life insurance trust?

If the goal is to exclude the life insurance proceeds from the nongrantor spouse's estate, the nongrantor spouse should not be given a general power of appointment over trust assets. Similarly, the nongrantor spouse should not also be a grantor (i.e., initiator) of the trust.

If both spouses are grantors of the trust, any rights that either one has to receive the income from the trust will cause all or a portion of the trust proceeds to be taxable in the other person's estate. [IRC § 2036] Even if under certain circumstances the nongrantor spouse is considered a grantor, the estate tax consequences can be avoided by having the trust provide that the nongrantor spouse's rights to income are discretionary with a third-party trustee. [IRC § 2036]

To satisfy the requirement that the surviving spouse not have a general power of appointment, the surviving spouse should not be given a power to appoint trust assets to himself or herself, or to his or her creditors, estate, or the creditors of the estate. The surviving spouse should not be given the right to invade trust principal unless such a right is limited to either (1) an ascertainable standard relating to health, education, support, or maintenance or (2) the greater of $5,000 or 5 percent of the principal in the trust for the calendar on a cumulative basis.

Q 7:38 Should the surviving spouse act as trustee of an irrevocable life insurance trust?

The surviving spouse can act as trustee of an irrevocable life insurance trust provided that (1) he or she is not a grantor, and (2) he or she has no administrative power over the trust that would constitute a general power of appointment.

Q 7:39 Can life insurance be used in a buy/sell agreement as an estate planning device?

Yes, it can and usually is. A buy/sell agreement is a contract between owners of a business providing, among other things, for the uninterrupted continuation of the business in the event one of the owners dies (see chapter 9). Use of life insurance to fund a buy/sell agreement is advantageous to the decedent-seller's estate because the insurance proceeds become available to pay the full purchase price of his or her ownership interest. If little or no insurance is available and most of the purchase price is paid with a long-term note, the decedent's estate incurs the risk that the note will not be paid. In effect, then, the note holder shares in the risk that the business will collapse and that his or her note will not be paid, yet the note holder does not share in the opportunity to receive business profits if the business does well. The advantage of life insurance is that it provides the necessary funds to consummate the purchase.

Buy/sell agreements are usually divided between entity and cross-purchase agreements. In an entity agreement, the corporation owns and is the beneficiary of the life insurance used to purchase the stock from the estate of a deceased stockholder. In a cross-purchase buy/sell agreement, each stockholder owns life insurance on the other stockholders. When one stockholder dies, the surviving stockholder purchases the stock from the deceased stockholder's estate. The advantage of a cross-purchase agreement is that the remaining stockholder obtains a step-up in the cost basis of his or her stock

Q 7:40   Estate and Retirement Planning Answer Book

equal to the insurance proceeds used to purchase the stock of the deceased stockholder.

Q 7:40   Are the optional settlement provisions in insurance agreements adequate substitutes for trusts?

Optional settlement provisions are settlement options under which an insurance company makes installment payments over time. One difficulty with these payments, which are typically fixed in amount, is that their value can be eroded by inflation. Insurance proceeds are usually paid into a trust that invests them on behalf of the trust beneficiaries.

Q 7:41   What are the disadvantages of making insurance payable to the insured's estate?

The amounts payable to the estate become subject to the claims of the estate's creditors. If insurance is paid directly to a trust or to a beneficiary, state law may protect the proceeds from creditors. If the estate is the beneficiary of the insurance policy, the executor may be able to claim a fee for collecting the insurance, and in some cases estate inheritance tax exemptions for insurance may be lost.

Q 7:42   How can a trust be designed so that insurance proceeds can be paid into it and used to buy estate assets without the risk of incurring estate taxes?

If the trust provisions authorize but do not specifically direct a trustee to purchase estate assets, insurance proceeds may be used for the purchase without the risk of incurring estate taxes. If, however, the trustee is directed to buy estate assets, the insurance proceeds will be includible in the estate on the theory that the insurance proceeds were receivable for the benefit of the estate. Also, the trust provisions can permit the trustee to provide loans derived from the insurance proceeds to the estate at arm's-length interest rates when, as, and if the estate is in temporary need of funds.

Example 7-10: The majority owner of a manufacturing company creates an irrevocable insurance trust and funds it with an insurance policy in the amount of $3 million. His intent is that his children will use the proceeds of the policy to purchase his majority interest in the manufacturing company when he dies. The proceeds from the sale will be used to pay estate taxes and to provide for the owner's wife. No estate tax will be payable on the insurance proceeds if the trust gives the trustee the discretion to purchase company assets but does not require this purchase.

Q 7:43 May insurance be disqualified and therefore treated as taxable income?

Code Section 7702 sets forth a series of tests for income, estate, and gift tax purposes. If the contract fails to meet the qualifications established, the cash surrender part of the contract's income will be treated as income in the year the contract fails to meet the qualifications. Furthermore, all income earned in previous years will be included in gross income and will be taxed as ordinary income.

Q 7:44 What is income for purposes of inclusion under Code Section 7702?

Income is the amount by which the increase in net surrender value and the cost of the life insurance provided exceed the amount of premiums paid, less any dividend credit.

Q 7:45 What is the cost of the insurance provided?

The cost of the insurance provided is the lower of the mortality charge stated in the contract or the cost of the insurance on the insured's life.

Q 7:46 What is the effect of a disqualification of the policy under Code Section 7702?

If the policy is disqualified, only the excess of the death benefit over the net surrender value will qualify for the income tax exclusion under Code Section 101.

Q 7:47 How should one evaluate which type of insurance policy to invest in?

Although each individual's circumstances are different and this list may vary, some of the factors that should be taken into consideration are as follows:

1. Return on the investment and whether it is taxable,
2. Tax bracket of the insured (if the return is taxable), and
3. Premium cost and net cost.

Q 7:48 What is the taxable effect for a policy owner if he or she dies before the insured?

Under Code Section 2033, if a policy owner dies before an insured, the value of the unmatured policy is included in the policy owner's gross estate.

Q 7:49 How is the value of the unmatured policy determined?

The insurance company will provide what is called an *interpolated terminal reserve figure* as of the date of death. This figure is added to the proportionate part of the gross premium last paid before the date of the decedent's death covering the period extending beyond that date.

Q 7:50 What recommendations can be made when naming a beneficiary?

First, if the beneficiary dies before the insured, the value of the policy will be included in his or her estate. It may therefore be best to name a young person as beneficiary or to place the insurance policy in a trust.

Q 7:51 How much insurance should be taken out on an individual?

Some factors to be considered when taking out an insurance policy and attempting to determine policy limits are as follows:

1. *Family.* Gather as much personal information about the individual as possible. Determine what the individual's objectives are in obtaining the insurance policy.
2. *Assets.* Look at the value of the individual's current and anticipated assets and liabilities.
3. *Liquid assets.* Liquid assets will be necessary to pay off liabilities and death expenses. The insured will need to provide adequate compensation to pay off these expenses.
4. *Financial needs.* Look at what the family will need in the way of income.

Q 7:52 Should an insured replace an old policy if he or she determines that the selected policy does not meet the insured's objectives?

Changing the type of policy is always an alternative. The insured must, however, consider factors such as the following:

1. New acquisition costs,
2. Value of the existing policy,
3. Whether the new policy can be contested,
4. Current return on the new policy as opposed to the old policy,
5. Cash value of each policy, and
6. Needs of the insured in purchasing the policy.

Q 7:53 What factors should be taken into consideration when transferring an insurance policy for value?

When an individual purchases a life insurance contract for value, the proceeds are includible in taxable income. The amount included will be the net proceeds of the policy less the consideration paid for the transfer and the premiums paid.

Q 7:54 Is a transfer for valuable consideration recommended as an investment?

Not usually. The purchaser is better off purchasing the policy directly from the insurance company or receiving the policy as a gift. These will not generally result in includible income for the purchaser.

Q 7:55 What are the advantages to a settlement option as opposed to a trust?

A settlement option provides a guaranteed fixed income with no direct management fee.

Q 7:56 What are the advantages of a trust as opposed to a settlement option?

A trust contains several advantages that a settlement option does not, as follows:

1. It is better equipped to meet the changing needs of the beneficiary.
2. It provides a hedge against inflation.
3. The rate of return is generally higher.
4. The insured has the final say as to the disposition of the proceeds of the policy.
5. If a beneficiary is later deemed incompetent, the trustee will automatically assume the duties of guardian or conservator.

Q 7:57 Can there be a tax-free exchange of insurance policies?

Code Section 1035 permits three types of exchanges of insurance policies:

1. An exchange of a life insurance policy for another life insurance policy or for an endowment or annuity contract;
2. An exchange of an endowment contract for an annuity contract or for another endowment contract that provides for payments beginning not later than the date payments would have begun under the exchanged contract; and

3. An exchange of an annuity contract for another annuity contract.

All these policies assume exchanges involving the same insured. Furthermore, Code Section 2035 triggers ordinary income if a policyholder exchanges an endowment or annuity contract for a whole life policy. The IRS has recently announced its position that a tax-free exchange is unavailable under Code Section 1035 where a single life policy is exchanged for a second-to-die policy because such exchange does not involve the same insured. [Ltr Rul 9542037]

Chapter 8

Annuities

Annuities are contracts designed to provide retirement income. This chapter describes the features of an annuity (including investment and payment options), issues to consider when purchasing annuities, and taxation of annuities. Noncommercial annuities, called private annuities, are also explained.

Overview	8-1
Purchasing an Annuity	8-4
Tax Treatment of Annuities	8-6
Private Annuities	8-7
Simplified Safe Harbor Exclusion	8-19

Overview

Q 8:1 What is an annuity?

An annuity is a contract under which the insurer is obligated to make periodic payments to the annuitant for the annuitant's lifetime. The basic purpose of an annuity is to provide a secure retirement income for the purchaser and, in some cases, for the purchaser's spouse.

Under a single life annuity, the annuitant is the person whose lifetime will govern the minimum duration of the payment. For a joint and last survivor annuity, there are two annuitants, usually a husband and wife, and the annuity income payments are made for as long as either of these persons survives.

Annuities may be commercial or private. A commercial annuity is an annuity purchased from an insurance company or an organization that sells annuity contracts. A private annuity is an annuity from any other source. A private annuity, for example, would result from a sale of assets, usually by one family member to another, in which the person would sell his or her assets to another family member and that family member would promise, in exchange, to pay the person (now the annuitant) yearly annuity payments.

Q 8:2   How are annuities invested?

There are two main ways of investing annuities. Annuities may be fixed or variable annuities.

Fixed-dollar annuities. Under a fixed-dollar annuity, the insurer guarantees both (1) the cash value of the annuity and (2) a fixed rate of interest from year to year and thus bears the investment risk. For this reason, fixed-dollar annuities are similar to savings accounts or certificates of deposit that have fixed interest rates.

Variable annuities. The owner of a variable annuity generally has the advantage of choosing among several investment funds in which to invest annuity premiums. Typically, the premiums in a variable annuity are converted into units in a fund that is managed by the insurer, which does not guarantee any particular rate of return.

Q 8:3   How does a variable annuity work?

Under a variable annuity, investors select investments they believe will produce returns that will allow them to stay ahead of the inflation rate. This practice does not always achieve the desired results; nevertheless, for investors who begin when they are young and want to ensure that they earn sufficient funds for retirement, it is the preferred method. The variable annuity is intended to offer the annuitant a hedge against inflation by providing an annuity measured by the investment results achieved by the insurance company.

Q 8:4 What different types of annuity payment options are available?

Annuity contracts usually offer the annuitant several methods of payment.

Straight life annuity. The simplest type of annuity is the straight life annuity, which makes annuity payments for the annuitant's lifetime. Upon the annuitant's death, those payment cease regardless of how few or many premium payments the deceased annuitant had made.

Refund life annuity. A refund life annuity is similar to a straight life annuity with one added feature: the insurance company will refund the balance of the payments due under the annuity contract to the annuitant's beneficiary or estate if the annuitant dies before the premiums paid for the annuity have been returned. This feature can be advantageous if the annuitant is concerned about protection of wealth for his or her estate and/or beneficiaries (in addition to his or her own lifetime income security) and wishes to protect the amount of money contributed to the annuity.

Certain term annuity. The life annuity with a certain term combines characteristics of a straight life annuity and those of a refund life annuity. This type of annuity provides for annual payments to be made during the annuitant's entire life, and it also provides that if the annuitant dies before the expiration of a period specified in the agreement (called the *certain term*), the payments will continue until the expiration of that term. For example, the agreement could provide that if the annuitant dies within the ten-year period following the beginning of the annuity payments, the annuity payments will continue for the remainder of that ten-year period.

Joint life and survivorship annuity. For this type of annuity, payments are made during the joint lives of two persons, typically spouses. When one of the two persons dies, payments continue for the life of the survivor. Joint life and survivorship annuity contracts can be written to provide either that the amount of payments made during the life of the survivor will continue to be made at the same level as prior to the death of the first of the two persons or that the amount of payments to the survivor will be reduced. Because of the additional cost of providing this survivorship benefit, joint life and survivorship annuities are more costly than straight life annuities providing comparable dollar amounts of benefits.

Purchasing an Annuity

Q 8:5 How are annuities purchased?

An annuity may be purchased either by making a single premium payment or by making periodic premium payments.

Single premium payment. If an annuity is purchased by a single premium payment, annuity payments often begin immediately. This kind of immediate annuity is usually purchased at retirement by someone ready to start receiving retirement benefits at that time. Even with a single premium payment for an annuity, however, payments may be deferred to a future date if the annuitant so chooses. Those deferred annuities can be used to accumulate a retirement fund prior to retirement age.

Periodic payments. Under the periodic premium payment approach, an annuity owner has the discretion of paying periodic premiums to the annuity in order to build up the annuity's cash value until a retirement date sometime in the future.

Q 8:6 What are the advantages of purchasing an annuity?

The major advantage of an annuity is that it may be used to establish retirement income for a later date. Annuities are attractive for this purpose because the year-to-year increases in value from investment gains are not taxable to the individual until withdrawal from the annuity. Therefore, an annuity is an excellent way in which to build up tax-deferred cash value. In addition, an annuity is desirable for persons who want to ensure an income for their lifetimes without participating in investment management.

When offering fixed-dollar annuities (see Q 8:2), an insurance company will initially specify a credited interest rate that the company will pay on accumulations under the annuity. Many fixed-dollar annuities have a minimum guaranteed interest rate, and the insurance company cannot set its interest rate below this rate. Many fixed-dollar annuities also permit the annuitant to withdraw the funds in the annuity if the interest rate falls below a certain level, an obvious benefit for the annuitant.

The investment return realized on variable annuities (see Q 8:2) depends on the investment performance of the account in which the annuity funds are invested.

Q 8:7 What are some of the disadvantages of purchasing an annuity?

The fixed rate of interest paid on fixed-dollar annuities can be a disadvantage in periods of high inflation. As well, annuity payments are not as flexible as other kinds of payments and are generally made in accordance with a fixed schedule regardless of variations in the annuitant's need for money. Accordingly, a typical annuity, because it is a fixed amount, does not permit the annuitant to maintain his or her purchasing power so as to keep up with inflation.

Q 8:8 Are there any other costs or expenses involved in purchasing an annuity other than the annuity premium payment?

Yes, there are a number of expense charges that may be incurred in addition to an annuity premium.

The insurance company may impose a sales charge (often referred to as a *load*). If the insurance company imposes a load at the time of the purchase of the annuity (a front-end load), this charge is deducted from the premium when the annuity is purchased. In contrast, a back-end load occurs when the insurance company imposes a surrender charge on the annuitant if he or she withdraws a certain amount from the annuity or surrenders the annuity within a specified period of time after it is purchased. These charges are intended to discourage annuity owners from transferring or surrendering their annuities during fixed time periods.

Variable annuities are also subject to a number of typical charges. These charges significantly affect the yield on a variable annuity and should be considered before purchasing a variable annuity.

Tax Treatment of Annuities

Q 8:9 What is the tax treatment of annuities and annuity payments?

The taxation of annuities is covered by Section 72 of the Internal Revenue Code (Code) and its corresponding regulations. Usually, the increase in the cash value due to investments is not currently taxable to the annuitant.

Annuitants generally pay taxes only on that portion of the annuity payments that represents returns of accumulated income rather than return of their invested principal. Therefore, each annuity payment is partly a nontaxable return of the annuitant's investment in the contract and partly a taxable return of accumulated income.

The investment in the contract is the premium cost or the amount paid for the annuity contract. To determine the amount of taxable income, the investment in the contract is divided by the expected return of the annuity. The expected return is usually the total amount, including return of premium costs and investment income, under the contract.

Q 8:10 Are there any penalties for making withdrawals from annuities?

The distribution rules for annuities are similar to those for individual retirement arrangements (IRAs). For annuities issued after January 18, 1985, amounts withdrawn by the annuitant when the annuitant is under age 59½ will generally be subject to a 10 percent penalty tax on premature distributions. The exceptions to the 10 percent penalty tax also are similar to those for IRAs. An annuity contract can be exchanged for another annuity contract tax free, however. [IRC § 1035]

Partial withdrawals (ad hoc withdrawals of a portion of the value of the annuity) from annuities are viewed for tax purposes as a withdrawal of taxable investment earnings rather than a withdrawal of premium costs paid by the annuitant. Therefore, these partial withdrawals are taxed as ordinary income to the annuitant until the investment earnings are wholly distributed. In contrast, a portion of each regularly scheduled annuity payment is treated as a tax-free return of contributions.

Private Annuities

Q 8:11   What are private annuities?

A private annuity is an annuity contract between an annuitant and anyone other than an insurance company or other entity regularly engaged in the business of issuing annuity contracts. Private annuities usually are annuity contracts between the annuitant and a family member of the annuitant. In a private annuity contract, a family member promises to pay a life annuity to the annuitant in connection with the purchase of a business interest or other property from the annuitant. Usually an elderly family member will transfer assets to a younger family member, and the younger family member will promise to pay annuity payments for the lifetime of the transferor.

Private annuities are a common means of transferring wealth within a family. They have the tax advantage of eliminating assets from the taxable estate of the annuitant during the annuitant's lifetime. Moreover, this transfer of family wealth from one family member to another will not result in a gift tax treatment because the annuitant has transferred property and the other family member has provided the consideration by promising to pay the annuitant lifetime annuity payments. If, however, the value of the annuity payments is less than the fair market value of the property transferred, a gift tax will be applied.

Q 8:12   What are the advantages of private annuities?

The use of a private annuity is advantageous in estate planning because the property will be transferred out of the transferor's estate, intact and unaffected by estate taxes; and the transferor will still be able to receive an income from the private annuity payments during his or her lifetime. Moreover, an individual can transfer property in exchange for a private annuity without losing the estate tax credit.

Q 8:13   Estate and Retirement Planning Answer Book

There is usually no gift tax incurred when someone transfers his or her property in return for a private annuity unless the value of the property transferred is substantially greater than the amount of annuity payments that have been offered in exchange for the property. Furthermore, the annuitant will generally enjoy favorable tax treatment because the annuity payments will be partly a tax-free return of the annuitant's basis in the property. It is likely that the remaining portion of the payments will be taxed as capital gains.

Lastly, private annuities permit control of the assets to remain in the transferor's family and permit family members to acquire property sooner than if the property had been devised to them.

Q 8:13   What risks are associated with private annuities?

A family member who makes private annuity payments may ultimately pay more than the estate tax that would have been assessed on the property if the annuitant lives longer than his or her life expectancy. If the annuitant dies earlier than his or her life expectancy, the transferee may receive a lower basis in the transferred property than he or she would have received if he or she had inherited the property instead. This is because the transferee's basis in the property is the cost of the annuity payments made.

The transferee must also be sure that he or she can afford to make the annuity payments to the transferor. If the value of the transferred property is high, the annuity payments will be correspondingly high. The annuity payments also will be high if the annuitant has a short life expectancy. If the transferee cannot make the annuity payments, the annuitant may have no remedy because private annuities are generally unsecured promises. Difficulties in making the annuity payments also raise the possibility of creating bitter family feuds.

A potential tax problem exists for the transferee if the transferee decides to sell the property transferred. If the property is sold and the annuitant dies before the transferee has paid annuity payments that equal the value of the annuity, the transferee may have a taxable gain the year that the annuitant dies. Generally, the value of the annuity is the amount of money that was paid to purchase the annuity.

Difficulty in valuing the transferred property can create another risk. If a later determination is made that the value of the property is greater than what was originally estimated, the transferor may be subject to a gift tax on the excess of the value of the property over the value of the promised annuity payments.

Q 8:14 Are the payments that are received from a private annuity ever includible in the decedent's gross estate?

If the transferee is a trust or the payments are conditioned upon the income received from the property, the transaction may be includible in the grantor's estate.

Q 8:15 Can the yearly payments from a private annuity be given by the grantor in an amount not exceeding the annual gift tax exclusion, thereby avoiding gift tax or payments?

This may be done; however, there is no guarantee that the grantor will make the annual gift. Therefore, if the payments are high, the transferee may have higher payments than he or she can afford.

Q 8:16 What is the income tax treatment for a grantor of a private annuity where property is involved?

If the private annuity is unsecured, the annuitant will be taxed on the gain from the sale of the property over time. Therefore, the part of the payment attributable to the basis in the asset will be excluded from income; the part of the payment attributable to the gain from the sale of property will be capital gain; and the remainder will be investment or ordinary income. When the annuity is secured, the entire gain is taxable at the time the annuity is established.

Q 8:17 What is the income tax treatment for a grantee of a private annuity where property is involved?

The grantee will treat as ordinary income all income returned from the investment. The payments to the annuity, although not deductible, will increase the basis in the property, thereby allowing less capital gain treatment on the sale of the property as the annuity payments continue.

Q 8:18 What factors should be considered when considering establishing a private annuity?

The following factors should be considered: (1) valuation of the annuity, (2) value of the property, (3) insurance coverage for the taxpayer, and (4) health of the taxpayer.

Q 8:19 What is a deferred annuity?

Under a deferred annuity, the taxpayer invests pretax funds to be received at a later date. This is especially helpful if the taxpayer currently has a large income and wishes to reduce his or her current tax liability. The income is deferred to a time when the taxpayer will likely be in a lower income tax bracket.

Q 8:20 What happens to a deferred annuity if the taxpayer dies before he or she begins to receive payments?

If the taxpayer dies before the annuity begins to make payments, the proceeds generally must be distributed within five years of the taxpayer's death or must be payable to a beneficiary not in excess of that beneficiary's expected lifetime.

Q 8:21 What is a wrap-around annuity?

A wrap-around annuity focuses its income on one or more different types of investments, such as mutual funds. For this reason, a wrap-around annuity has a variable rate of return.

Q 8:22 What is the tax treatment of a wrap-around annuity?

Where the wrap-around annuity is a mutual fund of the type that is available to the public investor, taxpayers are treated as if they own the annuity and are taxed on the income from the annuity. [Rev Rul 81-225] Where a company sets up its own private mutual fund solely for the purpose of serving as a vehicle for its annuity, however, the income will be deferred.

Q 8:23 May an annuitant deduct unrecovered annuity investments on his or her tax return?

Code Section 72 allows a deduction of unrecovered investment upon two conditions. First, the payments must cease by reason of the annuitant's death. Second, there must be unrecovered investment on the date of the annuitant's death.

Q 8:24 When may a beneficiary deduct unrecovered annuity investments on his or her tax return?

The beneficiary must also meet a two-part test in order to deduct the unrecovered annuity investment. First, the contract must provide for annuity payments to be made to the estate of the annuitant or the beneficiary. Second, the payment must be the principal amount invested.

Q 8:25 When will an insurance contract under a qualified plan be treated as an annuity?

An insurance contract under a qualified plan will be treated as an annuity when the cash surrender value exceeds the contract's face amount.

Q 8:26 What is a single annuity contract, and why is it an important consideration?

Under a single annuity contract, an employee agrees in writing to contribute a certain sum and his or her employer agrees to match that sum. Under Code Section 72, the employee will not be able to offset his or her contribution against the employer's contribution in determining the taxable amounts—an important consideration.

Q 8:27 Can a person purchase an annuity for another individual?

Yes. Unless the value of the annuity is less than the annual exclusion (currently $10,000), however, gift tax will be levied on the premium paid for the annuity if the annuity is given at the time of purchase. If the annuity is given at a later time, the value for gift tax purposes is the single premium the insurance company would charge at that time.

Q 8:28 Are annuities includible in a decedent's gross estate for tax purposes?

Refund annuities, certain term annuities, and joint life and survivorship annuities are included in a decedent's gross estate to the extent of the fair market value of the survivor's interest in the annuity. A straight life annuity is not included in the decedent's gross estate.

Q 8:29 Is the entire amount of the fair market value of the survivor's interest included in the estate even if the payments go directly to a beneficiary after the death of the annuitant?

Code Section 2039 includes only that portion that the decedent paid for the annuity in the gross estate.

Q 8:30 May an annuitant make a withdrawal prior to the starting date of the annuity without paying income taxes on the funds?

Prior to 1982, deferred and wrap-around annuities often could be withdrawn tax free to the extent of the initial investment. The Code permitted the amounts withdrawn to be treated as principal, with investment income being the remainder. Code Section 72 now requires that the payments first be treated as a withdrawal of investment income and as a return of capital only after the income earned on the investment is fully used.

Q 8:31 What is the disadvantage of annuities with regard to estate taxes?

Evidently, under Code Section 1014, even though the annuity may be included in a decedent's gross estate, it does not receive a stepped-up basis.

Q 8:32 Are members of the armed forces allowed to exclude annuity payments received on account of personal injuries or sickness resulting from active service in the military?

Code Section 104 allows members of the armed forces to exclude payments from annuities from gross income if they are any of the following:

1. Individuals who were entitled to receive the annuity on or before September 24, 1975;
2. Individuals who were armed forces members or were under a binding agreement to become armed forces members on or before September 24, 1975;
3. Individuals who received the disability pay because of an injury related to combat; or
4. Individuals who were entitled to benefits for disability from the Veterans Administration.

Q 8:33 Must a certain type of injury have occurred in order for Code Section 104 to apply?

The injury must have in fact resulted from active service.

Q 8:34 If a taxpayer who is a member of the armed forces falls ill while on active duty and is paid for his or her leave time, will this be excludable?

The taxpayer must be compensated for disability as opposed to compensated for salary in order for Code Section 104 to apply.

Q 8:35 How much disability pay is excludable under Code Section 104?

Under Code Section 104, the maximum amount that may be excluded is the amount that the individual would receive by applying to the Veterans Administration for disability compensation.

Q 8:36 What is the maximum number of years over which an employee may receive installment payments from a tax-qualified plan?

Proposed Treasury Regulations Section 1.401(a)(9)-2 sets forth a maximum period for taxpayers to receive an annuity for a fixed period of years without a life contingency, as follows:

> Q-5. For calendar years after 1988, if an employee's benefit is being distributed in the form of a period certain annuity without a life contingency (e.g., installment payout), how must the benefit be distributed in order to satisfy the MDIB requirement?
>
> A. (a) *General rule.* If an employee's benefit is being distributed in the form of a period certain annuity without a life contingency, the period certain may not exceed the applicable period determined using the table below. In general, the applicable period is determined using the attained age of the employee as of the employee's birthday in the calendar year in which the annuity payments commence. However, if distributions commence after the end of the employee's first distribution calendar year and on or before the employee's required beginning date, the applicable period is determined using the attained age of the employee as of the employee's birthday in the employee's first distribution calendar year. Further, if distributions commence before January 1 of the employee's first distribution calendar year under a benefit option which provides for distributions in the form of a period certain annuity without a life contingency, the MDIB requirement will not be satisfied as of the date distributions commence unless the benefit option provides that, as of the beginning of the employee's first distribution calendar year, the remaining period under the annuity (including such calendar year) will not exceed the period determined under the table below using the attained age of the employee as of the employee's birthday in the employee's first distribution calendar year. For example, if distributions commence to an employee (X), born May 5, 1930, on January 1,

Annuities   Q 8:36

1990, and the benefit option provides for distribution in the form of a period certain annuity for 37 years, the MDDIB requirement is not satisfied when the distributions commence because the remaining period certain as the beginning of X's first distribution calendar year (year 2000) will be 27 years (37 minus 10) which exceeds 26.2. However, the benefit could provide for an automatic shortening of the period at age 70½ to conform to the MDIB requirement. Additionally, the amount of the annuity payments must satisfy F-3 of § 1.401(a)(9)-1 in order to satisfy the MDIB requirement. Of course, if the annuity payments commence after the employee's required beginning date, distributions before the annuity payments commence must satisfy Q&A-4.

(b) *Table.*

Age of Employee	Maximum Period Certain	Age of Employee	Maximum Period Certain
70	26.2	93	8.8
71	25.3	94	8.3
72	24.4	95	7.8
73	23.5	96	7.3
74	22.7	97	6.9
75	21.8	98	6.5
76	20.9	99	6.1
77	20.1	100	5.7
78	19.2	101	5.3
79	18.4	102	5.0
80	17.6	103	4.7
81	16.8	104	4.4
82	16.0	105	4.1
83	15.3	106	3.8
84	14.5	107	3.6
85	13.8	108	3.3
86	13.1	109	3.1
87	12.4	110	2.8
88	11.8	111	2.6
89	11.1	112	2.4
90	10.5	113	2.2
91	9.9	114	2.0
92	9.4	115 and older	1.8

Q 8:37   How is the initial year in which installment payments must be made determined for the taxpayer?

Under Proposed Treasury Regulations Section 1.401(a)(9)-2, the maximum period certain is determined by using the taxpayer's birthday in the year the payments start.

Q 8:38   Must the maximum defined injury benefit rules also meet the tests under a defined benefit plan?

Under Proposed Treasury Regulations Section 1.401(a)(9)-2, the annuity payments must be paid at intervals not longer than one year. Once payments have started over a period certain, the period certain may not be lengthened, and payments may not increase except for certain cost of living increases or increases in benefits under the plan.

Q 8:39   May the maximum defined injury benefit rules apply to a joint and survivor annuity?

The maximum defined injury benefit (MDIB) may apply where the beneficiary is someone other than the spouse and where the annual periodic annuity payments are not more than a certain percentage of the annuity payment payable to the employee after the employee's required start-up date. The maximum percentage is determined by using a table found in Proposed Treasury Regulations Section 1.401(a)(9)-2, which uses the difference in the annuitant's and beneficiary's ages in determining the applicable percentage.

Q 8:40   If there is more than one beneficiary, how is the difference in age determined for maximum defined injury benefit purposes?

Where the annuitant has more than one beneficiary, the youngest beneficiary's age is used to find the applicable percentage.

Q 8:41   Under Proposed Treasury Regulations Section 1.401(a)(9)-2, what is the effect on the maximum defined injury benefit percentage requirement of adding a new, younger beneficiary?

The applicable percentage must be adjusted to reflect the younger beneficiary in the calendar year following the change of beneficiary.

Q 8:42 How do the requirements of Proposed Treasury Regulations Section 1.401(a)(9)-2 change when the beneficiary is the annuitant's spouse?

The MDIB requirement is automatically satisfied.

Q 8:43 What if the annuitant and the annuitant's spouse are divorced and the court orders that a portion of the employee's annuity payments be paid to the spouse under a qualified domestic relations order?

Under Proposed Treasury Regulations Section 1.401(a)(9)-2, the ex-spouse is treated as a spouse for MDIB purposes.

Q 8:44 What is the expected return of an annuity?

The expected return is the total amount receivable as an annuity under the contract. If the contract is not for a period certain, but for the lifetime of the annuitant, then the expected return is determined by multiplying the expected payments by actuarial tables that are published by the Internal Revenue Service (IRS).

Q 8:45 Can an annuitant deduct a percentage of his or her return of capital from each payment and therefore exclude this percentage from income?

The taxpayer can exclude the percentage of each annuity payment from his or her income that represents return of capital. After the full amount of capital invested has been deducted, however, the remainder of the payments are fully includible in gross income.

Q 8:46 Are there any circumstances under which the percentage deductible may continue after the total amount invested has been excluded from income?

Under a qualified plan with a start-up date before January 1, 1987, a portion is partially excludable even after the total investment has been excluded. [Treas Reg § 1.402(a)-1(a)(1)(iii)]

Q 8:47   Estate and Retirement Planning Answer Book

Q 8:47 Was there a time when the exclusion ratio did not apply to annuity payments?

Yes. Treasury Regulations Section 1.402(a)-1(a)(1)(iii) provides for exclusion of the full investment before inclusion of the income from the investment where (1) the annuity is under a qualified plan; (2) the start-up date for the annuity is before July 2, 1986; and (3) the annuitant's investment in the contract did not exceed the annuity payments receivable in the first three years after the date of the first payment.

Q 8:48 What type of payments are considered annuities?

To be considered an annuity under Treasury Regulations Section 1.72-2(b)(2), the payments must be (1) received on or after the annuity starting date, (2) payable in period installments at regular intervals for a period of more than one full year from the annuity starting date, and (3) determined at the annuity starting date either from the terms of the contract or by the use of mortality tables.

Q 8:49 How much of an employer's contribution must be included in an annuitant's income?

The annuitant must include the amount in a plan that is derived from employer contributions in the year the amount is made available under Code Section 72.

Q 8:50 If an employee is given an option to receive a lump-sum payment or an annuity, how much is includible in the employee's income for the year in which the offer is made?

Under Code Section 72, the entire amount of the lump-sum payment offered is includible in income in the year in which it is offered, even if the annuity is chosen.

Q 8:51 Is there an exception to Code Section 72's harsh inclusion requirement?

Yes. Under Code Section 72, the lump sum is not includible in income if (1) the option to chose an annuity is exercised within 60 days from the date of the availability of the lump sum; (2) all of the lump sum would be includible in gross income as an amount received under an annuity; and (3) the option is irrevocable.

Q 8:52 How long must the option be irrevocable for the exception to Code Section 72 to apply?

The option must be permanently irrevocable. The annuitant must not have the option of changing the election from time to time.

Simplified Safe Harbor Exclusion

Q 8:53 What is the simplified safe harbor exclusion ratio?

The simplified safe harbor exclusion ratio applies to annuity payments that start after July 1, 1986. It simplifies the usual calculation of the amount of the annuity payment to be excluded from taxable income.

Q 8:54 Will the simplified safe harbor exclusion ratio comply with Code Section 72?

Annuitants who qualify for and use the simplified ratio are considered to have complied with Code Section 72 for calculation of the exclusion ratio.

Q 8:55 Who qualifies for the simplified safe harbor exclusion ratio?

Taxpayers who are less than age 75 when annuity payments begin or age 75 or older with less than five years of guaranteed payments qualify for this method. [IR Notice 88-118]

Q 8:56 What qualifications must a taxpayer meet in order to use the simplified safe harbor exclusion ratio?

In accordance with Internal Revenue Notice 88-118, the annuity payments must (1) begin after July 1, 1986; (2) depend on the life of the receiver or the joint life of the receiver and beneficiary; and (3) be made from a qualified plan under Code Section 401, an employee annuity under Code Section 403, or an annuity contract under Code Section 403.

Q 8:57 How is the simplified safe harbor exclusion ratio determined?

The amount excluded under the simplified safe harbor exclusion ratio is determined by dividing the investment in the contract by the number of expected annuity payments.

Example 8-1: Upon retirement, a chemist receives an annuity payment of $2,000 per month. The chemist has an investment in the contract of $48,000. Her expected number of payments is 480. The amount of the payment that is excluded from income is determined by dividing the investment ($48,000) by the number of monthly payments (480), or $100.

Q 8:58 Is the simplified safe harbor exclusion ratio modified for changes in the annuity payments such as cost-of-living increases?

No. The amount of the payment excluded from gross income remains the same whether or not the amount of the annuity payments increases.

Q 8:59 What if the amount determined to be excluded under the simplified safe harbor method is greater than the annuity payment received?

The entire payment will be excluded from gross income until the investment in the contract is fully recovered.

Q 8:60 How is the excludable portion determined under the simplified safe harbor exclusion ratio where there is more than one beneficiary to an annuity?

The excludable portion is determined with reference to the age of the oldest beneficiary. The excludable portion is calculated by dividing the amount of the beneficiary's monthly annuity by the total amount of the monthly annuity payments made to all beneficiaries.

Q 8:61 How is the investment in the contract determined under the simplified safe harbor exclusion method?

The total investment in the contract is determined by subtracting any amounts received before the annuity starting date from the after-tax payments into the annuity.

Q 8:62 Can the investment in the contract be increased by any method other than payments to the annuity?

Yes. Any death benefit exclusions under Code Section 101 also increase the investment in the contract.

Q 8:63 How does a taxpayer elect to use the simplified method?

The taxpayer must attach a signed statement to his or her income tax return stating that the taxpayer is electing to use the simplified method.

Q 8:64 How is the total number of monthly expected payments determined?

Internal Revenue Notice 88-118, Section II.B, includes a table that is to be used when determining the total expected monthly payments. For a taxpayer who is 55 years of age or under, for example, the total number of expected payments is 300. The taxpayer must refer to this table when determining the total expected monthly payments.

Q 8:65 Once the election to use the simplified method is made, can the taxpayer later decide to use the actual calculation of the exclusion ratio or vice versa?

If the taxpayer is allowed to amend his or her return under the Code, the taxpayer may change from the simplified method to an actual calculation of the exclusion ratio or vice versa.

Q 8:66 How does a taxpayer change from using the simplified exclusion method to the actual exclusion?

The change is made by filing Form 1040X, an amended income tax return for all years for which an amended return is allowed.

Q 8:67 How is the value of the taxpayer's annuity determined?

The value is determined by looking at the total assets in the account. For a defined benefit plan, the value is determined by taking the present value of the vested portion of the participant's total accrued benefit under the plan.

Q 8:68 May a taxpayer be required to include loans on annuities in gross taxable income in the year the loan is made?

A loan may be taxable if it is determined that in reality it is a distribution to the taxpayer. Unless an exclusion under Code Section 72 applies, the following are taxable as distributions:

1. The receipt, directly or indirectly, by a plan participant or beneficiary of any amount as a loan from a qualified employer plan;

2. The assignment or pledge by a plan participant or beneficiary of any portion of his or her interest in a qualified employer plan; or

3. The receipt of any amount as a loan under a contract that was bought under a qualified employer plan.

Q 8:69 Even if an exclusion applies, may a taxpayer later be required to treat the loan as a distribution?

Yes. If the taxpayer terminates his or her participation in the plan without repaying the loan, the balance of the unpaid loan and accrued interest payable on the loan are treated as part of the plan distribution on termination.

Q 8:70 Are payments contributed to an annuity by an employer on behalf of a self-employed individual excludable by the self-employed individual?

No. When computing the investment on the contact, the contributions made on behalf of a self-employed individual are treated as consideration paid by the employer.

Q 8:71 Is it true that the early withdrawals tax does not apply to some employee distributions made after separation from service if the employee has attained age 55?

If the distribution is made from a qualified plan and (1) the distribution is made after the employee has separated from service with the employer maintaining the plan and (2) the separation from service occurs during or after the calendar year in which the employee attains age 55, the early withdrawals tax may not apply, according to Code Section 72(t).

Q 8:72 Does the Section 72(t) exception apply even if the employee later returns to employment with the same employer?

Yes. There must be an actual physical separation from service before the distribution. Short-term separations are closely scrutinized by the IRS to determine whether the separations were in fact intended to be permanent.

Chapter 9

Valuation of Business Interests and Other Property

This chapter reviews the importance of valuing business interests and other property for estate planning purposes. It discusses how to establish value for estate tax purposes before a taxpayer's death in order to minimize the eventual estate tax bite. It also discusses permitted methods of valuation. Special issues in valuation include interest in closely held corporations, restrictive stock agreements, and real property.

Overview	9-2
Mortgages and Notes	9-3
Closely Held Securities	9-4
The Estate Tax Freeze	9-10
Restrictive Stock Agreements	9-15
Minority Interests	9-17
Real Estate	9-20
Penalties for Improper Valuation	9-24

Overview

Q 9:1 Why is valuation of business interests and other property an important aspect of estate planning?

The valuations assigned to interests in closely held business and other property can have a tremendous impact on the amount of estate tax that eventually will be paid. Business interests are valued by determining both the value of the assets of the business and the value of the interest in the business held by the shareholder. Some assets held by the business, such as notes, may be discounted because of changes in interest rates and the risk that the note cannot be collected. If a shareholder has a minority interest in a company, it is typically appropriate to discount the value of his or her interest in the company because of an inability to control the affairs of the company. If stock is not publicly traded, it is appropriate to discount the value of the stock to reflect this lack of marketability. To the extent possible, steps should be taken in advance to help establish and document the value of various types of interests and property.

Q 9:2 What are the basic valuation rules?

Estate and gift taxes are based on the fair market value of property. Fair market value is defined as the price at which property would change hands between a willing buyer and a willing seller, neither of whom is under any compulsion to buy or sell and both having reasonable knowledge of the relevant facts. [Treas Reg § 20.2031-1(b)] Property cannot be valued at the price it would bring at a forced sale. [Treas Reg § 20.2031-1(b)] Although the Internal Revenue Service (IRS) generally insists that property be valued at its highest and best use, the courts have occasionally disagreed with that approach when economic conditions precluded using the property in that way. [Sprenger Estate v Commr, 46 TCM 1295 (1983); Feutcher Estate v Commr, TCM 1992-97] The assessed value for real estate tax purposes is not used unless it is regarded as the fair market value of the real property. [Treas Reg § 20.201-1(b)]

Q 9:3 Is it always better to have property valued low?

Not necessarily. If no estate taxes are payable, a low value for property does not result in any estate tax savings. On the other hand, the low value will result in a lower basis for income tax purposes. Lower basis has two implications: (1) the amount that is potentially depreciable will be less, and (2) if the property is sold, a greater amount of income tax may be payable.

Q 9:4 What is the market approach to valuation?

The market approach to valuing property involves analyzing sales of other properties. It can be based on actual sales or comparable sales.

Actual sales. If actual sales are used, the sale must occur within a reasonable time before or after the valuation date. The IRS can (and does) disregard the sale price if there are indications that the sale was not at arm's length or if there were unusual circumstances. Unaccepted offers may be evidence of value.

Comparable sales. The second method of valuing property under the market approach is to consider comparable sales. This involves considering sales of similar property.

Q 9:5 What is the income approach to value?

The income approach is a method of determining the fair market value of property by determining the present value of the income that the property will produce in the future.

Q 9:6 What is the cost approach to value?

The cost approach to value involves determining the value of property on the basis of the cost required to replace it.

Mortgages and Notes

Q 9:7 How are mortgages and notes valued?

Mortgages and notes ordinarily are valued at their face value or the amount of unpaid principal plus the amount of accrued interest on the valuation date. [Treas Reg § 20.2031-4] The taxpayer has the burden of establishing a lower value. [Ltr Rul 8229001] Two important factors in establishing a lower value for mortgages are interest rates and the soundness of the security underlying the obligation.

Closely Held Securities

Q 9:8 What is the basic approach used in valuing closely held securities?

The basic approach for valuing closely held securities is set forth in Revenue Ruling 59-60, which recognizes that there is no one correct method. Instead, all of the facts and circumstances of each individual case must be analyzed by the appraiser, who is expected to use common sense and informed judgment and maintain "a reasonable attitude in recognition of the fact that valuation is not an exact science."

Q 9:9 Can developments subsequent to the valuation date be used in determining fair market value?

No, they cannot. The IRS recognizes that the appraisal must be based on facts that are available at the effective date of the valuation. In *Trust Services of America, Inc. v. United States* [885 F 2d 561 (9th Cir 1989)], the court disregarded evidence that the corporation had received an offer of merger four months after the decedent's death, finding it irrelevant that an offer to merge and an actual merger in fact took place after the decedent's death.

Q 9:10 What market should be used for valuation purposes if no market exists for the shares of a closely held corporation?

Revenue Ruling 59-60 suggests that where no market exists for the closely held securities, the selling price for shares of companies engaged in the same or similar lines of business that are traded on a free and open market may provide the best measure of value.

Q 9:11 What is the book value approach to valuating closely held securities?

Under the book value approach, the cost of all assets of the corporation is first determined. Then amortization and depreciation are subtracted, together with all liabilities. The resulting figure represents the company's book value. The values used are those shown on the corporate balance sheet at any given time. Because this method does not consider assets that appreciate or depreciate in value at any rate different from rates permitted by the Internal Revenue Code (Code), the economic value of the assets may not be accurately reflected. Book value may also fail to reflect the value of the intangible assets of the corporation such as goodwill, marketing lists, pricing lists, patents, and trademarks.

Q 9:12 What is the earnings approach to valuing closely held securities?

The earnings approach is based on a projection of the corporation's future earnings. The earnings approach to valuing closely held companies has several variations.

Discounted future returns. The discounted future returns method is based upon the assumption that the price an investor will pay for a share of stock is the present value of the future stream of income that he or she expects to receive from the investment. This method looks at the history of the corporation to determine expected future earnings over a selected period of years—generally five. After future earnings are projected for the selected period, each of the future year's expected earnings is discounted back to present value using a reasonable discount rate equivalent to the rate of return that an investor would expect to receive from investing in that business. The total of the present values of the corporation's expected future earnings represents the current fair market value of that corporation.

Capitalization of earnings. Typically, under the capitalization of earnings approach, a five-year history of the subject company's earnings is converted into present fair market value by using a multiplier factor. Frequently, the price/earnings ratio of comparable companies in the public sector is used as the multiple factor.

Q 9:13 What is the market approach to valuing closely held securities?

The market approach to determining the value of closely held corporations involves an analysis of similarly situated public companies in the same line of business on the theory that similar companies will have a similar value. For this analysis to work, the companies must be comparable. Factors relevant in determining comparability include the following:

1. The similarity of the markets in which the companies operate;
2. The structure and quality of the management of the companies;
3. The industry the companies operate in and their position within that industry;
4. The companies' earnings;
5. The product lines in which the companies are actively engaged; and
6. Industry-wide competition among comparable entities.

If these factors are comparable between the subject company and publicly traded companies within the same market, a basis exists for estimating what the closely held stock would sell for if it was also publicly traded.

Q 9:14 What factors does the IRS consider fundamental in valuing closely held corporations?

The IRS considers eight basic factors in valuing shares in a closely held corporation. It asserts that these factors apply in valuing corporate stocks for which market quotations are either unavailable or are of such scarcity that they do not reflect the fair market value. The relative weight given these factors depends upon the particular corporation being valued.

The eight factors listed in Revenue Ruling 59-60 are as follows:

1. *The nature and history of the business.* This includes such things as the nature of the business, the company's capital structure, plant facilities, sales records, management, income, and dividends. The corporate history provides indications of the degree of risk involved in the business, including the

stability, growth, and diversity of operations. [Rev Rul 59-60, 1959-1 CB 237, § 4.02(a)]

2. *Economic outlook.* The emphasis here is on the economic conditions both in the nation and in the business in which the corporation is engaged as of the date of the appraisal. The corporation's competitive success in relation to other entities in the industry is important. Prospective competition may also be significant; for instance, a corporation that has developed a novelty item resulting in significantly higher initial profit margins may face substantial future competition. Price trends in markets for commodities and securities are important indicators of general public approval or disapproval of competitive industries or competitors within a given industry. [Rev Rul 59-60, 1959-1 CB 237, § 4.02(b)]

3. *Book value and financial condition.* The book value of the stock of the business being valued is another factor. Revenue Ruling 59-60 suggests that investment property usually commands a lower rate of return than operating assets, presumably because of the risk factor. The ruling also recommends that the structure and ownership of the outstanding stock of the corporation be analyzed. If more than one class of stock exists, the corporation's articles of incorporation and bylaws should be carefully examined to determine the nature of variations in voting power, dividend preferences, and liquidation preferences.

   The value of a closely held business is not always equivalent to the value of its underlying assets. For example, the underlying assets would not take into consideration things such as goodwill and whether the company is a holding company or an operating company. The significance of book value depends on the type of company. If the company is a holding company, book value may be quite significant. If the company is operating a business, book value may be given little weight.

4. *Earning capacity.* Profit-and-loss statements should be considered for a representative period, preferably five or more years. Revenue Ruling 59-60 cautions that resorting to arbitrary five- or ten-year averages without regard to trends or future prospects will not produce realistic valuations.

5. *Dividend-paying capacity.* In valuing a closely held corporation, "[p]rimary consideration should be given to the dividend-

paying capacity of the company rather than to dividends actually paid in the past." Revenue Ruling 59-60 further states that the dividend factor is not material in the valuation of a controlling block of closely held stock because the payment of dividends is discretionary with the controlling shareholder and presumably dependent on the controlling shareholder's needs.

6. *Goodwill and intangibles.* Revenue Ruling 59-60 states that "in the final analysis, goodwill is based upon earning capacity. According to the ruling, the value to be placed upon intangibles and goodwill is the amount by which the appraised value of the tangible assets exceeds the net book value of such assets.

7. *Sales of stock.* All sales of stock for a closely held corporation should be carefully investigated to determine whether they represent arm's-length transactions. Revenue Ruling 59-60 states that all the evidence of fair market value should be considered, including the size of the block of the stock in question and the control or lack of control represented by that block. The ruling states that there is no basis for making an adjustment for blockage and that a control premium may be justified.

8. *Market price of comparables.* In valuing unlisted securities, the value of securities for comparable companies whose stock is listed should be considered. Revenue Ruling 59-60 states that comparable companies whose stocks are actively traded on the over-the-counter market may be used if sufficient comparable listed companies cannot be found. According to the ruling, two key issues are (1) whether the company is actually comparable and (2) whether the stock is actively traded. In determining comparability, other relevant factors besides being in the same line of business must be considered, including the structure of the outstanding stock (whether one or more classes of stock exist) and the historical profitability of the company.

Revenue Ruling 59-60 emphasizes that, although all of these eight factors are important in determining the fair market value of a closely held company, some of the factors may be more important than others in certain circumstances.

Revenue Ruling 59-60 further asserts that no universally applicable capitalization rate formula exists. Instead, it suggests taking into account a variety of factors in determining the relevant capitalization rate, including the nature of the business in general, the risks involved in investing in the business, and the stability of earnings.

Revenue Ruling 59-60 also rejects averaging factors to determine value. Rather, each factor's relative weight must be considered.

Agreements between a corporation and the shareholder or between two shareholders that restrict the sale of closely held securities do not conclusively establish fair market value, according to Revenue Ruling 59-60. Rather, those agreements are merely one factor to consider in analyzing the fair market value of closely held securities. Other factors such as the relationship between the parties to the agreement, the size of the block of stock subject to the agreement, and other material facts will determine whether the agreement represents a "bona fide business arrangement or is a device to pass the decedent's shares to the natural objects of his bounty for less than an adequate and full consideration in money or money's worth." (See Qs 9:23–9:26.)

Q 9:15 What factors does the federal Tax Court consider in determining the value of closely held corporations?

In *Newhouse Estate v. Commr* [94 TC 193 (1990), *nonacq*, 1991-1 CB 1], the Tax Court considered a number of valuation issues. It began by looking to Code Section 2031(b) and Revenue Ruling 59-60 to provide the appropriate criteria for determining fair market value. The court analyzed the factors of Revenue Ruling 59-60 and also addressed the following additional areas of concern with respect to the valuation of closely held securities: (1) the potential for extensive litigation in determining shareholders' rights, (2) the size of the corporation and the value of the stock involved as a deterrent to all but a relatively small number of potential buyers, and (3) the regulatory problems that may be incurred by a potential buyer of the block of stock in question. In *Newhouse*, the Tax Court heard testimony concerning general conditions of the national economy during the period 1979 to 1980. The court considered evidence of the national economy through the 1970s showing that, during the period immediately preceding the valuation date, the general economy was in a near recession with high interest rates and high inflation. The court relied heavily on expert testimony as to the willingness of a prospective buyer to purchase the stock of a newspaper company in the existing economy, and those economic factors played a significant role in the court's determination of a lower value for the corporation's stock than was claimed by the IRS.

The Estate Tax Freeze

Q 9:16 What is an estate tax freeze?

An *estate tax freeze* is a transaction involving a corporation or partnership in which the owner of a closely held business transfers an interest of the entity with anticipated future appreciation to a younger family member, while retaining rights in the income and principal of the entity having no anticipated future appreciation that have priority over the transferred interests. The value ascribed to the retained preferred rights has the effect of reducing the transfer tax value of the interest transferred. If the retained preferred rights are never exercised, however, any value attributed to those rights could potentially pass to subordinate owners without a taxable event occurring.

Q 9:17 How are estate freezes taxed?

Estate freeze transactions are addressed by a special gift tax valuation rule. [IRC § 2701] When an interest in a corporation or a partnership is transferred to a member of the transferor's family, the gift tax value of the transfer is determined, in part, by using the Section 2701 special valuation rules to value the interests in the entity retained by the transferor. Unless an exception applies, Section 2701 values certain retained interests at zero, thus increasing the value of the transferred interest (see Q 9:19).

Q 9:18 When do the special valuation rules of Code Section 2701 apply?

An estate tax freeze exists and the special valuation rules of Code Section 2701 will apply if the following occurs:

1. A transfer of an interest in a corporation or partnership to a family member of the transferor is made; and
2. Immediately after the transfer, the transferor or an applicable family member holds an *applicable retained interest.*

Both direct and indirect transfers (such as redemption or recapitalization) may be subject to Code Section 2701. [Treas Reg § 25.2701-1(b)(2)(i)] Although these special rules govern the valuation of certain transfers between related parties, in most instances the value of the entity itself (as opposed to the transferred interest alone) will still have to be determined using the traditional methods of determining fair market value and will be subject to the same type of analysis.

The following types of transfers are excluded from coverage under Code Section 2701:

1. Transfers for which market quotations on an established securities market are readily available on the date of transfer for either the interest transferred or for the interest retained by the transferor;
2. Transfers in which the retained interest is of the same class or proportionately the same class as the transferred interest; and
3. Transfers that proportionately reduce each class of interest held by the transferor and applicable family members immediately before the transfer.

The following terms will be used in the discussion of transfers and the special valuation rules of Code Section 2701.

Family members and applicable family members. The term *family member(s)* includes the transferor's spouse, any lineal descendants of the transferor or transferor's spouse, and the spouse of any such descendant. The term *applicable family member(s)* includes the transferor's spouse, any ancestor of the transferor or transferor's spouse, and the spouse of any such ancestor. Adopted relatives are treated as blood relatives for purposes of determining a family member and an applicable family member. [Treas Reg § 25.2701-1(d)]

Applicable retained interest. An applicable retained interest is an equity interest in a corporation or partnership for which there is either an *extraordinary payment right* or a *distribution right* in a *controlled entity.* When determining whether an applicable retained interest exists, special attribution rules apply. [Treas Reg § 25.2701-2(b)(1)]

Extraordinary payment right. An extraordinary payment right is a liquidation, put, call, or conversion right or any similar right in the controlled entity that has been retained by the transferor, whether exercised or not, that affects the value of the interests transferred to the family member. [Treas Reg § 25.2701-2(b)(2)]

Distribution right. A distribution right is the right to receive distributions with respect to an equity interest in a corporation or partnership. The right to receive distributions with respect to an interest that is of the same class or a class junior to the transferred interest is not a distribution right, however. [Treas Reg § 25.2701-2(b)(3)]

Controlled entity. A controlled entity is a corporation or partnership controlled by the transferor and applicable family members immediately before the transfer to a family member. For a corporation, that means holding 50 percent or more of either the voting rights or the fair market value of the corporation. For a partnership, that means holding 50 percent or more of either the capital interests or profit interests in the partnership. Control of a limited partnership means holding any interest as a general partner. [Treas Reg § 25.2701-2(b)(5)]

Family attribution rules. These rules treat an interest held by an individual's brothers, sisters, or lineal descendants as if it were held by that individual. *Entity attribution* exists to the extent that an individual is treated as holding any interest that is indirectly held by him or her through a corporation, partnership, estate, trust, or other entity. [Treas Reg § 25.2701-6]

Example 9-1: An investor is a 50 percent beneficiary of a trust that holds 50 percent of the preferred stock of a closely held corporation. Twenty-five percent of the preferred stock of the corporation is considered to be held by the investor.

Q 9:19 How are gifts subject to Code Section 2701 valued?

Gifts subject to Code Section 2701 are valued in two steps. First, the applicable retained interest is valued, and then the value of the transferred interest (the gift) can be valued.

Valuation of Business Interests and Other Property   Q 9:19

Step 1. If an interest in a corporation or partnership is transferred to a family member and the transferor or applicable family member retains an applicable retained interest (see Q 9:18), Code Section 2701 provides rules for valuing the applicable retained interests. If the applicable retained interest is an extraordinary payment right, it is valued at zero. If the applicable retained interest is a distribution right in a controlled entity, it is valued at zero, unless the distribution right is a qualified payment right. If the applicable retained interest of a transferor or applicable family member consists of one or more extraordinary payment rights and a qualified payment right, the value of all these rights is determined as if each extraordinary payment right is exercised in a manner that results in the lowest total value for all of the rights being valued, using a consistent set of assumptions and giving due regard to the entity's net worth, prospective earning power, and other relevant factors found in Treasury Regulations Sections 20.2031-2(f) and 20.2031-3. Any other retained right (including a qualified payment right whose value is not reduced by a corresponding extraordinary payment right) is valued at its fair market value.

For this purpose, a *qualified payment right* is the right to receive a preferred stock dividend or a preferred partnership distribution payable on a periodic basis and at a fixed rate or in a fixed amount. The stock dividend or partnership distribution must be cumulative; that is, any missed payments must be made up. A fixed rate includes a rate that bears a fixed relationship to a specified market rate. If an applicable retained interest is a qualified payment right, its value is determined using traditional valuation methods and not by Code Section 2701. Note that any transferor can elect to treat a payment right that is a qualified payment right as not being a qualified payment right (which would increase the amount of the gift) or, conversely, to have a payment right that is not a qualified payment right treated as a qualified payment right (which would decrease the amount of the gift). [Treas Reg § 25.2701-2(c)(2)]

Step 2. Once Code Section 2701 has been applied to value the applicable retained interest, the value of the transferred interest is measured using a subtraction method of valuation.

First, all the family members' interests in the entity are totaled and valued at fair market value (as if they were held by one individual).

Second, from the entity's value (determined in the first step), subtract the following:

a. The fair market value of all interests that have preferred rights to income or capital (other than an applicable retained interest held by the transferor and applicable family members);

b. The fair market value of any family held equity interests of the same or a subordinate class to the transferred interests held by persons other than the transferor and applicable family members; and

c. The value of any applicable retained interest held by the transferor and applicable family members, as determined under Code Section 2701.

The net amount remaining after these subtractions represents the total value of the transferred interest and all other equity interests of the same class or a class subordinate to the transferred interest (junior interests). To determine the amounts of the transferred interest and junior interests, the value of the junior interests is subtracted from the net amount. The total value of junior interests may not be less than the pro rata portion of 10 percent of the sum of (1) all equity interests in the entity and (2) the total indebtedness owed by the entity to the transferor and any applicable family member. The remaining amount is then allocated to the transferred interest and other junior interests held by the transferor and his or her family. Finally, the amount of the gift is determined by subtracting any discounts, such as minority discounts (see Q 9:27), from the total and reducing this amount further by the consideration paid by the transferee.

Q 9:20 What happens if a qualified payment is not made?

If the retained interest of the transferor or applicable family member includes a qualified payment right that was not valued at zero when the initial transfer occurred and there was a subsequent failure to timely pay the amount due, Code Section 2701(d) requires either an increase in the taxable estate or the taxable gifts of the transferor, depending on the circumstances.

Q 9:21 Does the lapse of rights result in a taxable transfer?

The lapse of a voting right or liquidation right created after October 8, 1990, in a corporation or partnership is treated as a taxable transfer by the holder of the right, if the holder and members of his or her family control the entity before and after the lapse. [IRC § 2704(a)] Such a lapse during the life of the holder will be a gift, and such a lapse upon the death of the holder will be a transfer includible in the holder's gross estate. The amount of the transfer is the difference between (1) the value of all interests in the entity held by the holder of the lapsed right determined as if his or her voting and liquidation rights were nonlapsing and (2) the value of those same interests in the entity immediately after the lapse.

Q 9:22 Does the lapse of a restriction on liquidation result in transfer tax?

No, not if certain conditions are satisfied. The effect of a lapse of a restriction barring liquidation of a closely held corporation (an applicable restriction) on the value of the interest transferred is disregarded if the restriction on liquidation was created after October 8, 1990, and either lapses, in whole or in part, after the transfer to the family member, or, after the transfer, the transferor or any member of his or her family, acting alone or together with other family members, has the right to remove the restriction on liquidation. [IRC § 2704(b)]

Restrictions on liquidation that are imposed by federal or state law, as well as commercially reasonable restrictions that are part of a financing transaction by the corporation or partnership with a person who is not related to the transferor, the transferee, or any family member of either, are not applicable restrictions.

Restrictive Stock Agreements

Q 9:23 What are the primary types of restrictive stock agreements?

The two primary types of restrictive stock agreements are (1) the stock redemption agreement in which the corporation agrees to purchase shares held by a shareholder and (2) the cross-purchase agreement in which other shareholders hold the option or obligation to purchase shares of a shareholder.

Q 9:24 What is the approach of the IRS to restrictive agreements?

The IRS has taken the following position regarding restrictive agreements: where the option or buy and sell agreement is the result of voluntary action by the stockholders and is binding during the life as well as at the death of the stockholders, the agreement may or may not, depending upon the circumstances of each case, fix the value for estate tax purposes. The agreement in any case is a factor to be considered, with other relevant factors, in determining fair market value. If the stockholder is free to dispose of shares during his or her lifetime and the option to purchase those shares becomes effective only upon his or her death, the fair market value is not limited to the option price. [Rev Rul 59-60]

Effective for restrictive agreements entered into or substantially modified after October 8, 1990, Congress has added requirements under the special valuation rules for an agreement to fix the value of a business for estate tax purposes. [IRC §§ 2701 *et seq.*]

Q 9:25 What threshold requirements must a buy/sell agreement meet to fix values for estate tax purposes?

The terms of a buy/sell agreement entered into after October 8, 1990, will fix values for estate tax purposes if the following four requirements are met:

1. The estate of the decedent must have a contractual obligation that is in effect at death to sell the shares. Restrictions that apply only during lifetime are not sufficient;
2. The buy/sell agreement cannot permit the decedent to sell his or her shares at a price during lifetime that is different from the price that governs at death;
3. The price included in the buy/sell agreement must be either fixed or determinable according to a formula; and
4. The buy/sell agreement and the price must not be devices to pass the decedent's interest to the natural objects of his or her

bounty for less than adequate and full consideration in money or money's worth. The agreement must be supported by adequate consideration and may not be a substitute for a testamentary disposition.

[IRC § 2703]

Q 9:26 Can restrictive agreements also fix the value of stock for gift tax purposes?

Generally not. The IRS asserts that restrictive agreements do not conclusively fix the value of stock for gift tax purposes, unless the restrictions apply immediately without action by the donee.

Minority Interests

Q 9:27 What is a minority interest discount?

A minority interest discount is based on a number of factors, including the inability of a minority owner to realize his or her pro rata share of the entity's net assets by liquidating his or her interests in the entity and his or her lack of control over corporate policy. The holders of the controlling shares can, and usually do, elect themselves or members of their families as directors and officers, thus enabling them to draw earnings out of the corporation as salaries and directors' fees and to control corporate policy. For these reasons, shares representing a minority interest in a closely held corporation are not readily marketable, and potential buyers, as a practical matter, may be limited to the group consisting of the controlling shareholders.

In most situations, more than 50 percent of the voting shares is a controlling interest, and less than 50 percent is a minority interest. If state law requires a greater percentage vote for corporate liquidation and liquidation control is considered significant, the higher percentage may be relevant. Similarly, if the corporate charter provides that a higher percentage is required for major corporate decisions, presumably that higher percentage would be necessary to constitute a control block.

Q 9:28 What happens if a noncontrol block is given away by the controlling stockholder with no one thereafter holding a majority of shares?

In *Heppenstall Estate v. Commr* [8 TCM 136 (1949)], the donor-taxpayer owned 2,310 of 4,233 outstanding shares of a closely held corporation and made a gift of 300 shares to each of four family members. As a result, the donor gave up control of the company. The total shares given away were not a controlling interest, however, even when aggregated, and no donee acquired control as a result of the gifts. The Tax Court applied a minority interest discount, adding by way of dictum that each 300-share gift must be valued separately: "In making the gifts [the donor] did lose, or surrender, his control over the Company, but he did not convey that control to any one of the donees or to all of them jointly. The gifts which he made, and which we must value, were of 300 shares of stock each."

In Revenue Ruling 81-253, the IRS espoused a unity of ownership theory and stated it would follow decisions that denied a minority discount in the context of a family controlling interest and would not follow cases such as *Heppenstall* that allowed the discount on similar facts. The IRS revoked Revenue Ruling 81-253 in Revenue Ruling 93-12 and ruled that a minority discount will not be disallowed solely because a transferred interest, when aggregated with interests held by family members, would be a part of a controlling interest.

Q 9:29 What is a control premium?

A *control premium* is an extra amount paid for a controlling interest in a company. It is appropriately asserted by the IRS if a decedent owns a majority interest. The IRS has further attempted to maintain that a control premium exists even when no one has a majority interest, using the *effective control* concept. Notwithstanding language in the regulations that purports to apply a control premium to the effective control of a corporation [Treas Reg §§ 20.2031-2(e), 25.2512-2(e)], the courts have rejected this concept. In *Trust Services of America, Inc. v. United States* [88-1 USTC ¶ 13,767 (SD Cal 1988)], the IRS attempted to apply a control premium to a minority interest that, it argued, constituted effective control of the corporation. The court noted that no previous decisions had "clearly" adopted the concept of a premium for effective control, as opposed to actual numerical control, and observed that premiums generally do not apply simply because the shareholder is a member of a control group.

Q 9:30 Is stock owned by a minority shareholder whose family owns a majority of the corporation's stock valued to include a control premium?

In *Bright Estate v. United States* [658 F 2d 999 (5th Cir 1981)], the Fifth Circuit concluded that the family holdings should not be taken into account when a minority shareholder transferred stock.

Q 9:31 Under what circumstances does a taxpayer want to assert the existence of a control premium?

If a majority interest in a corporation is given to the surviving spouse, the taxpayer may want to assert a control premium to enlarge the marital deduction. [Estate of Chenoweth, 88 TC 1577 (1987)]

Q 9:32 What is the lack of marketability discount?

The lack of marketability discount is based on the principle that, because the shares are not actively traded, an adjustment should be made in per share value. The basis for the discount is that shares that are not publicly held have no readily available market and therefore take longer to sell or may not be salable at all.

Q 9:33 What discounts have been allowed by the courts for minority interests and lack of marketability?

In *Sels v. Commr* [TCM 1986-501], the court discounted the per share book value by 60 percent, representing a combination of the minority interest discount and lack of marketability. In determining discounts, courts consider a number of factors affecting marketability, such as a substantial built-in capital gains tax liability on the investment portfolio, a potential accumulated earnings tax problem, the lack of professional management for the investment portfolio, the prospect that corporate income would not increase dramatically in the future, and the lack of a market for the shares. [Clark v United States, 75-1 USTC ¶ 13,076 (ED NC 1975) (40 percent discount)]

Real Estate

Q 9:34 Why is the valuation of real estate important in estate planning?

Real estate valuation is important in the planning stage so that the taxpayer can obtain the maximum tax advantages from the marital and charitable deductions. Real estate valuation is also important once someone dies in order to determine appropriate value of the decedent's gross estate. Many decisions arrive at a valuation that is in between those in the appraisals used by the taxpayer and by the IRS without really stating how the actual figure was determined. The Tax Court has recently rejected the concept of splitting the difference between the valuations used by the parties and has instead indicated that it will examine the analysis used by each party in determining values. [Buffalo Tool & Die Mfg Co v Commr, 74 TC 441, 452 (1980), *acq* 1982-1 CB 1]

Q 9:35 What happens if there is a dispute over real estate valuation between the IRS and the taxpayer?

The valuation is usually initiated by the taxpayer taking a position regarding the value of the real estate on an income or estate tax return. If that value is adjusted by the IRS after examination, the adjusted value is presumed to be correct, and the burden of proving the return value is correct is on the taxpayer. Even though the taxpayer has the burden of proof and his or her evidence falls short of competent expert proof, such evidence can shift the burden of going forward, however. This means that the taxpayer will prevail if the IRS fails to offer any contradicting evidence. [Byle v Commr, 24 TC 117 (1955)] Code Section 2512(c) provides that an individual has the right to obtain, upon request, a statement regarding any valuation made by the IRS pursuant to Code Section 7517. That section states that if the secretary makes a determination or proposed determination of the value of any real estate, for purposes of estate gift or generation skipping tax, the executor donor or person required to make the return can request a statement no later than 45 days after the later of the date of the request or the date of the determination. The contents of the statement must conform with Code Section 7517(b), which requires a statement of the basis on which the valuation was determined, the method of computation, and any expert appraisal made by or for the IRS.

Q 9:36 What is the definition of fair market value for real estate valuation purposes?

Fair market value is defined as the price at which property would change hands between a willing buyer and a willing seller, neither of whom is under any compulsion to buy or sell and both having reasonable knowledge of the relevant facts. [Treas Reg §§ 20.2031-1(b), 25.2512-1]

Q 9:37 Can local appraised values be used in determining fair market value of real estate?

The assessed value for local real estate tax purposes is not used unless it is regarded by the IRS as the fair market value of the real property. [Treas Reg § 20.2031-a(b)]

Q 9:38 Do any special valuation methods apply to real estate or closely held business property?

Executors may elect to value certain real estate under a special valuation method that produces a lower value for federal estate tax purposes. Rather than being valued at its highest and best use, real estate used in farming or in a closely held business is valued on the basis of its use as a farm or as a closely held business. A special valuation method cannot be used to reduce the decedent's gross estate by more than $750,000, however. The special valuation method must be elected, and the election is limited to estates of decedents who are U.S. citizens or residents at death. [IRC § 2032A]

Q 9:39 What are the qualification requirements for using the Section 2032A special valuation for real estate?

The following requirements must be satisfied for the real estate to be valued under Code Section 2032A:

1. The real estate must be located in the United States.
2. The real estate must have been acquired from or passed from a decedent to a qualified heir.
3. The real estate must have been put to a qualified use by the decedent or a member of the decedent's family. The pre-death qualified use requirement is met if the property was either used for farming purposes or used in a trade or business other than the trade or business of farming for an aggregate of five years during the eight-year period ending on the date of the decedent's death.
4. The decedent or a member of his or her family must have materially participated in the trade or business for five or more of the eight years before the decedent's death.
5. A 50 percent and 25 percent test must be met.

The 50 percent test is met if the adjusted value of the real estate that was acquired from the decedent and used for a qualified use is at least 50 percent of the adjusted value of the gross estate. [IRC § 2032A(b)(1)(A)] The 25 percent test is met if the adjusted value of the real estate that was acquired from the decedent satisfies the qualified use of material participation test and equals at least 25 percent of the adjusted value of the gross estate. [IRC § 2032(A)(b)(1)(B)]

The election to use the special valuation of Code Section 2032A must be made on the decedent's estate tax return.

Q 9:40 Who are qualified heirs for purposes of the special valuation tests?

Qualified heirs are members of the decedent's family who acquired property from the decedent. They may include the following:

1. Ancestors of an individual; and
2. The individual's spouse;

Valuation of Business Interests and Other Property   Q 9:42

3. Lineal descendants of the individual;
4. A spouse of a lineal descendant of the individual; and
5. Legally adopted children of an individual who are treated as related by blood. [IRC § 2032A(e)(2)]

Q 9:41 Does the special valuation apply to indirect ownership interests?

Yes, a special valuation does apply to real estate owned by a partnership or corporation in which the decedent has an interest. [IRC § 20.2032A-3(b)] The special use valuation applies to real property owned in this manner if any of the following ownership tests are met:

1. The decedent is a proprietor in a trade or business carried on as a proprietorship;
2. The decedent is a partner in a partnership carrying on a trade or business if 20 percent or more of the partnership's capital interest is included in the decedent's gross estate or if the partnership had 15 or fewer partners; or
3. The decedent holds stock in a corporation carrying on a trade or business if 20 percent or more of the corporation's voting stock is included in the gross estate or the corporation had 15 or fewer shareholders.

Interest in a trust carrying on a trade or business will meet the ownership qualification if the decedent's beneficial interest in the trust is 20 percent or more of the value of all beneficiary interest in the trust. [Treas Reg §§ 20.2032A-3(d), 6166(b)(1)(C)]

Q 9:42 Are tax benefits under Code Section 2032A(c)(1) subject to recapture?

Yes, all or a portion of the estate tax benefits from using Code Section 2032A in valuing real property for estate tax purposes will be recaptured if, within ten years after the decedent's death (but before the qualified heir's death), the real estate is disposed of to outsiders or, during any eight-year period after the decedent's death, there is an aggregate period of three years or more during which there is no

9-23

material participation in the operation of the farm or business by a qualified heir. [IRC § 2032A(c)(1)]

Penalties for Improper Valuation

Q 9:43 What penalties apply if a valuation is improper?

The penalties applying to an estate or gift tax return that understates the value of any property are as follows:

1. Code Section 6662(g) imposes a penalty for substantial underpayment if the value claimed on the estate or gift tax return is 50 percent or less of the amount determined to be the correct valuation. The penalty for substantial understatement imposed under Code Section 6662(a) is at a rate of 20 percent of the portion of the underpayment attributable to the undervaluation. Under Code Section 6662(g)(2), the penalty applies only if the underpayment exceeds $5,000 for the taxable period (or for the decedent's estate).

2. Code Section 6662(h)(1) doubles the penalty to 40 percent of the tax attributable to the undervaluation for gross valuation misstatements (i.e., valuations that are 25 percent or less of the amount determined to be correct).

Code Section 6664(c)(1) provides that penalties will not apply if there is reasonable cause for the underpayment and the taxpayer acted in good faith with respect to the underpayment.

Chapter 10

Charitable Contributions

The tax laws provide significant income tax and estate planning incentives designed to encourage both those who are charitably motivated and those who would not otherwise consider the role played by charitable giving in their estate planning.

Income Tax Deduction for Charitable Contributions	10-1
Charitable Organizations	10-9
Estate and Gift Tax Deductions	10-11
Gifts	10-11
Bequests	10-11
Charitable Trusts	10-13

Income Tax Deduction for Charitable Contributions

Q 10:1 Is there an income tax deduction for charitable gift giving?

Yes, an individual who makes cash gifts to a public charity can deduct up to 50 percent of his or her adjusted gross income (excluding any net operating loss carryback). This is known as the individual's *contribution base*. [IRC § 170(b)(1)]

Example 10-1: A physician who is a sole practitioner has an adjusted gross income of $180,000, including a $10,000 deduction for a net operating loss carryback. Because the physician has a net operating loss carryback, the contribution base is increased by

$10,000 and consequently, the physician can donate up to $95,000 to a public charity.

Q 10:2 What are the elements of a deductible charitable contribution?

In order to take an income tax deduction, there must be a voluntary transfer of money or property to an acceptable recipient (donee) without receipt by the donor of any return consideration. [IRC § 170]

Q 10:3 Must the transfer consist of a present interest in money or property?

Yes, the transfer must consist of a present interest in money or property. The transfer of an unsecured promissory note, for example, would be considered a promise to pay at a future date because most states consider such an instrument unenforceable unless the recipient relies on the note to his or her detriment. [Rev Rul 68-174, 1968-1 CB 81] Consequently, the transfer of an unsecured promissory note to a charity does not result in a deduction at the time of the transfer, but rather, when the note is paid. A similar rule is enforced with respect to pledges, making them not deductible until payment is actually rendered. [Treas Reg § 1.170A-1(a)]

Q 10:4 Does transfer of a partial interest in property qualify for a charitable deduction?

Generally no, the donor must part with complete *dominion and control* over the property transferred. [See Pauley v United States, 459 F 2d 624 (9th Cir 1972)] If the donor retains any *incidents of ownership* in the property, he or she will not be able to claim a Code Section 170 deduction. For example, the transfer of an undivided interest in property, such as a tenant-in-common, would qualify for the charitable deduction. [Treas Reg § 1.170A-7] Similarly, the contribution of a life insurance policy to a charity qualifies for a charitable deduction if the donor irrevocably surrenders all rights of ownership in the policy. If the donor continues to pay premiums on the policy after the transfer, he or she is allowed a deduction for the value of each premium payment as it is made. [See Hunton v Comm, 1 TC 821 (1943), *acq* 1943 CB 12] It is essential for the donor to consult state law before making such a transfer, however, because the IRS issued a private letter ruling suggesting that deductions for premium payments made subsequent to transfer may be disallowed where the transfer violates state insurance law. [Ltr Rul 9110016]

In contrast, the contribution of a partial interest in property will qualify for the charitable deduction if it consists of the donor's entire interest in the property. [Treas Reg § 1.170A-7(a)(2)(i)] For example, if the donor's entire interest in property is a life estate or remainder, that interest can be contributed to a charity and will result in a deduction.

Q 10:5 Does a donation of the taxpayer's services qualify for a charitable contribution deduction?

No, a deduction is not allowed for a taxpayer's performance of services on behalf of a charity. [Treas Reg § 1.170A-1(g)] For example, a taxpayer was not allowed a charitable contribution deduction for the value of uncompensated legal services performed for a charity. [Grant v Comm, 84 TC 809 (1985), *aff'd in unpublished opinion*, 800 F 2d 260 (4th Cir 1986)]

Q 10:6 Can the donor restrict the charitable contribution to a certain class of beneficiaries?

Yes, as long as the class of beneficiaries is not so small as to make the charity's purpose appear private rather than public. For example, a deduction was denied in a case in which a corporation gave money to a foundation established to provide funds for the education of the corporation's employees and their children. The court disallowed the deduction because the foundation's entire benefits went to four employees' children, and 30 percent of the benefits were paid to the son of the corporation's president. [Charleston Chair Co v United States, 203 F Supp 126 (EDSC 1962)]

In contrast, a charitable deduction was allowed in a case in which several companies contributed money to a foundation that they created to select and award scholarships to their employees. The court reasoned that the group of persons benefited was sufficiently broad based. [Chase v Comm, 19 TCM 234 (1960)] Similarly, deductions have been allowed to a foundation that awards scholarships solely to undergraduate members of a specified college fraternity. [Rev Rul 56-403, 1956-2 CB 307]

Q 10:7 Can a donor retain control to determine which individuals will receive the benefits from the donor's contribution?

Yes, the donor (or the donor's family members) can retain ultimate control over which individuals will receive the benefits resulting from the donor's contribution without jeopardizing the charitable deduction. [Hunton v Comm, 1 TC 821 (1943) *acq*, 1943 CB 12]

Q 10:8 Are tuition payments to tax-exempt private or parochial schools charitable contributions?

No, tuition expenses do not qualify for a charitable contribution deduction because the taxpayer receives a benefit as a result of his or her contribution in the form of education. Thus, tuition and school-related expenses paid to a parochial school for a child's education do not qualify for the charitable deduction. [McLaughlin v Comm, 69-2 USTC 9467 (1st Cir 1969)] Revenue Ruling 83-104 provides a number of factors to consider when determining if payments should be classified as tuition or charitable contributions. A parent's payment to a child's school will be treated as a charitable deduction only if: (1) the child could have attended the school without the parent's payment; (2) the payment was not part of an express or implied plan between the parent and the charity to allow the parent a charitable contribution deduction; (3) the child's receipt of educational services was not otherwise dependent on the parent's payment. [Rev Rul 83-104, 1983-2 CB 46, *superseding* Rev Rul 79-99, 1979-1 CB 108]

Q 10:9 For purposes of tax-deductible contributions, how does the Code define *charitable organizations*?

Public charities include such entities as churches, hospitals, and schools. [IRC § 170(b)] Some private foundations (referred to as *private operating foundations*) (see Q 10:19) and private distributing foundations (see Q 10:20) are treated as public charities for purposes of the contribution deduction, but generally donations to private foundations are subject to the special rule described in Q 10:10. [IRC § 508(d)]

Q 10:10 What is the income tax deduction for gifts to private foundations?

Cash contributions to private operating foundations (generally foundations that are actively engaged in charitable activities) are eligible for the 50 percent deduction limit. [IRC § 170(b)] Cash contributions to other private foundations are limited to 30 percent of the donor's contribution base.

Q 10:11 What limits apply if an individual makes contributions to both a public charity and a private foundation?

An individual's total deduction cannot exceed 50 percent of his contribution base. Gifts made to public charities are deducted first, and if these equal or exceed 50 percent of the individual's contribution base, no further deduction is available. If the gifts made to public charities do not equal 50 percent of the individual's contribution base, the individual can take a deduction for gifts to private foundations up to the 30 percent limit until the 50 percent limit is reached.

Example 10-2: An individual's contribution base is $100,000. She makes a gift of $30,000 to a public charity and a gift of $40,000 to a private foundation. The entire $30,000 gift to the public charity is deductible, and $20,000 of the gift to the private foundation is deductible.

Q 10:12 What happens if contributions to charity exceed the 50 percent limit?

An individual whose cash contributions to public charities exceed the 50 percent contribution limit can carry forward the excess contributions and treat them as contributions in each of the five succeeding years. In other words, if the individual makes a contribution to a public charity in 1990 that exceeds the 50 percent contribution limit, the individual can report a percentage of the excess in 1991, 1992, 1993, 1994, and 1995. [IRC § 170(d)] Excess contributions of long-term capital gain property (discussed below) may also be carried forward to each of the five succeeding taxable years. [IRC § 170(b)]

Q 10:13   Estate and Retirement Planning Answer Book

Q 10:13   What deduction is available for gifts of noncash property?

The amount of the deduction for gifts of noncash property depends upon whether the property has appreciated in value since the donor first obtained it. The treatment of appreciated and nonappreciated property is as follows:

Nonappreciated property. The donee may deduct the fair market value of gifts of noncash property.

Appreciated property. If the appreciated property is ordinary income property (i.e., would generate ordinary income if sold), the taxpayer may deduct only his or her own basis in the property. If the appreciated property is long-term capital gain property (i.e., would generate long-term capital gains if sold) and is given to a private foundation, the deduction is equal to the taxpayer's basis in the property. In some cases, however, the fair market value of gifts of stock to private foundations is deductible. The 50 percent and 30 percent deduction limits set forth in Q 10:11 apply. The fair market value of long-term capital gain property contributed to a public charity is generally deductible, but the applicable deduction limit is 30 percent rather than 50 percent of the contribution base. The taxpayer can, however, make a special election that permits the use of the 50 percent ceiling, but the consequence of making the special election is that only the taxpayer's basis in the property will be deductible. [IRC § 170(b)(1)]

Q 10:14   Does the donor recognize gain if appreciated property is contributed to a charity?

Gain is generally not recognized on charitable contributions of appreciated property. This general rule does not apply, however, for bargain sales and when the charity sells the property shortly after the transfer. [IRC § 1011(b); Rev Rul 60-370]

A bargain sale occurs when property is sold to a charity for less than its fair market value. The donor can take a charitable deduction for part of the value, but is taxed on part of the gain that occurs on the sale. [IRC § 1011(b)]

Example 10-3: A donor sells property with a fair market value of $10,000 to a church for $2,000. The donor's adjusted basis in the property is $4,000. The donor is treated as having made a deductible contribution to the charity of $8,000 ($10,000 fair market value − $2,000 purchase price). The $2,000 that the donor received from the charity is treated as part of a sale of a portion of the property. Section 1011(b) requires the donor to calculate a separate adjusted basis for determining gain on the sale, which in this case is $800 ($2,000 purchase price divided by $10,000 fair market value multiplied by $4,000 adjusted basis). The donor's gain on the transaction is $1,200 ($2,000 received from the charity − $800 of Section 1011(b) adjusted basis).

The second exception occurs when the charity sells the property shortly after the transfer, and it is determined that the sale was part of an overall plan between the charity and the donor. In this situation, the donor is treated as having sold the property for cash (and realizing and recognizing gain on this transaction) and then donating the cash from the sale to the charity. [Rev Rul 60-370]

Example 10-4: A donor gives watercolors in which she has a basis of $10,000 to a charity. Shortly thereafter, the charity sells the watercolors for $20,000. If it is determined that the sale was part of an overall plan between the charity and the donor, the donor will be treated as having sold the watercolors and will be taxed on the $10,000 gain from the transaction. Her charitable deduction will be calculated as if she had donated $20,000 in cash to the charity.

Q 10:15 What deduction is available for gifts of encumbered property?

A gratuitous transfer of encumbered property is treated as a sale or exchange in which the donor receives consideration equal to the value of the indebtedness transferred. [Treas Reg § 1.1011-2(a)(3)] In other words, it is treated as a bargain sale (see Q 10:14). This rule applies even if the indebtedness is nonrecourse or the charity does not agree to assume the indebtedness.

Example 10-5: A businessman contributed property, which had a fair market value of $25,000, an adjusted basis of $15,000, and was subject to a $10,000 mortgage, to a church. The contribution is treated like a bargain sale of the property to the church for $10,000 (the amount of the indebtedness). The portion of the transfer treated as a gift is $15,000 ($25,000 fair market value – $10,000 indebtedness (which is treated as consideration received)). The portion of the adjusted basis that determines the businessman's gain on the sale part of the transfer is $6,000 ($10,000 amount realized divided by $25,000 fair market value multiplied by $15,000 total adjusted basis). The businessman must thus recognize $4,000 of gain on the transfer ($10,000 amount realized – $6,000 adjusted basis for determining gain). [IRC § 1011(b)]

Q 10:16 What substantiation requirements are necessary to obtain the deduction?

For charitable contributions of $250 or more made after December 31, 1993, no deduction is available unless the taxpayer substantiates the contribution by a contemporaneous written acknowledgment of the contribution from the donee organization. [IRC § 170(f)(8)] The written acknowledgment must include the following information:

1. The amount of cash contributed and a description (but not the value) of property contributed.
2. A verification of whether or not the charity provided any goods or services as consideration for the contribution.
3. If the charity did provide goods or services, a description of the goods or services and an estimate of their fair market value.

Substantiation is not required if the donee organization files a return with the IRS reporting the information that has to be included in the written acknowledgment. [Treas Reg § 1.170A-13]

Q 10:17 When may penalties be assessed against a donor?

A donor who overvalues property for purposes of the charitable contribution deduction may be subject to an accuracy-related penalty or a fraud penalty. An accuracy-related penalty will be imposed if the donor underpays taxes based on (1) negligence or disregard of the rules; (2) any substantial understatement of income tax; or (3) any substantial valuation overstatement. [IRC § 6662(b)] A *substantial understatement* occurs if the understatement of tax is larger than the greater of (1) 10 percent of the tax that should have been properly paid, or (2) $5,000. A *substantial overstatement* occurs if the value of the property is 200 percent or more of the correct valuation. This penalty does not apply, however, unless the overstatement exceeds $5,000.

Further, if the IRS determines that any part of the underpayment is due to fraud, it will impose a penalty equal to 75 percent of the portion of the underpayment that is attributable to fraud. [IRC § 6663(a)] Interest is also payable on amounts determined under both of these penalties and runs from the date on which the tax return to which the penalty relates was due until the date the penalty is paid. [IRC § 6601(a)] In contrast to past years, the rate of interest is substantial; it is equal to the federal short-term rate plus three percentage points for underpayments. [IRC § 6621(a)(2)]

Charitable Organizations

Q 10:18   Which charities qualify for the 50 percent deduction?

Code Section 170(b)(1)(A) sets forth a list of institutions that qualify for the 50 percent deduction. This list includes public charities including but not limited to nonprofit schools, hospitals, churches, and charities receiving substantial public support.

Q 10:19   What is a private operating foundation?

A private operating foundation is a private foundation that has some of the advantages of a public charity. A private operating foundation may qualify for the 50 percent deduction of Code Section 170(b)(1) if it is actively engaged in a charitable purpose. That is to say that the activity may not be passive, such as making grants. [IRC § 4942]

Q 10:20   What is a private distributing foundation?

A private distributing foundation is an organization that distributes all of the funds it receives as contributions to public charities within 2½ months after the close of the year the gifts were made. This type of organization also qualifies for the 50 percent deduction of Code Section 170(b)(1). [IRC § 170(b)(1)(D)]

Q 10:21 What is the tax advantage of giving long-term capital gain property to a public charity?

As long as the property is related in use to the charitable purpose of the organization to which it was donated, the donor may deduct the full fair market value while avoiding capital gain treatment. [IRC § 170(e)(1)(B)]

Example 10-6: An individual purchases chairs, the value of which was $200 when purchased, but has now appreciated to $2,000. The individual sells these chairs and gives the proceeds to charity. The individual will receive the $2,000 deduction, but will also be taxed on $1,800 in capital gain. If that individual had contributed these chairs directly to the charity and the charity used the chairs for the period specified in Code Section 170, the taxpayer would not only avoid the $1,800 capital gain tax, but would still be entitled to the $2,000 deduction.

Q 10:22 What are the tax effects if an individual sells his long-term capital gain property to a charity at less than fair market value?

According to Code Section 1011(b), the individual may unexpectedly receive a gain, even if the sales price does not exceed the individual's basis. This rule treats the taxpayer as selling one portion of the property and contributing the remainder of the property to charity. To compute a taxpayer's gain, divide the sale proceeds by the fair market value of the property; then multipy that fraction by the taxpayer's cost, subtracting this net figure from the proceeds to determine the taxable gain.

Example 10-7: Assume the taxpayer purchased an asset for $200, which is now worth $800. The taxpayer wishes to make a contribution to charity, but would also like to recoup his initial investment of $200, so he decides to sell the asset to the charity for $200. The taxable gain is computed as follows:

Sale proceeds divided by fair market value: $\frac{$200}{$800}$ =		25%
Adjusted cost (25% × $200):		$ 50
Proceeds		$200
Less adjusted cost		$ 50
Taxable gain		$150

The taxpayer's deductible charitable contribution is $600 (i.e., 75% × $800).

Q 10:23 May an individual contribute a life insurance policy to a public charity?

Yes. Usually the value of the policy at the date of the contribution is the figure used for the deduction. If the value of the policy exceeds the premiums paid, the taxpayer will need to be aware that there may be ordinary or capital gain ramifications as set forth above. If the contributor continues to pay the premiums after the policy is transferred, these premiums will be deductible as a charitable contribution. [IRC § 170]

Estate and Gift Tax Deductions

Gifts

Q 10:24 What are the gift tax ramifications for contributions to a public charity?

If the amount of the gift exceeds the annual exclusion, the taxpayer must file a gift tax return in accordance with Code Section 6019; however, there is no limitation to the estate tax deduction for qualifying charities. [IRC § 2522]

Q 10:25 What is the advantage of donating assets to a charity during the individual's lifetime as opposed to devising them to a charity in a will?

Where an individual donates property to charity during his or her lifetime, the donor receives a deduction on his or her income tax return. This deduction is not available to the estate. [IRC § 2055]

Bequests

Q 10:26 For purposes of determining the estate tax imposed by Code Section 2001, are charitable devises subtracted from the value of the gross estate?

Yes. To determine the taxable estate subject to the estate tax imposed by Code Section 2001, the value of the gross estate is reduced by "the amount of all bequests, legacies, devises, or transfers— . . . to or for the use of any corporation organized and operated exclusively for religious, charitable, scientific, literary, or educational purposes. . . ." [IRC § 2055(a)(2)]

The amount of the deduction is the fair market value of property transferred to the charity. [IRC § 2055(d)]

Q 10:27 Are transfers to charities resulting from disclaimers deductible?

Yes. Transfers to a charity resulting from an irrevocable disclaimer by the named beneficiary are deductible. [IRC § 2055]

Q 10:28 Can the amount of charitable deductions exceed the value of the property included in the gross estate?

No. The amount of the charitable deduction allowable for any transfer cannot exceed the value of the transferred property that is required to be included in the gross estate. [IRC § 2055(d)]

Q 10:29 Can estate taxes imposed by Code Section 2001 be paid out of charitable bequests?

If the terms of the will, the law of the jurisdiction in which the estate is administered, or the law of the jurisdiction imposing the estate tax provide that the estate tax is payable in whole or in part out of the charitable bequests, legacies, or devises deductible under Code Section 2055, the amount of such charitable bequests, legacies, or devices shall be reduced by the amount of such taxes. [IRC § 2055(c)]

Q 10:30 Are devises to a trustee or trustees or a fraternal order deductible from the gross estate when determining the value of the taxable estate subject to the estate tax of Code Section 2001?

Maybe. Devises "to a trustee or trustees, or a fraternal society, order, or association operating under a lodge system" are deductible from the gross estate when determining the value of the taxable estate if (1) the gifts or contributions are to be used exclusively for charitable purposes, (2) the trust or fraternal order is not disqualified for tax exemption under Code Section 501 for attempting to influence legislation, and (3) such trust, trustees, or fraternal order does not participate or intervene in any political campaign on behalf of, or in opposition to, any candidate for public office. [IRC § 2055(a)(3)]

Q 10:31 Are charitable deductions from estate taxes disallowed for certain transfers?

Yes. No charitable deduction from estate taxes is allowable for transfers to or for the use of a trust or organization described in and subject to the conditions of Code Section 508(d) (i.e., terminating private foundations) or 4948(c)(4) (i.e., foreign organizations engaged in prohibited transactions). [IRC § 2055(e)(1)]

As a general rule, when an interest in property is transferred from the decedent to a qualified charity for a qualified charitable use and an interest in the same property passes or has passed for less than adequate and full monetary consideration from the decedent to a noncharitable person or for a noncharitable use, no charitable deduction is allowed for the interest. [IRC § 2055(e)(2)]

The rule does not apply if:

1. The interest for which inadequate consideration is given is extinguished at the donor's death.
2. The interest given is a remainder interest in a personal residence or farm, the contribution of an undivided portion of the taxpayer's entire interest in property, or a qualifed conservation easement.
3. The interest given to the charity is a charitable remainder annuity trust, or a charitable remainder unitrust, or a pooled income fund.
4. The interest is in the form of a guaranteed annuity or is a fixed percentage distributed yearly of the fair market value of the property (to be determined yearly). [IRC § 2055(e)(2)]

Charitable Trusts

Q 10:32 Why do charitable trusts figure so prominently in estate planning?

The charitable trust has become a valuable estate planning tool among practitioners because it lends itself to a combination of tax-saving strategies through the interaction of an income tax deduction with the estate and gift tax deduction. It is not necessary to be charitably motivated to enjoy the tax benefits from a charitable trust; a charitable trust creates increased overall tax savings regardless of a donor's philanthropic intentions.

Q 10:33 How do tax-saving strategies interact in a charitable trust?

In Code Sections 2702, 663, and 664 Congress provided opportunities allowing a taxpayer to create a split-interest trust for the benefit of a charity, either as an income beneficiary or remainderman, while also permitting a private beneficiary (i.e., spouse, children, or even the settlor himself) to enjoy the benefit of such trust in either of those capacities.

For example, if a taxpayer creates a so-called charitable remainder annuity trust, he can reserve an annuity to himself for life or for a period of no more than 20 years, at the end of which a charity receives the balance in trust. If structured properly, the taxpayer obtains an immediate income deduction (subject to the percentage limitations of adjusted gross income), an unlimited gift tax deduction (no gift for a reserved interest to the taxpayer himself and a 100 percent charitable gift tax deduction), and a 100 percent charitable estate tax deduction for the transfer to charitable organizations upon the settlor's death for the fair market value of the trust property.

The reverse can achieve similar tax-saving results. If a so-called charitable lead trust is structured properly naming a charitable organization as the income beneficiary and a private person as the remainderman, the taxpayer receives an immediate income tax deduction for the value of the income interest in trust given to a charitable organization; this deduction can fund the gift tax, if any, thereby permitting a tax-free gift to the private beneficiary.

Q 10:34 What is a charitable trust?

A charitable trust is established to benefit a particular charity or charities either as current annuity beneficiaries (*charitable lead* trust) or as remainder beneficiaries (*charitable remainder* trust). There is also another kind of funding organization called a charitable pool fund that provides similar tax benefits but, unlike either the charitable lead or charitable remainder trust, the donor can have no control over the investments made by the trustee or the designation of the beneficiary.

Practice Pointer: Most pool funds are established by universities or medical research organizations, so that the donors generally know when they contribute who the ultimate beneficiary of their contribution will be.

Q 10:35 How does a charitable trust differ from a charitable foundation?

As indicated above, a charitable trust is essentially a funding medium for a donor that allows him or her, through a trust, to fund charities while at the same time providing for private beneficiaries.

A charitable foundation, which can be either a corporation or a trust, is generally a private organization established by a family to accomplish charitable goals. The foundation allows the family and other interested parties to make contributions, gifts, and bequests, which the foundation will then distribute to public charities. Many family foundations are created to perpetuate the family name in a charitable setting while simultaneously acting as a conduit for charitable distributions to be made to the ultimate public charitable beneficiaries. Private operating foundations differ from charitable foundations in that instead of merely collecting and distributing for charitable activities, they conduct charitable activities of their own. A foundation, properly organized and operated, is exempt from federal income tax as an organization described in Code Section 501(c)(3) and gifts and bequests made to it are deductible under Code Sections 2522 and 2055, respectively.

Practice Pointer: Foundations, as noted above, do not have to be created as corporations but can, in fact, be established as trusts.

Q 10:36 What are the rules for determining the nature and extent of a charitable contribution deduction for income, gift, and estate tax purposes?

An individual donor must make a contribution to a *charitable organization*—not to a particular individual—in order to claim a charitable deduction; however, a charitable foundation receiving contributions can make distributions to individuals as long as such distributions are governed by charitable criteria (e.g., a scholarship program based on merit and need). [Rev Rul 56-304]

Practice Pointer: There is an anomaly concerning the charitable income, gift, and estate tax deductions in the treatment of gifts to foreign charities. Code Section 170(c) requires that a donee charity be *created or organized* in the United States or any of its possessions, whereas gift and estate tax deductions allowed under Code Sections 2522 and 2055, respectively, have no such restriction and do allow deductions to foreign charitable organizations.

For income tax purposes, contributions of cash and/or property are limited to a percentage of gross income; whereas the charitable deduction for gift and estate tax purposes is unlimited. The ceiling limitations for income tax purposes are 20 percent, 30 percent or 50 percent of adjusted gross income; the particular ceiling depends on the type of property contributed and the type of donee organization. Also, if the amount of the charitable contribution exceeds any of the percentage ceilings, it may be carried forward, until exhausted, for five years. Cash contributions made to public charities and certain private operating foundations are eligible for the 50 percent limitation. Cash contributions to private nonoperating foundations are limited to the 30 percent limitation. Appreciated property contributions to public charities are limited to the 30 percent ceiling (unless the property has not appreciated) and to the 20 percent ceiling if the donee organization is a private nonoperating foundation.

Practice Pointer: Until 1993, charitable contributions of appreciated property created a tax preference to the extent of the appreciation in value and such appreciation would have entered into the calculation of the alternative minimum tax: a tax designed to ensure that income otherwise favored in determining income tax is subject to a minimum tax rate starting at 26 percent. Beginning in 1993, however, the appreciation is not considered a tax preference item subject to the alternative minimum tax.

Q 10:37 If contributions made to a charitable lead trust or charitable remainder trust are not made directly to the charity, how is the charitable contribution calculated?

The IRS has valuation tables under Code Section 7520 that provide factors that rely on the monthly discount rate to determine the valuation of a contribution. The IRS has two publications that are essential for every tax practitioner's library: IRS Publications 1457 and 1458. These publications contain valuation tables at the various discount rates determined under Code Section 7520 for valuing annuities and term of years and remainder interests.

Q 10:38   What is a charitable remainder trust?

A charitable remainder trust is an irrevocable trust that holds and invests assets for the benefit of at least one noncharitable income beneficiary and for one or more charitable remaindermen. Because the property held by the trust (its corpus) is destined to benefit one or more charities when the trust terminates, transactions involving capital gain or loss on the sale of trust property are generally nontaxable. Accordingly, a charitable remainder trust may sell or resell trust property without the imposition of a capital gains tax.

Q 10:39   What forms of charitable remainder trusts are recognized under the Internal Revenue Code?

There are two forms of charitable remainder trusts recognized under Code Section 2702: (1) the charitable remainder annuity trust and (2) the charitable remainder unitrust (hereinafter referred to as CRAT or CRUT, respectively. Their recognition under the Code allows the grantors of such trusts to receive a charitable deduction for the value of the charitable remainder interest on their income tax returns, subject to the income tax percentage limitations. The estate of the grantor also obtains an unlimited charitable deduction for estate tax purposes equal to the value of the trust includible in the grantor's gross estate, as a result of the grantor's reserving an annuity interest in the trust at the time of his death.

Q 10:40   What is the difference between a charitable remainder annuity trust and a charitable remainder unitrust?

The CRAT and CRUT are similar in many ways but are dissimilar in one significant factor: the annuity valuation base. Both trusts are required under Code Sections 664 and 663, respectively, and Treasury Regulations Sections 1.664-2(a)(2)(i) and 1.664-3(a)(2)(i) to make an annual payment to all beneficiaries in an amount of not less than 5 percent of their annuity base or unitrust base.

Q 10:40   **Estate and Retirement Planning Answer Book**

The annuity base is constant for the CRAT and is determined by the fair market value of the donated corpus at the time of the beginning of the CRAT's existence. Accordingly, a CRAT created with a $100,000 corpus, which under its terms is to provide a 5 percent annual annuity to its private beneficiaries for a period of ten years, must pay an annual amount of $5,000.

The annuity base for the CRUT is not constant but is determined by the fair market value of the CRUT's assets on the first day of its tax year. Accordingly, a 5 percent annuity in a CRUT that has a fair market value on the first day of each of its three succeeding years of $100,000, $110,000, and $120,000, respectively, would require annuity amounts to be paid to the private beneficiary of $5,000, $5,500, and $6,000 in each of the succeeding years, respectively.

The CRAT is the more conservative of the two since the amount of the annual annuity payments is known and fixed. The CRUT, on the other hand, is market sensitive, so that the annual annuity amounts may increase or decrease due to changes in the fair market value of the trust's corpus. The CRUT can be more expensive to maintain since it requires an appraisal of corpus as of the first day of each year.

Q 10:41   **How does a donor benefit from creating a charitable remainder trust?**

Through a charitable remainder trust, a donor can receive numerous tax benefits in addition to the satisfaction afforded by charitable giving. The benefits include an immediate income tax deduction in the year in which the trust is created, thereby reducing the cost of the gift and allowing cash availability to pay gift tax for the interests given to the private beneficiary(ies). The donor's estate tax will be reduced and the possibility exists that the removal from the donor's estate of the trust corpus will place the estate in a lower estate tax bracket.

A charitable remainder trust is the most economical method for making gifts to charity and should be considered even if the client is not charitably motivated. It allows an individual to transfer assets, retain or provide income for himself or herself or some other private person for the period of the trust, and retain unused income without incurring any estate tax. The donor can serve as his or her own trustee during his or her lifetime and retain the right to change ultimate charitable beneficiaries on death. The charitable remainder trust can be used to augment or supplant qualified deferred compensation arrangements. Further, the charitable remainder trust can be utilized to diversify a portfolio and avoid the capital gains tax.

Q 10:42 Is a charitable remainder trust exempt from federal income tax?

Yes. Code Section 664(c) exempts a charitable remainder trust from income tax. As a result, a charitable remainder annuity trust can therefore convert appreciated property into an annual payout based on the entire value of the property without diminution by federal and state income taxes. If the trust sells assets given to it by the grantor and reinvests the proceeds in tax-exempt bonds, the beneficiary will receive tax-exempt distributions (after first receiving any recognized capital gains on the trust's sales).

Practice Pointer: Revenue Ruling 60-370, 1960-2 CB 203 holds that a charitable remainder trust's sale of assets and reinvestment in tax-exempt bonds was held to be pursuant to an agreement with the grantor and was taxed on all of the capital gain immediately, as if he had first sold the assets and then contributed the proceeds of the sale.

Q 10:43 What are the factors to consider in choosing between a charitable remainder annuity trust and a charitable remainder unitrust?

There are a number of factors one must review before deciding on which to select. They are as follows:

- The amount of the income tax deduction is based upon the Code Section 7520 rate. This rate fluctuates monthly. The taxpayer is permitted to use the rate that is for the month of transfer, or the rate of any of the preceding two months.

- In the case of the CRAT (fixed payments), as the IRS rate increases, the value of the fixed annuity for the private beneficiary decreases. Therefore, the charitable annuity amount also increases.

- As the IRS rate decreases, the value of the annuity increases, and the charitable deduction decreases.
- In the case of the CRUT, the payout fluctuates each year based upon the changing market value of the underlying trust assets. Thus, changes in the Code Section 7520 rate will not affect the deduction materially. Therefore, when rates are falling, the use of a CRUT will result in a larger charitable income tax deduction than the use of a CRAT. Further, a CRUT, unlike a CRAT, can accept additional amounts and is also permitted to pay the lesser of the unitrust amount or the net income of the trust to the income beneficiary. This will provide significant planning opportunities. The unitrust may, but need not, provide for makeup of deficiencies. The CRUT is an inflation hedge; however it results in risk in a falling market.

Q 10:44 What types of assets should be used in funding a charitable remainder annuity trust or charitable remainder unitrust?

In the case of a CRUT, it is preferable to utilize nonliquid assets, such as vacant land. In the case of a makeup CRUT, if there is no accounting income, then there is nothing to be paid out currently. On the other hand, if vacant land were used to fund a CRAT, the payout would be a problem because the annual annuity amount would be required to be paid, notwithstanding the lack of income. Therefore, liquid assets, such as cash, stocks, and bonds should fund the corpus of a CRAT. No makeup provisions are allowed in the case of a CRAT.

Q 10:45 What are the tax consequences to a grantor in creating a charitable remainder annuity trust or charitable remainder unitrust?

Income taxes. There is an immediate income tax deduction produced for the present value of the remainder interest passing to charity subject to the percentage limitations measured by adjusted gross income. The appreciation element of the assets contributed to a charitable remainder trust is a preference for alternative minimum tax purposes; however, because the remainder interest is a gift only in part to a charity, only a part of the gift is subject to the alternative minimum tax.

Gift taxes. There is no gift tax if the grantor or the grantor and his or her spouse are the sole income beneficiaries; however, if a child or other beneficiary is named to take income following the death of the grantor or his or her spouse, a taxable gift can result. This can be avoided by giving the grantor a special power of appointment. This will make the gift to the child incomplete for gift tax purposes.

Estate taxes. There is no estate tax effect. If the grantor reserves a life estate, then the total value of the amount held in trust at his or her death is includible in his or her estate; however, it is completely offset by the estate tax charitable deduction, which is unlimited.

Q 10:46 What are the income tax consequences to the beneficiary of a charitable remainder trust?

The trust tier rules apply. These rules provide that distributions to the beneficiary will be taxed in the following manner and in order of priority: (1) ordinary income, (2) capital gain, (3) nontaxable return of capital (corpus distributions).

> **Planning Pointer:** If the trustee sells appreciated property and then reinvests in tax-exempts, the distributions will first be deemed capital gain to the beneficiary and then followed by nontaxable exempt income.

Q 10:47 How does a charitable remainder trust work?

> **Example 10-8:** On December 31, 1992, Joyce Brown established a charitable remainder annuity trust to which she contributed $250,000. The CRAT is to provide a quarterly annuity at a 14 percent annual rate to her adult daughter, Grace, for a period of seven years, at the end of which time the balance remaining in trust is to be distributed to tax-exempt charitable and educational organizations described in Code Section 501(c)(3) to which contributions, gifts, and bequests are deductible for income, gift, and estate tax purposes. The following is a detailed computation disclosing how a charitable deduction of $58,900, representing the

value of the charitable remainder interest as of December 31, 1992, was determined:

Transfer of $250,000 to charitable remainder trust on 12/31/92		
Annual annuity under charitable remainder trust = 14% of $250,000	=	$35,000
Quarterly payments required	=	$8,750
Code Section 7520 interest rate for December 1992	=	7.4%
IRS annuity factor @ 7.4% for seven years—IRS Publ. 1457	=	5.3149
Present worth of an annuity for seven years: $250,000 × 5.3149 = $186,021 × quarterly factor of 1.0273 (because annuity is being paid in four quarterly installments)	=	$191,100
Charitable deduction for income and gift tax purposes:		
Total gift in trust	=	$250,000
Less: present value of annuity	=	$191,100
Charitable income tax deduction	=	$ 58,900

Planning Pointer: Because the present value of the annuity represents a present interest gift to the donee, the donor can claim a $10,000 exclusion (or $20,000 if a married spouse splits the gift). Further, assuming the donor is in the 36 percent income tax bracket in 1992, she would have an income tax savings generated by the charitable income tax deduction of $21,204 (36 percent × $58,900) that can be used to pay the gift tax, if any. If the $58,900 charitable deduction exceeds her deduction limitation, she can carry the excess deduction forward against income for five succeeding years.

Q 10:48 What is a charitable lead trust and how does it differ from a charitable remainder trust?

The charitable lead trust (CLT) is a valuable planning technique for an individual who is charitably inclined and wishes to accelerate his or her charitable deductions. A CLT is the reverse of a charitable remainder trust in that it provides initially for a charity to receive an annuity for its term (unlike a charitable remainder trust which pays the initial annual annuity to a private beneficiary) and distributes on termination, its principal either in reversion to the grantor or to named beneficiaries (unlike a charitable remainder trust which distributes its principal on termination to the designated charity(ies)). Some of the highlights of CLTs are as follows:

1. The reversionary type of CLT can be beneficial to a charitably motivated grantor, who needs to shelter unusually high income in a given year by creating a charitable deduction in the year of its creation to offset the high income, while allowing the corpus to return to the grantor at the end of the CLT term.
2. Where the CLT is not to revert to the grantor at the end of its term, it can be equally beneficial by securing advantages, such as:
   a. Allowing a taxpayer to continue charitable giving with the help of funds that might otherwise be destined for taxes;
   b. Permitting a taxpayer to fund the CLT with potentially appreciating property and pass the appreciation to his or her beneficiaries without gift tax;
   c. Excluding the appreciation and gift taxes paid from the taxpayer's gross estate. This may reduce the estate's liquidity needs and permit the taxpayer's estate to retain other nonliquid assets that have growth potential;
   d. Allowing a taxpayer's family to control the CLT's assets. This can be especially important if closely held stock is contributed to the trust; and
   e. Providing a charity with funding for a term of years after which the remainder passes to the grantor's beneficiaries.

Q 10:49 **How may a charitable lead trust be used for accomplishing any of the purposes described above?**

Example 10-19: On December 30, 1993, George Preston established a charitable lead trust to which he contributed $150,000. The trust was funded with municipal bonds owned by George and was to provide an annual annuity of 7 percent for ten years to tax-exempt charitable and religious organizations described in

Q 10:50 Estate and Retirement Planning Answer Book

Code Section 501(c)(3) to which contributions, gifts, and bequests are deductible for income, gift, and estate tax purposes.

Computation of charitable income tax deduction for CLT annuity interest conveyed to tax-exempt charitable organization:

Transfer to CLT on 12/30/93

Annual annuity under CLT = 7% of $150,000 or $10,500 annual annuity payable over ten-year period to charity

Code Section 7520 applicable interest rate for Dec. 1993	=	6.2%
IRS annuity factor 26.2% for ten years under IRS actuarial tables in IRS Publication 1457	=	7.2908
Present value of annual annuity to charity for ten years ($10,000 × 7.2908)	=	$76,553
Charitable deduction for income and gift tax purposes	=	$76,553

Planning Pointer: There is no gift tax exclusion for the gift of the remainder interest to the daughter because the gift constitutes a future interest. Because the CLT is a grantor trust, the taxpayer is required to include income earned by the trust in his own tax return; however, because income earned by the trust is municipal bond interest exempt from tax, the taxpayer has no tax liability. Accordingly, the taxpayer has obtained a contribution deduction without being required to include any trust income in his return over the ten-year period. If the taxpayer died during the ten-year period and the trust reinvested in stocks or bonds earning taxable income, the taxpayer's estate would not be required to include the income in its income tax return.

Q 10:50 What is a pooled income fund?

Pooled income funds (PIF) are similar to CRTs but instead of being created by private individuals, they are created by the charities themselves and managed by trustees appointed by the charities. Further, unlike CLTs and CRTs, the income interest reserved by the private donor is a true income interest, rather than an annuity interest or a unitrust interest. The private donor makes a gift of money or property to a charitable fund (usually an educational institution or a public charity) in exchange for units of interest that entitle the donor or the named beneficiary(ies) to a ratable share of the charitable fund's actual income each year for life or for a series of joint lives. At the death of the income beneficiary, the donor's share of the fund's assets passes outright to the charity.

Q 10:51 What are the advantages to a potential donor of a pooled income fund over a charitable remainder trust?

There are several. First, the PIF is organized by the charitable recipient and thus eliminates the fees and disbursements that the donor would otherwise incur if he or she created his or her own CRT. Second, the donor has no responsibility for the management of the PIF since the charity has its own professional financial and legal advisors. Third, the donor is one of many who contribute to a PIF and obtain the benefit of diversification in the investment mix of the charity. Fourth, the donor receives a higher charitable income tax deduction for his or her reserved interest because the size of the deduction depends on the fund's highest rate of return during the three years immediately preceding the gift. Generally, the valuation of an income interest is slightly higher for a gift to a CRUT having a comparable payout rate, and smaller than the gift to a CRAT with a comparable payout rate.

> **Practice Pointer:** The IRS has provided safe-harbor forms in which tax practitioners are guided in the drafting of CRT agreements that comply with the provisions of Code Sections 2702 and 664. These forms can be found in Revenue Procedures 89-19, 89-20, 89-21, 90-30, 90-31, and 90-32.

Q 10:52 What are the disadvantages of a pooled income fund?

The donor's loss of control of his or her investment and of the ability to designate alternate beneficiaries are distinct disadvantages of PIFs. Furthermore, distributions from a PIF to the donor are generally taxed as ordinary income regardless of their derivation by the PIF; in addition, the PIF cannot invest in tax-exempt securities so as to allow its donor to enjoy greater after-tax advantages from the donation.

Q 10:53 What is a tax-exempt charitable foundation?

It is an organization, described in Code Section 501(c)(3), that is organized and operated exclusively for religious, charitable, and educational purposes, no part of the net earnings of which inure to the benefit of any private person. Furthermore, no substantial part of a tax-exempt charitable foundation's activities may be devoted to carrying on propaganda or otherwise attempting to influence legislation, nor may it participate in, or intervene in political campaigns.

Q 10:54 What are the tax benefits that may be derived from qualifying as a charitable foundation?

A charitable foundation is exempt from federal income tax under Code Section 501(a) unless it engages in an unrelated trade or business. Contributions, gifts, and bequests made to it are deductible for federal income, estate, and gift tax purposes. The contribution, for income tax purposes, is subject to percentage limitations under Code Section 170, but the charitable deduction is unlimited for gift and estate tax purposes under Code Sections 2522 and 2055, respectively.

Q 10:55 What is a private charitable foundation?

A private charitable foundation is defined, by exclusion, under Code Section 509. In substance it is generally defined as an organization that is supported by family or family-connected members and can be a funnel for receiving and then distributing its contributions to other charities that are actively operating, or can itself be an operating foundation described under Code Section 4942(j)(3) (i.e., a private foundation which itself is actively engaged in conducting charitable activities).

Q 10:56 Are there any restrictions in being classified as a private foundation?

Yes. In the Tax Reform Act of 1969, Congress registered its concern for what it perceived as abuses by certain family foundations that conducted proscribed activities under the umbrella of tax exemption. Accordingly, a private foundation must maintain in its trust instrument or certificate of incorporation (or other enabling document), the following conditions of operation (or similar language):

> The income of the Foundation shall be distributed at such time and in such manner as not to subject the Foundation to tax under IRC sec. 4942; the Trustees of the Foundation shall not engage in any act of self dealing, as defined in IRC sec. 4941(d), not make any taxable expenditures, as defined in IRC. sec. 4945(d), shall not make any investments that jeopardize the charitable purposes of the Foundation within the meaning of IRC sec. 4944 nor retain any excess business holdings, within the meaning of IRC sec. 4943.

Practice Pointer: These provisions, if violated, will cause the trustee and/or foundation to be subject to severe penalties and possible revocation of the foundation's tax-exempt status.

Q 10:57 Is a private foundation automatically tax-exempt and eligible to receive tax-deductible contributions if it complies with the provisions of the Internal Revenue Code?

No. Code Section 508 requires newly created charitable organizations to apply to the IRS for tax-exempt status on Form 1023, which contains a series of questions regarding the identity of the creators, trustees, and officers of the foundation, the compensation, if any, paid to them, the source of foundation contributions, financial statements, and so forth. A conformed copy of the foundation's trust instrument, certificate of incorporation, and bylaws (if a corporation) or other enabling instruments must also be furnished. Also, the foundation must complete a Form 8718 to which it must attach a check to the IRS for $465, which represents a user fee (cost of compliance) required under Code Section 7805.

Chapter 11

Funding for Liquidity

One of the major concerns of estate planning is determining how to provide the funds needed to pay anticipated federal and state estate taxes. This problem becomes particularly acute where the estate has little or no liquid assets and consists principally of closely held stock, interests in a sole proprietorship or partnership, real estate, and the like. The executor of an estate does not wish to be compelled to dispose of these assets through a forced sale in order to meet the estate's need to discharge its estate tax liabilities. This chapter describes (1) how a deceased shareholder's shares of stock in a company can be redeemed as a tax-free exchange and (2) how insurance can be used to provide liquidity to an estate. The chapter also discusses ways in which the payment of estate tax liabilities can be extended and explores the option of selling a business as a way of solving liquidity problems related to that business.

Tax-Free Exchange Under Code Section 303	11-2
Life Insurance	11-3
Deferral of Payments	11-4
Sale of Business	11-7

Tax-Free Exchange Under Code Section 303

Q 11:1 What help does Code Section 303 offer for resolving an estate's liquidity needs?

Section 303 of the Internal Revenue Code (Code) permits corporate assets to be withdrawn from a business free of tax to pay funeral and administrative expenses, federal estate taxes, generation skipping taxes, and state gift taxes. Code Section 303 provides that, if certain conditions are met, a corporation can redeem part of a deceased shareholder's shares without the redemption being treated as a dividend; instead, the redemption is treated as a tax-free exchange. Because the shareholder's basis in the stock is stepped up to the fair market value of the stock as of the date of death, the estate recognizes no taxable gain on redemption. The family attribution rules do apply to a redemption under Code Section 303.

Q 11:2 What requirements must be met for Code Section 303 to apply?

The following conditions must be met so that an estate may qualify for a special tax treatment under Code Section 303:

1. The stock that is to be redeemed must be includible in the decedent's gross estate for federal estate tax purposes;

2. The value for estate tax purposes of all the stock of the redeeming corporation that is includible in the decedent's gross estate must comprise more than 35 percent of the value of the decedent's adjusted gross estate; and

3. The amount that can be paid out by the corporation under Code Section 303 is limited to an amount that does not exceed the sum of (1) all estate and inheritance taxes and (2) funeral and administrative expenses. Any excess over this amount is treated as a dividend to the estate to the extent of the corporation's earnings and profits. If the corporation has no earnings and profits, excess distributions are considered a return of the cost of the stock, and any amount recovered over cost is a capital gain.

Q 11:3 Can asset distributions besides cash satisfy Code Section 303?

Yes, they can. Although Code Section 303 envisions a distribution of cash to help satisfy estate tax liabilities, nothing precludes the distribution of other assets. For example, corporate real estate could be distributed under Code Section 303. Any gain or loss on this property would, however, be recognized and subject to tax at the corporate level.

Q 11:4 What if the estate is paid with a promissory note of the corporation that is payable in five years?

This complies with Code Section 303, which mandates that payment in redemption of the stock be made within three years and ninety days after the filing of the estate's federal estate tax return.

A distribution by a corporation of its own note satisfies the requirement that property is distributed within this period, even though the note will not be paid by the corporation until some time after the period elapses.

Q 11:5 Do the proceeds of the stock redemption have to be used to pay federal and state death taxes and funeral and administrative expenses?

No. All that is required is that the amount of the redemption does not exceed federal and state estate and inheritance taxes and funeral and estate administrative expenses. The source of the payment of these taxes and expenses is not relevant.

Life Insurance

Q 11:6 How can life insurance be used to provide liquidity for an estate?

One of the basic uses of life insurance is to provide liquidity for estate tax purposes. An individual can create an irrevocable trust and transfer money to the trust with the assurance that the trustee will buy life insurance on his or her life. If the transferor retains no incidents of ownership in the trust and his or her children are the beneficiaries of the insurance proceeds, the children will receive the insurance proceeds to offset losses to the estate as a result of estate taxes. The proceeds will not be subject to estate taxes. The insurance proceeds could be payable to the individual's estate, but this would subject them to estate tax and would reduce the amount of proceeds available for use by the survivors (see chapter 7).

Q 11:7 What is survivorship insurance?

Survivorship insurance pays a death benefit when the second of two insured persons dies. For example, a survivorship policy insuring a husband and wife might provide for a $1 million payout when both are dead; this policy would pay nothing at the first death.

Q 11:8 How is survivorship insurance used in estate planning?

Because of the marital deduction, there is often no estate tax burden when one spouse dies; however, for large estates, a significant estate tax liability might exist at the second death. Survivorship insurance can provide the liquidity to offset that projected tax liability. Because survivorship insurance is written over two lives, the annual premiums are potentially reduced.

> **Example 11-1:** A married physician with a net worth of $4 million plans to give all but $600,000 of his assets to his wife on his death. He expects that his wife will survive him. Because of the $192,800 estate tax credit, the physician expects to pay nothing on his death, but he expects that when his wife dies her estate will incur an estate tax liability of approximately $750,000. To provide the funds needed to offset that liability, the physician purchases a $750,000 survivorship insurance policy that will pay $750,000 on the latter of his death or his spouse's death.

Deferral of Payments

Q 11:9 What extensions for paying estate taxes are available?

The Internal Revenue Service (IRS) has the authority to grant a 12-month extension of time for paying estate taxes upon a showing of reasonable cause. [IRC § 6161(a)(1)]

Example 11-2: An estate does not have sufficient funds to pay the estate tax when due and provide a reasonable allowance during the remaining period of estate administration for the decedent's widow and children. The estate executor has made reasonable efforts to convert estate assets into cash. Under these circumstances, an extension of time is warranted. [Treas Reg § 20.6161-1 Ex 4]

Further, if reasonable cause is shown, the IRS is authorized to grant an extension for paying taxes of up to ten years. The estate must still file an estate tax return and must pay interest on the amount owed at the current rate of interest as determined by Code Section 6621. [IRC § 6161(a)(2)]

Q 11:10 Can the personal representative of an estate elect to defer the payment of estate taxes if a substantial portion of estate assets consist of a closely held business or a farm?

If the decedent's interest in a closely held business or a farm is more than a designated percentage of the estate and if other requirements are met, the executor can elect to pay a portion of the estate tax and generation skipping transfer tax in installments extending over as many as fifteen years. The executor can elect to completely defer tax for five years and then pay the tax in ten subsequent equal annual installments. Interest is payable at a rate of 4 percent per year on the first $1 million of property subject to the deferral. Interest on any remaining property subject to the deferral is payable at the rates ordinarily applicable to tax deficiencies. [IRC § 6166]

Q 11:11 Does the business interest have to be included in the probate estate to qualify for the 15-year extension?

No. It is only required that the interest be included in the taxable estate. Accordingly, an interest that passes by operation of law (e.g., joint ownership with right of survivorship or interest contained in a revocable trust) can qualify for the deferral.

Q 11:12 What requirements must be met to take advantage of the election to defer estate taxes?

The estate must satisfy requirements concerning (1) percentage ownership, (2) closely held business status, and (3) the timing of the election. [IRC § 6166] Initially, the closely held business interest must be included in the gross estate of a decedent who was a U.S. citizen or resident at the time of his or her death. Specific requirements are as follows:

Percentage ownership. The value of the closely held business must be more than 35 percent of the value of the decedent's adjusted gross estate (gross estate less expenses, debts, and losses). If the decedent owns more than one business, the value of each business in which the decedent owns at least a 20 percent interest can be aggregated to satisfy the 35 percent requirement.

Closely held business. The business must be closely held. This requirement is met if the decedent is

1. A sole proprietor;
2. A partner in a partnership that has either 15 partners or less or the decedent owns at least 20 percent of the capital interest in the partnership; or
3. A stockholder in a corporation that has either 15 stockholders or less or the decedent owns at least 20 percent of the stock of corporation.

In determining whether these requirements are met, special rules apply for aggregating the ownership of family members.

When to elect. The election must be made within the time for filing the federal estate tax return (i.e., Form 706), including extensions. If the election is not made when the estate tax return is filed and a deficiency is assessed, an election to pay the deficiency in installments must be made within 60 days after the issuance of an IRS demand for payment of the deficiency. [IRC § 6166(h)]

Q 11:13 Does the conduct of a rent producing activity constitute a trade or business for purposes of the 15-year deferral of taxes?

Yes, if the decedent is actively involved in the day-to-day operation and management of the properties (e.g., rental advertising, leasing, billing, mortgages, repairs, screening of applicants, and checking of credit histories). It must be shown that the decedent's personal involvement was not merely the supervision of investment assets but rather consisted of activities at a level necessary to maintain and constitute an active conduct of the rental activity.

Sale of Business

Q 11:14 When is the sale of a business a realistic option for solving estate liquidity options?

If none of the options discussed in this chapter are applicable and if the estate liquidity problem is caused by the inclusion of the value of a business in the estate, a sale of the business may be the only available option. Although the sale of the business may increase the estate's liquidity, if the business is held until death, it will receive a new income tax basis equal to its fair market value for estate valuation purposes. If the business has appreciated greatly, it may be preferable to hold it until death to avoid substantial gains that are subject to federal income tax.

Chapter 12

Using Trusts in Estate Planning

A trust, when properly structured, provides opportunities for both tax and nontax savings. It can be used to avoid the costs of probate, protect assets from creditors, maximize overall income, gift and estate tax savings, and serve as a vehicle for family support. This chapter explores how a trust can accomplish each of these goals.

Overview	12-1
Estate Planning Trusts	12-6
The Grantor Retained Income Trust	12-6
Grantor Retained Annuity Trusts and Grantor Retained Unitrusts	12-24

Overview

Q 12:1 In the context of estate planning, are trusts feasible only for affluent taxpayers?

No, not at all. Today, the average middle-income taxpayer generally has an estate consisting of a residence (with an accompanying mortgage), life insurance, a modest stock and bond portfolio, a pension or profit sharing plan, and cash in the form of a combination of checking and savings accounts. When the values of these assets are aggregated, the total surprisingly may often exceed $600,000. This is the amount exempt from federal estate tax. Any amount in excess of $600,000 is taxed at a rate of 37 percent. This rate increases gradually to 55 percent as the amount of the taxable estate increases. Accordingly, in the absence of constructive estate planning, 37 percent and more of an individual's assets (not income) in excess of $600,000 that a decedent intends for his or her designated beneficiaries can instead be inadvertently removed from his or her estate for the payment of estate taxes—and not merely by federal estate taxes, but by state estate and inheritance taxes as well.

An important part of estate planning consists of reducing the potential impact of income, gift, and estate taxes on both the creation of an estate (during an individual's lifetime) and the retention of an estate (at death). When properly designed, trusts constitute a significant estate planning tool that can be of considerable value to both high- and middle-income taxpayers.

Q 12:2 What benefit does a trust provide that a direct gift does not?

Once a direct gift is made, the donor generally loses all dominion, control, and economic enjoyment over and from the donated property. This is not the case where a property is transferred in trust. The trust allows the donor to retain a *real* economic benefit during the term of the trust while obtaining a *real* immediate opportunity to save estate and gift taxes when the trust is created.

Q 12:3 What is a trust, and why is one generally used?

Treasury Regulations Section 301.7701-4(a) defines a trust as an "arrangement by a will or by an inter vivos [during one's life] declaration whereby trustees take title to property for the purpose of protecting it for the beneficiaries . . ." The person who creates the trust—generally known as a *grantor* or *settlor*—can also be its beneficiary.

As a general rule, a trust is established by a grantor as a protection for a beneficiary who may be a minor, disabled, or incompetent or who may simply be unsophisticated in matters of money. By appointing a trustee to control, manage, and protect the assets placed in trust, the grantor intends to assure the safety of what he or she has placed in trust and the likelihood that such contributed property will be administered by the trustee (generally an individual, financial institution, or both) to produce a reasonable rate of return. The grantor will provide in the trust agreement that (1) the trust terminates at a specific date, (2) the trust property is to be paid to the beneficiary in periodic installments until the trust property is exhausted by a particular date, and/or (3) trust assets may be distributed by the trustee to or for the beneficiary on the occurrence of specified events (e.g., medical emergency and educational opportunity).

Where the grantor names himself or herself as both grantor and beneficiary, the grantor generally seeks to protect his or her assets through the use of a trust that will provide security against the grantor's potential disability (the trustee can manage the assets at that time) or death (thereby avoiding the time and expense of a probate proceeding), and that will place such assets in the hands of a trustee capable of managing and protecting the grantor's property in a way that the grantor cannot.

Q 12:4 How does the Internal Revenue Service view trusts that are established for the benefit of a pet?

In Revenue Ruling 76-486, the Internal Revenue Service (IRS) advised that if a trust is invalid under state law, as where it violates the rule against perpetuities, it cannot be a trust for income tax purposes. The *rule against perpetuities* is a rule of law in effect in most states that requires a time period for a trust to terminate and distribute its property to a person (e.g., a life in being plus 21 years). The IRS ruling holds that animals cannot be considered beneficiaries of a trust for income tax purposes because they are not persons. Accordingly, distributions made from a trust for the care of an animal are disregarded by the IRS, and the trust is taxed as if no distributions are being made. Because a trust pays the maximum tax rate of 39.6 percent on taxable income exceeding $7,900, the care of a pet through the establishment of a trust can be a costly undertaking.

Q 12:5 Do the legal and other professional fees incurred in creating a trust warrant the tax savings to be generated?

There is no blanket answer to this question. Creating a trust to satisfy both the nontax and tax motivations of the grantor will require an experienced tax attorney (or one experienced in trusts and wills) who will draft a trust tailored to satisfy the grantor's requirements. At the same time, the tax lawyer must be sufficiently sophisticated to advise as to the benefits and pitfalls, both tax and nontax, of the trust that is being contemplated. Also, an accountant or financial planner is often consulted in designing a trust. The costs for these professional services must be weighed against the income, gift, and/or estate taxes that may be avoided.

Q 12:6 When does a trust begin its life?

Although there is no exact authority, a trust is considered to commence its life for income tax purposes when property is first transferred to the trustee, rather than when the trust instrument is executed. [Bibby v Commr 44 TC 638 (1965)] Grantor trusts (see Q 12:7), which have no independent tax significance as long as they retain that status, only become separate entities for income tax purposes when the grantor dies, or if earlier, when the tainted powers (e.g., a power to revoke retained by the grantor) that caused them to be grantor trusts lapse or otherwise terminate (e.g., by death).

Q 12:7 What is a *grantor* trust?

Under certain conditions specified in the Internal Revenue Code (Code), the income of a trust is taxed to the grantor who created it rather than to the trust or its intended beneficiaries. These Code provisions justify tax to the grantor or even to certain other persons because the grantor is deemed to retain or possess substantial dominion or control over the trust property or income. For example, the grantor or others are each taxed as owners under the following circumstances:

1. The grantor or spouse has a reversionary interest exceeding 5 percent of the value of the transferred property. [IRC § 673]

Using Trusts in Estate Planning Q 12:9

2. The grantor or a nonadverse party has the power over beneficial interests of the trust [IRC § 674], can revoke the trust or return the corpus to the grantor [IRC § 676], or can distribute the income to or for the benefit of the grantor or the grantor's spouse. [IRC § 677]
3. Administrative powers exist in the provisions of the trust agreement that would be beneficial to the grantor. [IRC § 675]

Q 12:8 Once a trust is established upon reliance of competent professional advice, can the grantor be assured that the IRS and the local taxing jurisdiction will not challenge the tax results expected to be derived from the trust?

Because the success of an estate plan can be determined only after death, it is most important that assurances be provided that the estate plan will be carried out as intended. Unfortunately, although death is a certainty, there are no guarantees regarding taxes; however, a trust resulting from competent legal advice will generally achieve the benefit sought to be attained without challenge by the IRS. An opinion letter from the professional retained by a client should generally be obtained so as to assure the client and his or her family that what is sought is what is being accomplished. Where the tax provisions relied upon for creating the trust seem uncertain or unsettled, a competent lawyer will advise the client to seek a ruling letter from the IRS that will provide the assurance that is needed to prevent a challenge from the IRS after death. The ruling letter process generally takes from 90 to 180 days between the date that the request is submitted to the IRS and the issuance of a ruling. The premium paid for requesting the ruling from the IRS is a user fee that can be as high as $3,000. [IRC § 7805]

Q 12:9 How can a taxpayer be certain that his or her personal, emotional, and business needs are being properly attended to when he or she is caught up in the urgency of trying to save on taxes?

A person must first determine, without regard to taxes, the property and beneficiary to whom his or her assets are to be distributed on death. After having established answers to the foregoing, the taxpayer can seek legal and financial professional advice with the certainty that he or she knows exactly what is to be accomplished. The purpose of professional advice is to determine the most feasible and least costly tax method for accomplishing the taxpayer's estate planning goals.

Q 12:10 What are the different kinds of trusts currently being considered by estate planning practitioners in the framing of an estate plan?

The provisions of the Code currently favor a number of different types of trusts that can achieve meaningful tax savings if structured properly. Some estate plans also use trusts that have no material tax significance but nevertheless are designed to preserve an estate. Each of these trusts is reviewed separately below under the heading Estate Planning Trusts (i.e., trusts that carry tax saving as well as estate planning characteristics).

Estate Planning Trusts

Grantor Retained Income Trust

Q 12:11 What is a grantor retained income trust?

A grantor retained income trust (GRIT) is a generic term applied to personal residence trusts. A GRIT in use today under Code Section 2702 has *nothing* to do with a grantor reserving an interest in income from property placed in trust, but, rather, has *everything* to do with a grantor retaining an interest in his or her personal residence while it is in trust.

Q 12:12 How is a personal residence defined for GRIT purposes?

A personal residence includes the principal residence of the grantor and one other residence of the grantor (or an undivided fractional interest in such residence (e.g., as a tenant-in-common) and thus includes a vacation home. [Treas Reg §§ 25.2702-5(b)(2)(i), 25.2702-5(c)(2)(i)]

Q 12:13 Why would one transfer a personal residence merely to save on taxes?

A residence should not be placed in trust merely to save taxes; however, if a taxpayer believes that at some time in the foreseeable future it is likely that he or she will move from or sell the residence or that it will not be used as a principal residence, then a GRIT will permit a person to transfer the residence in trust to family members at a minimum or no gift tax cost. At the same time, the taxpayer can continue to use the residence during the term of years specified in the trust, and if he or she survives the trust term so as to cause the appreciation in the value of the residence from the date the trust was created, the taxpayer can escape estate tax.

Q 12:14 What other reasons are there for creating a GRIT?

When recommending a GRIT, most professional tax advisors put forth the "what have you got to lose" concept. To do nothing is to concede the value of a taxpayer's residence to the IRS at the time of death and the impact of estate taxes thereon, thereby reducing the amount of estate assets otherwise available to beneficiaries. By creating a GRIT, the value of the residence can be substantially reduced; furthermore, the residence will be affected only by a gift tax, thus allowing the estate to accrue more savings and to make more of its assets available to its beneficiaries.

Q 12:15 If a married person owns a residence jointly with right of survivorship to a spouse or owns it solely but provides that the residence be devised to the surviving spouse, the marital deduction will effectively keep the residence from being subject to an estate tax. Why then should a GRIT be considered?

The marital deduction certainly will cause the residence to escape estate tax in the estate of the first spouse to die; however, the surviving spouse, assuming that no subsequent marriage occurs, will have no marital deduction to exhaust against the value of the residence on death. When aggregated with other assets inherited on death, the presence of a residence in the estate will cause an estate tax impact that otherwise could have been avoided.

Further, the key to a successful GRIT is the survival of the grantors; if a grantor dies prior to the end of the trust term, the residence will be included in the grantor's estate at its fair market value on the date of death. Accordingly, it is most beneficial for both spouses to consider a GRIT because, if the surviving spouse's life expectancy is already diminished by age when the death of his or her spouse occurs, it may be too late for a GRIT to have any real tax saving advantages.

Q 12:16 Practically speaking, how does a GRIT work?

Example 12-1 illustrates the application of a GRIT to an unmarried person.

Example 12-1: A widow owns two residences: a principal residence worth $700,000 with no mortgage in New England where she and her deceased husband raised their two daughters (both now adults, married with children) and a condominium apartment in Florida worth $250,000 with a mortgage of $100,000 where she resides during the winter months. She is 82 years of age and wishes to reduce the value of her estate through the use of a GRIT. She has sufficient liquidity to live comfortably. Her life expectancy, based upon the IRS actuarial tables, is 8.4 years, and the IRS discount rate for the months in which she intends to create the trust is 7.4 percent. She will reserve the right to continue living in both residences for a period of six years and has named one daughter to own the New England residence and the other to own the Florida residence at the end of the trust term. Each of the valuations to be submitted to the IRS in attachments to the gift tax return would be substantiated as follows:

New England Principal Residence

On May 6, 1992, the taxpayer (age 82) created a qualified personal interest trust (*copy attached*) reserving her interest therein for a

Using Trusts in Estate Planning   Q 12:16

period of six years, at the end of which the remainder interest is to be conveyed to her adult daughter. The personal residence located at 125 Jerome Avenue, Engleton, CT, is mortgage-free and has a fair market value on the date of the trust's inception of $700,000 based upon the attached appraisal report dated May 1, 1992.

The computation of the taxable value of the gift of the remainder interest to the taxpayer's daughter is based on the full fair market vale of the property minus the values of the retained income interest and the reversion as follows:

Term of GRIT	=	6 years
Value of residence on May 6, 1992	=	$700,000
IRS applicable interest rate under Code Section § 7520 for the month of May 1992	=	8.6%
IRS remainder factor for six-year term under actuarial tables contained in IRS Publication 1457	=	.609566
Value of remainder to daughter if the grantor had not retained a reversionary interest is $700,000 × .609566	=	$426,696

Then:

Find the number in Table 80 CNSMT (IRS Publication 1457) listed for taxpayer's age at end of trust term	19,235
Find the number in Table 80 CNSMT listed for taxpayer's age at beginning of trust term	37,132
Divide: $\frac{19235}{37132}$ =	.51

Multiply the decimal obtained (.51) by the value of the remainder ($426,696). The resulting amount is the value of the remainder interest for gift and estate tax purposes:

$426,696 × .51 = $217,615

Result: The taxpayer, if she lives out the six-year term of the GRIT, will have avoided estate tax on the difference between $700,000 and $217,615 (i.e., $482,385) plus any subsequent appreciation after the creation of the trust.

Practice Pointer: The computation of the value of the Florida vacation home gift would be made under the same method, as described above, except the fair market value of the condominium

TABLE 80CNSMT: IRS's Underlying Mortality Table, Used to Calculate Factors Involving Life Contingencies

Age x (1)	l(x) (2)	Age x (1)	l(x) (2)	Age x (1)	l(x) (2)
0	100000	37	95492	74	59279
1	98740	38	95317	75	56799
2	98648	39	95129	76	54239
3	98584	40	94926	77	51599
4	98535	41	94706	78	48878
5	98495	42	94465	79	46071
6	98459	43	94201	80	43180
7	98426	44	93913	81	40208
8	98396	45	93599	82	37172
9	98370	46	93256	83	34095
10	98347	47	92882	84	31012
11	98328	48	92472	85	27960
12	98309	49	92021	86	24961
13	98285	50	91526	87	22038
14	98248	51	90986	88	19235
15	98196	52	90402	89	16598
16	98129	53	89771	90	14154
17	98047	54	89087	91	11908
18	97953	55	88348	92	9863
19	97851	56	87551	93	5032
20	97741	57	86695	94	6424
21	97623	58	85776	95	5043
22	97499	59	84789	96	3884
23	97370	60	83726	97	2939
24	97240	61	82581	98	2485
25	97110	62	81348	99	1598
26	96982	63	80024	100	1150
27	96856	64	78709	101	815
28	96730	65	77107	102	570
29	96604	66	75520	103	393
30	96477	67	73846	104	267
31	96350	68	72082	105	179
32	96220	69	70218	106	119
33	96088	70	68248	107	78
34	95951	71	66165	108	51
35	95808	72	63972	109	33
36	95655	73	61673	110	0

apartment on the date of the gift would be reduced by the amount of the mortgage.

Q 12:17 What if the term of a GRIT is for a period longer than the grantor's life expectancy?

Although the longer trust term produces a lower remainder value and, therefore, a lower valued gift upon which the gift tax is determined, there is a risk that the grantor might die during the trust term, thus resulting in the inclusion of the residence in the grantor's estate at its fair market value at her death. This would violate the entire purpose for which the QPRT was established.

Q 12:18 How would a GRIT be employed for a married couple as compared to a single person?

Example 12-2 illustrates the application of a GRIT for a married couple.

Example 12-2: George, age 69, and his wife Laura, age 66, own their family residence, worth $600,000, as joint tenants with right of survivorship. They cause a change in ownership in the residence to tenants-in-common, and each establishes a ten-year residence GRIT, with their daughter Paula as the remainderman. If either spouse dies prior to the ten-year term, that spouse's trust reverts to his or her estate. Using life expectancy tables and a 8.6 percent interest rate, the value of George's retained interest (i.e., his right to continue residing in the residence for ten years) is $145,000, and, under the same conditions, Laura's right is valued at $150,000. The reversionary interest for each is valued at $68,000 and $56,000, respectively. The total value of the retained interest is therefore $419,000. Accordingly, the value of the gifted remainder interest to their daughter is $181,000. If both George and Paula live beyond the ten-year trust term, $419,000 of value has escaped estate tax, the savings of which will be determined on their respective deaths.

Q 12:19 Does any part of the gift of the remainder interest qualify for the $10,000 annual gift tax exclusion?

No. Only gifts of present interests qualify for the $10,000 annual gift tax exclusion. A gift of a remainder interest is not a present interest because it is not enjoyed until some future time. As a result, the grantor is compelled to use his or her unified credit to remove or reduce the potential gift tax.

Q 12:20 How can a grantor use the $10,000 annual gift tax exclusion and still maximize the prospective benefit of a qualified personal residence trust?

Treasury regulations permit a qualified personal residence trust (QPRT) to own an undivided interest in a residence and thus provides the grantor with an opportunity to reduce his or her gift tax when establishing the QPRT. The grantor can transfer an undivided interest in the residence to the QPRT and simultaneously transfer outright undivided interests in the residence to the grantor's children. The direct transfers to the children may be made without gift tax by taking advantage of the $10,000.00 ($20,000 for split gifts by husband and wife) annual exclusion. Accordingly, a married couple with a residence having a fair market value on the date that the QPRT is established of $1 million can each transfer a 30 percent interest ($300,000 each) in the residence to their respective QPRT and start giving interests in the remaining 20 percent fractional interest to each of their children over the next five years (each taking an annual gift tax exclusion of $40,000 equals an aggregate annual total of $80,000); assuming, of course, that there is no increase in the fair market value of the residence during the four-year period. If structured properly, these gifts can be completed in two years and one day (12/31/96, 1/1/97, 1/1/98 and 1/1/99).

Q 12:21 What is a personal residence trust?

Code Section 2702 describes a personal residence trust (PRT) as a trust that allows a taxpayer to transfer his or her residence to a trust, with the retention of the right to use the residence for the term of years specified in the trust, and, if the taxpayer survives the trust term, the trust causes the residence to escape estate tax. The provisions of the PRT must expressly prohibit it from holding any assets other than one residence to be used as a personal residence by the grantor during the PRT's express term of existence. In addition, the provisions of the PRT must specifically prohibit the sale or other transfer of the residence and its use for any purpose other than as the grantor's personal residence. A PRT cannot hold cash or other assets or even any of the furnishings of the residence. Expenses for maintaining the residence must be paid by the grantor (or anyone else for that matter) inasmuch as the PRT is precluded from holding cash.

Practice Pointer: The IRS recently announced that a PRT interest cannot be commuted. Prior to this policy change by the IRS, the term holder (grantor) and the remainderman were able to commute their interests by mutual agreement in the event of an appealing sales offer.

Q 12:22 What is the difference between a personal residence trust and a qualified personal residence trust?

Both trusts involve the transfer of a personal residence. The principal difference is that the only asset that can be held by a PRT is the personal residence of the grantor whereas the QPRT may hold incidental amounts of other assets, and, where applicable, may nevertheless continue to qualify as a QPRT if it pays qualified annual annuities to its grantor.

Q 12:23 Inasmuch as a personal residence trust is precluded from holding cash, what is the effect of such a trust receiving cash as a result of destruction of the residence by fire or its condemnation by local government?

Treasury Regulations Section 25.2702-5(b) anticipates this problem and provides that a PRT can hold *qualified proceeds* from the disposition of a residence under such circumstances. Qualified proceeds are proceeds payable "as a result of damage to, or destruction or involuntary conversion (within the meaning of Code Section 1033) of the residence held by" the PRT; however, the provisions of the PRT must expressly require that such proceeds (and any income generated from their investment) be reinvested in a personal residence within two years from the date on which the proceeds are received. [Treas Reg § 25.2702-5(b)(3)]

Practice Pointer: In view of the above, it appears logical to assume that a PRT can hold an insurance policy or policies on the residence held in trust or, perhaps, the grantor can amend the policy, on establishing the PRT, to provide that insurance proceeds shall be paid to the grantor or to the PRT as their interest may appear.

Q 12:24 Qualified personal residence trusts are not described in Code Section 2702 or under any other provisions of the Code. What authority is there to provide the tax benefit expected from the creation of such a trust?

In fact, a QPRT is not authorized under any provision of the Code, but is approved by the IRS in its regulations under Code Section 2702. It is generally broader in scope than a PRT in that it allows cash—in addition to the personal residence—to be included in the trust corpus under specified circumstances. A QPRT is regarded as the more favorable estate planning tool and is recommended by estate planners.

IRS regulations require that the following provisions be contained in a QPRT:

- Mandatory distribution of income at least annually to the grantor/term holder
- A prohibition against distributions of income or principal to anyone other than the grantor except principal distributions on termination
- A prohibition against the trust's holding excess cash although some cash for defined purposes can be distributed
- A prohibition on commutation of the QPRT
- The required termination or conversion of the trust into a grantor retained annuity trust on the cessation of the QPRT's use as a personal residence

A QPRT can hold cash to meet certain short-term needs, although the trustee must hold the cash in a separate account and in an amount that, when added to the existing cash held for these purposes, does not exceed the amount needed:

- For payment of trust expenses (including mortgage payments) already incurred or reasonably expected to be incurred within the next six months
- For improvements to the residence to be paid for within six months
- On creation of the QPRT, to purchase a personal residence or thereafter to buy a replacement residence within three months, even then only if the trust prohibits any additions being made to the trust for this purpose unless there is an existing contract to purchase the residence

Practice Pointer: A QPRT is entitled to (1) the beneficial provisions of Code Section 1034 that allow it to purchase a residence within two years from the sale of the residence held by the QPRT, (2) the over 55 years of age exclusion of up to $125,000 in gain, and (3) the involuntary conversion rules of Code Section 1033, as long as the replacement is accomplished within two years of the involuntary conversion. If a QPRT holds a vacation residence, then the rules of tax-free rollover under Code Section 1034 within two years would not apply because that section only applies to a principal residence; furthermore, the over 55 years of age exclusion might not apply because, to qualify, a taxpayer must have used the vacation home as his or her principal residence for periods aggregating three years or more during a five-year period ending on the date of the sale or exchange.

Q 12:25 Why is a grantor entitled to the advantages of Code Sections 1034 and 1033, and the over 55 years of age exemption under Code Section 121, if the taxpayer does not own the residence during the years it is held in trust?

Because a PRT or a QPRT must be a *grantor trust*, the grantor is deemed the owner of the entire trust property and is treated as such for purposes of Code Sections 1033, 1034, and 121.

Q 12:26   Estate and Retirement Planning Answer Book

Q 12:26   What does it signify that commutation of the grantor's interest is prohibited under a QPRT and a PRT?

Commutation is the payment of the actuarial value of the income interest to the grantor at some point during the trust term. It is proscribed because it tends to prevent the QPRT and the PRT from functioning for the very reason that the regulations sanctioned its use. [Treas Reg 25.2702-5(c)(6)]

Q 12:27   Can a residence encumbered by a mortgage be transferred to either a PRT or QPRT?

Absolutely. The effect of the mortgage is beneficial from an estate planning viewpoint because it reduces the fair market value for purposes of valuing the gift of the remainder interest.

Q 12:28   Does a QPRT lose its special status if the residence held by it ceases to be the grantor's residence for any reason (e.g., sale, destruction, or condemnation, or change in use)?

No, it does not if its governing instrument (the trust itself) contains *any one* of the following three provisions:

1. The trust provisions require that the trustee distribute all of the trust assets to the grantor. Accomplishing this makes no sense from an estate planning perspective because it undoes the very reason for creating the QPRT (i.e., seeking to remove the appreciation in the residence—and, in many cases, the value of the residence itself—from the gross estate of the grantor).

2. The trust provisions require the trustee to convert the trust into a qualified grantor retained annuity trust (GRAT), which must meet all of the requirements of a GRAT (see Q 12:49, *et seq.*) and must function exclusively as a GRAT from the earlier of the date of sale, involuntary conversion, or cessation of use of the residence as a personal residence. The trustee can defer paying the annuity to the grantor until 30 days after converting the QPRT to a GRAT so long as the grantor receives the back payments plus interest at a rate set by Code Section 7520. Such a circumstance could occur if, after two years from the sale of

the residence held in the QPRT, the trustee was unable to find suitable replacement property. Here, annuity payments do not commence until 30 days after the expiration of the two-year period, but the grantor has the interest on the back payments going back two years on the date that the sale proceeds were received by the trustee.
3. The trustee has the option to convert the trust into a GRAT or to terminate and distribute all of the trust funds to the term holder. This permits the trustee to make a decision with full knowledge of the facts on the date that the property ceases to be a personal residence, not just those known on the trust's creation.

Q 12:29 Will using a portion of the residence on a regular basis exclusively for business purposes preclude transferring the residence to a PRT or a QPRT?

No. Treasury Regulations Secton 25.2702-5(d) provides an example in which a PRT or QPRT holding a residence in which a taxpayer maintains a principal place of business in one room is allowed to qualify. [IRC § 280A(c)(1)]

Q 12:30 Can anyone other than the grantor occupy the residence during the trust term?

When the grantor is not occupying the residence and it is being held for the grantor's use, it cannot be occupied by any person other than the grantor's spouse or dependent and must be available at all times for the grantor's use as a personal residence. Otherwise, this will cause a cessation of use as a personal residence and adversely affect the tax favored attributes of a PRT or QPRT. [Treas Reg § 25.2702-5(c)(7)(i)]

Practice Pointer: A live-in housekeeper, girlfriend or boyfriend, or nondependent relative cannot occupy the residence when it is not being used by, but is held for the use of, the grantor.

Furthermore, the grantor, not the PRT or QPRT, can rent out his residence for part of the year and occupy it for the other part because the grantor is exercising his use right in renting the residence. If the trust leased the residence, the trust would be disqualified as a PRT or QPRT because the residence would no longer be available for the grantor's use at all times.

Q 12:31　What is the effect on either a personal residence trust or a qualified personal residence trust arrangement if the grantor is required to move to a nursing home during the trust term?

None. If the grantor is compelled by circumstance to move to a nursing home during the trust term, the residence continues to be held for the grantor's use as long as the residence is available at all times for the grantor's use during the trust term, without regard to the grantor's ability to actually use the residence. [Treas Reg § 25.2702-5(d), Ex.5]

Q 12:32　Can a grantor establish more than one trust for each residence he or she owns?

A grantor can establish individual trusts to hold two of the residences he or she owns; however, trusts holding fractional interests in the same residence are treated as one trust. [Treas Reg § 25.2702-5(a)]

Q 12:33　Can the grantor be the trustee of his or her own personal residence or qualified personal residence trust?

Yes. There is nothing under Code Section 2702 or its regulations that precludes a grantor from being his or her own trustee in the PRT or QPRT he or she has established.

Q 12:34　What are the gift and estate tax advantages of a qualified personal residence trust?

There are several gift and estate tax benefits. For gift tax purposes, the transfer to a QPRT is a gift of the remainder interest valued under the discounted interest rate specified under Code Section 7520. The effect is that a residence that has substantial potential for appreciation may be transferred at a relatively low gift tax cost. There are two separate advantages: (1) the discount for the time value of money (use of the home) and (2) the fact that the value of the residence is captured at current market value, rather than at some future, hopefully appreciated value.

Q 12:35 How is the amount of the gift determined?

Although the property is valued at fair market value, only the value of the remainder interest is subject to gift tax. The remainder interest is determined by deducting from fair market value the present value of the grantor's retained contingent reversionary interest.

Q 12:36 What is the grantor's retained reversionary interest?

The contingent reversionary interest is the possibility that the residence transferred to the QPRT will revert to the grantor in the event that the grantor dies before the term specified in the trust. For example, if the trust term is fifteen years and the grantor dies in the tenth year, the residence will revert to the grantor, or more precisely to the grantor's estate. The value of the reversionary interest must exceed 5 percent of the fair market value of the residence placed in trust in order for the PRT or QPRT to qualify as a grantor trust eligible for the special benefits available to individual ownership of a principal residence.

Q 12:37 Are there changed circumstances where a married couple owns a residence jointly as tenants by the entirety?

It is generally more efficient for spouses each to own an undivided interest in the residence. This can be easily accomplished by having the husband transfer his undivided share to his QPRT and the wife transfer her undivided share to her QPRT.

Q 12:38 What are the benefits of such undivided interest?

A major benefit is to allow for marketability and minority discounts that further reduce the value of the gifts. The Tax Court has allowed a 15 percent minority discount where a fractional interest was transferred. [Mooneyham v Commr TCM 1991-78]

Q 12:39 Are there any situations when only one of the spouses should create the trust?

If one spouse has a health problem and is not expected to live out the trust term, then the healthier spouse should own the residence and create the QPRT. Otherwise, if the spouse in poor health dies before the end of the trust term, the property is included in his or her estate, thus causing unnecessary potential tax.

Practice Pointer: If the spouse with health problems does not survive the trust term, the result may not be as severe as it appears because the transferee of the deceased spouse's interest in may be the surviving spouse, which would allow for the use of a 100 percent marital deduction.

Q 12:40 Can a married couple owning a residence in joint name create a QPRT jointly, and, if so, what are the pitfalls?

Yes, a married couple can create a joint QPRT; however, the QPRT must preclude anyone else from living in the residence. A provision contained in the QPRT should read as follows:

> The trust will cease to be a qualified personal residence trust if the residence ceases to be used or held for use as a personal residence of the Grantors. The residence will be held for use as a personal residence of the Grantors so long as the residence is not occupied by any other person (other than a dependent of the Grantors) and is available at all times for use by the Grantors as a personal residence.

Practice Pointer: The difficulty created by transferring undivided interests to children is that, unless they pay rent, the IRS could claim that the parents retained a reserved life estate and thus could include the interests given to the children in the parents' estates. Of course, if rent is received, the property is eligible for depreciation, reducing cost basis and causing gain if the property is sold. Conversely, upon the parents' deaths, basis creates no problem because the children are entitled to claim their interest in the residence at fair market value at the date of death.

Q 12:41 Are any discounts available for these gifts?

Marketability and minority discounts may be available for gifts to children.

Q 12:42 What are the income tax consequences of the QPRT?

No gain or loss is recognized on the transfer to the QPRT. Because the QPRT is taxed as a grantor trust, the grantor is entitled to all the income tax deductions otherwise available to them, such as mortgage interest and real estate taxes. If the QPRT sells the residence, gain is not recognized if the proceeds are used by the QPRT to purchase another principal residence within two years, assuming, of course, that the cost of the new residence equals or exceeds the sales proceeds derived from the sale of the old residence. The QPRT is also entitled to the one-time $125,000 exclusion for those over age 55. The fact that the property is in the name of a trust does not affect these tax benefits. [Ltr Rul 8239055]

Q 12:43 May a grantor create more than one QPRT?

Yes. A grantor may create QPRTs for a principal residence and another residence. For this purpose, fractional interests in the same residence held by different trusts count as one trust. For example, if a husband and wife own undivided interests in the principal residence and a vacation home, they may create four QPRTs between them that count as two residences. Alternatively, they could create multiple QPRTS of various terms. This would allow them to hedge their bets against dying during the trust term, while still taking advantage of some long-term QPRTs where the remainder value subject to gift tax would be much lower.

Q 12:44 Is there a tax strategy that can be employed to obtain a step-up in basis while the residence is owned by a qualified personal residence trust?

If the residence has a low basis in relation to its fair market value, prior to the end of its trust term, the grantor can purchase the residence from the trust at its then fair market value without any gain being taxed. The trust obtains the cash and, if the grantor retains the residence until his or her death, it will be included in the grantor's estate at its fair market value. Naming the grantor's surviving spouse as the estate beneficiary of the residence qualifies it for the marital deduction, and if the surviving spouse chooses to sell the residence during his or her lifetime, the capital gain, if any, will be minimized. This becomes particularly attractive when the surviving spouse decides to rent an apartment using the proceeds from the sale of the residence (perhaps tax free with the use of the $125,000 exemption for being over 55 plus the step-up in basis) to fund the monthly rent payments.

Q 12:45 Can the grantor continue living in the residence if he or she survives the trust term?

Yes. The grantor may lease the property after the term expires. The property will not be included in the grantor's estate if the lease provides for a fair market rental. The grantor will obtain no deduction for the rent paid, and his or her children will have rental income subject to tax based upon the expense of owning the residence plus a presumably low depreciation deduction.

Practice Pointer: It is important that the lease be entered into at the end of the trust term. If a lease is executed at the time of the creation of the trust, the IRS could argue that the grantor has reserved a life estate in his or her residence and include the residence in the grantor's taxable estate. [IRC § 2036]

Q 12:46 What are the disadvantages in establishing a qualified personal residence trust?

Under the "what have you got to lose concept" of estate planning, there are no disadvantages. If the grantor dies during the trust term, then the residence is included in his or her estate as it would have been if no QPRT had been created. There are, however, nontax issues to consider, such as the cost of creating the QPRT (e.g., legal fees and disbursements for drafting the trust and preparing deeds to conform to the trust); the location of the grantor's residence if he or she survives the trust term; whether the grantor wants to rent his or her residence from his or her children; and the likelihood that property values may decline so that the whole purpose of creating the QPRT may be lost (i.e., if property values decline, there will be no appreciation to escape estate tax).

Q 12:47 What are the tax effects to the donee who receives the personal residence at the end of the trust term?

There is no gift tax effect because gift tax liability generally follows the donor. The donee, for income tax purposes, is required to take as a cost basis in the residence the cost basis of the donor at the time of the transfer in trust of the personal residence plus any gift tax that was incurred by the donor in giving the remainder interest to the donee.

Practice Pointer: This result to the donor should be weighed against the overall tax effect to both the donor and donee. If the donor dies owning the personal residence, then the estate tax (assuming there is a taxable estate) must be balanced against the potential capital gains income tax of 28 percent to the donee-legatee, who, on receiving the personal residence as a result of it passing to him or her on death, obtains an income tax basis equal to its fair market value on the date of death. [IRC § 1014]

Q 12:48 Should a qualified personal residence trust or a personal residence trust be considered if a gross estate, including a personal residence, does not exceed $600,000?

As a general rule, neither of these trusts should be considered where it is likely that no federal estate tax will be paid. The principal reason for creating these residence trusts is to avoid the federal estate tax. It is generally more beneficial to the overall economic welfare of the decedent and his or her family members that, under such circumstances, the estate beneficiaries obtain a stepped-up cost basis in the inherited basis that eliminates or reduces the impact of capital gains tax (currently 28 percent) on a subsequent sale by them.

Grantor Retained Annuity Trusts and Grantor Retained Unitrusts

Q 12:49 What are grantor retained annuity trusts and grantor retained unitrusts?

Under both a grantor retained annuity trust (GRAT) and a grantor retained unitrust (GRUT), the grantor has reserved a right to receive an annuity for a term of years at the end of which the trust property is transferred to named beneficiaries. The principal estate tax saving purpose of the GRAT and GRUT is to allow the grantor to enjoy the benefits from his property contributed to these trusts for a designated period of years; if he survives this period, the grantor can eliminate the then current balance in trust from his or her estate.

Both of these trusts should be compared to the GRIT, the charitable remainder annuity trust (CRAT) and the charitable remainder unitrust (CRUT) (see chapter 10). In the case of the GRIT, the grantor has reserved an interest in his personal residence for a term of years. If he survives at the end of the term, the trust property is transferred to named beneficiaries. Like the CRAT and CRUT, the GRAT and the GRUT achieve a gift tax advantage because the gift tax is not computed on the entire value of the property when placed in trust but only the value of the trust property being conveyed to the grantor's designated beneficiaries. Unlike the CRAT and CRUT, however, the GRAT and the GRUT achieve no offsetting charitable deduction that the grantor can use for income tax purposes, so that the income tax savings can be employed to pay the gift tax, if any. (The IRS's actuarial tables are used for this purpose.)

Practice Pointer: It should be noted that a GRIT leaves a grantor nothing but the use of a residence for a term of years and, if the grantor survives the term, his or her estate has been depleted to the extent of the value of the residence. In contrast, during the term for which a GRAT or GRUT is in existence, the grantor is having his or her estate replenished by his or her annual reserved annuity. Accordingly, there is a kind of trade-off in that, by surviving the term of a GRAT or GRUT, the grantor has eliminated from his or her estate the property he or she has contributed to the trust; however, the grantor has augmented his estate with the total of the annuities received during this period. Obviously, calculations should be made prior to the creation of the GRAT or GRUT clearly demonstrating the economic feasibility of such trusts and their overall potential estate tax saving to the grantor.

Q 12:50 **Would it not be easier for the grantor to keep the property otherwise placed in the GRAT or GRUT, enjoy its economic benefits for a period equaling the trust term, and then make a direct gift to the intended beneficiaries?**

Yes, from a practical viewpoint it would be easier to make a direct gift; however, estate planning and tax savings opportunities permit overall benefit to the grantor by employing a GRAT or GRUT. Although a direct gift allows the use of the $10,000 annual gift tax exclusion per donee ($20,000 if married and consent to gift splitting is given by the nongifting spouse), the total value of the gift, except for the gift tax exclusions, would be subject to gift tax. On the other hand, where a GRAT or GRUT is used, a discounted value is placed on the remainder interest because the value of the gift in either of these trusts is reduced by the actuarily determined value of the grantor's reservation of his interest in an annuity for the term of years stipulated in the trust. This actuarily determined value is measured by the annual annuity reserved by the grantor and the IRS discount rate in effect at the time that the GRAT or GRUT is established.

> **Practice Pointer:** Unlike a direct gift, a gift made of a remainder interest conveyed to a designated beneficiary in a GRAT or GRUT is not eligible for the gift tax exclusion because a remainder interest is a future interest (i.e., the beneficiary's enjoyment of the trust property is not immediate but is postponed until the end of the trust term). Only present interests are eligible for the annual gift tax exclusion.

Q 12:51 **Why should a taxpayer consider using a GRAT or GRUT in his or her estate planning?**

These trusts serve at least three beneficial estate tax savings purposes:

1. The grantor, as his or her own trustee, continues to retain control of the trust property during its term;
2. The grantor continues to obtain the benefit of an income stream or cash flow so that he or she does not necessarily cede this retained economic benefit from the property merely because he or she has created the trust; and
3. The grantor has predetermined the kind and destination of the property he or she has placed in trust, with a potential minimum of gift or estate consequences.

Q 12:52 What did Congress have in mind when it enacted Code Section 2702 permitting the use of GRATs and GRUTs?

Congress was willing to permit this form of estate planning as long as the transfers were capable of realistic valuation. Accordingly, Code Section 2702 applies to a transfer of an interest in trust to or for the benefit of a member of the grantor's family, if the transferor or an applicable family member has retained an interest in the trust. A retained interest will be valued at zero unless it is a *qualified interest*. In this connection, the retention of all income from a trust is *not* a qualified interest. Under such circumstances, the value of the income interest retained is zero and would compel the grantor to value the gift to his or her intended remainderman at 100 percent of the fair market value at the date that the transfer is made to the trust.

Practice Pointer: There is a significant difference between a retained income interest and a retained annuity interest. Where one retains an income interest, he or she is entitled to receive only the income earned by the property placed in trust; however, reserving an annuity interest requires payment to the grantor of a fixed amount (based on a percentage of the fair market value of the trust at its inception—a GRAT; or a percentage of the fair market value of the trust property valued annually—a GRUT). As a result, a grantor may receive an annuity represented by all the income earned by the trust; a carving out entirely of corpus to comply with the reserved annuity where no income is earned by the trust; or a combination of income and corpus where there is trust income but it is insufficient to meet the reserved annuity required. Congress has thus decreed that a qualified interest reserved by the grantor must take the form of either a GRAT or a GRUT.

Q 12:53 How does a GRAT work?

Under a GRAT, the grantor reserves a specific dollar amount to be paid each year (e.g., a trust funded with $800,000, in which the grantor reserves the right to receive $40,000 annually, will entitle the grantor to receive just that amount; it does not matter whether it comes from income, corpus, or both). The mandatory requirements required of a GRAT are as follows:

1. The annuity must be payable at least annually to the transferor for each taxable year of the term and may be paid following the close of the taxable year but not later than the due date (not including extensions) for filing the trust's return.

2. The annuity amount may be stated in dollars or as a fixed percentage of the value of the property transferred to the trust. Increases in the annuity are allowed, but only to the extent that the increased amount does not exceed 120 percent of the amount payable in the preceding year. [Treas Reg § 25.2702-3(b)(1)(ii)] Such increase will either reduce the taxable gift or reduce the term of the grantor's interest if the taxable gift remains the same. Conversely, the annuity amount may be decreased in future years, thus allowing for flexibility in future years where decreasing cash flow with respect to an asset is anticipated. [Treas Reg § 25.2702-3(c), Ex. 3]

3. The trust instrument must contain provision for short tax years (e.g., a trust created September 1 and the last tax year of the term. [Treas Reg § 25.2702-3(b)(3)]

4. If the annuity is stated as a percentage of the initial fair market value of the trust property, the trust must contain provision regarding adjustments for incorrect valuations. [Treas Reg § 25.2702-3(b)(2)]

5. The trust must contain a provision prohibiting additional contributions to the trust.

Q 12:54 What are the requirements that must be met by a GRUT?

A GRUT is a unitrust wherein the grantor reserves a specific percentage of the trust corpus (e.g., a trust funded with $500,000 in which the grantor reserves the right to receive 7 percent of the corpus, which must be revalued annually). A unitrust must meet all the requirements of the regulations [Treas Reg § 25.2702-3(c), 25.2702-3(d)], as follows:

1. The unitrust payment must be made at least annually to the transferor for each taxable year of the trust term and may be paid following the close of the taxable year but not later than the due date (not including extensions) of the trusts's return. [Treas Reg § 25.2702-3(c)(1)(i)]
2. The unitrust payment must be a fixed percentage of net fair market value of trust property determined annually.

Practice Pointer: As the Code Section 7520 rate decreases, the advantage of using a GRAT increases.

Q 12:55 Are there any other additional rules pertaining to a GRAT or a GRUT?

Yes, and they are as follows:

1. The trust instrument must prohibit distribution of trust property to anyone other than the transferor or an *applicable family member* retaining a qualified interest, prior to the termination of the qualified interest. [Treas Reg § 25.2702-3(d)(2)]
2. The term of the trust must be fixed in the trust instrument as the life of the transferor, a specified term of years, or the shorter of those two periods. [Treas Reg § 25.2702-3(d)(3)]

Practice Pointer: If the term of the trust is expressed as being the life of the grantor, Code Section 2036(a) requires that the full fair market value of the trust at the time of death be included in the transferor's estate.

3. The governing instrument must prohibit commutation of the qualified interest. [Treas Reg § 25.2702-3(d)(4)]

4. The trust is permitted to make payment of the greater (but not the lesser) of an annuity or unitrust amount. In that case, the retained interest is valued at the higher of the values of the two interests. [Treas Reg § 25.2702-3 (d)(1)]

5. Use of a contingent reversion does not operate to further reduce the value of the gift, as in the case of GRITs. The grantor may reserve the contingent reversion in order to qualify the corpus for the marital deduction should the grantor not survive the trust term.

6. The trust is also permitted to value a qualified annuity or unitrust interest by basing it upon the value of the interest for the shorter of the fixed term or the earlier death of the grantor, even though the annuity or unitrust interest is to be paid to the grantor's estate for the balance of the fixed term if the grantor dies during the term. [Treas Reg § 25.2702-3(e), Ex. 5] Most professional estate planners seek to *zero out* the remainder interest, thus avoiding a taxable gift to the grantor, by a combining a high annuity and a short term. This can only be accomplished with a GRAT because a GRUT is incapable of zeroing out.

Example 12-3: To zero out a ten-year GRAT using a 8.6 percent rate, the annuity would be 15.4 percent of the trust's value; however, if the term of the annuity is ten years or the earlier death of the grantor, the annuity increases to 22 percent with an 80-year-old grantor.

Q 12:56 How is a gift zeroed out in the case of an annuity trust?

The concept of zeroing out applies not only to a GRAT but also to a charitable lead trust. The value of a gift is depends on the duration of a trust and the amount reserved by the grantor. The amount of the gift therefore, is the difference between the value of the gift on the contribution to trust corpus and the value of the retained interest. The following table shows the minimum value of a retained annuity that will produce a taxable gift of zero, assuming a 10 percent IRS discount rate and various periods for which the annuity is payable:

Number of Years	Annuity as Percent of Original Value
2	57.6%
5	26.4%
10	16.3%
15	13.2%
20	11.7%
25	11.0%

Example 12-4: Grantor transfers $1,000,000 face amount of securities to a GRAT in a month that the IRS prescribes a discount rate under Code Section 7520. The trust is to have a duration of ten years and requires annual payments of the annuity.

To zero out the value of the gift, an annuity of 16.275 percent must be paid. As a result, the reserved annuity is valued at $1,000,000.

The GRAT can also be structured to consume the grantor's unified estate and gift tax credit (up to $600,000) so no current gift tax is payable. This would require a smaller annuity payment or a shorter term for the trust's existence. Thus, a 6.510 percent annuity ($65,100 annual annuity) creates a taxable gift of $599,987. Structuring a GRAT in this manner may be initially attractive but it violates the very reason for creating a GRAT because the grantor will be replenishing his or her estate and, at death, could conceivably have a larger gross estate than he or she had at the time the GRAT was created.

To determine how many years to zero out a gift at an assumed interest rate, divide the fair market value of the trust corpus by the anticipated annuity amount. Look at the IRS annuity tables that contain prescribed factors (assume 10 percent), and locate the corresponding annuity factor. The year listed next to the annuity factor will indicate the number of years required to zero out the gift.

Chapter 13

Asset Protection Trusts

Asset protection trusts are an important estate planning tool for protecting assets from personal liabilities such as personal creditor claims, alimony and child support claims, professional malpractice suits, and tax liability. Both offshore and domestic trusts are discussed.

Overview	13-1
Traditional Methods for Limiting Liability	13-2
Using Trusts as Protection from Creditors	13-3
Domestic Trusts Used as Protection from Creditors	13-5

Overview

Q 13:1 What does estate planning have to do with protecting an individual from his or her creditors?

Most of us think of estate planning as dealing exclusively with taxation and what has to be accomplished to mitigate or eliminate the impact of taxation on our income or assets, thereby allowing more income or unencumbered assets to be transferred. Although estate planning certainly does occupy itself with asset preservation by means of minimizing taxation, it must also take into account other means of asset preservation that are not influenced by taxes. One such crucial consideration is the preservation of assets and retention of income from creditors or creditors-to-be where the creditors are *not* connected with a taxing authority (e.g., trade creditor and judgment creditors).

Traditional Methods for Limiting Liability

Q 13:2 How do individuals generally protect their personal assets from creditors?

Typically, most individuals seeking shelter from creditor liability organize corporations to conduct their business. In satisfying a business judgment against a corporation, a creditor's claim against the corporation is limited to the assets owned by the corporation and does not implicate the assets of stockholders, unless, of course, a stockholder has personally guaranteed a corporate liability, or the law of a particular jurisdiction, as a matter of public policy, thrusts personal liability on a stockholder. Professionals such as physicians, dentists, and attorneys, who operate their professional practices through personal service corporations, are mandated by law to face personal liability in connection with legal actions brought against them for malpractice. In most cases, the professional corporation and the professional individual will carry malpractice insurance to anticipate such situations; however, there is always the possibility that a judgment may be rendered that exceeds the malpractice insurance being carried or that the insurance carrier will disallow the claim.

Q 13:3 Are there other forms under which business may be conducted that will also protect individuals from liabilities created by the businesses they have organized?

There are several forms of business entities that, like corporations, are designed to protect their individual creators from having their personal assets threatened by the liabilities incurred by their business. The organizational forms that clearly *do not* offer such protection are the sole proprietorship or the general partnership; however, the limited partnership and the recent addition to the selection of methods for conducting business—the limited liability company (LLC) and its offshoot, the limited liability partnership (LLP)—offer the same liability protection to the limited partner and LLC member as a corporation does to its stockholder. In a limited partnership, the general partner retains general liability to the creditors of the partnership while the limited partners' liability is generally restricted to their capital investments in the partnership. In an LLC, the members' liability is also generally restricted to the members' capital investment in the LLC.

Q 13:4 Why have LLCs and LLPs become increasingly popular?

LLCs were first given legal recognition with the advent of legislation introduced in Wyoming in 1977. They were intended to provide the best nontax feature of a corporation—limited liability—with the best nontax feature of a partnership: allowing income and loss to pass through, without an intervening corporate tax, directly to the partner. Today, 49 states (plus the District of Columbia) have enacted LLC legislation (Hawaii is the sole exception). The reason for the growth of professional LLPs is that, unlike a partner in a general professional partnership, a partner in a professional LLP is not personally liable for the professional misfeasance of another partner, so that his or her personal assets are not threatened by the liability created by misfeasance of another partner.

Using Trusts as Protection from Creditors

Q 13:5 Why should a trust be used for protection from creditors instead of a corporation, limited partnership, LLC, or LLP, all of which are intended to accomplish the same purpose?

Corporations, limited partnerships, LLCs, and LLPs are traditional methods for protecting personal assets from business creditors: each of these entities acts as a shield against personal liability. None of these entities, however, can protect an individual from such personal liabilities as personal creditor claims, alimony and child support claims, personal tort liability, tort liability of officers and directors of organizations that face potential environmental liability, professional malpractice suits, and personal federal, state, and local tax liabilities.

Q 13:6 Is there any method currently being used to thwart personal liability claims?

An editorial in *The Wall Street Journal* (March 1, 1996) described a method used by lawyers to shelter their personal assets by transferring them overseas to such places as the Cook Islands in the South Pacific. Many professionals have been making such overseas transfers to places such as the Bahamas, the Turk and Caicos Islands, Belize, and Gibraltar, and these transfers are perfectly legal. In all these cases, the vehicle used for the transfer of the assets overseas is an offshore asset protection trust (OAPT).

Q 13:7 What is an OAPT?

Generally, an OAPT is a trust created under the laws of certain foreign jurisdictions designed to shield the assets transferred to the trust from future creditors. The foreign jurisdiction selected for creating the trust has enacted favorable legislation intended to attract U.S. funds to its shores for such purpose. Once established, the OAPT is irrevocable and may terminate in a relatively short period, such as ten years, with the grantor of the trust retaining a reversionary interest. Alternatively, the trust term may be tied to the lives of the grantor or to one or more beneficiaries, usually children and spouse of the grantor, and the grantor. The trustee is a foreign trust company or financial institution. Ordinarily, the trust vests the trustee with unfettered discretion over distribution of income or principal among the beneficiaries named in the trust; however, the settlor typically reserves some measure of control over the trust, either through membership in a committee of advisors or as a self-designated protector of the trust with authority, among other things, to replace the trustee.

Q 13:8 Why use an OAPT?

An OAPT is used principally for two reasons: (1) it offers added protection from creditors when compared to other creditor avoidance structures, and (2) it offers this added protection without compelling the grantor to lose total control over the assets transferred to the OAPT.

Domestic Trusts Used as Protection from Creditors

Q 13:9 Why not use a domestic trust instead of an OAPT to protect assets from creditors?

There are several kinds of domestic trusts, such as spendthrift trusts and discretionary trusts, that a grantor may use to protect his or her assets or the income and assets of a trust beneficiary from creditor claims (see Qs 13:10–13:18), but none of these trusts can achieve creditor-proof results as successfully as an OAPT.

Q 13:10 What is a spendthrift trust?

The key provision contained in the typical spendthrift trust reads as follows:

> No interest of any beneficiary in the income or principal of this trust shall be assignable in anticipation of future payment or be liable in any way for the beneficiaries' debts or obligations and shall not be subject to attachment.

The intended effect of this provision is that the beneficiary's interest is not subject to the claims of his or her creditors. Accordingly, a creditor cannot attach, garnish, or use other legal processes to reach a beneficiary's interest in the spendthrift trust; however, once trust income is paid to the beneficiary by the trustee, the funds lose their trust character and may be attached by creditors. Of course, if the beneficiary spends the assets before a creditor attaches them or another of the beneficiary's creditors is quicker to respond with a claim, then a creditor is left with no opportunity to enforce the collection of the debt. Thus, the key virtue of the spendthrift provision is that the creditors' most effective remedies for collection—attachment and garnishment—are rendered useless.

Q 13:11 Can a spendthrift trust also be used by the person who created it (the grantor) to ward off creditor claims?

No. It has generally been held that a grantor cannot use a self-serving provision in a domestic trust of his or her own creation as insulation from creditors. Accordingly, a spendthrift provision included by a grantor as protection against creditors would be of no effect. It has generally been held that it is against public policy to permit the owner of property to create for his or her own benefit an interest in that property (through a trust created by such owner) that cannot be reached by his or her creditors.

Q 13:12 What is a forfeiture clause in a trust?

A forfeiture clause is inserted by a grantor in a trust to ensure that the trust beneficiary's interest is protected by providing that a trust terminates upon (1) an attempt by the beneficiary to transfer such interest, (2) an attempt by the creditors of the beneficiary's creditors to reach the interest, or (3) the beneficiary's bankruptcy. The forfeiture clause is self-triggering in that it automatically terminates the trust upon the occurrence of any of these three events. Forfeiture clauses are not as popular as spendthrift clauses because they conclude the trust and prevent the trust beneficiary from the continued enjoyment of the trust—the principal purpose for which the grantor created the trust.

Q 13:13 What is a support trust?

A support trust is commonly used as a means of allowing an independent entity—the trustee, who may be an individual, a trust company or financial institution, or a combination of both—to keep a watchful eye on the trust beneficiary so as to apply as much of the trust income or principal as may be necessary for the education or support of the beneficiary. Accordingly, standards of education or support as well as other standards that may be set forth by the grantor in the trust (e.g., maintenance, welfare, and comfort are also used, sometimes with adverse tax consequences) prevent creditors from compelling payment from the trustee because the trustee's discretionary authority to distribute trust assets to a beneficiary can only be exercised by reference to the standards contained in the trust.

Q 13:14 What is a discretionary trust?

Under a discretionary trust, a beneficiary is entitled to only as much of the income or principal of the trust as the trustee, in his or her controlled discretion, determines is fit to be distributed. Accordingly, a creditor cannot compel a trustee to distribute trust assets to a beneficiary because the beneficiary has no right to compel a trustee to make a distribution to the beneficiary. The grantor, in establishing the trust, has provided only the trustee with the discretion as to when and how much should be distributed to a beneficiary at any given time.

Q 13:15 Are spendthrift and forfeiture provisions also contained in discretionary trusts?

Yes. Both these provisions guard against creditors' attaching or obtaining trust funds the trustee has decided (in his or her discretion) to distribute to the debtor/beneficiary before the distribution. Accordingly, even a trustee's discretion to distribute is handcuffed by a spendthrift or forfeiture provision, and such restrictions preclude a creditor from imposing an attachment on a beneficiary's interest in a trust in violation of these provisions.

Q 13:16 Are there circumstances under which a creditor can reach the interest of a beneficiary in a trust despite its being discretionary or containing spendthrift or forfeiture provisions?

There is a general rule that, despite inhibiting provisions contained in a trust, the interest of the trust beneficiary can be reached in satisfaction of an enforceable claim against the beneficiary under the following circumstances:

1. By the wife or child of the beneficiary for support, or by the wife for alimony;

2. For necessary services rendered to the beneficiary or necessary supplies furnished (e.g., a trust beneficiary whose sole source of income is from the trust is negligently injured in a car accident by a driver with no insurance so that the hospital becomes a necessity provider to the trust beneficiary and entitled to perfect its claim against the trust);

3. For services rendered and materials furnished that preserve or benefit the interest of the beneficiary;

4. By the United States or a state to satisfy a claim against the beneficiary; or
5. Where none of the items listed in 1 through 4 apply, but considerations of public policy require it.

Q 13:17 What effect, if any, does the bankruptcy of a beneficiary have on the status of a spendthrift provision contained in a trust in which he or she is the beneficiary?

Section 541(c)(2) of the Bankruptcy Code provides that "a restriction on the transfer of a beneficial of the debtor [the bankrupt beneficiary] in a trust that is enforceable in a case under applicable nonbankruptcy law is enforceable in a case under this title." The term *applicable nonbankruptcy law* has been interpreted to include spendthrift provisions recognized under state laws. States vary as to how spendthrift provisions are affected by this bankruptcy provision (e.g., in Maryland the income of a spendthrift trust can be reached by the trustee in bankruptcy for up to 180 days after bankruptcy, but not thereafter, whereas New York allows bankruptcy claims to reach trust income for the duration of the trust). Governing state law takes into account a testator's domicile, where the trust is administered, or where land held in trust is located.

Q 13:18 Can a fraudulent conveyance be protected in a trust with a spendthrift provision?

No. The Uniform Fraudulent Conveyance Act, which many states have adopted, provides that a transfer made "with actual intent . . . to hinder, delay, or defraud either present or future creditors, is fraudulent as to both present and future creditors." Accordingly, a transfer to a trust under such circumstances would be treated as void and without effect.

Q 13:19 How does one distinguish under UFTA between a fraudulent conveyance affecting present creditors and one affecting future potential creditors?

In a decision rendered over 40 years ago, a Wyoming court held that "[i]f there were no creditors . . . the conveyance could not be fraudulent as to them." [Wantulok v Wantulok, 214 P 2d 477 (Wyo

1950)] The general consensus is that without creditors at the time of the transfer, there can be no fraud committed in regard to them. In a Florida case, a doctor transferred assets in his sole name to himself and his wife as tenants by the entireties (joint tenants with rights of survivorship). Some four months later, he committed malpractice, was sued, and won in a lower court that determined that the transfers in joint name took place before the debt arose thus rendering the patient merely a *possible* future creditor who was not protected by the fraudulent transfer law. A higher court sent the case back to the lower court to address more carefully whether the physician "harbored actual fraudulent intent at the time any of the transfers were made." [Hurlbert v Shackleton, 560 So 2d 1276 (Fl Dist Ct App 1990)] Accordingly, the key to any determination of a fraudulent transfer is to determine whether in fact the transferor had an intent to defraud at the time he or she made the transfer.

Q 13:20 Can a grantor of an OAPT reserve a reversionary interest so that, at the termination of the OAPT, its property reverts to the grantor?

It is not advisable for the grantor of an OAPT to reserve a reversionary interest. In a significant bankruptcy decision, a grantor established an OAPT in Bermuda in which he served as trust protector and retained a reversionary interest. Two years after the trust was created, the grantor petitioned for bankruptcy and neglected to list his reversionary interest in the OAPT as an asset on his bankruptcy schedules, indicating when later questioned that he valued the reversionary interest at zero. The Bankruptcy Court responded that "a debtor may not omit the existence of an asset because he believes it to be worthless." Therefore, the court concluded that the nonlisting by the grantor on the schedule indicated his intent to hinder or delay creditors making claims on his reversionary interest in the OAPT, and the grantor was denied discharge from bankrutpcy. [Peoples Bank of Charlestown v Colburn, 145 BR 851 (Bankr ED Va 1992)] This case may represent an exaggerated instance of greed, but nevertheless connotes possible adverse consequences where a grantor retains a connection to the property that would allow him or her to reel it in after the OAPT has served its purpose.

Q 13:21 How can an individual avoid fraudulent conveyance laws when making a transfer from his or her name?

The transfer must be shown to be motivated for purposes other than protecting the transferor from creditors. Reasons for a transfer may derive from motives as varied as any of the following: estate planning, adhering the provisions of a premarital agreement, bona fide tax avoidance, or foreign and investment management. Also, it is imperative that the transferor not become insolvent as a result of the transfer.

Q 13:22 What is the distinction between protection from creditors through use of an OAPT and protection through use of domestic trusts, which include spendthrift provisions and forfeiture provisions?

Most notably, an OAPT, properly structured, allows the grantor protection from his or her creditors, whereas the domestic trust does not allow a grantor to create a trust with self-serving provisions, such as spendthrift or forfeiture provisions that are intended to shield the grantor from creditors. Such provisions in a domestic trust are only applicable to—and are only intended to protect and benefit the beneficiary of—the domestic trust.

Q 13:23 How does an OAPT protect a grantor from his or her creditors?

Most of the foreign havens (e.g., Belize, the Cook Islands, Gibraltar, and the Cayman Islands) are doing their best to encourage the placement of funds in their financial institutions. To facilitate this goal, they have created laws that protect the assets contained in OAPTs created under their jurisdiction from being attached or levied. In a typical case, a creditor, after lengthy and costly litigation in the United States, searches for and finds the assets of the judgment debtor who has them tied up in the arcane provisions of the laws of a foreign jurisdiction, all intended to frustrate the creditor. Under these circumstances, it would be extremely time-consuming, costly, and perhaps ultimately pointless for a harried creditor to continue to pursue the collection of the judgment. Further, many foreign jurisdictions do not respect judgments entered in other jurisdictions, so that in many cases a creditor will have to renew his or her claim against the creditor in the foreign jurisdiction.

Q 13:24 How long does a creditor usually have to press his or her domestic judgment in a foreign jurisdiction that serves as a haven for OAPTs?

The foreign OAPT havens also create difficulty for the beleaguered creditor by the manner in which their statutes of limitations are intended to apply. In the Cayman Islands, which is most favorable to creditors, a creditor must initiate collection proceedings against the grantor or the OAPT within six years from the date of transfer. Cyprus and the Bahamas permit a creditor to initiate proceedings for only two years from the date of transfer. The Cook Islands provides an even greater shield for the debtor by requiring a creditor to commence litigation against the debtor within two years after the creditor's right to bring a suit has accrued or within one year of the transfer of assets.

Q 13:25 Has the IRS taken a position on OAPTs?

The IRS, in a private letter ruling, addressed certain income, estate, and gift tax issues involved in the creation and transfer of assets to an OAPT. [Ltr Rul 9332006] In the ruling, two U.S. citizens, who were siblings and trust grantors, created a 100-year irrevocable trust in a foreign jurisdiction. The trust beneficiaries included the two grantors, one of their parents, and the heirs of the grantors. An unrelated protector was authorized to channel trust distributions for the benefit of either grantor. The IRS was asked to resolve the gift and estate tax questions and relied on the taxpayers' claim that, under the law of the foreign country, neither a creditor or beneficiary (including the grantors as beneficiaries) could mandate to the trustee that trust assets could be distributed to them or for their benefit. Accordingly, the IRS ruled that there was a completed gift and that no part of the trust assets is includible in the estates of either of the grantors. The IRS also ruled that the trust was a "grantor trust," which meant that, for income tax purposes, the grantors are required to include the trust income on their individual income tax returns.

Q 13:26 What is a protector of an OAPT?

There is no role of a protector in domestic trusts. The domestic trust only requires three roles: (1) the grantor or settlor who creates the trust, (2) the trustee who manages the trust based on provisions contained in the trust document, and (3) the beneficiary who is intended to be the recipient of trust assets and income. A grantor may hold dual roles as grantor-trustee or grantor-beneficiary but may not hold all three roles; otherwise all three roles would merge, and the trust would not have legal validity.

The role of protector is unique to foreign trusts and may be granted broad powers by the grantor under the provisions of the trust, including the following powers:

1. To oversee the activities of the trustees;
2. To remove and replace the trustees;
3. To authorize payouts to beneficiaries;
4. To vary beneficiaries; and
5. To change jurisdictions or applicable law.

Many foreign jurisdictions do not allow the grantor of a trust to also act as its protector, so that in these jurisdictions, the grantor would name a trusted family member, a friend, his or her lawyer, or a trusted professional as the protector; however, two jurisdictions, the Cook Islands and Belize, presently allow the grantor to act as his or her own protector without endangering the assets to claims of creditors.

Q 13:27 What are some of the risks and expenses in the creation and operation of OAPTs?

Individuals should be very aware of the political instability of many of the tax havens offering hospitality to OAPTs. It was not so long ago that Cuba and Nicaragua expropriated the property of both nationals and noncitizens without providing any compensation to those affected by the expropriation. Many OAPTs contain flight clauses that provide that a trustee can relocate the assets to another foreign jurisdiction if any event threatens the trust or its assets. Also, there is no requirement that the assets of an OAPT be located in the foreign jurisdiction under which the trust was created. In this connection, individuals should be wary of retaining the OAPT assets in the United States because U.S. courts could find reasons to justify their attachment by a creditor in spite of the existence of the OAPT.

Furthermore, attorneys and accountants who specialize in the creation of OAPTs within the tax and estate planning sector do not come cheaply: the professional fees can be significant.

Q 13:28 What are the ethical and policy considerations that a professional person should entertain before being linked to an OAPT?

This is a nagging question for professionals because in many instances, a client is creating an OAPT for the purpose of avoiding potential creditor claims against his or her property. The American Bar Association in Rule 1.2(d) of the Model Rules of Professional Responsibility states that a lawyer "shall not counsel a client to engage, or assist a client, in conduct that the lawyer knows or reasonably should know is criminal or fraudulent." Certified public accountants and other professionals are subject to the same kind of proscriptions. In the case of an OAPT, conveyances made to thwart possible future creditor claims so as to limit one's potential liability to what is in his or her own name should not be considered fraudulent. It is clear to anyone who seeks refuge from personal liability that corporations, limited liability companies, and limited partnerships are chosen by those entering a new business or professional practice to avoid personal liability. Therefore, in the right circumstances, a U.S. person should be able, with proper professional representation, to create an OAPT that will protect the assets placed in it from future creditor claims.

Chapter 14

Tax and Estate Planning in Marital Settlements

A marital split-up is an exhausting experience, draining both emotional and financial resources. Among the controversial issues on which separating spouses frequently contend are: (1) the amount, frequency, and duration of alimony payments; (2) the division and allocation of property; (3) the amount, frequency, and duration of child support payments; and (4) establishing the duration, ownership, and beneficiaries of security obligations, such as life insurance policies.

These are but a few of the considerations around which controversy may arise, and each is fraught with tax consequences. For example, it generally is the divorcing husband who, when required to pay alimony, seeks to maximize his tax deduction in paying it. Conversely, the divorcing wife looks to minimize the tax impact on the settlements she receives. Each spouse realizes that the only income that really matters is the income remaining after taxes.

Another issue that may arise, sometimes years after the divorce, relates to dealing with the Internal Revenue Service when an innocent spouse learns that his or her spouse has unreported income with respect to a joint tax return that the innocent spouse signed without knowledge of such income having been received by the other spouse and without having derived any economic benefit from it.

Estate and Retirement Planning Answer Book

An extensive body of case law has been created that can provide useful insights for the innocent spouse who becomes enmeshed in a situation of this kind.

Owing to these complexities, the preservation and accumulation of income and assets—the goals of responsible estate planning—play an integral role for each of the divorcing spouses. The questions and answers that follow anticipate and highlight tax considerations connected with the dissolution of a marriage and are based on the significant changes made by Congress in 1984 in the Internal Revenue Code provisions governing the transfer of property between spouses, payment of alimony, separate maintenance, and the entitlement to the child dependency exemption.

Alimony and Separate Maintenance Payments	14-3
Child Support	14-12
Taxability of Property Transfers	14-15
Alimony Trusts	14-17
Employee Retirement Benefits	14-19
Annulments and Sham Divorces	14-21
Filing Status	14-22
Selling the Marital Home	14-23
Deductibility of Legal and Accounting Fees	14-24
The Innocent Spouse Rules	14-25
Estate Tax Considerations	14-26

Alimony and Separate Maintenance Payments

Q 14:1 In structuring a separation agreement or legal instrument for incorporation into a divorce decree, do the laws of the state in which the separation or divorce takes place determine the tax effects governing the provisions of the agreement?

No. The IRS and the courts agree that the provisions of the Internal Revenue Code determine whether a payment is deductible and includible as to the payer and payee spouse, respectively. "State law may control only when the Federal taxing act, by express language or necessary implication, makes its own operation dependent on the State law." [Burnet v Harmel, 287 US 103, 110 (1932); Rev Rul 58-192, 1958-1 CB 34]

Q 14:2 How are alimony or separate maintenance payments treated for federal income tax purposes?

Alimony or separate maintenance payments are defined under the provisions of Code Sections 71 and 215 and are included in the gross income of the payee spouse and allowed as a deduction from the gross income of the payor spouse, under each of those provisions, respectively.

Q 14:3 What is an alimony or separate maintenance payment?

An alimony or separate maintenance payment is any payment received by or on behalf of a spouse, which for this purpose includes a former spouse, of the payor under a divorce or separation instrument that meets all of the following requirements:

1. The payment is in cash and can be received by or on behalf of the payee spouse. The IRS regulations provide, in part:

   For example, cash payments of rent, mortgage, tax or tuition liabilities of the payee spouse made under the terms of the divorce or separation instrument will qualify as alimony or separate maintenance payments even if made to third parties

Q 14:3   **Estate and Retirement Planning Answer Book**

on behalf of the spouse. Any payments to maintain property owned by the payor spouse and used by the payee spouse (including mortgage payments, real estate taxes and insurance premiums) are not payments on behalf of a spouse even if those payments are made pursuant to the terms of the divorce or separation instrument. Premiums paid by the payor spouse for term or whole life insurance on the payor's life made under the terms of the divorce or separation instrument will qualify as payments on behalf of the payee spouse to the extent that the payee spouse is the owner of the policy. [Temp Treas Reg § 1.71-1T(b), Q&A 6]

2. The payment is not designated as a payment that is excludable from the gross income of the payee and nondeductible by the payor. Accordingly, if the divorce or separation agreement does not designate a payment as being excludable in gross income under Code Section 71 and not deductible under Code Section 215, then it is considered a taxable alimony payment.

Example 14-1: Ed and Sue enter into a separation agreement that provides that Ed will pay Sue the sum of $24,000 per year, in monthly installments of $2,000 unallocated as between alimony and child support. The unallocated support is to terminate on Sue's death, remarriage, or cohabitation with another unrelated male and thereupon, Ed is to pay for the support of the unemancipated (i.e., a child who has not yet reached majority age) children of the marriage the sum of $6,000 per child per year. The agreement also includes a provision regarding taxation that states that the agreement has been negotiated and executed on the assumption that payments made by Ed will be deductible to him and taxable to Sue, and if not determined as such by a binding legal determination, then the agreement is to be renegotiated.

Because the agreement between Ed and Sue does not designate Ed's payment as being excludable from Sue's income or nondeductible to Ed, it is construed as a deductible and includible alimony payment to Ed and Sue, respectively. Indeed, in the example, the parties make clear their intention that Ed's payment is to be construed as alimony; however, if the parties made no mention in the agreement as to how they intend to treat Ed's payment, the payment would nevertheless still be treated as alimony. Code Section 71 requires that the parties specifically

14-4

designate in the agreement their intention that Ed's payment not be includible in Sue's income and not be deductible by Ed. In the absence of such a specific provision, Ed's payment is alimony.

3. In the case of spouses legally separated under a decree of divorce or separate maintenance, the spouses are not members of the same household at the time the payment is made.
4. The payor has no liability to continue to make any payment after the death of the payee (or to make any payment as a substitute for such payment) and the divorce or separation instrument states that there is no such liability; however, a different rule applies if the payee spouse remarries.
5. The payment is not treated as child support.
6. To prevent the parties from converting a property settlement agreement (nondeductible payments) into an alimony agreement that provides the payor spouse with a deduction for each payment made, Code Section 71 creates rules designed to inhibit excess front-loading of alimony payments. These rules provide that if the alimony payments in the first year exceed the average payments in the second and third years by more than $15,000, the excess amounts are recaptured in the third year. The payor spouse includes the excess in income and the payee spouse, who had previously included the alimony in income, deducts the excess amount in computing his or her adjusted gross income.

Worksheet 1 should be used to determine the application of the alimony recapture rules.

Q 14:4 Are there any exceptions to the recapture rule?

Yes. Payments under a temporary (i.e., *pendente lite*) order or decree are not subject to the recapture rules. Furthermore, the recapture rules do not apply if the alimony or separate maintenance payments cease owing to the death of either spouse before the close of the third post-separation year, or because the payee spouse remarries before the close of that year. The recapture rules do not apply if the payor spouse experiences a continuing liability (over a period of at least three years) for the payment of a fixed portion(s) of his or her income from a business or property, or from compensation for employment or self-employment.

Worksheet 1: Alimony Recapture Rules

Note: Do not enter less than zero on any line.

1. Alimony paid in **2nd year** .... _____
2. Alimony paid in **3rd year** .... _____
3. Floor $15,000
4. Add lines 2 and 3 .... _____
5. Subtract line 4 from line 1 .... _____
6. Alimony paid in **1st year** .... _____
7. Adjusted alimony paid in **2nd year** (line 1 less line 5) .... _____
8. Alimony paid in **3rd year** .... _____
9. Add lines 7 and 8 .... _____
10. Divide line 9 by 2 .... _____
11. Floor $15,000
12. Add lines 10 and 11 .... _____
13. Subtract line 12 from line 6 .... _____
14. **Recaptured alimony.** Add lines 5 and 13 .... *_____

*If you deducted alimony paid, report this amount as income on line 11, Form 1040. If you reported alimony received, deduct this amount on line 29, Form 1040.

Q 14:5 What is the *divorce or separation instrument,* required under Code Section 71, under which an alimony payment must qualify in order to be deductible?

A divorce or separation instrument must be one of the following:

- A final decree of divorce or separate maintenance or a written instrument incident to such a decree
- A written separation agreement

14-6

- A temporary (in legal terminology, *pendente lite*) support order requiring one spouse to make alimony or separate maintenance payments to the other spouse

Q 14:6 If the divorce decree or written separation agreement providing for a continuation of the alimony payments after remarriage conflicts with a state law that precludes such payments from constituting alimony, are the alimony payments nondeductible for federal income tax purposes?

No. Code Section 71 does not disqualify a payment represented between the parties as alimony where, for example, the payee spouse remarries. There is no requirement that a payment represented as alimony be made pursuant to an obligation of support. Indeed, the IRS has taken the position that alimony income and the corresponding deduction are mandated even though they are made after remarriage of the payee-spouse, as long as the legal instrument required the continuation of payments and all other compliance provisions of Code Section 71 are satisfied. [Ltr Rul 8644061]

Q 14:7 In order to be treated as alimony or separate maintenance payments, must the payments be *periodic*, as that term was defined prior to enactment of the Tax Reform Act of 1984, and be made in discharge of a legal obligation of the payor to support the payee arising out of a marital or family relationship?

No. The Tax Reform Act of 1984 replaces the old requirements with the requirements described in Q 14:3, above. The requirements that alimony or separate maintenance payments be periodic and be made in discharge of a legal obligation to support arising out of a marital or family relationship have been eliminated.

Q 14:8 May alimony or separate maintenance payments be made in a form other than cash?

No. Only cash payments (including checks and money orders payable on demand) qualify as alimony or separate maintenance payments. Transfers of services or property (including a debt instrument of a third party or an annuity contract), execution of a debt instrument by the payor, or the use of property of the payor do not qualify as alimony or separate maintenance payments.

Q 14:9 May payments of cash to a third party on behalf of a spouse qualify as alimony or separate maintenance payments if the payments are made to the third party at the written request of the payee spouse?

Yes. For instance, instead of making an alimony or separate maintenance payment directly to the payee, the payor spouse may make a cash payment to a charitable organization if such payment is pursuant to the written request, consent or ratification of the payee spouse. Such request, consent, or ratification must state that the parties intend the payment to be treated as an alimony or separate maintenance payment to the payee spouse subject to the rules of Section 71, and must be received by the payor spouse prior to the date of filing of the payor's first return of tax for the taxable year in which the payment was made.

Q 14:10 How may spouses designate that payments otherwise qualifying as alimony or separate maintenance payments shall be excludable from the gross income of the payee and nondeductible by the payor?

The spouses may designate that payments otherwise qualifying as alimony or separate maintenance payments shall be nondeductible by the payor and excludable from gross income by the payee by a provision in the divorce or separation instrument. [IRC § 71(b)(2)] If the spouses have executed a written separation agreement [IRC § 71(b)(2)(B)], any writing signed by both spouses that designates otherwise qualifying alimony or separate maintenance payments as nondeductible and excludable and that refers to the written separation agreement will be treated as a written separation agreement (and thus a divorce or separation instrument) for purposes of the preceding sentence. If the spouses are subject to temporary support orders [IRC § 71(b)(2)(C)], the designation of otherwise qualifying alimony or separate payments as nondeductible and excludable must be made in the original or a subsequent temporary support order. A copy of the instrument containing the designation of payments as not alimony or separate maintenance payments must be attached to the payee's first filed return of tax (Form 1040) for each year in which the designation applies.

Q 14:11 What are the consequences if, at the time a payment is made, the payor and payee spouses are members of the same household?

Generally, a payment made at the time when the payor and payee spouses are members of the same household cannot qualify as an alimony or separate maintenance payment if the spouses are legally separated under a decree of divorce or of separate maintenance. For purposes of the preceding sentence, a dwelling unit formerly shared by both spouses shall not be considered two separate households even if the spouses physically separate themselves within the dwelling unit. The spouses will not be treated as members of the same household if one spouse is preparing to depart from the household of the other spouse, and does depart not more than one month after the date the payment is made. If the spouses are not legally separated under a decree of divorce or separate maintenance, a payment under a written separation agreement or a decree described in Code Section 71(b)(2)(C) may qualify as an alimony or separate maintenance payment notwithstanding that the payor and payee are members of the same household at the time the payment is made.

Q 14:12 Assuming all other requirements relating to the qualification of certain payments as alimony or separate maintenance payments are met, what are the consequences if the payor spouse is required to continue to make the payments after the death of the payee spouse?

None of the payments before or after the death of the payee spouse qualify as alimony or separate maintenance payments; this would be tantamount to allowing a deduction for a property settlement rather than a payment of alimony; however, payments made as alimony under a legal instrument between the parties will continue as such where the payee spouse remarries (see Q 14:6).

Q 14:13 What are the consequences if the divorce or separation instrument fails to state that there is no liability for any period after the death of the payee spouse to continue to make any payments that would otherwise qualify as alimony or separate maintenance payments?

If the instrument fails to include such a statement, none of the payments, whether made before or after the death of the payee spouse, will qualify as alimony or separate maintenance payments.

Example 14-2: A is to pay B $10,000 in cash each year for a period of 10 years under a divorce or separation instrument that does not state that the payments will terminate upon the death of B. None of the payments will qualify as alimony or separate maintenance payments.

Example 14-3: A is to pay B $10,000 in cash each year for a period of 10 years under a divorce or separation instrument that states that the payments will terminate upon the death of B. In addition, under the instrument, A is to pay B or B's estate $20,000 in cash each year for a period of 10 years. Because the $20,000 annual payments will not terminate upon the death of B, these payments will not qualify as alimony or separate maintenance payments; however, the separate $10,000 annual payments will qualify as alimony or separate maintenance payments.

Q 14:14 Will a divorce or separation instrument be treated as stating that there is no liability to make payments after the death of the payee spouse if the liability to make such payments terminates pursuant to applicable local law or oral agreement?

No. Termination of the liability to make payments must be stated in the terms of the divorce or separation instrument. The provisions of a state law or an oral understanding between the parties do not determine deductibility of an alimony payment or its inclusion in income.

Tax and Estate Planning in Marital Settlements   Q 14:16

Q 14:15   What are the consequences if the payor spouse is required to make one or more payments (in cash or property) after the death of the payee spouse as a substitute for the continuation of pre-death payments that would otherwise qualify as alimony or separate maintenance payments?

If the payor spouse is required to make any such substitute payments, none of the otherwise qualifying payments will qualify as alimony or separate maintenance payments. The divorce or separation instrument need not state, however, that there is no liability to make any such substitute payment.

Q 14:16   Under what circumstances will one or more payments (in cash or property) that are to occur after the death of the payee spouse be treated as a substitute for the continuation of payments that would otherwise qualify as alimony or separate maintenance payments?

To the extent that one or more payments are to be initiated, increased, or accelerated as a result of the death of the payee spouse, such payments are treated as a substitute for the continuation of payments terminating on the death of the payee spouse and are not deductible or includible as alimony. The determination of whether or not such payments are a substitute for the continuation of payments that would otherwise qualify as alimony or separate maintenance payments, and of the amount of the otherwise qualifying alimony or separate maintenance payments for which any such payments are a substitute, will depend on all of the facts and circumstances.

> **Example 14-4:** Under the terms of a divorce decree, A is obligated to make annual alimony payments to B of $30,000, terminating on the earlier of the expiration of six years or the death of B. B maintains custody of the minor children of A and B. The decree provides that at the death of B, if there are minor children of A and B remaining, A will be obligated to make annual payments of $10,000 to a trust, the income and corpus of which are to be used for the benefit of the children until the youngest child attains the age of majority. These facts indicate that A's liability to make annual $10,000 payments in trust for the benefit of his minor

14-11

children upon the death of B demonstrates that $10,000 of the $30,000 annual payments to B are a substitute for child support; thereby preventing the $10,000 from being deductible or includible as alimony during B's lifetime.

Example 14-5: Under the terms of a divorce decree, A is obligated to make annual alimony payments to B of $30,000, terminating on the earlier of the expiration of 15 years or the death of B. The divorce decree provides that if B dies before the expiration of the 15-year period, A will pay to B's estate the difference between the total amount that A would have paid had B survived, minus the amount actually paid. For instance, if B dies at the end of the 10th year in which payments are made, A will pay to B's estate $150,000 ($450,000 − $300,000). These facts indicate that A's liability to make a lump-sum payment to B's estate upon the death of B is a substitute for the full amount of each of the annual $30,000 payments to B. Therefore, none of the assumed payments are alimony. The result would be the same if the lump sum payable at B's death were discounted by an appropriate interest factor to account for the prepayment.

Child Support

Q 14:17 What are the consequences of a payment which the terms of the divorce or separation instrument fix as payable for the support of a child of the payor spouse?

A payment which, under the terms of the divorce or separation instrument, is fixed (or treated as fixed) as payable for the support of a child of the payor spouse does not qualify as an alimony or separate maintenance payment. Thus, such a payment is not deductible by the payor spouse or includible in the income of the payee spouse.

Q 14:18 When is a payment fixed (or treated as fixed) as payable for the support of a child of the payor spouse?

A payment is fixed as payable for the support of a child of the payor spouse if the divorce or separation instrument specifically designated some sum or portion (which may fluctuate) as payable for the support of a child of the payor spouse. A payment will be treated as fixed as payable for the support of a child of the payor spouse if the payment is reduced (1) on the happening of a contingency relating to a child of the payor, or (2) at a time that can clearly be associated with such a contingency. A payment may be treated as fixed as payable for the support of a child of the payor spouse even if other separate payments specifically are designated as payable for the support of a child of the payor spouse.

Q 14:19 When does a contingency relate to a child of the payor?

For this purpose, a contingency relates to a child of the payor if it depends on any event relating to that child, regardless of whether such event is certain or likely to occur. Events that relate to a child of the payor include the following: the child's attaining a specified age or income level, dying, marrying, leaving school, leaving the spouse's household, or gaining employment.

Q 14:20 When will a payment be treated as to be reduced at a time which can clearly be associated with the happening of a contingency relating to a child of the payor?

There are two situations, described below, in which payments that would otherwise qualify as alimony or separate maintenance payments will be presumed to be reduced at a time clearly associated with the happening of a contingency relating to a child of the payor. In all other situations, reductions in payments will not be treated as clearly associated with the happening of a contingency relating to a child of the payor.

The first situation is where the payments are to be reduced not more than six months before or after the date the child is to attain the age of 18, 21, or local age of majority. The second situation is where the payments are to be reduced on two or more occasions that occur not more than one year before or after a different child of the payor spouse attains a certain age between the ages of 18 and 24, inclusive. The certain age referred to in the preceding sentence must be the same for each such child, but need not be a whole number of years.

The presumption in these two situations (i.e., that payments are to be reduced at a time clearly associated with the happening of a contingency relating to a child of the payor) may be rebutted (either by the Service or by taxpayers) by showing that the time at which the payments are to be reduced was determined independently of any contingencies relating to the children of the payor. The presumption in the first situation will be rebutted conclusively if the reduction is a complete cessation of alimony or separate maintenance payments during the sixth post-separation year or upon the expiration of a 72-month period. The presumption may also be rebutted in other circumstances, for example, by showing that alimony payments are to be made for a period customarily provided in the local jurisdiction, such as a period equal to one-half the duration of the marriage.

Example 14-6: A and B are divorced on July 1, 1985, when their children, C (born July 15, 1970) and D (born September 23, 1972), are 14 and 12, respectively. Under the divorce decree, A is to make alimony payments to B of $2,000 per month. Such payments are to be reduced to $1,500 per month on January 1, 1991, and to $1,000 per month on January 1, 1995. On January 1, 1991, the date of the first reduction in payments, C will be 20 years, 5 months, and 17 days old. On January 1, 1995, the date of the second reduction in payments, D will be 22 years, 3 months, and 9 days old. Each of the reductions in payments is to occur not more than one year before or after a different child of A attains the age of 21 years and 4 months. (Actually, the reductions are to occur not more than one year before or after C and D attain ANY of the ages 21 years, 3 months, and 9 days through 21 years, 5 months, and 17 days.) Accordingly, the reductions will be presumed to clearly be associated with the happening of a contingency relating to C and D. Unless this presumption is rebutted, payments under the divorce decree equal to the sum of the reduction ($1,000 per month) will be treated as fixed for the support of the children of A and therefore will not qualify as alimony or separate maintenance payments.

Taxability of Property Transfers

Q 14:21 What are the tax consequences of property transfers between spouses in a marital separation?

In 1962, the United States Supreme Court issued a landmark decision [United States v Davis 370 US 65 (1962)], involving a husband who transferred certain shares of stock that had appreciated in value to his wife. The transfer was in exchange for a waiver of marital claims by the wife. The Supreme Court held that this transfer constituted a taxable event and the value of the release of marital claims by the wife was equal to the fair market value of the stock surrendered to her by the husband. Accordingly, the husband had a taxable gain measured by the difference between the cost of the stock to him and its fair market value at the time of transfer to his wife. The wife, on the other hand, was enabled to have a cost basis in the stock she received equal to its fair market value at the time of receipt and was not adversely affected by the transaction. This caused major problems in negotiating property transfers between the parties because of the differing tax consequences; and, in many cases, caused unanticipated adverse tax effects to the transferring spouse who was unfamiliar with the *Davis* decision. As indicated below in Q 14:22, Congress acted in response to the *Davis* decision.

Q 14:22 Is the above rule of the *Davis* case still in effect?

No. Congress enacted IRC § 1041 in 1984 based on the premise that it was inappropriate to tax transfers between spouses and former spouses. Accordingly, all transfers similar to the *Davis* case transfers have, since 1984, been nontaxable events. Under § 1041 it is provided that:

1. No gain or loss is recognized on a transfer of property to a spouse or in trust for the benefit of a spouse; and

2. No gain or loss is recognized on the transfer of property to a former spouse or in trust for the benefit of a former spouse if the transfer is incident to a divorce.

Q 14:23 Does the rule of nontaxability of transfers of property between spouses apply only to those spouses involved in the divorce process?

No. This nontaxability rule also applies to any property transfers between the spouses that arise by reason of gift or sale and purchase; it would also extend to property transfers between a spouse and a sole proprietorship owned by the other spouse. In contrast, a sale arrangement and transfer between a spouse and a closely held corporation owned by the other spouse is treated as a taxable event.

Q 14:24 Does the nontaxability of property between divorcing spouses also apply where one of the spouses assigns income to which he or she is entitled?

No. The rule is that if someone entitled to receive income transfers the entitlement to that income to another person, the transferor will be taxed because the attempt to transfer is a prohibited assignment of income and, as such, is not insulated by the nontaxability provisions of Code Section 1041.

Q 14:25 Will the nontaxability rules also apply where one spouse transfers U. S. Savings Bonds with accrued but unrecognized interest to the other spouse?

The IRS holds that such a transfer represents an assignment of interest income that becomes taxable to the transferor when paid. It is not a property right that is being transferred. [Rev Rul 87-112]

Q 14:26 Who and what is excepted from the nontaxability rules of transfers between spouses?

Nonresident aliens are not entitled to the nontaxable benefits of Code Section 1041. Accordingly, if a U.S. spouse transfers property to his nonresident alien spouse, the transferring spouse would realize gain under the old rules. Also, where a spouse transfers property that has liabilities in excess of its adjusted basis to a trust, gain is recognized to the transferor and its recognition would cause an upward adjustment to the cost basis of the property to the recipient spouse. Also excepted are transfers of installment obligations to a trust. The gain will be accelerated to the transferor measured by the difference between its adjusted cost basis on the date of transfer and its fair market value.

Q 14:27 What is the effect of a transfer of property after the divorce?

Code Section 1041 provides nontaxability between the divorced spouses if the transfer is incident to divorce. To be *incident to divorce*, the transfer has to be made pursuant to the terms of a divorce or separation instrument as defined under Code Section 71(b)(2) and the transfer occurs no later than six years from the marriage termination date. A divorce or separation agreement is defined as a final decree of divorce, separate maintenance or written instrument incident to such a decree; a written separation agreement; or, a *pendente lite* order requiring one spouse to make alimony or separate maintenance payments to the other spouse.

Only two instances of former spouse transfers qualify:

- If the transfer occurs within one year after the date on which the marriage ceases, or
- If the transfer related to the cessation of the marriage.

Alimony Trusts

Q 14:28 What is an alimony trust?

An alimony trust is a secured commitment on the part of the payor spouse to place funds in trust that will provide the payee spouse with the alimony that he or she would otherwise receive directly from the other spouse. If an alimony trust is properly drafted, no part of the income that it earns annually (except the portion used for child support) will be taxed to the payor spouse, but instead, will be taxed to the payee spouse.

Example 14-7: Under a divorce decree, a husband is required (1) to pay his ex-wife monthly support of $1,000 for five years, subject to earlier termination upon her death or remarriage and (2) $200 monthly support for their minor child until the child reaches majority or graduates from college, whichever comes first. To fund his obligation, the husband transfers property in trust naming his lawyer as trustee: $1,000 per month from trust income to his former wife for the period of five years provided in the divorce decree, and if insufficient income is produced, then from trust principal; and $200 per month for child support under the same circumstances.

Under normal trust rules, the income from this trust would be taxed to the husband as grantor of the trust since it is being used to discharge the husband's legal obligation. However, under Code Section 682, the trust income is taxed to the ex-wife. The income from the trust fixed for the support of the child would be taxed to the husband because it discharges his legal obligation to support his minor child. [IRC §§ 677, 662]

Q 14:29 When does Code Section 682 apply to an alimony trust to keep the paying spouse from being taxed on the trust income and cause said trust income to be taxed to the payee spouse?

Code Section 682 applies where a spouse is divorced or legally separated under a decree of divorce or separate maintenance, or where one spouse is separated from the other under a written separation agreement. It also applies when a trust, formed as the result of a prenuptial agreement, continues after a divorce and the other substantive requirements of Code Section 682 are met.

Q 14:30 What purpose does an alimony trust serve?

An alimony trust is essentially a substitute for the typical unsecured alimony obligation of the payor spouse who obtains a deduction under Code Section 215 and requires the payee spouse to include the deductible amount in income under Code Section 71. Because the alimony trust is funded, it provides the payee spouse with the financial security of knowing that the payor spouse's obligation to pay alimony is not dependent upon an unsecured promise of the payor spouse to fulfill the payment commitment. It is often used by those who have sufficient assets to fund such a trust, because the overall tax consequences to the divorcing parties will be the same as an unsecured commitment to make alimony payments.

Q 14:31 It appears that Code Sections 71 and 682 cover the same situations by providing the payor spouse a deduction for alimony (IRC § 71) that is essentially the same as avoiding tax on the trust income received by the payee spouse (IRC § 682). Do these two Code sections cover the same situations?

No, there are some significant differences between them. Code Section 682 applies to a trust created before the divorce or separation and not in contemplation of it, while Code Section 71 applies only if the creation of the trust or payments by a previously created trust are in discharge of an obligation imposed upon or assumed by the payor spouse (or made specific) under the court order or decree divorcing or legally separating the spouses, or a written separation agreement.

Q 14:32 What is the effect to the payee spouse where the income from the alimony trust is derived exclusively from tax-exempt municipal bond interest?

The payee spouse is not required to include the tax-exempt municipal bond income in taxable income. [Stewart, 9 TC 195 (1956)] Accordingly, where an alimony trust is used, the trustee's investments, where appropriate, should be applied toward municipal bond investments since the trust beneficiary has no tax to pay on it and the payor spouse is not adversely affected.

Employee Retirement Benefits

Q 14:33 Why are retirement plans an integral part of the property division process?

During the course of a divorce proceeding, many states typically require that property be equitably distributed to the parties. Equitable distribution is the process by which the husband and wife agree (and if they do not agree, the divorce court will impose its decision) to divide all the assets accumulated during their marriage on an equitable basis. An equitable basis may be a division of 50/50, 60/40, or whatever is determined under the specific facts relating to the marriage. If one of the parties is the major earner and is a participant in a pension, profit sharing, or other form of retirement plan, then it is usually required that its value to him or her at the time of divorce be determined so that an equitable share can be made payable to the other.

> **Example 14-8:** John and Mary are divorcing and John is a participant in his employer's tax-qualified employees' profit sharing plan. Under the state law that has jurisdiction over the divorce, John's entire account balance in the profit sharing plan is marital property subject to equitable distribution. The only other significant asset acquired by John and Mary during their marriage is their residence. John and Mary agree to divide equally the values in both the residence and the profit sharing plan. The transfer of a one-half interest in the residence (assuming it was in John's name only) from John to Mary will be a nontaxable event and Mary will acquire a cost basis equal to one-half of John's cost basis in the residence; however, the assignment of John's one-half present interest in the profit sharing plan to Mary can only be accomplished with a qualified domestic relations order (QDRO).

Q 14:34 What is a qualified domestic relations order?

Under the Retirement Equity Act of 1984, an assignment of a participant's interest in an employees' benefit plan can be made pursuant to a court order to his or her alternate payee. An alternate payee is defined as any spouse, former spouse, child or other dependent of a participant that a QDRO recognizes as having a right to receive all or a portion of the benefits payable to the participant under the employees' benefit plan.

To be a QDRO, the order must clearly specify:

- The name and last known mailing address of the participant and the name and mailing address of each alternate payee covered by the order

Tax and Estate Planning in Marital Settlements   Q 14:36

- The amount or percentage of the participant's benefits to be paid by the plan to each alternate payee, or the manner of determining the amount or percentage
- The number of payments or period to which the order applies
- Each plan to which the order applies

Q 14:35 Are there any proscriptions by which the qualified domestic relations order is limited?

Yes. The QDRO may not:

- Require the plan to provide any type or form of benefit, or any option not otherwise provided under the plan
- Require the plan to provide increased benefits, determined on the basis of actuarial value
- Require the payment of benefits to an alternate payee that are required to be paid to another alternate payee under another order determined to be a QDRO

Note: The subject of QDROs is briefly outlined above to make readers aware that it can be a meaningful tool in negotiating a marital settlement. For a full and complete discussion of QDROs, see the *Qualified Domestic Relations Order Answer Book*, which is published as part of the Panel Answer Book Series.

Annulments and Sham Divorces

Q 14:36 What are the income tax consequences of an annulment?

If a state court with competent jurisdiction annuls a marriage and rules that no valid marriage ever existed, the hitherto "married" couple is required to file amended returns as unmarried individuals for all the years that have not been closed by the statute of limitations. This would also include the tax year in which they were married because they are considered single as of the close of that year. [Rev Rul 76-255, 1976-1 CB 40] There would likely be no delinquency penalty for any additional tax that might be due on the filing of the returns as single or head of household since a reasonable cause for the amended filing could be demonstrated.

Q 14:37 Can a married couple achieve tax savings by divorcing before the end of the year to file separate returns as single taxpayers—with the expectation of tax benefit from such filing—and subsequently remarry early in the next year?

Not according to the IRS. [Rev Rul 76-255, 1976-1 CB 40] In a subsequent letter ruling, the IRS emphasized the importance of the intent of the couple for divorcing prior to year-end, by holding that a married couple divorcing to avoid tax, had no intent to remarry although they would be living together much of the time after their divorce. [Ltr Rul 7835076] Accordingly, a divorce before year-end cannot be used as a cosmetic device for achieving tax savings where the couple's intent and conduct are clearly tax motivated.

Filing Status

Q 14:38 Can a married couple file a joint return if they are legally separated?

A married couple separated pursuant to a written separation agreement must file either a joint return or as married filing separately; however, if they are separated by December 31st of the tax year under a decree of divorce or a court order of separate maintenance—but not by a written separation agreement—they are treated as single taxpayers. There seems to be no logical basis for differing between legal separation by written agreement or legal separation effected by a court order of separate maintenance; however, the Code provisions are not necessarily intended to be logical.

Q 14:39 Can a married person qualify for head of household status?

Yes. Either or both spouses can qualify for head of household if that spouse meets all four of the following tests:

1. The spouse files a separate return.
2. The spouse furnished more than half of the maintenance costs of his or her household for the taxable year.
3. The spouse did not live with the other spouse during the last six months of the taxable year.
4. For over six months during the taxable year, the spouse's home was the main home of his or her child (including a legally adopted child, stepchild or foster child) who:
   a. Is claimed as a dependent or
   b. The child's other parent claims as a dependent.

Head of household filing status, while generally not as tax beneficial as a joint return, often provides tax savings greater than those made available by filing a single return or as married filing separately.

Q 14:40 **In connection with the filing status of the separated or divorced parties, who is entitled to claim the child dependency exemption?**

Amendments made by Congress in 1984 to the Internal Revenue Code provide that the parent having custody of the child is entitled to the dependency exemption unless the custodial parent releases the exemption claim to the noncustodial parent. IRS Form 8332 must be signed by the custodial parent releasing the claim for the dependency exemption to the noncustodial parent who attaches the form to his or her return to support the claim for the dependency exemption. Divorce decrees and separation agreements effected prior to 1985 are subject to different rules for claiming the dependency exemption.

Selling the Marital Home

Q 14:41 **What must a divorcing couple consider when selling their marital residence in connection with or as a result of their divorce?**

There are two significant issues to consider, both of which deal with the potential tax benefits that accompany the sale of a principal residence. If the couple or one of the spouses is at least 55 years of age at the time of the sale of the residence and they have lived in the property as a principal residence for at least three years of the five-year period ending on the date of the sale, then they may elect to exclude up to $125,000 of gain on the sale. If they file returns as married filing separately, then each spouse may claim up to $62,500 as excludable gain. This is a one-time election and therefore, once made, cannot be made again. Also, if only one spouse is at least 55 years of age and the principal residence is sold after the divorce, the other spouse, who has not yet reached age 55, cannot exclude his or her share of the $125,000 gain on his or her return. Since no marital status existed as of the close of the year, this spouse would be required to file a return as a single person or head of household. [IRC § 121]

Another relief provision is contained in Code Section 1034, which permits gain on the sale of a principal residence to be deferred if a new principal residence is purchased within a period beginning two years before or ending two years after the date of the sale. The cost of the new residence must equal or exceed the adjusted selling price of the old residence in order to permit deferment of the gain. This deferral provision applies separately to the gain realized by a husband and wife who agree to live apart, sell their jointly owned residence and purchase separate replacement residences. [Rev Rul 74-250, 1974-1 CB 202]

Also, the deferral provision and the provision allowing the one-time exclusion for taxpayers age 55 or older can be combined for taxpayers who qualify for both.

Deductibility of Legal and Accounting Fees

Q 14:42 Can a separated or divorced couple deduct the legal and accounting fees incurred in connection with their marital split?

No. the Supreme Court has ruled that because a divorce is rooted in matters of a personal nature, the professional fees in connection with the divorce cannot be deducted. [United States v Gilmore 372 US 39 (1963)] This rule, however, has not been applied to that portion of a professional fee that is properly allocated to tax advice or estate planning in connection with the divorce. Code Section 212(3) permits the ordinary and necessary expenses paid in connection with the determination, collection, or refund of any tax to be deductible. The amount available for deduction, however, must exceed, together with other applicable itemized deductions, 2 percent of the taxpayer's adjusted gross income.

Also, that part of a lawyer's fee for services rendered to collect alimony is deductible by the payee spouse under Code Section 212(1), because it is an ordinary and necessary expense related to the collection of income. [Jane U. Elliott 40 TC 304 (1963)] Such deductible expense, however, is only available if it exceeds 2 percent of the taxpayer's adjusted gross income, as explained above.

It is important, in both of the above described cases, that the professional's bill clearly differentiate between the fee charged for services rendered in connection with the separation or divorce and the fee charged for tax advice or collecting alimony (or both) and that this allocation of fees can be substantiated in the event of a tax examination by the IRS.

The Innocent Spouse Rules

Q 14:43 How is a spouse who innocently signs a joint return protected from tax liability, interest, and potential penalties as a result of income omissions or fictitious or exaggerated deductions claimed by the other spouse on the joint return?

Code Section 6013(e) grants innocent spouse protection where an innocent spouse did not enjoy significant economic benefits from the tax savings generated by the spouse at fault. The liability for filing a joint return is joint and several between the spouses; this means that the IRS can pursue either of the signing spouses for all or part of the tax, interest, and penalty liability unless innocent spouse relief is available.

Q 14:44 How does one qualify for innocent spouse relief?

To qualify for innocent spouse relief, a taxpayer must have filed a joint return that has a substantial understatement of tax attributable to a grossly erroneous item of the spouse at fault. The taxpayer must then establish that in signing the return, he or she did not know, and had no reason to know, that there was such substantial understatement. In addition, it must be shown that, taking into account all facts and circumstances, it is inequitable to hold the taxpayer liable for the deficiency in tax to the extent the deficiency is attributable to a grossly erroneous item.

Q 14:45 What is a *grossly erroneous item* for purposes of the innocent spouse provisions?

A grossly erroneous item is an item that is incorrectly omitted from gross income. Such an item also includes any claim of a deduction or credit for which there is no basis in fact or law. A substantial understatement for purposes of the innocent spouse provisions is any understatement that is more than $500.00.

Example 14-9: Husband and wife filed a joint return. Husband was the sole proprietor of a construction business who filed a Schedule C for the business with the couple's Form 1040 in which he claimed a substantial amount for cost of goods sold—which he could not substantiate to the IRS on its audit of the return. The wife, claiming innocent spouse status, argued that she did not know nor did she benefit from this omission from gross income which was grossly erroneous. The court held that the wife qualified for innocent spouse relief since she did not have access to information with respect to her husband's unsupported claim as to the cost of goods sold and did not benefit from the tax savings generated thereby. [Comm v Lilly, Ct of App 4th Cir (02/20/96)]

Estate Tax Considerations

Q 14:46 Can the estate of a deceased payor-spouse claim a deduction, for federal estate tax purposes, for the deceased individual's obligation to make future alimony or support payments to his or her former spouse, pursuant to a divorce decree?

Yes. Such an indebtedness constitutes a valid deductible claim for estate tax purposes. In addition, if the decedent was in arrears for alimony due under a divorce decree at the time of death, such arrears

Tax and Estate Planning in Marital Settlements   Q 14:46

are also deductible. Furthermore, where the divorce decree orders that support payments are to continue for the other spouse's life or until remarriage and the payor's estate is thereby obligated for such payment, then the estate can claim the present value of its obligation, based on IRS actuarial tables, as a deductible claim against the estate. This deduction can lead to a significant estate tax savings since the estate tax rates begin at 37 percent once the $600,000 exemption available to all estates for federal estate tax purposes has been consumed.

Chapter 15

Post-Death Estate Planning

Once a person dies, decisions must be made by the executor regarding the filing of an estate tax return and a final income tax return for the deceased. The Internal Revenue Code also permits executors to make a number of elections. This chapter describes the relative merits of those elections and the pros and cons of allocating expenses and deductions to either the estate tax return or the decedent's final income tax return. Also discussed in this chapter are various strategies the executor can use when distributing the assets of the estate in order to minimize the tax burden on the estate, the beneficiaries, or both.

Overview	15-2
Required Tax Returns	15-2
Deductions	15-4
Valuation of Assets	15-8
Elections	15-10
Distribution Income Planning	15-13
Disclaimers	15-15

Q 15:1   Estate and Retirement Planning Answer Book

Overview

Q 15:1   What is post-death estate planning?

Many decisions remain to be made after death occurs. Post-death estate planning centers around filing the appropriate tax returns, making the proper elections, planning estate distributions, and determining whether any disclaimers can and should be made. Both estate income and estate tax returns must be prepared and filed on time. The executor must consider whether to take a deduction for administrative expenses against the estate tax or the estate's income tax. Because estate assets can be valued as of the date of death or on an alternate valuation date, the estate executor must decide which of those dates to use.

Required Tax Returns

Q 15:2   Which federal tax returns must be filed by the executor?

The executor must file the decedent's final income tax return (Form 1040), the estate fiduciary tax return (Form 1041), and the federal estate tax return (Form 706). [IRC §§ 6012(b)(1), 6012(b)(4), 6018(a)]

Q 15:3   What requirements apply to the filing of the decedent's final income tax return?

The decedent's final income tax return is due three and one-half months after the close of the decedent's taxable year. [IRC § 6072(a)]

Q 15:4   When must the estate fiduciary tax return be filed?

The estate fiduciary tax return is due three and one-half months following the end of the fiscal year of the estate. The executor has the authority to select from a variety of fiscal years. A return is required for any taxable period during which the estate's gross income is $600 or more. The estate tax return is computed in a similar manner to the individual income tax return, except that beginning in 1993 the top bracket for the estate income tax return occurs at $7,500, an amount much lower than for personal income tax. Furthermore, a personal exemption of only $600 is allowed for the estate tax return, and deductions are allowed for distributable net income that is distributed to beneficiaries and for charitable contributions. [IRC § 6072(a)]

Q 15:5 When must the federal estate tax return be filed?

A federal estate tax return must be filed if the gross estate exceeds $600,000. It is due nine months after the estate owner's death. [IRC § 6075(a)]

Q 15:6 What time period is covered by the decedent's final income tax return?

The decedent's final income tax return includes only the portion of the income earned for the year up to the date of death. The balance is taxed to the estate when received. [IRC §§ 451(a), 451(b)]

Q 15:7 Can the executor, on behalf of the decedent, file a joint income tax return with the surviving spouse?

Yes, the executor and the decedent's surviving spouse can elect to file a joint income tax return for the decedent and the decedent's surviving spouse in the year in which the decedent died. [IRC § 6013(a)(2)] A joint return is allowed only if the surviving spouse does not remarry before the close of his or her tax year and only if the taxable years of the spouses begin on the same day. A joint return includes the income earned by the decedent up to the date of death and the income of the surviving spouse up to the end of the year.

Q 15:8 What kinds of taxable years can be used for the estate's tax reporting purposes?

The executor for an estate can elect to report income on a fiscal year rather than a calendar year. The election must be made within three and one-half months after the close of the fiscal year selected. [IRC § 1441]

No election. If no timely election is made, the estate must report income on a calendar year basis, and the first taxable year of the estate will end on the December 31 following the date on which the decedent died.

Election of fiscal year. By electing a fiscal year, the executor has the opportunity to select an ending date for the year, which must end on the last day of the month, and cannot be more than 12 months from the decedent's death. This permits the executor to extend the time for reporting income. For example, if the decedent died on October 30, the executor could elect a fiscal year with a last day up to the following September 30. [IRC § 441(e)]

Multiple estate tax filings. With the exception of the first year, additional years for which an estate tax return is filed must consist of a full 12 months. The final estate tax year terminates on the date of final distribution of the estate even if it is less than 12 months, however. [IRC § 443(a)(2)]

Deductions

Q 15:9 What is the medical deduction election?

A fiduciary may elect to deduct the decedent's unpaid medical expenses, which are paid by the estate within one year after death, on either the decedent's final income tax return or the federal estate tax return. [IRC § 213(c)(1)] If those medical expenses are deducted on the final income tax return, the fiduciary must file a waiver of the right to claim an estate tax deduction. [IRC § 213(c)(2)] The waiver statement must be filed either with the return for the year in which the deduction is taken or with the district director of the Internal Revenue Service (IRS) for the district in which the return was filed. [Treas Reg § 1.642(g)-1]

In deciding whether to make a medical deduction election, the fiduciary should consider the following:

1. The effective income and death tax rates;

2. That the income tax deduction is limited to the amount of medical expenses that exceeds 7.5 percent of adjusted gross income [IRC § 213(a)]; and

3. If the decedent leaves a maximum marital deduction bequest, the medical expense deduction should be taken on the decedent's income tax return. The deduction will be wasted if taken on the estate tax return because no estate tax is payable.

Q 15:10 What deductions are available for administrative expenses and casualty losses?

Administrative expenses and casualty losses during the administration of an estate may be deducted on either the estate tax return (Form 706) or the estate tax income tax return (Form 1041). A double deduction is available only in a few instances (see Q 15:12). Accordingly, the executor must decide on which return to take these deductions.

Q 15:11 How are deductions taken on the estate's income tax return?

Deductions may be taken on the estate's income tax return provided a waiver of the estate tax deductions allowed under Code Sections 2053 and 2054 of the Internal Revenue Code (Code) is filed with the IRS (see Q 15:13).

Q 15:12 Is a double deduction against the estate tax and estate income tax ever available?

The prohibition against double deductions does not apply to deductions with respect to a decedent under Code Section 691(b). Those deductions are accrued and unpaid as of the date of death, are paid after death, and can include such things as interest, taxes, and business expenses. [IRC § 642(g)]

Q 15:13 When must the election to waive the estate tax deduction be made?

The waiver of the estate tax deduction can be filed with the applicable income tax return, or the executor may wait to file a waiver until the statute of limitations expires for that tax year, which normally (but not always) occurs three years from the due date of the return. Prior to the filing of the waiver, the executor can tentatively claim the deductions against the estate tax. So long as these deductions against the estate tax are not allowed by the IRS, the estate can preserve the opportunity to take the deductions against income tax rather than estate tax. Once the waiver is filed, however, the option to use the estate tax deductions against the estate tax return is lost.

Q 15:14   What factors should be taken into account when deciding on which return to deduct administrative expenses?

The following factors should be considered when determining on which return to deduct administrative expenses:

1. Administrative deductions can be split between the estate tax return and the estate income tax return. Individual items also can be split.

2. If the decision is made to elect the income tax deduction, the income tax deductions should be maximized. This can be done by taking income tax deductions in that year in which the estate is in the highest marginal tax bracket or by paying administrative expenses of the estate in those years in which the estate is in the highest marginal income tax bracket.

3. The estate tax rates and the income tax rates of the estate and the estate beneficiaries should be considered. If the estate tax rate exceeds the income tax rate for the estate, a deduction should normally be taken on the estate tax return. If the reverse is true, the deduction should be taken on the estate's income tax return. The projected income tax rates of beneficiaries should also be factored into the calculations. If the marginal income tax brackets of the beneficiaries exceed the marginal income tax bracket for the estate, administrative deductions should be taken in the last possible tax year of the estate because estate assets are distributed in that year. As a result, when the distribution is made, these deductions will either reduce the income reportable by beneficiaries or, if there are excess deductions, the loss can be used by beneficiaries to offset high income on their individual tax returns.

4. The effect of the marital deduction (see chapter 4) should be considered. If administrative expenses are deducted on the estate income tax return, the effect of the marital deduction must be considered. If an unlimited marital deduction is taken and the administrative expenses exceed the exemption equivalent (i.e., $600,000), the result could be that estate tax could be payable if the administrative expenses are deducted on the income tax return. If this is the case, it must then be decided whether it is preferable to pay the estate tax or income tax.

Example 15-1: A businessman's gross estate is $5 million; administrative expenses for the estate are $1 million. The businessman's wife survives him, and he leaves her his entire estate. If the $1 million in expenses is taken against income, the maximum marital deduction becomes $4 million. This is because $1 million has been paid out, leaving $4 million to go to the surviving spouse. This leaves a taxable estate of $1 million. Because the exemption equivalent is limited to $600,000, estate tax on $400,000 must be paid. To eliminate this result, $400,000 of administrative losses and expenses should be deducted from the estate tax return. Such a deduction, when added to the marital deduction of $4 million, totals $4.4 million and leaves a taxable estate of $600,000. The result is that, due to the exemption equivalent, there is no estate tax.

Even if administrative expenses are less than the exemption equivalent of $600,000, it may still make sense to deduct these items on the estate tax return. That would make sense, for instance, if a decedent leaves an optimum marital deduction bequest to his or her spouse but also creates a bypass trust designed to receive assets up to the equivalent exemption (i.e., $600,000). If this is done, taking the administrative expenses on the income tax return rather than the estate tax return would reduce the amount payable to the beneficiaries of the bypass trust and increase the amount payable to the surviving spouse.

Example 15-2: A businessman leaves a gross estate of $2 million and has administrative expenses of $200,000, leaving estate assets of $1.8 million. The estate plan calls for the optimum marital deduction with the remaining assets being left to a bypass trust for the businessman's children. If the $200,000 of administrative expenses are deducted on the income tax return, the optimum marital deduction necessary to eliminate the estate tax will be $1.4 million. If $1.4 million is passed to the surviving spouse, only $400,000 is left to be passed to the children as beneficiaries of the bypass trust (whereas, had no administrative expenses been incurred, they would have received $600,000). On the other hand, if the $200,000 in administrative expenses are instead deducted on the estate tax return, the taxable estate becomes $1.8 million. In this case, only $1.2 million is needed to satisfy the optimal marital deduction, and the equivalent exemption would be $600,000. The amount of $600,000 would be paid to the children as beneficiaries of the bypass trust.

When deciding on which return to take the deduction, the executor must consider not only the relative effects on the spouse and the other beneficiaries, but also whether the income tax reduction upon the decedent's death is worth the potential estate tax increase upon the surviving spouse's death.

Q 15:15 If the estate tax deduction is waived, must the tax savings be allocated to beneficiaries?

Yes; if an election is made to deduct administrative expenses on the estate's income tax return rather than on the estate's tax return, a portion of the income tax savings must be allocated to the remainder beneficiaries (i.e., the persons who will receive trust income or property when a present interest terminates) to compensate for the increased estate tax burden. This allocation rule does not apply if the will contains a specific provision giving the executor complete discretion in allocating deductions and waiving all rights to compensatory adjustments. [IRC §§ 691(b)(1)(B), 2053(a)(2)]

Valuation of Assets

Q 15:16 What factors should be considered when selecting a valuation date for estate assets?

Although the value of the gross estate is generally determined as of the date of death, the executor can elect to value the assets of the estate as of six months after the date of death. [IRC § 2032] The election is irrevocable and can be made only if the election results in a lower valuation of assets. If an alternate valuation date is elected, all assets of the gross estate are valued as of the alternate date, except that any assets sold, distributed, or disposed of during the six-month period between the date of death and the alternate valuation date are valued as of the date of disposition.

In deciding whether to elect the alternate valuation date, the executor should consider the following factors:

1. A result of electing an alternate valuation date is to lower asset value for both estate tax purposes and income tax purposes because the income tax basis of assets is equal to the federal estate tax value of assets. Accordingly, the executor must decide whether to pay a larger estate tax and obtain a higher income tax basis or pay a lower estate tax and accept a lower income tax basis.

2. The lower value associated with the alternate valuation date can result in a smaller portion of the assets going to the surviving spouse, which reduces the estate tax on the surviving spouse's death.

Example 15-3: A businesswoman's gross estate has a value at the date of death of $2 million. The value of the estate as of the alternate valuation date is $1.5 million. Under the estate plan, $600,000 goes to a bypass trust and the remainder goes to the surviving spouse. If the estate assets are valued as of the date of death, $1.4 million will be allocated to the surviving spouse. On the other hand, if estate assets are valued using the alternative valuation date, only $900,000 will be allocated to the surviving spouse. In other words, if the alternate valuation date is used in this example, 60 percent of the assets goes to the surviving spouse; however, if the date of death valuation is used, 70 percent of the assets goes to the surviving spouse.

Q 15:17 Is there a penalty for overvaluing assets to obtain a higher income tax basis?

Yes; the Code penalizes a taxpayer who uses a substantial overvaluation for income tax purposes. [IRC § 6662] For this purpose, a substantial valuation overstatement occurs if the value or adjusted basis of any property claimed on a return is 200 percent or more of the correct value or adjusted basis. The penalty applies only if the amount of the underpayment of income taxes attributable to a valuation overstatement exceeds $5,000.

The penalty is a percentage of the underpayment computed as follows:

Table 15-1. Incorrect Valuations and Penalties

Claimed Valuation as a Percentage of Correct Valuation	Penalty Percentage
Under 200%	-0-
200% to 400%	20
More than 400%	40

Note: Penalties can also be imposed for undervaluing assets.

Elections

Q 15:18 What special elections can an executor make?

An executor can make the following elections to reduce taxes:

1. A special valuation election under Code Section 2032A for real estate used in farming or by other closely held businesses; and

2. An election under Code Section 6161 to defer paying estate taxes. The deferral can extend up to 12 months for reasonable cause and up to 10 years for special reasonable cause (i.e., undue hardship). An even longer extension of the time for paying taxes can be obtained if a substantial portion of the estate consists of interests in closely held businesses or farm property.

Q 15:19 When should the executor elect to waive his or her fees?

Executor fees can be taken as the deduction against either the estate income tax or the estate tax. In each case, the executor reports his or her fees as ordinary income. [IRC § 61(a)(1)] If the executor is also the sole beneficiary of the estate or family members are the other estate beneficiaries, he or she should consider waiving fees if his or her personal income tax bracket exceeds the estate bracket.

Example 15-4: The executor for the estate of a deceased inventor is also the residuary legatee of the decedent's estate. The executor is entitled to a fee of $50,000 and is in the 39.6 percent income tax bracket. If the executor takes the fee, the net benefit to him or her is $30,200 ($50,000 less $19,800 in income tax payable). Assuming the maximum tax bracket for the estate is 37 percent, the executor will benefit by waiving the fee because the net benefit to him or her then would be $31,500 ($50,000 less the $18,500 estate tax).

Q 15:20 What post-death partnership elections should be considered?

If the decedent owned an interest in a partnership, the partnership should consider the possibility of making a Section 754 election. This election adjusts the income tax basis of the deceased partner's share of partnership assets so that it equals the value of the deceased partner's interest in the partnership that is used in preparing the decedent's estate tax return. [IRC §§ 734, 743] The election is often advantageous.

Example 15-5: A deceased attorney owned a 50 percent interest in a partnership. His adjusted income tax basis in that interest immediately before his death is $500,000. Following his death, the estate tax value (i.e., fair market value) of the partnership is $1 million. Just before the lawyer's death, the partnership owned an asset worth $1 million that had an adjusted basis of $100,000. If no Section 754 election is made and the partnership sells the asset for $1 million, a taxable gain of $900,000 would occur, and one half of it would be taxable to the attorney's estate. If the Section 754 election is made, however, the basis of the estate's share of partnership assets would be increased to $500,000 (the estate tax value of his partnership share). Accordingly, there would be no gain to the attorney's estate on the sale of the asset. Had the election not been made, the gain to the estate would have been $450,000.

Example 15-6: Consider the same facts as in Example 15-5 except that the asset is worth $1.4 million so that, when it is sold, a taxable gain of $1.1 million occurs. Without the election, one half of the gain ($550,000) is taxable to the attorney's estate; with the election, $200,000 ($700,000 – $500,000) is taxable to his estate. If the estate tax value of a partner's interest is lower than the adjusted basis of his or her interest before death, making the Section 754 election would result in a reduced basis and a greater gain if partnership assets are sold. Under these circumstances, there would be no reason to make a Section 754 election.

Q 15:21   How is the Section 754 election made?

The Section 754 election (see Q 15:20) is made by the partnership, not by the deceased partner's estate. Sometimes the partnership is unwilling to make the election because the decision is irrevocable and is binding on the other partners.

Q 15:22   How is income collected by an estate taxed?

Income collected by an estate (e.g., dividends on stocks in the estate) is generally taxable to the estate and not to the beneficiaries. [IRC § 641] The estate is allowed a deduction equal to the total income required to be distributed currently plus any other amount paid or credited during the taxable year, not to exceed the estate's distributable net income. [IRC § 661] Distributions of bequests are treated as distributions of income unless the bequest is (1) of a specific sum of money or specific property that is not payable out of current or prior estate income and (2) the bequest is paid in not more than three installments. [IRC § 663(a)(1)] The distributions are also taxable income to the beneficiary. [IRC § 662]

Example 15-7: The estate of a deceased heiress earns $50,000 of net income and distributes the decedent's home to a residuary legatee. The home is worth $20,000. The estate has a deduction of $20,000, and the residuary legatee has taxable income of $20,000. If, however, the home is distributed to a specific devisee, the $20,000 is not treated as an income distribution and is not deductible by the estate.

Distribution Income Planning

Q 15:23 What is distribution income planning?

Distribution income planning minimizes income taxes by apportioning distributions to those in low tax brackets. Ways to effect this are as follows:

1. If the estate beneficiaries are in a lower tax bracket than the estate, distribution of income producing assets should be made to them to take advantage of their lower rates.

2. If the beneficiaries are in different brackets, income producing assets should be distributed to those beneficiaries having lower personal income rates.

3. Capital gain properties should be distributed to a beneficiary who has a capital loss or to a beneficiary who can use the capital gain to offset a net operating loss carryover.

4. If the estate has a lower effective income tax rate than the beneficiaries, the executor should delay closing the estate as long as possible to take advantage of the lower bracket. This permits the estate to pay taxes at a lower rate and thus accumulate more property than would be possible if the assets were distributed. The period of administration cannot be unduly prolonged, however. [Treas Reg § 1.641(b)(3)]

Q 15:24 How can deductions from estate income be maximized?

Among the options for maximizing deductions from estate income are the following:

Q 15:25 Estate and Retirement Planning Answer Book

1. An estate is entitled to a personal annual exemption of $600 during administration. [IRC § 642(b)] An extra personal exemption can be created through the use of a short initial tax year. Furthermore, the estate can retain sufficient taxable income after taking into account expense deductions to take advantage of the full exemption amount.

2. Net operating loss carryovers or capital loss carryovers of the estate can be deducted by the beneficiary in the year the estate terminates. Losses can also be carried over by the beneficiary into future years. Because beneficiaries can carry only the loss forward, an executor should consider early termination if the beneficiary is in a sufficiently high income tax bracket so as to use the carryovers more effectively.

3. The excess of the deduction in the year of termination over the estate's income is available to succeeding beneficiaries as a deduction. [IRC § 642(h)] If the beneficiaries are in a higher tax bracket than the estate, an executor should consider paying administrative and other expenses in the year of termination, electing to take the deductions on the estate tax return, and passing the loss on to the beneficiaries as excess deductions on their own income tax returns.

Q 15:25 How can additional taxpayers be created by the use of a trust?

One planning technique is to fund beneficiary trusts by estate distributions as soon as possible to create additional tax entities. This is desirable if the trusts are taxed at lower rates than would be the case if all income was taxed to the estate.

Q 15:26 How should installment obligations arising after death be treated?

If an estate asset is to be sold and an installment obligation taken back, the estate fiduciary should consider either holding the installment obligation for an extended period of time or distributing the asset to the estate beneficiaries instead and having them sell it. Distributing the installment obligation would accelerate the tax on the obligation and require the estate to report the entire untaxed profit at the time of distribution. [IRC § 453B(a)] Therefore, it is desirable for the executor to delay distributing the installment note until it is collected in full. Executors are limited in how long they can hold such a note, however, because of the requirement that estates cannot remain open for unreasonable periods of time. It may be better to distribute the assets to beneficiaries who can then make a sale on an installment basis.

Disclaimers

Q 15:27 What is a disclaimer?

A *disclaimer* is the refusal to accept benefits conferred by a will or by operation of law. For example, a beneficiary who does not want his or her share of an estate because he or she is in both high estate tax and income tax brackets may disclaim the interest. Gift taxes may apply, however, unless a qualified disclaimer is made.

Q 15:28 When should a disclaimer be used?

A disclaimer can make sense if a married couple is not sure whether they want to take advantage of the $600,000 exemption by creating a trust for the benefit of others. This could occur, for example, if the couple is childless and is somewhat indifferent about whether nephews and nieces inherit from them. Under those circumstances, the couple can provide that the surviving spouse has the option to disclaim all or a portion of the inheritance.

A disclaimer may also make sense if the couple's total assets are about $600,000. Here, no estate tax advantage results from giving an inheritance to others at the death of the first spouse. Furthermore, it may very well be desirable to concentrate assets in the hands of the surviving spouse. In this situation, the use of a disclaimer permits the best of both worlds. If assets grow beyond $600,000 at the death of the first spouse or if there is some other reason to give a portion of the inheritance to someone else, the surviving spouse can disclaim the excess assets.

If a spouse has the disclaimer, he or she can disclaim the assets in favor of a trust in which he or she has a beneficial interest. Only spouses have this opportunity. Others can disclaim in favor of a trust, but they cannot have an interest in the trust.

The generation skipping transfer tax should also be considered in conjunction with making a disclaimer. Here the main concern is whether the disclaimer would result in the imposition of the generation skipping transfer tax.

If a disclaiming party disclaims an interest, the interest is deemed to pass from the creator of the interest directly to the person receiving it as a result of the disclaimer. If the distributee is more than one generation below that of the transferor, a generation skipping transfer occurs.

Q 15:29 What are the requirements for a qualified disclaimer?

A *qualified disclaimer* is one in which the disclaimed interest is not deemed to have been owned by the disclaiming party for gift tax purposes. As a practical matter, this means that the disclaimer does not result in a potential gift tax to the disclaiming party.

The requirements for a valid disclaimer under Code Section 2518 are as follows:

1. The refusal must be in writing;
2. It must be made within nine months of the time that the interest is irrevocably transferred;
3. The disclaiming party must not have accepted the interest or any of its benefits before making the disclaimer; and
4. The interest must pass to a person other than the disclaiming party without any direction on the part of the disclaiming party.

If the disclaiming party is under age 21, the time for making a disclaimer is extended until nine months after he or she reaches 21.

Q 15:30 How are joint tenancies treated for disclaimer purposes?

The interest of a joint tenant (see Qs 2:25–2:41) is treated as a completed irrevocable gift on the date the joint tenancy was created.

[Treas Reg § 25.2418-2(c)(4)(i)] This means that to avoid gift tax, a surviving joint tenant must file a qualified disclaimer no later than nine months after the establishment of the joint tenancy, rather than nine months from the deceased joint tenant's date of death. There is an exception to this rule, however, for joint tenancy bank accounts. The surviving joint tenant on a bank account has nine months from the decedent's death in which to disclaim that portion of the account attributable to the decedent's contributions. [Treas Reg § 25.2518-2(c)(5)]

Q 15:31 Can a power of appointment be disclaimed?

A beneficiary can disclaim a power of appointment without the disclaimer's being treated as a taxable transfer. Such disclaimers are made to avoid having the property be subject to the general power of appointment includible in one's estate under Code Section 2041.

Q 15:32 Are there any exceptions to the rule that a disclaimed interest must pass to a person other than the disclaiming party?

Yes, if the disclaiming person is the surviving spouse of the decedent, that spouse may disclaim an interest in the property even if the disclaimed property passes to a trust that the spouse has an interest in. [IRC § 2518(b)(4)] The spouse cannot disclaim an interest that passes into a trust that gives the spouse the power to direct to whom the interest will go, however.

Q 15:33 What other factors should be considered in making a disclaimer?

The chief issue for consideration when making a disclaimer is the generation skipping transfer tax—whether the disclaimer would result in the imposition of the generation skipping transfer tax.

If a party disclaims an interest, the interest is deemed to pass from the creator of the interest directly to the person receiving it as a result of the disclaimer. If the distributee is more than one generation below that of the transferor, a generation skipping transfer occurs.

Q 15:34 Can a disclaimer be made in favor of a charity?

A bequest may be disclaimed to increase a charitable deduction. The will should make it clear, however, that if the bequest is disclaimed, it will go to a named charity. This preserves the charitable deduction for the estate. Under certain circumstances, it is preferable for the beneficiary to accept the bequest and donate it to the charity. If the value of the estate is less than $600,000, no disclaimer should be made because no estate tax savings occur as a result of the disclaimer; the beneficiary should accept the bequest and donate it to charity to receive an income tax deduction.

Part II

Benefit Plans and Other Sources of Retirement Assets

Chapter 16

Benefit Plans

This chapter sets forth the fundamental retirement planning issues for small business owners, owners of professional practices, and executives. Because owners must focus on the effect of a retirement plan on the operations of the business as well as on themselves, the essential issues for them differ from those for executives of large companies, although there is some degree of overlap. Small business owners will be concerned about legal liability, which they may incur as a result of adopting a plan, while executives will be concerned with their rights under the retirement plan.

Overview	16-2
Labor Law Requirements	16-3
ERISA	16-4
Fiduciary Responsibility	16-8
Age and Sex Discrimination	16-22
Veterans' Rights	16-24
WARN	16-25
Taft-Hartley Act	16-25
Multiemployer Plans	16-26
Collective Bargaining	16-27

Overview

Q 16:1 What are the crucial retirement planning issues for small business owners and executives?

For entrepreneurs and owners of small businesses and professional organizations, the essential retirement planning issues are as follows:

1. How will the business benefit from establishing a retirement plan?
2. How will a retirement plan fit in with estate planning objectives?
3. What kind of retirement plan should be adopted?
4. What legal barriers and risks exist if a particular kind of retirement plan is adopted?
5. Which employees should and must be included in the plan?
6. What are the costs of establishing a retirement plan?

For executives, the crucial retirement issues are as follows:

1. When should a distribution be taken from the plan?
2. What right does the executive have to obtain information about the plan?
3. What protection exists for the executive's benefits under the plan?
4. What is the effect of the plan on the executive's estate?
5. How are distributions calculated?

Q 16:2 What are the basic types of retirement plans?

The two basic types of retirement plans are tax-qualified plans and nonqualified plans. Tax-qualified retirement plans provide favorable tax treatment for contributions to the plan, for plan earnings, and for distributions from the plan, but must comply with the complex requirements of Section 401 of the Internal Revenue Code (Code). Those rules specify funding requirements and require that minimum numbers of employees benefit under the plan. Nonqualified plans can avoid those rules but do not offer the tax advantages that qualified plans can provide.

Q 16:3 What are the advantages of tax-qualified retirement plans?

Tax-qualified retirement plans have a number of significant tax advantages. A company adopting a tax-qualified retirement plan is allowed a current deduction for its contributions to the plan, and the plan participants pay no tax on the money contributed for their benefit until the plan pays them. Moreover, earnings on plan assets accumulate tax-free, and payments (e.g., distributions) from the plan may get favorable income tax treatment. The assets in tax-qualified retirement plans are generally protected from creditors.

Q 16:4 What are the advantages of nonqualified retirement plans?

Nonqualified retirement plans can be subject to less onerous regulation than qualified plans. Accordingly, the legal costs of establishing and maintaining such plans can be less. Further, such plans can avoid the minimum coverage requirements imposed upon tax-qualified plans and, as a result, employers can focus retirement benefits on a select group of key persons. Nonqualified plans are often used to retain key executives in certain positions.

Labor Law Requirements

Q 16:5 What labor laws play a significant role in the administration of employee benefit plans?

A number of labor laws affect the administration of employee benefit plans and have the effect of protecting the employee's accumulation of wealth under retirement plans. These laws must be observed when adopting and maintaining an employee benefit plan. The most significant of these labor laws are as follows:

1. The Employee Retirement Income Security Act of 1974 (ERISA). This law generally applies to all types of plans maintained by employers;
2. The labor laws prohibiting discrimination on the basis of age and gender; and
3. The labor laws that apply to veterans.

Two other relevant labor laws apply primarily to larger employers:

1. Worker Readjustment and Retraining Act (WARN). This law applies when plants are shut down.
2. Taft-Hartley Act. This law applies when plans are established as a result of the collective bargaining process.

ERISA

Q 16:6 What is the Employee Retirement Income Security Act of 1974?

ERISA is a federal law specifically aimed at providing protection to participants in employee benefit plans and their beneficiaries. The most important parts of ERISA for retirement plan purposes are the following: Title I, which imposes eligibility, coverage, vesting, and fiduciary responsibility requirements on retirement benefits; Title II, which amended parts of the Code to impose eligibility, coverage, and vesting requirements on tax-qualified retirement plans; and Title IV, which established the Pension Benefit Guaranty Corporation (PBGC) and plan termination insurance. Title I of ERISA lists which plans are covered by ERISA, outlines the claims procedures applicable to ERISA plans, preempts much state law, provides standards of fiduciary responsibility, imposes reporting and disclosure requirements, and contains the legal remedies available to individuals. ERISA is the most significant source of relief for a executive who believes that he or she is being treated unfairly with respect to a plan.

ERISA regulates a variety of employee benefit plans, although some significant classes of plans are exempted from its coverage. Both ERISA and the Code contain comprehensive restrictions on the ability of the business owner to design a plan entirely at his or her own discretion. To some extent, the burden of these requirements can be lightened by using standardized plans.

Q 16:7 What is the Pension Benefit Guaranty Corporation, and what retirement plans does it insure?

The Pension Benefit Guaranty Corporation (PBGC) is a federally chartered corporation whose primary function is to provide minimum benefit guarantees for participants in, and beneficiaries of, tax-qualified defined benefit pension plans or plans that in practice have met the requirements for tax-qualified defined benefit pension plans during the past five years. [ERISA § 4021(b)] Insured plans pay premiums to the PBGC each year based upon the number of participating employees. The PBGC provides federal protection for a portion of the wealth accumulated under the pension plans that it insures. The PBGC does *not* insure the following types of plans:

- Defined contribution plans [ERISA § 4021(b)(12)]
- Plans established by professional service corporations that do not at any time after September 2, 1974, have more than 25 active participants in the plan [ERISA § 4021(b)(13)]
- Certain plans for highly compensated executives, known as top-hat plans
- Plans established exclusively for sole proprietors or more than 10% partners or shareholders [ERISA § 4021(b)(9)]
- Federal, state, and local government plans [ERISA § 4021(b)(2)]
- Church plans that have not elected to have PBGC coverage apply [ERISA § 4021(b)(3)]
- Plans that provide benefits in excess of Section 415 limits, known as excess benefit plans [ERISA § 4021(b)(8)]
- Plans covered by the Railroad Retirement Acts of 1935 and 1937 [ERISA § 4021(b)(2)]
- Certain plans to which only employees can contribute [ERISA § 4021(b)(1)]
- Plans to which no employer contributions have been made since September 1, 1974 [ERISA § 4021(b)(5)]

- Other miscellaneous plans [ERISA §§ 4021(b)(4), 4021(b)(7), 4021(b)(10), 4021(b)(11)]

Q 16:8 What benefits are guaranteed by the Pension Benefit Guaranty Corporation?

To be guaranteed by the PBGC, a benefit provided by an employer-sponsored retirement plan must be the following:

1. A pension benefit; that is, a benefit payable as an annuity to a participant who terminates employment that provides, either alone or in connection with Social Security and other retirement benefits, a level income;
2. Nonforfeitable;
3. Payable directly or indirectly to a living person or to a trust or estate for the benefit of a natural person; and
4. In pay status or payable when a lapse of time occurs or the participant satisfies a waiting period or makes an election.

There is also a statutory limit on the amount of benefits that are guaranteed by the PBGC. In 1995, the basic limit on single employer plan benefits guaranteed was $2,573.86 per month. Benefits provided by multiemployer plans are also guaranteed by the PBGC, subject to certain limits that approximate the limits on guarantees for single employer plan benefits.

Example 16-1: An engineer is entitled to a monthly pension benefit of $1,000 from a plan maintained by an aircraft manufacturer. This is the kind of plan that is protected by PBGC guarantees. If the benefit were payable from a money purchase pension plan or a profit sharing plan, PBGC protection would not be available.

Q 16:9 What rights does ERISA give plan participants and beneficiaries?

ERISA gives plan participants and beneficiaries the following rights:

1. To sue for benefits promised by the plan;
2. To sue to enforce rights under the plan;
3. To clarify rights to future benefits under the plan;

4. To obtain an injunction or other equitable relief for violations of Title I of ERISA;
5. To sue to recover damages on behalf of the plan if a plan fiduciary breaches his or her fiduciary duty;
6. To compel the secretary of labor to take actions required by Title I of ERISA, to stop the secretary of labor from taking actions contrary to Title I of ERISA, or to review a final order of the secretary of labor;
7. To sue to obtain a $100-per-day penalty if the plan administrator fails to provide plan documents within 30 days of receiving a request for them [ERISA § 502]; and
8. To sue to assure receipt of amounts to be provided by an insurance contract or annuity that was purchased in connection with the termination of an individual's status as a participant in a pension plan. The purchase must violate either the terms of the plan or the fiduciary responsibility provisions of ERISA. [ERISA § 502 (a)(9)]

Example 16:2: The plan administrator for a terminating defined benefit plan purchases a group annuity contract from an insurance company that has a poor rating. The purchase is not prudent under ERISA fiduciary standards. A plan participant brings suit under ERISA Section 502(a)(9) to force the administrator and the insurance company to rescind the contract.

ERISA makes it unlawful for any person to discharge, fine, discipline, expel, or discriminate against a participant or beneficiary for exercising any right he or she is entitled to under a covered employee benefit plan or under Title I of ERISA. It is also unlawful for any person to discharge, fine, discipline, expel, or discriminate against a participant or beneficiary for the purpose of interfering with the attainment of any right that the participant may become entitled to under ERISA or the plan. [ERISA § 510]

Q 16:10 Under ERISA, is the prevailing party entitled to an award of attorneys' fees?

Perhaps. Title I of ERISA provides that courts have the discretion to award the prevailing party attorneys' fees for lawsuits brought under Title I of ERISA. [ERISA § 502(g)] As a practical matter, the courts have generally exercised their discretion more liberally in favor of plaintiffs than defendants.

Fiduciary Responsibility

Q 16:11 What is a fiduciary?

A person is a fiduciary for purposes of Title I of ERISA to the extent he or she meets the following requirements:

1. The person exercises any discretionary authority or discretionary control regarding the management of the plan or exercise of authority or control of the management or disposition of plan assets;
2. The person renders investment advice for a fee or other compensation, direct or indirect, regarding any plan asset or has the authority or responsibility to do so; or
3. The person has discretionary authority or discretionary responsibility in the administration of the plan.

[ERISA § (3)21(A)]

A person is, however, subject to fiduciary liability only to the extent that he or she is acting as a fiduciary.

Example 16-3: A plan trustee that is appointed by the board of directors of an aerospace firm negligently invests plan funds and commits a breach of fiduciary duty. The directors' only involvement with the plan is to appoint the trustee. Unless they were negligent in appointing the trustee (i.e., they appointed the trustee when a prudent investigation would have shown that he was likely to behave negligently), the directors are not liable under ERISA for the trustee's bad investment decisions.

Q 16:12 What are the duties of ERISA fiduciaries?

ERISA fiduciaries must perform the following duties:

1. Act solely in the interest of plan participants. [ERISA § 404(a)(1)(A)]

2. Act for the exclusive purposes of providing benefits to participants and their beneficiaries and of defraying reasonable expenses of administering the plan. [ERISA § 404(a)(1)(A)]
3. Exercise the same care, skill, prudence, and diligence that a prudent person acting in a like capacity and familiar with such matters would use in the conduct of an enterprise of like character and with like aims. [ERISA § 404(a)(1)(B)]
4. Adequately diversify plan assets. ERISA requires that plan fiduciaries diversify plan investments so as to minimize the risk of large losses, unless under the circumstances it is clearly prudent not to do so. [ERISA § 404(a)(1)(C)]
5. Discharge his or her duties in accordance with the documents and instruments governing the plan, to the extent the documents do not violate ERISA. [ERISA § 404(a)(1)(D)]

Q 16:13 What legal responsibilities and requirements pertain to ERISA fiduciaries of retirement plans?

Retirement plans are subject to the two general types of fiduciary responsibility rules:

1. General fiduciary duties are imposed on the fiduciaries of retirement plans.
2. Individuals and entities involved with retirement plans are prohibited from engaging in certain types of prohibited transactions.

If the fiduciary responsibility provisions are violated, plan fiduciaries may be individually responsible for making up any losses to the plan or participants. Under the Code, excise taxes may also be imposed on any disqualified person who participates in a prohibited transaction with respect to a tax-qualified plan or individual retirement account (IRA). [IRC § 4975(d)] The secretary of labor can impose a similar penalty on parties in interest who engage in such transactions in connection with nonqualified plans. [ERISA § 5029(i)] The initial penalty tax equals 5 percent of the amount involved in the prohibited transaction; the tax is cumulative and can be assessed annually. If the prohibited transaction is not corrected within a period defined by statute, an additional 100 percent penalty tax may be imposed.

Q 16:14 To which assets do the fiduciary responsibility rules apply?

The fiduciary responsibility rules apply to plan assets. Plan assets generally include assets actually owned by a plan, such as securities, cash, and perhaps real estate. In some instances, however, through the application of "look-through" rules, plan assets may also include the assets of an entity in which a plan has invested. For example, plan assets could include the assets owned by a limited partnership in which the plan owned a limited partnership interest. [Lab Reg § 2510.3-101]

Q 16:15 Do assets in a tax-qualified plan have to be held in trust?

Not always. Assets in a tax-qualified pension, profit sharing, or stock bonus plan that are held in trust must be held in a trust created or organized in the United States. [IRC § 401(a)] Instead of a trust, a custodial account, whose assets are held by a bank or another entity permitted by IRS regulations, can be used; however, the assets are invested by some other entity. [IRC § 401(f)] The trust requirement does not apply to a plan in which all participants are self-employed individuals under Code Section 401(c)(1). If all plan assets are annuity or insurance policies, a trust is not required. [Treas Reg § 1.404(a)-3(a); ERISA § 403(b)(1)]

Q 16:16 Does ERISA permit retirement plans to hold employer securities and property as plan assets?

Title I of ERISA permits retirement plans that are eligible individual account plans to acquire and hold certain kinds of an employer's real property and securities. [ERISA § 404(a)(2)] An eligible individual account plan is a profit sharing, ESOP, stock bonus, money purchase, or thrift savings plan that explicitly permits investment in qualifying employer real property or employer securities. IRAs are not included in this definition. [ERISA § 407(d)(3)]

Example 16-4: The trustee for a profit sharing plan for a tractor distributor wants to invest 10% of the plan's assets in the distributor's common stock. Neither ERISA nor the Code preclude this investment.

Q 16:17 How may a plan limit the liability of plan fiduciaries and trustees?

Trustees and other plan officials are subject to fiduciary duties with respect to plan investments. Under certain circumstances, however, these officials can be relieved of most of their fiduciary duties. Fiduciaries for individual account plans (i.e., plans that have individual accounts for participants such as profit sharing, 401(k), or money purchase pension plans) but not defined benefit pension plans can be relieved of most of their fiduciary duties if participants are to exercise control over their accounts and to invest in a wide range of investment options. The criteria for meeting these requirements are specified in regulations issued by the Department of Labor (DOL).

Example 16-5: A pathology laboratory decides to create a profit sharing plan that offers every participant the opportunity to instruct the plan trustee to invest in any publicly traded security. This plan clearly provides for investment direction from participants. If the requirements of the statute and regulations are met, the plan will relieve the trustee and other plan officials of most of the liability that may arise from bad or unsuccessful investments.

The protection provided by this exemption is limited in the following respects:

1. It does not protect against the tax imposed on disqualified persons for engaging in a prohibited transaction under the Code.
2. Fiduciaries are not insulated from liability resulting from instructions that:
   - Are not in accordance with plan documents and instruments
   - Cause a fiduciary to maintain the indicia of ownership of any plan assets outside of the jurisdiction of U.S. district courts

Q 16:18   Estate and Retirement Planning Answer Book

- Jeopardize the plan's status as a tax-qualified plan
- Could result in a loss in excess of the participant's account balance
- Result in a direct or indirect exchange or lease of property between the plan sponsor (or any of its affiliates as defined in the regulations, including, among others, officers, employees, and directors of the employer) and the plan
- Result in a direct or indirect loan to a plan sponsor (or any affiliate of the sponsor as defined in the regulations) or the acquisition, sale, or lease of any employer real property or (with certain exceptions) securities

3. Fiduciaries are not protected where losses are attributable to intervening breaches of fiduciary responsibility as opposed to breaches caused by the investment instructions. [Lab Reg § 2550.404(c)-1]

Example 16-6: A participant instructs a plan fiduciary to invest in a certain stock. The plan fiduciary is unreasonably slow in executing the instructions, which results in a loss. The plan fiduciary would not be insulated from liability by the investment direction statute and regulations.

Example 16-7: A participant chooses an investment manager pursuant to the investment direction provisions. The investment manager makes imprudent investments. The investment manager is not relieved of liability, because the imprudent investments were not the result of the participant's exercise of control. The only control the participant exercised was to choose an investment manager. Had the participant directed the investment manager to make an investment that turned out be imprudent, the manager would be relieved of liability. [Lab Reg § 2550.404c-1(f)(3)]

Q 16:18   What general requirements must plans that offer individually directed accounts satisfy to avoid fiduciary liability?

In general, to avoid the fiduciary responsibility requirements of ERISA Section 404(c) the plan must provide an opportunity for a participant or beneficiary to exercise control over the assets in his or her individual account and choose from a broad range of investments in which some or all of the assets in his or her account are to be invested. [Lab Reg § 2550.404(c)-1(b)(1)]

Q 16:19 How can a plan fiduciary determine whether it is providing plan participants and beneficiaries with sufficient exercise of control to satisfy the ERISA requirements?

The exercise of control requirement is met if the following is true:

1. The terms of the plan give the participant or beneficiary a reasonable opportunity to give investment instructions to an identified plan fiduciary who is obligated to comply with these instructions. The instructions do not have to be in writing.
2. The participant or beneficiary is given sufficient opportunity to receive information with which to make informed decisions about possible investments he or she might choose to make. [Lab Reg § 2550.404(c)-1(b)(2)]

Q 16:20 How can a plan determine whether it is providing plan participants and beneficiaries with sufficient opportunity to receive information to satisfy ERISA's requirements regarding informed decision making?

Participants or beneficiaries will not be considered to have sufficient opportunity to obtain information to make informed decisions unless an identified plan fiduciary provides the following information:

1. An explanation that the plan is intended to constitute a plan described in ERISA Section 404(c) and Labor Regulations Section 2550.-404(c)(1) and that fiduciaries may be relieved of any losses that are the direct and necessary result of investment decisions given by the participant or beneficiary.
2. A description of the investment alternatives available under the plan and a general description of the investment objectives and risk of return of each investment alternative.
3. Identification of designated investment managers.

Q 16:20   Estate and Retirement Planning Answer Book

4. An explanation of when and how investment instructions may be given with any limitations, including restrictions on transfer to or from designated investment alternatives.
5. A description of any transaction fees and expenses that affect the participant's or beneficiary's account balance in connection with the purchase or sale of interest in investment alternatives.
6. The name, address, and telephone number of the plan fiduciaries who will provide certain information on the request of a participant or beneficiary.
7. If the plan offers investment securities as an investment alternative, a description of the procedures established to provide for the confidentiality of information relating to the purchase, holding, and sale of the employer's securities in the exercise of voting tender and similar rights by participants and beneficiaries, as well as the name, address, and telephone number of the plan fiduciary responsible for monitoring compliance with those procedures.
8. A prospectus provided to the employer or beneficiary prior to or immediately following the initial investment of assets subject to the Securities Act of 1933.
9. Subsequent to the investment in an investment alternative, any materials provided to the plan relating to the exercise of voting tender or similar rights incidental to that investment alternative, to the extent that such rights are passed through to the participant or beneficiary under the terms of the plan, as well as a description of a reference to plan provisions relating to the exercise of voting tender or similar rights.

In addition, the following information must be provided on request:

1. A description of the annual operating expenses of each designated investment alternative that reduced the rate of return to participants and beneficiaries.
2. Copies of any prospectuses, financial statements and reports, and any other material relating to investment alternatives available under the plan, to the extent such information is provided to the plan.

3. A list of assets that make up the portfolio of each designated investment alternative. The list should include the value of each asset and, with respect to each such asset that has a fixed rate investment contract issued by a financial institution, the name of the issues or the contract and the term and rate of the contract.

4. The value of shares or units in a designated investment alternative available to participants and beneficiaries under the plan, as well as the past and current investment performances of such alternatives determined net of expenses on a reasonable and consistent basis.

5. Information concerning the value of shares or units in the designated investment alternatives held in the account of the participant or beneficiary. [Lab Reg § 2550.404(c)-1(b)(2)]

Q 16:21 What opportunities for giving investment instructions must be available to plan participants to satisfy the requirements of ERISA and the Code?

Plan participants must be given a reasonable opportunity to give investment instructions. The instructions need not be given in writing. The instructions must be given to an identified plan fiduciary who is obligated to comply with them. [Lab Reg § 2550.404c-1(a)(2)(B)] The plan may, however, do the following:

1. Impose charges for reasonable expenses. Participants and beneficiaries' accounts may be charged for reasonable expenses incurred in carrying out investment instructions. The plan must establish procedures to periodically inform the participants and beneficiaries of actual expenses incurred.

2. Permit plan fiduciaries to decline to implement instructions that:
   - Result in prohibited transactions under the ERISA or the Code
   - Generate taxable income
   - Cause plan fiduciaries to lose the protection provided by the participant direction regulations

Q 16:22 What opportunities for a broad, diversified range of investment alternatives must be made available to the plan participants to satisfy the requirements of ERISA?

A plan is viewed as having a broad range of investment alternatives if the investment options give the participants a reasonable opportunity to materially affect the return and degree of risk of the accounts over which they have discretion. Participants must also be able to diversify in order to minimize the risk of large losses. [Lab Reg § 2550.404c-1(b)(3)] A plan must offer at least three diversified categories of investments that have materially different risk and return characteristics. The investment options offered must in the aggregate enable the participant to select a combination of risk and return characteristics throughout the range that is appropriate for the participant.

Q 16:23 How are plan fiduciaries shielded if the participant direction regulations are complied with?

If a participant or beneficiary exercises independent control over plan assets in accordance with the ERISA regulations, plan fiduciaries will not be liable to the participant or beneficiary for any loss with respect to Part IV of Title I of ERISA (the basic fiduciary responsibility provisions) that is a direct and necessary result of each participant's exercise of control. A disqualified person is not relieved, however, from excise taxes for prohibited transactions under Code Section 4975(c)(1). [Lab Reg § 2550.404(c)-1(d)]

> **Example 16-8:** An attorney who participates in a profit sharing plan that provides for investment direction in accordance with DOL regulations directs the plan trustee to invest in Acme Rocket stock. Shortly after the investment is made, the stock plummets from $50 to $2 a share. If the participant direction regulations were complied with, the plan trustee does not have any liability under ERISA for this loss.

This protection is limited in some rather important ways. It does not protect against the imposition of prohibited transaction taxes under the Code, and it does not apply to the following types of instructions:

1. Instructions that are inconsistent with the plan documents (insofar as the plan documents conform with Title I of ERISA);
2. Instructions that cause the fiduciary to retain indicia of ownership outside of the United States;
3. Instructions that would jeopardize a plan's tax-exempt status;
4. Instructions that could result in a loss in excess of a participant's account balance;
5. Instructions that result in sales or exchanges between the plan and the plan sponsor or one of its affiliates (an exception exists for funds managed by the plan sponsor);
6. Instructions that result in a loan to a plan sponsor;
7. Instructions that result in acquisition or sale of an employer's real property (as defined in ERISA Section 407(d)(2);
8. Instructions that result in acquisition of employer securities (as defined in ERISA Section 407(d)(5)), except that employer securities may be acquired if they meet the following requirements:
   a. They are qualifying employer securities under ERISA Section 407(d) (stock or certain types of marketable obligations).
   b. They are stock or equity interests in certain publicly traded partnerships.
   c. They are publicly traded on a national exchange or on another generally recognized market with sufficient trading volume to assure that participant or beneficiary directions to buy or sell the securities may be acted on promptly and efficiently.
   d. Voting tender and similar rights are passed through to participants and beneficiaries.
   e. Certain steps are taken to safeguard trading information. [Lab Reg § 2550.404(c)-1(b)(1)]

Q 16:24 What are prohibited transactions?

The Code and ERISA contain prohibited transaction provisions that are very similar but not identical. In determining whether a provided transaction provision exists, it is therefore important that both sets of provisions be reviewed.

Prohibited transactions are specifically defined within the Code and ERISA to include the following:

1. The sale, exchange, or leasing of any property between a plan and a disqualified person or party in interest (see Q 16:27). [IRC § 4975(c)(1)(A); ERISA § 406(a)(1)(A)] The transfer of real or personal property to a plan by a disqualified person or a party in interest will be treated as a sale or exchange if the property is subject to a mortgage or similar lien that the plan assumes or that a disqualified person or party in interest placed on the property within a ten-year period ending on the date of transfer.

2. The lending of money or other extension of credit between the plan and any disqualified person or party in interest. [IRC § 4975(c)(1)(B); ERISA § 406(a)(1)(B)]

3. The furnishing of goods, services, or facilities between the plan and a disqualified person or party in interest. [IRC § 4975(c)(1)(C); ERISA § 406(a)(1)(C)]

4. The transfer to or the use by or for the benefit of a disqualified person of the income or assets of a plan. [IRC § 4975(c)(1)(D)] The corresponding ERISA section applies only to the assets of a plan, not its income. [ERISA § 406(a)(1)(D)]

5. An act by a fiduciary whereby the fiduciary deals with the income or assets of a plan in his or her own interest or for his or her account. [IRC § 4975(d)(1)(E); ERISA § 406(b)(1)]

6. The receipt of any consideration for his or her personal account by a fiduciary from any person dealing with the plan in connection with the transaction involving the income or assets of the plan. [IRC § 4975(c)(1)(f)] Under Title I of ERISA, a fiduciary may not receive any consideration for his or her own personal account from any party dealing with a plan in connection with a transaction involving the assets of a plan. [ERISA § 406(b)(3)]

7. Under Title I of ERISA, a fiduciary may not personally or in any other capacity participate in any transaction involving the plan on behalf of a party (or representing a party) whose interests

| Benefit Plans | Q 16:26 |

are adverse to the interests of the plan or the interests of its participants or beneficiaries. [ERISA § 406(b)(2)]

8. Under Title I of ERISA, the acquisition or holding of employer securities or real property on behalf of the plan in violation of ERISA Section 407(a). [ERISA § 406(a)(1)(E)] ERISA Section 407(a) basically requires a plan to hold employer stocks or securities that are marketable obligations and real property parcels that are dispersed geographically and suitable for more than one use.

Q 16:25 Do any exceptions exist to the prohibited transaction rules?

The Treasury and the DOL, after consultation, can waive the prohibited transaction rules under some circumstances; a number of statutory exclusions to the prohibited transaction rules do exist. [IRC § 4975(d); ERISA § 408]

Q 16:26 What penalties apply if a prohibited transaction occurs?

The prohibited transaction provisions of the Code provide for a tax equal to 5 percent of the amount involved in a prohibited transaction for each year in which the transaction occurs. [IRC § 4975(a)] The 5 percent tax is cumulative.

> **Example 16-9:** The amount involved in a prohibited transaction is rent of $10,000 per year under a four-year lease. The initial amount of prohibited transaction tax is $5,000 ($2,000 for the first year ($10,000 × 4 × 5%), $1,500 for the second year ($10,000 × 3 × 5%), $1,000 for the third year, and $500 for the fourth year).

If the prohibited transaction is not corrected within the taxable period, an additional tax equal to 100 percent of the amount involved is imposed. The taxable period begins the day the prohibited transaction occurs and ends on the earliest of the following: (1) the date of mailing a notice of deficiency, (2) the date on which the tax imposed by the prohibited transaction provisions is assessed, or (3) the date on which the correction of the prohibited transaction is completed.

Q 16:27 Who are parties in interest and disqualified persons for prohibited transaction purposes?

Parties in interest may include a variety of individuals, trusts, estates, partnerships, sole proprietors, joint ventures, and corporations. [ERISA § 3(14)] The definition of disqualified persons is virtually identical to the definition of parties in interest. [IRC § 4975(e)(2)] There are, however, minor differences between the two terms.

The terms *party in interest* (used in the Code) and *disqualified person* (used in ERISA) refer to the following:

1. Any fiduciary (including, but not limited to any administrator, officer, trustee, or custodian), counsel or employee of the plan. A fiduciary is not liable for the excise tax imposed by the Code unless he or she participates in the transaction in a nonfiduciary capacity.

2. A person providing services to the plan.

3. An employer, any of whose employees are covered by the plan.

4. An employee organization, any of whose members are covered by the plan.

5. An owner, directly or indirectly, of 50 percent or more of an employer, any of whose employees are covered by the plan, or an employee organization, any of whose members are covered by the plan.

6. A spouse, ancestor, lineal descendent, and spouse of a lineal descendent of any person described in Numbers 1 through 5 of this list.

7. A corporation, partnership, trust, or estate in which 50 percent or more is owned directly or indirectly or held by persons described in Numbers 1 through 5 of this list.

8. An officer, director (or individuals with similar powers or responsibilities), 10 percent shareholder, or an employee of an entity described in Numbers 2, 3, 4, 5, or 7 of this list. For this purpose, the Code limits employees to highly compensated employees earning 10 percent or more of the yearly wages of

the employer. The Code's definition of disqualified persons for this purpose excludes persons described in Number 2 of this list.

9. A 10 percent or more (in capital or profits) partner or joint venturer of a person described in Numbers 2, 3, 4, 5 or 7 of this list. The Code's definition of disqualified persons for this purpose excludes persons described in Number 2 of this list.

Q 16:28 What reporting and disclosure rules apply to ERISA plans?

The administrators of ERISA employee benefit plans must provide plan participants and beneficiaries receiving benefits under the plan with the following information:

Summary annual report. This report contains basic information about the plan, such as the value of plan assets, increases or decreases in net assets, plan income, and the amount of employer contributions. [Lab Reg § 2520.104b-10]

Summary plan description. This is a summary of plan provisions that must contain the plan's procedures for processing benefit claims. It must be written in a manner calculated to be understandable to the average plan participant. [Lab Reg § 2520.102(a)] The summary plan description is often an important document in litigation concerning tax-qualified plans and should be carefully prepared.

Summary of material modifications. This is a description of material changes made to the plan during the plan year.

Statement of benefits. Upon receipt of a written request for benefit information, the plan will furnish plan participants and beneficiaries with a statement of benefits. Only one such request may be made in any 12-month period. [ERISA §§ 105(a), 105(b)]

Retirement plans must also file annual reports with the IRS on Form 5500. Some types of retirement plans, generally those for key employees, are exempt from these requirements.

Substantial penalties may be imposed for failure to file these reports. ERISA contains additional provisions requiring plan administrators to provide copies of plan documents and instruments to the participants within 30 days of a request for these items. A failure to provide documents within the 30-day period can result in the imposition of a $100-per-day penalty for each document that is not provided on time. The penalty is not imposed if the failure to provide the documents results from matters beyond the control of the plan administrator. [ERISA § 502(c)(1)] These documents can help plan participants and their advisors determine the benefits to which they are or may become entitled and are thus an important source of information about potential retirement benefits. Further, both the plan document and the summary plan description create enforceable legal rights for plan participants.

Practice Pointer: Requests for these documents should be made by certified mail, return receipt requested, or other means by which the dates of mailing and receipt by the plan administrator can be established.

Age and Sex Discrimination

Q 16:29 What sex discrimination laws apply to retirement plans?

Title VII of the Civil Rights Act of 1964 prohibits discrimination in employment practices (including the provision of fringe benefits) on the basis of gender. It has been applied to retirement plans to prohibit the use of separate male and female mortality tables to pay lower annual pension benefits to women than to men or to require greater pension contributions for women (due to their greater life expectancy). [City of Los Angeles Dept of Water & Power v Manhart, 435 US 702, 98 S Ct 1370 (1978)] Pension plans that pay smaller retirement annuities to women over a longer time period than are paid to men violate Title VII. [Arizona Governing Comm v Norris, 463 US 1073 (1983)]

Title VII covers employers engaging in interstate commerce with at least 15 employees for each working day in at least 20 calendar weeks in the current or preceding calendar year. [29 USC § 630(b)]

Q 16:30 What age discrimination laws apply to retirement plans?

The Age Discrimination in Employment Act of 1967 (ADEA), as amended, protects employees who are 40 years of age and older against discrimination on the basis of age. [29 USC § 631] The ADEA protects former employees from discrimination relating to employment issues (including fringe benefits), but it does not protect independent contractors.

The ADEA covers employers affecting interstate commerce with at least 20 employees for each working day in at least 20 calendar weeks in the current or preceding calendar year. [29 USC § 630(b)]

Q 16:31 What protections does the ADEA give participants in retirement plans?

The ADEA contains the following provisions:

1. A retirement plan cannot require or permit the involuntary retirement of any individual protected by the ADEA because of the individual's age. [29 USC § 623(f)]
2. A defined benefit pension plan cannot require or permit the cessation of an employee's benefit accrual or the reduction of the rate of an employee's benefit accrual because of age. [29 USC 623(i)]
3. A defined contribution plan cannot require or permit the cessation of allocations to an employee's account or the reduction of the rate at which amounts are allocated to the employee's account because of age. [29 USC 623(i)]

Both defined contribution and defined benefit plans can cease benefit accruals, however, if a participant attains the maximum amount of service that can be credited under the plan.

Example 16-10: An engineering firm's profit sharing plan provides that no allocations will be made to participants who have 30 years or more of service. This plan complies with the ADEA. [29 USC 623(i)]

If a distribution of benefits is made to an employed participant who has attained normal retirement age (typically age 65), the amount of benefits that the participant accrues under the plan can be offset (i.e., reduced) by the actuarial equivalent of the distributions made while the participant is still employed. [29 USC § 623(i)]

If a participant has attained normal retirement age under a defined benefit plan and the distribution of benefits has not commenced because the participant is still employed, any adjustment in benefits because of the delay in payout will count in determining whether the ADEA requirements for benefit accruals are met. [29 USC § 623(i)]

Veterans' Rights

Q 16:32 What impact do the labor laws that apply to veterans have on retirement plans?

The Uniformed Service Employment and Retirement Act (USERA) determines the rights of reemployed veterans to retirement benefits. It applies to plans sponsored by private employers (including pension plans under ERISA) as well as to rights to retirement benefits established under state and federal law. [38 USC § 4304] In general, it treats reemployed veterans as if they had continued to be employed while on military duty. Military service counts as service for vesting purposes and for the accrual of benefits. [38 USC § 4318(a)(2)] The employer is liable for funding the cost of any benefit accrual during the period the participant is on active duty, except for forfeitures and earnings on plan assets. [38 USC § 4318(b)(1)] The law applies to both qualified and nonqualified retirement plans.

> **Example 16-11:** A telephone lineman is called to active duty and completes two years of military service. He is then reemployed by the telephone company. The lineman is entitled to credit for his military service for purposes of determining which portion of his pension benefits is nonforfeitable and for determining the amount of his benefits. If the lineman participated in a 401(k) plan, he is entitled to make salary reduction contributions to the plan for the period during which he was on active duty, and he will be entitled to any matching contributions made by the employer for that period.

WARN

Q 16:33 How does WARN affect retirement plans?

The possible applicability of the Worker Adjustment and Retraining Notification Act (WARN) [29 USC § 2101 *et seq.*] to retirement issues must be considered when employees are terminated. WARN requires employers to give 60 days notice for plant closings (basically a shutdown of a single job site involving 50 or more employees) or mass layoffs (a reduction in force that can involve as few as 50 employees if that number of employees constitutes 33% or more of the workforce). The notice must be given to the affected employees (or their union officials if the employees are unionized) and to certain state and local officials. If the notice required by WARN is not given, employees can recover benefits and pay for the period during which notice is not given, up to a maximum of 60 days. Under some circumstances (e.g., if the employer maintains a plan that requires employment on the last day of the year in order to be eligible for a contribution), this can result in the employer's incurring an additional contribution obligation. Small employers (generally those with fewer than 100 employees) are not required to provide this notice.

Taft-Hartley Act

Q 16:34 What retirement plans are governed by the Taft-Hartley Act?

The Taft-Hartley Act applies to retirement plans involving employer contributions if a union or union representative has any authority in the administration of the plan or management of its assets. [29 USC § 186]

> **Example 16-12:** A trucking firm enters into a collective bargaining agreement that, among other things, requires it to contribute to a pension plan maintained by a union. The retirement plan is governed by the Taft-Hartley Act.

Q 16:35 What concerns does an employer have with respect to plans governed by the Taft-Hartley Act?

The Taft-Hartley Act requires that a union and an employer have a written agreement that specifies the detailed basis on which payments are to be made. A failure to comply with this requirement could result in an employer's incurring a criminal conviction. [Moglia v Geoghegan, 403 F 2d 110 (2d Cir 1968) *cert denied* 394 US 919 (1969)] It is not always necessary that the employer sign the agreement; some courts have determined that an employer adopts the agreement by implication by complying with an existing collective bargaining agreement if the employer's conduct manifests an unequivocal intent to be bound. [Labbe v WM Heroman & Co, 521 F Supp 1017 (MD La 1981)]

Multiemployer Plans

Q 16:36 What are multiemployer plans?

Generally, multiemployer plans receive required contributions from and are maintained pursuant to one or more collective bargaining agreements between one or more unions and more than one employer. [ERISA § 4001(3)]

Q 16:37 Does ERISA specifically address multiemployer plans?

Yes, there are specific ERISA sections that apply to multiemployer plans. Key regulations deal with the collection of delinquent employer contributions, the provision of benefit guarantees by the PBGC, and the treatment of insolvent plans. [ERISA §§ 4022A, 4041A]

Q 16:38 Should an employer be concerned about the withdrawal liability that applies to multiemployer plans?

Yes. An employer that withdraws from a multiemployer plan may incur withdrawal liability. In some cases this liability may be significant; it is equal to the employer's proportionate share of the plans unfunded vested benefits. Because of withdrawal liability, an employer should be cautious about participating in multiemployer plans. [ERISA § 4202]

Collective Bargaining

Q 16:39 Must an employer bargain with a union over retirement benefits?

Yes. The National Labor Relations Act (NLRA) requires that an employer negotiate in good faith with a union over retirement benefits. [29 USC § 158 (d)]. A union can, however, waive the right to bargain over retirement benefits. [Ador Corp, 150 NLRB 1658 (1965)] The employer does not have to agree with the union, but must bargain with a view to reaching an agreement if possible. An employer cannot proceed with a fixed resolve to not enter into an agreement with a union even on matters on which there is no disagreement. [NLRB v Highland Park Mfg Co, 110 F 2d 632 (4th Cir 1940)] As part of its duty to bargain in good faith, an employer has a duty to supply information necessary for informed bargaining to occur. [Cone Mills Corp, 169 NLRB 59 (1968)] A union that is in effect in control of an employee benefit plan has a duty to supply information that is necessary for informed bargaining to the employer. [NLRB v AMAX Coal Co 453 US 322 (1981)]

> **Example 16-13:** A toy manufacturer refuses to supply union representatives with the actuarial assumptions used in administering its retirement plan as well as information on the costs of administering the plan. This refusal is a violation of the manufacturer's duty to bargain in good faith.

Q 16:40 What effect does ERISA have on collective bargaining?

Collective bargaining for contract provisions that violate ERISA (or other federal and nonpreempted state laws) violate the NLRA. [NLRB v Wooster Division of the Borg-Warner Corp, 356 US 342 (1958)] Unions and employers can bargain for benefits that are more generous than the minimum ERISA requirements, but they cannot bargain for plan provisions that do not meet these minimun requirements.

Q 16:41 Does the NLRA limit coverage of retirement plans?

Yes, to a certain extent. The NLRA forbids discrimination against employees in the terms and conditions of their employment as a result of lawful union activities. [29 USC §§ 157, 158] This means that an employer cannot use plan eligibility requirements as a device to discourage unionization.

> **Example 16-14:** A company establishes a profit sharing plan providing retroactive coverage to all full-time employees who are not union members prior to an election to determine if employees are to be represented by a union. This is a violation of the NLRA. [Melville Confections, Inc, 142 NLRB 1334]

The National Labor Relations Board has held that provisions in plans that exclude union members are per se illegal [Motor Wheel Corp 180 NLRB 354 (1969)]; however, an employer can exclude unionized employees from coverage under a retirement plan provided the employer bargains in good faith on this issue. An employer cannot notify employees that their eligibility to participate in a retirement plan has terminated as a result of their becoming unionized. [Goodyear Tire & Rubber Co 170 NLRB 539 (1968)]

Q 16:42 Can an employer subject to a collective bargaining agreement unilaterally amend a retirement plan?

No. Retirement benefits are mandatory subjects for collective bargaining. Unilateral changes to these subjects are per se violations of the NLRA. [NLRB v Katz, 369 US 736 (1962)]

Q 16:43 Does an employer have an obligation to continue to provide retirement benefits after the collective bargaining agreement expires?

Yes. An employer has an obligation to abide by the terms of a collective bargaining agreement even after the agreement has expired. This means that the employer must maintain the status quo and continue to provide retirement benefits until either a new agreement is negotiated or there is an impasse in the bargaining. [Atlas Tack Corp, 226 NLRB 222 (1976), *enf'd* 559 F 2d 1201 (1st Cir 1977)]

Q 16:44 Can an employer discontinue accrued benefits during a strike?

No. Although an employer need not provide striking employees with benefits that depend on the continuation of services (i.e. unearned wages), the employer must provide benefits that have accrued at the time the strike begins. [Texaco, 285 NLRB No 45 (1987)]

Chapter 17

Tax-Qualified Retirement Plans

Tax-qualified retirement plans are employee benefit plans that meet the requirements of Section 401 of the Internal Revenue Code. The main purpose of tax-qualified plans is to offer retirement benefits; however, they can also provide death and disability benefits. Although tax-qualified plans are subject to complex regulations, hundreds of thousands of employers have adopted them because they offer impressive tax advantages.

Employers that adopt tax-qualified plans may choose from a variety of options. They can either have plans designed for them from scratch or can adopt standardized plans. Customized plans provide the most flexibility and may be the only practical choice for employers with special needs. Standardized plans are usually less expensive than customized plans to install, but the benefits paid to rank-and-file employees under them may be greater than benefits paid to rank-and-file employees under customized plans, increasing the employer's salary expense.

Overview	17-2
Design Considerations	17-5
Defined Contribution Plans	17-14
Defined Benefit Plans	17-21
Actuarial Factors	17-27
Keogh Plans	17-42
General Considerations	17-43

Overview

Q 17:1 How do tax-qualified retirement plans generate retirement income?

Tax-qualified retirement plans generate retirement income by taking advantage of a number of significant tax advantages for employees and employers. An employer that adopts a tax-qualified retirement plan is allowed a current deduction for its contributions to the plan. Plan participants pay no tax on the money contributed on their behalf until the plan makes a distribution to them. Moreover, earnings on plan assets accumulate tax free under the plan, and payments (e.g., distributions) from the plan may get favorable income tax treatment. The assets in tax-qualified retirement plans are generally protected from creditors.

Example 17-1: A physician, age 30, adopts a profit sharing plan for his professional corporation. He is the only employee and throughout his career occupies the 36 percent tax bracket. Each year, the physician contributes $30,000 to his profit sharing plan and then retires at age 65. Throughout this period the physician earns 10 percent on plan assets. At retirement, the physician has $8,130,871 in the plan. If he withdraws all the funds in the plan at retirement and is taxed at 36 percent, the physician still has $5,366,282. Had he allocated those amounts of money outside the tax-qualified plan for investments, the physician would have had $2,433,419 because taxes would have been assessed immediately, leaving less money to invest and grow. This dramatic difference occurs because, by using a tax-qualified plan, the physician avoids the 36 percent tax that would have been levied each year on the $30,000 available for investment (the tax would have reduced the amount available for investment to $19,200). Furthermore, when the 36 percent tax rate that is imposed on earnings outside the plan is applied to the earnings on those amounts, it reduces the rate at which earnings compound to 6.4 percent as compared with a rate of 10 percent for earnings on assets in the plan.

Tax-qualified retirement plans are particularly attractive to working owners of closely held corporations and to self-employed individuals who typically have the longest periods of service with their companies and receive the highest salaries. Accordingly, they receive the most generous benefits, although benefits must be provided for other employees as well. Tax-qualified retirement plans also may help businesses attract and retain desirable employees.

Q 17:2 What favorable tax treatment exists for payments from tax-qualified retirement plans?

Payments (e.g., distributions) from tax-qualified retirement plans receive the following kinds of favorable tax treatment:

1. Reduced tax rates may apply to lump-sum distributions made to certain participants.
2. Income taxes on certain distributions may be deferred by rolling over the distribution to an individual retirement account (IRA) or to another tax-qualified plan.
3. Income taxes on a partial or qualified total distribution to a deceased participant's spouse may be deferred by rolling over the distribution to an IRA.
4. Installment or annuity payments are taxed only when they are received.

Q 17:3 What is an insured tax-qualified retirement plan?

An insured tax-qualified retirement plan is a plan that is funded in whole or in part through the purchase of life insurance policies. If the plan is funded partially through the purchase of insurance policies, the remaining portion of the plan is funded through investments held by a trust. One significant advantage of a plan that invests only in insurance policies is that the plan can qualify for an exemption from provisions of the Internal Revenue Code (Code) that require plans to be funded at minimum levels each year.

Q 17:4 When should a plan have insurance as a plan asset?

Insurance may be a good investment for tax-qualified retirement plans if the participant needs large amounts of insurance and lacks sufficient funds outside the plan with which to pay the premiums, because the premiums paid by the employer in the form of plan contributions are deductible by the employer.

There are some drawbacks, though. Each insured participant must report as taxable income an amount that represents the cost of current life insurance protection, determined under tables created by the Internal Revenue Service (IRS). [Rev Rul 55-747, 1955-2 CB 228] Moreover, the effective rate of return of insurance products is reduced by various loads and commissions charged in connection with those products. Because the income earned by tax-qualified plans is not subject to federal income tax, the exemption from federal income tax on insurance policy earnings (i.e., tax-free inside buildup) does not provide a significant benefit.

Q 17:5 What are master and prototype retirement plans?

A master retirement plan is a standardized retirement plan in which the funding vehicle is specified in the sponsor's application. A prototype retirement plan is a standardized retirement plan that permits each employer that adopts the plan to select the funding vehicle it wishes to use. [Rev Proc 89-9, 1989-1 CB 780, as modified by Rev Proc 90-21, 1990-1 CB 499] As a practical matter, this usually means that the employer that adopts a prototype plan can choose the trustee for the trust or the life insurance policy that the plan is to invest in, while the employer that adopts a master plan cannot make these choices.

Companies, mutual funds, banks, brokerage firms, law firms, and other types of firms have created master and prototype plans that have already been approved by the IRS. These plans may be adopted by executing an adoption agreement and electing certain available options. If the participating employer adopts a standardized plan (i.e., a plan that contains certain restrictions), the employer need not obtain a separate determination from the IRS that the plan is tax qualified, which saves time, expense, and attorneys' fees. The IRS restrictions that pertain to a standardized plan prevent it from conditioning the receipt of a contribution or the accrual of a benefit on employment as of the last day of the plan year or on more than 500 hours of service in the year of termination.

Employers may also adopt prototype plans that are not subject to the restrictions on standardized prototype plans. These plans are known as nonstandardized plans. Nonstandardized plans are not preapproved by the IRS. If the plan sponsor wants to obtain IRS approval, it must obtain a determination letter.

Q 17:6 Can a nonstandardized plan be converted into a standardized plan?

A nonstandardized plan cannot be converted into a standardized plan of a different type. For example. a nonstandardized money purchase pension plan cannot be converted into a standardized profit sharing plan. A nonstandardized plan can, however, be converted into a standardized plan of the same type. For example, a nonstandardized profit sharing plan can be converted into a standardized profit sharing plan.

Design Considerations

Q 17:7 How does a retirement plan achieve tax-qualified status?

A retirement plan is deemed to be a tax-qualified plan if the plan document meets certain requirements set forth in Code Section 401(a) and if the plan is operated in accordance with Code Section 401(a). For a user fee, the IRS will review a plan and determine whether the plan document meets the requirements for tax-qualified status. Although this IRS review is not necessary to obtain tax-qualified status, almost all plans are submitted to the IRS for review, even though the IRS review does not guarantee that the plan will not be disqualified. Instead, the IRS review provides protection in the event that the IRS later asserts that the plan is disqualified because the plan document does not meet the requirements for tax-qualified plans. Most practitioners believe that in almost all cases the potential costs of plan disqualification greatly outweigh the costs of obtaining a determination letter. Some types of plans (e.g., standardized master and prototype plans) obtain a generic determination letter that applies to all plans of that type. These generic letters relieve employers of the cost of obtaining individual determination letters for standardized master and prototype plans and are one of the reasons why small employers often use those types of plans. Nonstandardized master and prototype plans must obtain determination letters, but the costs of obtaining these letters are usually relatively small in comparison to the costs of obtaining letters for individually designed plans.

Q 17:8 What happens if a plan is disqualified?

If a plan is disqualifed, the employer loses its income tax deduction for plan contributions for each year in which the plan is disqualifed. In all likelihood, this means that the employer will incur additional income tax. It is possible that the employer will also be liable for additional FICA and FUTA taxes. The trust for the plan will lose its income tax exemption on trust income for all years in which the plan is disqualified.

There are also adverse consequences for plan participants. A participant in a disqualifed defined benefit plan is taxed on the increase in his or her accrued benefit in the plan for all years that are open (i.e. subject to increased tax) to the extent he or she is vested in it. [Treas Reg § 1.402(b)-1(a)]

The favorable tax treatment for distributions from a tax qualified plan may also be lost. The consequences of this can be serious. For example, rollover status could be lost. Some courts have decided that distributions from a plan that becomes disqualifed are not entitled to favorable tax treatment. [Woodson v Commr, 73 TC 779 (1980), *rev'd* 651 F 2d 1094 (5th Cir 1981)] Other courts have reached a contrary conclusion. [Greenwald v Commr 44 TC 137 (1965) *rev'd* 366 F 2d 538 (2d Cir 1966)]

Only highly compensated individuals are affected by some plan disqualifications. If a plan is disqualifed solely because it fails to satisfy the nondiscrimination requirements of Code Section 410(b) (i.e., the minimum coverage requirements) or Code Section 401(a)(26) (i.e., the minimum participation requirements), non-highly compensated employees do not recognize income as result of the disqualification. In contrast, highly compensated employees have to recognize as taxable income the entire value of their vested account balances or vested accrued benefits when disqualification occurs. [IRC § 402 (b)(4)]

Q 17:9 What alternatives exist to plan disqualification if a tax-qualified plan violates the requirements for tax-qualified status?

Because the effects of plan disqualification are so great, the IRS has developed three administrative alternatives to plan disqualification: (1) the Administrative Policy Regarding Sanctions (APRS) program, (2) the Voluntary Compliance Resolution (VCR) program, and the Closing Agreement Program (CAP) program.

APRS program. This program is available for taxpayers who have incurred onetime, minor violations. It is available only for operational defects. Unless a newly qualified plan is involved, this program is available whether the IRS or the taxpayer discovers the defect. The only action that is taken is that the defect is corrected. Because there are no sanctions, this is the most favorable program for the taxpayer.

VCR program. This program permits the correction of operational problems solely. It is available only if the taxpayer discovers the defects and the plan is not being audited. All defects must be corrected and the taxpayer must pay a fixed user fee based on the amount of plan assets and the number of participants in the plan. The program is not available if the violations are consistent and repeated or if the violation is egregious. Certain types of violations, such as failures to file Form 5500, cannot be corrected through this program. Specific operational problems can be resolved through the standard VCR program using simplified procedures by paying a $356 compliance fee. All defects must be corrected. Cases that are submitted to the VCR program but that are inelgible are returned to the plan sponsor for submission under the CAP program.

CAP. This program applies both to defects in plan documents and to operational defects whether the IRS or the plan sponsor discovers the defect. If the plan sponsor discovers the defect, it may "walk in" or voluntarily approach the IRS. This can be done anonymously until the production of specific documents is necessary. CAP requires the correction of all defects and the payment of a negotiated dollar sanction. These sanctions can be 100 percent of the income tax

Q 17:10   Estate and Retirement Planning Answer Book

liability for plan disqualification. [Rev Proc 94-16] If the plan sponsor discovers the defect and the plan is not under examination, the sanction is limited to 40 percent of the income tax liability for plan disqualification. A lesser sanction can be negotiated, however, and it may be helpful to point out that the taxpayer informed the IRS about the problem.

Q 17:10   What are the vesting requirements for tax-qualified plans?

Vesting refers to the percentage of a plan benefit that the participant cannot forfeit for such things as terminating employment. A tax-qualified plan must provide for 100 percent vesting after five years of service or for vesting according to the following schedule:

Years of Service	Percentage Vested
3	20
4	40
5	60
6	80
7	100

A special rule applies to participants in a collectively bargained multiemployer plan. [IRC § 411]

Tax-qualified plans can be designed so that a new employee cannot participate in the plan until he or she completes two years of service. If the plan contains that feature, the employee must be 100 percent vested after two years of service.

Q 17:11   Must a tax-qualified retirement plan include all employees?

No. A tax-qualified retirement plan may exclude certain classes of employees on the basis of age, length of service, and union status. [IRC § 410] Nevertheless, there are rules that require tax-qualified plans to cover minimum numbers of employees. These rules are designed to ensure that the plan benefits a broad spectrum of employees, not just highly compensated employees.

Q 17:12 What are the most common eligibility requirements for participation in a tax-qualified retirement plan?

Most plans have minimum age and length of service requirements. A plan may exclude any employee who has not yet reached age 21, and may also require an employee to complete a certain period of service before becoming eligible to participate. The service requirement usually may not exceed one year [IRC § 410(a)(1)(A)(i)] and is defined as 1,000 hours of creditable service. A two-year service period may be required, however, if the plan immediately vests benefits at 100 percent once participation begins. Creditable service, for which the employee is entitled to payment, includes both on-the-job service and paid leave. [IRC § 410(a)(1)(A)(ii)] If the plan requires more than one year of service for eligibility, the plan must provide full and immediate vesting of benefits. [IRC §§ 401(k)(2)(D), 410(a)(1)(A)(ii), 410(a)(1)(B)(i)]

Q 17:13 Can a tax-qualified plan give credit for an employee's service in years prior to the adoption of the plan?

An employer can credit an employee with service for years of employment in which a tax-qualified plan was not in effect. The employer can also give credit for years of service in which the employee was not eligible to participate in the plan even though the plan was in existence (pre-participation service) or for imputed service. Imputed service is service that was not performed for the plan sponsor by an employee who is currently a participant in the employer's plan.

Example 17-2: An engineering firm acquires a two-person consulting firm in a merger. The new employees are given credit in the engineering firm's defined benefit pension plan for their service with the consulting firm.

If imputed service credit or pre-participation service credit is given to highly compensated employees, the same credit must be given to similarly situated non-highly compensated employees. [Treas Reg § 1.401(a)-11(d)(3)]

Q 17:14 Which nondiscrimination rules apply to tax-qualified plans?

The Code generally prohibits tax-qualified plans from providing benefits or contributions that discriminate in favor of highly compensated employees. [IRC § 401(a)(4)] These plans must be nondiscriminatory with respect to either contributions or benefits, but not both. [Treas Reg § 1.401(a)(4)-1(b)(2)(i)] The Treasury Department issued final nondiscrimination regulations in August 1993, replacing regulations issued in 1991. The new regulations contain safe harbors that permit plans that have certain design features to automatically pass the nondiscrimination tests.

Example 17-3: A medical professional service corporation adopts a profit sharing plan in which contributions to the plan are allocated in proportion to income. All participants in the plan have the same normal retirement age and are subject to the same vesting schedule and definition of years of service. The plan automatically satisfies the nondiscrimination requirements.

The regulations also contain general tests that must be passed by plans that do not satisfy the safe harbor tests. Plans that do not pass the nondiscrimination tests can sometimes be retroactively amended to pass those tests. [Treas Reg § 1.401(a)(4)-11(g)]

Q 17:15 May a tax-qualified plan discriminate against rank-and-file employees on the basis of benefits, rights, and features?

No. Benefits, rights, and features must be made available to participants in a nondiscriminatory manner. [IRC § 401(a)(4)] This requirement is not met if the benefits, rights, or features substantially favor the highly compensated group. [Treas Reg § 1.401(a)(4)-4(c)(1)]

Example 17-4: A profit sharing plan provides that only employees who have attained age 55 and have 30 years of service with the employer are entitled to obtain a payment from the plan while still employed there. All highly compensated employees can meet the 30-year requirement by the time they reach age 55, but only 10 percent of the non-highly compensated employees can meet this requirement by the time they attain age 55. The plan fails the nondiscrimination test.

Assuming the nondiscrimination test is met, however, age and service requirements are generally not taken into account unless the requirement is linked with a specific time period.

Example 17-5: A profit sharing plan provides that only employees who have reached age 55 and have ten years of service with the employer are entitled to obtain a payment from the plan while still employed there. This plan complies with the nondiscrimination requirement for benefits, rights, and features. The plan would not necessarily comply with that requirement if only persons who attained age 55 in 1994 and had ten years of service could obtain the distribution. It would comply with the requirement only if the benefit was available to a sufficient number of non-highly compensated employees. [Treas Reg § 1.401(a)(4)-4(b)(2)]

Moreover, certain conditions do not count in determining whether the nondiscrimination rules are met. These include the following:

- Family status
- Disability
- Hardship
- Default on a plan loan secured by a participant's account balance
- Minimum loan amounts up to $1,500

[Treas Reg § 1.401(a)(4)-4(c)(1)]

Example 17-6: A plan provides that plan loans will be made only to persons who are disabled. This condition does not violate the nondiscrimination rules.

Q 17:16 What kind of benefits can be provided under a tax-qualified retirement plan?

Besides retirement benefits, qualified plans may provide death benefits, disability benefits, and benefits on termination of employment. Profit sharing and 401(k) plans can provide for hardship distributions. A profit sharing plan may also permit distribution of all or a part of a participant's vested interest that has remained in the plan for at least two years prior to distribution. [Rev Rul 71-224, 1971-1 CB 124]

Q 17:17 May a tax-qualified plan provide for plan loans for participants?

Yes, but the loans are subject to certain restrictions. If a loan exceeds a certain dollar amount, the amount loaned will be treated as a distribution. [IRC § 72(p)] Keogh plans may not make loans to owner-employees under Code Section 401(c)(3), and plan loans from tax-qualified plans may not be made to shareholder employees in S corporations (i.e., individuals deemed to own more than 5 percent of an S corporation). [IRC § 4975(d)]

Q 17:18 Can an employer provide different tax-qualified plan benefits for participants in different lines of business?

Yes, an employer can provide different tax-qualified plan benefits for employees in separate lines of business. The employer must meet certain tests to establish the existence of a separate line of business, and it must establish that it is a qualified separate line of business. [IRC § 414(r)] If an employer can establish those things, it does not have to take into account the employees in the qualified separate lines of business in determining whether a tax-qualified plan maintained by one line of business meets the nondiscrimination tests. As a practical matter, this means that an employer that can establish a qualified separate line of business can provide a greater differential in benefits between the different qualified separate lines of business than would otherwise be possible. The employer must, however, still satisfy a liberalized version of the nondiscriminatory classification test.

Example 17-7: An employer has 500 employees who are employed in its construction subsidiary and 1,000 employers who are employed in its banking subsidiary. The banking subsidiary maintains a defined benefit pension plan that provides substantial benefits.

The construction subsidiary maintains a profit sharing plan that provides minimal benefits. If the employer can meet the requirements for qualified separate line of business status, it may disregard the employees of the construction subsidiary in determining whether or not the defined benefit plan for the employees in its banking subsidiary meets the nondiscrimination tests.

Q 17:19 May a tax-qualified retirement plan provide health insurance?

Pension plans may provide health insurance only for retired employees. [IRC § 401(h)] A profit sharing plan may provide health insurance benefits for all plan participants and their families. If the insurance is purchased with funds that have been in the plan for more than two years, there is no limit on how much the plan may pay for insurance coverage. If the plan uses other funds to buy the insurance, the amount of the premiums must be incidental. [Treas Reg § 1.401-1(b)(1)(ii)]

Q 17:20 Can a company take Social Security benefits into consideration in designing its tax-qualified retirement plan?

Yes. Tax-qualified retirement plans can be designed so that Social Security benefits are taken into account in determining participants' benefits, by subtracting a portion of Social Security benefits when calculating the benefit due under the tax-qualified retirement plan. As a practical matter, this means that higher-paid employees receive a greater portion of benefits than would otherwise be the case. The rules governing how and when a retirement plan may subtract (or offset) Social Security benefits are quite complex. [IRC § 401(l)]

Example 17-8: A law firm has two employees, a lawyer and a secretary. The lawyer's compensation is $140,000 per year, and the secretary's compensation is $30,000. The firm has a profit sharing plan. Under the plan, Social Security benefits are taken into account by integrating the plan at $30,000 of compensation per year. The integration factors permitted by federal law that are most favorable to the lawyer are used. The law firm makes a yearly contribution of $10,000 on behalf of both employees. Under these circumstances, the lawyer receives a contribution of $8,928, and the secretary receives a contribution of $1,072. Had integration not been used, the lawyer would have received $8,235, and the secretary would have received $1,765.

Q 17:21 What is adequate consideration for the sale of stock held by tax-qualified plans?

Adequate consideration for a security that is listed on a national exchange is the prevailing price for the security on that exchange. [DOL Prop Reg § 2510.3-18] Adequate consideration for securities that are not listed on national exchanges but that have a market is the offering price established by the current bid and asked price quoted by persons independent of the issuer and parties in interest. For securities that have no generally recognized market, adequate consideration is the fair market value as determined in good faith by the trustee or named fiduciary pursuant to the terms of the plan and in accordance with regulations issued by the Department of Labor (DOL).

Defined Contribution Plans

Q 17:22 What is a defined contribution plan?

A defined contribution plan is a retirement plan that has individual accounts for each participant. The amount in the account depends, in part, on the investment performance of the plan.

Example 17-9: A software distribution company maintains a profit sharing plan. The plan records state that the president of the company has an account balance of $50,000. The plan records show that similar account balances exist for other participants in the plan. This plan is an individual account plan.

Example 17-10: A firm's pension plan states that the president of the company is entitled to a pension of $1,000 per month when she reaches age 65. The participant has no account balance in her name that is available to pay the benefit. This pension plan is not an individual account plan.

The amount of benefits in a defined contribution plan is based solely on the amount contributed to the participant's account, plus the combined income, expenses, gains, losses, and forfeitures from the accounts of other plan participants that can be allocated to the account. [ERISA § 3(34); IRC § 414(i)] In general, there is no guarantee that a particular level of benefit will be provided upon retirement; instead, whatever is in the individual account at retirement is the amount of the retirement benefit. The contributions to the account (and other amounts allocated to the account), not the benefit ultimately payable, are what is "defined" under a defined contribution-type retirement plan. Defined contribution plans include the following kinds of plans:

- Money purchase pension
- Target benefit
- Profit sharing
- Thrift or savings
- 401(k)
- Stock bonus
- Employee stock ownership

Q 17:23 Are benefits in a defined contribution plan guaranteed?

No. The amount of benefits a participant receives from a defined contribution plan depends on the size of a participant's account balance. This balance, in turn, depends on the amount of contributions an employer makes and on the plan's investment performance. Some defined contribution plans' participants have seen their account balances become worthless as a result of poor investment decisions. The insurance program administered by the Pension Benefit Guaranty Corporation (PBGC) does not apply to these plans.

Q 17:24 What is a money purchase pension plan?

A money purchase pension plan is a defined contribution plan to which the company makes mandatory contributions. These contributions are usually based on the amount of each participant's compensation. For example, a money purchase pension plan might require that the company contribute an amount equal to 10 percent of each participant's compensation to the plan. This obligation to contribute to the plan distinguishes money purchase pension plans from profit sharing plans. In profit sharing plans, the amount of the contribution is usually left to the discretion of the employer. Forfeitures that occur in a money purchase pension plan may be used either to reduce future employer contributions or to increase the benefits of the remaining participants.

To be a valid money purchase pension plan, the plan's document must state that it is a money purchase pension plan. [IRC § 401(a)(27)] Often this statement is contained within the definitions section of the plan.

Q 17:25 What is a target benefit plan?

A target benefit plan has certain elements in common with both defined benefit plans and with defined contribution plans. The resemblance to a defined benefit plan is that the annual contribution amount depends on the payment of a projected retirement benefit to the participants; the resemblance to a money purchase plan (a type of defined contribution plan) is that the benefits paid out by the plan depend on the plan's investment success and may fluctuate because the employer's contributions remain stable and do not compensate for irregular earnings.

If favorable actuarial assumptions are used to compute the target benefit, a greater proportion of benefits can be paid to older employees than under profit sharing (another type of defined contribution plan) or money purchase pension plans. If the group that the employer wants to benefit consists of older employees, a target benefit plan may be preferable to a profit sharing or money purchase pension plan.

A target benefit plan is like a defined benefit plan in that the annual contribution is determined by the amount needed each year to accumulate a fund sufficient to pay a projected retirement benefit to each participant upon reaching retirement age. The interest rate needed to accumulate this amount is assumed. A target benefit plan may contain a projected benefit that (e.g., 30 percent of compensation) that is similar to the promised benefit contained in some defined benefit plans and, like those benefits, is funded on the basis of actuarial assumptions.

Funding for a target benefit plan remains constant when the plan's actual investment experience differs from the plan's actuarial assumptions. This means, for example, that the employer continues to make contributions to a target benefit plan at the rate implied by the plan's actuarial assumptions, even if the actual rate of return on investments would justify a lower rate of contribution.

A target benefit plan is like a money purchase pension plan in that if a favorable investment performance continues over the life of the plan, the actual benefits provided by the plan will exceed the projected (target) benefit. The benefit provided by a target benefit plan depends on the actual experience of the plan, and the contributions made to the plan are not adjusted because the plan's actual experience differs from its actuarial experience. Thus, if the earnings in a target benefit plan differ from the original assumptions, the employees' contributions to the plan do not fluctuate; instead, the benefits paid out will fluctuate.

Target benefit plans are classified as defined contribution plans for purposes of determining whether Section 415 limits on annual benefits or contributions are exceeded. [Rev Rul 76-46, 1976-2 CB 115]

In a defined benefit plan, in contrast to a target benefit plan, if the actual experience of a defined benefit pension plan differs from the actuarial assumptions for the plan (e.g., if earnings are higher or turnover is greater than the actuarial assumptions predicted), the employer either increases or decreases its subsequent contributions to the extent necessary to provide the promised benefit.

Q 17:26 What is a profit sharing plan?

A profit sharing plan is a defined contribution plan that can give an employer complete discretion to vary the contributions it makes to the plan. Some profit sharing plans, however, require employers to make contributions pursuant to a formula. For example, a employer might be required to contribute 2 percent of its profits to the profit sharing plan. Amounts contributed to the plan are invested and accumulate tax free for distribution to participants or to their beneficiaries at retirement, after a fixed number of years or upon the occurrence of some specified event. Contributions to a profit sharing plan do not have to be based on profits. [IRC § 401(a)(27)] Most profit sharing plans have discretionary formulas that permit the employer to forgo or limit its contributions in a particular year.

Q 17:27 What is an age-weighted profit sharing plan?

An age-weighted profit sharing plan allocates employer contributions among plan participants on the basis of age and compensation. Age-weighted profit sharing plans are designed so that older participants receive larger contributions than younger participants. Because the owners and top executives of a company tend to be older, age-weighted profit sharing plans have the effect of allocating a greater proportion of their assets to these participants than other types of plans. [Treas Reg § 1.401-1(b)(ii)]

Q 17:28 What is a thrift plan?

A thrift plan is a defined contribution plan that requires the employer to make contributions only if the employee makes contributions. Employee contributions are made on an after-tax basis (i.e., income tax has already been paid on the amounts contributed to the plan). For instance, an employer may pledge a contribution that is 50 percent of the contribution made by an employee out of his or her own compensation. Although it was formerly the case that financial institutions often established these plans, they have been supplanted to a great extent by 401(k) plans. This occurred because 401(k) permits pretax contributions that allow the plan participant to avoid paying tax on the amounts he or she contributes until the plan makes a distribution of the participant's account balance.

Q 17:29 What is a 401(k) plan?

A 401(k) plan is a defined contribution plan that gives participants an election to forgo a direct cash payment from the employer as compensation and instead have the employer contribute to the plan on behalf of the employees. Section 401(k) of the Code provides an express exception to the constructive receipt rule (see Q 24:4); a plan participant is not considered to have received the cash, and it is treated for tax purposes (other than for Social Security tax purposes) as an employer contribution. As a result, the participant does not have to include in income the employer's contributions to the plan merely because the participant could have elected cash instead. [IRC §§ 401(k)(2), 402(a)(A)] This represents a significant tax benefit because, under constructive receipt principles (see chapter 24), the mere opportunity to elect cash would cause the amount subject to the election to be counted as taxable income.

Section 401(k) plans may take the form of salary reduction arrangements. In this type of arrangement, a participant elects to have a portion of his or her salary contributed to the 401(k) plan. [Treas Reg § 1.401(k)-1(a)(3)(i)]

Benefits attributable to employer contributions to a 401(k) plan that are made because of a participant's election cannot be distributed without penalty until the employee retires, becomes disabled, dies, or reaches age $59\frac{1}{2}$. Contributions made by the employer to the plan because of the employee's election are 100 percent vested, which means that the employee will not lose the benefit if he or she terminates employment. [IRC § 401(k)(2)(B)(1)]

Q 17:30 What practical problems can an employer expect if it establishes a 401(k) plan?

The amount that can be contributed on behalf of highly compensated employees through salary reduction is limited by the average amount that is contributed through salary reduction by rank-and-file employees. Sometimes rank-and-file employees do not elect sufficient salary reductions to permit the highly compensated employees to defer the maximum amount possible. If the highly compensated employees have been taking the maximum possible deferrals, it may be necessary for the plan to distribute to them a portion of the amount that was contributed on their behalf. This is a taxable distribution that results in an increase in income. If the highly compensated employee has filed an income tax return, he or she may have to file an amended return. This means additional time and trouble. The risk of this occurring can be reduced by testing at periodic intervals throughout the year and by having the highly compensated employees reduce their salary reduction contributions. Insufficient rank-and-file employee contributions can also be corrected by the employer's making supplemental contributions on their behalf. These contributions must be 100 percent vested.

Another solution to this problem is to create a nonqualifed plan that mirrors the terms of the 401(k) plan. Accounts are created in the nonqualified plan that replicate those in the 401(k) plan. Salary reduction contributions on behalf of the highly compensated employees are made to the nonqualifed plan. At the end of the year these contributions are transferred to the 401(k) plan to the extent possible. The residual amounts are left in the nonqualified plan where they continue to accrue benefits at the same rate as the 401(k) plan.

Q 17:31 Is it a good idea to allow multiple investment options?

As a practical matter, it may be a good idea to limit investment options to five or fewer mutual funds. Many employees may be interested in only one type of investment option such as a bond fund or a money market fund. Administrative costs mount as the number of investment options increases. Morever, regulations issued by the DOL require that investment information on the investment options be made available to plan participants. [DOL Reg § 2550.404(c)-1(b)(3)] If the number of options is too great, this burden becomes onerous. A minimum of three investment options should be offererd, however. Each option must be diversified and have materially different risk and return characteristics. In the aggregate, the options must afford participants and beneficiaries a range of portfolios with varying risks and returns. Each option, when combined with the others, must tend to minimize risk by providing diversification. [DOL Reg § 2550.404(c)-1(b)(3)

Q 17:32 What is a stock bonus plan?

A stock bonus plan is like a profit sharing plan except that benefit payments must be made in the stock of the company if the participant requests a stock distribution. A stock bonus plan may distribute cash to a participant if the participant requests a cash distribution; however, the participant has the right to demand a distribution of the employer's stock. [Treas Reg § 1.401-1(b)(iii)] Employers who wish to establish a market for their stock sometimes create stock bonus plans.

Q 17:33 What is an employee stock ownership plan?

An employee stock ownership plan (ESOP) is a type of defined contribution plan that can borrow money from the employer or can obtain loans that are guaranteed by the employer (see chapter 18).

Q 17:34 How may an ESOP or stock bonus plan benefit a corporation or its shareholders?

A stock bonus plan may be beneficial to a company or to its shareholders in the following ways:

1. By providing a market for the owners' closely held stock as a tax-favored alternative to stock redemption;
2. By giving the company tax deductions without affecting its cash flow; and
3. By keeping the company's stock in friendly hands in the event of a hostile takeover.

Defined Benefit Plans

Q 17:35 What is a defined benefit plan?

A defined benefit plan is a plan other than a defined contribution plan that generally promises to pay a specific benefit at a certain age. For instance, a defined benefit plan may promise plan participants a lifetime payment of $500 per month commencing when they reach age 65. The key distinction between a defined benefit plan and a defined contribution plan is that a defined benefit plan predetermines the benefit payable upon the employee's termination of employment, retirement, disability, or death. The sponsoring employer then must take steps to assure that the plan will be adequately funded to provide the defined benefit at the time it becomes payable. In contrast, a defined contribution plan defines the amount that is contributed to the plan each year and allocated to each participant's individual account. No guarantee is made about how much the individual account will be worth upon termination of employment, retirement, death, and the value of the individual account will fluctuate due to investment gains and losses. From a retirement and estate planning perspective, a defined benefit plan provides a more easily measurable and predictable amount of retirement income (assuming that the plan's age and service requirements are satisfied). [ERISA § 3(35); IRC § 414(j)]

Unlike defined contribution plans, defined benefit plans do not have accounts in the names of individual plan participants that are available to pay benefits to those participants. Instead of being determined by an account balance, the amount of benefits paid is determined by a formula stated in the plan.

Q 17:36 What is a flat benefit plan?

A flat benefit plan is a type of defined benefit plan in which the benefit for each participant depends solely on compensation. It may, for example, be structured according to a formula that entitles each participant to a monthly pension that commences at a normal retirement date and is payable for life in an amount equal to 25 percent of the participant's average monthly compensation.

Q 17:37 What is a unit benefit plan?

In a unit benefit plan, the amount of the benefit depends on and increases in proportion to the employee's amount of service. A unit benefit plan could be structured according to a formula that entitles each participant to a monthly pension that commences at a normal retirement date and is payable for life in an amount equal to 1 percent of the participant's average monthly compensation multiplied by the participant's number of years of service with the company.

Q 17:38 Are benefits in a defined benefit plan guaranteed?

Not always. In theory, the employer that establishes a defined benefit pension plan is obligated to pay the benefits promised. The possibility exists, however, that the plan may terminate before the benefits are fully funded; for example, the employer may go into bankruptcy. Additional protection is afforded participants in these plans by the PBGC, a U.S. government corporation. The PBGC protection does not cover all defined benefit plans, however, and there are maximum limits on PBGC benefits.

Q 17:39 What are the advantages of defined benefit plans?

From the employee's point of view, defined benefit plans can be better than other types of plans both because the benefit is not subject to the results of investment performance and because defined benefit plans do not impose fixed limits on the amounts of employer contributions. In a defined benefit plan, the employer contribution may be whatever is necessary to fund the projected benefit, and this amount can far exceed the allowable contributions to a defined contribution plan.

Defined benefit plans are attractive to small employers that become highly profitable and whose key employees are age 45 or older. This is because defined contribution plans limit the amount that can be contributed on behalf of the employees to the greater of $30,000 or 25 percent of compensation. Employees who are 45 and over have only a limited time to save for retirement, and the contribution limits for defined contribution plans may preclude these employees from reaching their desired level of retirement savings. In contrast, defined benefit plans are not subject to these limits. Accordingly, they can be designed to provide for a hefty retirement benefit for older key employees and can be funded at levels far in excess of the contribution limits on defined contribution plans.

Example 17-11: A professional corporation owned by a physician, age 55, obtains a lucrative hospital contract. The physician's income jumps from $130,000 to $600,000 per year. If the professional corporation adopts a profit sharing plan, contributions made on behalf of the physician are limited to $30,000 per year; however, if the corporation adopts a defined benefit plan, annual contributions made with respect to the physician may exceed $150,000, depending on the level of benefits and the funding assumptions used.

Defined benefit plans also provide employees with a definite retirement benefit. This makes such plans attractive to employers (especially large employers) that wish to provide employees with predictable retirement benefits.

Q 17:40 Does a plan sponsor of a defined benefit pension plan have to be concerned about overfunding?

Yes. Small business owners in particular have to be concerned about overfunded defined benefit plans. If the excess funds are taken out, they could be subject to a 50 percent excise tax as well as state and federal income taxes. In a state that imposes a high income tax rate, virtually all of the distribution may need to be used for taxes.

Q 17:41 What actions should a plan sponsor take if a defined benefit pension plan is overfunded?

If a defined benefit pension plan is overfunded, a plan sponsor may take the following actions:

1. Terminate the plan and roll the excess funds over to an IRA. This works best if the amount of overfunding is relatively small. The money can still accumulate in the IRA on a tax-deferred basis. This option forces the payment of penalty and tax on the excess; however, if this action is taken while the overfunded amount is still relatively small, the penalty and tax are not significant.

2. Amend the plan so that increases in employee benefits will absorb the excess funding. For example, joint and survivor provisions and cost of living provisions can be added.

3. Share the excess with employees. If 20 percent of the excess is shared with employees, the penalty is reduced from 50 percent to 20 percent on the portion of the excess that is not shared. If the entire excess is shared with employees, the penalty disappears.

4. Transfer at least 25 percent of the excess to a qualified replacement plan. This will reduce the penalty from 50 percent to 20 percent.

5. Sell the business to another business that has an underfunded plan. The plans can then be merged without penalty. The acquiring business has an incentive to buy the business because it can use the overfunded plan of the acquired business to reduce its own liability on its existing plan. If the purchasing entity is a not-for-profit corporation, the sale becomes even more attractive because such an entity does not receive a deduction for contributions to tax-qualified plans. An aggressive owner might reduce his or her corporation to a shell corporation that has few assets other than the pension plan before making the sale. This action could, however, be challenged by the IRS.

Q 17:42 What are the advantages of a defined benefit plan with regard to service?

Unlike other types of plans, a defined benefit plan permits a company to consider previous years of service, which allows people to catch up for years in which they made no contributions.

Example 17-12: An entrepreneur creates a company when he graduates from high school and works there for 30 years. During that time the company grows from two employees to six. If the entrepreneur creates a defined benefit pension plan, he can base his pension benefit on his 30 years of service. The employee who has the most seniority with the company after the founder has five years of service. The plan provides that each participant gets an annual pension of 1 percent of his or her final pay for each year of service to the company. Because of the method used to credit service, the entrepreneur is entitled to an annual pension equal to 30 percent of his pay, while the nearest employee is entitled to a pension equal to 5 percent of his or her pay. The entrepreneur can use this rule to direct most of the pension benefits to himself.

Q 17:43 What is the wear away method of calculating benefits?

The so-called wear away method of calculating benefits for defined benefit pension plans is the result of the reduction of the amount of compensation that can be counted for benefit accrual purposes to $150,000, a benefit limitation set by the Code provisions. Employers are generally given a choice whether to compute accrued benefits using the wear away method. This choice affects how rapidly pension benefits will accrue in future years. If the wear away method is used, the entire accrued benefit is based on the new lower compensation limit. No new benefits are accrued until accrued benefits under the new compensation limit exceed existing benefits under the old limit.

Example 17-13: A pension plan provides a benefit equal to 1 percent of compensation multiplied by years of service. Under the old compensation limit ($235,340), an executive accrues a benefit of $50,000 a year. If the new $150,000 compensation limit is applied to all of the executive's years of service, the executive accrues a benefit of $43,000 per year. The wear away method is applied. Under this method, the executive retains his accrued benefit of $50,000 a year but does not accrue any new benefits until five years elapse, and his benefit under the $150,000 limit for all of his years of service is $50,500. At that time, his accrued benefit of $50,000 increases $500 to $50,500.

Q 17:44 How are benefits calculated without the wear away method?

If benefits are calculated without the wear away method, a participant's accrued benefit equals the current benefit based on the old compensation limit plus future accruals using the new compensation limit.

Example 17-14: Assume the same facts as in Example 17-13, except that benefits are calculated without using the wear away method. The executive's accrued benefit increase using the $150,000 limit is $1,500. Accordingly, after one year, the executive's accrued benefit increases from $50,000 to $51,500.

The effect of calculating benefits without the wear away method is that accrued benefits continue to increase; under the wear away method, accrued benefits may not increase at all for a substantial length of time.

Q 17:45 What is annuity value?

Annuity value is the present value of a dollar of benefits paid over an assumed life.

Example 17-15: Under certain PBGC tables, the annuity value of a $1 monthly benefit payable at age 65 is $120.43, which means that a lifetime annuity starting at age 65 and paying a benefit of $1 per month can be purchased for $120.43.

Actuarial Factors

Q 17:46 What is the importance of actuarial assumptions to defined benefit pension plan participants?

Actuarial assumptions are used to determine the basis on which defined benefit pension plans are funded. Some of these assumptions concern the mortality rates of plan participants and the expected investment return for the plan. If the assumptions are accurate, the plan will be appropriately funded in the sense that the amount of funds available to pay benefits will closely match the amount of benefits owed. If they are inaccurate, the plan may become overfunded or underfunded, and the plan sponsor will have to take corrective measures. The actuarial assumptions used help to determine the amounts that plan participants will receive in plan distributions; using a high expected investment return or interest rate can significantly affect the value of a participant's benefit.

Example 17-16: A bank president, age 55, is entitled to a benefit of $4,000 per month beginning at age 65. By applying an interest rate of 8.5 percent instead of an interest rate of 5 percent, the single sum value of the president's benefit at age 65 drops from $600,000 to $400,000.

Q 17:47 What are the common mortality tables used to administer defined benefit pension plans?

The Society of Actuaries publishes a number of common mortality tables for use in administering defined benefit pension plans. Tables often used include the following:

1971 Group Annuity Mortality (GAM). This table is based on the life expectancies of persons covered by group annuities.

1971 Individual Annuity Mortality (IAM). This table is based on the life expectancies of people who buy individual annuities. This table gives higher present values than a group mortality table because the life expectancies used in this table are greater. This means that benefits calculated under this table will be larger than those derived from a group annuity table.

1983 Group Annuity Mortality. This table gives a higher present value than the 1971 table because the life expectancies it uses are greater than those in the 1971 table. Benefits calculated under the 1983 table will be larger than those derived from the 1971 table.

1983 Individual Annuity Mortality. This table gives a higher present value than the 1971 table because the life expectancies it uses are greater than those in the 1971 table. Benefits calculated under the 1983 table will be larger than those derived from the 1971 table.

There is a table that provides data for males and a table that provides data for females. The table containing data on females gives the largest benefits.

The following table, based on blended male and female mortality rates, is often used:

Unisex Pension 1984 (UP). This table blends male and female mortality rates and is the basic table the PBCG uses. A single payout of benefits calculated under this table benefits males: although men and women of the same age receive the same single sum amount, a man is, in effect, buying a bigger annuity for the money because male life expectancies are shorter than those of females.

Example 17-17: A male executive and a female executive, both age 65, receive $125,000 payouts of their accrued benefits under a pension plan. With this sum, the male executive can purchase a lifetime annuity paying $10,000 a year; with the same amount, the female executive can purchase an annuity paying only $9,000 a year.

Actuaries use these tables to obtain actuarial assumptions for plan administration. If the actuary's goal is to obtain the greatest single-sum value at normal retirement age, he or she should use the female

1983 IAM. This table gives the largest single-sum values because it has the longest projected life spans for the following reasons: (1) its database comprises individuals who buy annuities (purchasers of annuities are credited with longer expected life spans than participants in group annuity contracts); (2) it lists women (women's life spans tend to exceed those of men); and (3) in general, life spans have increased over time.

Q 17:48 Can a table containing data exclusively on males be used to approximate a unisex table?

Yes. Actuaries sometimes use a set-back with a table containing data on males to give a closer approximation of a unisex table.

Example 17:18: An actuary using the 1983 Individual Annuity Table for males wishes to more closely approximate a unisex table. He therefore uses the 1983 Individual Annuity Table for males with a three-year set-back. This means that participants aged 65 are assigned life expectancies under the table for persons who are 62. This results in the use of longer life expectancies for plan participants and is a way of allowing for the fact that females, on average, outlive males.

Q 17:49 Does the choice of mortality tables affect the amount of money that must be paid into a defined benefit pension plan to fund it?

Yes. The choice of mortality tables can significantly affect the amount that must be set aside to purchase annuities; this amount in turn affects the amount that must be paid into the plan.

Example 17-19: The actuary for a defined benefit pension plan decides to use the 1983 IAM female table. According to this table, the cost of purchasing a $1 monthly annuity for a participant age 65 is $153.65. In contrast, if the actuary uses a Unisex Pension 1984 table, the cost of purchasing a $1 monthly annuity for a participant age 65 is $120.43. The cost of funding the plan under the second set of actuarial assumptions is signficantly lower than funding it under the first set of assumptions.

Q 17:50 Can a tax-qualified plan use an actuarial table containing data on males to compute benefits for males and an actuarial table containing data on females to compute benefits for females?

No. The U.S. Supreme Court has held that a unisex table must be used to compute benefits or that either a male table or a female table must be used for both sexes. [Florida v Long, 487 US 223 (1988)]

Thus, a plan sponsor could use a table containing data on males for both sexes or a table containing data on females for both sexes, instead of using a combined table. In any case, the same table must be used for both male and female participants in a plan.

Q 17:51 What actuarial assumptions are used to determine the amounts of plan distributions?

Plan distributions are determined by comparing the distribution amount that would be payable under two different interest rates: those developed by the PBGC and those contained in the plan's actuarial assumptions. The greater of the two amounts is paid to the participant. Thus, the PBGC's rates provide a floor for the amount of benefits payable. The amount payable using PBGC rates is paid if that amount is greater than the amount determined using plan rates; however, if the plan rates yield a larger amount, that is the amount paid.

Q 17:52 How are defined benefit pension plans funded?

The plan actuary determines the projected value of benefits. That value is discounted by an appropriate interest rate to determine the present value of those benefits. The plan actuary then determines the amount that must be paid yearly to fund those benefits over the time that remains until the individual's retirement.

Example 17-20: A physician, age 55, establishes a defined benefit pension plan for himself and two of his nurses. The projected value of benefits provided by the plan when the physician reaches age 65 is $865,000. The actuary determines the appropriate actuarial assumptions to use and calculates that the present value of the projected benefits is $440,000. This is the sum that the company would have to pay at the time the plan is established if it wishes to fully fund the expected benefits. The actuary then determines that the company must contribute $62,600 a year for the next ten years to fund the projected benefit.

Q 17:53 How are the funding calculations made for defined benefit pension plans that own life insurance?

Under traditional funding methods, as opposed to envelope funding (see Q 17:54), the insurance is treated as a separate investment that is used to fund a separate portion of the projected retirement benefits. In practical terms, this means that the current cash value of the insurance policy is disregarded in determining funding requirements for the portion of the projected benefits that is not covered by insurance.

Example 17-21: Apply the same facts as in Example 17-20, except that insurance is purchased and the traditional method of funding is used. Insurance with a projected cash surrender value in ten years of $125,000 is purchased by the plan for $40,000. The current cash surrender value of the policy is $8,000. Because $125,000 of the projected value of benefits is funded by insurance, the projected value of benefits that must be funded by plan assets other than insurance is $740,000. The plan actuary concludes that the present value of this $740,000 benefit is $376,000. The actuary also concludes that over the next ten years, $53,000 must be contributed to the plan annually to achieve the funding objective. Thus, the employer initially contributes $40,000 to the plan to pay for insurance and $53,000 to the plan to fund that portion of the benefit not funded by insurance. It is expected that these contributions will continue over the next ten years, resulting in an insurance policy with a cash surrender value of $125,000 and a so-called side fund with a value of $740,000.

Q 17:54 How are the funding calculations made if the envelope funding method is used?

In envelope funding, the insurance policy is aggregated with other plan assets to determine the amount that must be contributed to meet the funding requirements of the plan. The current cash surrender value of the policy is treated as a plan asset for purposes of funding.

Example 17-22: Apply the same facts as in Example 17-20, except that envelope funding is used. For funding purposes, a projected benefit of $865,000 is used. The plan actuary determines that the present value of this $865,000 projected plan benefit is $440,000. The plan actuary further concludes that the employer must contribute $62,600 per year to the plan over a ten-year period to fund the projected benefit. Of this $62,600 initial contribution, $40,000 is used to purchase insurance, while the remaining $22,600 is used to purchase other plan assets.

Q 17:55 What is the effect of using envelope funding instead of traditional funding methods?

Once an adjustment is made for earnings on contributions, the actual amount of funding under envelope funding and traditional funding is the same over time. In later years, the funding obligation under traditional funding will be less than that of envelope funding because the initial contribution is greater and no portion of the initial contribution is diverted to pay for insurance premiums. In Examples 17-20 and 17-21, under the traditional method plan funding remains constant at $93,000 per year ($40,000 for insurance each year and $53,000 for funding the remainder of the benefit). By contrast, a plan that implements envelope funding will experience a lower initial contribution with an increasing funding amount needed for each subsequent year.

Example 17-23: Same facts as in Example 17-22 concerning envelope funding, in which the amount of assets to be placed in the plan in the first year was $62,600. After the first year, however, the value of assets in the plan is not $62,600, but $30,600. This is because the current cash surrender value of the life insurance policy is $8,000. Consequently, in the next year, a larger amount of funds must be placed in the plan to make up this $32,000 deficit. Thus, under envelope funding, in the second year of plan operations the actuary determines that the yearly contribution should be increased to $75,000. These increases will continue until eventually they will exceed the total yearly contribution obligation under the traditional approach. Because the initial contributions under the envelope funding approach are less than those of a traditionally funded plan, the total contributions under both methods will equal out once an adjustment is made for the ability of earlier plan contributions to earn an investment return.

Q 17:56 What are the individual aggregate method and group methods of funding?

Under the individual aggregate method, plan funding is determined by ascertaining the funding needed for each individual participant. These funding requirements are then aggregated to arrive at the total amount of plan funding required. In contrast, under the group method, the funding requirements are determined for the group by taking into account such group characteristics as average age of the group members. In comparison to the individual aggregate method of funding, the group method of funding method tends to result in level contributions because group characteristics tend to change less rapidly than individual characteristics. For example, the average age of a group might remain constant, but every individual ages. If the individual aggregate method is used, contributions tend to increase over time because as participants age and accrue additional years of service, they require greater contributions. Thus, the individual aggregate method of funding can require lower levels of initial funding; however, the funding obligation will tend to increase over time.

The need to increase contributions over time associated with the individual aggregate method is not necessarily a negative factor. The real issue is when a taxpayer prefers to incur the bulk of the funding obligation. Higher income tax deductions are associated with a greater funding obligation. Those deductions may be more advantageous in later years than in earlier years, if, for example, the corporation becomes more profitable over time.

Q 17:57 What is the relation of the normal retirement benefit to plan funding?

The normal retirement benefit is the benefit that a defined benefit pension plan attempts to fund. It is based on the assumption that a participant will reach normal retirement age (typically age 65). The normal retirement benefit for small pension plans is commonly based on a single life annuity because the sole owner is often at the Section 415 limits, which cap the maximum amounts of benefits and are based on a single-life annuity. Accordingly, if a plan funds for a joint and survivor annuity benefit, which is more expensive, the plan risks overfunding because more funds are put into the plan than can be taken out by the owner in a single payment as a result of Section 415 limits.

Example 17-24: A physician, age 55, funds his defined benefit pension plan for a joint and survivor annuity of $120,000 for himself and a $60,000 annual annuity benefit for his wife if she survives him. The physician retires at age 65. The single-sum value of his benefit is $1.5 million if it is not paid to him in a single payment but is instead paid to him and his wife in a series of payments over their lives. Because of the effect of Section 415 limits, however, the physician is entitled to only $1.2 million if he takes his benefits out in a single payment. If the plan is funded for the joint and survivor annuity, the excess $300,000 that was used to fund the physician's benefit remains in the plan if the physician is paid in a single payment.

Q 17:58 How are the sums paid by defined benefit pension plans prior to normal retirement age determined?

To compute a benefit prior to normal retirement age, first compute the value of the benefit at normal retirement age. This is done on a payment-by-payment basis. Each payment is discounted for interest and for mortality, as follows: At normal retirement age each person has a life expectancy. For example, a male age 65 has a life expectancy of 17 years. Pension plans, by their nature, make payments over a person's lifetime. To determine the single-sum value, each of those payments is discounted for interest and for mortality. The interest rate used to make these calculations is known as the postretirement interest rate.

Example 17-25: A plan promises to pay an executive, now age 55, $100,000 per year for his life starting when he attains age 65. At age 65, his life expectancy is 17 years. To determine the single-sum value of his pension when the executive attains age 65, each

$100,000 payment is discounted by appropriate actuarial factors. The value of the payments for the executive when the executive turns age 65 is $1 million.

Next, the single-sum value of the benefit at normal retirement age must be discounted by the preretirement interest rate. The plan document for small employers often provides for a 5 percent interest rate for computing preretirement benefits. This maximizes the amount that a business owner can take as a single-sum distribution. Typically, there is no discount for mortality (i.e., the risk that someone might die).

Example 17-26: Same facts as in Example 17-25. Using a 5 percent discount rate, the plan actuary determines that the executive is entitled to $500,000 at age 55.

If the plan were to provide for a higher rate, such as 8 percent, the PBGC rates might come into play to force the plan to make a distribution of a minimum size. The effect of applying PBGC rates is to prevent the plan sponsor from excessively reducing the single-sum payout amount by using high interest rates.

The rates used by the PBGC are graduated rates. For example, the PBGC graduated interest rate for a 40-year-old man is 6.75 percent for the first seven years, 5.5 percent for the next eight years, and 4 percent for the next ten years. If the single sum is over $25,000, the single-sum amount can be computed using rates that are equal to 120 percent of the PBGC rates. Use of these rates results in a smaller distribution. In determining whether the single-sum amount exceeds $25,000, the PBGC rates are used.

Recent legislation in the form of the General Agreement on Tariffs and Trade (GATT) will change this result. GATT is likely to result in the use of higher interest rates derived from returns on long-term Treasury notes. These higher rates, coupled with the use of an actuarial table required by the federal government, will normally result in the use of higher interest rates and in lower minimum single-sum payments.

Q 17:59 What postretirement interest rate should be used?

In small plan design, the typical postretirement interest rate is 5 percent. This is the lowest rate permitted by the IRS in determining single-sum payments. The use of the 5 percent postretirement interest rate (as opposed to a higher rate of interest) increases the present value of the single-sum payment. Use of a higher rate reduces the amount of the payment. The 5 percent interest rate is often advantageous to a small business owner because he or she typically receives the largest payout and thus benefits the most from the use of the 5 percent rate.

If the 5 percent interest rate is used, the owner of a small business often has an incentive to take a single-sum distribution at retirement if he or she can obtain a return greater than 5 percent elsewhere. If this can be done, the owner can increase his or her overall wealth by taking a distribution and investing the amount distributed in other investments that have an investment return that is greater than 5 percent. It may be possible, for example, for the owner to roll over the amount distributed to an IRA so that taxation on the new investments is deferred. Alternatively, the owner can take the single-sum amount and use it to purchase an annuity. Because the actuarially assumed 5 percent interest rate is relatively low, the owner has a good chance of buying an annuity that has a return of more than 5 percent. This means that the owner can use his or her single-sum payment to obtain an annuity that is greater than the projected benefit under the plan or that the owner can obtain an equivalent annuity using only a portion of his or her single-sum payout.

Example 17-27: An entrepreneur reaches age 65 and decides to retire. He can receive yearly payments from his firm's pension plan of $100,000 per year. Using a 5 percent discount rate, the plan's actuary calculates that the entrepreneur is entitled to a single-sum distribution of $1 million. The entrepreneur believes that he can earn at least 15 percent per year by investing in an IRA that holds mutual funds, and he calculates that if he invests the $1 million in the IRA, over an eight-year period, the $1 million will grow to $3 million. Even if income tax on the $3 million is factored in, he will still have about $1.8 million left. In contrast, if the entrepreneur takes the $100,000 yearly distribution, he calculates that he will have $61,000 after taxes and that if he invests this amount at 15 percent he will have about $740,000 after eight years. The entrepreneur decides to cash out his retirement benefit from the plan and place it in an IRA.

GATT is expected to have a significant effect on this kind of activity because it will place limitations on the lowest interest rate that can be used. These limitations will be based on long-term interest rates. If those rates are relatively low, maximum single sums can be relatively large. If they are high, the maximum single sum rate will reduced.

Q 17:60 Are there limits on the interest rates that can be used for single-sum payments?

There are upper limits on interest rates that can be used in determining the minimum single sum payable. These limits exist to prevent plan sponsors from unduly reducing retirement benefits by using high rates. For distributions of $25,000 or less, the interest rate cannot exceed the PBGC rate; for distributions of more than $25,000, the interest rate cannot exceed 120 percent of the PBGC rate. These limitations apply to postretirement distributions as well as preretirement distributions. PBGC interest rates are used in determining the $25,000 threshold. If the 120 percent rate is used, the distribution cannot be less than $25,000 even if use of that rate would imply a distribution of less than $25,000.

Example 17-28: The PBGC rate is 6.0 percent. If that rate is used, the distribution amount is $25,500. If 7.2 percent is used (120 percent of the PBGC rate), however, the distribution amount drops to $21,165. The required benefit payment is $25,000.

Example 17-29: A defined benefit pension plan has a postretirement interest rate of 8 percent. Using the appropriate PBGC rate, the plan actuary determines that the participant's benefit is $10,000. The PBGC interest rate that is applicable to the participant is 6.75 percent. If the participant takes a single-sum distribution at retirement, the PBGC rate applies, resulting in a greater distribution. Had the 8 percent rate applied, the participant would have received $9,560. Under the PBGC rate, he receives $10,000.

Example 17-30: A participant who retires after normal retirement age receives an actuarial increase in her monthly benefit from $200 to $210. The PBGC rates are applied in determining the amount that is payable in a single sum. The plan rate is then compared with the PBGC rate to determine the amount distributed. If the

Q 17:61   Estate and Retirement Planning Answer Book

PBGC rate is 9 percent, the participant's $210 monthly payment is discounted by 8 percent.

The interest rates associated with Code Section 415 also limit the amount of the lump-sum distribution.

Q 17:61   What effect do Section 415 limits have on single-sum distributions from defined benefit pension plans?

Code Section 415 limits the amount of single-sum distributions in several ways. Under Code Section 415, the lump-sum distribution is limited by the actuarial equivalent of a $120,000 life annuity. The Section 415 single-sum distribution limit is either the greater of 5 percent or the discount rate specified in the plan. The result of using the higher of these two interest rates is that the distribution amount is minimized for the participants whose benefits are at Section 415 limits. Eventually the interest rate needed to satisfy the Section 415 limit will be based on the interest rate for 30-year Treasury bills.

Example 17-31: A veterinarian, age 65 in 1995, is entitled to a retirement benefit that consists of $120,000 per year for her life (this benefit is at the Section 415 limit for that year). The veterinarian decides to take a single-sum distribution. The plan provides that postretirement distributions are discounted by 3 percent. Applying this discount rate to the veterinarian gives a projected single-sum distribution of $1.4 million. If instead the Section 415 rate of 5 percent is used, the projected single-sum distribution amount is $1.2 million. Because 5 percent exceeds 3 percent, the Section 415 limit applies, and the veterinarian is limited to a single-sum distribution of $1.2 million.

Section 415 limits may also restrict the use of the joint and survivor annuity as the normal form of retirement benefit when determining lump sums. If an employee is at the Section 415 limit, the joint and survivor annuity cannot be used in making the single-sum calculation. This is because Section 415 limits are based on a single life annuity, which is less valuable than a joint and survivor annuity providing the participant the same amount of benefits.

Example 17-32: A physician is entitled to receive his pension plan benefits in the form of an annuity that pays him $120,000 per year.

If his wife survives him, she receives an annuity of $60,000 a year. The single-sum value of this benefit is $1.5 million. If, however, the physician takes a single-sum benefit, he will obtain a lesser amount, $1.2 million. Because Section 415 limits are based on a $120,000 single life annuity, the value of the wife's benefit is disregarded.

Conversely, Section 415 limits permit the use of a joint and survivor annuity as the normal form of retirement benefit in circumstances where a single-sum distribution is not permitted. An employee who has reached the Section 415 limits can receive a joint and survivor annuity that places him at the Section 415 maximum even if a single-sum distribution of that benefit would be precluded.

Example 17-33: Same facts as in Example 17-32, except the physician intends to receive his retirement benefits in the form of a lifetime annuity for him and a 50 percent survivor annuity for his spouse (i.e., his surviving spouse receives a benefit that is 50 percent of the benefit payable when both spouses were alive). The physician can receive a benefit of $120,000 a year that pays his surviving spouse $60,000 a year if he predeceases her.

Q 17:62 What actuarial factors apply if a participant elects one type of annuity instead of another?

If a plan participant elects one type of annuity instead of another, plan actuarial factors are used. These factors must be reasonable.

Example 17-34: A commercial airline pilot is entitled to an annuity that pays him $60,000 year and that pays his wife $30,000 a year if she survives him. He decides to change the benefit to one in which his wife receives a survivor benefit that is one quarter of his retirement benefit. Under the new annuity, which is determined by actuarial factors specified in the plan, the pilot's life benefit increases to $68,000, and his wife's survivor benefit drops to $17,000.

Q 17:63 What interest rates should be used in plan administration?

For funding purposes, the actuary must use his or her best judgment regarding the expected performance of plan investments. For

Q 17:64   Estate and Retirement Planning Answer Book

postretirement benefits, the actuary can use the plan rate because that rate determines the lump sum value (i.e., 5 percent). GATT will eventually affect plan funding by requiring the use of 30-year Treasury bill rates in determining plan funding obligations.

For benefits paid before retirement, the actuary's focus is different; he or she attempts to fund for the normal retirement benefit (i.e., the actuary determines the amount of money at normal retirement age that is needed to pay for the annuity that the plan participant is entitled to at normal retirement age). The actuary looks at the plan's earnings history and estimates future earnings. If the actuary thinks the plan will earn 8 percent or 9 percent, that rate is used to determine the amounts to be contributed to the plan to pay for benefits.

There is a self-correcting aspect to this process. If the actuary estimates that the plan will earn 6 percent and it in fact earns 16 percent, the amount of assets is greater than expected, and the amount of funding required for future years drops. This results in a reduction in the next year's contribution computation.

The existing funding limits create problems for plans by limiting the amount of the deduction an employer can take for contributions to defined benefit plans. The value of plan assets cannot exceed 150 percent of the present value of the accrued benefit. This present value is computed using published IRS rates. A problem arises because the present value of the accrued benefit is based on IRS interest rates, which are typically higher than the interest rates used by plans. As a result, the present value of the accrued benefit is smaller, and 150 percent of the accrued benefit is sometimes less than the plan assets. The amount of benefit payable is based on the interest rate used by the plan, however. This may mean that some employers must make additional contributions to the plan to pay for plan benefits.

Q 17:64   What is the effect of using the unit credit method of funding?

The unit credit method of funding results in an increase in dollar contributions over time—as a plan participant ages, the benefit costs more. The older a participant gets, the fewer years of employment he or she has left in which to fund the benefit.

17-40

Q 17:65 How must service after retirement affect the accrued benefit under a tax-qualified plan?

Before the Tax Reform Act of 1986 (TRA '86), the accrual of benefits could stop at normal retirement age provided the participant was given the actuarial equivalent of his or her normal retirement benefit if he or she continued to work past normal retirement age. TRA '86, however, requires that a participant who works past normal retirement age must be given the greater of the benefit increase for each year or the actuarial equivalent for that year.

Example 17-35: A banker reaches normal retirement age on April 1, 1993. At normal retirement age the banker has an accrued pension benefit of $100,000 per year. The banker terminates service on March 31, 1994. Under the plan's actuarial assumptions, the value of the banker's benefit increases to $106,000 per year. If benefit accruals for the additional year of service are taken into account, the banker's benefit increases to $112,000 per year. The banker receives the greater amount or $112,000. Under prior law, the banker would have received only $106,000 per year.

Q 17:66 What is the significance of the method of accrual used in determining benefits?

In defined benefit plans, the total benefit is determined as of normal retirement date. The method of accrual comes into play in determining benefits if a participant terminates employment before reaching normal retirement age. The method of accrual used can have a significant effect on the amount of benefit payable.

Example 17-36: A defined benefit pension plan provides that a participant's benefit at normal retirement age is 2.9 percent times years of benefit service (up to 15 years) times the average of the participant's high three years of compensation. The participant terminates after 10 years of service, and the average for his highest 3 years of compensation is $150,000. Had the participant remained on the job until he attained normal retirement age, he would have had 30 years of service. At normal retirement age, the participant is entitled to 29 percent times $150,000 or $43,500 per year. If benefits are accrued on a unit basis, the benefit at termination is $43,500 per year. If the fractional method of accruing benefits is used, however, the participant is entitled to only $21,750 (43.5 percent × $150,000 × 10 ÷ 30 = $21,750) (43.5 percent is derived by multiplying 15 by 2.9 percent).

Q 17:67 Should career average compensation be used to determine benefits in a defined benefit plan?

Career average compensation (i.e., compensation averaged over the employee's years of employment with the employer sponsoring the plan) can result in an inadequate pension because salary normally goes up over one's lifetime. Career average compensation is an average of a participant's compensation in that job and therefore may not provide a sufficient benefit to sustain the participant's lifestyle if that participant's compensation increased markedly over his or her career.

Example 17-37: An executive with 30 years service with a company had a beginning salary of $5,000 per year and now has a salary of $150,000 per year. His average salary with the company is $45,000. The company's pension plan provides a yearly benefit for this executive equal to 30 percent of career average compensation or $15,000. Had the plan provided a yearly benefit equal to 30 percent of final pay, the executive would have received a pension equal to $45,000 per year. The higher amount would better enable the executive to maintain his lifestyle.

Keogh Plans

Q 17:68 What are Keogh plans?

Unincorporated entities such as proprietorships and partnerships can establish tax-qualified plans. These plans (which have historically been known as Keogh or HR-10 plans) are similar to those established by corporations with the following two exceptions:

1. Tax-qualified plans can loan money from the plan to the plan participants. Keogh plans cannot make such loans to owner-employees as defined in Code Section 401(c)(3).

2. A self-employed individual under a Keogh plan must take into account all deductions, including the deduction for contribu-

tions by a trade or business to a qualified plan, when he or she calculates the compensation on which his or her Keogh plan benefit is based. An employee benefiting from a corporate tax-qualified plan, however, does not have to deduct the corporation's contributions to the plan in determining his or her compensation for contribution purposes. The result is that the tax-qualified plan employee can receive a larger deductible contribution for the year than the Keogh plan employee receives.

General Considerations

Q 17:69 What type of plan should a new business consider adopting?

A new business should consider adopting a defined contribution plan such as a profit sharing plan, which can be designed so that contributions are discretionary. Accordingly, an employer whose cash position fluctuates markedly from year to year or an employer that is just starting up may be well advised to adopt this type of plan.

Because the adoption of a defined benefit pension plan requires a funding commitment, regardless of the employer's cash position, a new company probably should not establish this type of plan. If, however, an employer is in a strong cash position and has senior, highly compensated, key employees for whom no pension plan was previously established, a defined benefit pension plan may be a good way to quickly accumulate retirement funds for those key employees. On the other hand, if the rank-and-file employees are older, a defined benefit plan may be disadvantageous to the employer: because benefits for older employees must be funded over a shorter period, a cash flow problem could arise for the employer.

Q 17:70 What should be done with a benefit if the plan participant cannot be located and the participant's plan terminates?

If the plan is insured by the PBGC and is terminated under ERISA Section 4041(b), the plan administrator must either transfer the participant's benefit to the PBGC or purchase an irrevocable annuity

Q 17:71   Estate and Retirement Planning Answer Book

from an insurer for the missing participant. [ERISA § 4050] In other cases, the law is much less definite. Apparently the missing participant's benefit cannot be escheated to the state (see Q 25:18). Often it is impractical to maintain a trust for the benefit of missing participants. One solution used by practitioners is to buy postal money orders in the participant's name and hold them.

Q 17:71   What is the plan year?

The plan year is the period over which a plan keeps its accounting records. Typically, the plan year coincides with its sponsoring employer's tax year, although the plan year can begin on or end on any date.

Q 17:72   Can the plan year be changed?

Yes. If the plan year for a tax-qualified plan is changed, however, the plan participants need to be protected for vesting and eligibility purposes by creating overlapping plan years, and special limitations apply during the short plan year. If automatic IRS approval is desired, the plan amendment must be made before the end of the short plan year. Sometimes, IRS Form 5308 must be filed. [Rev Proc 87-27, 1987-1 CB 769]

> **Example 17-38:** An engineering firm wants to change the plan year for its profit sharing plan from a fiscal year ending July 31 to a year ending December 31. To accomplish this change, a short plan year that begins August 1, 1994, and ends December 31, 1994, is created. Because the plan sponsor wants to take advantage of the automatic approval procedures, the plan amendment is made before the ending date for the short plan year, December 31, 1994. Beginning January 1, 1995, the plan is on a calendar year. Reduced Section 415 limits ($30,000 × 5 ÷ 12 or $12,500) apply to the short plan year. Moreover, persons who have certain levels of service must be credited with a year of service for the period that begins August 31, 1994, and ends on July 31, 1995, and for the period that begins on January 1, 1995, and ends on December 31, 1995.

Chapter 18

Employee Stock Ownership Plans

Employee stock ownership plans (ESOPs) provide special opportunities for retirement and estate planning, particularly for small or family-owned businesses. ESOP participants may defer recognition of capital gains on distributions, and special stock redemption provisions permit an estate to generate cash to cover estate taxes and administrative taxes without forcing the sale or liquidation of the business. This chapter describes the tax considerations in adopting and funding an ESOP, how an ESOP works, and the special rights accorded plan participants.

Overview	18-2
Establishing an Employee Stock Ownership Plan: Funding Requirements	18-5
Plan Design Parameters	18-14
Dividends	18-21
Distributions	18-23
Sale of Employer Securities	18-27
Estate Planning Implications	18-33

Overview

Q 18:1   What is an employee stock ownership plan?

An employee stock ownership plan (ESOP) is a defined contribution plan that must have its funds invested primarily in employer securities. The funds, which may come from an exempt loan to the ESOP, are held in trust for, and are used to buy employer securities from stockholders or from the sponsoring company. When a participant retires, dies, or terminates employment, the participant receives his or her benefits in the form of cash or employer securities. A participant generally can demand that he or she receive a distribution of employer securities, unless the employer's corporate charter or bylaws limits the ownership of substantially all employer securities to employees or trusts for tax-qualified plans or imposes a right of first refusal. [IRC §§ 409(h)(1), 409(h)(2); Treas Reg § 54.4975-7(b)(9)]

A key distinguishing feature of an ESOP is that participants who receive benefits in the form of employer securities must be given the right to sell (put) the employer securities to the employer for their fair market value within a specified time period after receipt of the distribution if the securities are not readily tradable on an established market. Either the ESOP or the employer may be given the right of first refusal if the participant attempts to sell the securities.

Q 18:2   Why would an employer want to establish an employee stock ownership plan?

Use of an ESOP allows employees to become owners of the business, which in turn may increase productivity and reduce labor costs and disruptions. ESOPs can also provide a source of deferred compensation, retirement income, and capital accumulation to employees. An ESOP can purchase newly issued shares of corporate stock, allowing for tax-deductible capitalization of the company without immediate taxation to the employees. Furthermore, ESOPs provide a friendly way of holding large blocks of corporate stock and have been used as anti-takeover tools (see Q 18:8). Many corporations also use ESOPs as a corporate financial tool (see Q 18:18).

Q 18:3 Why would an employer not want to establish an employee stock ownership plan?

ESOPs are subject to ERISA rules on fiduciaries, which can cause a privately held company to be subject to the type of scrutiny generally reserved for publicly held companies. Similarly, any transactions that arise between the corporation and its controlling officers and shareholders must meet certain defined standards of reasonableness and care. Existing shareholders may resist the establishment of an ESOP because the ESOP's acquisition of newly issued corporate stock could dilute the shares and the ownership rights of the existing stockholders.

Q 18:4 How is an employee stock ownership plan different from a stock bonus plan?

A stock bonus plan permits, but does not require, current investments of plan funds in employer securities. In contrast, an ESOP must invest primarily in employer securities. This *primarily* rule has been interpreted to mean that the ESOP must invest at least 50 percent of the plan assets in qualifying employer securities over the life of the plan. [DOL Ad Op 83-6A, Jan 24, 1983] A plan will not lose its ESOP status if it temporarily drops below this 50 percent rule.

Q 18:5 What are the basic types of employee stock ownership plans?

The two basic kinds of ESOPs are leveraged ESOPs and nonleveraged ESOPs. The key distinction between the two types is the source of plan funds.

Q 18:6 What is a nonleveraged employee stock ownership plan?

In a nonleveraged ESOP, the employer contributes cash or stock directly to the plan's trust. The contributions are tax deductible up to 15 percent of payroll. If cash is contributed, the trust can buy shares of the employer's stock from existing shareholders. Plan participants are not taxed on contributions made on their behalf until distribution. [IRC §§ 72, 402, 404]

Q 18:7 What is a leveraged employee stock ownership plan?

In a leveraged ESOP, the ESOP borrows funds from a bank or other qualified lending institution and uses those funds to buy stock from existing shareholders. The employer then makes tax-deductible contributions to the ESOP trust, and the ESOP uses the employer contributions to repay the loan. [IRC § 4975(e)(7)] A leveraged ESOP must be either a tax-qualified stock bonus plan or a combination stock bonus and purchase money pension plan. A leveraged ESOP is subject to more qualification requirements than a nonleveraged ESOP. [IRC §§ 409(h), 409(o), 409(l)]

Q 18:8 Can employee stock ownership plans be used by publicly traded companies to defend against unwanted takeovers?

Yes. By establishing an ESOP that purchases stock on the open market, management hopes to place a block of stock in the presumably friendly hands of its employees. To the extent that publicly traded stock (i.e., a registration-type class of securities) is allocated to the individual accounts of participants, however, each participant must be given the opportunity to direct the ESOP with regard to the voting of the allocated shares. Stock that has been purchased by the plan but that has not been credited to the individual accounts of plan participants yet (unallocated stock) is voted by the trustees or other fiduciaries, who must vote the unallocated stock proportionately to the way participants vote their allocated stock. [IRC § 409(e)(5)(b)]

Q 18:9 Can an S corporation establish an employee stock ownership plan?

Trusts can hold S corporation stock only under limited circumstances. [IRC § 1361(c)(2)] Because an ESOP trust must generally hold employer stock, an S corporation could lose its S corporation status if it establishes an ESOP. Under a bill pending in Congress, an ESOP will be entitled to own stock of an S corporation.

Establishing an Employee Stock Ownership Plan: Funding Requirements

Q 18:10 What are employer securities?

The assets of an ESOP must be invested primarily in employer securities (see Q 18:4). Employer securities include common stock issued by the employer that is readily tradable on an established securities market. If the employer has no readily tradable common stock, employer securities include employer-issued common stock that has a combination of voting power and dividend rights at least equal to the class of common stock with the greatest voting power and the class of common stock with the greatest dividend rights. Noncallable preferred stock that is convertible into common stock that meets the requirements of employer securities also qualifies if the conversion price is reasonable. Employer securities also include stock issued by a member of a controlled group that includes the employer if the stock meets the same requirements as qualifying employer-issued stock. [IRC § 409(1); Ltr Rul 8610082]

ESOP assets will be considered invested in employer securities in a variety of circumstances. If an ESOP receives cash or other assets for employer securities as part of a reorganization, the assets will satisfy the requirement if they are invested in employer securities within 90 days (or an extended period if granted by the Internal Revenue Service (IRS)) of the acquisition of cash or other assets. Cash received by an ESOP as the result of an exempt loan, earnings, dividends, or other cash contributions will satisfy the requirements if invested in employer securities within 60 days of the contribution. Cash or cash equivalents allocated to a participant's account will be deemed to be invested in employer securities if the value of those benefits does not exceed 2 percent of the value of the allocated securities. Also, amounts transferred to an ESOP following a reversion from a terminated defined benefit plan will meet the investment requirements if the amounts are invested in employer securities within 90 days of the transfer. [IR Notice 88-56, 1988-1 CD 540, Q 18; IRC § 4989(c)(3)]

Q 18:11 How much may an employer contribute to an employee stock ownership plan each year on a tax-deductible basis?

Generally, the limitation on deductions for employer contributions to an ESOP is 15 percent of aggregate compensation of the plan beneficiaries. [IRC § 404(a)(3)(A)] Money purchase pension ESOPs have a 25 percent limitation. In all cases, the overall limitation on deductible contributions to all defined contribution plans in combination is 25 percent of covered compensation. [IRC § 404(a)(7)] The employer may deduct up to 25 percent of covered compensation for contributions to a leveraged ESOP (an ESOP that borrows to acquire employer securities) used to repay loan principal and an unlimited amount for contributions used to pay interest on the loan. [IRC § 404(a)(9)]

Q 18:12 Can a company obtain a tax deduction for stock contributions to its employee stock ownership plan?

Yes. One of the basic advantages of using an ESOP is the ability to use either cash or employer securities for the company's contributions. A company that is short of cash can make its contributions in authorized but unissued securities (treasury stock) and still get a tax deduction for the full amount of the contribution. The amount of the contribution will be the fair market value of the employer securities even though there is no cost to the company (because it used treasury stock rather than buying back its issued stock in order to contribute it to the ESOP). The contribution in the form of employer securities not only keeps cash in the corporation but also provides additional cash flow from the tax savings realized by the deduction.

Example 18-1: Company XYZ has an annual payroll of $500,000. It contributes $75,000 (15 percent of $500,000) to its ESOP in the form of employer securities. XYZ is allowed a tax deduction of $75,000.

Q 18:13 What tax incentives are provided to encourage commercial lenders to make loans to employee stock ownership plans or to employers sponsoring employee stock ownership plans?

If a bank, insurance company, corporation actively engaged in the business of lending money, or regulated investment company under

Employee Stock Ownership Plans Q 18:13

Section 851 of the Internal Revenue Code (Code) makes a securities acquisition loan (see Q 18:14), 50 percent of the interest received by the lender in connection with the loan is excluded from income tax. The lender may make the loan directly to the ESOP or to the employer (which in turn lends the money to the ESOP). Interest on loans between related persons or entities does not qualify for the exclusion from income tax. [IRC §§ 133(a), 133(b)]

Entities eligible for the 50 percent interest exclusion are often referred to as qualified lenders. [IRC § 133(a)] A corporation is actively engaged in the business of lending money if it meets all of the following conditions:

1. It is not an S corporation;
2. It lends money to the public on a regular and continuing basis (other than in connection with the purchase by the public of goods and services from the lender or a related party); and
3. A predominant share of such loans is not made up of securities acquisition loans. [Temp Treas Reg § 1.133-1T, Q&A 2; Ltr Rul 9119065]

A holder of a securities acquisition loan may sell or transfer the loan to another lending institution. A subsequent holder of the debt instrument may qualify for the 50 percent interest exclusion if the holder is a qualified lender. Further, a qualified lender will be eligible for the 50 percent interest exclusion even if the previous holder of the debt instrument was not a qualified lender. [IRC § 133; Rev Rul 89-76, 1989-1 CB 24] The 50 percent interest exclusion does not apply to interest income received while the ESOP's stock ownership percentage is 50 percent or less. The 50 percent ESOP stock ownership requirement is reduced to 30 percent for loans made after July 10, 1989, but before November 18, 1989.

The interest exclusion is allowable for the excludable period that begins on the date of the original securities acquisition loan. The excludable period generally is seven years or the term of the original securities acquisition loan, if longer. For immediate allocation loans and back-to-back loans with more rapid repayment provisions for the ESOP than for the employer, however, the excludable period is only seven years. The refinancing of an original securities acquisition loan

Q 18:14   Estate and Retirement Planning Answer Book

does not extend the excludable period for the original securities acquisition loan. [IRC § 133(e)]

Q 18:14   What is a securities acquisition loan?

A loan to an ESOP or to the sponsoring employer will be a securities acquisition loan eligible for the 50 percent interest exemption if either of the following occur:

1. The proceeds are used to acquire employer securities for the ESOP or are used to refinance an exempt loan that was used to acquire employer securities; or
2. Employer securities are transferred to the ESOP within 30 days in an amount equal to the proceeds of the loan, and such securities are allocable to accounts of participants within one year of the date of the loan.

Additionally, a loan will not be considered to be a qualifying securities acquisition loan (and thus eligible for the interest exemption) unless the following requirements are met:

1. For loans made after November 18, 1989, the ESOP owns more than 50 percent of the issuing corporation's stock immediately after the ESOP receives the employer securities acquired with the loan proceeds (certain nonvoting, nonconvertible preferred stock is disregarded, and the IRS may provide that warrants, options, and convertible debt interest may be counted as stock for the purposes of this 50 percent rule);
2. The term of a securities acquisition loan made after July 10, 1989, does not exceed 15 years; and
3. The ESOP permits participants to vote stock allocated to their accounts that was acquired with a post-July 10, 1989, securities acquisition loan on a one share, one vote basis on all issues put to a shareholder vote.

A loan made to an employer sponsoring an ESOP may also qualify as a securities acquisition loan if the employer in turn uses the loan proceeds to make an exempt loan (see Q 18:16) to the ESOP on substantially similar repayment terms or on more rapid repayment terms than the loan to the employer if allocations of employer securities within the ESOP attributable to the difference in payment schedules do not result in discrimination in favor of highly compensated employees and the total commitment period for the ESOP does not exceed seven years.

For amounts realized on dispositions of employer securities acquired with a securities acquisition loan made after July 10, 1989, in a transaction to which Code Section 133 applied (see Q 18:13), a nondeductible 10 percent excise tax will be imposed on the employer if any of the following events occur:

1. Within three years after acquisition, the total amount of employer securities held by the ESOP decreases;
2. Within three years after acquisition, the value of the ESOP's employer securities drops below 50 percent of the value of all employer securities; or
3. The ESOP disposes of employer securities not allocated to participants and does not allocate the proceeds to participants.

Certain distributions to participants, including distributions pursuant to a diversification election, exchanges in corporate reorganizations, and dispositions required by state law, are not treated as dispositions for purposes of the 10 percent excise tax. [IRC §§ 133, 4978B; Treas Reg §§ 54.4975-7, 54.4975-11]

Q 18:15   What is a mirror loan?

A mirror loan occurs when a bank or other lending institution makes a loan to a company that then makes a loan to the ESOP. Both loans have the same terms.

Q 18:16   Do employer loans or guarantees of loans to employee stock ownership plans violate the Code's prohibited transaction provisions?

Employer loans or guarantees of loans to tax-qualified plans are generally prohibited transactions subject to an excise tax under Code Section 4975. An employer's loan or guarantee of a loan to an ESOP is not a prohibited transaction, however, if the loan satisfies the requirements for an exempt loan status. Those requirements include the following:

Q 18:17   Estate and Retirement Planning Answer Book

1. The loan must be primarily for the benefit of participants and beneficiaries of the ESOP;
2. The loan proceeds must be used to acquire qualifying employer securities or to repay an exempt loan;
3. The interest rate for the loan must be reasonable;
4. The loan must be without recourse against the ESOP (i.e., the ESOP is not the entity that is liable if the loan is in default) and without collateral other than qualifying employer securities acquired (or refinanced) with the proceeds of the exempt loan; and
5. The loan must provide for the release of employer securities used as collateral as the loan is repaid. [IRC § 4975 (d)(3); Treas Reg § 54.4975-7(b)]

Q 18:17   Is a loan from a shareholder to an employee stock ownership plan a prohibited transaction under ERISA?

Not necessarily. Although ERISA generally prohibits loans (or loan guarantees) between a qualified retirement plan and a disqualified person (e.g., a 10 percent or more shareholder), a loan (or a loan guarantee) by a disqualified person to an ESOP is not a prohibited transaction if the loan qualifies as an exempt loan under Code Section 4975 (see Q 18:16). [ERISA § 408(b)(3); IRC § 4975(d)(3)]

Q 18:18   How can an employee stock ownership plan be used to finance a business?

Typically, a company that decides to raise $1 million in working capital for expansion purposes would borrow the funds from a bank or other lender and repay the loan with after-tax dollars. Under this conventional method of financing, the interest component of each debt payment is a deductible expense to the company, but the principal repayment is not deductible by the company (i.e., it is paid on an after-tax basis).

By using an ESOP, it is possible to arrange the financing so that both the interest and principal repayments are tax deductible. This is accomplished either by having the ESOP rather than the company borrow the $1 million or by having the corporation take out the loan and reloan the proceeds to the ESOP. The ESOP then would use the loan proceeds to purchase $1 million worth of newly issued stock from the company. The company would have the $1 million needed for working capital for expansion purposes, and the ESOP would own $1 million worth of company stock. Thereafter, the company may make an annual tax-deductible contribution to the plan consisting of an amount of up to 25 percent of covered payroll for the purpose of repaying the loan principal, plus an unlimited amount used to pay interest on the loan. [IRC § 404(a)(9)]

The lending institution often will demand both a pledge agreement (pledging the shares of stock as collateral or security for the loan) and a guarantee agreement from the company under which the company agrees to make annual contributions to the ESOP sufficient to allow the ESOP to repay the loan and, if the company fails to make such contributions, to repay the loan directly.

Q 18:19 What actions can be taken to prevent a depletion of employee stock ownership plan assets as a result of market conditions?

A problem sometimes faced by ESOPs is the risk that employees will withdraw their funds if they believe that the ESOP stock is overpriced. This could occur, for example, if the company experienced sudden financial difficulties that were not yet reflected in the ESOP valuation. One solution to this is to delay the payout period for preretirement terminations other than death or disability.

> **Example 18-2:** An employer whose stock is volatile is concerned that employees will resign and seek employment elsewhere when the stock is doing well. To reduce this risk, the employer amends the ESOP to provide a five-year waiting period before payouts begin and to provide that once payouts do begin, they are paid out over a five-year period. The ESOP stock is valued as of the date payouts begin, not the date of termination.

Q 18:20 How can an employee stock ownership plan be used to facilitate a buyout of shareholders in a closely held corporation?

An ESOP can be used to repurchase all or a portion of the stock of minority shareholders, inactive shareholders, and outside sharehold-

Q 18:21   Estate and Retirement Planning Answer Book

ers. The primary advantage of these transactions is that the corporation repurchases the shares with deductible contributions to the ESOP. Minority shareholders should generally consider it irrelevant whether their stock is purchased by the company or by the ESOP, inasmuch as the shareholder would generally be entitled to the same tax treatment in either case. The sale of the stock to the ESOP should be treated as a sale, however. In contrast, a risk exists that a sale of stock to the company could be treated as a dividend distribution rather than a sale. This would deprive the seller of capital gains. [Ltr Rul 8931040]

The purchase of stock from existing shareholders can be financed in a number of ways, depending on the size of the payroll, the assets in the ESOP, and the needs and objectives of the selling shareholder. If the selling shareholder needs immediate liquidity, the ESOP may use any cash on hand and borrow funds either from the company or from an outside lender to purchase the shareholder's stock for cash. If the selling shareholder does not need immediate liquidity, the shareholder may prefer to receive interest by selling the stock to the ESOP in an installment sale in return for an interest-bearing note. An installment sale has the advantages of spreading out the income tax over a number of years while fixing the price of the shares at the time of sale. Alternatively, a shareholder may simply sell a portion of the shares each year on a serial-sale basis. This is the approach usually taken when the shareholder is not yet ready to sell a block of stock at one time.

In any of these transactions, in order to meet ESOP qualification requirements and avoid a prohibited transaction under Code Section 4975, an independent appraiser must determine the purchase price for each transaction on the basis of the stock's fair market value at the time of sale. [IRC §§ 401(a)(28)(C), 4975(d)(13); ERISA § 408(3)]

Q 18:21   **How can an employee stock ownership plan be used to provide a market for the stock of controlling shareholders in a closely held corporation?**

An ESOP is a mechanism that enables controlling shareholders to sell all or a portion of their shares to the employees, who would be the logical buyers if they could obtain financing. The controlling shareholders thus are able to cash out their interests in a company. This is advantageous if the shares are not publicly traded or have no readily available market. The ESOP is also advantageous for the corporation because the shares may be purchased with pretax dollars (i.e., annual deductible cash contributions to the ESOP), resulting in a substantial reduction in the cash required to finance the transaction. Further, if the ESOP is a leveraged ESOP, a commercial lender may charge a reduced rate of interest due to the tax advantages it receives in return for making loans to ESOPs.

Another advantage of the ESOP mechanism is that it provides for the continuity of management by enabling new employees to acquire stock as older employees and shareholders retire without diluting the equity of the remaining shareholders. In other words, the ESOP, by purchasing outstanding shares from existing shareholders and allocating them to other ESOP participants, avoids purchasing newly issued shares from the company (which would increase the total shares outstanding and dilute or reduce the voting power, and possibly also the value, of each shareholder's interest).

There may, however, be some dilution of earnings to the extent that the ESOP creates expenses that the company would not otherwise have. Even this may not be the case if the company previously had a profit sharing plan and the ESOP is installed simply as a replacement for the profit sharing plan. An existing buy/sell agreement between two related controlling shareholders, giving each the option to buy the other's shares at a below-market price, may pose a problem. The IRS ruled that a father's sale of some of his shares to an ESOP at market value (after his son's waiver of his rights under the agreement) would be a taxable gift by the son to his father to the extent the ESOP's purchase price exceeds the option price under the buy/sell agreement. [Ltr Rul 9117035]

Q 18:22 How do ERISA and the Code regulate employee stock ownership plans?

Because an ESOP is a qualified retirement plan, it is subject to many of the same requirements that profit sharing plans face. These requirements include the following:

1. The ESOP must have a written plan document pursuant to ERISA.
2. ESOP contributions must be administered for the sole benefit of the plan participants. [IRC §§ 401(a)(1), 401(a)(2)]
3. The plan must have a fiduciary who serves as plan administrator and a trustee who has sole authority to manage plan assets. One person may serve in both capacities, if desired.
4. The plan cannot discriminate in favor of officers, shareholders, or highly compensated employees in terms of either benefits or participation.
5. The employer can contribute cash, property, or employer stock (or a combination of these three) to the plan within certain limitations. [IRC § 404(a)(3)]
6. The employer contributions must be allocated in a nondiscriminatory manner to individual participant accounts.

Plan Design Parameters

Q 18:23 How much can be added to an employee stock ownership plan participant's account each year?

The amount that can be added to a participant's account each year (annual addition) is the lesser of $30,000 or 25 percent of the participant's compensation. [IRC §§ 415(c)(1), 415(c)(2)] If no more than one third of the employers' contributions for the year are allocated to highly compensated employees, certain items (e.g., contributions applied to pay interest on a loan, as well as forfeitures of ESOP stock acquired through a loan) are disregarded for purposes of computing the amount of each participant's allowable annual addition. [IRC § 415(c)(6)] It seems that dividends on employer securities held by an ESOP are not considered part of the annual addition, so contributions to an ESOP may be effectively increased. [IRC § 404(k)] For limitation years that began before July 13, 1989, the dollar limit was doubled to $60,000 if no more than one third of the employer's contributions for the year was allocated to highly compensated employees. [IRC § 401(a)(17)]

Q 18:24 Are employee stock ownership plan participants entitled to the voting rights of the employer securities allocated to their individual accounts under the plan?

In certain circumstances, yes. If the employer securities are registered with the Securities and Exchange Commission, participants must be given full voting rights with respect to stock allocated to their ESOP accounts. An ESOP maintained by an employer that does not have registration-type securities (e.g., a closely held corporation) is required to pass through voting rights to participants for stock allocated to their accounts only with respect to any corporate merger, consolidation, recapitalization, reclassification, liquidation, dissolution, sale of substantially all assets of a trade or business, or other similar transaction prescribed by regulations. The plan may authorize the trustees of an ESOP maintained by such an employer to exercise the voting rights of such allocated stock on a one-vote-per-participant basis. [IRC § 409(e)] Participants do not have any voting rights regarding stock held by the ESOP in a suspense account (i.e., stock that has not yet been allocated to participants). The trustees have discretion in exercising the voting rights of allocated stock not subject to the pass-through rule, but they must exercise the voting rights of such stock in accordance with their ERISA-mandated fiduciary duties to plan participants and beneficiaries.

If an ESOP has a loan that qualifies for the partial exclusion of interest under Code Section 133, the right of participants to direct voting must be extended to all corporate matters involving shareholder approval even if the corporations stock is not publicly traded and the one-vote-per-participant rule normally permitted in the absence of registration-type securities cannot be applied. [IRC § 133(b)(7)(A)]

Q 18:25 Are employee stock ownership plan participants entitled to be involved in decisions to tender plan stock in response to a tender offer?

No, the Code does not require the pass-through of decisions regarding the tendering of the ESOP's stock in response to a tender offer. In some instances, participants have been given the opportunity to direct the ESOP trustee. If this is done, the trustee still nevertheless has a duty to independently evaluate the participants' directions rather than to follow them blindly. [Martin v Nationsbank of Georgia, 16 EBC (BNA) 2138 (ND Ga 1993)] ESOP trustees cannot vote stock in response to a tender offer in an effort to retain control of the company.

Q 18:26 What are the fiduciary obligations of an employee stock ownership plan trustee with regard to unallocated stock?

ESOP trustees cannot vote stock to retain control of the company. In an effort to avoid the potential fiduciary liability that could exist for voting ESOP stock the wrong way, ESOPs sometimes require the ESOP trustee to vote unallocated shares in the same proportion as allocated shares for which instructions have been received. The Department of Labor (DOL) takes the position that these provisions do not entirely relieve the trustee from making an independent judgment regarding the advisability of tendering or voting unallocated shares. By letter, a DOL official took the position that tender decisions with respect to unallocated shares are the exclusive responsibility of an ESOP trustee and that a trustee may follow pass-through instructions only to the extent that they are consistent with his or her independent fiduciary duties. [Polaroid Stock Equity Plan (DOL 1989)]

Q 18:27 Must an employee stock ownership plan allow participants to diversify the investment of any portion of their individual accounts?

Yes, in certain circumstances, it must. During the 90-day period following the close of each plan year in the qualified election period, any employee who has completed at least ten years of participation in the ESOP and has attained age 55 (a qualified participant) must be permitted to direct the ESOP as to the investment of at least 25 percent of his or her account (50 percent for the last election period). [IRC § 401(a)(28)(B)] For this purpose, the qualified election period is the six-plan-year period beginning with the first plan year in which the participant is a qualified participant. [IRC § 401(a)(28)(B)(iv)]

The ESOP must distribute or invest the portion of the participant's individual account as directed by the participant's diversification election within 90 days after the end of the period during which the election could be made for the plan year. Thus, the deadline for the ESOP to comply with the qualified participant's diversification election is 180 days (90 days of the election period plus 90 days after the election period). [IRC § 401(a)(28)(B)(ii); IR Notice 88-56, 1988-1 CB 540, Q 13]

Q 18:28 If an employee stock ownership plan participant elects to diversify a portion of his or her plan account, what special rules apply to the amounts so diversified?

Amounts invested in an investment option pursuant to a diversification election are generally treated as amounts not held by an ESOP and, as a result, are no longer subject to the statutory provisions governing amounts held by an ESOP. Thus, for example, a qualified participant cannot demand that the distribution of diversified amounts be made in the form of employer securities. [IR Notice 88-56, 1988-1 CB 540, Q 16]

Amounts that consist of employer securities distributed to the participant pursuant to a diversification election are subject to a participant's put option (see Q 18:41). Distributions in satisfaction of the diversification requirements do not violate the general restrictions regarding distributions before a participant's termination of employment or certain other events. [IR Notice 88-56, 1989-1 CB 540, Q&A 14; IRC § 409(h)]

Q 18:29 Is the entire amount allocated to the participant's individual account under the employee stock ownership plan subject to diversification?

Not necessarily. The diversification election does not apply to the following:

1. Employer securities acquired by or contributed to the ESOP on or before December 31, 1986; and
2. Dividends paid on or before December 31, 1986.

Q 18:30   Estate and Retirement Planning Answer Book

In addition, if an ESOP holds and allocates to a qualified participant's account a *de minimis* amount of employer securities acquired after December 31, 1986, the ESOP is not required to offer diversification to that participant. A fair market value of $500 or less is deemed to be a *de minimis* amount for this purpose, although an ESOP may elect to use a lower threshold. If the *de minimis* amount is exceeded later in the qualified election period, however, all employer securities allocated to the qualified participant that were acquired or contributed after December 31, 1986, are subject to diversification. [IR Notice 88-56, 1988-1 CB 540, Qs 7, 8]

Dividends paid after December 31, 1986, in the form of employer securities, cash, or other property used to acquire employer securities are subject to the diversification rules. This will be true even though the dividends are paid with respect to employer securities acquired by the ESOP before January 1, 1987. [IR Notice 88-56, 1988-1 CB 540, Q 1] The diversification rules do not apply, however, to securities acquired with cash dividends paid before January 1, 1987, if the acquisition occurred within 60 days of the date of payment of the dividend. [IR Notice 88-56, 1988-1 CB 540, Qs 1, 3]

Employer securities acquired by or contributed to an ESOP after December 31, 1986, are subject to the diversification requirements. Employer securities allocated to participant accounts after December 31, 1986, will not be subject to diversification requirements if they were acquired or contributed before that date. [IR Notice 88-56, 1988-1 CB 540, Q 1] If an ESOP received cash contributions prior to January 1, 1987, and thereafter—but within certain time limits—used the contributions to acquire employer securities, those securities would be deemed to have been acquired before January 1, 1987, and would not be subject to the diversification rules. [IR Notice 88-56, 1988-1 CB 540, Q 3]

Q 18:30   How does the employee stock ownership plan determine which employer securities allocated to the participant's account are counted for purposes of the participant's diversification election rights?

A participant's diversification election does not necessarily apply to the entire amount of stock and dividends allocated to his or her individual account under the plan (see Q 18:29). It is therefore necessary to be able to isolate the amount of stock allocated to the account that is counted when applying the diversification election rule (see Q 18:27).

Note that the shares diversified need not be those shares actually acquired after 1986. The number of shares that must be available for diversification is nevertheless determined by the number of shares acquired or contributed after December 31, 1986. The diversified shares, however, must be employer securities that, immediately prior to diversification, were subject to the put option and right to demand requirements of Code Section 409(h). [IR Notice 88-56, 1988-1 CB 540 Q 10]

Two methods may be used to determine the amount of stock to allocate to a participant's ESOP account when applying the diversification rule: separate accounting or formula.

Separate accounting method. An ESOP may separately account for employer securities contributed or acquired after December 31, 1986, and those contributed before January 1, 1987. If the ESOP does not maintain separate accounts for securities based on the date of acquisition, any securities allocated after 1986 will be presumed to consist, first, of securities acquired or contributed after 1986, and, second, of securities acquired or contributed before 1987. [IR Notice 88-56, 1988-1 CB 540, Q 4]

Formula method. An ESOP may, under certain circumstances, use an alternative formula to determine the portion of a qualified participant's account attributable to employer securities acquired or contributed after December 31, 1986. Under this formula, the number of securities in a qualified participant's account deemed acquired or contributed after December 31, 1986, is determined by multiplying the number of shares allocated to a qualified participant's account by a fraction representing, as of the plan valuation date closest to the date on which the individual becomes a qualified participant, the portion of the total shares that were acquired by or contributed to the ESOP after December 31, 1986. This formula is available only if certain IRS model plan amendments were adopted by the ESOP sponsor on or before January 1, 1989. [IR Notice 88-56, 1988-1 CB 540, Q 5; IR Notice 87-2, 1987-1 CB 396]

Example 18-3: A manufacturing corporation adopted the model plan amendments with respect to its ESOP. On January 1, 1991—the plan's valuation date—the ESOP holds 100,000 shares of the corporation's stock. Of those 100,000 shares, 75,000 were acquired by the ESOP after December 31, 1986. Carol, a participant in the ESOP with 40 shares allocated to her account, became a qualified participant on January 15, 1991. The number of shares allocated to Carol's account that are subject to the diversification requirements is 30 (75,000/100,000 × 40). If Carol does not elect to diversify within 90 days after the close of the 1991 plan year and eight more shares are allocated to her account on January 1, 1992, the number of shares in her account subject to diversification increases to 36 (75,000/100,000 × (40 + 8)). [IR Notice 88-56, 1988-1 CB 540, Q 9]

Q 18:31 May an employee stock ownership plan permit a qualified participant to elect diversification of amounts in excess of that required by statute?

Yes, an ESOP may permit diversification of amounts in excess of the minimum requirements. Such amounts, however, are not treated as available for diversification or as diversified in accordance with Code Section 401(a)(28)(B). Amounts in excess of the minimum diversification requirements remain subject to the participant's right under Code Section 409(h) to demand distribution in the form of employer securities. [IR Notice 88-56, 1988-1 CB 540, Q 11]

Q 18:32 Can benefits payable under an employee stock ownership plan be integrated with Social Security?

A qualified retirement plan designated as an ESOP after November 1, 1977, may not be integrated with Social Security benefits (that is, the plan may not offset or reduce benefits payable under the plan by any portion of the Social Security benefits expected to be received by the participant). An ESOP established and integrated before that date can remain integrated, but the plan cannot be amended to increase the integration level or the integration percentage.

Q 18:33 Can a profit sharing plan be converted to an employee stock ownership plan?

Yes. If the company currently has a profit sharing plan and wants to replace it with an ESOP, the company can adopt the ESOP as a continuation of the profit sharing plan without triggering the full ownership of benefits that would otherwise be required upon termination of the profit sharing plan. Employer securities must be purchased with plan assets because an ESOP must invest primarily in employer securities.

Q 18:34 Is a bankrupt participant's interest in an employee stock ownership plan exempt from a creditor's claims?

Yes. The U.S. Supreme Court has held that a participant's interest in tax-qualified plans such as ESOPs is excluded from bankruptcy claims. [Patterson v Shumate, 112 S Ct 2242 (1992)]

Dividends

Q 18:35 Is the company permitted to deduct dividends paid on employer securities held by an employee stock ownership plan?

Yes. An employer is allowed to deduct dividends it pays on employer securities held by an ESOP that it maintains or by an ESOP maintained by another member of a controlled group (as defined under Code Section 1563(a)) that includes the employer, if one of the following criteria is met:

1. The dividend is paid in cash to the ESOP participants or their beneficiaries;
2. The dividend is paid to the ESOP and distributed to the participants or beneficiaries not later than 90 days after the close of the plan year in which paid; or
3. The dividend is used to make payments on an exempt loan. (For employer securities acquired by the ESOP after August 4, 1989, the deduction for dividends used for loan repayment is

18-21

applicable only if the dividends are on employer securities acquired with the proceeds of the loan being repaid.)

The deduction is allowed for the taxable year of the employer during which the dividend is paid, distributed, or used to repay an exempt loan. [IRC §§ 404(k), 409(1)(4); Ltr Rul 9124038] (See Q 18:16.) If dividends on employer securities allocated to a participant are used to repay an exempt loan, the ESOP must provide that employer securities with a fair market value equal to the dividends be allocated to such participant in lieu of the dividends. [IRC § 404(k)(2)(B)] The IRS may disallow the dividend deduction if it determines that the dividends constitute an evasion of taxation. [IRC § 404(k)(5)(A)]

Q 18:36 Are dividends paid to participants deductible by the company even if participants can elect whether to receive them in a current cash payment?

Yes. Dividends actually paid in cash to plan participants are deductible by the company even if the plan contains a provision that permits participants to elect to receive or not receive dividend payments. [IRC § 404(k); Temp Treas Reg § 1.404(k)-1T] Employers must report deductible dividends on Form 1099-DIV.

Q 18:37 How are dividends paid to employee stock ownership plan participants taxed?

Dividends either paid in cash directly to ESOP participants by the employer or paid to the ESOP and then distributed in cash to participants are deductible by the company (see Q 18:12) and are treated as a taxable distribution to the employee. As a result, they are included in the employee's gross income. They are treated as paid separately from any other payments from the ESOP. Thus, a dividend is treated as a plan distribution and as paid under a separate contract providing only for payment of dividends. A dividend is a fully taxable distribution to the employee even though the employee has basis, but the distribution is not subject to the 10 percent tax on early distributions. [IRC §§ 72(t)(2)(A)(vi), 402; Temp Treas Reg § 1.404(k)-15] Participants must report the distribution on their tax returns as a plan distribution and not as investment income. Additionally, a distribution of a participant's entire account balance from an ESOP will still be eligible for treatment as a lump-sum distribution even if the participant received dividend distributions with respect to employer securities held by the ESOP in earlier years. [Ltr Ruls 9045048, 9024083]

Distributions

Q 18:38 Must distributions under an employee stock ownership plan commence by specified dates?

Yes. As a qualification requirement, with regard to distributions attributable to stock acquired after December 31, 1986, an ESOP must provide that, if a participant elects (and, if applicable, the participant's spouse consents), the distribution of the participant's account balance will begin no later than one year after the end of the plan year

1. In which the individual terminates employment by reason of reaching retirement age, disability, or death; or
2. That is the fifth plan year following the plan year in which the individual otherwise terminates employment (unless the individual is reemployed by the employer before such time).

For purposes of this rule, the individual's account balance is deemed not to include any employer securities acquired with the proceeds of an exempt loan until the end of the plan year in which such loan is repaid in full. The ESOP must also comply with the minimum distribution requirements. [IRC §§ 401(a)(9), 409(o)(1)(A), 409(o)(1)(B)]

Q 18:39 Must distributions under an employee stock ownership plan be made at certain intervals?

An ESOP must provide that (unless the participant elects otherwise) the distribution of the account balances attributable to stock acquired after December 31, 1986, will be in substantially equal periodic payments (not less frequently than annually) over a period not longer than five years. If the participant's account balance exceeds $500,000, the distribution period may be extended one year for each $100,000 (or part thereof) by which the account balance exceeds $500,000. The distribution period cannot exceed ten years, however. [IRC § 409(o)(1)(C)]

Q 18:40   What can be distributed?

The ESOP can distribute cash, property, or employer stock, but the participant usually has the right to demand that the distribution be in employer stock. [IRC § 409(h)]

Q 18:41   When can an employee stock ownership plan participant exercise his or her put option?

An ESOP participant who receives his or her plan benefits in the form of employer securities must be given the right to sell (put) the securities to the employer for their fair market value within a specified time period after the date of distribution (see Q 18:1). This so-called put option must last for a period of at least 60 days following the date of distribution of employer securities. If the put option is not exercised, the participant must be given the opportunity to sell the stock to the employer during a 60-day period in the following plan year. [IRC § 409(h)(4)] The nature of the employer's obligation to pay for the stock depends upon whether the participant's stock was received as a total distribution (that is, the balance of the participant's account was distributed to him or her within one calendar year) or whether the stock was distributed to the participant in installments. If a put option is exercised for stock distributed in a total distribution, the employer must pay for the repurchased stock in substantially equal periodic payments (not less frequently than annually) over a period beginning no later than 30 days after the exercise of the put option and ending no later than five years thereafter. Reasonable interest and adequate security must be provided for unpaid amounts. [IRC § 409(h)(5)] If the stock is distributed in installments, the employer must pay for the stock no later than 30 days after the put option is exercised. [IRC § 409(h)(6)] Put options are an important consideration in leveraged buyouts because they represent a potential cash drain on a highly leveraged employer.

Q 18:42 What steps should be taken to ensure an employee stock ownership plan has sufficient cash to pay for required distributions?

An important aspect of ESOP planning is providing sufficient cash to pay distributions. ESOP distribution liability can vary markedly from year to year, and an ESOP may very well have small initial liability that greatly increases over time.

Example 18-4: An equipment manufacturing company created an ESOP in 1980. Up to the present, the only turnover in the company has involved rank-and-file employees, and the amount distributed by the ESOP each year has averaged $10,000. In the next three years, however, three of the four founders of the company expect to retire. Each of these founders has an account balance of $300,000. As a result, the ESOP will have to locate $900,000 to pay for these distributions.

Because of the serious effect a few large distributions may have on an ESOP, it is often advantageous for a company to try to predict future ESOP distributions by determining when various classes of persons are likely to retire. Moreover, a number of steps can be taken with respect to plan design to minimize the cash effect of large distributions. For example, the ESOP could be designed to provide that any distribution in excess of $25,000 will be paid over a ten-year period. Other solutions are as follows:

1. Purchasing life insurance on the lives of key employees to provide funds should a key employee die prematurely.
2. If large distributions are foreseeable, cash contributions can be made to an ESOP so that the ESOP has sufficient cash.

Q 18:43 How are distributions from an employee stock ownership plan taxed?

Distributions from an ESOP are generally taxed like similar distributions from other tax-qualified retirement plans. If appreciated employer securities are included in a lump-sum distribution, the recipient may defer tax on the net unrealized appreciation until the securities are sold. [IRC § 402(e)(4)(B); Treas Reg § 1.402(a)-1(b)(1)]

Distributions from ESOPs are subject to the 10 percent additional tax on early distributions. [IRC § 72(t)(2)(C)] Distributions before January 1, 1990, were exempt from this additional tax if the distributions were attributable to assets that had been invested in employer securities for the five-plan-year period preceding the plan year in which the distributions were made.

Q 18:44 When must employee stock ownership plan assets be valued?

ESOP assets must be valued at least once a year. [Rev Rul 80-155, 1980-1 CB 84] This is generally done as of the last day of the plan year. For transactions involving a disqualified person, the valuation must be done on the day of the transaction. For all other transactions, the most recent valuation can be used. [Treas Reg § 54-4975-11(d)(5)]

Q 18:45 What factors are used to appraise employer securities that are not readily tradable?

Employer securities that are not readily tradable must be appraised by an independent appraiser. [IRC § 401(a)(28)(C)] The valuation must be reasonable, written, made in good faith, and based on all relevant factors used to determine fair market value. Those relevant factors include the following:

- Nature of the business and history of the enterprise
- Economic outlook in general and condition of specific industry
- Book value of securities
- Earning capacity of the company
- Dividend-paying capacity of the company
- Existence of goodwill
- Market price of similar stocks

- Marketability of securities, including an assessment of the company's ability to meet its put obligations
- Existence of a control premium

The last factor refers to a block of securities that provides actual control of the company (control must be actual control that is not dissipated within a short period of time). [Prop Treas Reg § 2510.3-18]

Sale of Employer Securities

Q 18:46 May gains on the sale of securities to an employee stock ownership plan be deferred?

Yes. A shareholder who sells his or her qualified securities to an ESOP may elect to defer recognition of all or part of the gain, which would otherwise be recognized as long-term capital gain, by purchasing replacement property within the replacement period. Alternatively, the shareholder is permitted to elect immediate taxation of the gain, in which case the gain will be taxable only to the extent that the amount realized on the sale exceeds the cost of the replacement property. [IRC § 1042] All taxpayers (including grantor trusts) other than C corporations can elect to defer the recognition of gains on the sale of securities to an ESOP. [IRC § 1042(c)(7); Ltr Rul 9041027]

Additionally, in order for the deferral of gain to be permitted, after the sale the ESOP must own at least 30 percent of either (1) each class of outstanding stock of the corporation or (2) the total value of all outstanding stock of the corporation. Also, for sales after July 10, 1989, the selling shareholder must have held the stock for at least three years. As part of the election, the selling shareholder must file with the IRS a verified written statement of the corporation sponsoring the ESOP consenting to the application of the excise taxes on early dispositions and prohibited allocations of the qualified securities. [IRC § 1042(b); Temp Treas Reg § 1.1042-1T, Q&A 2(a)]

Qualified securities. For these purposes, qualified securities are employer securities (1) that are issued by a domestic corporation that for one year before and immediately after the sale has no readily tradable stock outstanding and (2) that were not received by the seller as a distribution from a qualified retirement plan or pursuant to an option or other right to acquire stock granted by the employer. Shares of the employer's common stock are not qualified securities if the employer's stock had been traded over the counter on NASDAQ within one year of the sale of the ESOP. [IRC § 1042(c)(1); Temp Treas Reg § 1.1042-1T, Q&A 1(b); Ltr Rul 9036039]

Qualified replacement property. For these purposes, qualified replacement property is any security issued by a domestic operating corporation that did not have passive investment income (e.g., rents, royalties, dividends, or interest) exceeding 25 percent of its gross receipts in its taxable year prior to the purchase. Securities of the corporation that issued the ESOP stock and of any corporation that is a member of a controlled group of corporations with such corporation cannot be qualified replacement property. An operating corporation is a corporation that uses more than 50 percent of its assets in the active conduct of trade or business. Banks and insurance companies are considered operating corporations. [IRC §§ 409(I), 1042(c)(4)]

Replacement period. For these purposes, the replacement period, is the period beginning three months before the date of sale to the ESOP and ending 12 months after the sale. The qualified replacement property must be purchased during this period. [IRC § 1042(c)(3); Temp Treas Reg § 1.1042-1T, Q&A 3(c)]

Q 18:47 How does the selling shareholder elect to defer recognition of gain on the sale of employee stock ownership plan stock?

The election to defer (i.e., not to recognize) the gain realized on the sale of the qualified securities is made in a statement of election attached to the selling shareholder's income tax return filed on or before the due date (including extensions) for the taxable year in which the sale occurs. The election is irrevocable. If the selling shareholder does not make a timely election, the shareholder may not subsequently make an election on an amended return or otherwise. [Ltr Rul 8932048]

The statement of election must provide that the selling shareholder elects to treat the sale of securities as a sale of qualified securities and must contain the following information:

1. Description of the qualified securities sold, including the type and number of shares;
2. Date of the sale of the qualified securities;
3. Adjusted basis of the qualified securities;
4. Identity of the ESOP to which the qualified securities were sold; and
5. Names and taxpayer identification numbers of the others involved if the sale was part of a single interrelated transaction that includes other sales of qualified securities and the number of shares sold by the other sellers. [Treas Reg § 1.1042-1 T, Q&A-3]

If the selling shareholder has purchased qualified replacement property at the time of the election, a statement of purchase must be attached to the statement of election. The statement of purchase must describe the qualified replacement property, give the date of the purchase and the cost of the property, declare such property to be the qualified replacement property, and be notarized within 30 days after the purchase of the qualified replacement property. If the selling shareholder has not purchased qualified replacement property at the time of the filing of the statement of election, the notarized statement of purchase described above must be attached to the shareholder's income tax return filed for the following taxable year. The statement of purchase must be filed with the IRS district where the election was originally filed, if the return is not filed with such district. [IRC § 1042(a)(1); Temp Treas Reg § 1.1042-1T, Q&A 3]

The IRS has ruled that an election that substantially complied with the rules was valid even though the notarized statement did not declare that the property purchased with the sale proceeds was intended to be qualified replacement property. [Ltr Rul 9028082]

Q 18:48 What is the basis of qualified replacement property?

If the selling shareholder makes an election not to recognize the gain (see Q 18:47), the basis of the qualified replacement property purchased during the replacement period (which equals the purchase price of the property) is reduced by an amount equal to the amount of gain that was not recognized. If more than one item of qualified replacement property is purchased, the basis of each item is reduced by an amount determined by multiplying the total gain not recognized by a fraction whose numerator is the cost of such item of property and whose denominator is the total cost of all such items of property. [IRC § 1042(d); Temp Treas Reg § 1.1042-1T, Q&A 4; Ltr Ruls 9102021, 9102017]

Q 18:49 What happens if the taxpayer who elects nonrecognition treatment later disposes of the qualified replacement property?

If the taxpayer disposes of any qualified replacement property, gain must be recognized at that time. This is so even if other parts of the Code might apply and permit the deferral of recognition of gain. A special recapture rule applies if the taxpayer controls the corporation that issued the qualified replacement property and the corporation disposes of a substantial portion of its assets other than in the ordinary course of its trade or business. [IRC § 1042(e)]

Q 18:50 Do all dispositions of qualified replacement property result in the recapture of gain?

No. The following dispositions are exempt from the recapture provisions:

1. Disposition upon death. If the selling shareholder is holding the qualified replacement property, a subsequent disposition of the qualified replacement property may not be taxed at all.

Example 18-5: A businessman sells stock with a basis of $100,000 and fair market value of $1 million to an ESOP in a qualifying transaction. Replacement property costing $1 million is purchased by the businessman, who holds that replacement property until his death. When he dies, the replacement property is worth $1.2 million and, because a step up in basis, has a basis in the hands of the businessman's heirs of $1.2 million. If the property is subsequently sold by the heirs for $1.2 million, there is no income tax payable on this subsequent sale. There could, however, be estate tax payable on the replacement property upon death of the businessman.

2. Dispositions by gift.

Employee Stock Ownership Plans Q 18:52

3. Subsequent sales of the qualified replacement property to an ESOP pursuant to Code Section 1042.
4. Transfers in a corporate reorganization, provided no corporation involved in the reorganization is controlled by the taxpayer holding the qualified replacement property. [IRC § 1042(e)(3)]

Q 18:51 What is the statute of limitations when a selling shareholder elects nonrecognition of the gain on the sale of qualified securities?

If any gain is realized, but not recognized, by the selling shareholder on the sale of any qualified securities, the statute of limitations with respect to such nonrecognized gain will not expire until three years from the date the IRS receives one of the following:

1. A notarized statement of purchase that includes the cost of the qualified replacement property;
2. A written statement of the selling shareholder's intent not to purchase qualified replacement property within the replacement period; or
3. A written statement of the selling shareholder's failure to purchase qualified replacement property within the replacement period.

If the selling shareholder files a statement of intent not to purchase or of failure to purchase qualified replacement property, the statement must be accompanied, if appropriate, by an amended return for the taxable year in which the gain from the sale of the qualified securities was realized. The amended return must report any gain from the sale of qualified securities that is required to be recognized in the taxable year in which the gain was realized due to a failure to meet the nonrecognition requirements. [IRC § 1042(f); Temp Treas Reg § 1.1042-1T, Q&A 5]

Q 18:52 What happens if an employee stock ownership plan disposes of qualified securities within three years of their acquisition?

An excise tax is imposed on the amount realized on the disposition of qualified securities if the following requirements are met:

18-31

Q 18:53   **Estate and Retirement Planning Answer Book**

1. The ESOP acquires any qualified securities in a sale for which nonrecognition treatment was elected.
2. The ESOP disposes of any of such qualified securities during the three-year period after the date on which any qualified securities were acquired.
3. Either the total number of shares of employer securities held by the ESOP after such disposition is less than the total number of shares of employer securities held immediately after the sale for which nonrecognition treatment was elected or the value of the employer securities held by the ESOP immediately after such disposition is less than 30 percent of the total value of all employer securities outstanding at that time. [IRC § 4978(a); Temp Treas Reg § 54.4978-1T, Q&A 1]

Q 18:53   What is the amount of excise tax on the disposition of qualified securities?

The excise tax is 10 percent of the amount realized that is allocable to qualified securities that are disposed of within the three-year period following their acquisition. [IRC § 4978(b); Temp Treas Reg § 54.4978-1T, Q&A 2]

A disposition is any sale, exchange, or distribution. The excise tax will not, however, apply to any distribution of qualified securities that is made by reason of the following:

1. Death of the employee;
2. Retirement of the employee after the employee has attained age 59;
3. Disability of the employee; or
4. Separation from service by the employee for any period that results in a one-year break in service.

Dispositions necessary to comply with the diversification requirements and exchanges pursuant to corporate reorganizations will not trigger the excise tax. [IRC § 4978(d); Temp Treas Reg § 54.4978-1T, Q&A 3]

The excise tax is imposed on the corporation or corporations that made the verified written statement of consent to the application of such excise tax on the disposition of employer securities. [IRC § 4978(c); Temp Treas Reg § 54.4978-1T, Q&A 4]

Q 18:54 Are there any restrictions on the allocation of employer securities acquired by the employee stock ownership plan in a transaction in which the seller elected nonrecognition of gain?

Yes. None of the stock acquired by the ESOP in a nonrecognition transaction may be directly or indirectly allocated to or accrued to the benefit of the selling shareholder or a member of the shareholder's family during the three-year nonallocation period (see Q 18:52) or to an owner of more than 25 percent of any class of employer stock at any time.

In determining whether the prohibition against an accrual of qualified securities is satisfied, the allocation of any contributions or other assets that are not attributable to qualified securities sold to the ESOP must be made without regard to the allocation of the qualified securities. [IRC § 409(n); Temp Treas Reg § 1.1042-1T, Q&A 2(c); Ltr Rul 9041071]

The prohibited allocation is treated as a distribution to the person receiving it, and there is an excise tax imposed on the employer equal to 50 percent of the amount involved in a prohibited allocation of qualified securities acquired by an ESOP after October 22, 1986. [IRC §§ 409(n), 4979A]

Estate Planning Implications

Q 18:55 How can an employee stock ownership plan be used as an estate planning tool for the owner of a closely held corporation?

If an individual's estate consists mostly of the stock of a closely held corporation, his or her estate might not have enough liquid assets to pay the estate taxes and administration expenses of a deceased majority shareholder of a closely held corporation. This is of special concern when the individual wishes to preserve a family business intact for his or her heirs, rather than having it sold or liquidated to raise the necessary cash for such taxes and expenses. The Code provides various solutions to the liquidity problems of an estate that consists mostly of the stock of a closely held corporation. If the estate fails to qualify for that special treatment, however, it may be able to raise the cash through a permitted sale of stock to the ESOP.

> **Example 18-6:** The estate of a deceased shareholder fails to meet certain conditions under which it is permissible to pay the estate tax in installments over a period of up to fifteen years. As a result of this failure, the estate tax would be due within nine months of the shareholder's death. The estate can raise the cash it needs by selling the deceased shareholder's stock to the ESOP.

An ESOP can also benefit the estate of a deceased shareholder that cannot avail itself of the benefits of Code Section 303, which permits the redemption of a portion of a deceased shareholder's stock (i.e., the issuing corporation pays cash in return for getting back the shares) for the express purpose of paying estate taxes and administration expenses. If the estate cannot take advantage of Code Section 303, all the proceeds of the redemption are likely to be taxed as a dividend. This means that the taxable amount is not limited to the gain and that capital gains treatment is not available. If a Section 303 tax-free exchange cannot be used, the ESOP could buy the stock from the estate and the sale to the ESOP also would not be in danger of being treated as a dividend. Generally, a sale to the corporation or to the ESOP will result in no gain at all because the estate's basis for the stock it sells will equal the fair market value of the stock on the deceased shareholder's date of death, and the purchase price paid by the corporation or the ESOP will likely be this amount. [IRC §§ 303, 1014, 6166]

Q 18:56 Is there an estate tax deduction for sales of employer securities to an employee stock ownership plan?

Prior law permitted an estate tax deduction for sales of employer securities to ESOPs, but such deduction is no longer available.

Q 18:57 Can an employee stock ownership plan enter into an agreement obligating itself to purchase stock when a shareholder dies?

No. An ESOP may, however, be given an option to buy stock when the shareholder dies if the stock is not widely traded on an established market. [Treas Reg § 54.4974-11(a)(7)(i)] The corporation itself can be given a right of first refusal. [Treas Reg § 54.4975-7(b)(9)]

Q 18:58 Is it a good idea to require that an employee's stock be sold to an employee stock ownership plan when the employee terminates employment?

The advantage of requiring the sale of stock on termination of employment is that it eliminates the possibility of a significant block of stock being out on the market that will be turned in once the company stock appears valuable, thus reducing cash reserves of the company.

Chapter 19

Nonqualified Retirement Plans

Nonqualified retirement plans are an option for employers who wish to retain and reward key employees. Although they do not enjoy the favorable tax treatment accorded qualified plans, nonqualified plans offer a number of benefits that make them an attractive choice in certain situations. Nonqualified plans, for example, usually have lower administrative costs than qualified plans. Also, although qualified plans do not provide benefits to independent contractors, nonqualified plans are accessible to these individuals.

Many employers prefer nonqualified retirement plans because these plans are not necessarily subject to the same nondiscrimination rules that apply to qualified plans. Similarly, through the use of noncompetition provisions and extended vesting schedules, nonqualified retirement plans can be designed to give a company's key employees an incentive to remain with their employer. Nonqualified plans may also be used to encourage employee performance by tying benefits provided by the plan to the attainment of certain performance objectives. Through careful planning, employers can establish a nonqualified retirement plan and avoid the complex requirements of the Employee Retirement Income Security Act of 1974.

Nonqualified retirement plans can also benefit employees. They can provide benefits beyond those permitted by tax-qualified plans and can be used to replace benefits that highly skilled workers would otherwise forfeit when transferring from one employer to another. Security for those benefits can be provided through the use of trusts. Employees may be subject to immediate taxation unless careful planning is done, however.

Overview	19-2
Applicable Tax Principles	19-4
Supplemental Executive Retirement Plans (SERPs)	19-10
Rabbi Trusts	19-11
Surety Bonds	19-13
Secular Trusts	19-13
ERISA Implications	19-17

Overview

Q 19:1 What are nonqualified deferred compensation plans?

Nonqualified deferred compensation plans are arrangements (other than the tax-qualified plans described in chapter 14) providing for the payment of income to an employee (or an independent contractor in some cases) in a year following the year in which the individual enters into the arrangement or otherwise becomes a participant in the plan or arrangement and performs services.

Example 19-1: In 1993, a cartographer enters into an agreement providing that, starting in 1999, when the cartographer reaches age 62, she will receive payments of $50,000 per year for ten years.

Q 19:2 Why do organizations establish nonqualified deferred compensation arrangements?

Nonqualified deferred compensation arrangements are established for the following reasons:

1. A nonqualified deferred compensation arrangement that is not subject to Title I of the Employee Retirement Income Security Act of 1974 (ERISA) is not subject to the spousal consent rules under the Retirement Equity Act of 1984 that apply to qualified retirement plans.

2. A nonqualified deferred compensation arrangement can provide benefits to independent contractors who cannot be covered by a qualified retirement plan.

3. A nonqualified deferred compensation arrangement usually has lower administration costs than qualified retirement plans.

4. A nonqualified deferred compensation arrangement can be used to encourage employees to retire early during an early retirement window program. Such programs can be used to reduce an employer's labor force without layoffs.

5. A nonqualified deferred compensation arrangement can replace benefits that a highly skilled employee often forfeits when transferring from one employer to another.

6. An employer can use a nonqualified deferred compensation arrangement as a means of retaining key employees. The plan can be designed so that the employee forfeits benefits if he or she terminates employment before a certain age. As well, a nonqualified deferred compensation arrangement can be used to provide the retirement income increment that cannot be obtained under a tax-qualified retirement plan due to the restrictions on the benefits available to highly compensated employees under tax-qualified plans.

7. A nonqualified deferred compensation arrangement can be used to encourage performance by tying benefits under the plan to the achievement of certain performance objectives.

8. A nonqualified deferred compensation arrangement can be used to provide key employees with some security against the possibility of a change in ownership or control that may result in their premature dismissal. Payments under these plans are often referred to as golden parachute payments.

Applicable Tax Principles

Q 19:3   When is an employer entitled to a deduction for contributions to a nonqualified deferred compensation arrangement?

An employer should be entitled to a deduction when the payments are includible in the employee's gross income for federal income tax purposes.

Q 19:4   Are amounts deferred in a nonqualified deferred compensation arrangement subject to Social Security and Medicare tax?

Yes, amounts deferred under nonqualified deferred compensation arrangements are subject to Social Security and Medicare tax. The tax applies at the later of (1) the time the amount deferred is earned or (2) the time at which it becomes nonforfeitable. Often, individuals covered by nonqualified deferred compensation arrangements have income in excess of the Social Security tax wage base ($62,700 in 1996) taxed at 12.4 percent. In 1994, the cap on the amount of compensation subject to Medicare tax was removed; the amount deferred under the arrangement will be subject to a Medicare tax of 2.9 percent for participants on the total amount of compensation.

Q 19:5   When is an employee subject to income tax on benefits received under a nonqualified deferred compensation arrangement?

As a general rule, an employee is not taxed on the economic benefits received under a nonqualified deferred compensation arrangement until there is no substantial risk that he or she will forfeit the benefit or until he or she receives a payment. More specifically, an employee may be taxed under the following four doctrines or Internal Revenue Code (Code) provisions:

1. The constructive receipt doctrine (see Q 19:6);
2. The economic benefit doctrine (see Q 19:8);

Nonqualified Retirement Plans — Q 19:7

3. Code Section 83 (see Qs 19:10, 19:11); and
4. Code Section 402(b) (see Q 19:12).

Q 19:6 What is the constructive receipt doctrine?

The constructive receipt doctrine concerns the time at which items must be taken into income. Under this doctrine, a taxpayer will be taxed on income that he or she has an unconditional right to receive regardless of whether or not the taxpayer actually reduces the income to his or her possession.

> **Example 19-2:** A participant in a nonqualified deferred compensation arrangement is given the opportunity to receive a $1,000 income payment on December 31, 1993. The participant declines and asks that a check for $1,000 be given to him on January 4, 1994. The participant is potentially subject to income tax in 1993 on the $1,000 under the constructive receipt doctrine because he could have received the $1,000 but turned his back on it.

Q 19:7 Will the Internal Revenue Service provide a favorable private letter ruling that an unfunded nonqualified deferred compensation arrangement will defer compensation without running afoul of the constructive receipt doctrine?

Yes, the Internal Revenue Service (IRS) will give a favorable private letter ruling on a nonqualified deferred arrangement if the following requirements are met:

1. The decision to defer must occur before the beginning of the calendar year for which the compensation is payable. [Rev Proc 92-65, 1992-2 CB 428]

   There are two exceptions to this rule:

   a. In the initial year of the plan's operation, the eligible participant may make an election, within 30 days after the date the plan is effective for eligible employees, to defer compensation for services performed subsequent to the election.

Q 19:7   Estate and Retirement Planning Answer Book

      b. In the participant's first year of eligibility in the plan, the participant must make an election, within 30 days after the employee's eligibility date, to similarly defer compensation for services performed after the election. [Rev Proc 92-65]

2. If, after the initial election, an employee makes additional elections to defer the payment of income, the payment must be subject to a forfeiture provision. The substantial forfeiture provision must impose upon the employee a significant limitation or duty that will require a meaningful effort by the employee to fulfill the provision's requirements, and there must be a definite possibility that the forfeiture of compensation could occur. [Rev Proc 92-65]

      The nonqualified deferred arrangements also must define the time and method for the payment of the deferred compensation for each event that entitles a participant to receive benefits (e.g., termination of employment, regular retirement, disability retirement, and death). The arrangement may specify the date of payment or provide that payments begin within 30 days after the occurrence of a stated event. [Rev Proc 92-65]

3. The arrangement must provide that participants have the status of general unsecured creditors of the employer and that the plan constitutes a mere promise by the employer to make benefit payments in the future. [Rev Proc 92-65]

4. If the arrangement uses a trust, the arrangement must also provide that any trust created by the employer and any assets held by the trust to assist it in meeting its obligation under the arrangement will conform to the terms of a model rabbi trust, as described in Revenue Procedure 92-64.

5. The arrangement must state that the parties intend for it to be unfunded for tax purposes and for purposes of Title I of ERISA.

6. The arrangement must provide that a participant's rights to benefit payments under the plan are in no way subject to anticipation, alienation, sale, transfer, assignment, pledge, encumbrance, attachment, or garnishment by creditors of the participant or the participant's beneficiary. [Rev Proc 71-19, 1971-1 CB 928, as amplified by Rev Proc 92-65, 1992-33 IRB 16]

Q 19:8 What is the economic benefit doctrine?

Under the economic benefit doctrine, an employee is taxed on money or other property set aside in a way that gives the employee an unrestricted, nonforfeitable right to receive the money or other property at some future date, even though he or she is not currently able to receive the money or other property. [E.T. Sproull, 16 TC 244 (1951), *aff'd* 194 F 2d 541 *per curiam* (6th Cir 1952)]

Q 19:9 Does the making of a promise to make a future payment result in taxation under the economic benefit doctrine?

An unsecured promise to make a payment in the future does not result in giving an economic benefit to the employee because the source of funds for paying the benefit is subject to the creditors of the corporation.

Q 19:10 How does Code Section 83 affect nonqualified deferred compensation arrangements?

Code Section 83 generally requires that a taxpayer performing services must include the excess of the fair market value of such property transferred in connection with the performance of those services over any amount paid for the property in income when rights in the property are either transferable or no longer subject to a substantial risk of forfeiture.

Example 19-3: An executive becomes entitled to stock in a company worth $10,000 because the company earns record profits. The executive directs that the stock be distributed to his favorite nephew. The executive is subject to income tax on the $10,000 stock distribution.

Q 19:11 Is an employer's promise to make a future payment a taxable event under Code Section 83?

No. The mere promise by an employer to make a future payment is not treated as property transferred in connection with the performance of services for purposes of Code Section 83. [Treas Reg § 1.83-3(e)]

Q 19:12 How are employees taxed under Code Section 402(b)?

Contributions made to a nonqualified employees' trust pursuant to a nonqualified deferred compensation arrangement are taxed under Code Section 402(b). That section states that contributions to an employees' trust made by an employer during a taxable year of the employer ending within or with a taxable year of the trust for which the trust is not exempt from tax under Code Section 501(a) are included in the gross income of the employee in accordance with Code Section 83 (relating to property transferred in connection with performance of services). This implies that the participant can incur tax even though the participant does not receive a distribution from the trust. This could happen once the participant becomes vested, even though he or she does not receive a distribution. [IRC § 402(b)]

Q 19:13 Can a favorable private letter ruling be obtained for a nonqualified deferred compensation arrangement that provides for the payment of benefits if an unforeseen emergency occurs?

Yes, a nonqualified deferred compensation arrangement that provides for the payment of benefits in the case of an unforeseeable emergency can obtain a favorable private letter ruling. The key is avoiding current taxation of the deferred compensation under Code Section 83 on the grounds that funds are available now and are not subject to a substantial risk of forfeiture. To avoid such a characterization, the *unforeseeable emergency* must be defined in the plan as an unanticipated emergency that is caused by an event beyond the control of the participant or beneficiary and that would result in severe financial hardship to the individual if early withdrawal was not permitted. The plan must also provide that any early withdrawal approved by the employer is limited to the amount necessary to meet the emergency. The plan may use language similar to that required under Treasury Regulations Sections 1.457-2(h)(4) and 1.457-2(h)(5) concerning nonqualified deferred compensation arrangements for employees of state and local governments and tax-exempt organizations.

Q 19:14 Will the IRS issue favorable private letter rulings for nonqualified deferred compensation arrangements for controlling shareholders?

No. The IRS refuses to issue rulings in connection with nonqualified deferred compensation arrangements for controlling shareholders in the same manner that it does for other types of plans. [Rev Proc 93-3, IRB 1993-1, 71, § 3.01(32)] The employer thus must rely on the preparing attorney's opinion that the plan produces the desired tax effect.

Q 19:15 Can a participant in a nonqualified deferred compensation arrangement make the decision to defer compensation after the services have been performed?

The courts have been more liberal than the IRS in permitting this type of action. Although the IRS will not give a favorable private letter ruling under similar circumstances, the courts have allowed employees to make the decision to defer after the services were rendered, but before the amounts were determined. [James F Oates, 18 TC 570 (1952), *aff'd* 207 F 2d 711, 53-2 USTC ¶ 9596 (7th Cir 1953)] The IRS acquiesced in that case. [1960-1 CB 5] The decision to defer after the amount has been determined but before the employee is entitled to payment has also been allowed. [Howard Veit, 8 TCM 919 (1949)]

Q 19:16 Will an employee be subject to current taxation if he or she has the right to decide whether to accept nonqualified deferred compensation payments in a single sum rather than in installments?

Evidently not. The Tax Court addressed this issue in a case in which two employees who were participants in an unfunded nonqualified deferred compensation arrangement were permitted to select between a single-sum payment and installment payments before they terminated their employment and became entitled to payment. Furthermore, the employees made their elections before the amounts became due and ascertainable. The Tax Court held, based upon the facts of the case, that the ability to make such an election did not result in the amounts deferred being constructively received; therefore, the payments were not currently taxable. [Martin v Commr, 96 TC No 39 (1991)]

Supplemental Executive Retirement Plans

Q 19:17 What are supplemental executive retirement plans?

Supplemental executive retirement plans (SERPs) are nonqualified deferred compensation plans designed to supplement the retirement income that an executive receives from tax-qualified retirement plans.

Q 19:18 What are excess benefits plans?

Excess benefits plans are SERPs that are designed solely to provide benefits in excess of those permitted in a tax-qualified retirement plan because of Section 415 limitations on the maximum permissible plan benefit for any participant. [ERISA § 3(36)]

Q 19:19 What are the reasons for establishing a supplemental executive retirement plan?

SERPs are often established for the following reasons:

1. A SERP may be used when the compensation cap under Code Section 401(a)(17) ($235,840 in 1993, $150,000 in 1995) limits the annual benefit or annual addition that may be provided under a qualified retirement plan. SERPs may be used to compensate highly compensated individuals who incur a reduction in benefit accruals because of the $150,000 limitation on compensation.

2. An employer may adopt a SERP to provide benefits to highly compensated employees in amounts that would violate the nondiscrimination rules applicable to qualified retirement plans under Code Section 401(a)(4).

3. SERPs permit highly compensated employees to defer additional compensation when they are limited by the actual defer-

ral percentage test or the dollar limit on deferrals (currently $9,240 per calendar year) under a 401(k) cash or deferred plan.

4. SERPs may be used as a means of lowering taxes, a subject of particular interest to highly paid executives.

5. Nonqualified deferred compensation plans that are not subject to ERISA are not subject to its vesting rules. Accordingly, these plans may be used to lock executives into employment positions by not vesting benefits until a specified, privately set service period has elapsed.

Rabbi Trusts

Q 19:20 What is a rabbi trust?

A rabbi trust is typically an irrevocable trust that holds assets for the benefit of one or more employees to pay promised deferred compensation. The trust assets can be reached by the employer's creditors. The employer is taxed on the income of the trust. [Ltr Rul 8113107]

Rabbi trusts are created to give employees some security that their deferred compensation benefits will be paid. An employee may be concerned about whether the employer will have a change of heart and refuse to comply with the deferred compensation agreement. If this happens, the employee could have to enforce his or her right to the deferred income through lengthy and costly litigation against the employer. An employee may also be concerned about a takeover by another company that would refuse to comply with the deferred compensation agreement. A rabbi trust will provide protection against both of these risks by setting aside the funds necessary to honor the deferred compensation agreement. A rabbi trust will not protect the employee if the employer goes bankrupt, however, because, as noted, the assets in the trust must be subject to the claims of the employer's creditors. A rabbi trust typically meets this requirement by containing a provision saying that its assets cannot be reached except by the employer's judgment creditors.

Q 19:21 Will the IRS issue private letter rulings for rabbi trusts?

The IRS has stated that, with the exception of rare and unusual circumstances, it will no longer issue rulings on unfunded nonqualified deferred compensation arrangements that use any rabbi trust other than the model rabbi trust set forth in Revenue Procedure 92-64. The IRS promulgated the model rabbi trust to serve as a safe harbor for taxpayers who adopt and maintain rabbi trusts in connection with unfunded nonqualified deferred compensation arrangements.

Q 19:22 Is a rabbi trust subject to the vesting requirements of Title I of ERISA?

No. Because rabbi trust assets are subject to the claims of the employer's creditors, they are not considered funded for purposes of Title I of ERISA. Accordingly, they are not subject to the vesting requirements of Title I of ERISA.

Q 19:23 What are the tax effects of using the model rabbi trust?

If the model rabbi trust is used, the IRS will not treat an employee as being in constructive receipt of income or as incurring an economic benefit solely on account of the adoption or maintenance of the rabbi trust. [Rev Proc 92-64, 1992-2 CB 422]

Q 19:24 What are the requirements for using the model rabbi trust?

The following requirements must be met in order to obtain the tax benefits that the model rabbi trust provides:

1. The model language contained in Revenue Procedure 92-64 must be adopted verbatim except where substitute language is expressly permitted. Additional sections not inconsistent with the model language may be added.
2. The trust must be valid and its terms enforceable under state law.

3. The trustee must be an independent third party that may be granted corporate trustee powers under state law, such as a bank trust department.

4. The trustee must be given some investment discretion, such as the authority to invest within the broad guidelines established by the parties. [Rev Proc 92-64, 1992 CB 422]

Surety Bonds

Q 19:25 How are surety bonds used in connection with nonqualified deferred compensation arrangements?

Surety bonds are a means by which an employee can protect his or her rights under a nonqualified deferred compensation arrangement. If the employer cannot meet its obligations under the nonqualified deferred compensation arrangement, the surety will make the payments required by the arrangement. The IRS has held that an employee receives no current taxable income when the employee purchases a surety bond from an independent insurance company to protect his or her deferred compensation. [Ltr Rul 8406012] If the employer pays the premium on the surety bond, the premium will be treated as compensation paid to the employee, and the deferred income may also be currently taxed to the employee.

Secular Trusts

Q 19:26 What is a secular trust?

A secular trust is another type of irrevocable trust that holds assets for the benefit of one or more employees to pay promised deferred compensation. In contrast to a rabbi trust, the assets of a secular trust cannot be reached by the creditors of the employer. Because trust assets cannot be reached by the employer's creditors, a substantial risk exists that secular trusts will be considered funded for purposes of Title I of ERISA. If this occurs, certain reporting, disclosure, vesting, fiduciary, and other requirements may have to be satisfied.

A secular trust can use a graduated vesting schedule that complies with Title I of ERISA, but vesting must occur within specified periods.

Q 19:27 Why is a secular trust used?

The primary reason for using a secular trust is to avoid the risk that the employer will become insolvent. Funds are deposited in a secular trust so that the funding of deferred compensation is protected from claims for payment by the company's creditors.

Q 19:28 What is the tax treatment of a secular trust?

Because the employee's benefit is not subject to the creditors of the employer, the employee is taxed when he or she vests in the benefit. This vesting occurs either at the time the employer makes the contribution or at a later date, when the employee's right to the benefit is no longer subject to a substantial risk of forfeiture, depending upon how the deferred compensation arrangement that the trust accompanies is structured. Because the deferred compensation arrangement is not tax qualified, the employer is unable to protect employees from taxation until retirement. [IRC § 402(b)] As a result, the employer sometimes agrees to pay an additional amount to the employee equal to the tax on the amount the employee must report as current income (including the additional amounts paid to the employee to compensate for the taxes he or she incurs). This additional amount is treated as compensation. The employee obtains a tax basis in the benefit equal to the amount reported as taxable income.

Under some circumstances, highly compensated employees who participate in a secular trust may receive less favorable tax treatment than non-highly compensated employees who participate in such trusts. To qualify for tax-exempt status under Code Section 501(a), a trust must meet the requirements of Code Sections 401(a)(26) and 410(b). Code Section 401(a)(26) states that the plan must benefit the lesser of 50 employees of the employer or 40 percent or more of all employees of the employer; Code Section 410(b) requires that the plan benefit a percentage of nonhighly compensated employees equal to at least 70 percent of the highly compensated employees who benefit from the plan. If these requirements are not met, the amount currently included in an employee's income depends on whether the employee is a highly compensated employee as defined in Code Section 414(q). A highly compensated employee must include in gross income an amount equal to his or her vested accrued benefit, rather than the value of the employer's contribution to the trust. [IRC §§ 402(b)(1), 402(b)(2)(A); Treas Reg § 1.402(b)-1(a)(1)] Consequently, a highly compensated employee who is fully vested (see Q 19:35) in his or her benefit will always have a tax basis in the vested benefit equal to the value of his or her accrued benefit under the deferred compensation arrangement. A highly compensated employee will also be taxed on the value of any earnings that increase the value of his or her benefit, even though the trust is also taxable on the same earnings. [IRC § 402(b)(2)]

Although the trust will not be subject to income tax on unrecognized gain or on tax-free buildup in the cash value of life insurance contracts, the highly compensated employee will be taxable on both because the gain or buildup increases the value of the employee's benefit. [IRC § 402(b)(2)]

In contrast, when a non-highly compensated employee's benefit becomes substantially vested, that employee reports income equal to the employer's contribution to the secular trust on the employee's behalf. Consequent earnings and gains on the employer's contributions to a secular trust on behalf of a non-highly compensated employee will not be taxed to the employee when the employee becomes vested in them pursuant to the terms of the nonqualified deferred compensation arrangement.

Because secular trusts are primarily established to benefit key employees, most of them are likely to fail to satisfy the requirements of Code Sections 401(a)(26) or 410. As a result, highly compensated employees will be subject to less favorable tax treatment than non-highly compensated employees under the rules described above.

Q 19:29 When does the employer receive a deduction for amounts contributed to a secular trust?

The employer receives a deduction for amounts contributed to the secular trust at the time the employee is required to include the benefit in gross income. This deduction is available only if separate accounts are maintained for each participant in the plan. [IRC § 404(a)(5)] The IRS has held that separate accounts did not exist when the income generated by the assets in the accounts was paid to the employer or was subject to allocation to the accounts of other participants in the plan. [Ltr Ruls 9206009, 9207010]

Q 19:30 Who is taxed on income generated by secular trust assets?

The employee reports the income on secular trust assets on the employee's own return pursuant to the grantor trust rules if the employee is treated as the settlor of the trust. The employee will be treated as the settlor of the trust if the contributions of the employee are not incidental. Contributions made by the employee are not considered incidental if the employee's total contributions at any date exceed the employer's total contributions. [Treas Reg § 1.402(b)-1(b)(6)] Because the trust income is not taxable to the trust in this situation, the trust cannot obtain a deduction for amounts distributed to participants or their beneficiaries. On the other hand, if the employee's contributions are considered incidental, the trust income will be taxed to the trust. In this case, the trust can obtain a deduction for amounts distributed to participants or their beneficiaries. The deduction, however, will be limited to the distributable net amount for each account.

The IRS has held that Code Sections 402(b) and 404(a)(5) preclude a secular trust from being treated as employer-owned (which would shift the tax on the income generated by the trust to the employer), even though the employer was entitled to receive income generated by assets held in the accounts of participants who were not in pay status. [Ltr Ruls 9206009, 9207010, 9212019, 9212024]

Q 19:31 How are distributions from a secular trust taxed?

The IRS has held that distributions from a secular trust are taxed under Code Section 72, which deals with the tax treatment of annuities. That section provides that amounts received in the form of an annuity are includible in the recipient's taxable income to the extent they exceed a pro rata portion of the employee's investment in the contract. The employee's investment in the contract as of the annuity starting date is generally (1) the aggregate amount paid in by the employee less (2) the aggregate received under the contract before that date to the extent such amount was excludable from gross income. Code Section 72 further provides that amounts received before the annuity starting date are includible in gross income to the extent that the value of the employee's vested accrued benefit exceeds the employee's basis. This means that the potential tax burden is imposed on the first payments made from the trust.

Example 19-4: An employee who has a vested accrued benefit in a secular trust of $100,000 and a basis in the trust of $20,000 receives a payment of $40,000 before the annuity starting date for the plan. The entire amount of the distribution is taxable to the employee.

Under these rules a senior executive who is classified by the Code as a highly compensated employee and who receives benefits from a trust that fails the Section 401(a)(26) test should recognize no income because his or her basis in the trust should always equal the value of the assets in the trust, at least to the extent he or she is vested. (The employee's basis in the trust equals the highly compensated employee's accrued benefit because the employee is subject to tax on the amount of his or her vested accrued benefit.)

ERISA Implications

Q 19:32 How does Title I of ERISA apply to nonqualified deferred compensation arrangements?

Title I of ERISA applies to all pension plans, including plans that are not designed to qualify under Code Section 401(a). These pension plans are established or maintained by employer or employee organizations or both that either provide retirement income to employees or result in a deferral of income until the termination of covered employment or beyond. [ERISA § 3(2)(A)]

Q 19:33 Does Title I of ERISA apply to excess benefit plans?

Excess benefit plans, if unfunded, are exempt from ERISA. [ERISA § 4(6)] The Department of Labor (DOL) has stated that excess benefit plans that do not have mandatory employer contribution provisions are not funded for purposes of ERISA, even if a rabbi trust is used to pay the benefits. [DOL Adv Op 92-13A (May 19, 1992)] If an excess benefit plan is funded, ERISA will, correspondingly, apply.

Q 19:34 Does ERISA apply to top-hat plans?

Yes, in part. Top-hat plans are unfunded plans for management and highly compensated employees. Such plans are exempt from the participation, vesting, funding, and fiduciary rules of ERISA, but are subject to reporting and disclosure requirements. They can satisfy the ERISA reporting and disclosure requirements by a one-time filing of a statement with the DOL that sets forth the name and address of the employer, the employer identification number, a declaration that the employer maintains one or more such plans, and the number of employees in each plan. [DOL Reg § 2520.104-23] The DOL has stated that top-hat plans are not funded for purposes of Title I of ERISA, even if a rabbi trust is used to pay the benefits. [DOL Adv Op 92-13A (May 19, 1992)]

Q 19:35 What are the ERISA vesting requirements?

The vesting requirements under Title I of ERISA are similar to those under the Code for tax-qualified plans. [IRC § 411] Under Section 203 of ERISA, a plan must guarantee 100 percent vesting after five years of service or vesting according to the following schedule:

Years of Service	Percentage Vested
3	20
4	40
5	60
6	80
7	100

A special rule applies to participants in a collectively bargained multiemployer plan.

Chapter 20

Personal Investing

Retirement planning also includes personal investing. This chapter begins by discussing capital gains and moves on to investment principles. A variety of commonly asked, and not so commonly asked but equally important investment questions are answered. The needs of two types of investors, small business owners and executives, are considered; the majority of the questions apply to both categories, however. Finally, guidance is given for selecting the right professional to manage an individual's asset needs.

Overview	20-1
Capital Gains and Losses	20-2
Investment Principles	20-7
Investment Terms and Concepts	20-8
Tax-Qualified Retirement Plans	20-16
Choosing an Investment Advisor	20-19

Overview

Q 20:1 How does personal investing relate to estate planning?

Investing should be an integral part of estate planning. With proper selection and diversification of investment goals, investors can assure themselves of retirement income as well as a buildup of wealth. If the investment time horizon will be longer than three years, investment planning should be considered during the estate planning process.

Capital Gains and Losses

Q 20:2 Why is the tax rate for capital gains important to consider when planning for retirement?

One of the key concepts of retirement planning is the preservation of financial assets. This includes taking advantage of favorable tax treatment. Tax planning for individuals should include consideration of capital gains because tax rates on capital gains are presently less than those on ordinary income. Long-term capital gains are taxed at a maximum of 28 percent, whereas ordinary income is taxed at a maximum rate of 39.6 percent. (The cap on capital gains for corporations is 35 percent.)

Q 20:3 What are capital gains and losses?

Capital gains and losses result from taxable sales and exchanges of capital assets held six months or more. There are two categories of capital gains or losses: realized and unrealized. Simply stated, if an asset is sold, there can be an increase or decrease from the original invested amount. If an increase occurs, a capital gain is realized; if a decrease occurs, a capital loss is realized. The amount by which the value of an asset that is not sold increases or decreases on an open market is the unrealized gain or loss.

Q 20:4 What are capital assets?

Capital assets include any property except the following:

1. Inventory or other property held for sale to customers;
2. Accounts or notes receivable from the sale of property or generally for the performance of services as an employee or in connection with a business;

3. Depreciable property used in a trade or business;
4. Real estate used in a trade or business;
5. Copyrights, music, books, and similar artistic properties that are (a) created by the taxpayer, (b) produced for the taxpayer, or (c) received by the taxpayer from their creator or a person for whom they were created by gift (or in another way in which the taxpayer was entitled to use the tax basis of the former owner); and
6. Generally, U.S. government publications received from the government other than by purchase at the normal sales price.

Certain items may be difficult to categorize as property for capital gains purposes, which would entitle them to the favorable tax treatment at the lower rate applicable to capital gains. For instance, sales of streams of ordinary income are not entitled to capital gains treatment, but a stream of income may not be easy to identify.

In a recent case, a taxpayer bought and subsequently sold the rights to a best-seller that permitted the taxpayer to (1) produce a play based on the book and (2) get a percentage of the proceeds from a movie based on the book. The court concluded that the right to produce the play was a capital asset, reasoning that there was no equivalence between the amount obtained from selling the right to produce the play and its sale price. On the other hand, the court reasoned that selling the right to receive a portion of the movie proceeds was not the sale of a capital asset because it was in effect a sale of a right to ordinary income. [Commr v Ferrer, 304 F 2d 125 (2d Cir 1962)]

Q 20:5 What are long-term and short-term capital gains and losses?

Long-term capital gains and losses are those resulting from the sale or exchange of capital assets held for more than one year. Short-term capital gains and losses result from the sale or exchange of capital assets held one year or less.

Q 20:6 How are capital gains and losses treated for income tax purposes?

Each year, a taxpayer's short-term capital gains and losses are combined; the result is either a net short-term capital gain or a net short-term capital loss. A similar calculation is performed for long-term capital gains and losses. These two net results are combined and taxed as follows:

1. If the combined result is a loss, the loss may be deducted from ordinary income, subject to certain limits.
2. If there are no net long-term capital gains and if short-term capital gains exceed short-term capital losses, the net gains are taxed like ordinary income.
3. If there are net short-term capital gains and net long-term capital gains, the net long-term capital gains must be separated out. The long-term capital gains are taxed at 15 percent to the extent the taxpayer's ordinary income is insufficient to reach the 28 percent bracket (which starts at $22,100 for unmarried individuals). Any remaining portion of the long-term capital gains is taxed at 28 percent.

Example 20-1: A single attorney has ordinary income of $120,000 in 1993. She also has long-term capital gains of $15,000, long-term capital losses of $3,000, short-term capital gains of $5,000, and short-term capital losses of $2,000. The attorney has a net long-term capital gain of $12,000 and a net short-term capital gain of $3,000. The $3,000 of short-term capital gain is treated as ordinary income. The first $22,100 of the taxpayer's ordinary income is taxed at 15 percent, the next level of income ($22,101 to $53,500) at 28 percent, the third level ($53,501 to $115,000) at 31 percent, and the final level of income (to $123,000, including the $3,000 of short-term capital gains) at 36 percent. The $12,000 of net long-term capital gain is taxed at 28 percent because the taxpayer's ordinary income was sufficient to reach the 28 percent bracket.

Example 20-2: A single student has ordinary income of $10,000 and $30,100 of long-term capital gains from the sale of property. The first $22,100 of the student's income is taxed at 15 percent, including $12,100 of long-term capital gains. The remaining $18,000 of long-term capital gain income is taxed at 28 percent.

Q 20:7 What capital losses cannot be deducted from ordinary income?

Capital losses from the sale or exchange of property generally are not deductible if the sale or exchange is between any of the following:

1. Family members;
2. A corporation and an individual owning more than 50 percent of the corporation's stock (unless the loss is from a distribution in complete liquidation of the corporation);
3. The grantor (creator) and fiduciary (e.g., a trustee) of a trust;
4. A fiduciary and beneficiary of the same trust;
5. A fiduciary of one trust and beneficiary of another trust created by the same grantor; and
6. An individual and a tax-exempt organization controlled by the individual or the individual's family.

Q 20:8 Can gains from the sale of small business stock be excluded from income?

Noncorporate investors can exclude up to 50 percent of the gain they realize from the disposition of small business stock that has been held for more than five years after August 10, 1993. There is a cumulative limit on the gain from any single issuer that the taxpayer may exclude. [IRC § 1202]

Q 20:9 If capital assets are held for personal use, what is the income tax treatment when they are sold or exchanged?

If capital assets held for personal use are sold or exchanged, any gain therefrom is taxable as a capital gain. Losses from the sale or exchange of such property are not deductible.

Q 20:10 What kinds of transactions are accorded special treatment for capital gains purposes?

The following kinds of transactions involving capital assets are accorded special treatment under the Internal Revenue Code (Code) for capital gains purposes:

1. Transactions by securities dealers. [IRC § 1236]
2. Wash sales of stock or securities (a wash sale involves a sale or exchange of securities within a short time in order to create an artificial tax loss). [IRC § 1233]
3. Sale or exchange of bonds and other debt instruments. [IRC § 1233]
4. The sale of certain subdivided real estate that may be considered a capital asset. [IRC § 1237]
5. The sale of depreciable property to a more than 50 percent owned entity or to a trust in which the taxpayer is a beneficiary, if the sale generates a gain. [IRC § 1239]
6. Disposition of stock in an interest charge domestic international sales corporation (DISC) if a gain is generated thereby. [IRC §§ 995-996] Code Section 995(f) requires that each shareholder of a DISC shall pay interest on his or her deferred tax liability. An interest charge DISC is a domestic corporation whose income is predominantly derived from export sales and rentals.
7. Sale or exchange of stock in certain foreign corporations. [IRC § 1248]
8. Transfer of property to a foreign corporation, as paid-in surplus or as a contribution to capital, or to a foreign trust or partnership. [IRC § 1491]
9. Transfer of property to a partnership that would be treated as an investment company if it were incorporated. [IRC § 721]
10. Transfer of appreciated property to a political organization. [IRC § 84]
11. The sale, exchange, or worthlessness of small business stock. [IRC § 1244]
12. The transfer of property from an individual to a spouse or a former spouse if the transfer is incident to a divorce (in general, no gain or loss is recognized at such time). [IRC § 1041]
13. Retiring a debt instrument (amounts received therefrom are generally treated as received in exchange for the debt instrument). [IRC § 1271]

14. The disposition of converted wetland or highly erodible cropland that was first used for farming after March 1, 1986. [IRC § 1257]
15. Gifts of property and inherited property. [IRC §§ 1015, 1014]
16. Corporate liquidations resulting in payments to shareholders.
17. A stock split or stock dividend that results in the receipt of cash in lieu of fractional shares of stock.

Investment Principles

Q 20:11 What are some basic investment principles?

Although there are many opinions about the best way to invest, there do seem to be investment principles that are widely accepted or at least regarded as factors to consider when developing an investment program. These principles include the following:

Maintain liquid assets. A cash reserve can provide a buffer against emergencies. If there is no cash reserve, assets may have to be sold at distress prices to raise funds immediately.

Determine risk tolerance. Different people have different tolerances for risk. Because higher returns are generally associated with higher levels of risk, an individual with a low tolerance for risk may be more comfortable forgoing some returns in exchange for a lower risk level. There are a number of tests that provide some measure of an individual's risk tolerance. In part, a tolerance for risk is determined by economic factors. An elderly widow with a modest savings account should be less tolerant of risk than a young executive earning $200,000 per year. The risk that inflation will increase at a faster rate than asset values is often overlooked. Options such as bank accounts that nominally seem to have no risk are, in fact, not without risk: the rate of inflation can increase faster than the value of those accounts, particularly when after-tax returns are considered.

Minimize taxes where possible. By placing investments in tax-qualified plans or IRAs, an individual can defer income tax on investment earnings until the funds are actually paid to the individual. If the funds are held by the plan or the IRA for a long period of time, the gains can be substantial. There are limits on the amounts that can be placed in tax-qualified plans and IRAs. Additional amounts can, however, be placed in tax-deferred annuities. In evaluating these annuities, it is important to consider fees and commissions charged. Sometimes those expenses nearly offset the gains from tax deferral.

Deposit liquid assets where their earnings will at least match inflation. Investors should consider placing their assets in a money market mutual fund, money market deposit account, bank certificates of deposit, or (for those in high income tax brackets) tax-exempt money market funds. All of these provide relatively good yields and security.

Money market mutual funds invest in such things as large bank certificates of deposit, short-term corporate debt obligations, and government securites. Money market mutual funds permit investors to write checks, although usually the amounts of the checks cannot be less than a minimum amount (e.g., $250). Although money market mutual funds do not provide a guarantee against a loss of principal, their record in protecting principal has been excellent. In evaluating competing money market mutual funds, it is advisable to compare their expenses. Differences in these expenses can markedly affect the return to the investor.

Money market deposit accounts are bank accounts insured by the federal govenment that earn interest rates comparable to money market mutual funds. Their yields tend to be lower than those for money market mutual funds, and they typically limit the number of checks that can be written.

Commissions and other charges are not uniform. Different firms charge different amounts for the same services. Discount brokers are available. Some mutual funds charge commissions (known as loads) for participating in the funds, some do not; moreover, these charges vary from fund to fund. Administrative fees also vary significantly among mutual funds.

Investment Terms and Concepts

Q 20:12 What is an investment time horizon?

An *investment time horizon* is the time during which assets will be in use. This period can extend through the end of the retirement years or through the continuation of the estate.

It is important to understand that the need for investment planning does not end when the assets are put to their intended use (e.g., retirement). The reasons for holding the assets may have changed, but the time horizon should remain throughout the life of the assets. Many people plan for their retirement but fail to plan their investments after they retire.

When an individual retires, the investment objective is likely to change from growth or preservation of principal to production of income. This means that the assets in a retiree's portfolio must produce a certain level of income to meet that individual's financial needs without depleting the principal. One of the largest fears faced by retirees today is that they will outlive their money. To avoid that possibility, investors should never invade principal (the retirement amount) unless it is absolutely necessary.

Example 20-3: An executive, age 45, is planning to retire at age 60. She currently has $1.2 million of investable assets. Because there is a significant period prior to retirement in which to invest, she invests the assets in a blended portfolio consisting of 80 percent stock and 20 percent fixed-income instruments in an attempt to achieve maximum growth potential. Over the next ten years, the portfolio does well and grows to $4.5 million. The executive's retirement is now imminent, and her income and investment needs will change. The portfolio allocation is changed to 30 percent stock and 70 percent fixed-income instruments and continues to grow by an additional $2,225,000 over the next five years.

The executive's lifestyle has expanded to meet her earned income over the years, and her financial planner anticipates that she will wish to continue this lifestyle. The portfolio is allocated to provide 4 percent income for the next 30 years (her expected period of retirement) because it will generate at least 4 percent in income plus additional growth. The executive should be able to live comfortably on the 4 percent income, and her financial planner anticipates that she will never invade the principal and, thus, not outlive her assets.

Q 20:13 What are investable assets?

Investable assets are any monies (currency) that are not needed as current operating capital. They may have a short-term (e.g., six

Q 20:14   Estate and Retirement Planning Answer Book

months) or a long-term (e.g., 40 years) investment time horizon (see Q 20:12).

Q 20:14 What is a portfolio?

A portfolio is another name for a single individual's or company's asset account.

Q 20:15 What is risk tolerance?

Risk tolerance is a term used in the investment industry to describe a particular level of comfort with specific investments. Investors must tolerate a certain amount of risk in order to receive the high returns that are often associated with high-risk investments. Sometimes, a better-than-average chance exists that a high-risk investment will decline in value before (if ever) it increases in value; however, a well-diversified portfolio (holding 30 or more stock and bond issues) will help the investor achieve consistent returns without experiencing significant volatility and also will reduce the inherent risk of equity investing.

Q 20:16 How is risk tolerance measured?

Brokers and investment managers often have clients complete questionnaires to determine their levels of risk tolerance. A better gauge, however, is simply the client's degree of knowledge about the inherent risk factors of the investments. The more knowledgeable an investor becomes, the more comfortable he or she will be with risk tolerance and portfolio diversification.

Q 20:17 What is tax-free investing?

Tax-free investing produces income from the investment that is never taxed. The most commonly used vehicle for tax-free investing is municipal bonds because the interest earned on them generally is not subject to federal or state income tax. The instruments are backed by the particular municipality that offers them, so familiarity with the balance sheet of the issuing city is just as important as familiarity with the finances of a company in which a client is planning to invest. Municipal investing is not without its pitfalls; some municipalities have been known to default on their bonds.

Q 20:18 What is an investment policy statement?

An investment policy statement (IPS) is a statement specific to an investor's needs and goals that clearly states the type of investments that should be placed in an investor's portfolio; the investor's income requirements, if any; and which issues, if any, should be excluded. The IPS clarifies the investor's financial position and goals for the investment manager who will be investing on the client's behalf.

Q 20:19 What is compounding?

Compounding is earning interest on both the principal amount and the interest already accrued on that amount (see Tables 20-1 and 20-2).

Q 20:20 What are compounded annualized returns?

Compounded returns are the principal amount plus the interest already earned. Compounded annualized returns consist of the annual growth rate over a specified number of years needed to achieve the compounding value.

A compounded annualized return should not be confused with an average annual return. As indicated in Tables 20-1 and 20-2, compounding adds another dimension to earning money. An illustration of noncompounded returns may help in understanding this concept.

The aggregate (average) return and a compounded annualized return for the total assets in Year 4 displayed in Tables 20-1 and 20-2 are as follows:

$157,505.18
    Average annual return = 16.68%
    Compounded annualized return = 16.35%

$150,050.00
    Average annual return = 16.68%
    Compounded annualized return = 14.48%

Table 20-1. Noncompounded Return

Initial investment	$100,000.00
Growth of assets in Year 1 ($11,500.00)	11.5%
Total assets in Year 2	$111,500.00
Initial investment	$100,000.00
Growth of assets in Year 2 ($9,250.00)	9.25%
Total assets in Year 3	$120,750.00
Initial investment	$100,000.00
Growth of assets in Year 3 ($29,300.00)	29.3%
Total assets in Year 4	$150,050.00

Table 20-2. Compounded Return

Initial investment	$100,000.00
Growth of assets in Year 1 ($11,500.00)	11.5%
Total assets in Year 2	$111,500.00
Growth of assets in Year 2 ($10,313.75)	9.25%
Total assets in Year 3	$121,813.75
Growth of assets in Year 3 ($35,691.43)	29.3%
Total assets in Year 4	$157,505.18
A difference of	$ 7,455.18

Q 20:21 What is the difference between a broker and an investment manager?

A stockbroker must broker something to earn a commission (see Q 20:26). Whenever a broker buys or sells something, a commission is incurred and must be paid by the investor. Accordingly, commissions received by the broker increase as the volume of buying and selling increases; if assets are not touched, no commissions are generated. In contrast, investment managers charge fees that are a percentage of assets for managing the assets, regardless of how many individual purchases or sales occur. Fee schedules vary, but the normal schedule is 1 percent of assets up to $1 million, 0.75 percent of assets to $3 million, and 0.5 percent of assets over $5 million. As the schedule indicates, the more the assets grow, the more compensation the manager receives.

Q 20:22 What is discretion?

Discretion is the authority to trade (buy or sell) within an account without the client's prior permission. Brokers must secure the authority of the client before each and every transaction to purchase or sell any issues in his or her account. Investment managers who have been given discretion over their clients' accounts may trade the issues as they deem necessary.

Q 20:23 What is the difference between equity and fixed income?

Equity, or stock, represents a contract between the issuing corporation and the owner that gives the owner an interest in the management of the corporation, the right to participate in its profits, and, if the corporation is dissolved, a claim upon the assets remaining after all debts have been paid. According to the New York Stock Exchange, an individual who owns a share of stock owns a share of the business. The value of the stock may fluctuate based upon the performance of the business or for other reasons (e.g., economic upturns and downturns, rumors or fears about a stock exchange).

Fixed income, also known as bonds, refers to such items as certificates of debt issued by corporations, municipalities, and the U.S. government and its agencies. These instruments bear a stated interest rate that is payable periodically until the instrument matures at a fixed price on a stated future date (maturity date).

The salient difference between stocks and bonds is the ability of stocks to participate in the growth of the company. Because bonds (debts) have a stated interest rate, this fixed income is less volatile.

Q 20:24 What is the difference between Treasury bills, Treasury bonds, and Treasury notes?

Treasury bills, bonds, and notes are differentiated by the length of time each one is to be held. Treasury bills are short-term investments that mature in 60 or 90 days. Treasury notes are slightly longer-term and will mature in three to five years. Treasury bonds are the longest debentures offered by the U.S. government, with maturities that range from 5 to 30 years. Although these types of securities have stated maturity dates and interest coupons that are paid throughout the time they are owned until the maturity date, there is a secondary (open) market for Treasury bills, bonds, and notes; thus, they can be readily sold at any time.

If a bond is held in a Street name, it is automatically liquidated on the date of maturity. Investors who actually hold these bonds have a statutory period of limitations in which to redeem them; however, interest will cease to be paid as of the maturity date.

Q 20:25 What are asset classes?

Investment asset classes are any of the following: domestic stocks, domestic bonds, international stocks, international bonds, or tangible assets. These classes, which are quite broad in nature, can be defined more specifically; for example, domestic stocks can be divided into value stocks, growth stocks, market-oriented stocks, or small capitalization stocks.

Q 20:26 What is a commission?

Commissions are charges for conducting transactions. If a client has stock to sell on the open market, for example, a broker will sell it, and, in fact, must sell it for the client. The fee charged for doing so is a commission.

Q 20:27 What is an investment advisory fee, and how is it different from a broker's commission?

An investment advisory fee is a payment made to a money manager in exchange for the manager's investment experience and advice, similar to a fee paid to an attorney or an accountant. A broker's commission is only generated from the buying or selling of an investment, and the commission reflects neither the broker's expertise and experience nor the wisdom of the purchase or sale from which it derives.

Q 20:28 What is bundling?

Bundling is aggregating costs and fees into one set fee. This may include money management fees, transaction costs, custodial fees, monitoring fees, and administration costs.

Unbundling is separating fees and costs. Unbundling assists in determining what the actual costs are for each service.

Bundling can prove expensive for investors who are unfamiliar with all of the specific costs and services provided by an investment manager. Such investors should carefully read the marketing literature and the prospectus or contract. If any of the fees are unclear, investors can request an accounting of the fee.

Q 20:29 What is a wrap fee?

An all-inclusive fee is commonly referred to as a wrap fee. For one set fee, all of the client's separate fees—including the money manager's fee, the custody fee (if any), broker transaction fees (buy and sell commissions), reporting fees, and monitoring fees—are paid for. The current range for wrap fees (determined annually) is 2.25 percent to 3 percent of the value of the investment account. It takes an extremely active investment manager, trading the portfolio very regularly, to earn fees equal to the wrap fee. Many investors come out ahead if they choose to have the manager direct individual transactions to the broker and pay the resulting commission fees as they arise. Some managers' transaction fees may be as low as 0.30 percent annually. This means that the monitoring must have a value of 0.95 percent to the client.

Management fee	=	1.00%
Transaction costs	=	.30%
Wrap fee	=	2.25%
		2.25
		−1.30
Monitor fee	=	.95

Tax-Qualified Retirement Plans

Q 20:30 Should employees be given the opportunity to direct their investments?

Professionals in small professional corporations often wish to direct their own investments. In larger companies, management sometimes believes that morale will improve if employees are given the opportunity to direct investments with a resulting increase in productivity; however, when employees assume responsibility for directing investments, it often creates additional administrative complexity and expense for employers. Furthermore, investment decisions may be questionable. In many cases, the investment decision is better left to the company official who has the most experience in this realm.

A 401(k) savings plan (a type of tax-qualified retirement plan) allows an employer to shift almost all of the fiduciary responsibility for directing the investment of employee monies to the employees. Employees are supplied with information about their investment choices and are expected to design an investment program specific to their individual needs. Unfortunately, the information supplied by the retirement plan administrator to employees is often confusing. Furthermore, many employers erroneously believe that by allowing employees to direct their own investments, they will be relieved of all fiduciary liability. This presumption is inaccurate; residual liability remains, even if a plan provides for investment direction.

Q 20:31 What resources should an investment advisor have?

An administrator and an investment advisor must be able to share on-line access to certain information, including an employee's personnel data (e.g., date of hire, years of service), investment choices (e.g., switches among investment options, if offered), and other information such as valuation of accounts and sales of plan assets. Having on-line data available will help the investment advisor streamline plan administration and make the process of gathering necessary data less expensive.

Q 20:32 What are the different types of accounts (portfolios) an investor should have?

There are four different options that investors should look at for inclusion in a portfolio: (1) equities, (2) fixed income (bonds), (3) international, and (4) derivatives.

Equities and fixed income (bonds) have been discussed previously (see Q 20:23). The international asset class includes the equities and fixed income instruments of both industrialized nations and third-world emerging markets. Derivatives include the highly volatile issues of futures, options, and commodities.

Portfolios may consist of any of these investment options. Typically, portfolios are described as equity (all stocks and/or derivatives), fixed income (all bonds), or balanced (a blend of both equity and fixed income).

Q 20:33 Under what circumstances should an investor have an equity account, fixed-income account, or balanced account?

A number of factors must be considered before deciding which type of portfolio should be developed. These include the following:

1. Risk tolerance or avoidance. (Can the individual tolerate significant declines in portfolio value?)
2. Current income considerations. (Is the individual receiving income from another source such as employment, pension, or government entitlements?)
3. Liquidity needs. (Is the individual planning to buy a house with the funds in the next year or so?)
4. Stability of valuations. (Is invasion of principal—the initial invested amount—acceptable to the individual?)
5. Maintenance of purchasing power. (Purchasing power is the individual's protection against inflation.)
6. Total return. (This includes income dividends or interest as well as netting out fees.)
7. Time horizon. (This includes the time until the individual retires, life expectancy, and expected occurrence of other major life events.)

Other factors will contribute to the development of the initial investment portfolio that are specific to the plan sponsor or employer and will come to light as investment sophistication increases.

Q 20:34 When should a mutual fund (an open-ended investment company) be used in place of an individual stock/bond portfolio?

The primary consideration is the size of the asset base with which a client is working. Many investment managers have minimum account sizes of $1 million or more. The large brokerage houses have coordinated their efforts with some investment managers and, by using economies of scale, have been able to lower the minimum asset base that managers will require from their clients to as little as $250,000 or even $100,000. Those investment managers do not really offer individual money management in the traditional sense; rather, the investment manager used by the brokerage firm often will have a so-called clone account for brokerage firm clients because the investment manager cannot achieve a level of diversification with any meaningful impact for the portfolio. More accurately, individual money management begins to be conducted for accounts with asset bases of $500,000 or more.

Mutual funds also can offer diversification through large economies of scale. Because these funds represent a pool of investors, mutual funds can purchase blocks of stock or bonds in round lots (100 shares or more). An initial cost savings can be realized because investors will not incur an odd-lot share cost. Clients will also save on commissions to the investment manager because large blocks are being purchased. A client can use a variety of funds to achieve not only diversification among stocks and bonds, but also among manager styles. Investors should steer clear of investing entirely within one family of funds. Even with good performance in general, all the managers in a family of mutual funds are subject to the same rules and company policies. By choosing funds from different families of funds, diversification is increased and risk can be avoided.

Choosing an Investment Advisor

Q 20:35 What are the different investment manager styles?

There are eight widely recognized investment styles, as follows:

1. *Income.* The primary goal in security selection is to achieve a current yield significantly higher than the Standard and Poor's (S&P) 500 Index. The stability of the dividend and its rate of growth are also of concern to the income buyer.

2. *Value.* The primary motivation is to select securities based on known information. This information may take the form of price/earnings screens or screens for various financial characteristics. In a P/E screen, "P" is today's price and "E" is the trailing 12 months' earnings. This style is frequently associated with a strong emphasis on discipline based on the forgoing selection methods. At times, a value manager may use earnings projections; however, these projections frequently occur after the screening process has been completed.

3. *Core/Growth.* These terms, while not synonymous, are used here to describe management strategies that have a common style: they typically do not buy overly aggressive stocks but do rely heavily on earnings forecasts. This is a style that is usually devoid of extremes—not too much income and not too much risk. An investor who wishes to place all of the fund's assets with one manager is likely to select this style.

4. *Timers.* This management style places more emphasis on asset allocation than on stock selection. The primary decision is whether or not to own stocks and to what extent the total portfolio should be committed.

5. *Contrarians.* Using this style, managers purchase stocks that are currently out of favor with the investment community. These are usually stocks of companies that are cyclically out of favor while still being leaders in their industries. Some contrarians, however, will automatically purchase stocks on the new low list regardless of industry leadership or quality.

6. *Rotators.* Here, primary emphasis is on finding industries that will outperform the market as a whole. This style begins with a top-down approach that requires managers to make projections and forecasts on general economic conditions. This macro approach leads rotators to over- or underweight certain industries that are consistent with their economic scenarios. The industry categories are filled with the individual stocks believed to be the strongest in each industry.

7. *Aggressive Growth/Small Caps.* As the name suggests, managers with this style tend to buy stocks that have a high degree of price volatility. This is a bottom-up approach—the primary motivation for buying a particular stock is inherent in the stock itself. Managers with this approach are stock pickers. There may or may not be any similarities in the methods used by one or another of these stock pickers. Some buy based on price momentum or earnings momentum or (in addition to other factors) changes in the way a company is perceived.

8. *Index.* The primary purpose is to replicate the performance of the market. An example would be a market value-weighted index such as the S&P 500 Index.

Q 20:36 How is the performance of an investment manager or mutual fund reviewed?

Performance is the most difficult of all aspects of investing to monitor. An entire segment of the investment industry is devoted to the evaluation of investment managers, indexes, and funds. The Association for Investment Management and Research (AIMR) published guidelines and standards to assist the investor in determining manager performance. Many investment managers have adopted those guidelines and present their performance figures in compliance with the published standards, but some have not. The most simplistic evaluation of an investment manager's performance is to take the fund balance at the beginning of the period and subtract it from the ending balance (taking into consideration contributions, withdrawals, and fees). This calculation should give a rough estimate of the performance for that period (quarter, semiannual, annual). If the figure does not match the investment manager's own representation of its investment management performance, the investment manager should be requested to review the figures, in writing, to assist in deriving the performance figures. Whether the figures are net or gross of management fees and expenses (i.e., calculated before or after such fees and expenses are subtracted) must also be determined.

Mutual fund performance is more difficult to ascertain. The mutual fund will report the net asset value for the period, and, although those figures will be reported net of expenses, they will not net out management fees. Investment evaluation services such as Morningstar and Lipper both produce information on mutual funds and make it easier to assess the performance of a specific fund (and they offer comments regarding the pros and cons of these funds).

An important consideration is to compare the performance of the fund currently under consideration against funds or investment managers that have similar investment strategies and philosophies. The following list of indexes can assist when making such comparisons. Because these indexes do not include management fees or transaction costs, these costs must be netted out of the index to produce a true comparison.

Russell 1000	Value Managers
Standard & Poor 500	Value Managers
Dow Jones Industrial	Value Managers
Lipper Growth & Income	Growth and Income Managers
Russell 2500	Growth Managers
Lipper Equity Income	Value Managers
MSCI EAFE Index	International Managers
Lipper International	International Managers
Lipper Real Estate	Real Estate (REIT) Managers
NAREIT Equity	Real Estate (REIT) Managers
Lehman Brothers Aggregate Bond	Fixed Income Manager
Salomon Brothers three-month Treasury Bills	Money Market Fund

Q 20:37 How does an investor evaluate the costs of an investment manager or a mutual fund in view of the performance of the portfolio?

Investment managers are generally expected to outperform the management fee significantly (that is, the net return is expected to be significantly higher than the management fees charged). An investment manager who is unsuccessful over a sufficient period of time should be replaced.

Q 20:38 What factors should be considered in deciding whether to hire an investment manager or use mutual funds?

There are several reasons to consider hiring an investment manager rather than choosing a mutual fund. An investment manager is going to buy issues specific to the needs and goals of the client. An investor will not own a unit (as in a mutual fund), but will own 200 or 300 shares of an actual stock or other investment vehicle.

An investment manager is cognizant of the needs and goals of a client. While mutual funds have specific styles and strategies similar to those of individual investment managers, they cannot be concerned with an individual's needs, such as those of an employee who will be retiring in the near future or one whose daughter is heading for college. The mutual fund, by its very nature, is a pool of investors' assets managed collectively for the intent of the fund. Investment managers, on the other hand, offer more personalized service in structuring an investment approach (within a spectrum of investment philosophies and disciplines) to address needs and goals. They design individualized portfolios, taking into account the client's risk tolerance, liquidity, income needs, and a variety of additional pertinent information. These professionals are constantly reviewing the investments in specific portfolios and adjusting the allocation of assets and types of investments accordingly.

Recently, some investors have expressed a desire not to invest in specific issues or industries. Physicians sometimes wish to avoid tobacco stocks or issues of questionable benefit; environmentalists may wish to find companies that have both a good balance sheet and are sensitive to the impact their products have on the environment. This so-called socially responsible investing can be found in some mutual funds, but an investment manager can tailor the portfolio to the client's needs.

There are, of course, drawbacks to hiring an investment manager. Like mutual funds, investment managers have defined investing styles. Those styles are likely to rotate in and out of favor with different market conditions. All markets are cyclical in nature: stocks or bonds do not go up all the time. Given an expected rotation of styles, a manager who had good or above average performance last year or several years in a row is likely to experience below average returns in the following one or more years. This is simply a function of market trends. A manager's style can be in phase or out of phase for an extended period, which is when unwary, unsophisticated investors learn hard lessons.

Most managers who use a value-oriented investing style are naturally cautious managers: it often takes a long time (six to eight months) to fully invest assets, so a client should plan to have a long and comfortable relationship with the manager. It can be expensive and frustrating to change managers more often than every three years. A long-term relationship will provide the manager with the opportunity to invest assets, allow the assets to perform as expected, and educate the client concerning the manager's investing process and style. Most managers will encourage an open dialogue with their clients, and they should also provide the opportunity to speak directly to the portfolio manager handling the account.

Q 20:39 Why not use certificates of deposit or other investments provided by banks?

Although some banks have hired prominent investment managers, banks are not regulated by the same authority as are other investment managers and therefore are not required to divulge the same information regarding performance numbers. Historically, banks have managed their clients' assets with a focus only on preservation of principal. They continue to have certificates of deposit (CDs) for a finite period of time, at a specific interest rate. When interest rates are very low, CDs are unattractive for investors with more than a six-month time horizon.

One must always consider the economics of inflation and its impact on future purchasing power.

Example 20:4: In 1994, a loaf of bread costs $1.00. Also in 1994, a tailor invests $1.00 in a ten-year CD earning 4 percent. Ten years later, with an average inflation rate of 4 percent (inflation has averaged 3.5 percent from 1920 to 1993), a loaf of bread costs $1.48. Luckily, the CD matures and $1.48 is available to buy the bread. If the tailor wishes to purchase butter to go with his bread, however, he is out of luck.

It is not only essential that investments exceed the inflation rate; it is vital to have a portfolio grow at a rate significantly higher than inflation (in Example 20:4, the portfolio growth rate should be 8 percent).

Q 20:40 What is the harm in earning less than the inflation rate if the money is safe?

Over a long period of time, the purchasing power of money will erode. Whether the assets are intended to be used for retirement, travel, or bequests, the investment return must exceed the inflation rate over an extended period of time in order to maintain purchasing power.

Table 20-3 shows what happened to the value of $1.00 from 1960 to 1980:

Table 20-3. Inflation: 1960–1980

1960	$1.00
1965	.94
1970	.78
1975	.57
1980	.37

Q 20:41 What is the difference between mutual funds purchased from a broker and those purchased directly from the fund company?

A mutual fund purchased from a broker includes a *sales load*, that is, a sales commission. Many brokers believe that they follow these mutual funds more closely than individuals could, and often they are correct. Using the Morningstar Report or other investment reports currently available, however, close monitoring may be something individuals can do for themselves. A critical factor in properly reviewing investments is the amount of time that must be spent in researching and analyzing data, and some investors prefer having a broker monitor and review investment opportunities because of the time involved.

Q 20:42 Why would a broker recommend an investment manager?

Investment managers and brokers are not in competition with one another. If a broker feels that it would benefit a client to have an investment manager, the broker often will assist the client in evaluating those managers who have an affiliation with the broker's firm to find the best match (or matches) with the client's investment needs. A client's lack of sophistication, time, or availability may constitute good reasons for considering an investment manager.

Q 20:43   Estate and Retirement Planning Answer Book

It is important to emphasize that brokerage firms have been able to put downside pressure on managers' minimum investment requirements. This is not always in the client's best interest. For example, if $100,000 is invested with one manager, that amount may not allow the manager to diversify properly within the portfolio. Small portfolios simply become clones of one another and can be equated to a mutual fund, which might be a less expensive alternative. It would be wise to give the manager sufficient capital, if it is available, to make a difference in the individual's portfolio.

A broker can be of tremendous service in evaluating clients' needs and matching them to specific managers. The broker will be compensated by receiving directed trades and custody of the account, as well as continued contact with clients.

Q 20:43   Why pay a wrap fee?

Investors who engage extremely active managers would do well to pay a wrap fee. If a manager with a less active buy/hold strategy is employed, the wrap fee generally is not advisable. It is impossible to forecast how active a particular manager will be in any given situation (owing to the stock market's cyclical nature). Knowing that commission charges are prepaid under a wrap fee arrangement provides some comfort to the investor. Investors who expect to change managers frequently may find the wrap fee will help defray the costs associated with any moves, because the new manager may decide to liquidate the old portfolio and incur transaction charges (buying and selling fees).

Q 20:44   Are bonds purchased commission-free?

No. Bond prices already reflect a built-in commission. Usually the commission is approximately 0.1675 percent for institutional trades, but it might be much higher for retail buyers. This commission is rarely disclosed, and investors who want to know the commission charge must request a breakdown of specific charges.

Q 20:45 When should investors pick individual stocks for a portfolio?

Investors should pick individual stocks when they feel comfortable about a specific company's balance sheet and management team. Investors who plan to build a portfolio of individual issues (stocks or bonds) should diversify among asset classes and industry classes (sectors). It is important to be aware of the characteristics of the issues intended for purchase. For example, putting utility stock issues and bond issues in the same portfolio is not a proper diversification because both of those asset classes are sensitive to changes in interest rates. If the interest rate increases, the value of both of the issues will decline; the performance of one will not counterbalance the negative performance of the other.

Another consideration is the time factor. It takes a lot of time to monitor and invest in an individual portfolio. To some investors, investing is a hobby, and they do very well at understanding the nuances of investing properly in a portfolio. There are also "armchair investors" who take a small portion of their investable assets and invest in highly speculative ventures. The entire invested portion can be lost in a day, however.

Q 20:46 How can a portfolio be diversified?

When a portfolio is diversified, the assets can show a mixed response to a specific investment environment. A selection of at least 30 different stock or bond issues should be placed in the portfolio. Among the general guidelines used by professionals are that no more than 5 percent should be invested in any one company and no more than 10 percent in any one sector.

Another option is to use available mutual funds. The inclusion of several different types of mutual funds or funds with different styles is important to achieve balance within the portfolio. Adding a fixed-income mutual fund to reduce the volatility of a portfolio may also be desirable. This is an area where a full-service broker could assist the individual investor in developing asset allocation among mutual funds.

Q 20:47 What is the advantage of using pretax dollars for investing purposes?

Using pretax assets benefits investors because they start out with more investable capital. If a tax-qualified retirement plan is used, income earned by its assets (income that would otherwise be used to pay taxes) is compounded on a tax-free basis while the assets remain in the plan. The secret to taking advantage of such compounding is to leave the money invested in the plan and not withdraw it prior to retirement (see Tables 20-4 and 20-5). This does not necessarily mean that the assets must remain locked into the original investments; rather, the money remains in the qualified retirement plan.

Table 20-4. Compounding Interest

Year	$ Investment	$ Value @ 10%	$ Investment	$ Value @ 10%
1	0	0	2,000	2,000
2	0	0	2,000	2,000
3	0	0	2,000	2,000
4	0	0	2,000	2,000
5	0	0	2,000	2,000
6	0	0	2,000	2,000
7	0	0	2,000	2,000
8	0	0	2,000	2,000
9	2,000	2,200	-0-	27,675
10	2,000	4,620	-0-	30,442
20	2,000	47,045	-0-	78,960
25	2,000	89,198	-0-	127,165
29	2,000	140,806	-0-	186,183
30	2,000	157,086	-0-	204,801
TOTALS	44,000	157,086	16,000	204,801

Table 20-5. Comparison of After-Tax and Pretax Savings

After-Tax Savings		Pretax Savings
1.00	$ Earned	1.00
−.28	Taxes	-0-
.72	$ Saved	1.00
.75	Year 1: 6%	1.06
.79	Year 2: 6%	1.12
.83	Year 3: 6%	1.19
.87	Year 4: 6%	1.26
.90	Year 5: 6%	1.34
.95	Year 6: 6%	1.42
1.00	Year 7: 6%	1.50
. . .	. . .	. . .
1.25	Year 12	2.00

Q 20:48 How does a financial planner differ from a stockbroker?

A financial planner helps design an individual's investment plan. Stockbrokers may also assist in formulating an investment plan, but they are more focused on creating trades.

Fee-only financial planners design investment plans using a variety of asset classes (Q 20:25) and/or insurance products.

Commissioned financial planners, who are similar to stockbrokers, design investment plans using the type of investments for which they receive a commission. The inherent risk to investors is that the commissioned financial planner may design a plan using those investments on which the planner receives the highest commissions, regardless of whether such investments are appropriate for the investor's needs.

Some financial planners charge a fee to design a plan that includes products for which they will also receive a commission, such as investment or insurance products managed by the company with which the investment manager is affiliated. In ascertaining the total fees paid, it is important to keep the issue of compensation versus service in the forefront.

A stockbroker can serve as a clearinghouse for investments (some also offer a wide range of insurance products) and can provide individuals with information about estate or pension plans. Generally, however, brokers are order takers, solicitors, and salespersons, not individually oriented financial planners.

Q 20:49 How would an insurance agent assist with investments?

Insurance agents may be able to introduce the individual investor to a wide variety of investment products because insurance companies have some quite sophisticated investments. Insurance products often, however, have loads (sales commissions), high transaction and managerial costs, back-end loads (commissions charged if the investor withdraws funds before a specified time), and surrender charges (for withdrawing the initial investments before a defined period of time). These charges may make it difficult to cancel an insurance contract and reinvest the assets in some other type of investment. Discount insurance agents are available in some geographic areas, however. Some of these discount insurance agents accept an hourly fee rather than a commission.

Despite the possibility of insurance loads hampering investment flexibility, insurance has a place in estate planning. One of the primary functions of insurance is to provide the liquidity needed for estate taxes.

Q 20:50 What is the difference between a stockbroker who is also a consultant and other stockbrokers or individual consultants?

A broker who is also a consultant can assist in determining the client's investment needs and goals. The broker will also provide myriad investment options and will receive a commission on any investments the client agrees to make. Another facet the broker/consultant brings to the table is the ability to assist in reviewing investment managers. This may not be an altogether objective review, however, especially if the portfolio is not paying a wrap fee (see Q 20:29). Some brokers have attempted to switch managers for clients because a particular account is not trading (and providing broker commissions) often enough.

A true consultant receives compensation only for the information and service he or she provides. Fee-based consulting may be the best alternative for investors who cannot find a stockbroker they trust.

Q 20:51 Who can be a trustee?

A trustee is a person who has been charged with the responsibility of reviewing investments and monitoring performance. Often the treasurer, CFO, or investment committee are named as the trustee of an organization.

There are also firms that can be hired to be the trustees. Some single-source provider mutual funds and banks offer trusteeship, and some attorneys will take on that role.

Q 20:52 What is the advantage of having fees unbundled?

Unbundled fees allow the investor to see exactly what fees are paid and how these fees were incurred. If an investment manager is retained and a bank is the account custodian, three separate fees will be incurred: one for the investment manager, one for broker commissions, and one for the bank. If these fees are bundled into a wrap fee, only one fee will be apparent to the investor.

Many single-source providers (large mutual funds or investment houses) have a bundled fee for providing their in-house administration and investment funds as well as for their service as custodian of the funds. The best way for an investor to learn about the fee schedule is to ask the contact person to spell out, in writing, what each fee is. Investors may want to request the information by letter, even if they have a prospectus. Prospectuses are difficult to read if one is not familiar with them. Even with the advent of user-friendly examples, fee schedules may still be confusing.

Q 20:53 Should a broker be granted discretion on an account?

Discretion is the ability to trade (sell or buy issues for a portfolio) without the client's explicit permission for each trade. Money managers are registered investment advisors (RIAs) with the SEC and have passed a series of examinations to indicate their ability to manage assets. Managers are granted discretion because they trade accounts to benefit the client and do not benefit directly from the trades themselves (they do not receive a commission). Clients sign an authorization that provides the investment manager with blanket authority over the trading activities of the account.

A broker who requests discretion may in fact be acting as an investment manager. There is an inherent conflict of interest, however, especially if the manager brokers the trades, because there is always the opportunity to trade accounts just to generate commissions. For this reason, investors must be careful when authorizing such discretion. If, in fact, discretion is granted to the broker, it is important to ascertain that the broker holds an RIA license.

Q 20:54 What are soft-dollar fees?

Soft-dollar fees are trades that are used to pay for a variety of items through trading activity reimbursement for these items. Soft-dollar arrangements are typically double the cost of the item. For example, if an investor hires a consultant through a brokerage firm, a broker may indicate his or her willingness to arrange for soft-dollar compensation to pay the consulting fee. This arrangement will be provided through the managers the broker recommends. Those managers will make any portfolio trades within the account through that particular broker. Again, double the amount in soft-dollar trades is usually required to offset the original fee. As the trades must be done, however, an investor may benefit by having the trades pay for the consulting fee.

If used wisely, soft-dollar trades can be a prudent use of trading dollars.

Q 20:55 What are sectors, and where are they found?

Sectors are categories of potential investments that are characterized by major industry groups. There are nine industries (sectors) defined within the S&P 500 Index and numerous subsectors:

1. Capital goods;
2. Consumer durables;
3. Consumer nondurables;
4. Banking and finance;
5. Energy;
6. Intermediate goods;
7. Raw materials;
8. Transportation; and
9. Utilities.

Chapter 21

Business Transfers

The transfer or sale of a business can be an important source of retirement funds and funds for payment of estate taxes. Indeed, because of the limits on the amount of benefits that can be provided by tax-qualified retirement plans, assets from the sale of a business may be the primary source of retirement benefits and funds for future generations. A business transfer can be effected either by sale of the business to outsiders or by transfer of ownership to insiders. The adroit division of a business may result in estate tax savings and may reduce family conflict.

Overview	21-2
ESOPs	21-2
Sales to Outsiders	21-5
Buyouts	21-9
Stock Redemptions and Direct Sales of Stock	21-12
Stock Sales	21-13
Sales of Assets	21-14
Stock Split-Offs and Spin-Offs	21-19

Overview

Q 21:1 Why are business transfers important to retirement and estate planning?

Transfer of a business is a useful means of accumulating a large amount of wealth. For an entrepreneur, the sale of a business may be the sole source of retirement funds. This wealth can, in turn, be used for retirement, for estate funds, or for the payment of estate taxes. Skillful division of a business can result in substantial tax savings. A business transfer can also be used to augment any funds available from tax-qualified retirement plans. This becomes important if those funds are modest.

Q 21:2 What is basis?

Basis is an important factor when selecting from the different methods of transferring a business. It is the baseline for the amount of the proceeds from the transfer of an asset that will be subject to taxation and the baseline for measuring loss in value as well. Any sale proceeds in excess of the basis amount will be taxed as gain. Similarly, if proceeds from the sale do not reach the basis, the difference between the two amounts represents loss. Thus a high basis is often desirable because less of the asset's value will be subject to taxation.

An individual's basis in a particular asset is the acquisition cost assigned to that asset for income tax purposes. Acquisition cost is the consideration paid for the asset by the purchaser. [Treas Reg § 1.1060-1T(b)(1)] In most situations, gain and loss are measured by the cost of the asset to the purchaser; however, special rules apply when determining the basis of property acquired by gift or through inheritance. An individual's basis in an asset will be increased by, for example, capital improvements and reduced by depreciation.

ESOPs

Q 21:3 How can an ESOP be used in succession planning?

An employee stock ownership plan (ESOP) has the following advantages:

1. *Tax-free rollovers.* If the ESOP owns at least 30 percent of the outstanding shares of the corporation after a sale of stock to the ESOP by the departing owner, the sale proceeds will not be currently taxable to the owner if he or she invests them in the domestic stocks or bonds of certain qualifying companies within a specified 15-month period. This 15-month period begins three months before the sale date and ends 12 months after the sale date. [IRC § 1042(c)(3)] Any domestic corporation can be a qualifying corporation except for the corporation that issued the ESOP stock and corporations that are operated solely for investment. [IRC § 1042(c)(4)] The owner's basis in stock for tax purposes is reduced by the as yet untaxed amount equal to the increase in value of the stock since the date the ESOP first acquired the shares, called unrecognized gain. Despite this reduction, the rollover transaction gives the owner two important advantages. First, it permits the owner to exchange his or her stock in the company for a more diversified and presumably less risky portfolio. Second, in contrast to a stock redemption (see Qs 21:19, 21:20), the owner has more proceeds to invest because there is no initial imposition of taxes.

Example 21-1: The owner of a medical supply company sells his stock back to the company (a redemption) and has a gain of $1 million on the redemption. If the owner is taxed at a rate of 39.6 percent, he pays $396,000 in taxes and keeps $604,000. He can then invest the $604,000. In contrast, if the owner sells the stock to an ESOP and then uses the proceeds to make a tax-free rollover, the owner has the full $1 million gain to invest in a stock or bond portfolio. If the owner holds this portfolio until his death, no income tax will be paid on the $1 million gain. Should the owner sell a portion of the portfolio prior to death, he will be taxed on the unrecognized gain in the value of the shares sold at that point. Nonetheless, he will have had the use of the full $396,000 up until that point and will continue to earn income on the portion of the $396,000 that corresponds to the remaining portion of the portfolio.

2. *Tax-favored borrowing.* In a conventional ESOP, the ESOP borrows money to purchase employer stock from the employer. As loan payments become due, the employer makes deductible

contributions to the ESOP and thus, in effect, receives a deduction for principal payments as well as for the interest payments. Furthermore, if the ESOP owns more than 50 percent of each corporate class of stock or more than 50 percent of the value of all outstanding stock, half of the interest earned by the lender (e.g., the bank) on the loan to the ESOP is excluded from income. This makes ESOP loans attractive for banks, insurance companies, actively engaged lending corporations, and regulated investment companies, and permits the ESOP to negotiate for lower interest rates than would otherwise be the case. [IRC § 133]

3. *Dividend deduction.* Corporations can deduct dividends paid to an ESOP trust holding the employer stock to which the dividends relate, and the ESOP trust passes the dividends through to participants. [IRC § 404(k)]

4. *Employee morale.* By giving employees a share of the company, ESOPs are thought to promote morale. There is anecdotal evidence to support this assertion. Because ESOP shares are allocated proportionately to compensation, highly compensated employees tend to benefit most from an ESOP.

In addition to the advantages that ensue from the use of an ESOP, the following consequences may be of concern to some owners:

1. An ESOP has the potential to alter a company's response to certain events. Employees holding shares in an ESOP have the right to vote on the following corporate transactions:

   — Mergers

   — Consolidations

   — Recapitalizations

   — Liquidation of the business

   — Sale of the business or of substantially all of its assets

[IRC § 409(e)(3)]

2. If new stock is issued to an ESOP, the interest of the existing shareholders is diluted; if stock is purchased from existing shareholders, their interest in the corporation is also diminished.

3. An ESOP trust must be able to purchase employer stock from retiring employees if the employees wish to sell the stock to the ESOP trust.

4. The creation of an ESOP will terminate a corporation's subchapter S election. [IRC § 1361]

Sales to Outsiders

Q 21:4 How can a transfer of the business to an outside party be structured?

The transaction can be structured either as a taxable sale or as a tax-free transaction involving the exchange of stock for stock in the acquiring company. One risk in obtaining the stock of the acquiring company is that securities law may require that the stock in the acquiring company be held for a fixed period of time and, as a result, the value of such stock may go down before it can be sold.

Q 21:5 Is a stock sale preferable to an asset sale?

Buyers generally prefer asset sales. An asset sale exposes the buyer to fewer liabilities because the liabilities of a company are generally not transferred to the buyer when an asset sale occurs. In contrast, a buyer of stock will inherit the liabilities of the selling company by operation of law. The buyer can reduce this risk to some extent by indemnification agreements and representations and warranties in favor of the buyer. These may be difficult to enforce, however, or the buyer may lack sufficient resources to back up the representations or warranties.

In addition to considering which form of transaction (stock or asset sale) is preferable based upon the assets and liabilities that can be retained or transferred to the buyer, the seller must also consider the tax effect of each type of transaction from a retirement and estate planning perspective. The seller of a C corporation will usually prefer a stock sale if all else is equal because the seller is taxed only once. Furthermore, the seller may be able to avoid current taxation by structuring it as a tax-free exchange (see Q 21:3). An asset sale, on the other hand, results in income taxation when the assets of a C corporation are sold and again if the corporation is liquidated. In contrast, if the assets of an S corporation are sold and the S corporation is liquidated, only one tax is imposed when the stock is sold. One strategy for the owners of a C corporation contemplating an asset sale is to attempt to elect S corporation status, but this may not always be possible.

Q 21:6 How is a sale of stock taxed?

Corporate shareholders usually are taxed on gain or loss when they sell their stock at the capital gains rate of 28 percent instead of the higher rate applicable to ordinary income, providing the stock has been held for more than one year. If the corporation is a collapsible corporation, income from the sale of shares by its shareholders will be taxed as ordinary income. [IRC § 341(b)(1)] Generally, a collapsible corporation is a corporation that is intended to convert ordinary income into capital gains through the liquidation or early sale of the stock. To prevent this result, however, Congress enacted Section 341 of the Internal Revenue Code (Code), which requires that certain income items that would otherwise be treated as ordinary income be treated as capital gains. A collapsible corporation must be formed or used primarily for the manufacture, construction, or production of property or for the purchase of assets defined in Code Section 341 (generally inventory, receivables, or depreciable property used in the trade or business) with a view to sale, liquidation, or distribution *before* both of the following occur:

1. The corporation has realized two thirds of the taxable income to be derived from the property, and
2. The shareholders have realized the gain attributable to the property.

[IRC § 341(b)(1)]

Example 21-2: A corporation is created to make a movie about grizzley bears. The movie is a hit and the royalties start to appear. At that point, the owners of the corporation decide to sell their stock. It is possible that this corporation might be treated as a collapsible corporation and that the gains on the sale to the selling shareholders are taxable as ordinary income.

Q 21:7 Is an exchange of stock preferable to an asset or stock sale?

Instead of purchasing stock or assets, an acquiring company might offer to exchange its stock for stock in the company being acquired. In such a stock exchange, the buyer will get the seller's basis plus the gain recognized in the assets. [IRC § 362(b)] If, however, the fair market value of the selling firm's assets is higher than its basis in those assets, the buyer will tend to prefer an asset sale to an exchange of stock because the buyer of assets will get the sales price of the assets as his or her basis in the assets. [IRC § 1012] The higher basis permits the buyer to obtain additional depreciation. It is not necessary that these benefits be captured by the buyer. These tax benefits can be wholly or partially passed back to the seller through an appropriate increase in the price if an asset sale is agreed to by the seller.

On the other hand, if the expected sale price for the assets is lower than the seller's tax basis in the assets, the buyer may prefer to exchange stock. Because a stock exchange allows the buyer to use the seller's basis in the assets for depreciation purposes, the buyer obtains a higher basis under these circumstances by electing a stock exchange over an asset sale.

Q 21:8 Can a buyer obtain an increased basis with a stock sale?

Yes, in certain circumstances. If it acquires at least 80 percent of the voting power and at least 80 percent of the value of the stock of the acquired corporation within 12 months, the purchasing corporation can make an irrevocable election under Code Section 338 to treat the acquisition of stock as a purchase of assets of the acquired corporation. If it makes that election, the purchasing corporation will have a basis in the acquired corporation's assets equal to its basis in the acquired corporation's stock. [IRC § 338] It is not necessary that the newly acquired subsidiary be liquidated; the acquired corporation that makes a Section 338 election will be treated as if it sold the assets of the newly acquired subsidiary for an amount equal to the purchasing corporation's basis in the stock (if the purchasing corporation owns less than 100 percent of the stock, a technical adjustment is made to take this into account), and the acquired corporation

Q 21:9 Estate and Retirement Planning Answer Book

recognizes the gain or loss associated with the election. Recognition of gain or loss under Code Section 338 occurs when the corporation first purchases the stock. [IRC § 338(a)] Because the corporation can make the election any time within nine months and fifteen days of its first stock purchase, the gain or loss is, in effect, retroactively recognized for tax purposes. [IRC § 338(g)(1)]

Q 21:9 What can be done with unwanted assets in a business?

If the corporation owns assets that are unattractive to buyers, it may experience difficulties in finding a buyer at the time the owners wish to sell the business. The following options can be used if a business contains unwanted assets:

1. The unwanted assets can be distributed to the shareholders, and the company can then be sold. Such distributions will probably be treated in the same manner as dividends, which means that the corporation will not get a deduction for, and the shareholders will incur income tax on, the proceeds.

2. The unwanted assets can be sold off piecemeal by the corporation, and the cash obtained can be distributed to the shareholders. The company can then be sold. The distribution of cash will probably be treated as a dividend.

3. Unwanted assets can be distributed to a controlled subsidiary, or a controlled subsidiary can be created and unwanted assets can be distributed to it. In a controlled corporation, another corporation, the parent, owns stock possessing at least 80 percent of the total voting power of the controlled corporation. [IRC § 1563(a)(1)] The parent corporation can distribute shares of stock in the subsidiary to the shareholders of the parent corporation in a spin-off transaction. If done correctly, the transaction will not result in income tax. At the conclusion of this transaction the shareholders of the parent corporation will hold shares in both the parent and in the subsidiary. Assuming the costs of the reorganization are not excessive, this option is preferable to the first option in this list because the unwanted assets are removed from the business that is being sold without the imposition of income tax.

Q 21:10 What other items need to be considered in selling a family business?

Members of the family will need to consider protection of their positions within the company if they wish to continue working in the business under its new management. If they do not wish to remain with the business or the new owner does not need them, family members need to protect their ability to continue to work in the same type of business. The new owner may be concerned with retaining individuals who are the driving force of the business or with being able to draw on their expertise if necessary. As well, the new owner may be concerned about members of the selling family engaging in a competing business. Sales of family businesses are often accompanied by employment, noncompete, and consulting agreements. These agreements often provide for accelerated payments to the seller if the buyer does not perform.

Q 21:11 When selling a business, what are the advantages of creating a family limited partnership?

Sometimes it is desirable to create a family limited partnership to hold business real estate. The business real estate can be retained and leased to the new owners, and the limited partnership can shift rental income to different family members. The lease can be designed so that the real estate can be sold to the new business owners upon the occurrence of certain events. The sales price can be based on the appraised value of the property at the time of the sale of the business as opposed to the later date of the actual sale of the property. This protects the seller against a decline in property values, although such a strategy can be disadvantageous if the property appreciates. It also gives the seller residual assets should the business fail before the purchaser of the business purchases the real estate.

Buyouts

Q 21:12 What constitutes an inside group?

An inside group comprises key employees and family members active in the business.

Q 21:13 How is a buyout used to sell the business to insiders?

A buyout by insiders transfers ownership of a departing owner's share of the business to an inside group by using business assets and earnings to pay for that share.

Q 21:14 What kinds of devices can be used to pay the departing owner?

The departing owner can be compensated for giving up the business by several methods that can be used alone or in combination, including stock redemptions, supplemental nonqualified pension agreements, employment agreements, consulting agreements, and noncompete agreements. These methods can help spread out the payments over time, thereby reducing the tax burden on the departing owner and the strain on the buyer's cash flow; they also may permit the company to obtain a deduction for the payments. The more traditional approach of using a stock redemption may be less effective from a tax standpoint because the company cannot obtain a tax deduction for those payments (see Q 21:19).

A stock redemption can result in capital gain treatment if (1) the redemption is not equivalent to a dividend; (2) after the redemption, the shareholder owns less than 50 percent of the total voting stock; (3) all of the shareholder's stock is redeemed by the corporation; or (4) for a noncorporate shareholder, the redemption is in partial liquidation of the corporation. [IRC § 302(b)]

Q 21:15 How is a noncompete agreement used in an insider buyout?

A noncompete agreement compensates the departing owner in return for not starting up or obtaining employment in a competing business for an agreed upon period after the buyout. It can be structured so that the departing owner receives yearly payments over a five- to ten-year period. The payments are taxable as ordinary income to the recipient and are a deductible expense for the company at the time they are made. The noncompete agreement must be differentiated from the redemption of stock so it is not treated by the Internal Revenue Service (IRS) as a stock redemption and cannot include any amount that constitutes payment for company goodwill. The noncompete agreement must be economically realistic in terms of the seller's age, skills, health, and ability to compete with the company.

Q 21:16 How is a nonqualified deferred compensation arrangement used in an insider buyout?

If future company earnings are to be used to pay a seller, a deferred compensation arrangement may be advantageous because the payments are deductible to the corporation. A nonqualified deferred compensation arrangement can be structured to provide for payouts over a fixed time period such as five years. If no trust is used, the payments are taxable to the departing owner when received and deductible by the company at that time. Sometimes, however, the departing owner wants the security that the payments will be made, particularly if he or she is concerned that the company might fail under the new management. If a trust is used to provide this security, the tax treatment is more complex.

Q 21:17 How can employment agreements and consulting agreements be used in an insider buyout?

Employment agreements and consulting agreements permit the departing owner to exchange services for compensation. The compensation paid must be reasonable in relation to the services provided. The employment agreement may be for full- or part-time employment. If a consulting agreement is used, the former owner will be an independent contractor and will be responsible for paying employment taxes. Because an employer pays a portion of employment taxes (i.e., FICA, FUTA, Medicare surcharge) and an independent contractor pays all employment taxes, a consulting agreement results in the former owner incurring a greater income tax burden.

Q 21:18 How can a rabbi trust be used in an insider buyout?

A seller who is concerned about the security of deferred compensation payments might want to have a rabbi trust created in connection with the deferred compensation arrangement. Money can be set aside in a rabbi trust to fund the deferred compensation arrangement for the seller. Deposits to a rabbi trust remain corporate assets but can only be reached under limited circumstances (e.g., if the company becomes insolvent). Payments from a rabbi trust are taxable to the recipient when received and deductible by the company at that time.

Stock Redemptions and Direct Sales of Stock

Q 21:19   What are the tax effects of a stock redemption?

A stock redemption occurs when a corporation repurchases stock held by a selling shareholder. The purchase price is usually at fair market value or at a price determined by a shareholder's agreement. The purchase price is often paid over time. A shareholder who has all of his or her stock redeemed will recognize gain equal to the amount received less his or her basis unless there is attribution of ownership pursuant to Section 318 of the Code (see Q 21:21). If there is attribution of ownership, the payment may be treated as a dividend. The basis of other shareholders in the corporation will not be affected. The corporation may not deduct amounts paid in a redemption. [IRC § 162(k)] For this reason, it is sometimes desirable to use employment or consulting agreements in connection with a transfer of ownership because payments made pursuant to such agreements may be deducted by the corporation when made. [IRC § 162(a)]

Q 21:20   What are the advantages of a stock redemption?

A direct sale of stock to insiders or to a purchasing corporation may not be possible because the acquiring shareholder may lack the funds to purchase the stock. Accordingly, a stock redemption (whereby the business repurchases its stock already owned by the acquirer) may be the only choice. Unlike the creation of an ESOP, a stock redemption will not terminate an election of S corporation status.

Q 21:21   What is family attribution?

The family attribution rules provide that shares of stock owned by spouses, children, grandchildren, or parents are deemed owned by the shareholder. The family attribution rules are significant if a redemption occurs because they may cause the selling shareholder to lose capital gains treatment upon the redemption of stock. [IRC § 318(a)(1)]

Stock Sales

Q 21:22   What is a direct sale of stock?

A direct sale of stock is a sale of stock from one shareholder to another.

Q 21:23   What advantages does a direct sale of stock have over a stock redemption?

A direct sale of stock between shareholders results in the purchaser obtaining a basis in the stock equal to the purchase price. An increased basis may be beneficial if the corporation subsequently distributes additional assets. In a redemption, the shareholders' basis is unchanged. If the stock redemption is funded with life insurance, the insurance proceeds may cause the corporation to incur alternative minimum tax. This will not occur with a purchase of stock funded by insurance proceeds.

Q 21:24   What arrangements should be made for the stock of a key employee if the key employee dies, becomes disabled, or terminates employment?

Spouses of key employees often have little knowledge of the business and, in the case of professional corporations, may not be able to be shareholders in the company. They may also, for whatever reasons, be difficult to deal with personally. Nonetheless, a spouse may inherit stock in the company when a key employee dies. To avoid having to deal with the spouse of a deceased key employee, the majority owner of a company can implement a repurchase agreement that covers this contingency, as well as disability or termination of employment. The repurchase agreement can provide a set price for the stock and thus avoid disputes over the valuation of the stock. Such an agreement gives a key employee a market for his or her shares of stock and also provide liquidity for his or her estate.

Sales of Assets

Q 21:25 Should all assets be sold in an asset sale?

Asset sales permit the buyer and seller to select which assets and liabilities will be transferred to the buyer and which of them will be retained by the seller. One approach is to sell operating assets and retain those assets that are not needed to operate the business, such as receivables, excess cash, and real estate. The real estate can be leased to the new owners. The new owners can either pay cash for the operating assets or else make a cash down payment and give back a note.

Q 21:26 How is an asset purchase financed?

An asset purchase can either be financed by a bank through a bank loan or by the selling corporation. The selling corporation can finance the purchase by entering into an installment sale in which payments are made over a period of time (e.g., five years).

Q 21:27 How is goodwill treated in an asset sale?

Goodwill is the excess of the purchase price of the assets over their value and is attributable to such intangibles as good customer relations, a well-recognized company name, and other attributes that make the business valuable and enhance its potential long-term success. Tangible assets (e.g., equipment) are depreciated, while intangible assets (e.g., goodwill) are amortized. [IRC §§ 167, 197] Depreciation and amortization have different time schedules. In an asset sale, the Code requires buyers and sellers to classify the assets of a business into different categories and determine the fair market value of the assets. One category consists of intangibles, like goodwill, and this category is assigned the residual value of the purchased assets (the purchase price of the entire business minus the fair market value of all other assets). [Treas Reg §§ 1.1060-T1(d)(1), 1.1060-T1(d)(2)] This information is reported to the IRS on Form 8594.

Q 21:28 What happens if assets are sold that were depreciated under an accelerated method?

If the assets sold were depreciated under an accelerated method permitted by Section 168(b)(1) of the Code instead of straight-line depreciation permitted by Code Section 168(b)(3), the sale may result in the excess depreciation (that is, the excess over the amount that would have been allowed had straight-line depreciation been used) being recaptured and imputed to the seller as ordinary income. This will happen if the sale price of the asset exceeds the adjusted basis of the depreciated property. [IRC § 1245(a)]

Q 21:29 What are the advantages of an asset sale?

Purchasers often prefer an asset sale because it can limit their liability for the past actions of the selling corporation. In contrast, a stock sale results in the purchaser acquiring by operation of law the liabilities of the corporation whose stock is sold.

Q 21:30 How can a tax-qualified retirement plan be used with an asset sale?

If the asset sale is accompanied by the lease of real property and equipment, the selling corporation will have income from the lease. The former owner can continue as an employee of the selling corporation, whose job is to manage corporate assets. The corporation can also set up a defined benefit pension plan for the owner. Assuming the owner is the only employee left so that all plan benefits accrue to him or her, it may make economic sense to create a tax-qualified retirement plan for the owner. Further, it may be possible to credit the owner with his or her past service in designing the plan so that substantial contributions have to be made on the owner's behalf.

Example 21-3: A businessman sells the operating assets in his company for $1 million and leases equipment and real estate used in the business to the new asset owners for $150,000 a year. The businessman continues as the owner of his old corporation and pays himself a salary of $30,000 a year for his activities as manager. If no tax-qualified retirement plan is established, the old corporation will be taxed on the remaining $120,000 per year. If, however, the old corporation establishes a defined benefit pension plan for the businessman and bases his benefit on his prior years of service to the company, a large amount, such as $100,000 a year, can be contributed to the defined benefit pension plan on behalf of the businessman, and the corporation pays income tax on the remaining $20,000. The benefit provided by the defined benefit pension plan in this example is expected to be worth $1 million in the next eight years. Because of the tax-deferred compounding of interest, the $100,000 per year contributed to the plan is expected to be sufficient to fund that benefit.

Q 21:31 What are the income tax consequences if a sale of corporate assets is followed by a liquidation of the selling corporation?

The impending retirement of the owner of a small business may result in a sale of assets followed by a liquidation. This will occur, for example, if the potential buyer of the business will only buy assets because of a concern about the transfer of liability. If the selling corporation is a C corporation, gains or losses occur at the corporate level when the assets are sold, regardless of whether a simultaneous liquidation occurs. On liquidation, gain or loss is also recognized at the shareholder level. Prior to the passage of the Tax Reform Act of 1986 (TRA '86), the rule under *General Utilities and Operating Co. v. Helvering* [296 US 200 (1935)] provided a method of selling corporate assets and simultaneously liquidating the corporation in which gain was not taxed at the corporate level and, thus, was taxed only once at the shareholder level. This concern does not arise for S corporations because gains are not taxed at the corporate level but are instead passed through to the shareholders, who then receive an increased basis. This basis increases the potential gains to the shareholders when they receive a distribution of assets from the liquidation of the corporation.

Q 21:32 What alternatives to liquidation exist if a C corporation sells its assets?

The following methods can be used to avoid the double taxation associated with the liquidation of a C corporation:

1. The stock of the C corporation can be contributed to a charitable remainder trust. The trust can liquidate the corporation and only pay tax at the corporate level. The shareholders can receive a charitable deduction for their contribution and can receive income from the trust for the remainder of their and their spouses' lives. At their death, the trust donates the principal to charity.

2. Nonqualified retirement plans can be used to take money out of the corporation.

3. The stock in the C corporation can be exchanged for stock of the acquiring company in a tax-free exchange. If the acquiring company is publicly held and traded on a stock exchange, the seller can liquidate the stock and diversify his or her investments. This liquidation may result in tax, but double taxation is avoided because there is no tax at the corporate level.

Q 21:33 Should a C corporation be converted to an S corporation if it is contemplated that the C corporation will sell its assets?

The attraction of converting a C corporation to an S corporation if an asset sale is contemplated is the avoidance of the double tax that can occur if a C corporation sells assets. A double tax occurs because when a C corporation sells assets it is taxed on the gain from the sale. If the sale proceeds are distributed to shareholders, a second tax may be imposed. In contrast, if an S corporation sells assets, the income tax burden falls on the shareholders, but it is imposed only once. If a C corporation is converted into an S corporation, the following tax issues arise, however, if the S corporation subsequently sells assets.

Q 21:33   Estate and Retirement Planning Answer Book

1. *Built-in gains tax.* A special tax on built-in gains applies if a corporation makes an election to become an S corporation after December 31, 1986. The S corporation is potentially liable for the tax if it has gains on the sale of assets within ten years from the first day of the tax year it became an S corporation. The effective result is that the S corporation is treated as if it were a C corporation for this purpose. The amount of the tax is determined by multiplying the highest applicable corporate tax rate by the net recognized built-in gains for the S corporation for the tax year. [IRC § 1374 (b)(1)] Recognized built-in gains are gains recognized by an S corporation upon the disposition of any asset except to the extent the corporation can show either the asset was not held by the S corporation at the beginning of the first tax year that the current S election is in effect, or the recognized gain on the asset is greater than the excess of the fair market value of the asset at the beginning of the first tax year over the adjusted basis of the asset at that time. These gains are offset by recognized built-in losses to determine net recognized built-in gains. [IRC 1374(d)(3)]

2. *Corporate tax preference.* The corporate preference reduction rules under Code Section 291 apply if the S corporation was a C corporation for any of the three preceding years. [IRC § 1363(b)(4)] These rules generally provide that the tax benefit derived from certain tax preferences, including Section 1250 property (i.e., depreciable property), is subject to a 20 percent reduction (30 percent in some cases). [IRC § 291]

Furthermore, passive income limitations may make conversion of a C corporation into an S corporation undesirable. S corporations that have accumulated earnings and profits from a prior C corporation are subject to passive income limitations. [IRC §§ 1362(d)(3), 1375] These corporations need to moniter their passive income (e.g., debt income) for two reasons:

1. If passive income for a taxable year exceeds 25 percent of gross receipts for the year, a tax on excess net passive income may be imposed under Code Section 1375(a). The tax is imposed at the highest corporate rate.

2. If the 25 percent limit is exceeded for three consecutive tax years, the corporation's S status will terminate at the beginning

of the next tax year under Code Section 1362(d)(3). An inadvertent termination of S corporation status for this reason can be waived by the IRS under Section 1362(f) if certain conditions are met.

Stock Split-Offs and Spin-Offs

Q 21:34 What is a stock split-off?

In a pure split-off, one owner retains an ownership interest in the original company and no stock in a newly formed company while another owner gives up all of his or her stock in the original company in exchange for shares of a newly created corporation. A split-off does not result in income taxation if all of the following requirements are met:

1. The division of the business has a valid business purpose;
2. Immediately after the division, both corporations conduct a valid trade or business;
3. The original business that is divided was actively conducted before the split-off occurs;
4. The parent corporation distributes all of its stock in the newly formed subsidiary and gives up all its interest in the new corporation; and
5. The distribution of the stock in the new corporation must not be a device for distributing earnings and profits.

[IRC § 355]

Example 21-4: An engineer and a lawyer own a company in the health food business with two locations. The engineer and the lawyer cannot agree whether the health food business should stock vitamin E and decide to split up the business. To do this, they create a subsidiary of the health food corporation and transfer one store into the subsidiary. The lawyer then gives up all of his stock in the original company in exchange for all the stock in the new subsidiary. After this transaction, the engineer owns 100 percent of the original company, and the lawyer owns 100 percent of the newly formed corporation. Each is then free to go his or her own way.

Q 21:35 How can a split-off help in succession planning?

A split-off can help in succession planning by permitting the owner to divide the company between two rivals so that each is free to develop his or her own business approach.

Example 21-5: A toy manufacturer's son and daughter work in the business. Each owns 10 percent of the company's stock. The daughter has been with the business for ten years and expects to become CEO when her father retires. The son, after pursuing a variety of interests, decides to try business and has been involved in the business for five years. A rivalry develops between the son and daughter over who will run the business when their father retires. To avoid further acrimony, the father creates a subsidiary to manufacture electronic games. The father then exchanges stock in the original company equal to 30 percent of the total for 75 percent of the stock in the new subsidiary, and the son exchanges all of his stock in the original company for 25 percent of the stock in the new subsidiary. The father continues to own about 80 percent of the original company while his daughter owns 20 percent. The father also now owns 75 percent of the stock in the second company while his son owns 25 percent. Son and daughter are now free to develop in the separate businesses, and their father can relinquish control to them at different times if that seems desirable.

Q 21:36 What is a stock spin-off?

In a spin-off, stock in a wholly owned subsidary of a corporation is distributed proportionately to the shareholders of the parent corporation. Those shareholders then hold stock in both corporations.

Example 21-6: A corporation that owns a string of coffeehouses has a wholly owned subsidiary that makes designer coffee cups. The parent corporation is owned by a 25 percent shareholder and a 75 percent shareholder. The shareholders in the parent corporation decide that the coffee cup business would grow faster if divorced from the coffeehouse business. Seventy-five percent of the stock in the coffee cup corporation is distributed to the 75 percent shareholder of the parent corporation, and 25 percent of the stock in the coffee cup corporation is distributed to the 25 percent shareholder.

Q 21:37 How can spin-offs be used to reduce estate taxes?

If a portion of the business is rapidly growing, estate taxes may be reduced by spinning off that portion of the business.

Example 21-7: A family owned dairy products company is headquartered in Ohio but has a fast-growing Florida subsidiary run by the family's oldest son, who owns 10 percent of the company. The Ohio portion of the company is stable but not growing. To minimize estate taxes, stock in the Florida subsidiary is distributed to all shareholders. Once this occurs, the parents have 90 percent of the stock in the Florida subsidiary, and the son has 10 percent of the stock in it. The parents can transfer most of the stock in the subsidiary to the son by making gifts using the unified credit. [IRC § 2010] Any future appreciation in the stock of the Florida subsidiary escapes gift and estate taxation. The parents retain control of the Ohio business.

Chapter 22

Individual Retirement Accounts and Simplified Employee Pensions

Individual retirement accounts permit individuals to set aside tax deductible funds toward retirement each year on a tax-deferred basis. This chapter discusses how such accounts are set up and funded, who can make contributions, and how much can be contributed on a tax-deferred basis. Spousal accounts and rollover accounts are also covered. The simplified employee pension, a type of retirement plan that uses individual retirement accounts for funding purposes, is also reviewed.

Individual Retirement Accounts	22-1
Simplified Employee Pensions	22-13

Individual Retirement Accounts

Q 22:1 What are individual retirement accounts?

Individual retirement accounts (IRAs) are individual non-qualified retirement plans similar to employer sponsored retirement plans that allow individuals an opportunity to set up their own tax-favored retirement plans subject to certain conditions and limitations. There are three types of IRAs: individual retirement accounts, individual retirement annuities, and group retirement annuities. An individual retirement account is a trust account established by an individual with a bank, brokerage firm, or similarly qualified firm that acts as a trustee of the investments. An individual retirement annuity is an annuity or endowment contract issued by an insurance company into which an individual pays premiums instead of contributions. Certain types of retirement accounts established by employers also qualify as IRAs.

Q 22:2 What requirements must a plan meet to qualify as an individual retirement account?

An individual retirement account must be established by a written governing document. [IRC § 408(a)] This document must contain the account's terms, the account owner's rights and obligations, and the rights and obligations of the trustee or custodian. There are two IRS-issued forms that may be used to establish an individual retirement account: Form 5305 is used to establish an individual retirement account trust, in which the funds or assets are deposited with a trustee, and Form 5305-A is used to establish a custodial agreement.

An individual retirement account must be created or established in the United States and must be maintained as a domestic trust or custodianship. [IRC § 408(a); Treas Reg § 1.408-2(b)] The document establishing the individual retirement account must contain language prohibiting the funding of the individual retirement account through investment in a life insurance contract. [IRC § 408(a)(3)] Finally, the document must expressly provide that the assets of the trust account cannot be commingled with other property.

Q 22:3 Who is eligible to establish an individual retirement account?

Anyone who receives compensation for work performed in a year, including wages, salaries, commissions, or professional fees, is eligible to establish an IRA. Furthermore, an individual may establish an IRA even if the individual is covered under an employer's retirement plan, subject to certain deduction limits based on the employee's adjusted gross income (or the combined adjusted gross income of the spouses). To be eligible for an IRA, an employee or a self-employed person must have earned income or received compensation for services actually performed by the individual. This earned income or compensation does not include investment income, such as interest, dividends, or capital gains made from investments, nor does it include any amount received as a pension or annuity.

Q 22:4 When may someone establish an individual retirement account?

An individual may establish an IRA at any time prior to the time his or her tax return is due for any given tax year. This rule also applies to spousal IRAs. Once established, the IRA can receive contributions for other years.

Example 22-1: A banker who establishes an IRA on April 15, 1996, can claim as deductions against his 1995 income any tax deductible contributions made into the IRA by April 15, 1996.

Q 22:5 What limits apply to contributions to an individual retirement account?

Limitations apply to (1) the type of property that may be contributed to an IRA, (2) when each year's contribution must be made, and (3) the age at which an individual may make tax-deductible IRA contributions.

What may be contributed to an IRA? All contributions to an IRA must be made in cash (i.e., currency or negotiable instruments) because an IRA deduction is not allowed for contributions of property other than cash. [IRC § 408(a)(1)] An IRA owner may take out a loan to make the contribution as long as the contribution is made in cash. [Pub L No 8617044] A noncash contribution will not disqualify the account or annuity as an IRA, but it will be considered an excess contribution subject to a 6 percent annual excise tax. [Michel v Commr, TCM 1989-670] This excise tax is payable until the excess contribution is withdrawn.

Timing of annual contribution to an IRA. An individual may make a contribution to an IRA for a particular year no later than the date his or her tax return is due for such year (April 15 of the following year). The time for making contributions cannot be extended by obtaining an extension on the filing of an income tax return. The contribution, if it is deductible (see Q 22:7), may be deducted from gross income in Year 1 even though it is not physically deposited in the IRA until Year 2, as long as it is deposited on or before the date that the individual's tax return for Year 1 is filed (and on or before the due date for such filing). [IRC § 219(f)(3)]

Age limit on IRA contributions. No deduction is available for any contributions made by an IRA owner who is over 70½ years of age at the end of the taxable year for which the contribution is made. [IRC § 219(d)(1)] An employer, however, is allowed to make a SEP contribution (see Qs 22:20–22:28) to the IRA of an employee pursuant to the employer's SEP arrangement or agreement, although the employee may have attained age 70½ by the end of the year for which the contribution is made.

Q: 22:6 Does an individual retirement account have to be standardized?

No. It is possible to modify an IRA to meet the individual needs of the IRA owner, provided the bank or financial institution agrees. The chances of a financial institution modifying its standard IRA are greater as the IRA balance becomes greater. As much as $500,000 may be needed for some financial institutions to consider a modification to their standard IRA. A taxpayer may want to have a customized IRA because he or she dislikes the distribution provisions of the standardized IRA or for estate planning purposes. For example, the IRA participant may want to modify the distribution provisions for his or her beneficiaries so that the IRA amounts are not included in the participant's taxable estate because of the operation of the power of attorney rules.

Q 22:7 What is the annual individual retirement account deduction limit?

The annual IRA deduction limit for an individual is the lesser of $2,000 or 100 percent of the individual's annual compensation. This annual $2,000 limit applies whether the contributions to the account were made by the individual or by his or her employer. [IRC § 408(a)]

Effect of participating in an employer's retirement plan. If a person or his or her spouse is covered under an employer's retirement plan, each of those persons may be able to make tax-deductible contributions to an IRA, subject to certain restrictions that apply to individuals who already are active participants in an employer's plan. [IRC § 219(g)(1)] Separate rules apply to determine if an employee is an active participant in a defined contribution plan or in a defined benefit plan. A quick way to determine an individual's active participant status is to check the IRS Form W-2 issued by the individual's employer. If the individual was an active participant for that calendar year, a box should be checked on the Form W-2 to indicate this participation. [IR Notice 87-16, Q&A A-1] The active participant restrictions apply if an individual, or, in the case of a joint return, either the individual or his or her spouse, is an active participant in a simplified employee pension plan; Section 403(b) tax-deferred annuity plan; tax-qualified retirement plan; or federal, state, or local government plan. Persons who are active plan participants may make deductible IRA contributions only to the extent that their incomes fall within certain limits. The full deduction is available for married tax payers filing joint returns if their combined adjusted gross income for federal income tax purposes is less than $40,000. The deduction is decreased under a formula until adjusted gross income reaches $50,000. Once that level is reached, there is no deduction. A contribution is fully deductible for an individual filing a single tax return if his or her adjusted gross income is below $25,000; a partial deduction is allowed if adjusted gross income is between $25,000 and $35,000; and there is no deduction if adjusted gross income exceeds $35,000. [IRC § 219(g)]

Nondeductible contributions. Individuals who are not entitled to a deduction (i.e., persons with adjusted gross incomes that exceed the $35,000 and $50,000 thresholds) are still permitted to make contributions to an IRA. Although the contributions themselves are not tax deductible, the earnings in the account will be tax deferred until withdrawn.

The deduction limits for active plan participants are as follows:

Full IRA deduction	Individual earning $25,000 or less	Married couple earning $40,000 or less, filing joint return	Married, filing separately, full deduction not available
Reduced deduction	Individual earning $25,000–$35,000	Married couple earning $40,000–$50,000, joint return	Married, filing separately, earning $0–$10,000
No deduction available	Individual earning $35,000 or more	Married couple earning $50,000 or more, joint return	Married, filing separately, earning $10,000 or more

Q 22:8 What are the advantages of making tax-deductible individual retirement account contributions?

Tax-deductible IRA contributions offer a number of advantages. The individual who contributes to an IRA may receive a current income tax deduction for the amount of his or her contribution provided certain limits are not exceeded (see Qs 22:5, 22:7). Income from investment earnings and capital gains in the IRA is not taxed currently and will be taxed only when it is actually paid out of the IRA. Over time, this deferral of taxation on the income of the IRA can result in a significant accumulation of income.

Example 22-2: A physician who is a participant in a tax-qualified retirement plan makes an after-tax contribution of $2,000 each year to an individual retirement account beginning at age 35 and continuing until he attains age 60. None of the deposits is withdrawn until the physician reaches age 60, and the individual retirement account investments earn 10 percent per year. The physician is in the 36 percent tax bracket throughout this period. At age 60, the physician will have $196,694 in his individual retirement account ($50,000 in contributions and $146,694 in investment income). When he withdraws the money at age 60, he will have $143,884 after taxes ($50,000 of the amount withdrawn is not taxed because it is a return of the physician's after-tax contributions, and, after income taxes are paid on $146,694 at the 36 percent rate, the sum of $93,884 is available). Had the physician simply invested the money and earned a 10 percent rate of return, he would have had $116,114 at age 60 because the income taxes payable on the investment income each year would have reduced the funds available for future growth.

Q 22:9 Is an individual retirement account available for a nonworking spouse?

Yes, an IRA may be established for a nonworking spouse. If an individual has a nonworking spouse, he or she may contribute an additional $250 into an IRA created for the nonworking spouse. Assuming the couple files jointly, the maximum total contribution to, and deduction for, both IRAs would be $2,250 ($2,000 contributed to the participant's IRA and $250 contributed to the spouse's IRA). [Rev Proc 87-50, 1987-2 CB 647]

A spousal IRA deduction cannot be taken unless one spouse has no compensation or elects to be treated as having no compensation. A spouse with less than $250 in compensation can make an election to be treated as having no compensation in order to establish a spousal IRA. A spousal IRA contribution is deductible only by the contributing, working spouse, and the spouses must file a joint return in order for the spousal IRA contribution to be deductible. Furthermore, a spouse may not make a contribution to a spousal IRA on behalf of a nonworking spouse if the nonworking spouse has attained age 70½ by the end of the taxable year for which the contribution is made. The age of the contributing spouse is irrelevant. [IRC § 219]

A bill pending in Congress would allow a spouse who does not work outside the home a full $2,000 deduction if the combined compensation of the spouses is at least equal to the contributed amount.

Q 22:10 How are excess individual retirement account contributions treated?

Any contribution in excess of the IRA deductible limits is an excess contribution that is subject to an annual nondeductible 6 percent excise tax. [IRC § 4973] The excess contribution is not tax deductible, nor will any income derived on any excess contribution accumulate on a tax-deferred basis. Furthermore, the 6 percent excise tax will continue to apply each year until the excess contribution is eliminated from the IRA.

Once an excess contribution has been made to an IRA, it can be handled in one of two ways: it can be carried forward or distributed.

Carrying forward excess IRA contributions. The first solution is to carry forward the excess contribution (i.e., apply it toward the following year's IRA deduction limit). The taxpayer would treat the amount of the excess contribution as an additional IRA contribution in a later taxable year. In other words, the excess is physically deposited in one taxable year, but it is deducted in a later taxable year. This carrying forward will occur automatically if the taxpayer does not contribute the maximum deductible amount to his or her IRA for a taxable year in which excess contributions remain in the IRA, and the excess will automatically be treated as deductible by Internal Revenue Code Section 219 (whether or not the taxpayer claims a deduction for the carrying forward amount) and thus is no longer subject to the excise tax for excess contributions. This solution is advantageous for smaller amounts of excess contributions because it avoids the need for an actual distribution from the IRA to correct the excess contribution situation. For larger amounts of excess contributions, however, the technique is disadvantageous because it will not be able to correct large amounts of excess contributions quickly, and the 6 percent excise tax will remain payable on the amount of excess contributions which remain in the IRA.

Distribution of excess IRA contributions. The second way to correct excess contributions is to distribute the excess contributions.

Q 22:11 How are individual retirement accounts funded?

There are three basic types of IRAs: individual retirement accounts, individual retirement annuities, and group retirement annuities. An individual retirement account is funded using a written trust or written custodial agreement (the custodial agreement is treated as a trust for IRA purposes [Treas Reg § 1.408-2(a)]). An individual retirement annuity that is issued by an insurance company is an annuity or endowment contract. The premium cannot be fixed, and the annual premium for any individual cannot exceed $2,000. [IRC § 408(b)(1)] Many financial institutions offer IRAs to the public, and many different types of investments can be used to fund IRAs, including common and preferred stock, money market accounts, annuity contracts (excluding life insurance policies), mutual fund shares, certificates of deposit, and bonds.

Q 22:12　How may individual retirement account funds be invested?

Funds contributed to an individual retirement account may be invested in such vehicles as stocks, bonds, annuities, or mutual funds. They may not, however, be used to buy life insurance policies. An individual retirement account may be established with a bank, brokerage firm, or insurance company. The individual owner of the individual retirement account decides how the funds in the account will be invested, and the brokerage firm or bank helps to set up the account and acts as trustee.

Q 22:13　When must distributions from an individual retirement account begin?

IRAs are subject to minimum distribution rules. The entire account balance generally must be paid, or periodic payments must begin, no later than April 1 of the year following the year in which the IRA owner becomes 70½. [Prop Treas Reg § 1.401(a)(9)-1 Q&A F-1(c)] This rule was adopted to encourage the use of IRA funds for retirement and to discourage the accumulation of IRA funds after age 70½. This distribution may be made in the form of a lump-sum payment or periodic payments. The minimum annual distribution is a periodic payment calculated on the basis of a period not exceeding the individual's life expectancy or the joint life expectancy of the individual and his or her designated beneficiary. The designated beneficiary is the person named in the IRA to receive the benefits upon the owner's death. If there is more than one designated beneficiary, the beneficiary with the shortest life expectancy is used for the purpose of measuring the minimum periodic distributions.

Q 22:14   Estate and Retirement Planning Answer Book

The individual retirement account owner must be very careful to meet the minimum distribution rules. If they are not met in any given year, the minimum amount that should have been distributed, minus what was actually distributed, is subject to a 50 percent penalty tax each year until the required excess is distributed. The IRS may waive the 50 percent penalty in cases involving reasonable errors.

Q 22:14   How are distributions from an individual retirement account taxed?

The actual distribution from an IRA to its owner generally is taxed as ordinary income in the taxable year in which the distribution is received by the IRA owner. These distributions are not eligible for capital gains treatment or forward income averaging, even if the IRA has been funded by assets that have been distributed from qualified plans (a so-called rollover IRA). If the contributions to the IRA were deductible when made, the distribution is fully includible in income. If nondeductible contributions have been made to the IRA, a portion of the distribution is treated as a tax-free return of those contributions. The portion of the distribution that is not taxed depends on how much of the value of the IRA is derived from these nondeductible contributions.

Q 22:15   Does a penalty apply to early withdrawals from an individual retirement account?

Yes, penalty-free withdrawals from an IRA may not be made prior to reaching age 59½. The penalty that applies to early IRA distributions is similar to the early-distribution penalty applied to tax qualified retirement plans. [IRC § 72(t)] This early-distribution penalty is 10 percent of the taxable amount of any IRA distribution. [IRC §§ 72(t)(1), 72(t)(2)] The amounts taken in an early distribution from an IRA are subject to income tax in addition to the penalty tax.

Example 22-3: An engineer, age 40, has a salary of $40,000 and withdraws $3,000 from an IRA established and maintained by her. Because she made an early withdrawal from the IRA, she will have to pay a penalty tax of $300 (10 percent of the $3,000 early withdrawal). She will also be subject to income tax on $43,000 (her salary plus the amount of the withdrawal).

Q 22:16 Are there any exceptions to the 10 percent penalty for early withdrawals from an individual retirement account?

Yes, there are some exceptions to the 10 percent penalty on early distributions from IRAs. These exceptions are made for the following reasons:

- Distributions made to a beneficiary or employee's estate on or after the employee's death
- Distributions attributable to disability
- Distributions made if the account owner has been declared mentally incompetent or the account owner has died
- Distributions made in substantially equal annual payments over the participant's lifetime or life expectancy or the joint lives or life expectancies of the participant and beneficiary

[IRC § 72(t)]

The exception for distributions made in substantially equal annual payments over the participant's lifetime is available only if the following conditions are met:

1. The substantially equal periodic payments to an IRA owner under age 59½ generally must be received for at least five years.
2. The IRA owner is prohibited from changing the method of distribution before age 59½.
3. The IRA owner must wait at least five years to change the distribution method even if he or she attains age 59½ before the end of that five-year period (unless the distribution change was because of the death or disability of the IRA owner). If this is not done, the exception from the 10 percent tax is canceled to the extent that the amounts were received before the IRA owner achieved age 59½. The 10 percent additional tax will be recaptured on all amounts received before the IRA owner attained age 59½, and the IRA owner will also be liable for interest on the additional tax. [IRC § 72(t)(4)(A)]

Q 22:17   Estate and Retirement Planning Answer Book

The IRS has authorized the following three ways to meet the substantially equal payment requirement:

1. An annual distribution of the required minimum distribution amount, based on either the life expectancy of the IRA owner or the joint life and last survivor expectancy of the IRA owner and a designated beneficiary;
2. Amortization of the IRA account balance over a number of years equal to the life expectancy of the IRA owner or joint life and last survivor expectancy of the IRA owner and a designated beneficiary, at an interest rate that does not exceed a reasonable interest rate on the date that payments commence; and
3. Dividing the IRA account balance by an annuity factor derived by using a reasonable mortality table at an interest rate that does not exceed a reasonable interest rate on the date that payments commence.

[IR Notice 89-25, 1989-1 CB 662]

Q 22:17   What is an individual retirement account rollover?

Rollovers permit an individual to move an investment from one type of tax-qualified retirement plan to another type of plan without incurring tax liability on the date of the transfer. A rollover occurs when an individual takes a distribution from a qualified retirement plan and puts it into a rollover IRA. A rollover also occurs when funds in a rollover IRA (i.e., an IRA that has received a rollover from a tax-qualified retirement plan) are transferred to another qualified plan.

Timing requirement. A distribution may be rolled over into an IRA (or into another IRA) if the assets are rolled over within 60 days of the date the distribution is received. A rollover from a given IRA to another IRA may be made only once a year.

Trustee-to-trustee transfers. If a check is not distributed to the IRA owner and the trustee of the first plan instead transfers funds directly to the trustee of the second plan, the direct transfer is considered a trustee-to-trustee transfer. In this case, there is no 60-day time requirement or any limitation on how often this may occur. Direct transfers can thus be used to avoid the one-year and 60-day rules. A trustee-to-trustee transfer can also be used by smaller employers to close out a superseded plan.

Q 22:18 What are the tax effects if part of an individual's individual retirement account balance is transferred to his or her spouse as a result of divorce?

The transfer of an individual's IRA interest to his or her spouse pursuant to a divorce decree or written separation agreement is not a taxable event. [IRC § 408(d)(6)] Once the transfer is made, the transferred interest is treated as an account owned by the spouse. Presumably this means that payment of this interest to the spouse is taxable to the spouse and not to the individual. The Internal Revenue Service (IRS) has ruled, however, that if an IRA is divided pursuant to a private separation agreement (as opposed to one entered into pursuant to a legal separation proceeding) and one half of the IRA is distributed to the owner's spouse, the IRA owner remains the owner of all IRA property and is taxable on the distribution to the spouse. [Ltr Rul 9344025]

Q 22:19 Can an irrevocable trust be a designated individual retirement account beneficiary without causing gift tax?

Yes, the IRS has ruled that the designation of an irrevocable trust as the beneficiary of an IRA is not a taxable gift as long as the IRA owner has sufficient retained powers to revest title to the transferred funds in himself or herself. In the fact pattern ruled on, the IRA owner retained the right to change the beneficiary designation and was until death the trustee of the trust and its sole beneficiary. The IRA owner also had the right to withdraw income and principal from the trust. Although the ruling was binding only on the taxpayer who requested it, the ruling indicates the IRS's interpretation of the applicable statutes.

Simplified Employee Pensions

Q 22:20 What is a simplified employee pension?

A simplified employee pension (SEP) is an IRA that can receive employer contributions under an arrangement set up by the employer that meets the SEP requirements. An individual must be an employee covered under a SEP arrangement before an IRA can be used as a SEP. SEPs may be established by sole proprietors and by partnerships. [IRC §§ 401(c)(4), 408(k)(7)] A SEP must be established by a written instrument executed by the employer. The written instrument must include the following items:

1. The name of the employer;
2. The requirements an employee must meet in order to receive an allocation of the employer's contribution;
3. The formula for allocating the employer contribution among the IRAs of the eligible employees; and
4. The signature of a responsible officer of the employer.

[Prop Treas Reg § 1.408-7(b)]

The easiest way to satisfy the written instrument requirement is to execute an IRS Form 5305-SEP. Although the form is not required to be filed with the IRS, it should be kept in the employer's records. Employer contributions under an SEP arrangement must be made pursuant to a written formula that specifies the formula for computing the amount allocated on behalf of each employee and the requirements an employee must meet to share in the contributions of the employer. [IRC § 408(k)(5)] The IRAs used in connection with a SEP can be individual IRAs or Section 408(e) IRAs sponsored by the employer or by a union. [Prop Treas Reg § 1.408-7(a)]

Q 22:21 Which employees must be covered by a simplified employee pension?

A SEP must cover all employees who are at least 21 years old and who have worked for the employer during three out of the five preceding calendar years. Contributions do not have to be made by the employer on behalf of an employee whose compensation for the calendar year is less than $300. The employer may make deductible contributions to a SEP, and such amounts are excludable from an employee's gross income. Whether or not an employer makes a contribution to the SEP is within the employer's discretion. If a contribution is made under the SEP, however, it must be allocated to all the eligible employees according to the SEP agreement. The contribution on behalf of each eligible employee must be the same percentage of compensation for all employees.

Q 22:22 Must a simplified employee pension cover employees other than those of the sponsoring employer?

Yes. The SEP must cover the employees of the sponsoring employer and the following:

1. Employees in a controlled group of corporations with the sponsoring employer;
2. All trades or businesses (whether or not incorporated) that are under common control with the sponsoring employer; and
3. All organizations that are members of an affiliated service group with the sponsoring employer.

[IRC §§ 408(k), 414(b), 414(c), 414(m)]

Q 22:23 What contributions can be made to a simplified employee pension?

An employer may contribute any amount each year up to the lesser of $30,000 or 15 percent of the employee's compensation. [IRC § 402(h)(2)] The employer makes these contributions directly to the appropriate IRA. The purpose of the SEP design established by Congress is to make it easier for employers to adopt a retirement plan for their employees by avoiding the complicated funding requirements that apply to other types of tax-qualified retirement plans.

Q 22:24 What is a salary-reduction simplified employee pension?

Small employers (those with 25 or fewer employees) may maintain SEPs that allow employees to elect to have their salary reduced and contributed on their behalf to the SEP or to receive cash. The amount is contributed to the SEP on the employee's behalf on a pretax basis. To qualify to use the salary reduction SEP alternative, at least 50 percent of the individuals employed must elect salary deferral. The deferrals are limited to $7,000 per year, adjusted for increases in cost of living (the limit was $8,994 in 1993). [IRC § 402(g)]

Q 22:25 Can employees who participate in a simplified employee pension also contribute to an individual retirement account?

An employee who is a SEP participant may still contribute the lesser of $2,000 or 100 percent of his or her compensation to an IRA. Any contribution that is more than the yearly limitation may be withdrawn without penalty by the due date for filing the tax return but will be included in the employee's gross income. Excess contributions left in the SEP-IRA account after that time may have adverse tax consequences.

Q 22:26 How are distributions from a simplified employee pension made?

Distributions from SEPs are subject to the same required distribution rules that apply to IRAs (see Q 22:13).

Q 22:27 Can a simplified employee pension provide a lump-sum distribution?

No, a SEP cannot provide a lump-sum distribution.

Q 22:28 Can an employee roll over funds from a simplified employee pension to another individual retirement account?

Employees can withdraw or receive funds from their SEP-IRAs and roll over such funds into another IRA if the rollover is made no more than 60 days from the date of distribution. These rollovers are subject to the same limitations as regular IRA rollovers and may not be made without penalty more than once a year. There are no restrictions on the number of trustee-to-trustee transfers (see Q 22:17) from SEP-IRAs to other IRAs.

Chapter 23

Distributions from Tax-Qualified Retirement Plans

Tax-qualified retirement plans can play a key role in retirement planning. This chapter discusses the tax consequences of distributions from such plans.

One option available to a distributee is a tax-free rollover, which defers both income tax and income tax withholding. An estate tax exclusion for benefits from tax-qualified retirement plans is also available in certain circumstances. Specific requirements must be met, however, to ensure that a distributee receives the tax benefits associated with qualified plan distributions. Therefore, it is essential that an individual be aware of the basic distribution rules. Once plan participants reach certain ages, tax-qualified plans must make distributions to avoid harsh penalties.

Overview	23-2
Distributions at Termination of Employment	23-4
Lump-Sum Distributions	23-13
Rollover Distributions	23-15
Required Distributions	23-19
Designation of Beneficiaries	23-21
Applicable Life Expectancies	23-25
Payments Following Death	23-25
Recalculation of Life Expectancy	23-31
Minimum Distribution Individual Benefit Requirement	23-32
Excise Tax	23-34

Special Cases	23-35
Witholding and Notices	23-37
Survivor Annuity Requirements	23-41
Estate Planning	23-46

Overview

Q 23:1 Are distributions from tax-qualified plans treated more favorably than distributions from other plans?

Yes. Tax-qualified retirement plans receive favorable tax treatment. The income that accumulates under a tax-qualified pension, profit sharing, or stock bonus plan is not taxed until distributed to the participant or his or her beneficiary. Alternatively, if the income is rolled over within 60 days of the distribution, it will not be taxed until a later date. [IRC §§ 401(a), 402(a), 501(a)] Employer contributions to tax-qualified plans are not taxable to the plan participant when made, even if the participant is vested in the plan; instead, taxation is deferred until distribution. Furthermore, distributions from tax-qualified retirement plans are sometimes taxed at favorable rates. In contrast, employer contributions made to funded nonqualified plans are taxable to participants when made if the participant is vested in the plan.

Generally, compensation paid by an employer is deductible only when such amounts are includible in the recipient's gross income. This general rule does not apply, however, to long-term compensation provided through tax-qualified retirement plans, which permit immediate employer deductions to be taken even though payments from the plan are made in a future tax year.

Q 23:2 Can an employee withdraw benefits from his or her vested account at any time without being subject to a penalty?

No. If an employee makes an early withdrawal from a qualified retirement plan, the employee's income tax equals 10 percent of the portion of the withdrawal that is includible in gross income. [IRC § 72(t)(1)] This penalty tax is in addition to any income tax on the

Distributions from Tax-Qualified Retirement Plans   Q 23:2

amount of distribution. There are, however, distributions that are not subject to this additional tax:

1. Distributions made on or after the date on which the employee attains age 59½;
2. Distributions made to a beneficiary (or the employee's estate) on or after the employee's death;
3. Distributions attributable to the employee's disability;
4. Distributions made as part of a series of substantially equal periodic payments (at least annually) made for the life (or life expectancy) of the employee or the joint lives (or life expectancies) of the employee and his or her designated beneficiary (this exception does not apply to any amount paid from a Section 401(a) trust that is exempt from tax under Section 501(a) of the Internal Revenue Code (Code) or from a Section 72(e)(5)(D)(ii) contract unless the series of payments begins after the employee separates from service);
5. Distributions made to an employee after separation of service and after attainment of age 55 (except where it is a distribution from an individual retirement plan); or
6. Dividends paid with respect to stock of a corporation that are described in Code Section 404(k).

[IRC 72(t)(2)(A)]

An additional tax may be imposed, however, on a distribution that is part of a series of substantially equal periodic payments where the series of payments are subsequently modified. [IRC § 72(t)(4)]

The additional tax is not imposed upon the following:

1. Distributions (other than distributions from an individual retirement plan) that do not exceed the amount allowable as a deduction under Code Section 213 to the employee for amounts paid during the year for medical care. [IRC §§ 72(t)(2)(B), 72(t)(3)]
2. Any distribution (other than a distribution from an individual retirement plan) made to an alternate payee under a qualified domestic relations order (QDRO). [IRC §§ 72(t)(2)(C), 72(t)(3)]

Q 23:3   Estate and Retirement Planning Answer Book

3. Dividend distributions from employee stock owership plans (ESOPs) that are deductible under Code Section 404(k). [IRC § 72(t)(2)(A)]

Q 23:3   Does the exception for distributions to employees who separate from service after age 55 apply even if the employee later returns to employment with the same employer?

Yes; however, there must be an actual physical separation from service before the distribution. Short-term separations may be closely scrutinized by the Internal Revenue Service (IRS) to determine whether the separations were in fact intended to be permanent.

Distributions at Termination of Employment

Q 23:4   How are distributions at retirement or earlier termination of employment taxed?

Distributions from tax-qualified plans are generally taxable under Code Section 72. [IRC § 402(a)] Certain distributions may be taxable as lump-sum distributions (see Qs 23:33–23:36). Other distributions may escape taxation through rollover treatment (see Qs 23:37–23:45). If an annuity contract is distributed from a qualified plan, the annuity contract will not be taxed until distributions are made from it. Those distributions, however, will be taxed in accordance with Code Section 72. [Treas Reg § 1.401(a)-1(a)(2)]

Code Section 72 does not apply to distributions that are specifically excluded from income by statute. Two types of distributions that fall in this catagory are (1) life insurance proceeds payable as a result of the participant's death (excludable from income under Code Section 101(a)(d)) and (2) compensation for sickness or personal injury (excludable under Code Section 104(a)).

Q 23:5 How are distributions taxed under Code Section 72?

Payments taxable under Code Section 72 are generally divided into taxable and nontaxable components. The taxable and nontaxable components are determined by applying an exclusion ratio. The exclusion ratio is determined by dividing the investment in the contract by the expected return from the plan. [IRC § 72(b)] Tax-qualified plans are treated as contracts for purposes of Code Section 72.

To determine the exclusion ratio, several steps must be performed, as follows:

1. Determine whether the amount is paid after the annuity starting date. The annuity starting date is the first day of the first period for which an amount is payable as an annuity.
2. Determine whether the amount is received as an annuity. An amount is received as an annuity if it is payable at regular intervals over more than one year measured from the annuity starting date, if received on or after the annuity starting date, and if the total amounts payable are determinable at the annuity starting date. [Treas Reg § 1.72-2(b)(2)]

If the payment is made after the annuity starting date and the payment is received as an annuity, the exclusion ratio is applied to each payment. If this is not the case, the amount received is treated as an amount not received under an annuity.

The exclusion ratio is determined by dividing the investment in the contract by the expected return. The expected return is the total amount receivable. If the annuity is payable over the participant's life, the expected return is generally derived by multiplying the expected monthly payment by the appropriate life expectancy factor. [Treas Reg 1.72-9, Table V] If the annuity is payable for a fixed period of time (i.e., term-certain annuity), the expected return equals each payment times the number of payments. [Treas Reg 1.72-4(a)(3)]

Investment in the contract consists generally of consideration paid by the employee or participant such as premiums or nondeductible employee contributions made to the plan. [IRC § 72(c)] (Some employer contributions otherwise excludable from income also count. [IRC 72(f)(2)] Investments in a contract count only against distributions from the same Section 72 contract. In general, a tax-qualified plan constitutes one Section 72 contract. A plan that contains several programs of interelated contributions and benefits (e.g., the plan has definitely determinable retirement benefits and definitely determinable disability benefits) contains several Section 72 contracts, however. [Treas Reg 1.72-2(a)(3)] Employee contributions and the associated income may be treated as made under separate contracts. [IRC § 72(d)]

Example 23-1: A retired engineer is to receive from a qualified plan a life annuity of $1,000 per month starting at age 65. His actuarial life expectancy is 20 years. [Treas Reg 1.72-9, Table V] Therefore, the expected return under the contract is $240,000. The engineer made after-tax employee contributions to the plan of $24,000. The exclusion ratio is the ratio of the investment in the contract ($24,000) to the expected return ($240,000), or 90 percent. Thus, each year the engineer excludes 10 percent of the payments made to him ($2,400) from gross income. The remaining $21,600 in payments is includible in gross income.

The exclusion ratio depends on the actuarial tables used. In Example 23-1, if the engineer had a life expectancy of 22 years beginning at age 65, the exclusion ratio would be less. The actuarial tables currently in use are gender neutral, but earlier tables were not. Under those tables, males had shorter life expectancies and higher exclusion ratios than females with the same investment in the contract. The earlier tables may still be used by some individuals. [Treas Decision 8115, 1987-1 CB 22)]

The IRS has also provided a simplied method to determine the exclusion ratio. [IR News Rel 89-31, Mar 20, 1989]

Q 23:6 Is the exclusion ratio ever redetermined?

Generally not. The exclusion ratio is not redetermined unless a new type of annuity becomes payable. [Treas Reg 1.72-4(a)(4)]

Example 23-2: A widowed physician receiving a life annuity from a pension plan remarries. Consistent with the terms of the plan, the physician converts his annuity option to a joint and survivor annuity. A new exclusion ratio will be determined for the joint and survivor annuity payments.

Q 23:7 Was there a time when the exclusion ratio did not apply to annuity payments?

Yes. If an employee's annuity starting date was before July 2, 1986, and if the annuitant's investment in the contract did not exceed the annuity payments received in the first three years after the date of the first payment, the employee could exclude the full investment before inclusion of the income from the investment. The last year amounts could be deducted using this rule was 1989. [Pub L No 99-514 1122(h)]

Q 23:8 What type of payments are considered annuities?

To be considered an annuity, payments must be (1) received on or after the annuity starting date, (2) payable in periodic installments at regular intervals for a period of more than one full year from the annuity starting date, and (3) determined at the annuity starting date either from the terms of the contract or by the use of mortality tables. [Treas Reg § 1.72-2(b)(2)]

Q 23:9 When must an employer's contribution be included in an annuitant's income?

The annuitant must include the amount in a plan that is derived from employer contributions in the year a distribution is actually made. [IRC § 402(a)]

Q 23:10 If an employee is given an option to receive a lump-sum payment or an annuity, how much is includible in the employee's income for the year in which the offer is made?

The entire amount of the lump-sum payment offered is includible in income in the year in which it is offered, even if the annuity is chosen. [Treas Reg § 1.72-11]

Q 23:11 Are there any exceptions to the harsh inclusion requirements referred to above?

Yes. A lump sum is not includible in income if (1) an option to chose an annuity is exercised within 60 days from the date of the availability of the lump sum, and (2) no portion of the lump sum is receivable by the annuitant. In lieu of immediately exercising an option to take an annuity, an annuitant can irrevocably agree within 60 days to take the proceeds as an annuity. [Treas Reg § 1.72-12]

Q 23:12 How long must the option to take payments as an annuity be irrevocable for this exception to apply?

The option must be permanently irrevocable. The annuitant must not have the option of changing the election from time to time. [Treas Reg § 1.72-12]

Q 23:13 What is the simplified safe harbor exclusion ratio?

The simplified safe harbor exclusion ratio applies to annuity payments that begin after July 1, 1986. It simplifies the usual calculation of the amount of the annuity payment to be excluded from taxable income. [IR Notice 88-118, 1988-2 CB 450]

Q 23:14 Will the simplified safe harbor exclusion ratio comply with Code Section 72?

Annuitants who qualify for and use the simplified ratio are considered to have complied with Code Section 72 for calculation of the exclusion ratio. [IR Notice 88-118, 1988-2 CB 450]

Q 23:15 Who qualifies for the simplified safe harbor exclusion ratio?

Taxpayers who are (1) less than age 75 when annuity payments begin or (2) age 75 or older with less than five years of guaranteed payments qualify for this method. [IR Notice 88-118, 1988-2 CB 450]

Q 23:16 What qualifications must a taxpayer meet in order to use the simplified safe harbor exclusion ratio?

The annuity payments must (1) begin after July 1, 1986, (2) depend on the life of the receiver or the joint life of the receiver and beneficiary, and (3) be made from a qualified plan under Code Section 401, an employee annuity under Code Section 403, or annuity contract under Code Section 403. [IR Notice 88-118, 1988-2 CB 450]

Q 23:17 How is the simplified safe harbor exclusion ratio determined?

The amount excluded under the simplified safe harbor exclusion ratio is determined by dividing the investment in the contract by the number of expected annuity payments. [IR Notice 88-118, 1988-2 CB 450]

Example 23-3: A geologist retires and receives an annuity payment of $2,000 per month. The geologist has an investment in the contract of $24,000, and his expected number of payments is 240. The amount of the payments that is excluded from income is determined by dividing the investment ($24,000) by the number of monthly payments (240) for a result of $100.

Q 23:18 Is the simplified safe harbor exclusion ratio modified for changes in the annuity payments such as cost-of-living increases?

No. The amount of the payments excluded from gross income remains the same regardless of whether the amount of the annuity payments increases. [IR Notice 88-118, 1988-2 CB 450]

Q 23:19 What if the amount determined to be excluded under the simplified safe harbor method is greater than the annuity payment received?

The entire payment will be excluded from gross income until the investment in the contract is fully recovered. [IR Notice 88-118, 1988-2 CB 450]

Example 23-4: A married retired commercial airline pilot receives monthly pension payments of $2,000. Fifty percent of each payment is excluded from income under the simplified method. The pilot dies. Under the terms of the plan, which provides for a 50 percent survivor annuity, his widow is entitled to a pension payment of $1,000 each month. Until the investment in the contract is recovered, each $1,000 monthly payment to the widow will be excluded from income.

Q 23:20 How is the excludable portion determined under the simplified safe harbor exclusion ratio when an annuity has more than one beneficiary?

The excludable portion is determined with reference to the age of the oldest beneficiary. The excludable portion for each beneficiary is calculated by dividing the amount of the beneficiary's monthly annuity by the total amount of the monthly annuity payments made to all beneficiaries. [IR Notice 88-118, 1988-2 CB 450]

Q 23:21 How is the investment in the contract determined under the simplified safe harbor exclusion method?

The total investment in the contract is determined by subtracting any amounts received before the annuity starting date from the after-tax payments into the annuity. [IR Notice 88-118, 1988-2 CB 450]

Q 23:22 May the investment in the contract be increased by any method other than payments to the annuity?

Yes. Any death benefit exclusion under Code Section 101 also increases the investment in the contract. [IR Notice 88-118, 1988-2 CB 450]

Q 23:23 How does a taxpayer elect to use the simplified method?

The taxpayer must attach a signed statement to his or her income tax return stating that the taxpayer is electing to use the simplified method. [IR Notice 88-118, 1988-2 CB 450]

Distributions from Tax-Qualified Retirement Plans   Q 23:28

Q 23:24 How is the total number of monthly expected payments determined?

Internal Revenue Notice 88-118, Section II. B, includes a table that is to be used when determining the total expected monthly payments. For example, for a taxpayer who is 55 years of age or under, the total number of expected payments is 300. The taxpayer must refer to this table in making the determination as to the total expected monthly payments.

Q 23:25 Once the election to use the simplified method is made, may the taxpayer later decide to use the actual calculation of the exclusion ratio or vice versa?

If the taxpayer is allowed to amend his or her return under the Code, the taxpayer may change from the simplified method to an actual calculation of the exclusion ratio or vice versa. [IR Notice 88-118, 1988-2 CB 450]

Q 23:26 How does a taxpayer change from using the simplified exclusion method to the actual exclusion?

The change is made by filing Form 1040X, which is an amended income tax return, for all of the years for which an amended return is allowed. [IR Notice 88-118, 1988-2 CB 450]

Q 23:27 How is the value of the taxpayer's annuity determined?

The value is determined by looking at the total assets in the account. For a defined benefit plan, the value is determined by taking the present value of the vested portion of the participant's total accrued benefit under the plan. [IR Notice 88-118, 1988-2 CB 450]

Q 23:28 Do payments contributed to an annuity by an employer on behalf of a self-employed individual count as investments in the contract?

No. When computing the investment on the contact, the contributions made on behalf of a self-employed individual are deemed employer payments that are not included in income but that would be included in income if paid directly to the individual. [Treas Reg § 72]

Q 23:29 How is investment under the contract allocated when a portion of plan benefits is paid out pursuant to a QDRO?

It depends on the identity of the payee. If the payee is a spouse or former spouse, the investment in the contract is prorated. If the payee is someone else, the participant retains the full investment in the contract. This is because only an alternate payee who is a spouse or former spouse is taxable on distributions made to the alternate payee. In all other cases, the participant is taxable on those distributions. [IRC § 72(m)(10)]

Q 23:30 How are amounts received before the annuity starting date taxed?

Amounts received before the annuity starting date are taxed under a pro rata rule. Under this rule, the portion of the distribution that is excludable from income is equal the ratio of the participant's investment in the contract to the total value of the participant's account balance or, in the case of a pension plan, accrued benefit as of the date of distribution. [IRC 72(e)(8)] Because this ratio is determined at the date of distribution, in contrast to the exclusion ratio that is used for post-annuity starting date distribution, this ratio is likely to vary from distribution to distribution. Only the vested portion of the participant's account balance or acrued benefit is considered in determining the total acrured benefit or account balance. [IRC § 72(e)(8)(C)] If the plan is a defined benefit plan, the present value of the participant's vested accrued benefit is determined by using the plan's actuarial factors for a total distribution. [IR Notice 87-13, 1987-1 CB 432, Q&A 11]

Prior to 1986, the rule was more favorable to plan participants. The rule then was that amounts received before the annuity starting date were excluded from gross income if the amount received was less than the investment in the contract (as reduced, of course, by prior tax-free distributions). This meant that any available exclusion

Distributions from Tax-Qualified Retirement Plans   Q 23:33

from income was concentrated in the first distributions. This rule, which was generally applicable to individuals with annuity starting dates beginning on or before July 1, 1987, is applicable to portions of other distributions attributable to pre-1987 employee contributions. [IRC § 72(e)(8)(D)]

Q 23:31 How are non-annuity payments received after the annuity starting date treated for tax purposes?

Non-annuity payments received as distributions from a qualified plan are fully includible in gross income. [IRC § 72(e)(5)(A)]

Q 23:32 How are increases in annuity payments from tax-qualifed trusts after the annuity starting date taxed?

Increases in annuity payments after the annuity starting date that are paid in a manner not specified in the annuity contract are treated as amounts not received as annuities. [Treas Reg § 1.72-4(a)(3)] The entire increase in benefits is taxable. [IRC § 72(e)(5)(A)] The exclusion ratio applicable to the basic annuity payments is not affected by the payment increase.

Example 23-5: An engineer receiving a monthly pension of $1,000 benefits from an unexpected retroactive increase in pension benefits of $50 per month. This $50 increase in benefits is taxable.

Lump-Sum Distributions

Q 23:33 What is a lump-sum distribution for purposes of income averaging?

For purposes of the income averaging rules, a *lump-sum distribution* means a distribution or payment of the balance to the credit of an employee that becomes payable to the recipient

1. On account of the employee's death;
2. After the employee attains age $59\frac{1}{2}$;
3. On account of the employee's separation from the service (does not apply to self-employed individuals); or

23-13

Q 23:34   Estate and Retirement Planning Answer Book

4. After the employee has become physically or mentally disabled (applies only to self-employed individuals) from a trust that forms a part of a plan described in Code Section 401(a) and that is exempt from tax under Code Section 501 or from a plan described in Code Section 403(a).

[IRC § 402(d)(4)]

The lump-sum distribution must be made within one taxable year of the recipient. This means that the lump-sum distribution may actually be a series of payments, as long as the payments occur within one taxable year. [IRC § 402(e)(4)]

No amount distributed to an employee from a plan may be treated as a lump-sum distribution unless the employee has been a participant in the plan for five or more taxable years before the taxable year in which the amounts are distributed. [IRC § 402(d)(F)]

Q 23:34   What interest rates are used to calculate lump sums?

Lump sums are calculated using the yield on 30-year Treasury bonds for employees that earn the maximum benefit. Previously, lump-sum rates were calculated using rates published by the Pension Benefit Guaranty Corporation.

Q 23:35   What is the effect on pension plans of the rules using the 30-year Treasury bond rate in determining the amount to be paid out in a single-sum distribution?

The new rules make it more difficult for actuaries to determine the appropriate funding for small defined benefit pension plans. [IRC § 417(e)] The 30-year Treasury bond yield is relatively volatile. If a company is large, the effect of one employee's departure on the entire fund is not significant. If a plan is small, however, slight fluctuations in interest rates can dramatically affect the amount of funding necessary.

Example 23-6: An employee in a two-participant plan is eligible for a benefit of $120,000 per year at her retirement at age 65. If an interest rate assumption of 5 percent is used, the participant would need a single sum of $1.38 million to obtain the maximum benefit. If an interest rate of 12 percent is used, the single-sum amount would be $861,800.

Q 23:36 What is five-year forward income averaging, and when can a forward averaging election be made?

Five-year forward income averaging allows the distributee to treat a lump-sum distribution from a tax-qualified retirement plan as though received over a period of five years. [IRC § 402(d)] This permits the individual to "smooth out" the tax impact of what can be a sudden jump in income due to receipt of the distribution: five-year forward income averaging might help a recipient avoid a higher tax bracket or the imposition of the alternative minimum income tax. The income averaging election is not limited to individuals. A beneficiary that is an estate or a trust may also elect five-year forward income averaging. [IRC § 402(d)(4)(B)]

Limitations. The five-year averaging rule generally may not be used unless the individual is age 59½ at the time of the distribution. In addition, the election to use the rule may be made only once by a taxpayer with respect to any employer. [IRC § 402(d)(4)(B); IRS Ann 87-2, IRB 1987-2, 38]

Grandfather rule for individuals aged 50 by January 1, 1986. Individuals who have reached age 50 by January 1, 1986, generally can elect to use the five-year income averaging provisions (using the tax rates in effect in the year of distribution) or the ten-year income averaging provisions that existed prior to the changes made by the Tax Reform Act of 1986 (TRA '86) (using the 1986 tax rates), and they may also elect to apply the pre-TRA '86 capital gains rules (using a 20 percent rate). Under those rules, the portion of a lump-sum distribution that was attributable to pre-1974 participation could be taxed as a long-term capital gain. [TRA '86 § 1122(h)(3); IRS Ann 87-2, IRB 1987-2, 38]

Rollover Distributions

Q 23:37 Is a distribution from an eligible retirement plan always taxed in the year it is distributed?

Not necessarily. Under certain circumstances, the distributee can avoid immediate taxation by making a tax-free rollover. The gross income of a distributee does not include any amount of an eligible rollover distribution that is transferred from a qualified trust to an eligible retirement plan. [IRC § 402(c)(1)] If this transfer occurs, the taxation is deferred beyond the date of distribution.

Q 23:38 What is a rollover?

A rollover is a distribution of plan assets to a participant or beneficiary that is subsequently contributed to another plan or to an individual retirement account (IRA). The rollover rules permit all or any part of the taxable portion of a distribution from a tax-qualified plan to be deposited tax free in another tax-qualified plan, 403(b) annuity, or IRA unless the distribution is a required minimum distribution under Code Section 401(a)(9) or unless the distribution is one of a series of substantially equal payments made (1) over the life or life expectancy of the participant (or the joint lives or joint life expectancies or the participant and his or her beneficiary) or (2) over a period of ten years or more. [IRC § 402(c)(1)(4)]

Q 23:39 What is the definition of an eligible rollover distribution?

An *eligible rollover distribution* is any distribution to an employee of all or any portion of the balance to the credit of the employee in a qualified trust. An eligible rollover distribution does *not* include the following:

1. Any distribution to the extent it is required under the minimum distribution rules of Code Section 401(a)(9); and
2. Any distribution that is one of a series of substantially equal periodic payments (at least annually) made for the life (or life expectancy) of the employee or the joint lives (or joint life expectancies) of the employee and the employee's designated beneficiary or for a specified period of at least ten years.

[IRC § 402(c)(4)]

The IRS has issued temporary regulations that expand the list of distributions that are not considered to be eligible rollover distributions. According to those temporary regulations, the following amounts also are *not* eligible rollover distributions:

1. Returns of Section 401(k) elective deferrals described in Code Section 1.415-6(b)(6)(iv) that are returned as a result of the Section 415 limitations;

2. Corrective distributions of excess contributions and excess deferrals under qualified cash or deferred arrangements and corrective distributions of excess aggregate contributions, together with the income allocable to these corrective distributions;
3. Loans treated as distributions under Code Section 72(p) and not excepted by Code Section 72(p)(2);
4. Loans in default that are deemed distributions (in contrast, the amount of the employee's unpaid balance that is treated as distributed when there is a termination of employment may be an eligible rollover distribution);
5. Dividends paid on employer securities as described in Code Section 404(k);
6. The costs of life insurance coverage; and
7. Similar items designated by the tax commissioner in revenue rulings, notices, and other guidance of general applicability.

[Temp Treas Reg § 1.402(c)-2T, Q&A-4, Q&A-8]

Q 23:40 What is an eligible retirement plan?

A distributee may elect to have an eligible rollover distribution paid directly to an eligible retirement plan, thereby deferring immediate tax on the distribution. An eligible retirement plan is any of the following:

1. An individual retirement account described in Code Section 408(a);
2. An individual retirement annuity described in Code Section 408(b) (other than an endowment contract);
3. A tax-qualified trust; and
4. An annuity plan described in Code Section 403(a).

[IRC § 402(c)(8)(B)]

Q 23:41 What is the maximum amount a recipient may roll over?

The amount that may be rolled over cannot exceed the portion of such distribution that otherwise would be includible in gross income. [IRC § 402(c)(2)]

Q 23:42 What is the time limit for making a rollover?

The distribution, or any part thereof, will be excluded from the distributee's gross income only if transferred to an eligible retirement plan within 60 days of receiving the distribution. [IRC § 402(c)(3)] The statutory language does not provide for any extensions of this time period. Nevertheless, the Tax Court allowed an extension of the 60-day period where, notwithstanding the distributee's reasonable efforts to complete the rollover within the 60 days, the IRA trustee made a bookkeeping error in recording the transaction. [Wood v Commr, 93 TC 114 (1989)]

Q 23:43 If a deceased employee's spouse receives a distribution after the employee's death, is the distribution eligible for rollover treatment?

Yes. For this purpose, however, neither a tax-qualified trust nor an annuity plan described in Code Section 403(a) is treated as an eligible retirement plan. [IRC § 402(c)(9)] As a result, the spouse is limited to rolling over the distribution into either an individual retirement account described in Code Section 408(a) or an individual retirement annuity described in Code Section 408(b) (other than an endowment contract). Otherwise, the spouse's distribution will be included in his or her gross income when it is received. [IRC §§ 402(a), 402(c)]

Q 23:44 Must a participant actually receive a distribution and roll it over to obtain rollover treatment?

No. A direct transfer to an IRA from a tax-qualified plan (or Section 403(b) annuity) can be treated as a rollover, but this treatment is allowed only in those instances where the participant could have received a qualifying rollover distribution from the plan and then could have made a tax-free rollover. [Ltr Rul 912269]

In contrast to IRA transfers, direct transfers to tax-qualified plans do not have to comply with the rollover requirements. Historically, these transfers have been known as plan-to-plan transfers. A plan-to-plan transfer permits, among other things, the amounts transferred to include nondeductible employee contributions. The transfer of a defined benefit or separate account cannot be made in most instances, however, because those benefits are protected by Code Section 411(d)(6). [Treas Reg § 1.411(d)-4, Q&A-3]

Furthermore, for distributions after December 31, 1992, qualified plans must allow plan participants to elect direct transfers of eligible rollover distributions to IRAs (provided they accept transfers) and qualified annuity contracts funded by insurance contracts. [IRC §§ 401(a)(31)(D), 402 (c)(8)(B)] Defined benefit pension plans are not eligible recipients. The participant can make the transfer by delivering the check to the recipient plan or IRA as long as the check is negotiable solely by the recipient plan. [Treas Reg § 1.401(a)(31)-1T, Q&A-3] Eligible distributions of less than $200 are excluded from this requirement. [Treas Reg § 1.401(a)(31)-1T, Q&A-11] The spousal consent rules of Code Section 417 apply to these distributions. Notice of participant rights must also be provided.

Q 23:45 What are the advantages of a direct transfer from a tax-qualified plan compared to those of a rollover?

The 60-day requirement that applies to rollover and sometimes causes a loss of the tax deferral does not apply to direct transfers. Furthermore, the 20 percent withholding requirement does not apply to direct transfers. [IRC § 3405(c)(2)]

Required Distributions

Q 23:46 What rules govern the timing of plan distributions?

Two kinds of rules govern the timing of plan distributions. One requires plans to make distributions at specified times unless the participant elects not to have them made at the times prescribed by the Code. This course is sometimes taken by plan participants so that they can continue to take advantage of the tax-free buildup of plan benefits. To prevent excessive tax-free accumulations, however, a second set of rules requires certain distributions to be made regardless of the participant's wishes.

Tax-qualified retirement plans must provide that distributions (payments) will begin no later than the 60th day after the latest of the end of the plan year

Q 23:47 Estate and Retirement Planning Answer Book

1. Containing the date on which the participant reaches age 65 or, if earlier, the normal retirement age specified in the plan;
2. Containing the tenth anniversary of the year in which the participant commenced participation in the plan; or
3. In which the participant terminates his or her service with the employer.

The participant can, however, elect to defer taking a distribution beyond this date subject to the rules requiring minimum distributions. [IRC §§ 401(a)(9), 401(a)(14)]

Q 23:47 When must a participant's distributions begin?

Mimimum distributions from tax-qualified retirement plans must begin no later than the required beginning date, which is April 1 of the calendar year immediately following the year in which the employee reaches age 70½. The participant's entire interest can be distributed in a single sum or annually but it must be distributed within specified time periods. Distribution options elected prior to the required beginning date must conform to the minimum distribution rules once the participant attains age 70½. [Prop Treas Reg 1.401(a)(9)-1 B-3A] If annual distributions are made, the initial annual distribution must be made by the April 1 that follows the date on which an employee attains age 70½, and each subsequent annual distribution must be made by December 31 of that calender year. This implies that if a participant does not receive a distribution in the calender year in which he or she attains age 70½, two distributions will be made in the subsequent calender year. [Prop Treas Reg 1.401(a)(9)-1 F-1C]

> **Example 23-7:** An engineer attains age 70½ on June 15, 1995. A minimum distribution from his qualified profit sharing plan must be made by April 1, 1996. An initial minimum distribution is made on behalf of the engineer on March 30, 1996. A second minimum distribution (for 1996) must be made by December 31, 1996.

Q 23:48 What is the time frame for making distributions from a tax-qualified plan?

Distributions must began no later than the required beginning date and must be paid over the life of the employee or over the lives of the employee and a designated beneficiary (or over a period not extending beyond the life expectancy of such employee or the life expectancy of the employee and a designated beneficiary). [IRC §§ 401(a)(9)(A)(i), 401(a)(9)(A)(ii)] Distributions may be paid over a fixed term provided that term is less than the relevant life expectancies.

Q 23:49   What is the required beginning date for plan distributions?

Generally, *required beginning date* means April 1 of the calendar year following the calendar year in which the employee reaches age 70½, regardless of whether the employee continues to be employed on that date. The required beginning date is different in the case of a governmental or church plan, however. [IRC § 401(a)(9)(C)]

Designation of Beneficiaries

Q 23:50   What factors should be considered in naming beneficiaries for tax-qualified plans?

Income tax on income earned by tax-qualified plans is deferred until plan assets are distributed. Accordingly, from a tax standpoint it is advantageous to defer the distribution of plan assets as long as possible. Because the time over which distributions must be made is determined in part by life expectancies, one planning strategy is to name beneficiaries with the longest life expectancies or to name beneficiaries that have an indefinite life expectancy, such as a trust. Participants do not have unlimited discretion in naming beneficiaries, however. The Treasury Department has issued extensive regulations concerning the designation of beneficaries. Thus, this planning issue is more complex than the mere designation of beneficiaries on the basis of life expectancy.

Q 23:51   Who can be a designated beneficiary?

Only an individual can be the designated beneficiary for receipt of benefit payments from a tax-qualified retirement plan. The employee's estate cannot be a designated beneficiary for purposes of the required distribution rules. [Prop Treas Reg § 1.401(a)(9)-1, Q&A D-2A(a)]

Q 23:52   Estate and Retirement Planning Answer Book

A trust may be named as the beneficiary to receive payments from a tax-qualified retirement plan. If a trust is so named, all beneficiaries of that trust with respect to the trust's interest in the employee's benefit are treated as having been designated as the employee's beneficiaries under the plan for purposes of determining the required distribution period, provided that the following requirements are met (1) on the later of the date on which the employee named the trust as beneficiary or the employee's required beginning date and (2) throughout all subsequent periods during which the trust is named as beneficiary:

1. The trust must be a valid trust under state law (or would be but for the fact that the trust has no assets);
2. The trust must be irrevocable;
3. The beneficiaries of the trust who are beneficiaries with respect to the trust's interest in the employee's benefit must be identifiable from the trust instrument (i.e., they must be individuals); and
4. A copy of the trust instrument must be provided to the plan.

[Prop Treas Reg § 1.401(a)(9)-1, Q&A D-5(a)]

When the employee dies, all beneficiaries of the trust with respect to the trust's interest in the employee's benefit will be treated as designated beneficiaries of the employee under the plan for purposes of determining the required distribution period if the above requirements are satisfied as of the employee's date of death. [Prop Treas Reg § 1.401(a)(9)-1, Q&A D-6(a)]

Q 23:52   Can a plan provide for discretionary payments among multiple beneficiaries?

A plan can provide that discretionary payments be made to a group of beneficiaries of varying ages. [Prop Treas Reg §§ 1.401(a)(9)-1 D-2(a)(1), 1.40(a)(9)-1 E-5(a)] Alternatively, separate accounts can be established, each using the life expectancy of the respective individual designated beneficiary. [Prop Treas Reg § 1.401(a)(9)-1 H-2(b)]

Q 23:53 When must separate accounts for each beneficiary be established?

A separate account or, for defined benefit plans, segregated share must be established by the participant's required beginning date. If the participant dies prior to the required beginning date, a separate account or segregated share must be established as of the participant's or spouse's date of death. [Prop Treas Reg § 1.401(a)(9)-1 H-2(b)]

Q 23:54 Does an employee have an absolute right to designate a beneficiary?

No. The plan may restrict the employee's right to designate his or her beneficiaries. [Rev Rul 70-173, 1970-1 CB 87] The plan itself may designate the beneficiary. If it does, the person specified in the plan is treated as having been designated by the employee for purposes of Code Section 409(a)(9). [Prop Treas Reg § 1.401(a)(9)-1, Q&A D-1] Both the plan and the beneficiary designations are subject to the requirements of Code Section 401(a)(11) (qualified joint and survivor annuity and qualified preretirement survivor annuity requirement rules), Code Section 414(p) (qualified domestic relation order rules), and Code Section 417 (minimum survivorship annuity requirements). [Prop Treas Reg § 1.401(a)(9)-1, Q&A D-5(a)]

Q 23:55 What is the applicable date for determining a designated beneficiary?

In calculating the Section 401(a)(9)(A)(ii) distribution period for distributions before death, the designated beneficiary is generally determined as of the employee's required beginning date. [Treas Reg § 1.401(a)(9)-1, Q&A D-3(a)] If there is no designated beneficiary as of that date, the period is limited to the employee's life (or a period not extending beyond the employee's death). There are, however, exceptions to this general rule provided in Proposed Treasury Regulations Section 1.401(a)(9)-1. Generally, the exceptions apply when a designated beneficiary is added or when he or she is replaced by another designated beneficiary during the calendar year in which the employee's required beginning date occurs, but on or before the employee's required beginning date.

In calculating the Section 401(a)(9)(B)(iii) and Section 401(a)(9)(B)(iv) distribution periods for distributions beginning after death in accordance with the alternative to the five-year rule, the designated beneficiary is generally determined as of the employee's date of death. If there is no designated beneficiary as of that date, distribution must be made in accordance with the five-year rule. [Treas Reg § 1.401(a)(9)-1, Q&A D-4(a)] There is also an exception to this general rule. It applies where the surviving spouse is the designated beneficiary and he or she dies after the employee and before distributions commence. In that case, the distribution rules are applied as if the spouse was the employee. Therefore, the designated beneficiary will be determined as of the surviving spouse's date of death. If there is no designated beneficiary as of that date, distribution must be made in accordance with the five-year rule. [Treas Reg § 1.401(a)(9)-1, Q&A D-4(b)]

Q 23:56 May designated beneficiaries be changed after the required beginning date?

If the plan permits, a participant may change designated beneficiaries even after the required beginning date. If the new designated beneficiary's life expectancy is longer than the life expectancy of the beneficiary used to determine the distribution period, the life expectancy of the old beneficiary is still used. If the new beneficiary has a shorter life expectancy than the old beneficiary, a new distribution period must be calculated based on the participant's life expectancy and the new beneficiary's life expectancy determined as of the calendar year in which the participant reaches age 70½. [Prop Treas Reg § 1.401(a)(9)-1 E-5(c)(1)] If the new beneficiary is not an individual or if no beneficiary is designated by the participant, the new distribution period is based solely on the participant's remaining life expectancy as if there were no designated beneficiary on the required beginning date. [Prop Treas Reg § 1.401(a)(9)-1 E-5(c)(2)]

Q 23:57 Can plans provide each beneficiary with an election regarding the period of distribution?

Yes, plans can provide this election for each beneficiary. [Prop Treas Reg § 1.401(a)(9)-1 c-4(c)]

Applicable Life Expectancies

Q 23:58 What life expectancy is used to determine the distribution period if a spouse, the designated beneficiary, dies on or after the applicable date for determining the distribution period?

If the designated beneficiary is the employee's spouse and the spouse's life expectancy is being recalculated (recalculating may be permitted pursuant to Code Section 401(a)(9)(D) other than in the case of a life annuity), and the spouse dies, the spouse does not have any remaining life expectancy. In any calendar year in which the last applicable life expectancy is reduced to zero, the plan must distribute the employee's entire remaining interest prior to the last day of such year in order to satisfy Code Section 401(a)(9). [Prop Treas Reg § 1.401(a)(9)-1, Q&A E-6, E-8(a)]

Q 23:59 How is the time frame for installment payments determined for the taxpayer?

The maximum time allowed is determined by using the taxpayer's birthday in the year the payment starts. [Prop Treas Reg § 1.401(a)(9)-2]

Payments Following Death

Q 23:60 What happens if a participant dies after his or her benefits commence?

The deceased employee's interest must be distributed at least as rapidly as under the method of distribution being used under Code Section 401(a)(9)(A)(ii) as of the date of the employee's death. [IRC § 401(a)(9)(B)(i)] Thus, in general, the designated beneficiary whose life or life expectancy was being used to determine the period described in Code Section 401(a)(9)(A)(ii) must be the designated beneficiary for the remaining portion. [Prop Treas Reg § 1.401(a)(9)-1, Q&A B-4] There are exceptions to this general rule, as follows:

1. *More than one designated beneficiary.* If there is more than one designated beneficiary as of the applicable date for determining the designated beneficiary, the beneficiary with the shortest life expectancy will be the designated beneficiary for purposes of determining the required distribution period. [Prop Treas Reg § 1.401(a)(9)-1, Q&A E-5(a)(1)] Two key points should be kept in mind:

    a. If the plan provides (or allows the employee to specify) that, after the employee's death, any person(s) have discretion to change the beneficiaries of the employee, then, for purposes of determining the distribution period for both distributions before and after the employee's death, the employee will be treated as not having designated a beneficiary. This discretion will not be found to exist simply because the employee's surviving spouse may designate a beneficiary for distributions pursuant to Code Section 401(a)(9)(B)(iv)(II). [Prop Treas Reg § 1.401(a)(9)-1, Q&A E-5(f)] This section applies to a surviving spouse who is the designated beneficiary and who dies before distributions to him or her have begun, in which case the required distribution rules are applied as if the surviving spouse was the employee.

    b. If a beneficiary's entitlement to the employee's benefit is contingent on the death of a prior beneficiary, this contingent beneficiary will not be considered a beneficiary for purposes of determining who is the designated beneficiary with the shortest life expectancy. This rule does not apply, however, if the death occurs before the applicable date for determining the designated beneficiary. [Prop Treas Reg § 1.401(a)(9)-1, Q&A E-5(e)(1)]

2. *Addition or replacement of beneficiary after applicable date.* The second exception applies when a new beneficiary is added or replaces a designated beneficiary after the applicable date for determining the designated beneficiary. If this occurs, the beneficiary with the shortest life expectancy will be used to determine the distribution period. Therefore, if the new beneficiary has a longer life expectancy than the old designated beneficiary, the life expectancy of the old designated beneficiary will continue to be used for purposes of determining the distribution period, even though the old designated beneficiary

Distributions from Tax-Qualified Retirement Plans   Q 23:61

is no longer a beneficiary under the plan. [Prop Treas Reg § 1.401(a)(9)-1, Q&A E-5(c)(1)] There is an exception to this exception, however. If the replacement occurs because the designated beneficiary dies on or after the applicable date for determining the designated beneficiary and the deceased beneficiary is someone other than the employee's spouse whose life expectancy is being recalculated, the life expectancy of the deceased designated beneficiary will be used for purposes of determining the distribution period, regardless of whether or not a beneficiary with a shorter life expectancy receives the benefits. [Prop Treas Reg § 1.401(a)(9)-1, Q&A E-5(e)(2)]

Example 23-8: The designated beneficiary of an unmarried businessman as of his required beginning date (April 1, 1988) is his sister. The businessman specified that if his sister dies, his brother will become the beneficiary. The sister's life expectancy as of her birthday in calendar year 1987 is 25 years. The brother's life expectancy as of his birthday in calendar year 1987 is 10 years. On the businessman's required beginning date, his sister is the designated beneficiary because his brother's entitlement to benefits is contingent on the sister's death. The sister dies on May 1, 1988. Her remaining life expectancy will continue to be used to determine the distribution period with respect to the businessman for purposes of determining the minimum distribution for the 1988 distribution calendar year and each succeeding distribution calendar year. [Prop Treas Reg § 1.401(a)(9)-1, Q&A E-5(e)(3), Ex]

Q 23:61 When are benefits deemed to commence?

Even though benefits may have begun before the participant's required beginning date, for purposes of applying the minimum distribution rules benefits are not treated as having commenced until the required beginning date. [Prop Treas Reg § 1.401(a)(9)-1 B-5(a)]

Example 23-9: A broadcaster receiving benefits from a qualified plan dies at age 65. Because his date of death occurs before his required beginning date, for purposes of determining the minimum distribution rules the broadcaster is treated as a participant whose benefit payments have not commenced.

Q 23:62 Estate and Retirement Planning Answer Book

Q 23:62 What if an employee dies before his or her benefit payments under a tax-qualified retirement plan commence?

If an employee dies before his or her benefit payments from a tax-qualified retirement plan begin, the plan generally must provide that the deceased employee's entire interest will be distributed within five years after his or her death. More precisely, the employee's entire interest must be distributed by December 31 of the calendar year that contains the fifth anniversary of the date of the employee's death. This general rule is known as the *five-year rule*. [IRC § 401(a)(9)(B)(ii); Prop Treas Reg § 1.401(a)(9)-1, Q&A C-2]

Example 23-10: An employee participating in a tax-qualified retirement plan dies on January 1, 1994, before any benefit payments have begun. His entire interest must be distributed by December 31, 1999. [Prop Treas Reg § 1.401(a)(9)-1, Q&A C-2]

Two alternatives to the five-year rule are available, as follows:

1. *Payments to a non-spouse beneficiary.* In lieu of the five-year rule, a plan may provide that any portion of an employee's interest that is payable to a designated beneficiary (other than the employee's spouse) may be distributed over the designated beneficiary's life (or over a period not extending beyond the life expectancy of such beneficiary), provided the distributions commence within one year of the employee's death. That is, distributions must commence on or before December 31 of the calendar year immediately following the calendar year in which the employee died. [IRC § 401(a)(9)(B)(iii); Prop Treas Reg § 1.401(a)(9)-1, Q&A C-1(a), C-3(a)]

Example 23-11: An employee dies on June 4, 1994, having designated his sister as beneficiary. The plan provides for making payments to a non-spouse beneficiary in lieu of the five-year rule. Distributions to the sister must commence on or before December 31, 1995. The same rule applies if the sister was designated beneficiary in addition to the employee's surviving spouse. If the employee's benefit is divided into separate accounts (or segregated shares, in the case of a defined benefit plan), however, special rules apply. [Prop Treas Reg § 1.401(a)(9)-1, Q&A C-3(a), H-2, H-2A]

Distributions from Tax-Qualified Retirement Plans   Q 23:63

2. *Surviving spouse as beneficiary.* In lieu of the five-year rule, any portion of an employee's interest that is payable to his or her surviving spouse as designated beneficiary may be distributed over the surviving spouse's life (or over a period not extending beyond the surviving spouse's life expectancy). Further, the distributions to the surviving spouse need not commence earlier than the date on which the employee would have attained age 70$\frac{1}{2}$ (unlike the one-year commencement rule for any other designated beneficiary). [IRC § 401(a)(9)(B)(iv)(I)]

Example 23-12: An employee who dies on August 1, 1994, would have reached age 71 on November 1, 2000. The employee designated his surviving spouse as beneficiary. The plan must provide that distributions will commence on or before the later of (1) December 31 of the calendar year immediately following the calendar year in which the employee died, which in this case would be December 31, 1995, and (2) December 31 of the calendar year in which the employee would have reached age 70$\frac{1}{2}$, which in this case would be December 31, 2000. Therefore, distributions must commence on or before December 31, 2000. [Prop Treas Reg § 1.401(a)(9)-1, Q&A C-3(b)]

If, however, the surviving spouse dies before receiving any distributions under Code Sections 401(a)(9)(B)(iii) and 401(a)(9)(B)(iv), then the surviving spouse will be treated as though she was the employee. [IRC § 401(a)(9)(B)(iv)(II)]

Example 23-13: An employee designates her surviving spouse as beneficiary and dies in 1990. The employee's surviving spouse remarries, but dies before distributions of plan benefits to him have begun. The distribution rules will be applied as though the surviving spouse was the employee. (The special rule for spousal beneficiaries provided in Code Section 401(a)(9)(B)(iv) is not available to the surviving spouse of the deceased employee's surviving spouse.) [Prop Treas Reg § 1.401(a)(9)-1, Q&A C-5]

Q 23:63 How is the five-year rule applied when there are designated beneficiaries and charitable beneficiaries?

Under Proposed Treasury Regulations Sections 1.401(a)(9)-1 D-2A, 1.401(a)(9)-1 E-5(a)(1), and 1.401(a)(9)-1 E-5(a)(2), if a nondesignated beneficiary (e.g., a charity) is a beneficiary, all distributions must be made within the five-year rule. This rule can be circumvented by having the charitable gift made through a separate account or through a segregated share. [Prop Treas Reg § 1.401(a)(9)-1 H-2] When there are both charitable beneficiaries and designated beneficiaries, the portion of the interest going to the charity must be placed in a separate account on or before the required beginning date in order to be excepted from the five-year rule. Failure to do so will result in the five-year rule applying to all distributions. [Prop Treas Reg § 1.401(a)(9)-1 H-2(b)]

Q 23:64 Is a participant constructively receiving income because of a plan's provision specifying that a discretionary power that allows a plan to provide that between a participant's *normal retirement date* and the April 1 of the calendar year following the participant's age 70½, a participant can request and receive ad hoc payments?

There is no constructive receipt because of this discretionary power. A participant will be taxed only when actual payments are made. Each ad hoc payment made from a defined benefit plan or a money-purchase plan is subject, however, to the Retirement Equity Act of 1984 (REA) waiver-and-consent rules in order to avoid the ad hoc payment being made in the form of a qualified joint and survivor annuity.

There is an exception to the general rule, however. If the MDIB rule of Code Section 401(a)(9)(G) applied to a distribution made after the required beginning date during the participant's life and there has been no recalculation of the participant's life expectancy, the amount remaining at the participant's death is payable on the date computed using the joint life and last survivor expectancy from Table VI of Treasury Regulations Section 1.72-9 and the participant's and the beneficiary's attained ages in the calendar year in which the participant reached age 70½, subtracting one year for each year that elapsed prior to the participant's death. [Prop Treas Reg §§ 1.401(a)(9)-1 E-1(a), 1.401(a)(9)-1 F-1(d)]

Recalculation of Life Expectancy

Q 23:65 Can a participant's or spouse's life expectancy be recalculated?

A participant's or spouse's life expectancy can be recalculated annually. [IRC § 401(a)(9)(D)] Recalculation of life expectancy is an elective procedure. [Prop Treas Reg § 1.401(a)(9)-1 E-6]

Q 23:66 Why would one want to recalulate life expectancies?

Recalculating life expectancies permits one to delay distributions longer and obtain the beneifts of tax deferrals on income for a longer period of time.

Q 23:67 Can the life expectancy of a non-spouse designated beneficiary be recalculated?

No, only the life expectancy of a participant's spouse can be recalculated. The recalculation of life expectancy election applies only to spousal designated beneficiaries. [IRC § 401(a)(9)(D)]

Q 23:68 How is the life expectancy of the designated beneficiary determined when the designated beneficiary is not the participant's spouse?

When the designated beneficiary is not the participant's spouse and the designated beneficiary's life expectancy is determined using the beneficiary's attained age on his or her birthday in the calendar year in which the participant attains age $70\frac{1}{2}$ and there is an annual recalculation of life expectancy, every year the joint life and last survivor expectancy must be determined using the participant's age in that year and an adjusted age of the non-spouse beneficiary. [Prop Treas Reg § 1.401(a)(9)-1 E-8(b)]

Q 23:69 If recalculation is elected, what effect does the participant's or spouse's death have on distribution?

If recalculation is elected, upon the participant's or spouses death the decedent's life expectancy becomes zero, therefore requiring accelerated distribution in the calendar year following the calendar year of the decedent's death. [Treas Reg § 1.401(a)(9)-1 E-5(e)(2)]

Q 23:70 What is the result of the death of both the participant and the spouse on recalculating life expectancies?

When both the participant and the spouse recalculate life expectancies, upon the survivor's death there is no remaining life expectancy for the year following the survivor's death; therefore, the plan must distribute the balance prior to the last day of the calendar year during which the life expectancy was reduced to zero. [IRC § 1.401(a)(9)-1 E-8(a)]

Minimum Distribution Individual Benefit Requirement

Q 23:71 Is there any restriction limiting a qualified plan's payment of nonretirement benefits such as life, accident, or health benefits?

Yes. The incidental benefit requirement requires that death and other nonretirement benefits be incidental to the primary purpose of the plan, which is to provide retirement benefits. The incidental benefit requirement has two components, the mimimum distribution incidental benefit (MDIB) requirement and the preretirement incidental benefit requirement. [Prop Treas Reg § 1.401(a)(9)-2]

Q 23:72 What does the preretirement incidental benefit requirement do?

Under the preretirement incidental benefit requirement, preretirement distributions such as life, accident, or health insurance benefits that are not retirement benefits must be incidental to the plan's primary purpose to provide retirement benefits. It restricts the use of a qualified plan as a device to pay benefits other than retirement benefits. [Prop Treas Reg § 1.401(a)(9)-2]

Q 23:73 What does the minimum distribution individual benefit requirement do?

The MDIB requirement places limits on the use of a qualifed plan to build up substantial death benefits to be passed on to beneficiaries instead of providing retirement benefits. Failure to satisfy the MDIB requirement can result in plan disqualificiation. [Prop Treas Reg § 1.401(a)(9)-2, Q-1A]

Q 23:74 How does the minimum distribution individual benefit requirement work?

The requirement works as follows:

Nonannuity distributions. The minimum amount that must be distributed every year to satisfy the requirement is determined by dividing the employee's benefit in the plan by a divisor that is based on the employee's age. Divisors exist for all ages between 70 and 115. The divisor for an employee age 70 is 26, while the divisor for an employee 115 or older is 1.8.

Annuity distributions for a fixed term. The term over which the annuity is distributed cannot exceed the divisor.

Joint and survivor annuity. A joint and survivor annuity with non-spouse beneficiaries is treated differently than a joint and survivor annuity with spousal beneficiaries.

Non-spouse beneficiary. The amount payable to the non-spouse beneficiary cannot exceed the applicable percentage of the annuity payment that would have been paid to the participant had he or she survivied. The applicable percentage is determined by table and is based on the excess of the age of the participant over the age of the beneficiary. For example, if the employee is 10 or less years older than the beneficiary, the applicable percentage is 100 percent. If the employer is 44 or more years older than the beneficiary, the applicable percentage is 52 percent.

Example 23-14: A machinist aged 65 is entitled to a fixed monthly pension benefit of $1,000. He designates his 21-year-old granddaughter as joint annuitant with him. The maximum amount that can be paid to the granddaughter is $520 per month.

Spousal beneficiary. The MDIB rules do not apply to a joint and survivor annuity with a spousal beneficiary.

Annuities payable over an employee's life automatically satisfy the MDIB requirement. [Prop Treas Reg § 1.401(a)(9)-2,Q&A 6]

Q 23:75   Estate and Retirement Planning Answer Book

Q 23:75   If there is more than one beneficiary, how is the difference in age determined for purposes of the minimum distribution individual benefit requirement?

Where the annuitant has more than one beneficiary, the youngest beneficiary's age is used to find the applicable percentage.

Q 23:76   Under Proposed Treasury Regulations Section 1.401(a)(9)-2, what is the effect on the minimum distribution individual benefit percentage requirement of adding a new, younger beneficiary?

The applicable percentage must be adjusted to reflect the younger beneficiary in the calendar year following the change of beneficiary.

Q 23:77   What if the annuitant and the annuitant's spouse are divorced and the court orders that a portion of the employee's annuity payments are to be paid to the spouse under a qualified domestic relations order?

Under Proposed Regulations Section 1.401(a)(9)-2, the ex-spouse is treated as a spouse for MDIB purposes.

Excise Tax

Q 23:78   What tax penalites are imposed for failure to adhere to the minimum distribution requirements?

A 50 percent nondeductible excise tax is imposed on the participant, estate, or beneficiary that is entitled to receive the benefits subject to the minimum distribution rules. The tax is imposed on the excess of the amount of the minimum required distribution from a qualified retirement plan for any calender year over the amount actually distributed during the calender year. For this purpose, a qualified retirement plan is an IRA, a tax-qualifed plan, or an annuity plan or contract under Code Sections 403(a) and 403(b). [IRC 4794(a)]

Special Cases

Q 23:79 What tax rules apply to the distribution of employer securities from a qualified plan?

Special tax rules apply if the distribution from a qualifed plan consists wholly or partially of employer securities. The general rule is that the net unrealized appreciation on employer securities is not taxed on distribution from a qualified plan to the extent that the unrealized appreciation is attributable to contributions other than employee contributions deductible under Code Section 72(o)(5). [IRC § 402(e)(4)(B)] (The unrealized appreciation is, however, taxed when the securites that are distributed are subsequently sold or otherwise disposed of.) If employer securities are distributed as part of a lump-sum distribution, the entire appreciation is untaxed whether attributed to employer or employee contributions unless the taxpayer elects immediate taxation.

Q 23:80 How are distributions of life insurance proceeds taxed?

Distributions of death benefits from a life insurance contract held by a plan are excludable from income whether the proceeds are paid to the employee's estate or to another beneficiary. The amount excluded is equal to the excess of the total death benefits over the cash surrender value of the insurance contract. Benefits attributable to the cash surrender value of the policy are treated like other distributions, but they may be eligible for the $5,000 death benefit exclusion. [IRC § 72(m)(3)(C)]

Q 23:81 May a plan participant obtain a loan from a tax-qualified plan?

A plan participant or beneficiary may obtain a loan from a tax-qualified plan if the loan is secured by the participant's vested account benefit. Loans from a tax-qualified plan maintained by proprietors or partners (i.e., a Keogh plan) to owner-employees under Code Section 401(c)(3) are prohibited transactions, however. The same holds true for loans to officers or employees (and their families) who are 5 percent shareholders in an S corporation on any day of the corporation's tax year. [IRC § 4975(d)] For this purpose, family members are brothers, sisters (including half brothers and half sisters), spouses, ancestors, and lineal descendants. [IRC § 267(c)(4)] In determining whether the 5 percent ownership test is met, a person is treated as owing his or her stock and also as owning:

1. Stock owned directly or indirectly by his or her spouse (unless the individual is legally separated from his or her spouse);
2. Stock owned directly or indirectly by his or her children, grandchildren, and parents;
3. Stock owned directly or indirectly by a partnership or an estate in proportion to the individual's interest in the partnership or interest in the estate (S corporations are treated as partnerships for purposes of this rule);
4. Stock owned directly or indirectly by a trust in proportion to the individual's interest in the trust;
5. Stock owned directly or indirectly by a grantor trust that the individual is considered the owner of; and
6. Stock owned by a corporation if 50 percent or more of the stock of the corporation is owned directly or indirectly by the individual.

Stock options are counted as stock in determining if the 5 percent test is met. [IRC § 318] In general, stock that is constructively owned is treated as actually owned, but there are some exceptions. [IRC § 318(a)(5)]

Q 23:82 Are loans made to participants from a tax-qualified plan under Code Section 401(a) treated as distributions?

A loan (other than a home loan used to acquire a principal residence) that, by its terms, does not have to be repaid within five years will constitute a distribution for tax purposes. [IRC § 72(p)(2)(B)] If a loan is not repaid within five years, the amount that remains payable at the end of the five-year period will be treated as a distribution. Also, a loan that does not require substantially level amortization (with payments of principal and interest at least quarterly) over the term of the loan will be treated as a distribution for tax purposes. [IRC § 72(p)(2)(C)] Even a loan that must be repaid within five years and requires substantially level amortization will be treated as a distribution to the extent it exceeds a prescribed amount. There is a formula for determining the amount treated as a distribution. In general, the excess of the loan over $50,000 will be treated as a distribution. In some cases, however, a smaller loan amount will be treated as a distribution. [IRC § 72(p)(2)(A)] Generally, the portion of a plan loan that is deemed a distribution is not eligible for tax-free rollover. An amount equal to an employee's unpaid loan balance may, however, be an eligible rollover distribution when such amount is treated as distributed upon a termination of employment. [Temp Treas Reg § 1.402(c)-2T, Q&A-8]

Q 23:83 Is it true that even if an exclusion applies, a taxpayer may later be required to treat the loan as a distribution?

Yes. If the taxpayer terminates his or her participation in the plan without repaying the loan, the balance of the unpaid loan and accrued interest payable on the loan are treated as part of the plan distribution on termination.

Witholding and Notices

Q 23:84 What is a designated distribution for purposes of the income tax withholding provisions of Code Section 3405(c)(1)?

For purposes of income tax withholding, a designated distribution refers to any distribution or payment from an employer deferred compensation plan, an individual retirement plan (as defined in Code Section 7701(a)(37)), or a commercial annuity. [IRC § 3405(e)(1)(A)] The income tax withholding provisions [IRC § 3405(c)(1)] do not apply to distributions that are not designated distributions. Further, a designated distribution does not include the following:

1. Any amount that is wages without regard to Code Section 3405;
2. The portion of a distribution or payment that it is reasonable to believe is not includible in gross income;

3. Any amount that is subject to withholding under certain provisions of the Code relating to withholding of tax on nonresident aliens and foreign corporations by the person paying such amount or that would be subject but for a tax treaty; or

4. Any distribution described in Code Section 404(k)(2) (relating to dividends paid on certain employer securities).

A distribution (or payment) from an individual retirement plan does not fall within the second exception to a designated distribution, however, because such distribution (or payment) is treated as includible in gross income. [IRC § 3405(e)(1)(B)]

Q 23:85 Is a participant's consent needed before a tax-qualified plan may pay out benefits?

Usually, the consent of a tax-qualified plan participant is needed before his or her account balance can be paid out. This consent is not needed, however, if the participant attains the later of his or her normal retirement age under Code Section 411(a)(8) (generally, 65) or age 62. [Treas Reg § 1.417(e)-1(b)] A tax-qualified plan can also provide that a participant's account balance can be paid out to him or her without the participant's consent if the present value of his or her vested account balance is $3,500 or less. [IRC § 411(a)(11)] The present value of the account balance is determined using interest rates and mortality tables specified by law. [IRC § 417(e)]

Plans that are asked to provide qualified joint and survivor annuities (QJSAs) must generally provide that the consent of both the participant and the participant's spouse must be obtained before benefits can be paid out, unless the benefits are paid in the form of a QJSA. These consents are not needed, however, if the participant attains the later of his or her normal retirement age under Code Section 411(a)(8) (generally, 65) or age 62. [Treas Reg § 1.417(e)-1(b)] These consents are also unnecessary if the present value of the participant's vested accrued benefit has never exceeded $3,500. [Treas Reg § 1.417(e)-1(b)]

Q 23:86 Are distributions from tax-qualified retirement plans subject to the withholding provisions of Code Section 3405(c)?

Under some circumstances, yes. Distributions that are eligible rollover distributions are subject to the withholding provisions of Code Section 3405(c). The payor typically must withhold 20 percent of the amount of such distribution toward the payment of the employee's federal income tax, FICA, and FUTA on the amount of the distribution. [IRC § 3405(c)(1)] The distributee may elect out of the withholding provisions of Code Section 3405(c)(1) through direct rollover, however.

The distributee may elect to have the eligible rollover distribution paid directly to another tax-qualified retirement plan or to an IRA. If such an election is made, the payor does not withhold any portion of the distribution for income tax purposes. [IRC § 3405(c)(2)]

Q 23:87 What notice requirements apply to plan distributions?

The plan administrator must provide the recipient of a distribution that is eligible for rollover treatment with a written explanation of the provisions relating to the withholding of tax, the ability to make a direct rollover to certain plans, and the 60-day rollover option. [IRC § 402(f)(1)] The plan administrator may also be required to provide additional information, such as information on lump-sum distributions and distributions made pursuant to a QDRO. [IRC §§ 402(d), 402(e)]

When a participant's nonforfeitable accrued benefit with a present value in excess of $3,500 is immediately distributable (i.e., prior to the later of the time the participant has attained normal retirement age or age 62), the participant's informed written consent is required before commencement of the distribution. [IRC § 411(a)(11)(A); Treas Reg §§ 1.411(a)-11(c)(3), 1.411(a)-11(c)(4)] No consent is valid unless the participant has received a general description of the material features and an explanation of the relative values of the optional forms of benefit available under the plan. Further, such information must be provided in a manner that would satisfy the notice requirements of Code Section 417(a)(3) relating to a QJSA and

Q 23:88   Estate and Retirement Planning Answer Book

qualified preretirement survivor annuity (QPSA). Further, there are special rules applicable to consents to plan loans.

To satisfy the notice requirements of Code Section 402(f) when making an eligible rollover distribution, the plan administrator must provide such notice within a reasonable period of time. [IRC § 402(f)(1)] For this purpose, *reasonable period of time* is defined as no less than 30 days and no more than 90 days before making the distribution if it is a distribution for which the plan administrator is not required under Treasury Regulations Section 1.411(a)-11(c) to provide the general description of the distributee's distribution options and other rights under the plan. [Treas Reg § 1.402(c)-2T, Q&A-13] A plan must also provide participants with notice of their rights (when the participant's consent is required) no less than 30 days and no more than 90 days before the annuity starting date. [Treas Reg § 1.411(a)-11(c)(2)(ii)]

Q 23:88   What must this notice include?

The notice for a profit sharing plan must acknowledge the right, if any, to defer distributions and must describe the investment features. The notice for a profit sharing plan need not include the value of projected benefits.

Q 23:89   May a participant waive the 30-day or 90-day notice requirements associated with plan distributions?

The IRS has announced that a participant can waive the 30-day period for purposes of Code Sections 402(f) and 411(a)(11); it has not made any change with regard to the 90-day period. [IR Notice 93-26, IRB 1993-18] Moreover, this waiver does not apply to the 30-day notice period required under Treasury Regulations Section 417(e)-1(b)(3), which requires plans offering a joint and survivor annuity to provide a written explanation of the qualified joint and survivor annuity.

If a participant receives the Section 402(f) notice and affirmatively elects to make or not make a direct rollover, the reasonable time period requirement will not be violated merely because the election is implemented less than 30 days after the notice was given; provided, however, the following requirements are met:

Distributions from Tax-Qualified Retirement Plans   Q 23:92

1. The participant must be given the opportunity to consider whether to elect a direct rollover for at least 30 days after the notice is given; and
2. The plan administrator must provide information to the participant that clearly indicates the participant has a right to this 30-day period for making the decision. [IR Notice 93-26, IRB 1993-18; Treas Reg § 1.402(c)-2T, Q&A-13]

Survivor Annuity Requirements

Q 23:90   What is the purpose of the survivor annuity requirements?

These requirements are generally designed to protect the rights of participants' spouses to benefits. Plans covered by these requirements must provide benefit payments in the form of a QJSA (i.e. an annuity paying benefits over the participant's life and his or her spouse's life). These plans must also provide for a QPSA. This is an annuity payable to the surviving spouse of a participant with a vested interest in the plan who dies prior to his or her annuity starting date.

Q 23:91   What types of plans are subject the rules of the Retirement Equity Act of 1984?

The Retirement Equity Act of 1984 (REA) rules relate to QPSAs, QJSAs, defined benefit plans, money-purchase pension plans, and certain profit sharing plans. Generally, a profit sharing plan providing a surviving spouse with all a participant's accrued benefit at the participant's death is not subject to the REA rules. [Treas Reg § 1.401(a)-20 Q&A-3, Q&A-32, Q&A-33]

Q 23:92   May distribution deviate from a statutory QPSA?

Upon the prior waiver by the participant and consent by the spouse to a non-spouse beneficiary, a distribution may deviate from a statutory QPSA. In a QPSA, it is not necessary to obtain spousal consent to change the form of the preretirement benefit. [Treas Reg § 1.401(a)-20 Q&A-31(b)(2)] It has been held, however, that a death beneficiary designated by a participant prior to marriage was entitled to the proceeds of a retirement plan upon the participant's death even though there apparently was no waiver by the participant or spousal consent. [Estate of Bloom-Kartiganer, 599 NYS 2d 188 (1993)]

Q 23:93   When must the QJSA benefit be available?

The QJSA benefit must be available on the participant's earliest retirement date under the plan. [Treas Reg § 1.401(a)-20 Q&A-17(a)]

Q 23:94   In a QJSA, when must the participant's waiver and the spouse's consent be made to be effective?

To be effective, both the participant's waiver and the spouse's consent must be made during the 90-day election period preceding the participant's annuity starting date. [Treas Reg § 1.401(a)-20 Q&A-10(a), Q&A-31(c)] The participant must be allowed to change his or her election during the applicable election period. [Treas Reg § 1.401(a)-20 Q&A-30]

Q 23:95   Are alternatives to the QJSA available that allow the flexibility to change beneficiaries and the form of payment after the annuity starting date?

More flexible alternatives to the QJSA are available. Provided there is spousal consent, one alternative is to transfer the plan benefits into a rollover IRA—REA requirements do not apply to rollover IRAs. [Treas Reg § 1.401(a)-20 Q&A-3(c)] Another alternative is to name a revocable trust as the beneficiary because, under the REA rules, the participant's spouse need only consent to the designation of trust as beneficiary and need not consent to either the designation or changes of the trust beneficiaries. [Treas Reg § 1.401(a)-20 Q&A-31(a)] This alternative, however, might be valid only until the participant's required beginning date.

Q 23:96   Are payments made during the life of the participant subject to QJSA rules?

Every payment made during the participant's life is subject to the QJSA rules unless the appropriate waiver or consent is made. [Treas Reg § 1.401(a)-20 Q&A-10(a) and Q&A-9]

Q 23:97 Are there any special considerations for defined contribution plans subject to the REA statutory annuity rules?

If a defined contribution plan subject to the REA statutory annuity rules permits the participant to accelerate distributions, each distribution exceeding the minimum distribution requires either its own waiver by the participant or consent by the spouse, or it must be distributed as a QJSA. [Treas Reg § 1.401(a)-20 Q&A-10(e)]

Q 23:98 May a spouse choose the form of distribution under a deferred contribution plan subject to the REA rules?

If the plan so permits, a spouse entitled to a statutory annuity can choose any optional form of benefit that is available under the plan. [Treas Reg § 1.401(a)-20 Q&A-31(b)(3)]

Q 23:99 Is spousal consent to the QPSA or QJSA waiver revocable or irrevocable?

Spousal consent to the QPSA or QJSA waiver can be either revocable or irrevocable depending on the provisions of the plan. If the spousal consent is revocable, the spouse has the power to render the participant's prior election not to receive a QJSA or QPSA ineffective. [Treas Reg § 1.401(a)-20 Q&A-30]

Q 23:100 Is it necessary in a qualified joint and survivor annuity for a waiver/consent form to specify the optional form of benefit?

A waiver/consent must specify the optional form of benefit and once so designated, the form of benefit cannot be changed without spousal consent unless being changed back to a QJSA. [Treas Reg § 1.401(a)-20 Q&A-31(b)(1)]

Q 23:101 Is a waiver/consent required to specify an optional form of benefit in a QPSA?

A waiver/consent is not required to specify an optional form of benefit, and, therefore, a participant may be able to change a form of benefit without spousal consent. The non-spouse beneficiary, however, cannot be changed without spousal consent. Provisions in the consent, however, can limit the power to change a form of benefit without spousal consent. [Treas Reg § 1.401(a)-20 Q&A-31(b)(2)]

Q 23:102   What is a general consent?

General consents are governed by Treasury Regulations Section 1.401(a)-20 Q&A-31(c). Instead of a specific consent to a beneficiary and/or the form of benefit, a spouse can consent to the participant's power to change any such designations without further consent. A general consent document must state that the spouse has the right to limit the beneficiary and/or form of benefit designations and that the spouse voluntarily waives both rights.

Q 23:103   Can a general consent be limited?

A limited general consent is available. A limited general consent is restricted to certain beneficiaries and/or forms of benefit. [Treas Reg § 1.401(a)-20 Q&A-31(c)]

Q 23:104   Is a general consent available when the designated beneficiary is a trust?

If the beneficiary is a revocable trust, the spouse only needs to consent to the designation of the trust without further consent to a change in the trust beneficiaries. A spouse can make a specific consent whereby further consent is required for changes, however. [Treas Reg § 1.401(a)-20 Q&A-31(a)]

Q 23:105   Is spousal consent necessary for direct rollover to another qualified plan to an IRA?

Spousal consent is needed for the rollover. [Temp Treas Reg § 1.401(a)(31)-IT Q&A-14] Rollovers are treated as distributions and not as transfers of assets and liabilities. Therefore, the distributee-qualified plan is not required to have the same optional form of benefits as provided in the plan that made the rollover.

Distributions from Tax-Qualified Retirement Plans   Q 23:109

Q 23:106   Do rollover contributions subject the transferee plan to the survivor annuity requirements?

No. Rollover contributions are not transactions that subject the transferee plan to the survivor annuity requirements. [Treas Reg § 1.401(a)-20 Q&A-5]

Q 23:107   Are profit sharing plans subject to the REA, QPSA, and QJSA rules?

Profit sharing plans are not subject to the REA, QPSA, and QJSA rules or the waiver/consent procedures applicable to those rules if all the following conditions are met:

1. Under the provisions of the plan, the participant's entire nonforfeitable accrued benefit is payable to the participant's surviving spouse unless there is a waiver/consent for a payment to be made to a designated beneficiary instead.
2. The participant does not elect to have benefits paid in the form of a life annuity.
3. With respect to the participant, the plan is not an offset plan or a transferee plan.

[Treas Reg § 1.401(a)-20 Q&A-3(a)]

Q 23:108   Is spousal consent necessary for the profit sharing plans that are not subject to the QPSA and QJSA rules to make distributions to a participant or to make plan loans?

Spousal consent is not necessary for either distributions to a participant or for plan loans.

Q 23:109   When can the death benefit under profit sharing plan that is not subject to the QPSA and QJSA rules be waived?

The death benefit under such a plan is classified as the spousal benefit under Code Section 401(a)(11)(B). [Treas Reg § 1.401(a)-20

Q&A-32] The spousal benefit can be waived at any time. [Treas Reg § 1.401(a)-10 Q&A-33(a)]

Q 23:110 What must the waiver/consent under a nonsubject profit sharing plan that is not subject to the QPSA and QJSA rules state?

The waiver/consent under a nonsubject profit sharing plan must state the specific non-spouse beneficiary. [Treas Reg § 1.401(a)-20 Q&A-33(b)]

Q 23:111 Does naming a trust as a beneficiary satisfy the specificity requirement of Treasury Regulations Section 1.401(a)-20 Q&A-33(b)?

A trust qualifies as a specific beneficiary even if the participant can change the trust's beneficiaries. [Treas Reg § 1.401(a)-20 Q&A-31(a)]

Q 23:112 Is there a notice requirement with regard to the spousal consent for a waiver for a profit sharing plan that is not subject to the QPSA and QJSA rules?

The spouse must be notified that he or she does not have to consent to the waiver. [Treas Reg § 1.401(a)-20 Q&A-32(b)]

Estate Planning

Q 23:113 Does the gross estate of an employee include the value of distributions (other than life insurance proceeds) from a tax-qualified plan made to a beneficiary?

The gross estate includes the value of an annuity or other payment from a qualified plan receivable by any beneficiary by reason of surviving the decedent if the annuity or other payment was payable to the decedent or the decedent possessed the right to receive such annuity or payment for the decedent's life, for any period not ascer-

Distributions from Tax-Qualified Retirement Plans   Q 23:114

tainable without reference to the decedent's death, or for any period that does not in fact end before the decedent's death. [IRC § 2039(a)] Before the Tax Equity and Fiscal Responsibility Act of 1982 (TEFRA), there was an unlimited exclusion from estate tax for qualified plan annuity benefits attributable to employer contributions, includible in the employee's gross income under Section 402(b), and paid to the deceased employee's beneficiary on account of death. TEFRA limited the estate tax exclusion to $100,000 for decedents dying after December 31, 1982. [TEFRA §§ 245(a), 245(c)]

This $100,000 exclusion was eliminated by the Tax Reform Act of 1984 (TRA '84) for decedents dying after December 31, 1984. The $100,000 limitation still applies to decedents dying after December 31, 1984, however, if the decedent was a qualified plan participant in pay status on December 31, 1984, and irrevocably elected the beneficiary and form of benefit before July 18, 1984. [TRA '84, § 525(a)] In addition, TRA '84 provides an unlimited estate tax exclusion to the estate of any decedent dying after December 31, 1982, so long as such decedent was a qualified plan participant in pay status on December 31, 1982, and irrevocably elected the form of benefit before January 1, 1983. [TRA '84 § 525(b)(3), amending TEFRA § 245(c)]

Q 23:114   Are life insurance proceeds payable under a policy on a qualified participant's life includible in such participant's gross estate?

Life insurance proceeds from a qualified plan that are payable to the deceased participant's executor (or estate) are includible in the deceased participant's gross estate. [IRC § 2042(1)] If the proceeds are payable to a beneficiary, they are included in the deceased participant's gross estate only if the decedent possessed incidents of ownership in the policy at his or her death. [IRC § 2042(2)] Incidents of ownership include the power to change the beneficiary, to surrender or cancel the policy, to assign the policy, to revoke an assignment, to pledge the policy for a loan, or to obtain from the insurer a loan against the surrender value of the policy. [Treas Reg § 2042-1(c)(2)]

Chapter 24

Distributions from Nonqualified Plans

Payments from nonqualified deferred compensation arrangements receive less favorable tax treatment than payments from tax-qualified retirement plans. This chapter discusses the tax treatment afforded an employee with regard to nonqualified deferred compensation arrangement payments made from a plan's trust or made directly from the general assets of the employer.

Overview	24-1
Contractual Right to Future Payments	24-2
Trust Payments	24-3

Overview

24:1 How are distributions from nonqualified deferred compensation arrangements taxed?

Distributions from nonqualified deferred compensation arrangements do not receive the favorable tax treatment accorded to qualified plan distributions. Indeed, nonqualified deferred compensation arrangements must be carefully designed to avoid the premature receipt of income. The tax treatment varies depending on whether payments under the nonqualified deferred compensation arrangement are made from a trust or whether they are contract payments.

Q 24:2   Estate and Retirement Planning Answer Book

Contractual Right to Future Payments

Q 24:2   **How is a participant taxed under a deferred compensation arrangement consisting only of a contractual right to future payments?**

If a deferred compensation arrangement consists only of a contractual right to future payments (i.e., payments are to be made from the general assets of the employer rather than out of a trust associated with the arrangement), an employee who is a cash-basis taxpayer is not taxed until he or she actually or constructively receives income. [IRC § 61(a)]

Q 24:3   **If an employee participates in a deferred compensation arrangement consisting only of contractual rights to future payments, can he or she elect to defer a portion of salary prior to the beginning of the taxable year?**

The Internal Revenue Service (IRS) has ruled that an employee can elect, prior to the beginning of his or her taxable year, to defer a portion of his or her salary with the payment of the deferred amounts to be made after the employee attains age 55. [Ltr Rul 8021085] By making the election in advance, the employee keeps the portion of salary to which the deferral election applies from being included in gross income during the taxable year in which it is earned.

Q 24:4   **When is an employee in constructive receipt of income?**

Income not actually received is considered to be constructively received by an employee if it is credited to the employee's account, set aside for the employee, or otherwise made available to the employee, so that he or she can draw upon it at any time. [Treas Reg § 1.451-2(a)]

The IRS has ruled that an employee who is given the option at retirement to further defer income already earned is in constructive receipt of the income earned because the employee could also choose to receive the income rather than to defer it. [TAM 8632003]

Trust Payments

Q 24:5 Is an employee taxed on employer contributions made to a nonqualified trust?

Yes. If an employer makes contributions to an employee's trust that is not a tax-qualified trust under Section 401(a) of the Internal Revenue Code (Code), those contributions will be included in the income of an employee in accordance with Code Section 83. This means that the employee is taxed no later than the time at which his or her rights become nonforfeitable or transferable, and taxation will occur even if the employee is not yet entitled to receive any money.

Q 24:6 How is an employee taxed when he or she receives distributions from a nonqualified trust?

Code Section 72 provides that distributions from a nonqualified trust (see Q 24:5) are taxable when they are paid or made available to an employee. [IRC § 402(b)] This is true even if the employee's interest in the trust is not substantially vested yet. If the trust funds are subject to the claims of general creditors (as is often the case with most nonqualified deferred compensation arrangements), they are subject to income taxation once the money is paid to the employee or made available to the employee (even if the money is not yet nonforfeitable or transferable).

If the employee has previously been taxed on amounts contributed to the trust and he or she receives payments from the nonqualified trust in the form of an annuity, a portion of each payment is treated as a return of the amount that was already included in the employee's gross income. The portion of each payment that has not previously been taxed to the employee will be taxable. [IRC § 72] If, on the other hand, the distribution is not in annuity form (e.g., if payment is made in a single lump sum), the payment is taxed under Code Section 72(e). This means that the distribution is taxable to the extent that the value of the amount distributed exceeds the value of trust assets that have already been included in the gross income of the participant. [IRC § 402(b)(1)] Any remaining amount is not taxed because it derives from employer contributions that have not been previously taxed to the employee. [IRC § 72]

Chapter 25

Protection of Retirement Income

Most retirement planning involves the creation of an appropriate retirement plan and consideration of potential tax consequences. A significant but sometimes neglected concern, however, is the preservation and protection of accumulated assets from creditors. This chapter explores a number of devices that can be used to protect assets from creditors and some of the advantages and disadvantages of those devices. It also discusses the concept of fraudulent conveyance and how such a conveyance fails to protect assets from creditors.

Asset protection has attracted increasing attention in recent years, particularly from professionals earning high incomes who are concerned about the possibility of malpractice judgments depleting their assets. The basic tools of asset protection are not new; trusts have long been used to protect assets. Other devices include tax-qualified retirement plans in some states, individual retirement accounts, family limited partnerships, trusts, and foreign trusts.

Qualified Retirement Plan Assets	25-2
IRA Assets	25-6
Life Insurance Proceeds	25-14
Fraudulent Conveyances	25-14

Qualified Retirement Plan Assets

Q 25:1 Can qualified retirement plan assets be reached by judgment creditors?

Generally, no. Tax-qualified retirement plans must provide that participant benefits under the plan may not be assigned or alienated. [IRC § 401(a)(13)] The courts have held that these provisions protect plan assets against judgment creditors, even if the plan participant has committed an act of malfeasance against the employer. [Ellis National Bank of Jacksonville v Erving Trust, 786 F 2d 466 (2nd Cir 1986)]

Q 25:2 What is asset protection?

Asset protection consists of a series of actions taken by an asset owner to protect the asset from future creditors who may appear and place claims against it. This planning for potential creditors must be distinguished from a transfer of assets designed to actually defraud present creditors. The latter transfer—to defraud or illegally evade the rights of present creditors—is often referred to as a fraudulent conveyance. [In re Oberst, 91 BR 97 (Bankr CD Cal 1988); Hurlbert v Shackleton, 560 So 2d 1276 (Fla Dist Ct App 1990)]

Q 25:3 What is a fraudulent transfer?

A fraudulent transfer is a transfer made by debtor with regard to a creditor whose claim arose before or after the transfer was made, if the debtor made the transfer with actual intent to hinder, delay, or defraud the creditor. [UFTA § (a)(1), 11 USC § 548 (1984)] A transfer may also be presumed to be fraudulent, regardless of the debtor's intent, where it is made without receiving a reasonably equivalent value in exchange; that is, where the debtor transfers assets to a third party without receiving fair market or close to fair market value. Generally, the courts will find a fraudulent conveyance or transfer where the debtor's assets remaining after the transfer are unreasonably small in relation to the business liabilities normally expected to be incurred. [UFTA § (4)(a)(2)] Furthermore, a transfer is considered fraudulent under the Bankruptcy Code where the transfer is made without receiving a reasonably equivalent value and the debtor-asset owner was insolvent or became insolvent as a result of the transfer. [11 USC § 548]

Q 25:4 What are the most common methods used to protect assets?

The most common methods used to protect assets are as follows:

- Outright gift
- Gift in trust
- Co-tenancy
- Life insurance
- Homestead exemption
- Annuity exemption
- Qualified retirement plan or individual retirement account (IRA)
- Family limited partnership
- Trust
- Spendthrift trust
- Foreign trust

Q 25:5 How effective is a gift as a means of protecting an asset?

The obvious disadvantage of making a gift to a third party is that the donor loses control of the asset. If the asset owner attempts to limit this loss of control by making a gift of the asset to a family member, this transfer can also be open to attack by a creditor on the basis either of being a fraudulent transfer or that the recipient is a constructive trustee for the donor. In the case of a constructive trust, the courts will generally order that the asset be returned to the donor. Another consideration is that even family members can subvert control; for example, transferring an asset to a spouse can fail to provide control of the asset if a divorce ensues. Similarly, assets transferred to children may provide no more control over the asset than transferring the asset to any other third party. Furthermore, depending on the identity of the recipient and the nature of the asset, a potential gift tax arises that must be factored into the solution (see chapter 4). [IRC §§ 2523(a), 2523(i)]

Q 25:6 How does a gift in trust protect assets?

A donor may protect an asset by giving it to an irrevocable trust over which the donor retains no interest or power. A transfer of assets to an irrevocable trust has some of the disadvantages of a transfer to a third party: the transferor normally loses control over the asset and over the income from the asset and, depending on the beneficiaries of the trust, may incur gift tax.

Q 25:7 How do co-tenancies protect assets?

In general, co-tenancies protect assets by creating a transfer of an interest in the asset to another party. Co-tenancies such as joint tenants with rights of survivorship and tenants in common do not generally provide good asset protection because they merely transfer a portion of what the asset holder presently owns; generally, only this transferred portion is protected from creditors. Moreover, the present transfer can create other problems. If the person to whom the asset is transferred has creditors who seek to enforce their claims, for instance, those creditors may seek partition or sale of the asset. A tenancy by the entireties, a special form of joint tenancy that can only exist between husband and wife, will usually protect the property from the creditors of one spouse. If the individual is a creditor of both spouses, however, the tenancy by the entireties form will not protect the couple's assets. [First National Bank of Leesburg v Hecker Supply Co, 254 So 2d 777 (Fla 1971)]

Q 25:8 How does the homestead exemption protect assets?

Homestead exemptions are created by estate law and are intended to prevent a debtor's primary home from falling into the hands of creditors. The exemption may range from nothing to an unlimited value of the homestead restricted only by the size of the property. In some instances, this exemption can provide protection for very substantial values. The laws of the local jurisdiction must be carefully checked to determine the extent of the homestead exemption. In any event, the homestead exemption is generally limited solely to the dwelling or farm dwelling of the owner. For example, Florida has a homestead exemption of unlimited value for up to 160 acres of land located outside of a municipality and up to one half an acre if located inside the municipality. [Fla Const art X, § 4]

Q 25:9 How does an annuity protect assets?

Various state statutes create protection for the proceeds of annuity contracts that keep them safe from the claims of creditors. The scope of the exemptions varies significantly among the states. In Florida, for example, the annuity contract appears to be an absolute bar to creditors. [Fla Stat Ch 222.14; McCollam v McCollam, 986 F 2d 436 (11th Cir 1993)] Nebraska's annuity protection appears to be limited to $10,000. [Neb Rev Stat § 44-371(1)]

Q 25:10 Can qualified retirement plan assets be reached by judgment creditors?

Generally, no. Tax-qualified retirement plans must provide that a participant's benefits under the plan may not be assigned or alienated. [IRC § 401(a)(13)] The courts have generally held that these provisions protect plan assets against judgment creditors, even if the plan participant has committed an act of malfeasance against the employer. [Ellis Nat'l Bank of Jacksonville v Irving Trust Co, 786 F 2d 466 (2nd Cir 1986)]

Q 25:11 Can qualified retirement plan assets be reached if a participant is bankrupt?

If the participant is not the sole owner of the business sponsoring the qualified retirement plan, his or her benefits in the plan are generally protected from bankruptcy creditors. [Patterson v Shumate, 112 S Ct 2242; In re Lichstrahl, 750 F 2d 1488 (11th Cir 1985)]

Q 25:12 Can the qualified retirement plan benefits of the sole owner of a business be reached in bankruptcy proceedings?

Perhaps. The U.S. Supreme Court's decision in *Patterson* indicates that these benefits cannot be reached if the plan covers someone other than the owner of the business. [Patterson v Schumate, 112 S Ct 2242 (1992)] It is less certain whether, in a plan that covers only the sole owner of a business or his or her spouse, the benefits of the owners are protected.

In *Bernstein v. Greenpoint Savings Bank* [149 BR 760 (Bankr ED NY 1993] assets in a Keogh plan were not so protected. In *Greenpoint*, the court found that because Keogh plans covering only self-employed individuals are not subject to Title I of ERISA and because Patterson only protected plan assets that were subject to the antialienation provisions of Title I of ERISA, the Keogh plan assets in question could not be excluded from the bankruptcy estate. The court also found that the Keogh plan failed to meet the requirements for a state law exemption for qualified plans because the plan became disqualified by failing to make the minimum contributions for top-heavy plans.

IRA Assets

Q 25:13 Are IRA assets protected from creditors?

The Internal Revenue Code (Code) antialienation provisions do not protect IRA accounts from creditors. [IRC § 401(a)(13)] Many states have enacted legislation that protects IRA accounts from creditors, however. It is unclear whether these laws are valid. One Supreme Court decision can be read as suggesting that these statutes are preempted by federal law. [MacKey v Lanier Collection Agency & Service, 486 US 825 (1988)]

Q 25:14 What is the effect of a judgment creditor reaching IRA assets or qualified plan benefits?

When a judgment creditor reaches IRA assets or qualified plan benefits, the assets taken by the creditor are treated as a distribution to the participant. If the distribution occurs before the participant reaches age 59½, the premature withdrawal tax is triggered. [IRC §§ 72(t)(1), 72(t)(2)] This distribution is treated as ordinary income. [In re Kochell, 804 F 2d 84 (7th Cir 1986)]

Q 25:15 How does life insurance protect assets?

Many states provide exemptions for cash surrender values for the proceeds of life insurance contracts from the claims of creditors. [Fla Stat Ch 222.13(1)]

Q 25:16 How can a limited liability company be used to protect assets?

Limited liability companies are established by state law. Most have managers that administer the companies through an operating agreement. Limited liability companies are managed by either managers who are appointed by members or by member-managers. Like limited partnerships, limited liability companies restrict the creditor's ability to attach the personal assets of the members. Indeed, limited liability companies are similar to corporations in that their members, like shareholders of corporations, are generally protected from personal liability.

Q 25:17 Can qualified retirement plan assets be reached by a bankruptcy trustee?

No, they cannot. The Supreme Court has held that the antialienation provisions of ERISA preclude payment of plan assets in satisfaction of a bankruptcy claim. [Patterson v Schmate, 112 S Ct 2242 (1992)]

Q 25:18 Operating under its escheat laws, may a state take the unclaimed account balance of a plan participant?

No. The Department of Labor (DOL) has ruled that a Texas statute permitting the state to take possession of unclaimed property is preempted by ERISA when applied to a tax-qualified plan. As a result, the DOL concluded that Texas could not take the account balances of participants who had disappeared. [DOL Adv Op 94-41A]

Q 25:19 What exceptions exist to the rule that plan assets may not be attached?

Retirement plans are required by law to honor certain court orders that direct the plan to pay all or a portion of the participant's benefits to another individual. Although virtually all qualified domestic relation orders (QDROs) involve tax-qualified retirement plans, QDRO procedures also apply to nonqualified plans that are pension plans under Title I of ERISA. This would cover such plans as nonqualified retirement plans funded by trust assets that cannot be reached by employer creditors. In connection with family matters, such as divorce, a court order can be used to reach plan assets provided that the court order qualifies as a qualified domestic relations order. A QDRO is any judgment, decree, or order (including court approval of a property settlement agreement) that relates to child support, alimony payments, or marital property rights for a spouse, former spouse, child, or other dependent of a retirement plan participant pursuant to state domestic relations law. [IRC § 414(p)(1)(B), ERISA § 206(d)(3)(B)(ii)]

Q 25:20 What requirements must a domestic relations order meet to qualify as an exception to the rule that plan assets may not be attached?

A QDRO must include the following:

1. The name and last mailing address of the participant and the name and mailing address of each alternate payee covered by the order;
2. The amount or percentage of the participant's benefits to be paid by the plan to each such alternate payee or the manner in which such amount or percentage is to be determined;
3. The number of payments or period to which such order applies; and
4. Each plan to which such order applies.

To be a QDRO, a domestic relations order must specify certain facts and cannot require the plan to (1) provide increased benefits; (2) make benefit payments to an alternate payee[1] that are required to be made to another alternate payee under another order previously determined to be a QDRO; or (3) provide any type or form of benefits or any option not otherwise provided under the plan. [IRC § 414(p)(3)] The last requirement is not violated simply because the order requires that benefits be paid on or after the date the participant attains the earliest retirement age under the plan even if the participant has not separated from service by the date of the payment. In such event, the amount of the payment to be made by reason of the QDRO must be determined by taking into account only the present value of benefits actually accrued by the participant on the date of the first payment (early retirement subsidies cannot be considered). For this purpose, earliest retirement age is determined as follows:

1. Determine the later of (1) age 50 or (2) the earliest date on which a participant could receive benefits under the plan if the participant separated from service; and

2. Determine whether the date on which the participant is entitled to a distribution under the plan is earlier than the date identified in Step 1, and pick the earlier of those dates. That date is the earliest retirement age for QDRO purposes. [IRC § 414(p)(4)(B)]

Q 25:21 Who determines whether a domestic relations order is a qualified domestic relations order?

The plan administrator of the retirement plan initially determines whether a domestic relations order is a QDRO. [IRC § 414(p)(6)(A)(ii)] This determination is subject to review by the courts.

---

1. The alternate payee is a spouse, former spouse, child, or other dependent of the plan participant who is recognized by a domestic relations order as having a right to receive all or a portion of the benefits payable to the participant. [ERISA § 206(d)(3)(K)]

Q 25:22 Which plans are subject to the laws concerning qualified domestic relations orders?

The QDRO rules apply to all defined benefit, target benefit, money purchase pension, profit sharing, Section 401(k), and Section 403(b) annuity plans and, to a limited degree, to governmental and church retirement plans. [IRC §§ 401(a)(13), 414(p)(9)]

Q 25:23 What does a qualified domestic relations order do?

A QDRO allows a qualified plan to distribute benefits to a payee (alternate payee) without violating the antialienation provisions of the Code. The anti-alienation provisions prohibit the distribution of any portion of a participant's benefits to a third party. [IRC § 401(a)(3)]

Q 25:24 Who can be an alternate payee?

An alternate payee can be a spouse, former spouse, child, or other dependent of the plan participant. [IRC § 414(p)(8)]

Q 25:25 When does a qualified domestic relations order make payments?

Unless the plan contains specific language permitting immediate distributions to an alternate payee, QDRO payments are made when the plan participant reaches his earliest retirement age (see Q 25:20). [IRC § 414(p)(4)(B)] Immediate distribution is often desirable to allow for speedy completion of the property division. For this reason, many plans provide for the immediate distribution of benefits to the alternate payee.

Q 25:26 May a qualified domestic relations order require payment of the participant's entire plan account?

Yes. A QDRO may require payment of all or any portion of a plan participant's vested accrued benefit or of retirement payments the participant may already be receiving. [IRC § 414(p)(1)(A)]

Q 25:27 Who pays the income taxes due on qualified domestic relations order distributions?

If the alternate payee is the spouse or former spouse, the alternate payee pays any income taxes due on the distribution. [Patricia Eatinger v Commr, 59 TCM 954 (1990)] If the alternate payee is a child or non-spouse dependent, the plan participant is responsible for any income taxes due.

If the participant would be eligible to receive a lump-sum distribution that qualifies for income averaging, the alternate payee can elect income averaging for the QDRO distribution.

Q 25:28 Are qualified domestic relations order payments exempt from the 10 percent premature distribution penalties?

Yes. For example, QDRO payments to an alternate payee made before the participant reaches age $59\frac{1}{2}$ are exempt from the 10 percent premature distribution penalty that might otherwise apply under Code Section 72(t)(1). [IRC § 72(t)(2)(C)]

Q 25:29 Can qualified domestic relations order payments be rolled over?

In most cases, yes. The spouse or former spouse can roll over the QDRO payments to an IRA or to another qualified plan in order to defer payment of any income taxes. Some QDRO payments cannot be rolled over. These are retirement type payments that are substantially equal installment payments made (1) over the life or life expectancy of the participant (or the joint lives or joint life expectancies of the participant and his or her beneficiary) or (2) over a period of ten years or more. [IRC § 402(c)(1)(4)]

Q 25:30 Do the mandatory income tax withholding rules apply to qualified domestic relations order distributions?

Yes. QDRO distributions are subject to mandatory income withholding if the distributions are otherwise eligible for rollover to an IRA or to another qualified plan. [IRC § 3405]

Q 25:31 What happens to qualified domestic relations order payments pledged to prior payees if a second divorce occurs?

A second or subsequent divorce may result in additional QDROs and additional alternate payees. Subsequent alternate payees may not claim benefits already pledged to previous alternate payees. [IRC § 414(p)(3)(C)]

Q 25:32 May a participant be charged for the administrative costs of a qualified domestic relations order?

No. According to the DOL, the plan participant and the alternate payee may not be separately charged any fees or costs related to the determination or administration of the QDRO. Any administrative expenses paid by the plan are shared by all participants, not solely the individuals subject to the QDRO.

Q 25:33 If the retirement plan participant dies, should the participant's former spouse be treated as the participant's surviving spouse for joint and survivor and preretirement survivor annuity purposes?

Both the Code and ERISA contain provisions requiring spousal consent to any waivers of the joint and survivor annuity and the preretirement survivor annuity. [ERISA § 205(c)] A QDRO can provide that the surviving former spouse of a participant is to be treated as the surviving spouse of the participant for purposes of survivor and preretirement survivor provisions. To the extent this is done, any current spouse of the participant has no spousal rights under these provisions. This means, among other things, that if the participant dies before the earliest retirement date, his or her former spouse would be entitled to the preretirement survivor annuity. On the other hand, if the former spouse is not given surviving spouse status and if the participant dies before the earliest retirement date and before payments are made to the former spouse, the former spouse would not be entitled to survivor benefits. [IRC § 414(p)(5)]

Q 25:34 What actions should the plan administrator take if a domestic relations order is received by the plan?

The plan administrator must notify both the participant and each alternate payee (see Q 25:24) of the receipt of the order and the plan's procedures for determining the qualified status of the domestic relations order (see Q 25:21). Within a reasonable time after the receipt of the order, the plan administrator must determine whether the order is a QDRO and notify the participant and each alternative payee of that determination. [IRC § 414(p)(6)(A)]

While a determination is being made whether the domestic relations order is a QDRO (whether by the plan administrator, by a court, or otherwise), the plan administrator must separately account for the amounts that would have been payable to the alternate payee during that time period if the order had been determined to be a QDRO. [IRC § 414(p)(7)(A)] If during the 18-month period that begins when the first payment is due under the domestic relations order, it is either determined that the domestic relations order is not a QDRO or the issue as to whether the order is a QDRO is not resolved, the plan administrator must pay the segregated amounts (including any interest thereon) to the persons entitled to them had there been no domestic relations order. [IRC § 414(p)(7)(c)]

It is important for the alternate payee that a determination as to the qualified status of the domestic relations order be made within the 18-month period. Any determination that an order is a QDRO that is made after the close of the 18-month period must be applied prospectively. [IRC § 414(p)(7)(D)]

Q 25:35 What procedures must be established to handle domestic relations orders?

The plan must establish a reasonable procedure to determine the qualified status of any domestic relations order received and to administer plan distributions under these orders. [IRC § 414(p)(6)(B)] The procedure must be in writing and must permit the alternate payee to designate a representative to receive copies of any notices sent by the plan regarding the domestic relations order. The procedures must also provide that each person specified in the domestic relations order as entitled to payment of benefits under the plan be promptly notified of such procedures. [IRC § 414(p)(6)(A)]

Q 25:36 What fiduciary duties apply with respect to the processing of domestic relations orders?

If a plan fiduciary acts in accordance with the general ERISA fiduciary requirements in determining whether a domestic relations order is a QDRO or in segregating funds while determining the status of a domestic relations order, the plan's liability to the participant and each alternate payee is discharged to the extent of any payment made. [ERISA § 404]

Life Insurance Proceeds

Q 25:37 Are life insurance proceeds exempt from creditors?

The answer depends upon the applicable state insurance law. Some state laws provide that the proceeds of life insurance policies are exempt from the claims of creditors of the insured. [Fla Stat Ch 222.13(1)] Accordingly, purchasing life insurance in such states could protect a significant amount from creditors.

Fraudulent Conveyances

Q 25:38 What are fraudulent conveyance laws?

Fraudulent conveyance laws, which exist in some form in all states, are intended to protect present and subsequent creditors against transfers of property or assets made with an intent to hinder, delay, or defraud them. In general, under such laws the transferor's intent is a key factor. A transaction will not be set aside merely because it resulted in a creditor being hindered or delayed; instead, an intent or purpose to hinder or delay must be found.

Q 25:39 How can an intent to defraud be established?

An intent to defraud existing creditors can be established either by express statements or by inferences from facts and circumstances. There are certain conditions that sometimes create a presumption of an intent to defraud. They include the following:

- Insolvency
- A threat of litigation
- Lack of sufficient consideration
- A family or close relationship between the transferor and the transferee
- A transfer of one's entire estate

Q 25:40 How are subsequent creditors protected?

Under the fraudulent conveyance laws, subsequent creditors may be protected if they can show actual fraud. They generally cannot rely on presumptions, however.

In general, a person is a subsequent creditor of a transferor if the transferor knows the individual will be becoming a creditor and has an actual fraudulent intent at the time of transfer (including a present intent to act fraudulently in the future or to proceed with his or her affairs with reckless disregard for the rights of others). It does not include persons who some day may become a creditor of the transferor. The key distinction is the transferor's present intent.

Chapter 26

Incapacity and Other Retirement Issues

The prospect of a catastrophic illness or accident and the resulting disability or physical or mental incapacity during the retirement years is a sobering one for many individuals. Similarly, the possibility of having to reside in a nursing home is worrisome. This chapter discusses financial and estate planning for such eventualities.

Overview	26-1
Living Wills	26-3
Durable Powers of Attorney	26-3
Revocable Trusts	26-6
Long-Term Health Care Insurance	26-8
Medicaid Planning for Institutionalization	26-9
Estate Planning for Institutionalization	26-23

Overview

Q 26:1 Why is the possibility of incapacity an important issue in retirement planning?

Two factors make it extremely important for all individuals to consider the issue of incapacity. First, more elderly people are living longer than ever before—in nursing homes that provide the levels of care and service required by this segment of the population. It seems certain that, sooner or later, many people will face the problem of financing long-term health care, either for themselves or for an older family member.

The second important factor is the rising cost of health care. In 1992, Americans spent $800.2 billion on health care, a 10 percent increase over 1991. Similarly, in 1993, $950 billion was spent, and in 1994 expenditures were estimated at more than $1 trillion. The rate of health care inflation is 9 percent, compared to a 3 percent general rate of inflation.

Q 26:2   What is the cost of long-term health care?

Today, the average cost of care at a skilled nursing facility exceeds $3,800 per month, or more than $126 per day. These numbers are especially alarming given that one out of every four persons over the age of 65 will spend some time in a skilled nursing facility. This number increases to one out of every two people among individuals over age 80.

Q 26:3   What kind of estate planning can be done to prepare for a person entering a nursing home?

Persons about to enter nursing homes have special planning needs. Durable powers of attorney (financial and medical) can be helpful estate planning instruments because they allow family members or other trusted individuals to handle an individual's affairs. A revocable trust is another type of instrument that is helpful in financial planning for the infirm elderly. When considering how to pay for the costs of nursing homes, individuals may want to consider long-term care insurance. As well, persons who face the possibility of long-term health care are often vitally concerned with obtaining Medicaid benefits. To help achieve eligibility for Medicaid, several methods of transferring assets can be considered. Lastly, traditional (testamentary) wills and living wills should also be discussed.

Q 26:4   What estate planning can be done to mitigate the financial impact of catastrophic illness or accident?

Living wills and medical durable powers of attorney can save thousands of dollars in medical expenses by facilitating the cessation of unwanted health care should an individual become subject to a debilitating illness or injury. The availability of these instruments makes it possible to discuss and decide on options while an individual is still capable of expressing his or her wishes. If these instruments are used properly, they will generally allow family members to avoid prolonged legal disputes over the termination of care.

Living Wills

Q 26:5 What is a living will?

A living will instructs physicians to withdraw or withhold artificial life support under certain conditions. In most states, the patient's medical condition must be terminal before a living will becomes effective. Often, however, the statutory definition of terminal does not include comatose or vegetative states, strokes, or the occurrence of progressive degenerative diseases.

Durable Powers of Attorney

Q 26:6 What is a durable power of attorney?

A power of attorney gives another person (the agent) the power to make decisions regarding, and handle the affairs of, the person who signs the power of attorney (the principal). Unlike common-law powers of attorney, which expire if the principal becomes incapacitated, durable powers of attorney remain effective despite the principal's disability until the principal revokes it or dies. The Durable Power of Attorney Act recognizes both standing and springing durable powers. [UPC §§ 5-501-5-505] The former take effect upon execution, while the latter "spring" into existence if and when the principal becomes disabled. The durable power of attorney makes it possible for the agent to make financial and medical decisions on behalf of the disabled or incapacitated principal.

Q 26:7 What can durable powers of attorney be used for?

If permitted by applicable state law, durable powers of attorney can confer authority to claim a spouse's elective share; to disclaim gifts or inheritances; to make elections relating to, or directing distributions from, retirement plans (to the extent consistent with federal law governing the retirement plan); and to redeem or roll over certificates of deposit.

Q 26:8 What are medical durable powers of attorney?

Medical durable powers of attorney authorize an agent or proxy to provide or withhold informed consent on the patient's behalf to any form of medical treatment, not just artificial life support. For example, if a patient is comatose but not dying, the designated agent may assume authority to make decisions regarding all phases of the principal's medical treatment.

Q 26:9 What requirements must a durable power of attorney meet to be valid?

To be a valid durable power of attorney, the document must explicitly state that the agent's authority is not impaired by the principal's subsequent disability. Durable power of attorney statutes have been adopted in all 50 states. Accordingly, subject to the limitations of applicable state law, durable powers can be as broad or limited in scope as desired.

Q 26:10 Are there limits on the scope of durable powers of attorney?

Certain types of authority generally may not be delegated, such as the power to make or change the will of the principal or the power to exercise authority held by the principal in a fiduciary capacity.

Q 26:11 Can durable powers of attorney result in the imposition of gift or estate tax on the agent?

Express gift giving powers contained in a durable power of attorney may create gift tax exposure for the agent if the gift giving authority (1) is not limited by a prohibition against the agent's making gifts to himself or herself and (2) exceeds the greater of 5 percent of the aggregate value of the principal's assets or $5,000. Without these limitations, there is a risk the Internal Revenue Service (IRS) would treat the power as a general power of appointment (see Q 3:13), causing the inclusion of all the property subject to the power in the agent's gross estate under Section 2041(b)(2) of the Internal Revenue Code (Code).

Q 26:12 Must any special steps be taken if the durable power of attorney covers life insurance?

If the property subject to a durable power includes insurance on the life of the agent who has the authority expressly or implicitly under a durable power of attorney "to obtain, continue, modify, or terminate" such policies, that authority may be treated as an incident of ownership, subjecting the entire life insurance proceeds to inclusion in the agent/insured's estate. [IRC § 2042] To avoid this possibility, the document should expressly exclude from the scope of the agent's authority all powers over insurance on the agent's own life, including any such policies that are found to have been owned at the agent's death by the principal.

Q 26:13 What are the disadvantages of durable powers of attorney?

Broad durable powers of attorney are not easily monitored, and the risk exists that an agent may divest an incapacitated principal of his or her life savings. Further, durable powers of attorney are not always honored. Third parties may balk at instructions from an agent because the power creating the agent's authority is vague, or is more than a year old and thus is stale, or because it omits precise descriptions of the property or account numbers.

Q 26:14 What are the reasons for creating a living trust?

A living trust can protect the assets of a person who cannot look after them because of illness or incapacity. Because trusts are generally more widely accepted than powers of attorney, they are a superior vehicle for holding the assets of a person who is incapacitated.

Q 26:15   Estate and Retirement Planning Answer Book

A power of attorney that was signed many years in the past may very well be questioned by a broker or a banker who is asked to honor it; this is much less likely to happen with a trust.

Revocable Trusts

Q 26:15   Do revocable trusts have advantages in meeting the needs of individuals in nursing homes?

Revocable trusts are well suited to the needs of nursing home residents. These trusts typically designate the settlor as the lifetime beneficiary of distributions. These trusts avoid the uncertainties of durable powers of attorney and the formality and expense of conservatorship proceedings during periods of incapacity. When the settlor dies, the remaining trust assets pass to the designated remainder beneficiaries without the publicity, delay, and expense of probate.

Q 26:16   Do revocable trusts have to be funded immediately?

No, they do not. Revocable trusts can either be funded when they are created, or they can be dormant, serving as receptacles for future transfers.

Q 26:17   What is the income tax treatment of a revocable trust?

The typical revocable trust is a grantor trust under Code Sections 671 through 677, so all trust income is taxable to the grantor during his or her lifetime. As long as the grantor serves as trustee or co-trustee, the trust is not required to obtain a separate taxpayer identification number or to file annual income tax returns. [Treas Reg §§ 1.671-4(b)(1), 301.6109-1(a)(2)] Upon the grantor's death, the trust becomes irrevocable and a separate taxpaying entity with its own identification number and return filing responsibilities. [IRC §§ 6012(a)(4), 6072(a), 6109]

Q 26:18 What is the estate and gift tax treatment of a revocable trust?

No gift tax is due upon creation or funding of a revocable trust because transfers to a revocable trust are, by their nature, not completed gifts until distributions from the trust are made to beneficiaries other than the grantor, or until the trust becomes irrevocable at the grantor's death. The assets of a revocable trust are included in the grantor's gross estate for estate tax purposes under Code Sections 2036 (retained life interests) and 2038 (revocable transfers) and, to the extent the corpus includes insurance on the grantor's life, under Code Section 2042.

Q 26:19 How should a revocable trust be funded for a person who may go into a nursing home?

It is important to consider various means of funding a potential nursing home resident's revocable trust. When the trust is established, the resident should also execute a limited durable power of attorney giving an agent authority to marshal the client's assets and deposit them into the trust if the client becomes disabled and the trustee must step in. This step eliminates the need to fund the trust at its inception to avoid the risk of conservatorship proceedings in case of disability. After death, if a pour-over provision is included in the client's will, the remaining assets that were not conveyed to the trust during the client's lifetime can pass to the trust via the probate process.

Q 26:20 Who should be the trustee for a living trust?

If the person creating the trust is ill or in declining health, a third party may have to be appointed trustee from the beginning. If the person is still capable of handling his or her own affairs, that individual can be the initial trustee. The trust document can be drafted to provide that if a physician states that the individual has lost capacity, the trusteeship goes into the hands of others. The other trustees may be, for example, professionals or the trust creator's children.

Q 26:21 Should a co-trustee be named for a revocable trust?

If a revocable trust is used and the nursing home resident wishes to be both grantor and trustee, a co-trustee should be named or provisions for successor trustees should be included because of the grantor/trustee's expected potential future incapacity.

Long-Term Health Care Insurance

Q 26:22 What is long-term health care insurance?

Long-term health care insurance is a type of insurance policy that many insurance providers now make available. It provides for an individual in the event that he or she becomes incapacitated or otherwise needs lengthy, skilled health care, such as that provided by a nursing home. Long-term health insurance can be expensive, but this expense must be weighed against the fact that the daily cost of care in a nursing home now averages between $80 and $145 per day.

Q 26:23 What issues should be examined when considering long-term health care insurance?

Individuals should examine the following issues:

1. Are there any policy limitations for preexisting conditions?
2. What benefits are provided by the policy? It is important to consider the effects of inflation on health care costs. Examine the average daily rate of nursing homes and similar long-term care providers in the preferred area; then choose a benefit amount anywhere from 10 percent to 50 percent higher than the average daily rate. This range compensates for the length of time expected to elapse (and the consequent increases in inflation) before benefits are needed.
3. Does the policy contain an elimination period? Elimination period refers to the amount of time that the insured must wait before payments begin. Although a policy with a long elimination period may have lower premiums, it is important to consider the potential private pay cost of nursing home facilities

and services that could be incurred during the elimination period.
4. How long will payments continue? The average stay in a nursing home is thirty months, so it is advisable to choose a policy that offers a minimum of three years' coverage.
5. Does coverage depend on a period of prior hospitalization?
6. What are the renewal provisions in the policy? Potential purchasers should consider whether the policy offers automatic renewal and whether it reserves the right to change the amount of premiums payable.
7. Is there an inflation protection option in the policy? Potential purchasers should check to see if the policy provides for increases in benefit levels to coordinate with anticipated increases in health care costs.

Medicaid Planning for Institutionalization

Q 26:24 What is Medicaid planning?

Generally, the goal of Medicaid planning is to protect an individual's resources from short-run dissipation by nursing home expenses. This goal is accomplished by siphoning the assets either to family members or to a fund for the client's secondary needs (items other than food, clothing, and shelter). If this is done, the individual may be eligible for Medicaid.

Q 26:25 How do Medicare and Medicaid differ?

Medicare was intended to help elderly and disabled people pay for hospital and doctor bills, regardless of their financial situation. Medicare is financed and administered entirely be the federal government, and almost every American over the age of 65 is eligible. In contrast, Medicaid is a federal and state jointly funded program available to those states that choose to participate. The purpose is to provide medical care to financially needy persons. States that participate are required to adhere to general federal guidelines and must comply with the requirements imposed by the Social Security Administration and the Department of Health and Human Services. The states, however, have great latitude in determining the income and asset criteria that they choose to follow. Consequently, Medicaid eligibility requirements vary considerably from state to state. The Medicaid Institutional Care Program pays nursing home costs for people who need long-term care and who meet the financial requirements imposed by the state.

Q 26:26 Is Medicare limited, or does it pay for all of an individual's nursing home expenses?

Medicare is limited. It pays for approximately 2 percent of all annual nursing home costs. Specifically, Medicare pays for a maximum of 100 days of skilled care, provided that a number of conditions are met (see Q 26:27). Within this 100-day period, Medicare Part A only fully covers nursing home costs for the first 20 days after the individual enters a facility. The patient is then required to pay a coinsurance amount for days 21 through 100 of care. The current (1995) coinsurance amount that an individual must pay is $88 per day.

Q 26:27 What conditions must an individual meet to qualify for Medicare coverage?

The following conditions must be satisfied for an individual to be eligible for Medicare coverage of nursing home costs:

1. The individual must be hospitalized for medically necessary care for at least three consecutive days, not including the day on which he or she is discharged.
2. The individual must meet Part A eligibility requirements for the month in which he or she is discharged from the hospital.
3. The individual must be admitted to a skilled nursing facility within 30 days of his or her discharge from the hospital.
4. The individual's physician must order skilled care of a type that can only be provided in a skilled nursing facility.

It is often difficult for patients to meet these care requirements.

Q 26:28 How is Medicaid administered?

Medicaid is administered jointly by the federal Health Care Financing Administration of the Department of Health and Human Services and by the applicable state agencies. Many of the regulations governing the Medicaid program are issued by the states and can differ considerably from one state to another.

Q 26:29 Who is covered by Medicaid?

Medicaid generally covers persons 65 and over, disabled persons, and blind persons whose income and available resources do not exceed a specified level. [42 USC § 881396] Individuals generally must have monthly income less than the benefit rate provided under the Supplemental Security Income (SSI) program ($446 per month in 1994), although this amount may vary depending upon the state and the amount of the person's resources. [42 CFR § 435.831(b); 58 Fed Reg 58004 (1993)]

Specifically, most states' Medicaid programs provide for two categories of needy persons who can qualify for benefits: the *mandatorily categorically needy* and the *optionally categorically needy*. Mandatorily categorically needy persons include those who are currently receiving SSI or AFDC (Aid to Families with Dependent Children). Persons in this category are automatically eligible for Medicaid programs in most states. Optionally categorically needy persons include the elderly, blind, and disabled. States may elect to cover these individuals, and a number of states provide Medicaid programs specifically for them.

Q 26:30 What benefits are provided under Medicaid?

Medicaid generally provides the following benefits:

1. Payment of Medicare Part B premiums, deductibles, and coinsurances;
2. Inpatient hospital services with limitations and deductibles;
3. Outpatient hospital and rural health clinic services;
4. Nursing home care;
5. Physician services;

Q 26:31   Estate and Retirement Planning Answer Book

   6. Transportation;
   7. X-ray and laboratory services;
   8. Home health care services;
   9. Clinic services, subject to a copayment in some cases;
   10. Prescription drugs, also subject to a copayment;
   11. Preauthorized medical supplies and equipment in limited circumstances;
   12. Physical therapy and related services; and
   13. Emergency hospital services.

[42 USC § 1396d(a)]

Q 26:31 What resources are excluded in determining whether a person is entitled to Medicaid?

The following resources are not considered in determining an individual's eligibility for Medicaid:

1. The applicant's home is exempt as long as it is his or her principal residence. If the applicant lives alone, he or she must demonstrate an intent to return to the home, however unlikely that possibility might be, in order for the home to be excluded as a resource.
2. Household furnishings, such as furniture, paintings, appliances, and electronics, are excluded only while being used in the applicant's home.
3. Personal effects, including clothing, jewelry, photographs.
4. One automobile, regardless of value or use.
5. Property essential to the institutionalized person's self-support.
6. Any life estate interest held by the applicant, his or her spouse, or a specified relative.
7. Permanent life insurance, but only up to $2,500 of face value, and all life insurance with no cash surrender value (term insurance).
8. The value of an irrevocable burial contract, regardless of its value. A revocable burial contract, however, will only be excluded up to a value of $2,500. The applicant can further

exclude up to $2,500 for burial costs if the money is specifically earmarked for such use.

9. Cemetery plots, caskets, headstones, and the costs of the grave if they are to be used by the applicant, the applicant's spouse, or a member of the applicant's immediate family.

[42 USC § 1382b]

The home is treated as a resource after the owner has been institutionalized for six months unless (1) a spouse or a minor, blind, or disabled child continues to reside in the home, or (2) it can be shown that the patient will be able to leave the institution and return home. The state may impose a lien on the home of a Medicaid patient to recover the cost of nursing home care when either (1) the patient cannot reasonably be expected to return home and the home is not occupied by the patient's spouse or a minor, blind, or disabled child; or (2) the patient dies. [42 USC § 1396p(a)]

Q 26:32 What are 1634 states for Medicaid purposes?

States that adhere to the principles of the federal Supplemental Security Income program are known as 1634 states [42 USC §§ 1381 *et seq.*], while states that are allowed to deviate from SSI principles are called 209(b) states. [42 CFR § 435.121] Section 209(b) states are typically more restrictive and often have more stringent income requirements than 1634 states to qualify for Medicaid. There are currently 35 1634 states and 15 209(b) states. Regulations vary from state to state within these two broad catagories.

Q 26:33 What is the lookback rule?

Individuals in nursing homes frequently ask whether they can give all of their property to their children and then qualify for Medicaid. The lookback period is a significant obstacle to this proposal. The lookback rule attributes to a Medicaid applicant the value of all gratuitous transfers made to anyone by that individual within the 36 months immediately preceding his or her Medicaid application. [42 USC § 1396p(c)(1)] This 36-month period is a change from prior law and became effective August 11, 1993, as part of the Revenue Reconciliation Act of 1993 (RRA). The RRA also imposed a

60-month lookback period in cases involving payments from a trust or portions of a trust that are treated as assets disposed of by the applicant. Some states have indicated that they would not enforce the 36-month lookback rule immediately on the August 11, 1993, effective date. Florida, for example, issued a preliminary ruling that the 36-month lookback period would not become effective until July 1996. For this reason, it is important to check with local Health and Rehabilitative Services offices (or their counterparts) before making any transfer decisions.

For transfers made on or after July 1, 1988, and before August 11, 1993, the applicable lookback rule was 30 months. Similarly, prior to July 1, 1988, the lookback period was 24 months and was also optional under the federal statute, with the result that many states chose not to implement it. The Medicare Catastrophic Coverage Act of 1988 made the lookback rule mandatory for all states and established penalties for improper transfers of assets to achieve Medicaid eligibility.

Q 26:34   How do transfers of property affect Medicaid eligibility?

In determining the eligibility of a person for payment of nursing facility services by Medicaid, the applicant must fall within a certain resource level (see Q 26:29) and must not have made any improper transfers of assets within the lookback period (see Q 26:33). An improper transfer of assets for Medicaid purposes includes any transfer of assets by the applicant or by his or her spouse for less than fair market value. If such a transfer has occurred, the applicant will be deprived of Medicaid eligibility for a period of up to 36 months. [42 USC § 1396p(c)91)]

Q 26:35   How is the number of months of Medicaid ineligibility determined?

The number of months of Medicaid ineligibility resulting from a transfer of property is determined by dividing the uncompensated value of the property transferred (fair market value minus any compensation received by the applicant on the transfer of the property) by the state's average monthly charge for private pay nursing home care. The total number of months cannot exceed 36, however, regardless of the value of the property transferred.

Example 26-1: The average monthly charge for private pay nursing home care in a retiree's state of residence is $2,500. The retiree transfers an asset worth $50,000 to his daughter, receiving nothing in return. The retiree is not eligible for Medicaid-sponsored nursing home services for 20 months ($50,000 ÷ $2,500 = 20 months).

Q 26:36 What is the starting date of the lookback period?

If an individual is already institutionalized, the lookback period begins on the first day on which the individual is both institutionalized and has applied for state plan medical assistance. If the individual is not already institutionalized, the lookback period begins on either the date the individual applied for medical assistance under the state plan, or, if later, the date on which the individual transfers assets for less than fair market value.

Q 26:37 Are any transfers excluded from affecting Medicaid eligibility?

A transfer between a spouse who is receiving care in a nursing home and a spouse residing in the community is excluded if the community spouse does not transfer the resources to another person for less than fair market value. This interspousal transfer rule is unrestricted and unlimited. Similarly, the institutionalized spouse can transfer assets to another person for the sole benefit of the community spouse. This *sole benefit* language requires that the beneficiary—the community spouse—receive full payout of the asset within his or her life expectancy. The interspousal transfer rules do not, however, change the requirement that the community spouse may retain only $74,820 in assets (see Q 26:38).

Transfers to a blind or disabled child are also excluded, as are transfers to a trust established solely for the benefit of a disabled child. Spouses can also transfer assets to a trust that is established solely for the benefit of a disabled individual under the age of 65.

A Medicare applicant may transfer his or her home to the following people without adversely affecting his or her Medicaid eligibility:

1. A spouse;
2. A blind or disabled child;
3. A dependent child;
4. A sibling who (1) has an equity interest in the home and (2) has lived in the home for at least one year before the applicant's admission to the nursing home; or
5. A child of the applicant who (1) has lived in the home for at least two years before the applicant's institutionalization and (2) had cared for the applicant.

Asset transfers do not affect Medicaid eligibility if the Medicaid applicant can demonstrate through objective evidence that (1) he or she intended to receive fair market value or other valuable consideration; (2) he or she disposed of the asset exclusively for a purpose other than obtaining Medicaid eligibility; or (3) denial of eligibility would work an undue hardship. The undue hardship exemption is strictly construed. [42 USC §§ 1396p(c)(2)(C), 1396p(c)(2)(D)]

Q 26:38 Are the assets of both spouses considered in determining whether the institutionalized spouse satisfies the resource limitation?

The resources of both the husband and wife are considered in determining whether the institutionalized spouse satisfies the resource limitation. This determination, however, is made only once, at the beginning of the period of institutionalization. Resources that are acquired later by the community spouse (i.e., the noninstutionalized spouse) do not affect the Medicaid eligibility of the institutionalized spouse. The community spouse is permitted to retain the greater of $13,740 or one half of the value of the total nonexempt resources of the couple, but not in excess of $74,820. The $13,740 amount may be increased by state law up to $74,820, however. Both the $13,740 amount and the $74,820 amount are adjusted for cost-of-living increases. [42 USC § 1396r-5(f)(2)]

Q 26:39 What can be done to protect the noninstitutionalized spouse from impoverishment?

If the institutionalized spouse was the primary source of income for his or her family, the noninstitutionalized spouse (i.e., the "community spouse") can be left with meager resources. This occurs because of the need for the spouses to consume or transfer the majority of their assets in order to reach Medicaid resource eligibility limits. The community spouse would then have to spend the remaining resources for self-support. In order to avoid this result, the federal government allows the community spouse to retain a portion of the institutionalized spouse's income. This allowable portion of income is known as the Minimum Monthly Maintenance Needs Allowance (MMMNA) and consists of two components:

1. A portion of income that will raise the community spouse's total income to 150 percent of the federal poverty level rate for a two-person household; and
2. An excess shelter allowance, designed to cover high housing costs. The shelter allowance is determined by adding all of the community spouse's housing-related expenses: rent, mortgage payments (including principal, interest, taxes, and insurance), condominium maintenance fees, and utility costs. If the sum of the housing-related expenses is greater than 30 percent of the income allowance, the excess counts as an additional amount that the community spouse may also retain or receive from the institutionalized spouse's income.

Federal law restricts the total MMMNA (income allowance plus excess shelter allowance) to $1,871 for 1995.

Q 26:40 What rules apply in determining whether the assets of a trust will be treated as a resource of the beneficiary?

The assets of a trust will be treated as a resource of the beneficiary to the extent the beneficiary can withdraw the assets. [42 USC § 1396a(k)] If a trust was established by a grantor during his or her lifetime, the income and principal of the trust will be treated as available to the grantor or the grantor's spouse to the extent the trustee may pay out the income or principal to the grantor or the grantor's spouse, regardless of the purpose in establishing the trust, the revocability of the trust, or the trustee's record in using discretion. [42 USC § 1396a(k)]

Q 26:41 What are Medicaid qualifying trusts?

The statute governing Medicaid qualifying trusts (MQTs) [42 USC § 1396a(k)] applies the concept of *deemed availability* to any trust established by a Medicaid applicant or the applicant's spouse during their lifetimes for the benefit of either of them. According to the statute, the amount from an MQT deemed available to an individual is the maximum amount of payments that may be permitted under the terms of the trust to be distributed to the individual, assuming the full exercise of discretion by the trustee in favor of the individual. This provision means that the Medicaid applicant will be considered to be receiving money from the trust even if no distribution actually occurs. Establishing an MQT will likely result in disqualifying the beneficiary for Medicaid because, as a result of the deemed availability rule, the beneficiary will not be able to meet the income requirements.

Q 26:42 What makes a fund available for Medicaid purposes?

If the applicant or spouse is able to withdraw or liquidate a fund, regardless of the tax consequences, the fund is considered to be available for Medicaid purposes.

Q 26:43 What effect does an individual retirement account or Keogh plan have on Medicaid eligibility?

If the retiree or spouse requires nursing home care, an IRA or Keogh will be an available resource for purposes of Medicaid. This means that the IRA or Keogh plan might preclude Medicaid eligibility. State Medicaid regulations often treat an IRA as an available resource. In most states, the funds that are rolled over from a qualified retirement plan to an IRA are considered to be available for purposes of Medicaid eligibility and are required to be spent, in whole or in part, before Medicaid eligibility is allowed. Several states have an income limit. Under these limits, if monthly income exceeds a certain level (e.g., $1,200) regardless of monthly expenses, Medicaid eligibil-

Incapacity and Other Retirement Issues   Q 26:46

ity is denied. State laws often require the liquidation of Keogh plans to become eligible for Medicaid.

Q 26:44 Are tax-qualified plans treated differently than individual retirement accounts for purposes of Medicaid eligibility?

Although IRAs and Keoghs are treated as any other resource and may be required to be liquidated in order to achieve Medicaid eligibility, qualified pension plans are given preferential treatment under the Medicaid system. They are treated as unavailable due to the inability of the applicant to liquidate the qualified plan. Even if a Medicaid applicant is retiring and can liquidate the qualified pension plan, the state Medicaid authorities often do not require that the plan be liquidated in order for the individual to become eligible for Medicaid.

Q 26:45 Is a testamentary trust a Medicaid qualifying trust?

A testamentary trust is excepted from the statutory definition of an MQT, although not from the general rules relating to the availability of trust property and income. Although a testamentary trust will not be treated as a Medicaid qualifying trust, any income or principal that is required to be paid to a beneficiary will be included for purposes of determining whether that beneficiary satisfies the income or resource limit. [42 USC § 1396p(d)]

Q 26:46 What must be done to make an individual eligible for Medicaid?

Before becoming eligible to receive Medicaid, an individual must first consume virtually all privately available income and resources (with certain limited exceptions, such as the residence). Federal regulations define income as "anything you receive in cash or in kind that you can use to meet your needs for food, clothing, or shelter." A *resource* is cash or other liquid assets or any real or personal property that an individual (or spouse) owns or could liquidate and use for support and maintenance.

Q 26:47 How is a person's Medicaid eligibility determined?

Federal law requires that Medicaid eligibility be determined within 45 days of the date of application. [42 CFR § 435.911] It is rare, however, for applications to be processed within the required amount of time. Class action suits have been initiated in Nevada and in several other states to attempt to force the states to comply with this 45-day period. The problem for the Medicaid applicant is that nursing homes expect payment during the time that the Medicaid application is pending. If the applicant has depleted his or her resources to the level of Medicaid eligibility, there will not be any money left to cover costs during this interim period.

Q 26:48 What planning should be done to obtain Medicaid eligibility?

If a person has sufficient resources to produce enough income to pay for long-term care, the person need not consider eligibility for Medicaid. If a person lacks these resources, then it is appropriate to plan for Medicaid eligibility by consuming resources or transferring them.

Q 26:49 What reasons exist for not transferring assets to become eligible for Medicaid?

A number of reasons exist for not transferring assets in order to achieve Medicaid eligibility:

1. To become eligible for Medicaid, a person must demonstrate low levels of assets and income. Although some transfers can be made to relatives (perhaps with the understanding that the relatives will provide help), the low asset and income thresholds make this alternative risky because the transfers will deplete almost all of the available assets.

2. There is perceived (although illegal) discrimination in nursing homes with respect to the treatment of Medicaid patients.

3. The services available to a person on Medicaid are limited (see Q 26:30).

4. It may be difficult to locate a bed in a nursing home if the person will enter the nursing home as a Medicaid patient, even though such discrimination is illegal.
   5. The person's ability to care for himself or herself may improve to the extent the person no longer requires nursing care. If so, the person will be discharged and will return to the community impoverished.

Q 26:50 What asset planning can be done prior to institutionalization?

One way to protect assets from depletion due to institutionalization is to transfer the assets before the 36-month lookback period for Medicaid eligibility (see Qs 26:33, 26:51).

If this is done, enough assets should be retained to pay for the period of institutionalization until the expiration of the 36-month period (or for a shorter period if the fair market value of the transferred assets is less than 36 times the average monthly charge for private pay nursing home care).

Q 26:51 What techniques can be used to transfer assets if institutionalization is expected?

Several techniques are available to transfer assets in anticipation of institutionalization so that eligibility for Medicaid can be achieved (or maintained).

One technique involves retaining sufficient assets to pay for the nursing home costs during the lookback period associated with the asset transfer (see Q 26:49). As a starting point, the transferor should consider retaining assets with a fair market value equal to the fair market value of the assets transferred. This permits the transferor to use the retained assets to pay for the nursing home costs during the lookback period.

Example 26-2: A retiree lives in a state where the current average monthly charge for private pay nursing home care is $2,500. The retiree has nonexempt assets worth $50,000. If the retiree transfers an asset worth $25,000 and retains $25,000 of her nonexempt

Q 26:51 **Estate and Retirement Planning Answer Book**

assets, she will not be eligible for Medicaid for ten months ($25,000 ÷ $2,500). Because she has retained $25,000 for herself, however, she will be able to pay for her nursing home care for the ten-month period of ineligibility. Had she transferred the entire $50,000 at one time, she would have been ineligible for 20 months ($50,000 ÷ $2,500).

Consideration also should be given to transferring the home to the other spouse before institutionalization. Then, if it becomes necessary to sell the home later, the noninstitutionalized spouse can sell the home after the determination of Medicaid eligibility has occurred without having the proceeds from the sale of the home being taken into account for purposes of the institutionalized spouse's Medicaid eligibility. This advantageous result occurs because assets received by the other spouse after the determination of Medicaid eligibility for the institutionalized spouse are not considered to be resources available to the institutionalized spouse.

As a means of spending down to the Medicaid limits, nonexempt assets can be used to purchase exempt assets or to pay down debts on exempt assets. For example, cash or other liquid assets can be used to prepay a mortgage on a home or even used to purchase a new home. This use of funds to purchase exempt assets or to pay down obligations on exempt assets should occur after institutionalization but before the institutionalized spouse becomes eligible for Medicaid. In this way, funds are spent down before Medicaid eligibility is determined and will not count toward the total amount that will be used to determine the share the community spouse may retain.

Example 26-3: The total amount of resources available to a husband and wife is $100,000. The husband is admitted to a nursing home. An equal division of the couple's assets results in $50,000 being allocated to the wife. Their home is worth $80,000 and has a $10,000 unpaid mortgage. If the $10,000 is paid before Medicaid eligibility is determined, the wife can retain the home (now worth $90,000) and assets of $45,000 (one half of $90,000, the balance remaining after the mortgage payment). On the other hand, if the $10,000 is paid after the Medicaid eligibility is determined, the wife's initial share of $50,000 (one half of the $100,000 in total resources before the payment) is reduced by $10,000 as she pays off the mortgage, to $40,000.

The noninstitutionalized spouse could purchase an annuity. The annuity might not be considered a resource and, in that case, the income from the annuity would not be deemed available to the institutionalized spouse. The annuity should be nontransferable and not redeemable for cash.

Q 26:52 What gift tax consequences may occur in connection with property transfers?

To the extent that the value of the property transferred to a particular transferee in any year exceeds $10,000 (or $20,000 if the transferor is married and the couple elects to treat the gift as a split gift), the transfer will be treated as a taxable gift and will use up the transferor's unified credit. To the extent that the transferor has used up his or her unified credit, any additional transfers will be subject to gift tax (see chapter 6).

Q 26:53 What are Medicaid estate recovery programs?

These are programs promulgated by the individual states under the guidance of the federal government that allow individuals who have income that places them above the Medicaid maximum income limits to place their assets in a trust fund. The state then pays their nursing home bills until the individuals either die or are released from the nursing home. Upon the individual's death, the state receives the value of the trust fund as compensation. These programs became mandatory as part of the Revenue Reconciliation Act of 1993. Estate recovery can only occur at death, and will not occur if there are surviving children under the age of 21. Similarly, the state can waive estate recovery in situations in which an undue hardship would result.

Estate Planning for Institutionalization

Q 26:54 If a spouse is expected to be institutionalized, what are the estate planning considerations?

A spouse who expects the other spouse to be institutionalized should consider not bequeathing assets to the other spouse. Instead, assets could be placed in a trust with the surviving spouse as a discretionary beneficiary only to avoid having the assets in the trust treated as a resource or the income of the trust treated as available to the institutionalized spouse for Medicaid eligibility purposes. The healthy spouse should use a testamentary trust to avoid having the trust treated as a Medicaid qualifying trust (MQT) (see Qs 26:41, 26:45). Although a testamentary trust is excluded from the definition of a MQT, a similar exclusion for a revocable trust that becomes irrevocable at the death of a spouse is not available.

Life insurance proceeds and retirement plan benefits, as well as any other assets passing outside the probate estate, should not be made payable to the institutionalized spouse or to a spouse who is likely to be institutionalized. In the case of qualified retirement plan benefits, this course of action may not be possible if the spouse who is institutionalized or likely to be institutionalized is not the employee/participant and is not willing to sign a spousal consent, as required under the Equity Retirement Act of 1984, to validly waive his or her right to receive benefits.

Chapter 27

Estate Planning for Qualified Retirement Plan Benefits

Qualified plan benefits are often a major component of an individual's wealth; accordingly, they must be taken into account in preparing an estate plan. The main aspect of such planning is the designation of beneficiaries, those individuals who will receive the plan proceeds, either directly or indirectly.

Estate planning for qualified retirement plan benefits can occur at three different times: before retirement, at retirement, or at death. The time at which such planning takes place will affect both the individual's available options and decisions.

Overview	27-2
Estate Planning Before Retirement	27-4
Qualified Joint and Survivor Annuity	27-6
Estate Planning Considerations at Retirement	27-21
Estate Planning Considerations at Death	27-24

Q 27:1   Estate and Retirement Planning Answer Book

Overview

Q 27:1 What are the key estate planning considerations for qualified retirement plan benefits?

Both estate tax and income tax results should be considered in planning qualified retirement plan benefits. Such benefits are includible in a participant's gross estate; however, if those benefits are willed to the participant's spouse, the marital deduction will eliminate estate tax on such amounts at the time of the participant's death. Accordingly, estate planning for qualified retirement plan benefits centers around the designation of beneficiaries. Because large amounts of money are sometimes transferred from tax-qualified retirement plans, the choice of beneficiary can be very important.

> **Example 27-1:** A participant in a tax-qualified plan dies. Her husband is the beneficiary of the plan benefits, which equal $1.5 million. That amount is not includible in the participant's gross estate due to the operation of the marital deduction. If the plan benefits are paid to the participant's estate, however, the $1.5 million is includible in the participant's gross estate and potentially subject to estate tax (unless the participant's entire estate is bequeathed to her spouse).

Q 27:2 What is the basic tax treatment of benefits payable on death from tax-qualified retirement plans?

Death benefits payable from tax-qualified retirement plans are subject to two types of taxation: estate tax as a part of the deceased participant's gross estate and income tax to the recipient/beneficiary. Death benefits from tax-qualified retirement plans are income with respect to a decedent. [IRC § 691] The fair market value of these benefits at date of death (or alternative valuation date, if used) is includible in the decedent's gross estate. [IRC § 2033] The fair market value of these benefits is also includible in the gross income of the recipient. [IRC § 691] The impact upon the recipient is softened, however, by the recipient's ability to deduct against income the portion of the estate tax attributable to the income item. [IRC § 691(c)]

Example 27-2: A physician who previously used up his unified credit dies on September 19, 1993. His son receives a check for $1 million from the physician's profit sharing plan on November 5, 1993. The $1 million is includible in the physician's gross estate, and the estate tax attributed to it is $550,000. The son incurs income tax on $450,000 of the amount distributed ($1,000,000 − $550,000 = $450,000).

Two exceptions to the availability of the deduction for recipients exist. First, if the recipient is an estate or trust that distributes the income item in the year received, the deduction is not available. Second, if the qualified plan benefits exceed the statutory limits contained in Section 4980A of the Internal Revenue Code (Code), they are also subject to a special excise tax, and no income tax deduction is available for the portion of the increase in estate tax due to excess retirement accumulations. [IRC § 691(c)]

Example 27-3: A distribution from a profit sharing plan of $1 million to a deceased physician's son is subject to the penalty on excess retirement accumulations under Code Section 4980. The penalty tax is $50,000. Total estate taxes attributable to the profit sharing plan distribution are $550,000. The estate is further reduced an additional $50,000 by the penalty tax. Nonetheless, the son incurs income tax on $450,000, not $400,000.

Q 27:3 Are any benefits from tax-qualified plans and individual retirement accounts exempt from estate tax?

Participants who separated from service before 1983 may be entitled to exclude benefits from tax-qualified plans from their gross estates if they did not change the form of their benefits prior to death. Participants who separated from service before 1985 and did not change the form of benefit prior to death may be entitled to exclude $100,000 of benefit payments from their gross estate. [Ltr Rul 9221030]

The rules for exemption for individual retirement accounts (IRAs) are more rigorous. Complete exclusion is available only if the participant was receiving payments from the IRA on or before December 31, 1982, and had irrevocably elected a form of benefit payment before December 31, 1982. The $100,000 exclusion is available only if the participant was receiving payments from the IRA on or before

Q 27:4   Estate and Retirement Planning Answer Book

December 31, 1984, and had irrevocably elected a form of benefit payment before July 18, 1984. [Rev Rul 92-22, 1922-13 IRB 19]

Example 27-4: A petroleum engineer retires in 1981 and elects to receive his tax-qualified plan benefits in ten annual payments. In 1988, he changes his election and elects to receive his benefit payments in the form of a single future payment. The engineer dies before that payment is made. His entire account balance in his plan is includible in his gross estate.

Q 27:4   How should income tax on the plan benefits be handled?

One option is to have the beneficiary pay the tax out of his or her own funds. The beneficiary receives a distribution and pays the income tax on it from his or her other resources. Another option is to pay the tax out of the benefits themselves. In this situation, a grossed-up distribution has to be made to the beneficiary in order to cover the income tax that will be due on the distribution. [Ltr Rul 9132021] It is important to authorize such a distribution in the beneficiary designation (in the plan) because an authorization in the will is not binding on the plan administrator.

Example 27-5: A participant in a tax-qualified retirement plan designates his unmarried daughter as the beneficiary of the plan benefits. She receives a distribution of $10,000. The income tax on this distribution is $1,500. [IRC § 1(c)] The beneficiary pays the tax out of her own money, thus lowering the effective distribution to her to $8,500.

Example 27-6: The same beneficiary as in Example 27-5 receives a distribution of $11,765 from the retirement plan. This distribution includes $1,764.75 to cover the amount of income tax that will be payable on the distribution. [IRC § 1(c)] The beneficiary's net distribution is $10,000.25.

Estate Planning Before Retirement

Q 27:5   What estate planning should occur before retirement for qualified retirement plan benefits?

Before retirement, the primary task to be accomplished is designation of a beneficiary. The beneficiary designation must be consis-

Estate Planning for Qualified Retirement Plan Benefits Q 27:6

tent with the terms of the retirement plan. Qualified retirement plan benefits are includible in the participant's gross estate. If the participant's spouse is made the beneficiary of those benefits, however, the marital deduction (see chapter 4) will shelter those benefits from this inclusion in the participant's gross estate although, upon the subsequent death of the surviving spouse, the amounts received (but not consumed during the lifetime of the surviving spouse) will be subject to estate tax.

If the tax-qualified plan is subject to the Retirement Equity Act (REA) requirements (regarding the inclusion in the plan of a qualified preretirement survivor annuity payment feature and a qualified joint and survivor annuity requirement payment feature), the participants cannot designate a beneficiary other than his or her spouse, unless the spouse executes a consent thereto. If the spouse will not sign the consent, at least a portion of the benefits must go to the spouse. Except for certain kinds of profit sharing plans, all qualified retirement plans that are subject to REA requirements must pay the surviving spouse a qualified preretirement survivor annuity if the participant dies before the annuity starting date (generally, the first date on which a retirement annuity payment is made). [IRC § 401(a)(11)]

Q 27:6 What is a qualified preretirement survivor annuity?

A qualified preretirement survivor annuity is a survivor annuity for the life of the surviving spouse that is payable if the participant dies prior to retirement. For defined contribution plans (see Q 17:22), this is an annuity that is actuarially equivalent to 50 percent or more of the participant's nonforfeitable account balance as of date of death. For other types of qualified retirement plans, the payments cannot be less than those that would be payable to the spouse under a hypothetical qualified joint and survivor annuity (or its actuarial equivalent). If the participant dies after the earliest retirement age under the plan, the applicable hypothetical qualified joint and survivor annuity is the joint and survivor annuity that the participant would have, had he or she retired on the day before his or her death. If the participant dies before attaining the earliest retirement date under the plan, the applicable hypothetical qualified joint and survivor annuity is the joint and survivor annuity that the participant would have obtained had the participant separated from service at date of death, survived to the earliest retirement age, retired with an immediate qualified joint and survivor annuity at the earliest retirement age, or died on the day after the day the participant would have reached the earliest retirement age. [IRC § 417(c)] The surviving spouse must commence receiving the survivor annuity payments no later than the month in which the participant would have attained early retirement under the plan. [IRC § 417(c)(1)(B)]

This requirement of a preretirement survivor annuity furthers Congress's public policy goal of ensuring that surviving spouses will not be cut out of their participant spouses' plan benefits in the event that the participant dies first.

Example 27-7: A participant in a defined benefit pension plan dies at age 46, nine years before the earliest retirement age under the plan (age 55), but before he actually retires. His surviving spouse is entitled to a qualified preretirement survivor annuity. Had the participant retired the day before he attained age 46, his spouse would have been entitled to a benefit of $500 per month if she survived him. She is entitled to at least that amount as a preretirement survivor annuity.

Qualified Joint and Survivor Annuity

Q 27:7 What is a qualified joint and survivor annuity?

A qualified joint and survivor annuity is an annuity payable over the life expectancies of the participant and his or her spouse. The amount of the annuity payable to the surviving spouse may not be less than 50 percent nor more than 100 percent of the amount of the annuity that is payable during the joint lives of the participant and the spouse. [IRC § 417(b)]

A participant in a tax-qualified profit sharing plan generally is exempt from the REA joint and survivor annuity requirements and qualified preretirement survivor annuity requirements if the plan provides that, on the participant's death, the entire vested benefit is payable in full to the surviving spouse (or to the beneficiary if there is no surviving spouse or the surviving spouse consents to a designated beneficiary) and the participant does not elect an annuity benefit. [Treas Reg § 1.401(a)-20, Q&A-3(a)] IRAs, simplified employee pensions (SEPs), and certain salary reduction Section 403(b) arrangements are not subject to these requirements for benefits for surviving spouses. [IRC §§ 401(a)(11), 417]

> **Example 27-8:** A participant in a tax-qualified profit sharing plan can elect on retirement to obtain a single-sum payment or installment payments over a ten-year period. The plan provides that, on the participant's death, the entire vested benefit will be paid in full to the participant's surviving spouse. Because of this plan structure, the plan will be exempt from the REA requirements. As a result, the plan will not have to include a qualified preretirement survivor annuity payment feature, and the participant can designate a beneficiary other than his or her spouse without that spouse's consent.

Q 27:8 What exemptions are available from the qualified preretirement survivor annuity and qualified joint and survivor annuity requirements of the REA?

A participant in a tax-qualified profit sharing plan generally is exempt from the joint and survivor annuity requirements and qualified preretirement survivor annuity requirements if the plan provides that, on the participant's death, the entire vested benefit is payable in full to the surviving spouse (or to the beneficiary if there is no surviving spouse or the surviving spouse consents to a designated beneficiary) and the participant does not elect an annuity benefit. [Treas Reg § 1.401(a)-20, Q&A-3(a)] IRAs, simplified employee pensions (SEPs), and certain salary reduction Section 403(b) arrangements are not subject to these requirements for benefits for surviving spouses. [IRC §§ 401(a)(11),417]

> **Example 27-9:** A participant in a tax-qualified profit sharing plan does not elect an annuity benefit. The plan provides that on the participant's death, the entire vested benefit will be paid in full to his surviving spouse. Because of this organization, the plan will be exempt from the REA requirements. As a result, the plan will not have to include a qualified preretirement survivor annuity payment feature, and the participant may designate a beneficiary

for his retirement benefits other than his spouse without obtaining his spouse's consent.

Q 27:9 What is the annuity starting date, and what does it mean with respect to the frequency of waivers?

The annuity starting date is defined as: "the first day of the first period for which an amount is paid as an annuity or any other form." [Treas Reg § 1.401(a)-20, Q&A-10(b)] This definition and the definition for annuities suggest that every payment other than a periodic payment has its own annuity starting date so that, if a payment that is not in qualified and joint and survivor annuity form is made to a participant who is alive, waiver and consent must be executed for that payment. This does not apply to periodic payments.

Q 27:10 What is the effect of a divorce on benefit elections made by a participant and on the qualified joint and survivor annuity protections?

If a participant divorces his or her spouse prior to the annuity starting date, any elections made while the participant was married to the former spouse remain valid unless the participant changes them, a qualified domestic relations order (QDRO) provides otherwise, or the participant remarries. If the participant dies after the annuity starting date, the spouse to whom the participant was married on the annuity starting date is entitled to qualified joint and survivor annuity protection under the plan. That spouse is entitled to this protection even if the participant and the spouse are not married on the date of the participant's death, unless the QDRO provides otherwise or unless the spouse consents to a waiver of the benefit. [Treas Reg § 1.401(a)-20, Q&A-25]

Q 27:11 When must a waiver be signed?

The timing for execution of a waiver depends upon which REA requirement is at issue.

Qualified joint and survivor annuity. A participant's waiver of a qualified joint and survivor annuity and the associated spousal consent must be executed not more than 90 days before the payment date. [IRC § 417(a)(1)(A)]

Qualified preretirement survivor annuity. In contrast, a participant's waiver of the qualified preretirement survivor annuity and the associated spousal consent for it can be made on the first day of the plan year in which the participant reaches age 35 and remain effective until death with respect to amounts for which an annuity starting date has not yet occurred. [IRC § 417(a)(6)(B)]

> **Example 27-10:** A participant is due to receive a payment from a qualified joint and survivor annuity on June 1, 1996. She must execute a waiver, and her spouse must execute his consent to that waiver after March 2 of that year. If the waiver and consent are executed prior to March 2, they will not be effective with respect to that payment.

In contrast, if a qualified preretirement survivor annuity is at issue, the participant may execute a waiver and her spouse may execute his consent on the first day of the plan year in which the participant reaches age 35. This waiver and consent will then remain effective with respect to amounts for which an annuity starting date has not yet occurred, until the participant's death.

Q 27:12 Can a spousal consent to a waiver of benefits be irrevocable?

Yes, a spousal consent can be either revocable or irrevocable. If neither the plan nor the consent states whether the consent is revocable or irrevocable, the spouse's advisor should attempt to clarify the language in the consent to choose one or the other. [Treas Reg § 1.401(a)-20, Q&A-30] It is extremely important for the advisor to discuss with the spouses the consequences of making the consent either revocable or irrevocable.

> **Example 27-11:** An architect, age 40, is a participant in a tax-qualified profit sharing plan. He and his spouse are considering executing an irrevocable waiver of and spousal consent to a qualified joint and survivor annuity. At the time of this discussion, the benefit is worth $5,000. They decide instead to elect a life annuity. Twenty years later, the architect dies shortly after retiring, and the

waiver and consent become effective. At that time, a joint and survivor benefit would be worth $500,000, but the surviving spouse is entitled to nothing because the architect elected a life annuity.

Q 27:13 What constitutes a valid spousal consent?

Unless the plan document provides for a general consent, the spousal consent to the participant's waiver of a qualified preretirement survivor annuity or of a qualified joint and survivor annuity must state the specific non-spouse beneficiary who is to receive the benefit, and it must state that a new consent must be obtained if any change of beneficiary is made. [IRC § 417(a)(2)]

> **Example 27-12:** A tax-qualified plan does not allow for the execution of a general consent. The spouse's consent states that the couple's daughter, Sarah, is to receive the plan benefit. It also states that any change of this beneficiary designation will require a new spousal consent to be executed. The consent is valid. Had the consent permitted the plan participant to later designate any other beneficiary he chose, it would be an invalid general consent.

Q 27:14 Is spousal consent necessary if the spouse cannot be located?

No. Spousal consent to waive qualified joint and survivor annuities is not required if it is established to the satisfaction of a plan representative that the spouse cannot be located. [Treas Reg § 1.401(a)-20, Q&A 25]

Q 27:15 What happens if the non-spouse beneficiary is a trust?

In general, if the beneficiary is a trust, the trust can be amended without obtaining a new consent; that is, the consenting spouse will not be consulted again for any subsequent changes that are made to the trust by the trust's beneficiaries. A consent that names a trust as beneficiary is in many respects a general consent. If the consenting spouse really wants more control, that spouse should require his or her consent to all trust amendments (or to specified trust amendments). To avoid ambiguity, it also may be helpful to state that the consenting spouse wishes to permit any and all trust amendments, if the spouse wants to do this.

> **Example 27-13:** The participant in a tax-qualified plan and his spouse decide that plan benefits should be payable to a trust that they have established for their children. The spouse agrees to execute a spousal consent to implement this plan; however, she wants to retain some control over who the trust beneficiaries are. In her consent, then, the spouse specifically states that her consent will also be required for any future amendments to the trust that involve changing the trust beneficiaries. If she had not limited her consent in this way, it would have operated as a general consent, and the trust could have been changed without consultation with the spouse.

Q 27:16 What is a general consent?

A general consent permits a further change of beneficiary or of the form of payment of retirement benefits without further consent from the participant's spouse. For example, under a general consent, the form of payment can be changed from periodic payments to a single-sum payment without further spousal consent. A general consent must acknowledge that the spouse has the right to limit the scope of the consent and that the spouse voluntarily elects to relinquish that rights. [IRC § 417(a)(2)(A)]

Q 27:17 What is a limited general consent?

A limited general consent is a consent limited to certain beneficiaries or forms or payments but which is then general with respect to such stated category(ies). The consent might, for example, permit the plan participant to designate any of the spouse's children as death beneficiaries of the plan.

Q 27:18 Does a spousal consent to a waiver of REA rights constitute a taxable gift?

The argument has been made that a spouse's consent to a waiver of REA rights (see Qs 27:5–27:14) is a gift to the persons who receive the benefit as a result of the waiver. The Code, however, provides that such a waiver is not a taxable gift. [IRC § 2503(f)]

Q 27:19 What prenuptial planning can be done with respect to the qualified joint and survivor annuity and the qualified preretirement survivor annuity?

These spousal rights cannot be waived through prenuptial planning. In other words, if the participant's tax-qualified retirement plan is subject to these rights (see Q 27:5), a waiver of the nonparticipant spouse's rights in a prenuptial agreement will be ineffective. [Treas Reg § 1.401(a)-20, Q&A 28] Two reasons exist for this rule, as follows:

1. Because the objective of these agreements is for the nonparticipant spouse to waive his or her rights before marriage, the soon-to-be spouse is not in fact a "spouse" at the time of contracting.

2. Prenuptial agreements generally do not identify the specific non-spouse beneficiary who is to receive the benefit instead of the spouse, nor do they state that the participant may change beneficiaries without further spousal consent. Yet Code Section 417(a)(2)(A) requires that valid waivers either identify a specific non-spouse beneficiary or state that the participants may change beneficiaries without further spousal consent.

As a result, any attempted waiver of the nonparticipant spouse's qualified joint survivor annuity and qualified preretirement survivor annuity benefits in a prenuptial agreement is invalid.

Q 27:20 What are the advantages of having the spouse as the death beneficiary of a tax-qualified retirement plan?

The advantages of having the spouse as the death beneficiary are as follows:

1. The marital deduction generally should be available; thus no federal estate taxes will be payable on the retirement plan benefits, regardless of whether the payment is a lump sum or an annuity.

Estate Planning for Qualified Retirement Plan Benefits Q 27:21

2. No consent to waiver of REA rights (see Qs 27:5–27:14) by the spouse will be necessary.

3. The spouse as beneficiary has payment options that no other beneficiary has. For example, the spouse can roll the distribution over to an IRA. [IRC § 402(c)(9)] No other beneficiary may make this rollover. The Internal Revenue Service (IRS) has been generous in permitting a spousal rollover even though the spouse was not directly named as beneficiary. For example, the IRS permitted a decedent's spouse who was executrix and sole beneficiary of the estate to roll over to an IRA an amount for which there was no beneficiary designation.

   The IRA rollover will result in the postponement of income tax and permit the tax-free accumulation of income. Over time, this tax-free accumulation of income can result in a larger accumulation of wealth. If the spouse elects to treat the IRA as his or her own, the spouse need not start withdrawing funds until the year after the spouse reaches age $70\frac{1}{2}$.

4. The spouse as beneficiary may also elect to designate the benefits as his or her own for purposes of the 15 percent additional estate tax on excess accumulations under Code Section 4980A, thereby enabling the participant's estate to avoid the tax (see Q 27:43). If the spouse uses up a sufficiently large amount of the retirement assets while alive, the tax will be avoided all together.

Q 27:21 Under what circumstances is the marital deduction available?

The marital deduction (see chapter 4) is available if payments are made to the surviving spouse and if the terminable interest rule (see Q 4:6) does not apply. The main concern arises when the surviving spouse receives installment payments.

If the surviving spouse has the right to elect a lump-sum payment but instead chooses installment payments, the opportunity to elect the lump-sum payment satisfies the marital deduction requirements. If the surviving spouse has no choice but to receive installment payments, the marital deduction is available if the annuity or installment payments end with the surviving spouse's death. If, however, the payments continue after the spouse's death, either to his or her estate or to some third person, the payments are a nondeductible terminable interest, unless the qualified retirement plan could meet the requirements for a marital deduction trust.

Example 27-14: Under his wife's tax-qualified retirement plan, a widower has no choice but to receive installment payments. Upon his death, the payments terminate. The retirement plan benefits will not be subject to federal estate tax upon the death of the wife due to the operation of the marital deduction.

Example 27-15: The facts are the same as the one in Example 27-14 except that, on the widower's death, the payments continue to a beneficiary of his choice. In this situation, the payments conflict with the terminable interest rule, and the marital deduction will not be available. As a result, the retirement plan benefits will be subject to federal estate tax on the death of the participant spouse.

The reasoning behind this distinction lies in the government's desire to tax the passing of property from one person to another. In Example 27-14, the retirement plan payments pass from the participant to her spouse and then terminate upon the spouse's death. The transfer from the participant to her spouse is specifically exempted from federal estate taxes (or gift taxes, for that matter) as a matter of public policy. In Example 27-15, however, the benefits ultimately go to a third-party beneficiary of the spouse. It is this transfer to a non-spouse that the rules are designed to affect. As such, the marital deduction is disallowed because the participant is, in effect, transferring her benefits to the beneficiary. Because the federal estate tax rules are aimed at the transfer that occurs at the participant's death, the benefits must be included in her gross estate.

Q 27:22 Can a qualified retirement plan meet the requirements for a qualified terminable interest property or other marital deduction trust?

Yes, retirement plans can qualify as qualified terminable interest property or other marital deduction trusts (see chapter 4). [Treas Reg § 20.2056(b)-7(h)]

Estate Planning for Qualified Retirement Plan Benefits Q 27:24

Example 27-16: A advertising executive who has two children by his first wife wants to provide for both of those children and his second wife. He funds a qualified terminable interest property trust with the $2 million in benefits from his qualified retirement plan. The trust provides that the second wife will receive the income from the trust for her life, and (when she dies) the executive's children will receive equal shares in the plan benefits that were used to fund the trust.

Q 27:23 Is the 15 percent estate tax on excess retirement accumulations deductible from the decedent's taxable estate?

Yes, the 15 percent additional estate tax on excess retirement plan accumulations imposed by Code Section 4980(A)(d)(5) is deductible from the decedent's taxable estate. [IRC § 2053(c)(1)(b)]

Q 27:24 How can a surviving spouse avoid the excise tax on excess retirement plan accumulations or excess distributions relating to the decedent spouse?

If a surviving spouse rolls over the decedent spouse's IRA assets or qualified retirement plan payments into an IRA established in the surviving spouse's name, the rollover amounts are not counted for purposes of the tax on excess accumulations or excess distributions (see Q 27:43), provided that no other contributions or transfers are made to that IRA. Otherwise, the value of the IRA or the amount of the distributions will be counted in determining the decedent spouse's excess accumulation. If, for example, the surviving spouse rolls over the benefits to an IRA and commingles them with his or her own IRA contributions, the amounts contributed will count in determining excess accumulations. [Temp Treas Reg § 54.4981A-1T, d-10]

Example 27-17: The participant in a tax-qualified retirement plan dies, and his estate is subject to the 15 percent excess accumulations tax. In order to avoid the tax, his surviving spouse rolls over the plan payments into an IRA established in her name. She is not employed, so no other contributions or transfers are made to the

IRA. The amount that she rolled over will not be counted for the 15 percent tax on her deceased husband's estate.

Q 27:25 Should a marital trust be the named beneficiary?

Generally, a marital trust should be chosen as the named beneficiary of a qualified retirement plan benefit only if personal reasons preclude naming the spouse as beneficiary. There are several complications and potential drawbacks to naming a marital trust instead of naming the spouse. To obtain the marital deduction, installment payments must be such that all income earned by the account balance in the plan is paid out currently to the trust and treated as income by the trust. Where benefits are payable to a qualified terminable interest property trust, the IRS also requires, as a condition for the allowance of the marital deduction, that all administrative expenses normally allocable to the corpus be charged to the corpus and not to income. [Rev Rul 89-89]

The special retirement plan payout options available to a spouse as beneficiary (i.e., rollover to a spousal IRA, or, in the case of an IRA, treating the IRA as the spouse's own) are not available to a marital trust. Because the trust has no rollover option, it must take the entire distribution within five years. Accordingly, the income tax deferral that these options afford is not available to a marital trust.

Another potential drawback is that the marital trust will be unable to make a Section 4980A(d)(5) election for purposes of the 15 percent additional estate tax on excess accumulations (which, if it could be made, would permit the estate to avoid the tax). Similarly, assuming that the plan itself is subject to the qualified joint and survivor annuity and qualified preretirement survivor annuity requirements (see Q 27:7), the waiver and consent requirements will apply.

Example 27-18: The participant in a tax-qualified retirement plan names a marital trust as beneficiary of her plan benefits. When she dies, the trust must take the entire benefit distribution within five years, and income tax is payable on these distributions as they occur. If the total benefit equals $1 million, the trust will receive and pay taxes on $200,000 per year for the five-year period. In contrast, if the surviving spouse were the beneficiary of the plan benefits, the distribution could be made over a longer period, allowing for greater income tax deferral.

Q 27:26 Should a credit shelter trust be named as primary beneficiary of a qualified retirement plan?

Generally, no. Distributions from tax-qualified plans almost always create income tax liability, so part of the credit shelter would have to be used for those taxes. As a result, a credit shelter trust should be primary beneficiary only if there are otherwise insufficient assets to exhaust the entire unified credit.

Q 27:27 Can a spouse be named as primary beneficiary and a credit shelter trust be named as contingent beneficiary so the spouse can disclaim whatever amounts are needed to fund the credit shelter trust?

Yes. A surviving spouse may want to refuse or disclaim qualified plan benefits and have them paid instead into a credit shelter trust for the benefit of his or her children. This may be desirable, for example, so that $600,000 will pass to the children to take advantage of the unified credit. The IRS has recently ruled that qualified plan benefits may be disclaimed without violating antialienation provisions of Code Section 401(a)(13). [GCM 39858] Neither IRAs nor Section 403(b) annuities are subject to Code Section 401(a)(13), so a disclaimer is clearly permissible for them. [Ltr Rul 9037048]

Q 27:28 When must a disclaimer be made?

A surviving spouse's disclaimer of benefits transferred as a result of his or her spouse's death or made irrevocable as a result of death must generally be made within nine months of the date of death. [Ltr Rul 8922036] The disclaimer must be in writing and must be received by the executor of the estate within the nine-month period. [IRC § 2518(b)(2)(A)] The disclaimed benefits will be taxable to the actual recipient and not to the disclaiming spouse. [Ltr Rul 9319029] It is also a good idea to verify early on that the plan administrator will accept a disclaimer.

Q 27:29 Can qualified plan assets be paid to an irrevocable trust?

Yes, qualified plan benefits can be paid to a participant's irrevocable trust. That trust can be designed to divide after death into a marital trust and an A-B trust (see Qs 5:3–5:7).

Example 27-19: The participant in a tax-qualified retirement plan establishes an irrevocable trust into which he directs plan benefits to be paid. He wants to provide for his wife without incurring any estate tax on his death. As a result, he provides for the irrevocable trust to divide after his death in an A-B trust plan. The B trust contains up to $600,000 of assets that will qualify for the unified credit. The A trust serves as a marital deduction trust and contains the remaining assets of the participant. The surviving spouse can withdraw assets from the A trust, receive A trust income, and allocate A assets at her death. She can only receive B trust assets and income if they are needed for her support.

Q 27:30 What income tax concerns exist if a retirement plan death benefit is paid in installments to a marital deduction trust?

If the death benefit from a retirement plan is payable in installments or as an annuity to a pecuniary marital deduction trust, the right to receive future payments will be deemed to be transferred in satisfaction of a pecuniary obligation and will be taxed in the year of transfer to the trust, not as received by the spouse. [IRC §§ 691(a), 1014(c)]

Q 27:31 Why make a child or grandchild the beneficiary of a tax-qualified retirement plan?

Naming a child or grandchild as the beneficiary of a participant's tax-qualified retirement plan will maximize the tax-free buildup of funds by stretching out the payout period and deferring tax. This is because the plan can be designed so that payments may be made over the life expectancy of the beneficiary and in a manner that produces the smallest payments in the earliest years. For example, if the beneficiary has a 25-year life expectancy, 1/25 of the benefit must be paid out in the first year, 1/24 of the benefit must be paid out in the next year, and so forth. In naming a child or grandchild as

Estate Planning for Qualified Retirement Plan Benefits Q 27:34

beneficiary, however, the possibility of incurring the generation skipping transfer tax should be considered (see Qs 5:8–5:37).

Q 27:32 Should a charitable organization be the beneficiary of a qualified retirement plan?

Qualified retirement plan benefits are good assets to leave to a charity because, even though they may be income in respect to a decedent (see Q 3:44), the charity will not pay income tax on them. [IRC §§ 61(a)(14), 691] Naming a charity as beneficiary will not allow one to avoid the 15 percent additional excess accumulations tax, however. [IRC § 4980(A)(d)(5)]

Q 27:33 Is it advantageous to name a charity in the plan participant's will as a beneficiary?

Yes. It is a good idea to name the charity directly as the beneficiary of the plan benefits rather than to make a charitable bequest. If the charity is named as beneficiary of the plan benefits, the benefits will pass directly to the charity.

Example 27-20: A participant in a qualified retirement plan dies. The qualified plan benefits are part of a charitable bequest in her will. As a result, the plan benefits will be paid to the estate, which will then use them to fund the charitable bequest. Because the benefits are initially paid to the estate, the estate will be subject to income tax on the benefits under the income-with-respect-to-a-decedent rules. [IRC §§ 61(a)(14), 691] Similarly, the estate will not be entitled to a charitable deduction for the benefits unless the will specifically requires (or, at a minimum, allows) the charitable bequest to be funded by the qualified plan. [IRC § 642(c)] Had the charity been designated as beneficiary, these drawbacks would have been avoided.

Q 27:34 Can a charitable organization be named a beneficiary of a portion of the plan benefits and individuals be named as beneficiaries of the remaining benefits?

Yes, but if this is done, the taxpayer or the taxpayer's advisor must be very careful to ensure that, as of the participant's death or the required beginning date (see Q 23:49), whichever occurs first, the portion going to the charity is placed in a separate account. [Prop Reg § 1.401(a)(9)-1, H-2(a)] If the benefits are not separated, all of the benefits must be paid out over five years. [Prop Reg § 1.401(a)(9)-1, H-2(b)] Although this five-year rule is not a disadvantage for the charity, an extended payment period may be preferred for the individual beneficiaries.

Example 27-21: A participant in a tax-qualified retirement plan names a charity as beneficiary of a portion of the plan benefits and his children as the beneficiaries of the remaining benefits. At the participant's death, the portion going to the charity and the portions going to the children are commingled. The benefits to both the charity and the children must be completely paid out within five years. This is undesirable if the participant intended the benefits to provide income to his children over a longer period of time.

Q 27:35 Can plan assets be paid to a charitable remainder trust?

Designating a charitable remainder trust (i.e., a trust that provides for a life estate for an individual and the remainder for a charity) as the beneficiary of qualified retirement plan assets can effectively reduce the income tax liability resulting from the distribution of such benefits. The charitable remainder trust is exempt from income tax, although distributions to the beneficiaries are taxable in accordance with Code Section 664(b).

One drawback, however, is that the individual beneficiary will not be able to elect five-year averaging, even if the benefit is a lump sum, because payments will be made to him or her as an annuity.

Example 27-22: A participant wants his qualified plan benefits to provide for income to his daughter and the remainder to his favorite charity. If he sets up a charitable remainder trust, the income from the benefits will be paid to his daughter over the course of her life, with the corpus of the trust going to the charity upon her death. The participant's daughter will not be able to elect five-year income averaging even if the benefit is a lump sum; however, the difficulties associated with naming a charity as a beneficiary of a portion of the benefits and naming an individual as the beneficiary of the rest of the benefits will not exist.

Estate Planning Considerations at Retirement

Q 27:36 What estate planning should be done at retirement?

The key factors to consider at retirement are (1) the participant's need for funds and (2) the possible need to obtain a spousal waiver (see Qs 27:8, 27:11–27:12) within the 90-day period prior to the annuity starting date if payment is to be made in a form other than a qualified joint and survivor annuity. To the extent the participant is expected to use the qualified retirement plan payments during his or her lifetime, estate planning is unnecessary. From an income tax standpoint, it is probably preferable to spread the payment of retirement benefits out over the maximum period available under the retirement plan and take advantage of the tax-free buildup of assets in the plan. If benefits that are not paid out immediately are not expected to qualify for the marital or charitable deductions when finally paid, the impact of estate tax at the participant's death must be taken into account. This may be a particularly important consideration if the participant has no spouse (and, thus, no ability to shelter retirement plan benefits from estate tax by electing the marital deduction). If the asset accumulation in the plan as of the date of the participant's death is too great, the 15 percent penalty tax of Code Section 4980A will come into play. The source of funds to be used to pay taxes should be designated in the estate plan.

Q 27:37 What is the maximum permissible payout period for retirement plan benefits?

The maximum permissible payout period for retirement plan benefits depends on the identity of the designated beneficiary under Code Section 401(a)(9)(A). Qualified retirement plan distributions are permitted to be made over the life expectancies of the employee and the designated beneficiary, subject to the minimum distribution rules contained in Code Section 401(a)(9)(A).

If there is no designated beneficiary, payment of plan benefits may be made over the participant's life expectancy only. There will be deemed to be no designated beneficiary if an estate or charity is named as beneficiary. The same result will also occur in certain circumstances if a trust is named as beneficiary (see Q 27:41).

Q 27:38 What is the maximum payout period for retirement plan benefits if the spouse is the beneficiary?

If the spouse is the designated beneficiary for qualified retirement plan benefits, the life expectancies of the participant and spouse may be recalculated annually, thus slowing the rate of payment. [IRC § 401(a)(9)(D)] On the death of the participant, his or her recalculated life expectancy becomes zero and, thus, payments to the surviving spouse can be made over his or her life expectancy only. On the surviving spouse's death, both recalculated life expectancies become zero, and the payment of any remaining benefit must be made prior to the last day of the year following the year of the spouse's death. [Prop Treas Reg § 401(a)(9)-1, E-7(a)] Tax-qualified plans may adopt provisions specifying that the life expectancies of participants and spouses will or will not be recalculated and may permit the participant to elect or not elect recomputation and specify whether life expectancies will be recalculated in the absence of such election. In the absence of plan provisions, life expectancies must be recalculated. [Prop Treas Reg § 1.401(a)(9)-1, E-7]

Q 27:39 What are the advantages of electing not to recompute either spouse's life expectancy?

By electing not to recompute either of the spouses' life expectancies, the possibility that, upon the death of the surviving spouse, the plan is required to pay all remaining benefits prior to the last day of the year following the year of the spouse's death is avoided (see Q 27:37). In other words, this approach guarantees a lengthy payout period. The main disadvantage is that the fund may be completely exhausted during the participant's or the spouse's lifetime.

Q 27:40 What happens if the participant's life expectancy is recomputed and the spouse's life expectancy is not recomputed?

If the spouse dies first, the method of distribution will continue based on the participant's life expectancy, and the fund will not be exhausted during the participant's life. When the participant later dies, distributions will continue to the extent of the spouse's remaining life expectancy.

Estate Planning for Qualified Retirement Plan Benefits Q 27:41

On the other hand, if the participant dies first, larger payments will be made to the spouse over the course of his or her nonrecomputed life expectancy. In order to avoid exhaustion of the fund during the spouse's lifetime, he or she can roll over the payments into his or her own IRA and begin a new payout period with a younger generation of beneficiaries. This approach is probably the best way to ensure payment over the lives of both of the spouses and avoid the acceleration of payments into one year (see Q 27:37, Q 27:38).

Example 27-23: A participant in a tax-qualified retirement plan names his wife as designated beneficiary of the plan benefits. For payout purposes, his life expectancy is recomputed annually, but his wife's is not. He dies first. His wife will receive larger payments over the course of her nonrecomputed life expectancy. Because her life expectancy is not being recalculated each year, however, it is quite possible that the benefits will run out before she dies. In order to avoid this result, the widow rolls over the benefits into her IRA and begins a new payout period with her children as beneficiaries. Because they will have longer life expectancies than their mother, the payout period for the plan benefits will also extend over a longer period of time (although the total amount paid out will remain constant).

Q 27:41 What life expectancy applies if a trust is the beneficiary for qualified retirement plan benefits?

If a trust is named the beneficiary for qualified retirement plan payments, the life expectancy of the designated beneficiary with the shortest life expectancy will determine the applicable maximum payment period. In order to be the beneficiary of qualified retirement plan benefits, however, the trust must satisfy certain requirements. Those requirements must be met as of the later of (1) the date in that the trust is named as beneficiary or (2) the employee's required beginning date (that is, the date on which qualified retirement plan payments must begin if they have not already begun. [Prop Treas Reg § 1.401(a)(9)-1, D-5(a)] If the trust does not meet all the requirements, the participant is treated as having no designated beneficiary, and payments will be required to be made over the participant's life expectancy only. [Prop Treas Reg § 1.401(a)(9)-1, D-5(d)]

Q 27:42   Estate and Retirement Planning Answer Book

The requirements the trust must satisfy are as follows:

1. It must be a valid trust under state law;
2. It must be irrevocable;
3. The beneficiaries of the trust must be identifiable from the trust instrument; they may, however, be members of a class (i.e., the individual's children) if it is possible to determine the class member with the shortest life expectancy; and
4. A copy of the trust must be provided to the plan.

[Prop Treas Reg § 1.401(a)(9)-1, D-5(a)]

Q 27:42   Why is a child or grandchild named as beneficiary of a tax-qualified retirement plan?

A child or grandchild is often named as beneficiary of a tax-qualified retirement plan to maximize the tax-free buildup of income within the plan because of their greater life expectancies. These longer life expectancies permit an extended payout period for the plan benefits. During a participant's lifetime and after the required beginning date, however, the incidental benefit rules imposed on qualified retirement plans by Code Section 401(a)(14) will require a larger minimum payment than would be dictated by these life expectancies. On the participant's death, the incidental benefit rules no longer apply, and further payments may be made over the remaining joint and survivor life expectancies.

Estate Planning Considerations at Death

Q 27:43   What estate planning actions should be taken upon the participant's death?

The following estate planning actions with respect to assets in tax-qualified plans should be taken at death:

1. The beneficiaries should consider whether a disclaimer of all or part of the benefits is advisable and take any steps necessary to ensure the availability of the marital deduction (see chapter 4).

2. Spousal beneficiaries should consider whether to elect to have any excess accumulation tax that may be payable under Code Section 4980(A) shifted to them.
3. Beneficiaries of tax-qualified plans should consider the payment options available under the plan in which the decedent participated. Because income earned by tax-qualified retirement plans and IRAs is not taxed until benefits are actually paid, it may be advantageous to have these funds paid out as slowly as possible so that the income on unpaid amounts can accumulate tax free under the plan. Accordingly, the beneficiaries will want to examine the qualified retirement plan rules concerning required minimum payouts to determine what actions, if any, should be taken to slow the rate of plan benefit payments.
4. Beneficiaries of tax-qualified retirement plans will also want to determine if a lump-sum cash payment is available and, if so, whether it is desirable.

Q 27:44 Are any special estate taxes imposed on tax-qualified retirement plan distributions?

Yes, upon the death of an employee, an additional estate tax is imposed in an amount equal to 15 percent of the excess retirement accumulation. [IRC § 4980A(d)] The excess retirement accumulation essentially equals the total value of the decedent's interest in all retirement plans less the present value of a particular type of annuity. This annuity must have annual payments equal to the greater of $150,000 or $112,500 (adjusted annually for inflation). [IRC § 4980A(c)(1)] This additional estate tax is payable even if the decedent's estate is not large enough to be subject to the regular estate tax. In computing this additional tax, the unified credit, the marital deduction, the charitable deduction, and other estate tax deductions are not allowed. [IRC § 4980A(d)]

Chapter 28

Estate Planning for Nonqualified Retirement Plans

Nonqualified plans may include a variety of benefit options. Some plans may consist of only lifetime annuities, whereas others may have account balances that are payable at death. This chapter discusses the tax treatment of the various types of nonqualified retirement plan payments.

Overview	28-1
Treatment of Specific Benefits	28-2

Overview

Q 28:1 What is the basic tax treatment of benefits payable on death in nonqualified plans?

The fair market value of death benefits from nonqualified plans at date of death (or alternative valuation date, if used) is includible in the decedent's gross estate. [IRC § 2033] Death benefits from nonqualified plans are taxable income with respect to a decedent. [IRC § 691] Nevertheless, the recipient is entitled to a deduction for the portion of the estate tax attributable to the benefits. [IRC 691(c)] (If the recipient is an estate or trust that distributes the income item in the year received, this deduction is not available. An income tax deduction for the amount distributed may be available, however.)

Example 28-1: A physician dies on September 19, 1993. His wife receives a check from the physician's nonqualified salary deferral arrangement on November 5, 1993, in the amount of $200,000. The $200,000 is includible in the physician's estate, and the amount of estate tax attributed to it is $110,000. The physician's wife incurs income tax on $90,000 ($200,000 − $110,000 = $90,000).

Treatment of Specific Benefits

Q 28:2   How is a straight life annuity treated for estate tax purposes?

A straight life annuity (an annuity that pays benefits over a plan participant's lifetime only) is not includible in the participant's gross estate. Because benefits from this type of annuity cease at the participant's death, there is no passage of an interest on death for the government to tax.

Q 28:3   How is a participant's receipt of straight life annuity payments taxed?

A portion of any straight life annuity benefit payments will be subject to income taxes in the year received by the participant. [IRC § 61(a)(9)] Income tax liability will not be assessed against the entire amount of benefits received because the Internal Revenue Code (Code) allows for an exclusion from each benefit payment of an amount that represents what the individual paid to purchase the annuity. [IRC § 72(c)]

Q 28:4   How are refund annuities, term annuities, and joint and survivor annuities treated for estate tax purposes?

In general, the present value of the after-death payments from annuities is includible in the decedent's gross estate. If those amounts

Estate Planning for Nonqualified Retirement Plans   Q 28:6

are payable to the estate, the present value of all payments is includible in the gross estate. If the post-death payments are payable to a named beneficiary, the present value of such payments is includible in the gross estate to the extent that the decedent contributed to the value of the annuity.

> **Example 28-2:** A deceased businessman participated in a nonqualifi8d plan providing a joint and survivor annuity. The businessman contributed 75 percent of the value of the annuity. The survivor benefit is payable to his brother, who contributed 25 percent of the value of the annuity. Under these circumstances, 75 percent of the present value of the post-death payments is includible in the decedent's gross estate.

Q 28:5 What happens if an employee dies before all deferred payments have been made under a deferred compensation arrangement?

If an employee dies before all of the deferred payments have been made, the present value of the remaining payments to be made on or after death is includible in the gross estate. [IRC § 2039(a)]

> **Example 28-3:** A nonqualified deferred compensation arrangement provides that if a participant dies before retirement, $25,000 per year is to be paid for five years to the participant's beneficiary. Assuming the present value of the $125,000 of post-death payment is $94,770, the amount includible in the participant's estate is $94,770. [Treas Reg § 20.231-7(f)]

Q 28:6 What estate tax treatment occurs under a contract that permits no deferred payments to be payable to the employee during his or her lifetime and permits only a death benefit to be payable to a named beneficiary?

If the deferred compensation contract is drafted so that no deferred payments are payable to the employee during his or her lifetime and only a death benefit is payable to a named beneficiary, the likely result is that the value of the death benefit will not be includible in the employee's estate. [Estate of Henry Freed v Commr, 54 TC 805 (1970)] If as part of the same arrangement (but not

28-3

necessarily under the same contract) lifetime benefits are also payable to the employee, however, the death benefit will be includible in the employee's estate. For instance, if one contract provides for deferred compensation to be paid to an employee upon reaching age 65 and another contract provides that death benefits will be paid to the employer's sister, both contracts will probably be held to be part of one plan. It has been held that lifetime payments under a qualified retirement plan and payments to an employee under a disability plan after retirement but prior to death do not constitute payments that cause the payments under a death benefit only contract to be includible in the gross estate. [Estate of Shellberg v Commr, 612 F 2d 25 (2nd Cir 1979)]

The Internal Revenue Service (IRS) is continuing to attempt to include death benefit payments in an employee's estate, especially if the employee retains certain rights or benefits in the contract. [Rev Rul 78-15, 1978-1 CB 289] A factor to be considered in determining whether the death benefit will be taxable in the employee's estate is whether the employee has the right under the contract to revoke and change the beneficiary. If so, it is more likely that the proceeds will be includible in the estate. [IRC § 2038(a)(1); Rev Rul 76-304, 1976-2 CB 269]

Q 28:7 What are the tax effects where the insurance that funds a nonqualified plan is owned by the employer when the employee dies and the death benefits are paid to the employer?

The employer is subject to alternative minimum tax on the proceeds of the insurance policy. [IRC § 59] When the employer distributes the proceeds of the policy to the employee's designated beneficiary, the beneficiary becomes subject to income tax on the proceeds. [IRC § 61]

Example 28-4: An executive works for a manufacturing company. The manufacturer funds the executive's nonqualified retirement plan with insurance held by the company on the executive's life. When the executive dies, insurance proceeds of $1 million are paid to the company. The company incurs alternative minimum tax liability on the proceeds. When the company distributes the proceeds to the executive's wife, she incurs income tax liability in the amount of $372,528.50. [IRC § 1(a)]

Q 28:8 What are the tax effects where a nonqualified plan is funded by insurance, the insurance is owned by the employer when the employee dies, and the insurer pays the death benefits directly to the beneficiary?

The employer is not subject to the alternate minimum tax, and the beneficiary is not subject to income tax liability as a result of the operation of Code Section 101. The Department of Labor, however, in reviewing this fact pattern held that the nonqualified plan was funded for ERISA purposes due to the fact that the plan was to pay the benefits directly to the beneficiary. [DOL Op 81-11A] As a result, the plan is subject to the requirements of Title 1 of ERISA.

Example 28-5: Same facts as in Example 28-4, except that the death benefits are paid directly to the executive's wife. Neither the wife nor the company incurs tax liability on the transaction. Department of Labor Opinion 81-11A suggests, however, that the nonqualified plan would be subject to ERISA requirements.

Title I of ERISA sets out the rules for eligibility, coverage, vesting, and fiduciary responsibilities. Because nonqualified plans are often used expressly to avoid ERISA requirements, the imposition of those requirements can mean additional legal and administrative costs for the employer; furthermore, ERISA's coverage rules may prevent the employer from providing retirement benefits for specific key employees. Consequently, the manufacturer may decide that it is in the company's best interests to have the insurance proceeds payable to it, instead of to the executive's wife, even though this involves subjecting the company to alternative minimum tax liability.

Q 28:9 What should an employer do to help ensure that death benefits will not be taxable in an employee's estate?

The IRS will be more likely to include the benefits in the employee's estate if the employee has the right under the contract to change the beneficiary (see Q 28:6). It is important to draft the contract so that the employee does not have this ability. Difficulties can arise where the named beneficiary is a living trust that the employee has the right during his or her lifetime to revoke or amend. In such a case, the employee will be deemed to have this right even if the death benefits contract specifically excludes the right. In order to avoid that outcome, the trust itself should state that the employee's right to revoke or amend does not extend to benefits payable under a death benefits only contract.

> **Example 28-6:** An employee names a living trust as beneficiary of his $1 million death benefits only contract. The employee has the lifetime right to revoke or amend the trust; however, the death benefits contract specifically states that the employee cannot change the beneficiary designation. Because the death benefits contract is not binding on the trust, the IRS will most likely contend that the $1 million paid out according to the contract should be taxable as part of the employee's gross estate. To avoid this potentially disastrous result, the death benefits contract and the trust documents must state that the employee does not have the right to change the designated beneficiary.

Q 28:10 Does the fact that an employee owns stock in the employer corporation affect the taxability of death benefits?

No, it does not. The IRS stated in a private letter ruling that a death benefit payable to an employee's irrevocable beneficiary was not includible in the employee's gross estate even though the employee was a majority shareholder in the employer corporation. [Ltr Rul 8701003]

Q 28:11 Does a contract that provides only a death benefit create a gift?

The IRS contends that an employee who does not retain any rights or benefits in a contract providing death benefits has made a completed gift of the contractual benefits to the irrevocable beneficiary when the employee dies. [Rev Rul 81-301, 1981-1 CB 475] The Tax Court has taken a contrary position. [Estate of DeMarco, 87 TC 653 (1986)]

Estate Planning for Nonqualified Retirement Plans   Q 28:12

Example 28-7: An employee who has a death benefits only contract dies, and the benefits are paid to the irrevocable beneficiary of the contract, the employee's son. The IRS would consider this transaction a completed gift made by the employee (or, here, the employee's estate) to the son and would assess gift tax (if applicable) against the estate. The Tax Court, however, has held that this is not a taxable gift. Thus, the outcome would probably depend on whether and where the issue was litigated.

Q 28:12 When is a life estate includible in a decedent's gross estate?

Some decedents have life estate interests; that is to say, the decedent's interest in the property lasts only for his or her lifetime. Upon the death of the decedent, the life interest automatically terminates. Whether such interests are includible in the decedent's gross estate depends on whether the decedent is the transferor of the remaining interest. If the decedent transfers an interest to another but retains a life interest, that life interest is includible in the decedent's gross estate. [IRC § 2036] If, however, the decedent merely has a life interest in a life estate given to him by another, that interest is not includible in his gross estate.

Example 28-8: A stockbroker's will provides his nephew with an interest in a bank account for the nephew's life. Upon the nephew's death, the remainder of the bank account goes to the stockbroker's niece. When the nephew dies, the balance in the bank account is not includible in his estate because the donor was not the nephew but rather the stockbroker.

Chapter 29

IRA Distributions

Individual retirement accounts are popular methods for providing for retirement savings. Indeed, an IRA is the sole retirement vehicle for a great many workers. Even for workers who participate in tax-qualified plans and thus cannot get the IRA deduction, an IRA can be an excellent way to accumulate retirement savings because of the tax-free buildup of funds.

Taxation and Timing of Distributions	29-1
Transfers and Rollovers	29-10
Savings Incentive Match Plans for Small Employers	29-16

Taxation and Timing of Distributions

Q 29:1 Does the constructive receipt doctrine apply to IRAs?

No. Individual retirement account (IRA) assets and the income therefrom are taxable only when paid or distributed. IRA owners are not subject to income taxation merely because they have the right to withdraw their IRA amounts on demand.

Q 29:2 Are IRA distributions eligible for income averaging or capital gains treatment?

No. Distributions to IRA owners are generally taxed as ordinary income in the taxable year in which the distributions are received.

[IRC § 408(d)(1)] The distributions are not eligible for income averaging or capital gains treatment, even if the IRA has been funded with assets from a tax-qualified retirement plan. [IRC § 402(e)(4)(A)] In contrast, distributions from tax-qualified retirement plans are entitled to favorable tax treatment in two respects. Five-year or ten-year averaging may be available as well as favorable tax treatment on capital gains.

Q 29:3 Are IRA distributions fully includible in gross income?

Not always. Usually an IRA owner has a zero basis in the IRA, and therefore the distribution is fully includible in income. If nondeductible contributions have been made to one or more IRAs, however, a portion of the distribution is treated as a tax-free return on those contributions. The portion of the IRA distribution that is not taxed depends on the proportion of the IRA that is attributable to nondeductible contributions.

Q 29:4 Are IRA distributions subject to an early-distribution excise tax?

Yes, they are. IRA owners who receive distributions from the IRA before age 59½ are subject to an additional tax equal to 10 percent of the taxable amount of the distribution. [IRC §§ 72(t)(1), 72(t)(2)] The 10 percent additional tax does not apply to the extent the distribution is a nontaxable return of nondeductible contributions or is rolled over into another IRA or tax-qualified retirement plan.

Q 29:5 Are there any exceptions to the 10 percent additional tax on early distributions?

Yes. Distributions from an IRA whose owner who has not reached age 59½ are not subject to the 10 percent additional tax if they are any of the following:

1. A distribution that is made to a beneficiary or to the estate of the IRA owner after the death of the IRA owner.

2. A distribution that is attributable to the IRA owner's being disabled. For this purpose, the IRA owner is considered disabled if he or she cannot do any substantial gainful activity because of a medically determinable mental or physical condition that can be expected to result in death or to last indefinitely. [IRC § 72(m)(7)]
3. A distribution that is part of a series of substantially equal periodic payments made not less frequently than annually over the life (or the life expectancy) of the IRA owner or the joint lives (or joint life expectancies) of the IRA owner and the IRA owner's designated beneficiary. [IRC § 72(t)(2)(A)(iv)]

Q 29:6 Must an IRA owner receive distributions?

Yes, IRA owners generally must begin to receive distributions after reaching age 70½. [IRC § 219(d)(1)] An IRA owner need not take a full distribution of his or her interest at age 70½. The payout must begin by April 1 of the year following a calendar year in which the IRA owner attains age 70½ (required beginning date). A gradual payout is permitted in accordance with complex regulations. [IRC §§ 408(a)(6), 408(b)(3); Treas Reg §§ 1.408-8, 1.401(a)(9), 54.4974-2]

Q 29:7 What happens if an IRA owner fails to withdraw the minimum amount required by law?

If an IRA owner or an IRA beneficiary fails to withdraw the minimum amount required by law, an excise tax equal to 50 percent of the shortfall between the actual amount distributed and the minimum distribution required by law is imposed. [IRC § 4974]

Q 29:8 When must required distributions be made?

Distributions to an IRA owner must begin by the individual's required beginning date (see Q 29:6) and must be paid over one of the following periods:

1. The life of the IRA owner;
2. The lives of the IRA owner and a designated beneficiary; or

3. A period that can be a term certain, not extending beyond:

— The life expectancy of the IRA owner, or

— The life expectancy of the IRA owner and a designated beneficiary. [IRC § 401(a)(9)(A); Prop Treas Reg § 1.401(a)(9)-1, Q&A B-1]

Q 29:9 What happens if a designated IRA beneficiary exists at the required beginning date?

If a designated beneficiary is named by the required beginning date, the minimum required distributions to the IRA owner must begin by the required beginning date and must continue over the joint lives of the IRA owner and the designated beneficiary or over a period not exceeding beyond the joint life and last survivor expectancy of the IRA owner and the designated beneficiary.

In general, an IRA owner must designate a person to be his or her beneficiary for the person to qualify as a designated beneficiary. If, however, the IRA agreement or annuity contract specifies some person to be the owner's beneficiary if no actual designation has been made, the person identified would qualify as a designated beneficiary. [Prop Treas Reg § 1.401(a)(9)-1 Q&A D2]

Q 29:10 What are the minimum distribution requirements if no designated beneficiary exists at the required beginning date?

If there is no designated beneficiary on the required beginning date, the required minimum distributions to the IRA owner must begin by the required beginning date (see Q 29:6) and must be made over the IRA owner's life or a period not exceeding the IRA owner's life expectancy. As a practical matter, this means that there is a shorter period for making the required minimum distributions than there would be if a designated beneficiary existed on the required beginning date (see Q 29:9).

Q 29:11 How is the minimum distribution calculated for IRAs?

The required minimum distribution from an IRA that is paid over the life expectancy of the IRA owner or over the joint life expectancy of the IRA owner and the designated beneficiary is equal to the following: the account balance of the IRA as of December 31 of the calendar year immediately preceding the calendar year for which the required minimum distribution is being made, divided by the applicable life expectancy. [Prop Treas Reg § 1.401(a)(9)-1, Q&A F-1]

Q 29:12 Can life expectancies be recalculated?

Yes. IRA owners can decide whether to recalculate their life expectancies each year and whether to recalculate the life expectancy of their spouses, if the spouse is a designated beneficiary. The life expectancy of other designated beneficiaries cannot be recalculated. The recalculations cannot occur more frequently than once a year. [IRC § 401(a)(9)(D)]

Q 29:13 What happens if a beneficiary is added or substituted after the required beginning date?

If a beneficiary is added or substituted after the required beginning date and the new beneficiary's life expectancy is shorter than that of the person who was the designated beneficiary at the required beginning date, subsequent distributions must be made over the new beneficiary's shorter life expectancy. If the new beneficiary's life expectancy is longer than that of the prior designated beneficiary, the original distribution schedule is retained. If a designated beneficiary dies after the IRA owner's required beginning date, the deceased designated beneficiary's life expectancy continues in effect, even if the beneficiary next in line has a shorter life expectancy. [Prop Treas Reg § 1.401(a)(9)-1, Q&A G-2]

Q 29:14 How often must required minimum distributions be made?

A minimum distribution must be made at least once per calendar year. For an IRA owner's first distribution calendar year (the calendar year in which the IRA owner attains age $70\frac{1}{2}$), the distribution need not be paid until April 1 of the calendar year following the first distribution calendar year. For all other distribution calendar years, the required minimum distribution must be paid by December 31 of that year. [Prop Treas Reg § 1.401(a)(9)-1]

Q 29:15 Can the required minimum distribution amount be rolled over into another IRA?

No. The required minimum distribution amount for any particular distribution calendar year must be taken into gross income and cannot be rolled over to another IRA. [IRC § 408(d)(3)(E)]

Q 29:16 Is the owner of several IRAs required to make minimum distributions from each IRA?

Not necessarily. An IRA owner who has more than one IRA must calculate a minimum distribution for each IRA. It is possible, however, for the IRA owner to total those minimum distributions amounts and withdraw the total amount from any one or more of the individual IRAs. [IR Notice 88-38, 1988-1 CB 524]

Q 29:17 Are withdrawals of excess IRA contributions subject to excise tax?

Timely withdrawals of excess IRA contributions (see Q 29:18) can be made without penalty. The withdrawal is timely if it is made before the due date for filing the IRA owner's tax return for the taxable year in which the excess contribution is made, provided both of the following conditions are met:

1. The net income attributable to the excess contribution accompanies the withdrawal; and
2. No deduction is allowed for the excess contribution.

[IRC § 408(d)(4)]

If these rules are complied with, the 6 percent excise tax ordinarily applicable to the amount of any excess contributions is avoided. [IRC § 4973(a)]

Q 29:18 Can excess contributions to IRAs be withdrawn after the date of the tax return?

Yes, an IRA owner can withdraw the amount of any excess contributions after the due date of the tax return for the taxable year in which the contribution was made without incurring any excise tax if (1) the total IRA contributions for the taxable year did not exceed $2,250, and (2) no deduction is taken for the excess contributions. [IRC § 408(d)(5)] Because the due date for filing the tax return has passed, the second requirement may necessitate the filing of an amended return eliminating the deductions. A 6 percent excise tax will apply to the taxable year in which the excess contribution is made. [IRC § 4973(a)] When making such a withdrawal, earnings on the excess contributions do not need to be distributed. The $2,250 limitation is computed without regard to the amount of any rollover contributions made to the IRA during the tax year. [IRC § 408(d)(5)(A)]

Q 29:19 If the IRA owner dies, how are distributions made?

If the IRA owner dies, death payments are made from the IRA to the persons designated as beneficiaries by the IRA owner. If no designation is made, the IRA agreement typically has a fallback designation, such as the surviving spouse (if any).

Q 29:20 Are distributions to IRA beneficiaries on account of death taxable?

Yes, distributions to IRA beneficiaries on account of death are generally taxable to the beneficiary. [IRC § 408(d)(1)] In general, the same rules apply as for distributions during the life of an IRA owner.

Q 29:21 Must distributions to a death beneficiary be made at required times?

Yes, distributions to IRA beneficiaries must begin within a certain time after the IRA owner's death. The required timing of distribution after the IRA owner's death varies depending on whether the IRA owner died before or after the required beginning date (see Q 29:6).

Death prior to required beginning date. If the IRA owner dies before April 1 of the calendar year that follows the calendar year in which the IRA owner attains age 70½, the beneficiary generally must receive his or her interest in the IRA within five years after the IRA owner's death. [IRC § 401(a)(9)(B)(ii)] Exceptions exist if payments promptly commence or if the surviving spouse is the beneficiary.

1. *Prompt payment exception.* The five-year distribution requirement does not apply if (1) distributions begin not later than one year after the IRA owner's death, and (2) the amount paid to the designated beneficiary will be paid over the life of the beneficiary or over a period of years that does not extend past the beneficiary's life expectancy. This exception only applies to the portion of an IRA payable to a designated beneficiary. [IRC § 401(a)(9)(B)(iii)]

2. *Spousal beneficiary exception.* If the designated beneficiary is the IRA owner's surviving spouse, the surviving spouse is not required to receive all of the death benefit within five years if (1) the portion of the IRA to be distributed to the surviving spouse is paid over the surviving spouse's life or over a period of years that does not extend past the surviving spouse's life expectancy, and (2) the payments begin not later than the later of December 31 of the calendar year in which the IRA owner would have attained age 70½ or December 31 of the calendar year that follows the calendar year in which the IRA owner has died. [IRC § 401(a)(9)(B)(iv); Prop Treas Reg § 1.401(a)(9)-1, Q&A C-3(b)]

Death on or after the required beginning date. If the IRA owner lives past April 1 of the calendar year following the calendar year that he or she attained 70½, the beneficiary must receive his or her interest in the IRA at least as rapidly as the IRA owner would have received it under the method of distribution being used as of the date of the IRA owner's death. [IRC § 401(a)(9)(B)(i)]

Q 29:22 Can an IRA lose its tax-exempt status for failing to make regular distributions?

It could. Normally, the failure to make regular distributions results in the imposition of excise tax. A pattern or regular practice of failing

IRA Distributions   Q 29:26

to make the minimum distributions could cause loss of tax-exempt status. [Prop Treas Reg § 1.408-8, Q&A A-3A]

Q 29:23 Are excess retirement accumulations in an IRA subject to excise tax?

Yes. Like tax-qualified retirement plans, an IRA owner's estate becomes liable for an excise tax equal to 15 percent of the amount of any excess accumulations. [IRC § 4980A(d)]

Q 29:24 Can IRA beneficiaries disclaim their interest in an IRA?

Yes, IRA beneficiaries can make qualified disclaimers consistent with Code Section 2518 of the Internal Revenue Code (Code). If such a disclaimer is made, the disclaiming beneficiary will not be taxed on the interest in the decedent's IRA, and the payee or distributee (rather than the person named as primary beneficiary) will be taxed instead. [IRC § 408(d)(1)]

Q 29:25 Can a transfer be made to an IRA owner's ex-spouse upon divorce without incurring federal income tax?

If certain rules are followed, yes. To avoid tax, the transfer of the interest in the IRA must be made pursuant to a valid divorce decree or a written instrument incident to the divorce. [IRC § 408(d)(6)] The transfer can take the form of the execution of a separate document assigning the IRA owner's ownership rights in the IRA to the ex-spouse. [Ltr Rul 9016077] The IRA owner also has the option of making a direct transfer of assets from his or her IRA to an IRA already established and owned by the ex-spouse. [Ltr Rul 9006066] If these rules are followed, the amount transferred is not considered a distribution to either the IRA owner or to the ex-spouse, and no federal income tax is due. [Treas Reg § 1.408-4(g)(1)]

Q 29:26 Under what circumstances is an IRA owner treated as if a distribution is received even though no funds are paid?

An IRA owner is treated as if he or she received a distribution in the following situations:

29-9

Q 29:27   Estate and Retirement Planning Answer Book

1. The IRA is disqualified because of a prohibited transaction described in Code Section 4975(c)(1). If this occurs, the fair market value of the assets in the account on the first day of the first taxable year in which the prohibited transaction occurs is treated as being distributed on that day. [IRC § 408(e)(2)]
2. An IRA owner borrows from the IRA. If an owner borrows from the IRA, a distribution of the fair market value of the account as of the first day of the taxable year in which the borrowing occurred is deemed to have occurred. [IRC §§ 408(b), 408(e)(2)(A)]
3. Certain types of tangible personal property are purchased as IRA investments. In such cases, a deemed distribution to the IRA owner to occur. [IRC § 408(m)]
4. IRA assets are used to purchase an endowment contract for the IRA owner. If this occurs, a deemed distribution occurs to the extent the purchase goes towards life, health, accident, or other insurance. [IRC § 408(e)(5)]

Transfers and Rollovers

Q 29:27   What is a transfer between IRAs?

A transfer between IRAs is a transfer of assets by one IRA custodian directly to another IRA custodian. The funds transferred do not pass through the hands of the owner or beneficiary. In contrast, a rollover involves the receipt of cash or other property by the individual before it is contributed to another IRA or retirement plan.

Q 29:28   What are the advantages of IRA-to-IRA transfers over rollovers?

IRA-to-IRA transfers have the following advantages over rollovers:

1. The rule that only one IRA rollover can be made during a one-year period does not apply to transfers. [Ltr Rul 8651085]
2. The income tax withholding rules that apply to IRA distributions do not apply to transfers.

IRA Distributions   Q 29:31

Q 29:29   Are IRA-to-IRA transfers subject to the $2,000 annual contribution limit?

IRA-to-IRA transfers are not considered IRA contributions. Accordingly, the $2,000 annual contribution limit does not apply to the amount of the transfer. In addition, the amount of the transfer is not counted toward the IRA owner's contribution limit for the calendar year in which the transfer is made. [Ltr Rul 8228110]

Q 29:30   Can funds be moved directly from a tax-qualified retirement plan to an IRA?

Under some circumstances, a participant in a tax-qualified retirement plan can instruct the plan trustee to move assets or funds directly from the trust into the name of an IRA custodian for an IRA owned by the participant. This transaction is commonly referred to as a *transfer*. For tax purposes, however, this transfer must meet the same requirements as an eligible rollover if the transaction is to be tax free. [Ltr Rul 8340098]

Q 29:31   Can distributions from tax-qualified retirement plans be rolled over to IRAs?

Distributions that qualify as eligible rollover distributions can be rolled over into an IRA.

> An eligible rollover distribution is a distribution of any portion of the balance to the credit of the employee from a § 401(a) qualified plan, § 403(a) annuity plan, or § 403(b) tax-sheltered annuity, except: (1) a distribution that is one of a series of substantially equal periodic payments (not less frequently than annually) that is either (i) made for the life (or life expectancy) of the employee or the joint lives (or joint life expectancy) of the employee and the employee's designated beneficiary, or (ii) made for a specified period of 10 years or more; or (2) a distribution that is a required minimum distribution pursuant to § 401(a)(9).

[IRC § 402(c)(4)]

Q 29:32   What are the tax consequences if an eligible rollover distribution is not rolled over?

If an eligible rollover distribution from a tax-qualified retirement plan is not rolled over into an IRA or another tax-qualified retirement plan, the distributing plan must withhold 20 percent of any eligible rollover distribution paid to the participant. This obligation to withhold estimated federal income taxes is avoided if the amount to be distributed is moved directly from the tax-qualified retirement plan to the custodian for the participant's IRA. In those instances, the plan treats the transfer as a distribution for reporting purposes and for spousal consent purposes, and the IRA trustee treats the assets as a rollover contribution. [IRC § 3405(c)(2)]

Q 29:33   What basic rules apply to IRA rollovers?

The same basic rules that apply to tax-qualified retirement plan rollovers apply to rollovers:

1. The rollover must be made within 60 days after the funds are received [IRC § 408(d)(3)(A)(i)];
2. The required minimum distributions under Code Section 401(a)(9) (i.e., those that force the taxpayer to take distributions following the attainment of 70½) cannot be rolled over [IRC § 408(d)(3)(E)]; and
3. The portion of a distribution that is not rolled over is taxable under the usual rules applicable to distributions. [IRC §§ 401(a), 403(a), 403(b)]

Q 29:34   Can rollovers from a tax-qualified retirement plan be made to several IRAs?

Yes. There is no prohibition against rolling over a distribution from a tax-qualified retirement plan into one or more IRAs. [Rev Rul 79-2665, 1979-2 CB 186]

Q 29:35   Can IRA distributions be rolled over to other IRAs?

A distribution from one IRA generally can be rolled over as a contribution to another IRA if the rules generally applicable to rollovers (see Qs 29:28–29:34) are met. An IRA distribution cannot be rolled over as a contribution to a second IRA, however, if the IRA owner has used this rule to roll over an earlier distribution from the first IRA during the one-year period ending on the date of the distribution. [IRC § 408(d)(3)(B)] This restriction applies separately to each IRA an individual owns. A rollover of an IRA distribution from one IRA does not preclude a rollover of a distribution from another IRA owned by the same person. [Prop Treas Reg § 1.408-4(b)(4)(ii)]

Q 29:36   Can distributions from an IRA be rolled over into a tax-qualified retirement plan, Section 403(a) annuity plan, or Section 403(b) tax-sheltered annuity?

Yes, a distribution from an IRA can be rolled over to a tax-qualified retirement plan, a Section 403(a) annuity plan, or a Section 403(b) tax-sheltered annuity provided (1) the general rollover rules are followed, and (2) the IRA does not contain any funds derived from sources other than a rollover from a tax-qualified retirement plan, a Section 403(a) annuity plan, or a Section 403(b) tax-sheltered annuity. [IRC § 408(d)(3)(A)(ii)]

Q 29:37   If property is sold in the 60-day period following distribution, can the proceeds of the sale be rolled over if the distribution is from an IRA?

Unlike distributions from tax-qualified plans, it is not clear that the sale of proceeds of property distributed from an IRA can be rolled over even if the sale is made in the 60-day period following the distribution. [IRS Pub No 590]

Q 29:38   What is an inherited IRA?

An inherited IRA benefits an individual (other than a spouse) who acquired the IRA by reason of the death of another individual.

Q 29:39 Can distributions from an inherited IRA be rolled over into another IRA or to a tax-qualified retirement plan?

No. Distributions from an inherited IRA cannot be rolled over to another IRA or into any other tax-qualified retirement plan. Amounts directly transferred from an inherited IRA to another IRA are not exempt from tax. [IRC § 408(d)(3)(C)(i)]

Q 29:40 Can rollovers be made from a tax-qualified retirement plan into an IRA?

A tax-free rollover of a distribution from a tax-qualified retirement plan can generally be made into an IRA if a portion or all of the property received from the plan is contributed to the IRA no later than the 60th day after the distribution was received. If the distribution is made of property in kind (e.g., stock), the amount contributed to the IRA within the 60-day period must be the property in kind or proceeds from its sale. Distributions from tax-qualified plans, Section 403(a) annuity plans, and Section 403(b) tax-sheltered annuity plans can be rolled over to an IRA unless the distribution is one of the following types that are specifically prohibited from being rolled over from a tax-qualified plan, Section 403(a) annuity plan, or Section 403(b) tax-free annuity:

1. A distribution that is one of a series of substantially equal periodic payments made not less frequently than annually over (i) the life of the employee (or the joint lives of the employee and the employees designated beneficiary); (ii) the life expectancy of the employee (or the joint life expectancy of the owner and the owner's designated beneficiary); or (iii) a specified period of ten years or more.

2. A distribution that is made to the extent required under Code Section 401(a)(9), concerning the required minimum distribution rules.

3. A portion of any distribution that is already not includible in gross income (determined without regard for the exclusion for net unrealized appreciation under Code Section 402(e)(4)).

4. The portion of any distribution that is a return of 401(k) plan elective deferrals described in Treasury Regulations Section 1.415-6(b)(6)(iv). These are elective deferrals returned to a

participant to prevent a violation of the maximum contribution limits imposed by Code Section 415.

5. Corrective distributions of an excess contribution to a cash or deferred arrangement as described in Treasury Regulations Section 1.401(k)-1(f)(4).
6. Corrective distributions of an excess deferral to a cash or deferred arrangement described in Treasury Regulations Section 1.402(g)-1(e)(3) or a corrective distribution of excess aggregate contributions described in Treasury Regulations Section 1.401(n)-1(e)(3).
7. A loan treated as a distribution under Code Section 72(p) and not exempted by Code Section 72(p)(2).
8. Dividends paid on employer securities as described in Code Section 404(k).
9. The cost the life insurance coverage (PS 58 costs) provided under a qualified plan for the plan participants. [Treas Reg §§ 1.402(c)-2t, Q&As 3, 4, 1.403(b)-2t, Q&A 1]

For calendar years prior to 1993, distributions from tax-qualified plans, Section 403(a) annuity plans, and Section 403(b) tax-sheltered annuities could not be rolled into an IRA unless the distribution was either a qualifying distribution or partial distribution.

Q 29:41 When is the determination made as to whether a series of payments is a series of substantially equal payments?

The determination as to whether a series of payments is a series of substantially equal periodic payments over one of the prohibited periods is made at the time payments begin, without regard to contingencies or modifications that have not yet occurred. If distributions began before 1993, a determination of whether post-1992 payments are a series of substantially equal periodic payments over a specified period is made by taking into account all payments made, including payments before 1993. [Treas Reg § 1.402(c)-2T, Q&A 5(d)]

Q 29:42 What happens if a payment is significantly larger than other payments in a series?

An individual payment is eligible for rollover treatment if it is independent of a series of substantially equal payments that are themselves ineligible rollover distributions. A payment is treated as independent of the other payments in the series if it is substantially larger or smaller than the other payments in the series. [Treas Reg § 1.402(c)-2T, Q&A 6]

Q 29:43 What happens if a rollover fails to meet the legal requirements for rollovers?

A failed rollover into an IRA could result in an excess contribution with the attendant excise tax unless timely corrected. If the due date (including extensions) has not passed for filing the tax return for the taxable year in that the contribution was made, all of the contribution can be withdrawn without the distribution causing ordinary income. If the due date (including extensions) has passed, correction is more difficult.

Q 29:44 How are distributions made from a simplified employee pension taxed?

For tax purposes, distributions from a simplified employee pension (SEP) are generally treated the same as IRA distributions.

Q 29:45 How are rollovers from SEPs treated?

A distribution from a SEP is generally eligible for a tax-free rollover to an IRA in the same manner as a distribution from an IRA.

Savings Incentive Match Plans for Small Employers

Q 29:46 What is a savings incentive match plan?

As this book is going to press, Congress is considering a new kind of retirement plan, known as a savings incentive match plan for employees (SIMPLE). The essential components of the plan are summarized below.

Under existing law, the provisions involving the qualification of pension and profit sharing plans are rather complex and as a result, according to the Senate Committee, there are many small employers who, because of these complexities, are discouraged from establishing these plans.

The Senate Committee believes that the purposes of the complex nondiscrimination rules will best be served, in the case of small employers, if all full-time employees are given the opportunity to participate in the plan and the employer is required to match the employee contributions. These SIMPLE plans can be adopted by employers who employ 100 or fewer employees earning at least $5,000 in compensation for the preceding year and where such employers do not maintain another employer sponsored retirement plan. The SIMPLE plan can either be established as an IRA for each employee or as part of a qualified Section 401(k) plan. Moreover, if the SIMPLE plan is established in an IRA form, it is not subject to the nondiscrimination rules generally applicable to the qualified plans. Simplified reporting requirements will apply. The employee contributions to an IRA-type of SIMPLE plan has to be expressed as a percentage of the employee's compensation and cannot exceed $6,000 per year (which is indexed for inflation in $500 increments).

The SIMPLE provisions are intended to become effective for taxable years beginning after December 31, 1996.

Chapter 30

IRS Audits

Most taxpayers are concerned about the possibility that the Internal Revenue Service will audit them. This chapter discusses IRS audits, outlines some actions that taxpayers can take to protect themselves should an audit occur, and explains the audit appeal process.

Overview	30-1
Taxpayer's Response	30-2
Contesting Additional Assessments	30-5
Tax Returns	30-8
Tax Liability	30-10

Overview

Q 30:1   What is an IRS audit?

In an Internal Revenue Service (IRS) audit, the IRS examiner (in the case of estate taxes, an IRS attorney) examines the taxpayer's tax return and various supporting records. If the IRS examiner determines that the taxpayer has correctly reported his or her tax liability, the examination ends and the amount of tax shown on the return is accepted. If the IRS examiner makes a determination that the return is not correct and that the taxpayer owes additional tax, the IRS examiner sends a notice, known as the 30-day letter, to the taxpayer stating the amount of the proposed adjustments. The taxpayer then has the choice of agreeing with or disagreeing with the examiner's letter.

If the taxpayer agrees with the IRS examiner, the taxpayer pays the additional tax. If the taxpayer disagrees, the taxpayer can take any of the following actions: (1) appeal administratively within the IRS; (2) decline to pay the contested amount and file a petition with the Tax Court; or (3) pay the contested amount and seek a refund in federal district court or the federal Claims Court.

Example 30-1: The personal representative of an estate files an estate tax return. The IRS notifies the personal representative that it wants to audit the return and asks the personal representative to assemble the documents to be reviewed at the offices of the taxpayer's attorney. An appointment is arranged, and the IRS agent reviews the records on the appointed day. After the agent reviews the records, he sends a notice to the taxpayer's attorney declaring that an additional $50,000 in estate taxes are owed. The taxpayer has the option of appealing further within the IRS, paying the $50,000 and seeking a refund, or filing a petition in Tax Court challenging the IRS determination.

Q 30:2 Which estate tax returns are selected for audit?

The Internal Revenue Manual states that estate tax returns that are audited should contain at least one identified issue that is likely to result in a material change in tax liability.

Taxpayer's Response

Q 30:3 What rights do taxpayers have when audited?

In response to complaints that IRS agents were overzealous in dealing with taxpayers, Congress enacted the Taxpayer's Bill of Rights. [IRC § 7521] The provisions of Section 7521 of the Internal Revenue Code (Code) do not apply to criminal investigations or investigations into the integrity of any IRS employee. Among other things, Code Section 7521 gives the taxpayer the following rights:

1. The IRS must prepare a statement that sets forth, in simple and nontechnical language, the rights of the taxpayer and the obligations of an IRS agent during an audit, the IRS internal appeals procedures, the procedures for filing refund claims and taxpayer complaints, and the procedures the IRS may use to enforce the tax laws. In response to this enactment, the IRS issued three publications: (1) "Your Rights as a Taxpayer," (2) "Examination of Returns, Appeal Rights and Claims for Refund," and (3) "The Collection Process."

2. The taxpayer has the right to make an audio recording of any face-to-face interview with an employee of the IRS. The taxpayer must furnish the audio equipment and must provide 10 days' notice. The IRS can also tape-record the interview by giving the same 10-day advance notice. If the IRS makes a recording of the interview, it must provide the taxpayer with a transcript of the interview. The taxpayer must pay for the transcript.

3. The taxpayer has the right to have a representative at interviews with the IRS. The representative must be authorized to represent taxpayers before the IRS. The taxpayer may appear with the representative or, in most cases, can send the representative alone. The IRS can require the taxpayer to accompany the representative only when the interview is in response to an IRS administrative summons.

4. In any interview with a taxpayer, the IRS must explain the audit and appeals process, the collections process, and the taxpayer's rights.

5. The taxpayer is permitted to suspend the interview at any time for the purpose of consulting with a representative; however, this privilege cannot be abused. If the examiner believes that the taxpayer is calling for suspensions to delay the audit, the IRS can issue an administrative summons. This deprives the taxpayer of any suspension privilege and requires him or her to appear personally.

6. The IRS can abate any portion of a penalty or addition to tax that is attributed to reliance by the taxpayer on erroneous written advice by an IRS employee. The reliance has to be reasonable and in response to a specific written request by the taxpayer. The IRS official must be acting in an official capacity.

There is no abatement if the taxpayer fails to provide adequate information.

Q 30:4 What is a taxpayer assistance order?

A taxpayer assistance order is an order issued by the Office of Taxpayer Ombudsman. Such an order can prevent IRS agents from taking further actions to assess or collect taxes. Taxpayer assistance orders can be issued if the ombudsman concludes that the taxpayer is suffering or is about to suffer a significant hardship as a result of IRS administration of the Code.

Q 30:5 How is a taxpayer assistance order obtained?

A taxpayer can request a taxpayer assistance order by filing Form 911 (Application for Taxpayer Assistance Order to Relieve Hardship) with the Problem Resolution Office for the IRS district where he or she resides. It must be filed within a reasonable time after the taxpayer becomes aware of the hardship or potential hardship. [Treas Reg §§ 301.7811-1(b)(1), 301.7811-2]

Q 30:6 Can a taxpayer obtain damages for unauthorized IRS actions?

A taxpayer can maintain a civil action against the United States if any officer or employee of the IRS recklessly or intentionally disregards any provision of the Code or its regulations in connection with any collection of tax. [IRC § 7433] Damages are limited to the actual economic loss suffered plus the costs of the action, up to a ceiling of $100,000. Before filing suit under Code Section 7433, the taxpayer must exhaust all available administrative remedies. The taxpayer cannot recover any amounts that could have reasonably been mitigated. On the other hand, the United States can recover damages not to exceed $25,000 if the taxpayer initiates a frivolous or groundless action under Code Section 7433.

Q 30:7 When should a taxpayer seek help if he or she is audited?

Taxpayers who are being audited should seek help as soon as possible. In an audit, the control of information is sometimes critical, and an expert can advise the taxpayer about what information the taxpayer must reveal. Sometimes taxpayers reveal more than is necessary and pay additional taxes as a result.

Q 30:8 How should taxpayers approach an audit?

A taxpayer should provide an IRS agent with as much written documentation as possible. Where written documentation is unavailable, corroborating affidavits from third parties can be helpful. The IRS agent conducting the examination will have to determine whether the information is sufficient to support the deduction or the noninclusion of income.

Contesting Additional Assessments

Q 30:9 How does an appeal within the IRS work?

The taxpayer initiates an IRS appeal by filing a protest with the regional IRS appeals office for the taxpayer's district. [Treas Reg 26 CFR § 601.106(a)(1)(ii)] One or more conferences are then held between the appeals officer and the taxpayer or the taxpayer's representative. If the taxpayer disagrees with the results of the IRS appeals process, the taxpayer can either file a petition in Tax Court or pay the additional tax requested by the IRS and seek refund in federal Claims Court or in a federal district court.

Q 30:10 When must an appeal be filed with the IRS?

The taxpayer has 30 days after the receipt of the 30-day letter to file a notice of appeal with the IRS. If the taxpayer fails to respond to the 30-day letter, the IRS will then send a notice of deficiency (90-day letter) to the taxpayer. The taxpayer has 90 days after receiving the notice of deficiency to file a petition with the Tax Court to contest the notice of deficiency. If the taxpayer does not want to contest the deficiency in Tax Court, his or her other options are as follows:

1. Pay the deficiency.
2. Pay the deficiency, and file a refund claim. If the refund claim is denied, the taxpayer must file suit in either federal district court or the federal Claims Court if he or she wishes to pursue the matter further.
3. Permit the IRS to assess the tax and attempt to negotiate an offer in compromise with the IRS on the basis of an inability to pay the tax.

Q 30:11 What happens if the audit of an estate is settled?

If the estate audit is settled, a closing letter is sent to the executor of the estate. If this letter is sent, the estate audit cannot be reopened unless there is fraud, concealment, misrepresentation, or clearly defined error. With the receipt of the closing letter, the executor is also able to make final distributions of the estate's assets to the beneficiaries without being liable for any possible IRS claims for additional taxes.

Q 30:12 What factors does the IRS consider on appeal?

The appeals officer considers litigation hazards for the IRS as well as the facts and law related to issues raised by the IRS.

Q 30:13 Can the IRS reopen settled issues on appeal?

IRS policy is not to reopen an issue on appeal that it and the taxpayer have reached agreement on during the audit. [IR Manual 8651:(1)(1-22-90)]

Q 30:14 Can the IRS raise a new issue on appeal?

Yes, it may, but IRS policy is that a new issue should not be raised by the IRS that is detrimental to the taxpayer unless the ground for such action is substantial and the potential effect on tax liability is material. This seems to mean that the issue will not be raised unless the IRS will have a high probability of prevailing in litigation and the additional tax revenue to be gained thereby is significant. Materiality is determined from the government's viewpoint.

Q 30:15 What is an offer in compromise?

If the taxpayer either cannot pay or disputes the amount of the tax liability, the IRS and the taxpayer can enter into an agreement to reduce the tax liability. This is referred to as an *offer in compromise.*

The IRS can make an offer in compromise when criminal proceedings are not being considered and an analysis of the taxpayer's assets and liabilities indicates that the taxes due cannot realistically be fully collected. The offer must be submitted on a Form 656 with accompanying supportive paperwork. Once the IRS suggests an offer in compromise, it is up to the taxpayer to make the first specific offer of payment. The offer is not considered effective until the appropriate IRS official accepts it and the taxpayer is notified. The offer in compromise is binding on all parties. [IR Manual 57(10)(8)57(10)(2)]

Q 30:16 What courts handle federal tax disputes?

Disputes involving federal taxes can be litigated in federal district courts, the Tax Court, or the U.S. Court of Federal Claims (Claims Court).

Q 30:17 What is the advantage of litigating in Tax Court?

Litigation in Tax Court is advantageous to the taxpayer because the taxpayer does not have to pay the taxes owed until the litigation is resolved by the Tax Court. If the taxpayer loses, however, the taxpayer must pay interest on the taxes owed in addition to paying the deficiency. Cases are heard in the Tax Court by a judge because there are no jury trials in that forum.

Thus, even though payment of taxes may be delayed, it is not always preferable to litigate in Tax Court. A U.S. District Court or the Claims Court may be more favorably disposed to the taxpayer's claims than the Tax Court. Because these courts may disagree with one another, taxpayers sometimes try to predict which court will give them the most favorable result and attempt to file suit in that court. Federal district courts allow for a jury trial. They also require full payment of any asserted deficiency in the taxpayer's return before suit can be filed there. The Claims Court is often a taxpayer's last choice—it requires prepayment, like federal district courts, and conducts only bench trials, like the Tax Court. A taxpayer may choose to litigate in the Claims Court, however, if it appears that past decisions by the Claims Court favor the taxpayer.

Q 30:18 Does the Tax Court have a small tax case procedure?

Yes. The Tax Court has a procedure for cases of $10,000 or less. [IRC § 7463] This procedure must be elected by the taxpayer and approved by the Tax Court. These cases are heard by special judges, do not require briefs and oral arguments, and are informally tried. They also cannot be appealed.

Q 30:19 Can a taxpayer represent himself or herself in Tax Court?

Yes. Although it is generally advantageous to hire an attorney to present one's case in Tax Court, taxpayers can and do represent themselves in Tax Court.

Tax Returns

Q 30:20 If a return is being prepared that involves a gray area of taxation law, is there any way to know in advance whether the IRS will accept a particular position under specific facts?

Yes. Private letter rulings are issued by the IRS's national office to individual taxpayers in response to their particular requests. A user fee applies, ranging from $50 to $3,000. Revenue Procedure 90-17 sets forth specific provisions relating to private letter ruling fees.

An offer in compromise is also recommended under very specific circumstances.

Q 30:28 Once a taxpayer establishes an installment payment agreement with the IRS, is the IRS bound by the agreement?

Generally, the IRS is bound by the agreement. If, however, (1) the monthly payments are not made timely; (2) the taxpayer is delinquent on filing his or her income tax return (extensions are not permitted); or (3) the taxpayer has a significant change in income, the IRS may default on or alter the agreement. Also, if the taxpayer is found to have submitted false information to the IRS, the IRS may cancel the installment agreement.

Q 30:29 Once an installment agreement is defaulted on by the IRS, may it be reinstated?

An installment agreement may be reinstated. The IRS looks at the prior history of default with the installment agreement as well as payment history. If the taxpayer appears to be a good risk, the agreement may be reinstated; however, a $24 user fee is required.

Q 30:30 What is an IRS tax lien?

A lien attaches to property owned by the taxpayer. It is generally recorded at a local courthouse. It appears on all credit reports, affecting the ability of the taxpayer to pay the liability. Informally, a lien is generally always recorded on an individual taxpayer when the taxpayer owes in excess of $20,000 tax liability.

Q 30:31 When must a lien be released by the IRS?

Code Section 6325 requires a release within 30 days from the date the liability has been paid or is determined unenforceable.

Q 30:32 When may a taxpayer's assets be seized immediately without the usual administrative remedies?

This type of seizure is called a jeopardy assessment. Under Internal Revenue Regulations Section 1.6851, the jeopardy assessment is proper when (1) the taxpayer is leaving or appears to be leaving the United States; (2) the taxpayer is hiding or shifting assets; and (3) the taxpayer appears to be or is becoming insolvent.

Q 30:33 What is the advantage to filing a married filing separate return over a married filing joint return?

When a couple files a joint return, both become fully liable for the income tax liability. This makes it easier for the IRS to seize jointly held assets, such as the taxpayers' home.

Q 30:34 When one spouse is responsible for income tax liability, can the other avoid liability?

Generally, when a joint return is filed, both husband and wife are liable for the taxes due. Code Section 6013 provides relief on a joint return, however, if a substantial omission or overstatement is due to the acts of only one spouse and the other had no knowledge of these acts, and the imposition of liability would have unjust results.

Q 30:35 When a return has not been signed by one or both of the taxpayers, is the return considered filed?

The return is not considered filed by that person, and therefore liability from the return may not be imposed, except under very specific circumstances, such as the admission by the other spouse that he or she would have signed the return.

Q 30:36 Will Chapter 7 bankruptcy remove a taxpayer's federal income tax liability?

Bankruptcy may relieve all penalties and interest, and, if the return has been filed more than three years before the bankruptcy, may discharge the full tax liability.

Q 30:37 If the IRS prepares a return for a taxpayer based on informational returns it receives at year-end, may a taxpayer then file his or her own return?

The taxpayer may file, and should file, his or her own return. When the IRS prepares income tax returns for non-filers, it does not give any dependency credits, income tax deductions, or cost of assets before sold. In essence, the taxpayer is almost always in a worse situation than he or she would be if an independent return was filed.

Q 30:38 When a taxpayer is visited by a representative of the IRS who advises the taxpayer of his or her *Miranda* rights, should the taxpayer seek counsel?

If the taxpayer has been read *Miranda* warnings, the Criminal Investigations Division is almost certainly involved. The taxpayer should seek competent counsel immediately.

Q 30:39 What is the Criminal Investigations Division of the IRS?

The Criminal Investigations Division is the branch of the IRS that seeks criminal sanctions against such taxpayers as those who are involved in illegal activities or fraudulent activities. [IR Manual 52(10)1.2(1)]

Q 30:40 What is an IRS levy?

A levy attaches to specific assets of the taxpayer such as bank accounts and wages. Usually, a Notice of Intent to Levy will precede this type of action. This notice should prompt a taxpayer to take immediate action, such as contacting the Automated Collections Service or hiring counsel.

Q 30:41 How is a release of a levy obtained?

The taxpayer or counsel can contact the Automated Collections Service to make alternative payment arrangements. Usually, this is done by an Installment Payment Agreement reached with the IRS. The Automated Collections Service normally requires information from Form 433-A for individuals or Form 433-B for businesses at the time it is contacted. A taxpayer or his or her counsel should be prepared with this information.

Q 30:42 When a taxpayer dies leaving an estate and the beneficiaries are ready to close the estate but for the fact that the taxpayer did not file all of his or her returns, what options do the beneficiaries have in order to ensure that the IRS will not audit the returns after the estate is closed?

The estate may file the returns and submit a Form 4810. This form forces the IRS to make a determination as to the acceptability of the return in a shorter period of time than applies to a normal return.

Q 30:43 What is the benefit of filing a return and paying the total liability due on its due date?

If there is a liability for the tax year, filing a return on time will generally stop the compounding of interest and the addition of penalties. Interest is compounded on a daily basis, which can result in a large additional liability. Filing a return also avoids the failure to file penalty imposed by Code Section 6651 of 5 percent per month of the liability up to a maximum of 25 percent.

Q 30:44 If a taxpayer files a return under the guidance of his or her tax professional, who turns out to have advised the client incorrectly, does the taxpayer have any recourse?

The taxpayer may seek civil litigation against the tax professional for malpractice. The taxpayer may also prepare a Form 843 and request an abatement of the penalties assessed by the IRS.

Q 30:45 If a taxpayer receives a check from the IRS that he or she is not entitled to, what should the taxpayer do to avoid later liability?

The taxpayer should return the check to the IRS via certified mail after voiding the check. By using this procedure, the taxpayer will not be held liable for any interest that accrued on the funds.

Q 30:46 If a taxpayer filed an income tax return in one district, but later moved, does the taxpayer have to go to the area where the return was filed to be audited?

No. The taxpayer may request a transfer from the Examinations Division or Collections Division in the district where the taxpayer currently resides.

Q 30:47 May a taxpayer receive a tax refund for the current year even though he or she has an outstanding balance for an earlier year?

In most cases, the IRS will apply the funds received to the earlier year. In some cases, however, the IRS has not yet processed the earlier year liabilities or realized that the taxpayer owes the liability and will return the refund.

Q 30:48 If a taxpayer marries someone who owed a liability to the IRS from a year prior to the marriage, is the taxpayer liable, too?

The spouse is generally not liable for the debt. Where the taxpayer and his spouse would have been entitled to a refund on their current return, but for the taxpayer's prior liability, Form 8379 may be used to entitle the injured spouse to his or her portion of the refund.

Q 30:49 How long may the IRS pursue a taxpayer for the liability due?

Absent bankruptcy or another extension of the liability, the statute of limitations for collections is ten years from the date the return was filed or the liability was assessed, which ever is later.

Q 30:50 If a taxpayer submits a Form 433-A or Form 433-B, which is generally required for an installment agreement or offer in compromise, what risks does the taxpayer take?

These forms reveal all of the asset information for the taxpayer, including bank accounts, vehicle descriptions, and employment. All of these assets may be levied by the IRS, placing the taxpayer in a worse position than before he or she contacted the Automatic Collections Service.

Q 30:51   What benefit is served by Form 433-A or Form 433-B?

The Automatic Collections Service analyzes the income, expenses, and assets of the individual taxpayer. If the taxpayer is eligible for an installment payment agreement, the completion of this form will expedite the process and help in obtaining a release of any levies. The division will consider the market value of all assets and the amount of credit available to the taxpayer, however, and may demand immediate payment of the entire liability.

Q 30:52   If the taxpayer is about to reach the tenth year that the liability is due and the IRS levies the taxpayer's wages and demands an extension of the statute of limitations in order for the taxpayer to obtain a release, what should the taxpayer do?

The answer to this question varies depending on the individual. For most, if the taxpayer can hold out until the statute expires, he or she will be in a very good situation. For others, an extension may keep them from insolvency. Consultation with counsel will assist in this decision.

Q 30:53   The Automatic Collections Service has a tendency to send the monthly installment payment vouchers too late for the taxpayer to make monthly payments on time. What can a taxpayer do to avoid a default?

Far too many taxpayers default while waiting for their payment vouchers to reach them before sending the funds. To prevent taxpayers from complaining when the installment agreement defaults, the IRS makes a point of telling taxpayers to mail the payment ten days early and not to wait for the voucher. It is recommended that the taxpayer use the prior month's voucher statement in order to ensure that payment reaches the IRS in a timely manner. Simply cross off the prior month on the voucher and substitute the new month.

Q 30:54 **If a taxpayer is in the middle of an audit, does he or she have the right to request time to obtain counsel and a later appointment?**

The taxpayer has the right to be represented by counsel, certified public accountants, or other individuals authorized to practice before the IRS. Therefore, the taxpayer has the right to reschedule an appointment in order to obtain assistance from one of these individuals.

Q 30:55 **If the taxpayer terminates an appointment with the IRS to obtain representation, does the taxpayer have to appear or may his or her representatives appear at the next appointment?**

The representative should appear on behalf of the taxpayer. Usually this provides a buffer zone for the taxpayer. The representative will need to have completed a Form 2848, Power of Attorney, before he or she may appear for the taxpayer.

Q 30:56 **If a taxpayer's liability is determined to be uncollectible, does this mean that the taxpayer will not be liable for the debt?**

No. If the IRS later learns that the taxpayer is now capable of paying the liability, it may levy as it deems fit. The taxpayer will not be fully relieved of the liability until the amount is paid or the statute of limitations expires.

Q 30:57 **What criteria does the IRS use in determining when it will abate a penalty?**

The IRS looks at whether there was (1) a death, unavoidable absence, or serious illness of the taxpayer or the taxpayer's family; (2) fire, casualty, natural disaster, or other disturbance that destroyed the records or prevented compliance; (3) an inability on the part of the taxpayer to obtain records needed for the completion of the return; (4) advice of tax preparers; (5) advice of an IRS representative; (6) mistake or misinterpretation of the tax law; and (7) mistake or negligence.

Q 30:58 If the IRS refuses to abate a penalty, what options does a taxpayer have?

The taxpayer may appeal to a penalty appeals officer within 15 days of the notice that the penalty will not be abated.

Q 30:59 What is the difference between an offer in compromise based on doubt as to liability and an offer in compromise based on doubt as to collectibility?

An offer in compromise based on doubt as to liability provides the IRS with supporting documentation that states that the taxpayer is not liable for the debt owed. These are reviewed by the Examinations Division of the IRS. Doubt as to collectibility tells the IRS that the taxpayer accepts that he or she is liable, but, based on the taxpayer's financial situation (Form 433-A or Form 433-B is often used), he or she is unable to pay and will continue to be unable to pay the income tax liability. These are reviewed by the Collections Division.

Q 30:60 What are the chances that an offer in compromise will be accepted by the IRS?

Statistics show that the acceptance rate is increasing. Since the issuance of Internal Revenue Policy Statement P-5-100, the number of offers that are accepted has steadily increased. Before completing an offer in compromise, the taxpayer should look at the acceptance rate of the offers in his or her area.

Q 30:61 How is the amount to be submitted with an offer in compromise determined?

The taxpayer will need to factor in the quick sale value of his or her assets. Then the taxpayer takes the present value of his or her ability to pay, which is determined by analyzing income and expenses. These two figures are added to reach an amount that is generally acceptable to the IRS.

Q 30:62 How are pension plans valued for purposes of an offer in compromise?

Pension plans are valued on a case-by-case basis. Generally, if a taxpayer is required to contribute to a pension plan and does not have access to it until after retirement, this will not be an asset considered in the offer. If the pension plan may be borrowed against or is immediately accessible, which is often the case with individual retirement accounts, however, then the full value will be considered.

Q 30:63 How does the IRS value property owned as tenants by the entirety with a spouse who is not liable for the debt in determining the asset value for an offer in compromise?

The IRS usually requires that 20 percent to 30 percent be offered as part of the asset value.

Q 30:64 May an offer in compromise be rejected by the IRS after it is accepted?

The taxpayer must be current on all tax liabilities for five years after the offer is accepted. Even if the taxpayer has paid the amount due on the offer, the offer can still be revoked and the funds retained by the IRS.

Q 30:65 When can the IRS seize assets from a taxpayer's home?

Generally, if the assets are in what is considered to be a private area, such as inside the taxpayer's house or the taxpayer's garage, the IRS will need the taxpayer's permission or a court order to enter and seize the assets. If the assets are in a public area, such as a parking lot or on the street, they may be seized at any time after notice is given to the taxpayer that the assets may be levied.

Q 30:66 During the pendency of consideration of an offer in compromise, will collection activity such as levies and liens continue against the taxpayer?

Internal Revenue Manual Section 57(10)9.2(3) states that collection activity will cease while an offer is being considered if the taxpayer is not filing the offer solely to stay collection activity and if the government's interests are not placed in jeopardy by a staying of collection activity.

Q 30:67 What safeguards should a taxpayer use when preparing for an audit by the IRS?

The taxpayer should be prepared to cancel the audit at any time to obtain proper representation. Furthermore, under Code Section 7520, the taxpayer can tape-record the audit, provided advance notice is given to the IRS.

Q 30:68 May the IRS also tape-record the interview with the taxpayer?

Code Section 7520 also allows the IRS to tape-record a conversation with the taxpayer, but the IRS must provide the taxpayer with advance notice of its intent to tape-record the conversation. If the taxpayer receives this type of notice, it is advisable for him or her to obtain a representative to attend the session on the taxpayer's behalf. If the taxpayer has been summoned, he or she must attend the conference in person.

Q 30:69 Where might a taxpayer obtain tax forms?

The taxpayer may find the most common tax forms at a U.S. post office. The taxpayer may also visit the nearest taxpayer assistance office or call (800) 829-3676 to order forms.

Q 30:70 If a taxpayer takes his or her case to the Tax Court, can the taxpayer recover costs such as attorneys' fees and litigation costs?

The taxpayer may recover these costs if he or she shows (1) that the taxpayer prevailed, (2) that the IRS had no basis for its position, and (3) that he or she exhausted all administrative remedies prior to trial.

Q 30:71   How is a tax return selected for an audit?

Technically, all returns are electronically audited when received by the IRS. The other methods used by the IRS are random selection, matching of information received by employers (such as Forms W-2) to returns filed, and flagging by the computer (e.g., where expenses for a sole proprietor are unreasonable).

Q 30:72   How may a taxpayer check on the status of his or her tax return?

The easiest method for checking on a tax return 24 hours a day is through the Tele-Tax telephone system. Form 1040 gives instructions on how to use this system.

Q 30:73   How may a taxpayer learn of the different types of penalties that may be assessed against him or her and the penalty rates that would apply?

The taxpayer may look to the Code. The IRS also has a Consolidated Penalty Handbook found in the Internal Revenue Manual. This handbook is available by a request to the IRS's Taxpayer Services Division.

Q 30:74   Is it true that the IRS takes factors such as level of education into account when determining whether reasonable cause exists in abating taxation penalties?

The IRS does hold accountants and attorneys to a higher expectation as far as reasonable cause and knowledge are concerned. Often the average taxpayer will be successful in having his or her penalty abated due to ignorance of the law or mistake in situations where more educated individuals would be unsuccessful.

Q 30:75 How is the interest rate used by the IRS determined?

Code Section 6621 states that interest is determine by using the federal short-term rate plus three percentage points.

Q 30:76 What is the difference between simple and compound interest, and which does the IRS use?

Simple interest takes the interest rate and multiplies it against the principal debt only. Compound interest—which the IRS uses—takes the interest rate and multiplies it by not only the original debt, but by the accumulated interest as well.

Q 30:77 If a taxpayer timely files an extension, will interest accumulate on the liability that is eventually determined, even if good cause existed for not being able to file the return timely?

Interest will compound from the due date of the return on the total liability due. Reasonable cause will not relieve a taxpayer of the interest.

Q 30:78 If interest is compounded daily, does the running of interest stop on the date the payment of liability is sent or the date the payment is received?

Interest stops on the date the payment is received.

Q 30:79 If a taxpayer is a non-filer, what are the benefits of voluntarily filing his or her returns with respect to installment payments?

The Automatic Collections Service will be much more amenable to entering into an installment payment agreement and working with a taxpayer at arriving at a figure with a taxpayer who did not have to be tracked down and forced to file a return or had returns filed for him or her by the IRS.

Q 30:80 Is there an exception to the tax civil penalites for circumstances beyond the taxpayer's control?

Yes. Congress recognizes that a taxpayer should not be penalized for circumstances that are beyond his or her control. As a result, most of the civil penalties provide an exception if the required performance is not forthcoming as a result of reasonable cause. [IRC §§ 6651, 6652, 6664, 6676, 6686] Some of the penalties have other requirements (in addition to reasonable cause) before the penalty can be waived.

Q 30:81 Can the IRS partially waive a penalty for failure to show reasonable cause?

No. The IRS must either waive or impose the penalty in full. By requiring the penalty to be imposed unless the failure is due to reasonable cause, the statute precludes any partial waiver. [In re Sanford, 979 F 2d 1151 (11th Cir 1992)]

Q 30:82 What standards apply to the reasonable cause exception?

The determination of what elements must be present to avoid the penalty is a question of fact. [United States v Boyle, 469 US 241, 249 n 8 (1985)] The burden of proving the existence of such elements is on the taxpayer. [Hoefle v Commr, 114 F 2d 713 (6th Cir 1940)] If the penalty is asserted for the first time in the IRS's answer, however, the IRS bears the burden of proof. [Sarcone v Commr, TCM 1985-548; TC Rul 142(a)]

Q 30:83 When and how should the taxpayer request abatement of the penalty?

A taxpayer can request the nonassertion or abatement of a penalty by attaching a statement to his or her return or by responding after receiving a notice of assessment. [IR Manual (20)322:(1)] The request for nonassertion or abatement should be accompanied by documentary evidence, where possible. The request for waiver of a penalty should be made as soon as possible because the IRS has full authority to commence proceedings to collect the penalty ten days after the notice of assessment is sent.

The regulations generally require the taxpayer's request for waiver of the penalty be in writing and signed under penalties of perjury. [Treas Reg § 301.6651-1(c)(1)] In the interest of fairness, however, the IRS will consider oral and unsigned requests. [Consolidated Penalty Handbook, IR Manual (20)321, (20)322]

Q 30:84 What is the reasonable cause standard?

Reasonable cause is essentially any cause that arises despite the exercise of ordinary business care and prudence. [United States v Boyle, 469 US 241] In determining whether there is reasonable cause, the following questions must be asked:

1. Did the event occur as the result of an error made by a professional advisor retained by the taxpayer?
2. Does the length of time between the event cited as a reason and the due date for the required activity negate the event's effect?
3. Does the continued operation of a business after the event that caused the taxpayer's noncompliance negate the event's effect?
4. Should the event that caused the taxpayer's noncompliance have reasonably been anticipated?
5. Was the penalty the result of carelessness or forgetfulness, or did the taxpayer appear to have made an honest mistake?
6. Is a non-liable individual being blamed for the taxpayer's noncompliance? If so, what is the relationship between the taxpayer and the individual?
7. Has the taxpayer documented all pertinent facts?
8. Does the taxpayer have a history of being assessed the same penalty?
9. Could the taxpayer have requested an extension or filed an amended return?
10. Has the taxpayer provided sufficient detail to determine whether he or she exercised ordinary business care and prudence?

[IR Manual 4562.2, (20)333]

The ordinary business care and prudence standard, however, is only applicable to the ordinary person, that is, one who is physically and mentally capable of knowing, remembering, and complying with the statutory requirement. [United States v Boyle, 469 US 241 (1985) (concurring opinion)] If a taxpayer can show that because of incompetence or infirmity he or she is unable to meet the standard of ordinary business care and prudence, the IRS should not impose a penalty.

Q 30:85   What are common reasons given as reasonable cause?

For many of the major penalties, the IRS has prepared a list of the most common reasons given by taxpayers for many of the major penalties (e.g., the late filing and late payment penalties). [Consolidated Penalty Handbook, IRM (20)333] Some reasons commonly asserted by taxpayers to establish reasonable cause are as follows:

1. *Reliance on tax advisor.* Reasonable cause can be established if the taxpayer claims that he or she relied on the advice of a competent tax advisor (i.e., tax attorney, certified or licensed public accountant, or enrolled agent). The taxpayer must have received incorrect advice after (1) contacting a tax advisor who is competent on the specific tax matter and (2) furnishing necessary and relevant information. The taxpayer must also have exercised ordinary business care and prudence in determining whether to obtain additional advice, based on his or her own information and knowledge. In determining whether reasonable cause exists, the IRS considers the following factors: (1) when and how the taxpayer became aware of the mistake; (2) whether the taxpayer provided complete and accurate information to the tax advisor; (3) whether the taxpayer did actually rely on the advice of the tax advisor; and (4) supporting documentation, such as a copy of the advice requested, a copy of the advice provided, and a statement from the tax advisor explaining the circumstances. [Consolidated Penalty Handbook, IR Manual (20)333.6]

   The court has generally held that to qualify for a waiver of the penalty, the taxpayer's reliance on the tax advisor and advice must be both reasonable and in good faith. The tax advisor must be competent on the specific tax matter [Freytag v

Commr, 89 TC 849 (1987), *aff'd*, 904 F 2d 1011 (5th Cir 1990), *aff'd*, 111 S Ct 2631 (1991)], and the taxpayer must furnish the advisor with all necessary and relevant information to make a determination. [Given v Commr, 238 F 2d 579 (8th Cir 1956)] Moreover, the advice must be obtained timely, and the taxpayer cannot rely on the advice after it is withdrawn. [Stevens Bros Found, Inc v Commr, 39 TC 93 (1962), *aff'd in part, rev'd in part*, and *rem'd in part*, on other grounds, 324 F 2d 633 (8th Cir 1963)] The advice must directly address the issue. A taxpayer cannot rely on informal advice [Dwinell & Co v Commr, 33 TC 827 (1960), *acq*, 1960-2 CB 4] and cannot pick and choose from conflicting advice without good reason. [Condor Int'l, Inc v Commr, 98 TC 203 (1992)]

2. *Death, serious illness, or unavoidable absence.* The death, serious illness, or unavoidable absence of the taxpayer or the death or serious illness of a member of the taxpayer's family may constitute reasonable cause. For an entity, the incapacity must relate to an individual having the sole authority to take the required action or a member of his or her family. [M & F Holding Corp v Commr, 26 BTA 504 (1932)] In determining whether an illness constitutes reasonable cause, the courts focus on the severity and duration of the illness. The incapacity must be so severe that the taxpayer cannot function during the period, and so sudden that he or she could not reasonably have planned for it. For example, a court has waived the failure to file penalty imposed against a taxpayer whose sudden and continuing paralysis confined him to bed and required multiple blood transfusions. [United States v Isaac, 91-2 USTC ¶ 50,314 (ED Ky 1991)] In general, though, when a taxpayer continues to work or take care of other normal business matters during his or her incapacity, reasonable cause generally does not exist. [Hoefle v Commr, 114 F 2d 713 (6th Cir 1940); Hernandez v Commr, 72 TC 1234 (1979)]

Because a joint return involves two taxpayers, the test is applied separately to each. [Sanders v Commr, 21 TC 1012 (1954), *aff'd*, 225 F 2d 629 (10th Cir 1956), *cert denied*, 350 US 967 (1956)] Of course, the effect of one taxpayer's illness on his or her spouse, as well as the spouse's knowledge and experience, can be taken into account in making this determination.

3. *Records unavailable.* The unavailability of records is generally not considered reasonable cause for a taxpayer's failure to file a return. [Crocker v Commr, 92 TC 899 (1989)] Rather, the taxpayer must estimate his or her tax liability based on the best information available and, where necessary, obtain an extension of time to file. If, however, a proper return cannot be filed because information remains unavailable despite ordinary business care and prudence by the taxpayer, there is reasonable cause. [Connor v Commr, TCM 1982-302] For example, necessary records may have been destroyed by fire or other casualty, may not be timely supplied by a third party, or may not otherwise be available notwithstanding the taxpayer's exercise of ordinary business care and prudence. In the case of a significant disaster affecting numerous taxpayers, the IRS generally provides special guidance for penalty relief. [IR 93-30 (Mar 15, 1993) (1993 blizzard)]

4. *Lack of funds.* A claim of insufficient funds is not reasonable cause for failing to file a return. [Jones v Commr, 25 TC 1100 (1956), *rev'd* on other grounds, 259 F 2d 300 (5th Cir 1958)]

5. *Ignorance of the law.* In and of itself, ignorance of the law does not constitute reasonable cause. [Lammerts Estate v Commr, 456 F 2d 681 (2d Cir 1972)] This includes, for example, a taxpayer's erroneous belief (not based on advice of counsel) that no return is required to be filed; a lack of knowledge as to the correct due date; and an erroneous belief that the proceeds were not taxable. Ordinary business care and prudence requires taxpayers to be aware of their tax obligations.

    On the other hand, ignorance of the law in conjunction with other facts and circumstances, including the taxpayer's knowledge, may support a claim of reasonable cause. [IR Manual (20)333.5:(1), 4562.2:(4)] Where, for example, the IRS has not provided any guidance as to difficult and complex issues, reasonable cause may exist for a position taken in good faith. Similarly, a taxpayer may have reasonable cause if the failure is a result of a recent change in the tax law or forms of which the taxpayer could not reasonably be expected to know. [IR Manual (20)333.5]

6. *Mistake or forgetfulness.* A taxpayer's mistake, forgetfulness, or carelessness does not constitute ordinary business care and

prudence and is not a basis for reasonable cause. [Logan Lumber Co v United States, 365 F 2d 846 (5th Cir 1966)] Absent the affirmative advice of counsel, even a good faith but mistaken belief does not relieve the taxpayer from the penalty. [Fides v Commr, 137 F 2d 731 (4th Cir 1943)] The Tax Court has expressly rejected any assertion that a good faith dispute as to the proper treatment of a particular item constitutes reasonable cause for any failure to file a return [Stevens Bros Found, Inc v Commr, 39 TC 93 (1962), *aff'd in part, rev'd in part,* on other grounds, 324 F 2d 633 (8th Cir 1963)] (unless the failure is based on the advice of competent counsel).

7. *Misfeasance by employee or agent.* The neglect or misfeasance by the taxpayer's employee or agent is not reasonable cause. [United States v Boyle, 469 US 241 (1985)] In instances where the taxpayer's employee has failed to file timely tax returns or pay taxes, the courts have held that the taxpayer still has a duty to file, pay, and deposit taxes and cannot avoid responsibility by simply relying on the employee to comply with the statutes. Under such circumstances, a taxpayer can establish reasonable cause only if it can demonstrate that it was disabled from timely complying with the statutes. [Compare In re American Biomaterials Corp, 954 F 2d 919 (3d Cir 1992) (reasonable cause existed where corporate officers—who controlled corporation and were in charge of filing and paying taxes—embezzled funds, thereby "incapacitating" corporation and leaving it unable to comply with tax laws) with Conklin Bros of Santa Rosa, Inc v United States, 986 F 2d 315 (9th Cir 1993) (employee who failed to file timely payroll returns or deposit taxes was not beyond control of taxpayer, for unlike the officers in American Biomaterials, employee was not the control person and could have been supervised)]

8. *Erroneous advice from the IRS.* The portion of any penalty attributable to erroneous advice furnished to the taxpayer, in writing, by an IRS employee acting in his or her official capacity is waived if (1) the advice is reasonably relied on by the taxpayer; (2) the advice is issued in response to a specific written request for advice by the taxpayer; and (3) the taxpayer has provided adequate and accurate information in connection with the request. [IRC § 6404(f); Treas Reg

§ 301.6404-3(a), 301.6404-3(b)] A taxpayer is not considered to have reasonably relied on advice that he or she receives after the return or act to which it relates is filed or undertaken. [Treas Reg § 301.6404-3(b)(2)] If, however, the taxpayer files an amended return that conforms to the written advice, the taxpayer is considered to have reasonably relied on the advice. Moreover, reasonable reliance cannot continue after the taxpayer is put on notice that the advice no longer represents the IRS's position.

The IRS can also abate a penalty for reasonable cause where the taxpayer relies on oral advice from an IRS employee. [IRM (20)333.8] To claim the exemption, the taxpayer must show that he or she supplied the IRS with complete and accurate information and that he or she exercised ordinary business care and prudence in relying on that advice.

9. *Time and business pressures.* The taxpayer's heavy workload does not constitute reasonable cause for his or her failure to perform a required act. [Croker v Commr, 92 TC 899 (1989)] A person exercising ordinary business care and prudence does not take on assignments that would prohibit that person from fulfilling his or her own legal obligations within the prescribed time. Similarly, the time pressures of the taxpayer's agents cannot excuse the taxpayer's failure to file a return. [Nosek v Commr, TCM 1989-622; Dritz v Commr, TCM 1969-175, *aff'd per curiam*, 427 F 2d 1176 (5th Cir 1970)]

10. *Additional objections and religious beliefs.* Neither constitutional objections [Garner v United States, 424 US 648 (1976)] nor religious beliefs [United States v Lee, 455 US 252 (1982)] are valid reasons for failing to file a return or failing to pay the required tax.

11. *Miscellaneous.* The IRS accepts the following items as reasonable causes for the late filing of a return:
    — Where the taxpayer mails his or her return to the IRS (whether or not the envelope containing the return has sufficient postage) in time to reach the IRS service center or office within the prescribed period, given the normal handling of the mail. This rule is more lenient than the timely mailed, timely filed rule of Code Section 7502, which requires sufficient postage to be affixed.

- Where the taxpayer files his or her return within the legal period but with the wrong IRS office. This is also broader than Code Section 7502, which requires the envelope to be properly addressed.
- Where the taxpayer personally visits an IRS office before the return's due date for the purpose of securing information or assistance to file his or her return properly and, through no fault of the taxpayer's, is unable to see a representative of the IRS.
- Where the taxpayer applies to the IRS for the proper forms, but they are not furnished in sufficient time to permit the return to be filed timely. To rely on this exception, the taxpayer must have requested the forms sufficiently in advance of the due date to allow for processing his request, mailing the form, and completing his return. [Compare with IR Manual (20)362.2 (7-29-92) (requiring a five- to six-week advance request in connection with obtaining required FTD coupons)]

[IR Manual 4562.2:(1)]

Chapter 31

Family Limited Partnerships

The family limited partnership is a relatively recent arrival to the opportunities available for income, gift, and estate tax savings. It allows a family business to be transferred piecemeal to the next generation at a discounted gift tax valuation while the senior family members continue to control the business. This chapter explores its ramifications, both beneficial and adverse, by illuminating the various features of the family limited partnership.

General Characteristics and Benefits	31-1
Exercising Control	31-4
Transferability of Interests	31-6
Administrative Matters	31-9

General Characteristics and Benefits

Q 31:1 What is a family limited partnership?

A family limited partnership (FLP) is a limited partnership, formed under applicable state statutes, in which a familial relationship exists between the general and limited partners. An FLP is a partnership formed under state statute by two or more persons at least one of whom is a general partner and one is a limited partner. A limited partnership can be created only by virtue of the authority of an existing state statute. The Revised Uniform Limited Partnership Act

Section 303(d) notes that the surname of a limited partner can only appear in the name of the limited partnership if it is the same as the surname of the general partner or it was in the name of the old existing business.

Q 31:2 What are the intended benefits of a family limited partnership?

When structured properly, a family limited partnership can provide income, estate, and gift tax benefits.

Example 31-1: A husband and wife own a business and intend to transfer a significant interest in that business to their children. Accordingly, they transfer the business to an FLP in exchange for a combined 4 percent general partnership interest and a 96 percent limited partnership in the FLP (i.e., each spouse receives a 2 percent general partnership interest and a 48 percent limited partnership interest). Over a period of time, husband and wife gradually transfer their limited partnership interests to their children. The intended result is to allocate the partnership income among the parents and the children, who generally are taxed at a lower tax rate than the parents; furthermore, the fair market value of the gifts of the limited partnership interests to the children can be discounted at the 35 percent rate or higher for gift tax purposes because of lack of marketability due to the minority interests they represent. Meanwhile, husband and wife still retain control over the business and the FLP as its general partners.

Q 31:3 How does a family limited partnership achieve income shifting?

Because FLPs are taxable as partnerships, they are *pass-through* entities (i.e., they are vehicles through which gains, losses, deductions, and income flow directly to the partners in accordance with the allocation of their partnership interests). In Example 31:1, if the children ultimately obtained an overall limited partnership interest of 49 percent, then as much as 49 percent of the partnership income would be allocated to them.

Q 31:4 What are the estate planning advantages of a family limited partnership?

An FLP can be used to reduce the estate tax burden on a family by permitting parents (i.e., the general partners) to transfer their limited partnership interests during their lifetimes to their children and in so doing, to claim a significant minority and marketability discount so as to reduce the value of the transferred FLP limited partnership interest subject to gift tax. This discounted value would be included in the computation of *adjusted taxable gifts* when making a computation for estate tax purposes; however, the post-gift appreciation, over and above the discounted value reported for federal gift tax purposes, would not be subject to estate tax.

It is important to note that an FLP, unlike a corporation, is not subject to the provisions of Code Section 2036(b), which overrode a Supreme Court decision holding that a grantor retaining a controlling voting interest in shares transferred to a trust did not have a retained interest in the corporation requiring their inclusion in his estate. [Estate of Byrum, 408 US 125 (1972)] Congress reacted to the *Byrum* decision by enacting Code Section 2036(b), which provides that such a transfer as was involved in *Byrum* is includible currently in the estate of the transferor. The IRS has confirmed, however, that Code Section 2036(b) does not apply to an FLP (because it is not a corporation); therefore, parental control as general partners in an FLP will not cause the value of the transferred limited partnership interests to be included in the parents' gross estate. [Ltr Ruls 9415007, 9332006, 9310039, 9131006, and 8611004] Caution is required, however, if an FLP contains voting stock of a controlled corporation, because in this situation the possibility arises that the transferred FLP limited partnership interests could be challenged by the IRS and included in the donor's estate. To anticipate this IRS challenge, the donor (i.e., the general partner) should cause the controlled corporation to be recapitalized, so that only nonvoting stock is owned by the FLP.

Q 31:5 How does a family limited partnership facilitate a valuation discount?

The partnership agreement may place certain restrictions on the assets transferred to the partnership. These restrictions and limitations can reduce the value of the assets. Discounts may be given for lack of marketability, lack of transferability, minority interest, and lack of management participation.

Q 31:6 How vulnerable are partnerships to the attacks of creditors?

A creditor can obtain a charging order that entitles him or her to any distribution made to that particular partner; however, a creditor cannot reach the specific partnership assets because under state law, individual partners generally have no interest in specific assets.

Q 31:7 How many partners may a family limited partnership have?

Unlike a subchapter S corporation, which is limited to 35 stockholders (note that Congress is actively considering increasing the number to 75 stockholders), there is no limit to the number of partners permissible in a limited partnership; however, if the number of partners becomes so large as to create a public market for interest in the partnership, the partnership becomes a publicly traded partnership, and as such, would be treated as a corporation for federal income tax purposes. [IRC § 7704] This result would be highly unlikely in a family limited partnership.

Exercising Control

Q 31:8 Who generally controls family limited partnerships?

Limited partnerships are statutorily structured so that the general partner is responsible for the management of the partnership. As no statutory guidelines are provided for the percentage of interest that must be owned by partners, it is conceivable for a general partner to own 1 percent of the partnership and still have control over the assets of the partnership.

Q 31:9 How much control in a family limited partnership can be retained by the donor?

If the donor retains control of the interest that he or she has purported to transfer to the donee and if the controls are significant, he or she may, under Treasury regulations, be treated as remaining the owner of those interests. [Treas Reg § 1.704-1(e)(2)(ii)]

Q 31:10 What do the Treasury regulations mean by *significant controls*?

Control over the distribution of income, control of assets essential to the business, and management powers, either alone or combined, constitute significant powers. Retention of any of these controls by the donor may tend to show, in light of other facts, that the donor is really in control of the interest and is therefore the real owner. [Treas Reg § 1.704.-1(e)(2)(ii)(a)]

Q 31:11 Can a minor be a member of a family limited partnership?

Only if the minor child can demonstrate that he or she is competent to manage his or her own property. To prove competence in property management, the child will have to demonstrate, to the satisfaction of disinterested adults, that he or she possesses sufficient maturity and experience to be regarded as competent. In the absence of a showing of competency, a minor child will not be recognized as a partner unless control of the property is exercised by a fiduciary such as a guardian or custodian. [Treas Reg § 1.704-1(e)(2)(vii)]

Q 31:12 Are there any restrictions on the types of property that can be transferred to a family limited partnership?

Yes. The stock of an S corporation must be owned by an individual; therefore, by definition, it cannot be owned by a partnership. If S corporation stock is transferred to a family limited partnership, the S corporation election is terminated (although a bill pending in Congress is seeking to extend ownership of S corporation shares beyond individuals, estates, and certain trusts). An FLP can own any other type of asset.

Q 31:13 Can a family limited partnership own life insurance?

Yes, a life insurance policy, as an asset, can be owned by an FLP. Care should be taken that the insured under the policy retains no incidents of ownership in the policy and that the transfer for value rules do not apply.

Q 31:14 What is the difference between a general partner's liability and a limited partner's liability?

A limited partner is liable for debts and obligations only to the extent of his or her contribution or the amount he or she agreed to contribute to the partnership. In contrast, there is no such limitation for a general partner, who is subject to unlimited liability.

Transferability of Interests

Q 31:15 Is there free transferability of interests in a family limited partnership?

If the assignee of a limited partner's interest can be substituted only after unanimous consent, then there is no free transferability of the partnership interest [Rev Reg § 301.7701-3(b)(2)]; however, the Tax Court held that if the partnership agreement provides that such consent cannot be withheld unreasonably then this constitutes free transferability of a partnership interest. [Larson v Comm, 66 TC 159 (1979)] This becomes important because if an organization contains more than two corporate characteristics, the IRS will treat the organization as a corporation. Corporate characteristics are defined as any of the following: (1) continuity of life, (2) centralization of management, (3) limited liability, and (4) free transferability of interests. Such a holding would defeat the purpose of an FLP because income and losses would have tax consequences to the corporation and not to the partnership members (unless it was a subchapter S corporation).

Q 31:16 How does the Internal Revenue Service determine whether a family limited partnership has more corporate than partnership characteristics?

The Internal Revenue Service (IRS) analyzes the characteristics of an organization as follows:

1. *Continuity of life.* This does not exist if death, bankruptcy, or withdrawal of a general partner causes the dissolution of the partnership, even if the remaining general partners or a majority in interest of all the remaining partners can avoid dissolution by agreeing to continue the partnership. [Treas Reg § 301.7701-2(b)(1)]

2. *Centralized management.* For IRS ruling purposes, centralized management exists if the general partners own less than 20 percent of all partnership interests. [Rev Proc 91-13, 1991-1 CB 477]

3. *Limited liability.* For IRS ruling purposes, limited liability does not exist if a sole corporate general partner has net worth, excluding partnership interests, equal to 10 percent or more of total partnership contributions. [Rev Proc 92-88, 1992-2 CB 496]

4. *Transferability of interests.* If an organization restricts the free transferability of its interests then this constitutes a noncorporate characteristic. In this connection a right of first refusal will be treated as a modified or partial form of free transferability. [Treas Reg § 301.7701-2(e)(2)] On the other hand, there is no free transferability if a limited partner's assignee cannot become a substitute partner in all respects without the consent of the general partners. [Treas Reg § 301.7701-2(e)(1)] Also, for IRS ruling purposes, free transferability does not exist if the partnership agreement restricts the transferability of more than 20 percent of partnership interests. [Rev Proc 92-33, 1992-1 CB 782]

It should be noted that the IRS has issued proposed regulations intended to simplify its classification regulations to allow certain domestic unincorporated organizations to elect their own classifications. For instance, if A, B, and C create an unincorporated organization having all four corporate characteristics of limited liability, centralized management, free transferability of interests, and continuity of life, this organization could nevertheless elect partnership classification. The IRS's purpose in making this proposal is to reduce its administrative overload related to ruling on classifications of organizations. [Prop Treas Reg §§ 301.7701-1–301.7701-3, 301.7701-4(b), 301.7701-4(c)(1), 301.7701-4(c)(2), Example 1, 301.7701-4(f), 301.7701-6]

Q 31:17 What is a capital interest in a partnership?

A capital interest in a partnership is an interest in the assets of the partnership that gives rise to a distribution of the capital interest upon the partner's withdrawal or liquidation of the partnership. The mere right to participate in the earnings and profits of a partnership is not determinative of whether a partner has a capital interest. [Treas Reg § 1.704-1(e)(1)(v)]

Q 31:18 How does the Internal Revenue Service view a partnership?

Section 761(a) of the Internal Revenue Code (Code) defines a partnership to include a "syndicate, group, pool, joint venture, or other unincorporated organization through or by means of which any business, financial operation, or venture is carried on" that is not a corporation or a trust or estate.

This definition itself does not provide much direction on what will be considered a partnership by the IRS; however, there are several factors that have been used in the determination of a partnership. These factors include the following: joint contribution of capital or services; the purpose of carrying out a trade or business; joint ownership of the capital contributions and earnings of the enterprise; mutual control; representation of the business to others as a partnership; and conducting business, holding title to property, and filing tax returns in the partnership name. [Wheeler v Comm, 37 TCM 883 (1978)]

Q 31:19 How are family limited partnerships treated by the Internal Revenue Service?

If a limited partnership is formed under a state statute that is similar to the Uniform Limited Partnership Act, the IRS will ordinarily regard it as a partnership for federal tax purposes. In the case of FLPs, Code Section 704 should also be consulted. Revenue Procedure 91-13 provides a checklist that must accompany a limited partnership request for a ruling from the IRS seeking classification as a partnership and not a corporation. (See Appendix A.)

Q 31:20 Can a partner in a family limited partnership simply assign the income for services or from income-producing property to another taxpayer?

No. There can be no assignment of income whether by the provider of services of the income generated by his or her services or by the owner of property for the income produced by his or her property. An owner of income-producing property may achieve this result by conveying the ownership of the property.

Administrative Matters

Q 31:21 When does the Internal Revenue Service treat a partner as if he or she has received a distribution?

A partner is treated as having received a distribution of his or her share of the income, gains, deductions, credits, and similar items regardless of whether or not they are actually distributed or received by him or her. [IRC § 702] Losses are not recognized unless it is upon distribution in liquidation of the partner's interest. [IRC § 731(a)]

Q 31:22 What determines the taxable year of a partnership?

The partnership must adopt the taxable year of one or more partners having an aggregate interest in profits and capital in excess of 50 percent. If no such majority interest exists, then it must adopt the taxable year of all of its principal partners (those having a 5 percent or more interest in partnership profits or capital). If neither of the foregoing exists, the partnership must use the calendar year; or if the partnership satisfies the IRS by showing a valid business purpose for a taxable year, then such taxable year can be adopted by the FLP. [IRC § 706(b)(4)(A)(i)]

Q 31:23 What determines a family limited partnership's method of accounting?

Code Section 448(a) provides generally that the cash method of accounting is unavailable to (1) a C corporation, (2) a partnership that has a C corporation as a partner, or (3) a tax shelter. A personal service corporation (such as a professional corporation) is treated as an individual under Code Section 4489(b)(2), thus is eligible for the cash method, and does not prevent a FLP in which it is a partner from employing the cash method.

Q 31:24 Does a partnership file a tax return?

Yes. Even though the partnership is not a taxpayer and does not pay taxes, it is required to file a "U.S. Partnership Return of Income IRS Form 1065." This an informational return only and is due on April 15 for those electing calendar year accounting and by the 15th day of the fourth month after the end of the fiscal year for those electing otherwise. [IRC § 6072(a)]

Q 31:25 Does the Internal Revenue Service provide any other rules affecting FLPs other than those found in Code Section 702?

Yes. Code Section 704(e), often referred to as the FLP rules, must be followed to ensure recognition as an FLP.

The following Code Section 704(e) requirements must be met:

> the partnership must have capital as the material income-producing factor, if this requirement is met, a partner may have obtained his or her interest through a gift;

> income shifting by gift will work as long as partnership income bears a reasonable relationship to services rendered by the donor;

> the sale of partnership interest from one family member to another is presumptively a gift, unless there can be a showing of a bona fide purchase with the requisite characteristics of an arm's length transaction. [IRC § 704]

Q 31:26 How is the requirement that capital be a material income-producing factor satisfied?

This is generally determined on a case-by-case basis. Generally, capital is a material income-producing factor when a large part of the gross receipts of the business is attributable to the employment of capital in the partnership business; the business income does not consist mostly of compensation for services; and the business requires a large amount of inventory or a large investment in real estate or equipment. [Treas Reg § 1.704(e)(1)(ii)]

Q 31:27 Is the determination of partnership status by the Internal Revenue Service binding on all members of the partnership?

No. A partnership may be recognized for income purposes as to some partners but not to others. This is particularly important in FLPs because transactions between family members are closely scrutinized. [Treas Reg § 1.704-1(2)(e)]

Q 31:28 How does a gift transaction satisfy the complete transfer requirement for donees?

The transaction must be bona fide and there can be no evidence of tax-avoidance or evasion. The transferor must vest dominion and control over the partnership interest in the transferee. This will be determined by the facts and circumstances present in each case. If the transferor retains interest in ownership that deprives the transferee of dominion and control, the transfer will not be recognized. [Treas Reg § 1.704-1(e)(1)(ii)]

Q 31:29 How is ownership determined?

The IRS determines ownership on a case-by-case basis and the reality of the ownership is determined in the light of the transaction as a whole; however, there are certain basic tests that are employed to determine ownership. These tests generally look at retention of control, participation in management, income distribution, and conduct of partnership business. [Treas Reg § 1.704-1(e)(2)(i)]

Q 31:30 Is the motive of the transfer determinative of ownership?

No. Motive is generally immaterial. However, the IRS considers the presence or the absence of tax-avoidance as a factor that may be determinative of the reality of capital interest acquired by gift. [Treas Reg § 1.704-1(e)(2)(x)]

Q 31:31 What conduct on the part of the donee shows the donee's real ownership?

Consideration is given as to whether the donee is treated as a real partner, whether he or she has been held out publicly as a partner in business conduct, compliance with partnership statutes, and the recognition of the donee's interest in property, bank accounts, and insurance policies. [Treas Reg § 1.704(e)(2)(vi)]

Q 31:32 What is a limited liability company?

A limited liability company (LLC) is a new form of conducting business, first created by the State of Wyoming in 1977, in which the best nontax feature of being a corporation (i.e., limited liability) is combined with the best tax feature of being classified as a partnership (i.e., income and loss pass-through) without an intervening corporate tax, directly to the partner. There are now 49 states plus the District of Columbia that have enacted LLC legislation; Hawaii is the only state that does not yet recognize LLCs. The IRS has issued numerous rulings classifying most LLCs as partnerships. [Rev Proc 95-10, 1995-3 IRB 20]

Q 31:33 Can a limited liability company be used in the same way as an family limited partnership to create the same estate planning opportunities for discount valuations on transfers of minority interests?

Yes. An LLC member (similar to a partner in a partnership) can assign his or her interest to a child. In order for the child to enjoy full membership privileges in the LLC (i.e., the right to participate in management and the right to enjoy the economic benefits of LLC membership) consent to the assignment would typically be required unanimously by the existing LLC members. Without such unanimous consent, the assignee is only entitled to economic benefits. This feature, plus having only a minority interest in the LLC, would create a substantial discount in determining fair market value for the assigned interest, due to lack of marketability and the reduced benefit of a minority membership.

Q 31:34 What effect, if any, do the anti-abuse rules announced by the IRS have on family limited partnerships?

It is generally believed that the anti-abuse regulations [Treas Reg § 1.701-2] formulated by the IRS do not affect FLPs. These regulations require a partnership to have a *bona fide* business purpose and authorize the IRS to disregard the partnership and also to recharacterize the transaction if the partnership was "formed or availed of in connection with a transaction a principal purpose of which is to reduce substantially the present value of the partners' aggregate federal tax liability in a manner that is inconsistent with the intent of Subchapter K." (Subchapter K covers partnerships.)

The proposed regulations contain two examples concerning FLPs. Example 5 involved the contribution of income-producing real estate to an FLP followed by gifts by the FLP general partners of limited partnership interests to their children. The example concluded that this was not an abusive use of an FLP, absent other facts, such "as the creation of the partnership immediately before the gifts" were made. Example 6 covered a contribution of a vacation home to an FLP, followed "at a later date" by gifts of limited partnership interests by the general partners to their children. The IRS held in the proposed regulations that this was an abusive arrangement because the FLP was "not bona fide" and there was "no substantial business purpose for the purported activities" of the FLP. Subsequently, in IRS Notice 95-7, the IRS announced the amendment of the anti-abuse regulations to delete both of these examples and to advise that the regulations applied only for income tax purposes, meaning that they do not apply for estate and gift tax purposes.

Index

[References are to question numbers.]

A

A-B trust plan
  disclaimer, using, 5:8
  explained, 5:3
  structuring, 5:4–5:5
  taxation of B trust, 5:7
Accelerated depreciation, 21:28
Accrued interest and rents, 3:8
Acquisition cost, 21:2
Actual-sales method of asset valuation, 9:4
ADEA. *See* Age Discrimination in Employment Act of 1967
Administrative expenses
  marital deduction, allocating, 4:4
  post-death estate planning, 15:14
  tax deductibility of, 2:56, 15:10
Administrative Policy Regarding Sanctions (APRS) program, 17:9
Administrator, duties of, 2:13
AFDC (Aid to Families with Dependent Children), 26:29
Age discrimination, 16:5, 16:29–16:31
Age Discrimination in Employment Act of 1967 (ADEA), 16:30–16:31
Aid to Families with Dependent Children (AFDC), 26:29
AIMR (Association for Investment Management and Research), 20:36
Alien(s). *See* Non-U.S. citizens
Alimony and separate maintenance payments. *See also* Child support payments
  alimony trust. *See* Alimony trust
  deductibility
    designating, 14:10
    for estate tax purposes, 14:46
    governing laws, 14:1, 14:6–14:7, 14:14
    instrument required, 14:5
    while sharing a residence, 14:11
  defined, 14:3
  income tax treatment of, 14:2–14:3
  made after death of the payee spouse, 14:12–14:16
  made to a third party, 14:9
  must be cash, 14:8
  recapture rule, 14:3–14:4
Alimony trust
  Code Section 71 applicability, 14:31
  Code Section 682 applicability, 14:29, 14:31
  defined, 14:28
  purpose of, 14:30
  taxation of, 14:29, 14:31

Estate and Retirement Planning Answer Book

[*References are to question numbers.*]

Alimony trust (*cont'd*)
  using tax-exempt municipal bonds for, 14:32
Alternate valuation date, 3:21
Amortizing goodwill in an asset sale, 21:27
Anatomical gift(s), 6:52–6:56
Ancillary administration, explained, 2:6
Ancillary probate, 3:3
Annualized return, compounded, 20:20
Annuity. *See also* specific type
  asset protection through the use of, 25:9
  cost and buying, 8:5, 8:8
  deducting unrecovered investment, 8:23–8:24
  distribution rules, 8:10, 8:30, 8:68–8:69, 8:71–8:72
  employer contribution, 8:49, 8:70, 23:28
  expected return, defined, 8:44
  fixed-dollar and variable, 8:2–8:3, 8:6
  gifting, 8:27
  gross estate, inclusion in, 3:15, 8:28, 8:31
  joint life and survivor, 8:1, 8:4, 8:28–8:29, 8:39
  loans, 8:68–8:69
  maximum defined injury benefit, 8:38–8:43
  military service, 8:32–8:35
  overview and types of, 8:1, 8:4
  payments
    defined, 8:48
    lump-sum, 8:50–8:52, 8:54
    options, 8:4
    taxability of, 8:9, 8:45–8:47, 28:2, 28:4
  private annuity. *See* Private annuity
  pros and cons of, 8:6–8:7, 8:31
  simplified safe harbor exclusion, 8:53–8:66
  single annuity contract, 8:26
  starting date, defined, 27:9
  tax-free exchange, 7:57, 8:10
  tax-qualified retirement plan. *See* Tax-qualified retirement plan
  value of, determining, 8:67
Annulments and sham divorces, 14:36–14:37
Applicable retained interest
  defined, 9:18
  valuation of, 9:19
APRS program, 17:9
Ascertainable standard, 5:10
Asset classes, 20:25
Asset protection
  annuity, 25:9
  bankruptcy, 25:11–25:12, 25:17
  co-tenancies, 25:7
  definition and methods of, 25:2, 25:4
  escheat laws, 25:18
  gifts, 25:5–25:6
  homestead exemption, 25:8
  IRAs, 25:13–25:14
  life insurance, 25:15, 25:37
  limited liability company, 25:16
  qualified domestic relations order. *See* Qualified domestic relations order (QDRO)
  tax-qualified retirement plans, 25:1, 25:10–25:12, 25:14, 25:17
Assets
  managing through a trust, 2:47
  subject to probate, 2:10
  transferring by private annuity, 8:11–8:12
  transferring to a funded revocable living trust, 2:49
Assets, sale of
  accelerated depreciation, 21:28
  advantages of, 21:29
  business transfers, 21:25–21:26
  C corporation, 21:32
  corporate liquidation after, 21:31
  goodwill, 21:27
  S corporation, 21:33

Index

[References are to question numbers.]

tax-qualified retirement plan, 21:30
Asset valuation. *See* Valuation of assets
Association for Investment Management and Research (AIMR), 20:36
Audit, IRS. *See also* Internal Revenue Service (IRS)
  abatement of penalties, 30:3, 30:57–30:58
  appeals, 30:9–30:10, 30:12–30:14
  assistance order, 30:4–30:5
  bankruptcy, 30:27, 30:36
  estate closing, 30:11, 30:42
  installment payments, 30:27–30:29, 30:50–30:51, 30:53
  interest rate, 30:75–30:76
  joint return tax liability, 30:34–30:35
  litigation, 30:16–30:17
  location of, 30:24, 30:46
  obtaining previously filed returns and payment information, 30:21–30:23
  offer-in-compromise, 30:15, 30:27, 30:50–30:51, 30:59–30:64, 30:66
  preparing for, 30:8, 30:67
  process explained, 30:1–30:2
  representation and rights, 30:3, 30:7, 30:54–30:55
  seizures, 30:32, 30:65
  selection for, 30:71
  tape recording, 30:3, 30:67–30:68
  Tax Court. *See* Tax Court
  tax lien, 30:30–30:31, 30:66
  time limits for, 30:25
  unauthorized actions by the IRS, 30:6
Average annual return, 20:20

B

Bahamas, 13:24
Balanced portfolio, 20:32
Bank account(s)
  joint accounts, types of, 2:36
  record keeping, 2:39

Bankruptcy
  ESOP interest excluded from, 18:34
  reversionary interest, 13:20
  tax liability discharge in, 30:27, 30:36
  tax-qualified retirement plans, 25:11–25:12, 25:17
  trust beneficiary and, 13:17
Basis
  business transfers, 21:7–21:8, 21:19, 21:23
  community property, 3:43
  defined, 3:41, 21:2
  ESOPs, 21:3
  gifts, 3:45–3:46
  interspousal exchanges and sales, 3:47
  property acquired from a decedent, 3:41
  spousal residence, 3:42
  step-up in
    property acquired before 1976, 2:33, 3:11
    qualified personal residence trust, 12:44
    surviving joint tenant, 2:34, 3:11
Belize, 13:23
Bonds
  buying, 20:44
  distinguished from stocks, 20:23
  joint tenancy, 2:41
Book value approach of asset valuation, 9:11
Broker(s), 20:21, 20:42, 20:48, 20:50, 20:53
Bundling, 20:28
Business transfers
  assets, sale of, 21:5, 21:25–21:26, 21:29, 21:31–21:33
  assets, unwanted, 21:9
  basis, 21:7–21:8, 21:19, 21:23
  employment, noncompete and consulting agreements, 21:10, 21:17
  in estate planning, 21:1
  family attribution rules, 21:21

I-3

Estate and Retirement Planning Answer Book

[References are to question numbers.]

Business transfers *(cont'd)*
  family limited partnership, 21:11
  insiders, 21:12–21:13
  key employee repurchase agreement, 21:24
  stock, sale *vs.* redemption, 21:23
  stock redemption, 21:19–21:20
  stock sale, 21:4–21:8, 21:22
  stock split-offs and spin-offs, 21:34–21:37
  structuring, 21:4–21:5, 21:7, 21:10–21:11, 21:13–21:14, 21:19, 21:29
  taxation of, 21:5, 21:31–21:33
  using a tax-qualified retirement plan, 21:30
Buyouts
  ESOPs, using for, 18:20
  noncompete agreements, 21:15
  nonqualified deferred compensation, 21:16
  rabbi trust, 21:18
  structuring, 21:13–21:14, 21:18
Buy/sell agreement(s)
  ESOPs and, 18:21
  fixing value for estate tax purposes, 9:35
  life insurance in, 7:39
  transfer to a funded revocable living trust, 2:49
Bypass trust
  combining with a marital deduction trust, 5:3
  discretionary trust, 5:13–5:15
  explained, 5:1–5:2
  income tax consequences, 5:17
  invading principal, 5:10–5:11
  powers, 5:9
  special power of appointment, 5:12
Byrum decision, 31:4

C

Capital assets, defined, 20:4
Capital gains and losses
  assets held for personal use, 20:9
  charitable contributions, 10:13–10:14, 10:21
  charitable remainder trust, 10:46
  deductions and exclusions, 20:7–20:8
  estate planning and, 20:2
  explained, 20:3, 20:5
  holding periods, 3:48
  inherited assets, 3:48
  power of appointment trust, 4:25
  private annuity, 8:16–8:17
  sales of appreciated property to charities, 10:22
  special treatment of, 20:10
  taxes, 6:50, 20:6
Capitalization of earning valuation, 9:12
CAP program, 17:9
Cayman Islands, 13:23–13:24
Certain-term annuity, 8:4, 8:28
Charitable contributions
  appreciated property, 10:12–10:14, 10:21–10:22, 10:36
  cap on deductibility, 10:11
  carry forward of deductibility, 10:12, 10:36
  deductibility of, 6:3, 10:1–10:7, 10:36
  encumbered property, 10:15
  to foreign charities, 10:36
  fraud and negligence in valuing, 10:17
  gift tax, 10:24
  gross estate, 10:26, 10:28
  irrevocable disclaimer, 10:27
  life insurance, 10:23
  noncash property, 10:13
  penalties for overvaluing, 10:17
  private foundations, 10:9–10:10
  qualified organizations defined, 10:9
  restrictions on beneficiaries, 10:6–10:7
  substantiation requirements, 10:16
  taxpayer services, 10:5

Index

[References are to question numbers.]

Charitable foundation(s)
  defined, 10:53
  distinguished from charitable trust, 10:35
  private, 10:55-10:57
  tax benefits of qualifying as, 10:54
Charitable lead trust, 10:33-10:34, 10:37, 10:48-10:49, 12:56
Charitable organizations, defined, 10:9, 10:18
Charitable pool fund. *See* Pooled income fund
Charitable remainder annuity trust (CRAT), 10:39-10:40, 10:43-10:45
Charitable remainder trust
  benefits to donor, 10:41
  compared to pooled income fund, 10:51
  defined and explained, 10:33-10:34, 10:38
  income tax, 10:42, 10:45-10:47
  tax-qualified retirement plan benefits, 27:35
  types of, 10:39-10:40
  valuing contributions to, 10:37
Charitable remainder unitrust (CRUT), 10:39-10:40, 10:43-10:45
Charitable trust
  defined, 10:34
  distinguished from charitable foundation, 10:35
  in estate planning, 10:32
  tax saving strategies and, 10:33
Child dependency exemption, claiming, 14:40
Child support payments, 14:17-14:20
Church retirement plans, 25:22
CID (Criminal Investigations Division of the IRS), 30:38-30:39
Citizenship, effect of. *See* Non-U.S. citizens
Civil Rights Act of 1964, 16:29
Closely held securities and businesses
  control premium, 9:29-9:31
  ESOPs, 18:20-18:21, 18:24, 18:55
  estate tax deferrals and extensions, 11:10-11:12
  estate tax freeze, 9:16-9:19
  giving stock in, 6:6
  lack of marketability discount, 9:32-9:33
  minority interest discount, 9:27-9:28, 9:33
  property transfers between spouses, 14:23
  real estate valuation, 9:38-9:42
  restrictive stock agreements, 9:23-9:24, 9:26
  tax-qualified retirement plans, 17:1
  valuation of, 9:8, 9:10-9:15
Closing Agreement Program (CAP) program, 17:9
Collapsible corporation, 21:6
Collective bargaining, 16:5, 16:34-16:35, 16:39-16:40, 16:43
Commercial annuity, 8:1
Commissions, 20:26-20:27
Common disaster, planning for, 2:8
Community property, 3:9-3:10, 3:43
Comparable-sales method of asset valuation, 9:4
Compounding, 20:19-20:20
Condominium(s), 3:42
Confidentiality, 2:13
Constructive receipt doctrine, 19:6-19:7
Constructive trust, 25:5
Contribution base, 10:1, 10:11
Control block, 9:27
Controlled entity, defined, 9:18
Control premium
  explained, 9:29
  marital deduction, 4:14, 9:31
  minority shareholders and family ties, 9:30
Cook Islands, 13:23-13:24
Cooperative apartment(s), 2:38, 3:42
Copyright(s), 3:7
Corporate characteristics, defined, 31:15

[References are to question numbers.]

Corporate fiduciary, 2:63
Corporate tax preference reduction rules, 21:33
Cost-approach method of asset valuation, 9:6
CRAT (Charitable remainder annuity trust), 10:39–10:40, 10:43–10:45
Creditors
  claims by, 2:23
  estate planning, 13:1–13:2, 13:5, 13:9
  family limited partnership, 31:6
  funded revocable living trust and, 2:47
  insurance, 7:41, 25:15, 25:37
  IRAs, 25:13–25:14
  offshore asset protection trust, 13:6, 13:8, 13:22–13:24
  tax-qualified retirement plans, 17:1, 25:1, 25:10, 25:14
  trusts used as protection from, 13:6–13:16
Credit shelter trust, 27:25, 27:27
Crummey trust, 6:31–6:34
CRUT (Charitable remainder unitrust), 10:39–10:40, 10:43–10:45
Cuba, 13:27
Curtesy interest, 4:2
Custodian, duties of, 2:13
Cyprus, 13:24

D

Davis decision, 14:21
Death. *See* Post-death estate planning
Deferred annuity, 8:19–8:20
Deferred compensation. *See* nonqualified deferred compensation
Defined benefit pension plan
  actuarial factors, 17:46–17:51, 17:62
  age discrimination, 16:31
  annuity value, 17:45
  benefit calculation, 17:43–17:44, 17:66–17:67
  compared to target benefit plan, 17:25
  defined, 17:35
  distributions
    actuarial factors, 17:51, 17:62
    before normal retirement age, 17:57
    single-sum payments, 17:59–17:61, 23:35
    years-of-service eligibility rules, 17:42
  flat benefit plan, 17:36
  funding, 17:52, 17:57
    envelope funding, 17:54–17:55
    individual aggregate and group methods, 17:56
    life insurance, 17:53
    plan design and, 23:35
    unit credit method of, 17:64
  interest rates used, 17:59–17:60, 17:63
  normal retirement benefit, 17:57
  overfunding, 17:40–17:41
  pros and cons, 17:39
  qualified domestic relations order (QDRO), 25:22
  safety of, 17:38
  service after retirement, 17:65
Defined contribution retirement plan
  age discrimination, 16:31
  benefits, 17:23
  compared to target benefit plan, 17:25
  ESOP. *See* Employee stock ownership plan (ESOP)
  401(k) savings plan. *See* 401(k) savings plan
  overview, 17:22
  profit sharing plan. *See* Profit sharing plan
  survivor annuity requirements, 23:97, 27:6
  thrift plan, 17:28
Derivatives, 20:32

Index

[References are to question numbers.]

Direct skip, 5:23
DISC (Domestic international sales corporation), 20:10
Disclaiming bequests
  A-B trust plan, 5:8
  charitable contributions, 15:34
  estate planning, 4:15, 15:28
  explained, 15:27
  joint tenancies, 15:30
  power of appointment, 15:31
  qualifying, 5:8, 15:29
  spouses and, 15:32
  tax-qualified retirement plans, 27:27–27:28
Discounted future return valuation, 9:12
Discretionary trust(s)
  advantages of, 5:14
  explained, 5:13, 13:14
  power to appoint a trustee, 5:16
  spendthrift and forfeiture provisions in, 13:15–13:16
Distributees, defined, 2:20
Distribution income planning, 15:23–15:26
Distribution right, defined, 9:18
Diversification, 20:46
Divorce
  alimony. *See* Alimony and separate maintenance payments; Alimony trust
  annuity payments and, 8:43
  child dependency exemption, 14:40
  child support payments, 14:17–14:20
  innocent spouse rules, 14:43–14:45
  legal and accounting fees, 14:42
  liability for joint tax returns, 14:43–14:45
  qualified domestic relation orders. *See* Qualified domestic relations order (QDRO)
  retirement plans, 14:33, 23:77, 27:10
  selling the marital home, 14:41
  tax filing status during, 14:38–14:39
  transfers
    after the divorce, 14:27
    exceptions to nontaxability rules, 14:26
    IRAs, 22:18, 29:25
    nonresident aliens, 14:26
    right to receive income, 14:24–14:25
    tax consequences of, 14:21–14:23
Domestic international sales corporation (DISC), 20:10
Domicile, 2:3, 2:6, 3:2
Dower interest, 4:2
Durable power of attorney
  compared to funded revocable living trusts, 2:47, 2:62
  estate planning, 26:3–26:4
  explained, 26:6
  gift tax exposure, 26:11
  life insurance, 26:12
  limits on the scope of, 26:10
  medical, 26:8
  pros and cons, 26:13
  using, 26:7
  validity of, 26:9
Durable Power of Attorney Act, 26:6

E

Earnings approach to asset valuation, 9:12
Economic benefit doctrine, 19:8–19:9
Elective share (statutory), explained, 4:2
Employee Retirement Income Security Act of 1974 (ERISA)
  attorney fees, 16:10
  collective bargaining and, 16:40
  disqualified persons, 16:27
  employer securities and property, 16:16
  ESOPs, 18:3, 18:22
  exercise-of-control requirements, 16:19, 16:21
  fiduciaries, 16:11–16:14, 16:17–16:18, 16:23

Estate and Retirement Planning Answer Book

[References are to question numbers.]

Employee Retirement Income Security Act of 1974 (ERISA) *(cont'd)*
  informed-decision-making rules, 16:20
  investment options, 16:22
  multiemployer retirement plans, 16:37
  nonqualified deferred compensation plans. *See* Nonqualified deferred compensation plans
  overview, 16:6
  parties in interest, 16:27
  prohibited transactions, 16:24–16:26, 18:17
  rights, reporting and disclosure rules, 16:5, 16:9, 16:28
  top-hat plans, 19:34
  vesting rules, 19:35
  veterans, 16:32
Employee stock ownership plan (ESOP)
  asset and funding rules, 18:4, 18:10
  asset valuation, 18:44–18:45
  bankruptcy, 18:34
  basis, 21:3
  buy/sell agreements, 18:21
  closely held corporation, 18:20–18:21, 18:24, 18:55
  contributions, 18:11–18:12, 18:23
  defined, 17:33, 18:1, 21:3
  distinguished from a stock bonus plan, 18:4
  distributions, 18:38–18:43
  diversification election, 18:27–18:31
  dividends, 18:35–18:37
  leveraged buyouts, 18:41
  leveraged/nonleveraged, 18:5–18:7, 18:21
  loans, 18:13–18:17, 18:24
  nonrecognition transaction, 18:54
  payout strategies, 18:19, 18:42
  profit sharing plan, conversion of, 18:33
  pros and cons of, 17:34, 18:2–18:3, 18:21
  put option, 18:41
  qualified securities and replacement property, 18:46–18:53
  regulation of, 18:3, 18:22–18:23
  sale of shares to the ESOP, 18:56–18:57
  S corporations, 18:9
  Social Security integration, 18:32
  tender offers, 18:25–18:26
  termination of employment, 18:58
  trustee fiduciary obligations, 18:26
  unallocated stock, 18:26
  using, 18:8, 18:18, 21:3
  voting rights, 18:24
Encumbered property, 10:15
Endowment insurance, 7:2, 7:57
Equalizing estates in a marriage, 4:12
ERISA. *See* Employee Retirement Income Security Act of 1974
Escheat laws, 25:18
ESOP. *See* Employee stock ownership plan
Estate. *See* Gross estate; Probate estate(s); Taxable estate
Estate planning
  annuities, 8:11–8:12, 8:31
  buy/sell agreements. *See* Buy/sell agreement(s)
  catastrophic illness or accident, 26:4
  charitable trusts. *See* Charitable trust
  for children, 3:52–3:53, 6:27, 6:45–6:46
  consequences of failing to plan, 2:1
  creditors, 13:1–13:2, 13:5, 13:9
  defined, 3:1
  distribution income planning, 15:23–15:26
  equalizing estates in a marriage, 4:12, 6:24
  family limited partnership use in, 31:4
  gifts. *See* Gift(s)
  inflation, 20:11
  large estates, 4:15, 7:25, 7:30
  life insurance. *See* Life insurance

I-8

Index

[References are to question numbers.]

long-term health care, 26:3, 26:54
nontax considerations, 3:49
optimizing the marital deduction, 4:11
post death. *See* Post-death estate planning
at retirement, 27:36
state statutes, considering, 3:1, 7:21
tax-qualified retirement plans. *See* Tax-qualified retirement plan trusts. *See* Trust(s)
using the unified credit while alive, 6:16
Estate recovery programs, Medicaid, 26:53
Estate tax(es). *See also* Family limited partnership; Generation skipping transfer tax (GST)
   administrative expenses, 15:10, 15:14
   annuities, 28:2, 28:4
   on assets in a QTIP trust, 4:22
   bypass trust, using to reduce, 5:2
   charitable contributions, 10:24–10:25, 10:31
   credits against, 3:27–3:28
   debts, deductibility of, 2:57
   deductions, 14:46, 15:11–15:13, 15:15
   deferrals and extensions, 3:30–3:31, 11:9–11:13, 15:18
   determining, 3:29
   exemption equivalent, 3:26
   funded revocable living trust, 2:56
   income received after death, 3:44
   IRAs, 27:3
   joint tenancy property, 2:32
   liquidity, 11:2
   overview, 2:4, 2:11
   paying out of charitable bequests, 10:29
   rates, range of, 3:1, 15:4
   recapture rules, 9:42
   returns, 3:4, 15:2, 15:4–15:5
   revaluation of taxable gifts, 6:8
   state rules, 7:21
   tax-qualified retirement plans, 2:55, 27:2–27:3, 27:44
   unified credit, 3:25
Estate tax freeze, 9:16–9:22
Estate tax value clause(s), 4:31
Estate tax value pecuniary clause(s), 4:37–4:38
Estate trust, 4:26
Excess benefit plans, 19:18, 19:33
Excess depreciation, 21:28
Excess retirement accumulations, 27:23–27:24
Exclusion ratio
   distributions from a tax-qualified retirement plan, 23:5–23:7
   simplified safe harbor exclusion, 8:57–8:58
Executor
   activities and authority, 2:2, 2:7
   duties of, 2:13, 3:31, 15:2
   fees, 15:19
Exemption equivalent, 3:26
Extraordinary payment right, defined, 9:18

F

Fair market value, 3:21, 9:2, 9:36
Family attribution rules, 9:18, 11:1, 21:21
Family limited partnership
   accounting method, 31:23
   assignment of income, 31:20
   compared to a limited liability company, 31:33
   creditor protection, 31:6
   estate planning, 31:4
   exercise of control, 31:8–31:10
   gift transaction, 31:28–31:31
   income shifting through, 31:3
   IRS determination of, 31:15–31:16, 31:27
   IRS rules for, 31:19, 31:25–31:26, 31:34
   liability limits in, 31:14

Estate and Retirement Planning Answer Book

[References are to question numbers.]

Family limited partnership (*cont'd*)
  minor children, 31:11
  number of partners allowed, 31:7
  overview, 31:1–31:2
  tax year and returns, 31:22, 31:24
  transferability of interests, 31:15–31:16
  types of property that may be held by, 31:12–31:13
  using for business transfers, 21:11
  valuation of assets, 31:5
Farming, real estate valuation, 9:38–9:42
Fees
  for investment management, 20:21, 20:27
  soft-dollar, 20:54
  unbundled, 20:28, 20:52
  wrap, 20:29, 20:43
Fiduciary
  compensation, 2:17
  corporate fiduciary, 2:63
  durable power of attorney, 26:10
  duties of, 2:13–2:16
  ERISA. *See* Employee Retirement Income Security Act of 1974
  liability, 2:14–2:15, 2:61, 2:63
  qualified domestic relations orders, 25:36
Final distribution, 2:7
Financial planner, 20:48
First-to-die insurance policy, 7:33
Five-and-five power, 6:33–6:34
Fixed-dollar annuity, 8:2, 8:6
Fixed-income option, explained, 7:24
Flat benefit plan, 17:36
Flight insurance proceeds, 3:14
Foreign charities, 10:36
Foreign havens, 13:23–13:24, 13:27
Forfeiture clause in a trust, 13:12, 13:15–13:16
Formula clause(s), explained, 4:30–4:31

401(k) savings plan, 17:22. *See also* Savings Incentive Match Plan for Employees (SIMPLE)
  benefits allowed under, 17:16
  employer contributions, vesting of, 17:29
  highly compensated employees, 17:30
  investment management of, 20:30
  investment options under, 17:31
  overview, 17:29
  qualified domestic relations order (QDRO), 25:22
Fractional share clause(s), 4:31, 4:35–4:36
Fraudulent conveyance and transfer
  avoiding, 13:21
  conditions that create a presumption of intent, 25:39
  defined, 25:2–25:3, 25:38
  subsequent creditor defined, 25:40
  trusts, 13:18–13:19
Funded revocable living trust(s)
  compared to durable power of attorney, 2:62
  compared to probate, 2:54, 2:57
  cost of, 2:19
  debts, deductibility of, 2:57
  disadvantages of, 2:48
  estate taxes, 2:56
  fiduciary liability, 2:61
  overview, 2:45–2:47
  qualified plan death benefits, 2:55
  real property, out-of-state, 2:58
  taxation of a fixed sum, 2:60
  taxation of income earned by, 2:50–2:51
  transferring assets to, 2:49
Future interest, explained, 3:36, 6:9

G

General Agreement on Tariffs and Trade (GATT), 17:58, 17:63

Index

[References are to question numbers.]

General partnership, creditors and, 13:3
Generation skipping transfer, explained, 5:19
Generation skipping transfer tax (GST)
 amount, determining, 5:20
 avoiding, 5:29, 15:28
 direct skip, 5:23
 distribution and termination, 5:25–5:26
 exemptions and exclusions, 5:27–5:28, 5:30, 5:34–5:35
 explained, 5:18
 medical expenses, 5:35
 minimizing, 5:32, 5:36–5:37
 rate, 5:21
 tax-qualified retirement plan benefits, 27:31
 triggers, 5:22, 5:24
 tuition expenses, 5:35
Generation skipping trust, 5:31–5:33
Gibraltar, 13:23
Gift(s). *See also* Uniform Transfers to Minors Act (UTMA)
 appreciated assets, 6:28
 asset protection through, 25:5–25:6
 basis, 3:45–3:46
 capital gains, holding periods, 3:48
 gross estate, inclusion in, 3:16, 3:19–3:20, 6:18
 guidelines, 6:26
 life insurance, 7:10, 7:12, 7:14–7:15, 7:28, 7:35
 lifetime vs. testamentary, 6:51
 limits, 6:3–6:6
 made in trust, 6:10, 6:30
 made within three years of death, 3:16
 net gift explained, 6:13
 present interest, 6:9–6:10
 spousal consent, 3:33, 6:4
 to spouses, 3:37, 6:22–6:25
 tax advantages of making, 6:20, 6:24
 using planned, to reduce estate taxes, 4:11, 6:1–6:2, 6:17, 6:26
 valid, 6:21
Gift tax(es). *See also* Family limited partnership; Generation skipping transfer tax (GST)
 bypass trusts and, 5:15
 charitable contributions, 10:24
 computing and paying, 3:34, 3:38–3:39
 credit, 2:32
 discharge of a legal obligation, 6:11
 donee liability for, 3:39
 estate freeze transactions, 9:17–9:19
 exclusion
  annual, 3:36
  gifts losing, 6:40
  gifts qualifying for, 3:33, 6:9, 6:12, 6:31, 6:35, 7:15
 grantor retained income trust, 12:19
 gross estate, inclusion in, 3:17, 6:17–6:19
 joint tenancy, 2:27, 2:32, 2:43
 qualified personal residence trust, 12:20
 rates, range of, 3:1
 restrictive stock agreements, 9:26
 returns
  filing rules and deadlines, 3:5, 3:40, 6:14–6:15
  IRS examination of, 6:7–6:8
 transfers subject to, 3:33, 6:5, 26:52
 unified credit, 3:25, 3:35
Golden parachute payments, 19:2
Goodwill, defined, 21:27
Governmental retirement plans, 25:22
Grantor, defined, 12:3
Grantor retained annuity trust(s) (GRATs), 12:49–12:53, 12:55–12:56
Grantor retained income trust(s) (GRIT). *See also* Personal residence trust (PRT); Qualified personal residence trust (QPRT)
 gift tax, 12:19
 life expectancy and, 12:17
 for a married couple, 12:15, 12:18

[References are to question numbers.]

Grantor retained income trust(s) (GRIT) *(cont'd)*
  overview, 12:11, 12:16
  personal residence, definition of, 12:12
  uses of, 12:13–12:14
Grantor retained unitrust(s) (GRUTs), 12:49–12:52, 12:54–12:55
Grantor trust, 4:28, 6:49, 12:7
GRAT. *See* Grantor retained annuity trust(s)
GRIT. *See* Grantor retained income trust
Gross estate. *See also* Taxable estate
  administrative expenses, 3:22
  assets included, 3:7–3:9, 3:11–3:17, 3:19–3:20
  charitable contributions, 3:24, 10:26–10:28
  deductions, 3:22–3:24
  defined, 3:6
  devises to trusts or fraternal orders, 10:30
  durable power of attorney, 26:11
  life estate interests, 28:12
  life insurance, 6:18
  mortgages, 3:23
  nonqualified retirement plans death benefits, 28:1
  tax-qualified retirement plan benefits, 23:113–23:114, 27:1–27:2, 27:5
  transfers that take effect at death, 3:18
  trust assets, 2:53, 6:41–6:43
  valuation, 3:21, 15:16
Group retirement annuities, 22:1
GRUT. *See* Grantor retained unitrust(s) (GRUTs)

H

Hanging power, 6:33–6:34
Health Care Financing Administration, 26:28

Homestead exemption, 25:8

I

Incapacity, 26:1, 26:3, 26:14. *See also* Durable power of attorney; Medicaid; Medicare
Incident of ownership, 7:8–7:9
Income-approach method of asset valuation, 9:5
Income averaging, 23:33, 23:36
Income tax(es)
  annuity loans, 8:68–8:69
  annuity payments, 8:45–8:47, 8:50–8:54, 28:3
  bypass trusts and, 5:17
  charitable contributions, deduction for. *See* Charitable contributions
  charitable lead trust, 10:49
  charitable remainder trust, 10:42, 10:45–10:47
  child dependency exemption, 14:40
  employer contribution to an annuity, 8:49
  estates, 15:10–15:15, 15:22
  on estates, rates, 3:32
  final return, 15:3, 15:6–15:7
  grantor trust, 12:7
  on income collected by estates, 15:22
  income received after death, 3:44
  on insurance settlement options, 7:24
  interspousal gifts and, 6:25
  irrevocable insurance trust, 7:36
  legally separated couples, 14:38–14:39
  nonqualified deferred compensation plans, 19:5
  private annuity, 8:16–8:17
  rates, 3:1, 3:32
  tax-qualified retirement plan death benefits, 27:2–27:3, 27:30
  trusts, 3:32, 6:39, 6:49–6:50

Index

[References are to question numbers.]

Uniform Transfers to Minors Act, 6:29, 6:38
Independent contractors, 19:2
Individual Retirement Account (IRA). *See also* Savings Incentive Match Plan for Employees (SIMPLE); Simplified Employee Pension (SEP)
  contributions and deductibility, 22:5, 22:7
  creditors, 25:13–25:14
  death payments, 29:19–29:21
  disclaiming an interest in, 29:24
  distributions
    deemed though no funds are paid, 29:26
    failure to make, 29:22
    mandatory, 22:13, 29:6, 29:8
    minimum required, 29:7, 29:9–29:15
    taxation of, 22:14, 29:32
    when multiple IRAs are owned, 29:16
  divorce or separation, 22:18, 29:25
  early withdrawal, 22:15–22:16, 29:4–29:5
  eligibility, 22:3
  excess accumulations and contributions, 22:10, 29:17–29:18, 29:23
  funding, 22:11
  inherited, 29:38–29:39
  investment options, 22:12
  maintaining while participating in an employer's retirement plan, 22:7
  marital deduction, 4:2
  Medicaid eligibility, 26:43
  modifying, 22:6
  for nonworking spouse, 22:9
  overview, 22:1, 22:4, 22:8
  plan qualification, 22:2
  taxation, 29:1–29:3
  transfers and rollovers
    IRA-to-IRA, 29:27–29:29, 29:35
    penalty for illegal, 29:43
    rules, 22:17, 29:33
    from sale of property, 29:37
    from tax-qualified retirement plans, 29:30–29:32, 29:34, 29:40–29:42
    to tax-qualified retirement plans, 29:36
  trusts as beneficiaries, 22:19
  types of, 22:1
Individual retirement annuities, 22:1
Inflation, 2:13, 20:39–20:40
Innocent spouse rules, 14:43–14:45
Installment obligation, 2:52, 6:26
Installments-for-life option, 7:24
Insurance, long-term health care, 26:22–26:23
Insurance agents, 20:49
Interest option, explained, 7:24
Internal Revenue Service (IRS) audit. *See* Audit, IRS
  Automated Collections Service, 30:40–30:41, 30:50–30:51, 30:53, 30:79
  bankruptcy, 30:27, 30:36
  collections, statute of limitations, 30:49, 30:52, 30:56
  control premium, 9:29
  Criminal Investigations Division, 30:38–30:39
  family limited partnership. *See* Family limited partnership
  gift tax return, examination of, 6:7–6:8
  installment payments, 30:27–30:29, 30:50–30:51, 30:53
  interest on liability, 30:76–30:78
  interest rate, 30:75
  levy, 30:40–30:41, 30:52, 30:66
  minority interest discount, 9:28
  obtaining previously filed returns and payment information, 30:21–30:23
  offshore asset protection trust, 13:25
  partnership, 31:16, 31:18, 31:21

[References are to question numbers.]

Internal Revenue Service (IRS) audit *(cont'd)*
　penalties
　　abatement of, 30:44, 30:57–30:58, 30:74, 30:83
　　information on, 30:73
　　waiving, 30:80–30:82, 30:85
　private letter rulings, 12:8, 30:20
　rabbi trust, 19:21
　real estate valuation disputes, 9:35
　reasonable cause standard, 30:84–30:85
　refunds and checks from, 30:45, 30:47–30:48
　restrictive stock agreements, 9:24, 9:26
　returns
　　completing and filing, 30:37, 30:43
　　failure to file, 30:42, 30:79
　　filing, proof of, 30:26
　　joint liability, 30:34–30:35
　　joint vs. separate, 30:33
　　status of, 30:72
　seizures, 30:32, 30:65
　tax forms, 30:69
　tax lien, 30:30–30:31, 30:66
　unpaid prior-year liability, 30:47–30:48
　valuation of closely held securities, 9:14
　when to seek counsel, 30:38, 30:40, 30:52
Interpolated terminal reserve figure, 7:49
Inter vivos declaration, 12:3
Intestate estate, explained, 2:3
Investing, personal
　advisor, working with, 20:31, 20:35–20:38
　asset classes, 20:25
　basic principles, 20:11, 20:39–20:40
　commissions and fees, 20:21, 20:26
　estate planning and, 20:1–20:2
　insurance, 20:49
　mutual funds, 20:34
　picking your own stocks, 20:45
　portfolio diversification, 20:46
　portfolio options, 20:25, 20:32–20:33
　soft-dollar fees, 20:54
　terms and concepts, 20:12–20:29
　types of accounts, 20:32–20:33
　using pretax dollars, 20:47
Investment advisor, 20:31, 20:35–20:38
Investment advisory fee, 20:27
Investment management, 20:34–20:36, 20:38
Investment manager, distinguished from broker, 20:21, 20:42
Investment policy statement (IPS), 20:18
Investment risk, fiduciaries and, 2:13
Investment styles, 20:35, 20:38
Investment time horizon, 20:12
IPS (investment policy statement), 20:18
IRA. *See* Individual Retirement Account (IRA)
Irrevocable disclaimer, transfers to charities, 10:27
Irrevocable insurance trust(s)
　beneficiary and ownership considerations, 7:37
　explained, 7:34
　second-to-die policy, 7:32
　tax consequences of, 7:35–7:36
　trustees, choosing, 7:38
Irrevocable trust(s), 6:40–6:42, 7:27, 27:29
IRS. *See* Internal Revenue Service (IRS)

J

Joint ownership, 2:25–2:26
Joint tenancy
　compared to funded revocable living trust, 2:47
　converting to tenancy in common, 2:37

Index

[*References are to question numbers.*]

creation and dissolution of, 2:30, 2:43
creditors' claims and, 2:23
death of owners, simultaneous, 2:29
disadvantages of, 2:42
disclaiming bequests, 15:30
explained, 2:25
gift taxes associated with, 2:27, 2:43
gross estate, 3:11
husband and wife, 2:27, 2:33–2:34, 2:42, 3:42
probate, 2:10
selling an interest in, 2:28
stocks and bonds, 2:41
survivor, 2:34–2:35
taxation and, 2:31–2:32, 3:11
using, to avoid probate, 2:24

K

Keogh plans, 17:17, 17:68, 23:81, 26:43
Kiddie tax, 6:20

L

Labor laws, 16:5
Lack of marketability discount, 9:32–9:33
Letters testamentary, 2:2
Leveraged buyouts, ESOP put options and, 18:41
Leveraged ESOP, 18:7, 18:21
Life estate, 6:41, 28:12
Life insurance
  beneficiary and ownership considerations, 7:29–7:31, 7:37, 7:41, 7:50
  buy/sell agreement(s), 7:39
  changing policies, 7:52
  cost, 7:4, 7:45
  creditors, 25:15
  death of noninsured owner of, 7:13, 7:48
  disqualification, 7:43, 7:46
  durable power of attorney, 26:12

  estate planning, 7:1, 7:3, 7:21–7:23, 7:26–7:27, 11:6, 11:8, 20:49
  family limited partnership, 31:13
  first-to-die policy, 7:33
  gifts of, 7:10, 7:14–7:15, 7:19, 10:23
  gross estate, inclusion in, 6:18
  minimizing generation skipping transfer tax, 5:36
  policy loans, 7:19–7:20
  probate, 2:10
  second-to-die policy, 7:32
  selecting, 7:5–7:7, 7:47, 7:51
  settlement options, 7:24–7:25, 7:55
  split-dollar insurance, 7:17
  as taxable income, 7:43–7:44, 7:46
  tax-free exchange, 7:57
  transferring, 7:18, 7:27–7:28, 7:53–7:54
  treated as an annuity, 8:25
  trusts and, 7:11, 7:42, 7:56
  types of policies, 7:2
  value of unmatured policy, 7:49
Life insurance proceeds
  creditors, 25:37
  gross estate, inclusion in, 3:7, 3:14
  marital deduction, 4:2, 7:25
  payment option considerations, 7:41–7:42
  tax treatment of, 7:8–7:9, 7:12, 7:16, 7:18, 7:22
  testamentary trust, 2:64
Limited liability company (LLC), 13:3–13:4, 25:16, 31:32–31:33
Limited liability partnership (LLP), 13:3–13:4
Limited partnership, 13:3, 31:14
Liquidation, 21:31–21:32
Liquidity, 11:1–11:4, 11:6–11:8, 11:14
Living trust, 2:10, 2:19, 2:24, 26:14
Living wills, 26:4–26:5
LLC. *See* Limited liability company (LLC)
LLP. *See* Limited liability partnership (LLP)

Estate and Retirement Planning Answer Book

[References are to question numbers.]

Long-term health care, 26:2, 26:22–26:23. *See also* Nursing home care
Lookback rule, defined, 26:33
"Look-through" rules, 16:14
Lottery payments, 3:7
Low-load life insurance, 7:4
Lump-sum payments, options and distributions
  annuity, 8:50–8:52, 8:54
  income averaging, 23:33
  interest rates used to calculate, 23:34
  tax-qualified retirement plans, 23:10–23:12, 23:35, 23:79

M

Marital deduction
  $600,000 exemption equivalent, 4:10
  administrative expenses, 4:4
  citizenship, effect of, 4:1, 4:5, 6:24
  considerations in using maximum, 4:13
  control premium, using, 4:14, 9:31
  explained, 4:1
  gifts, 2:27, 3:37
  joint tenancy and gifts, 2:27, 2:33
  obtaining, 4:7
  optimizing, 4:11
  post-death tax planning, 15:14
  power of appointment trust, 4:23–4:24
  preserving in insurance settlements, 7:25
  property interests, 4:2–4:3
  QTIP trust, 4:20–4:21, 4:24, 4:27
  tax-qualified retirement plans, 27:21
  terminal interest rule, 4:6, 4:9
Marital deduction trust, 27:22, 27:25, 27:30. *See also* A-B trust plan
Master retirement plan, 17:5
Maximum defined injury benefit (MDIB), 8:38–8:42

MDIB. *See* Maximum defined injury benefit (MDIB); Minimum distribution individual benefit (MDIB)
MEC (Modified endowment contract), 7:7
Medicaid
  209(b) states, definition, 26:32
  1634 states, definition, 26:32
  administration, 26:28
  assets and eligibility, 26:3, 26:25, 26:31, 26:34–26:35, 26:37–26:38, 26:40–26:44, 26:46–26:47
  benefits available, 26:30
  distinguished from Medicare, 26:25
  estate recovery programs, 26:53
  IRA and Keogh plans, 26:43
  lookback rule, 26:33, 26:36–26:37
  Medicaid qualifying trust (MQT), 26:41, 26:45
  Minimum Monthly Maintenance Needs Allowance, 26:39
  planning, 26:24, 26:48–26:51, 26:54
  property transfers, 26:34–26:35, 26:37, 26:49–26:52
  tax-qualified retirement plans, 26:44
  who is covered by, 26:29
Medicaid Institutional Care Program, 26:25
Medical expenses
  deducting after death, 15:9
  generation skipping transfer tax, 5:35
  gift tax exclusion, 3:33, 6:12
Medicare
  assets and eligibility, 26:27
  distinguished from Medicaid, 26:25
  limits of, 26:26
Medicare tax, 19:4
Mental competence, 2:21
Military service annuity, 8:32–8:35
Minimum distribution individual benefit (MDIB), 23:71, 23:73–23:77
Minimum Monthly Maintenance Needs Allowance, 26:39

Index

[References are to question numbers.]

Minority interest discount, 9:27–9:28, 9:33
Minor's trust
  compared to Uniform Transfers to Minors Act custodianship, 6:38
  disadvantage of, 6:36–6:37
  explained, 6:35
  gift tax exclusion, 6:31
Miranda rights, 30:38
Mirror loan, 18:15
Modified endowment contract (MEC), 7:7
Money management. *See* Investment management
Money market mutual funds, 20:11
Money purchase pension plan, 17:22, 17:24–17:25, 25:22
Morningstar Report, 20:36, 20:41
Mortality tables, 17:47–17:50
Mortgages and notes, valuing, 9:7
MQT (Medicaid qualifying trust), 26:41, 26:45
Multiemployer retirement plans, 16:36–16:38
Mutual fund indexes, 20:36
Mutual funds, 20:34, 20:36–20:38, 20:41, 20:46

N

National Labor Relations Act (NLRA), 16:39–16:42
National Labor Relations Board, 16:41
Negligence, fiduciary, 2:16
Net gift, explained, 3:33, 6:13
Nicaragua, 13:27
NLRA, 16:40–16:42
Noncompete agreements, 21:10, 21:15
Nonleveraged ESOP, 18:6
Nonqualified deferred compensation plans
  Code Section 83 applicability, 19:10–19:11
  constructive receipt, 19:7, 19:23, 24:4
  contractual right to future payments, 24:2–24:3
  controlling shareholders, 19:14
  deductibility of employer contributions, 19:3, 19:29
  deferral option, timing of election, 19:15, 24:3
  emergencies, payments in, 19:13
  ERISA, 19:22, 19:26, 19:32–19:34
  excess benefit plans, 19:18, 19:33
  independent contractors, 19:2
  overview, 19:1
  payments to a nonqualified trust, 24:5–24:6
  rabbi trust, 19:20–19:24
  reasons for establishing, 19:2, 19:19
  secular trust, 19:26–19:31
  Social Security and Medicare tax, 19:4
  spousal consent rules, 19:2
  supplemental executive retirement plans (SERPs), 19:17, 19:19
  surety bonds, using in, 19:25
  taxation, 19:5, 19:11–19:12, 19:16, 19:31, 24:1, 28:5–28:6
  top-hat plans, 19:34
  using in a buyout, 21:16
  vesting, 19:22, 19:26–19:28
Nonqualified retirement plans. *See also* Individual Retirement Account (IRA)
  advantages of, 16:4
  death benefit as gift, 28:11
  overview, 16:2
  taxation of death benefits, 28:1, 28:7–28:10
  veterans, 16:32
Nonstandardized plans, 17:5–17:6. *See also* Prototype retirement plan
Non-U.S. citizens
  divorce and property transfers, 14:26
  estate tax return, 3:4
  gross estate, 3:7

Estate and Retirement Planning Answer Book

[*References are to question numbers.*]

Non-U.S. citizens (*cont'd*)
  joint tenancy, 2:33
  marital deduction, 4:1, 4:5, 6:24
  spousal gifts to, 6:23
Nursing home care, 26:3, 26:15, 26:19. *See also* Long-term health care

O

OAPT. *See* Offshore asset protection trust (OAPT)
Offer-in-compromise, 30:15, 30:27, 30:50–30:51, 30:59–30:64, 30:66
Offshore asset protection trust (OAPT)
  creditor protection through, 13:6, 13:8, 13:22–13:24
  ethical and policy issues, 13:28
  explained, 13:7
  IRS private letter ruling, 13:25
  protector, defined, 13:26
  reversionary interest, 13:20
  risks and expenses, 13:27

P

Partnership
  capital interest in, 31:17
  IRS anti-abuse rules, 31:34
  IRS treatment of, 31:21
  post-death elections, 15:20–15:21
  tax return rules, 31:24
  tax year, 31:22
  transferring to a funded revocable living trust, 2:49
Passive income, 21:33
Pecuniary clause
  estate tax value, 4:37–4:38
  explained, 4:31–4:32
  factors to consider in using, 4:34
  tax effects, 4:33

Pension Benefit Guaranty Corporation (PBGC), 16:6–16:8, 17:23, 17:38, 17:47, 17:51, 17:58, 17:60
Personal investing. *See* Investing, personal
Personal property, 3:7
Personal representative, duties of, 2:13
Personal residence trust (PRT). *See also* Grantor retained income trust; Qualified personal residence trust (QPRT)
  business use, 12:29
  commuting, 12:26
  compared to a qualified personal residence trust, 12:22
  defined, 12:21
  grantor ceases to live in the residence, 12:31
  IRS rules governing, 12:25
  mortgage on, 12:27
  number allowed, 12:32
  occupancy by others, 12:30
  pros and cons of, 12:48
  qualified proceeds, 12:23
  reversionary interest, 12:36
  trustee, who may serve as, 12:33
Pets, trusts for, 12:4
Plan-to-plan transfers, 23:44–23:45
Pooled income fund, 10:34, 10:50–10:52
Portfolio diversification, 20:46
Post-death estate planning
  administrative deductions, 15:14
  medical deductions, 15:9
  overview, 15:1
  partnership elections, 15:20–15:21
  special elections, 15:18
  tax returns, 15:2–15:3, 15:6–15:8
  tax year, 15:8
Power of appointment
  bypass trust, 5:12
  disclaiming, 15:31
  discretionary trust, 5:16
  gross estate and property subject to, 3:13

Index

[References are to question numbers.]

irrevocable insurance trust, 7:37–7:38
marital deduction, 4:2
Power of appointment trust
  access to trust principal, 4:29
  capital gains, 4:25
  compared to estate trust, 4:26
  compared to QTIP trust, 4:23–4:24, 4:27
  explained, 4:23
  income, payment requirements, 4:23, 4:26
  marital deduction, qualifying for, 4:23
Prenuptial planning, 27:19
Present interest, explained, 3:36, 6:9–6:10
Private annuity
  gifts, 8:15
  overview, 8:1, 8:11
  pros and cons of, 8:12–8:13
  tax treatment of, 8:11, 8:14, 8:16–8:17
  use in estate planning, 8:11–8:12, 8:18
Private charitable foundation, 10:55–10:57
Private distributing foundation, 10:20
Private letter rulings, 30:20
Private operating foundation, 10:9–10:10, 10:19, 10:35
Probate. *See also* Probate estate
  ancillary probate, 3:3
  assets not subject to, 2:46
  assets subject to, 2:10, 2:12
  avoiding, 2:24, 2:47
  compared to funded revocable living trust, 2:54
  costs of, 2:19
  creditors' claims, 2:23
  delays during, 2:20
  disadvantages of, 2:18
  and estate tax liability, 2:11
  process explained, 2:2, 2:7, 2:20
  publicity and, 2:22

purpose of, 2:11
for small estates, 2:9
tax advantages of, 2:54
when to use, 2:5
Probate estate
  administrative requirements, 2:54
  compared to funded revocable living trust, 2:57
  distinguished from taxable estate, 2:11, 4:8
  S corporation stock, 2:59
  taxation of fixed sum, 2:60
Professional corporation(s), 2:49
Profit sharing plan
  age weighting, 17:27
  benefits allowed under, 17:16, 17:19
  conversion to an ESOP, 18:33
  death benefit, waiving, 23:109–23:110
  health insurance, 17:19
  overview, 17:22, 17:26
  qualified domestic relations order (QDRO), 25:22
  rules governing, spousal consent, 23:107–23:110, 23:112, 27:7–27:8
  withholding and notice rules, 23:88, 23:112
Property interest, passing, 4:3
Protector, role in a trust defined, 13:26
Prototype retirement plan, 17:5
Publicity, probate and, 2:22
Public records, 2:22, 2:64

Q

QDOT. *See* Qualified domestic trust (QDOT)
QDRO. *See* Qualified domestic relations order
QJSA. *See* Qualified joint and survivor annuity

I-19

[References are to question numbers.]

QPRT. See Qualified personal residence trust
QPSA. See Qualified preretirement survivor annuity
QTIP property, 4:1
QTIP trust. See qualified terminal interest property trust (QTIP)
Qualified disclaimer, 5:8
Qualified domestic relations order (QDRO)
  annuity payments and, 8:43
  explained, 14:34
  proscriptions, 14:35
  retirement plans subject to, 25:22
  tax-qualified retirement plans, 23:29, 23:77, 25:19–25:21, 25:23–25:36
Qualified domestic trust (QDOT), 4:5
Qualified joint and survivor annuity (QJSA)
  availability, 23:93
  deferred contribution plan, 23:98
  defined contribution plan, 23:97
  exemptions to requirement for, 27:8
  explained, 27:7
  former spouse, 25:33
  notice requirements, 23:87
  plans required to have, 23:91
  purpose of rules on, 23:90
  spousal consent, 23:85, 23:94–23:96, 27:5
  waiver rules, 23:99–23:100, 27:11–27:14
Qualified payment right, 9:19–9:20
Qualified personal residence trust (QPRT). See also Grantor retained income trust (GRIT); Personal residence trust (PRT)
  business use, 12:29
  commuting, 12:26
  compared to a personal residence trust, 12:22
  discounts for gifts, 12:41
  expiration of the trust term, 12:45, 12:47
  form of ownership, 12:37–12:38, 12:40
  gift and estate tax, 12:20, 12:34–12:35
  grantor ceases to live in the residence, 12:28, 12:31
  health considerations, 12:39
  income tax consequences, 12:42
  IRS rules governing, 12:24–12:25
  mortgage on, 12:27
  number allowed, 12:32, 12:43
  occupancy by others, 12:30
  pros and cons of, 12:46, 12:48
  reversionary interest, 12:36
  step-up in basis, 12:44
  trustee, who may serve as, 12:33
Qualified preretirement survivor annuity (QPSA)
  estate planning, 27:5
  exemptions to requirement for, 27:8
  explained, 27:6
  former spouse, 25:33
  notice requirements, 23:87
  optional form of benefit, 23:101
  plans required to have, 23:91
  purpose of rules on, 23:90
  waiver rules, 23:92, 23:99, 27:11, 27:13
qualified terminal interest property trust (QTIP)
  A-B trust structured as, 5:5
  access to trust principal, 4:29
  compared to power of appointment trust, 4:23–4:24, 4:27
  disposition at death of survivor, 4:19
  estate taxes, 4:22
  explained, 4:18
  factors to consider in creating, 4:17
  irrevocable once elected, 4:18
  marital deduction, 4:20–4:21, 4:27
  remaindermen of, 4:18
  requirements, 4:18
  tax-qualified retirement plans, 27:22

Index

[References are to question numbers.]

R

Rabbi trust, 19:20–19:24, 21:18
REA. *See* Retirement Equity Act of 1984
Real estate valuation
   disputes with the IRS, 9:35
   in estate planning, 9:34
   fair market value defined, 9:36
   local assessment value, using, 9:37
   penalties for understatement, 9:43
   special valuation methods and rules, 9:38–9:42
Real property
   gross estate, inclusion in, 3:7
   inheritance taxes on, 2:58
   out-of-state, 2:58
   transferring to a funded revocable living trust, 2:49
Reasonable cause standard, 30:84–30:85
Recapture rules, 9:42
Redemptions, stock, 11:1–11:2, 11:4–11:5
Refund life annuity, 8:4, 8:28, 28:4
Registered investment advisors (RIAs), 20:53
Repurchase agreements, 21:24
Restrictive stock agreements, 9:23–9:24, 9:26
Retirement Equity Act of 1984 (REA)
   assignment of interest, 14:34
   exemptions, 27:7–27:8
   plans subject to, 23:91
   preretirement survivor annuity rules, 27:5
   spousal consent rules, 19:2, 26:54
   waiver rules, 27:11, 27:18
Retirement plans
   age and sex discrimination, 16:29–16:31
   collectively bargained, 16:5, 16:34–16:35, 16:39, 16:42–16:44
   divorce settlements and, 14:33
   for new businesses, 17:69
   overview, 16:2
   plan year, defined, 17:71–17:72
   Taft-Hartley Act, 16:5, 16:34–16:35
   tax-qualified. *See* Tax-qualified retirement plan
   termination and missing participants, 17:70
   vital issues, 16:1
   WARN applicability, 16:33
Revenue Reconciliation Act of 1993 (RRA), 26:33, 26:53
Reversionary interest
   gifts to an irrevocable trust, 6:41
   life insurance, 3:14, 7:8
   offshore asset protection trust, 13:20
   property transferred to a trust, 12:7
Revised Uniform Limited Partnership Act, 31:1
Revocable living trust
   advantages of in incapacity, 26:15
   estate tax treatment of, 26:18
   funding, 26:16, 26:19
   gift tax treatment of, 26:18
   income tax treatment of, 26:17
   probate, 2:10
   transfer of an installment obligation, 2:52
   trustee, successor, 26:21
   trustee, who should be, 26:20
RIAs (registered investment advisors), 20:53
Risk tolerance, 20:15–20:16
Rollovers. *See* specific retirement plan
Rule against perpetuities, explained, 12:4
Rule of contribution, 2:32–2:33

S

Safe deposit box(es), 2:40
Salary-reduction SEP, explained, 22:24
Sales load, explained, 20:41
Savings Incentive Match Plan for Employees (SIMPLE), 29:46

Estate and Retirement Planning Answer Book

[References are to question numbers.]

S corporation(s)
  consideration in electing, 21:33
  ESOPs and, 18:9, 21:3
  family limited partnership and, 31:12
  funded revocable living trust, 2:59
  gifts of stock, 6:26
  loans to shareholders, 23:81
Second-to-die insurance policy, 7:32, 7:57
Sectors, defined, 20:55
Secular trust, 19:26–19:31
Securities acquisition loans, ESOP, 18:13–18:14
SEP. *See* Simplified Employee Pension
SERPs (supplemental executive retirement plans), 19:17–19:19
Settlement options
  explained, 7:24
  pros and cons of, 7:40, 7:55
  using, 7:25
Settlor, defined, 12:3
Sex discrimination, 16:5, 16:29
SIMPLE (Savings Incentive Match Plan for Employees), 29:46
Simplified Employee Pension (SEP). *See also* Individual Retirement Account (IRA); Savings Incentive Match Plan for Employees (SIMPLE)
  contributions, 22:5, 22:23
  distributions, 22:26–22:27
  explained, 22:20
  IRA contributions, 22:25
  mandatory coverage rules, 22:21–22:22
  rollovers, 22:28
  salary-reduction SEP, 22:24
  tax treatment, 29:44
  transfers and rollovers, 29:45
Simplified safe harbor exclusion
  changing to an actual calculation, 8:65–8:66
  distributions from a tax-qualified retirement plan, 23:13–23:21
  electing, 8:63

exclusion ratio, 8:57–8:58
exclusion rules, 8:59–8:62
explained, 8:53–8:55
payments, calculating number of, 8:64
using, 8:56, 23:23
Single annuity contract, 8:26
Single life annuity, overview, 8:1
Single-sum distribution. *See* Lump-sum payments, options and distributions
1634 states, definition, 26:32
Skip person, 5:19
Small estates, probate procedures, 2:9
Socially responsible investing, 20:38
Social Security
  ESOPs integration, 18:32
  gross estate, inclusion in, 3:7
  nonqualified deferred compensation plans, 19:4
  tax-qualified retirement plans, 17:20
Society of Actuaries, 17:47
Soft-dollar fees, 20:54
Sole proprietorship, 13:3
Special power of appointment, 5:12
Spendthrift clauses
  bankruptcy of beneficiary, 13:17
  discretionary trusts, 13:15–13:16
  fraudulent conveyance, 13:18
Spendthrift trust, explained, 13:10–13:11
Split-dollar insurance, explained, 7:17
Split gifts, 3:33
Spousal bequests, 4:30
Sprinkling power, 5:15
SSI program (Supplemental Security Income), 26:29, 26:32
State estate taxes, 3:1, 7:21
State law(s)
  charitable contributions and, 10:4
  domicile and, 2:3, 2:6
  govern when an individual dies intestate, 2:3

I-22

Index

[*References are to question numbers.*]

Step-up in basis. *See* Basis
Stock(s)
  distinguished from bonds, 20:23
  gross estate, inclusion in, 3:7
  joint tenancy, 2:41
  redemptions, Code Section 303, 11:1–11:2, 11:4–11:5
  transferring to a funded revocable living trust, 2:49
Stock, sale of
  in business transfers. *See* Business transfers
  direct, 21:22
  family attribution, 11:1, 21:21
  key employee repurchase agreement, 21:24
  redemptions, 11:1–11:2, 11:4–11:5, 21:23
Stock bonus plan, 17:22, 17:32, 17:34
Stockbroker, 20:21, 20:42, 20:48, 20:50, 20:53
Stock redemption, 21:14–21:15, 21:19–21:20
Stock split-offs and spin-offs, 21:34–21:37
Straight life annuity, 8:4, 28:2–28:3
Strike(s), 16:44
S trust(s)
  characteristics of, 6:26
  holding S corporation stock, 2:59
Succession planning, 21:3, 21:35
Summary administration, 2:19
Supplemental executive retirement plans (SERPs), 19:17, 19:19
Supplemental Security Income (SSI) program, 26:29, 26:32
Support trust, 13:13
Surety bonds, using, 19:25
Surrogate's court
  explained, 2:2
  powers of, 2:3, 2:7
  simplified probate procedures for smaller estates, 2:9
Survivorship insurance, 11:7

T

Taft-Hartley Act, 16:5, 16:34–16:35
Target benefit plan, 17:22, 17:25, 25:22
Taxable estate
  annuities, 8:28–8:29
  deductions, excess retirement accumulations, 27:23
  distinguished from probate estate, 4:8
  what is included, 2:11, 2:46, 2:50, 6:17
Tax Court
  audit jurisdiction, 30:16
  pros and cons of litigating in, 30:17
  recovering costs, 30:70
  representation in, 30:19
  small-case procedure, 30:18
  valuation of closely held securities, 9:15
Tax Equity and Fiscal Responsibility Act of 1982 (TEFRA), 23:113
Taxes. *See also* specific type
  consequences of failing to leave a will, 2:3
  maximum rate on estate or trust income, 4:26, 4:28
  maximum rate on estates, 5:18
  rate for generation skipping transfer, 5:21
Tax-exempt status, charitable foundation(s), 10:57
Tax-favored borrowing from an ESOP, 21:3
Tax filing status, 14:38–14:39
Tax forms, 30:69
Tax-free investing, 20:17
Taxpayer assistance order, 30:4–30:5
Taxpayer's Bill of Rights, 30:3
Tax-qualified retirement plan
  actuarial factors, 17:50
  ad hoc payment election, 23:64
  advantages of, 16:3, 20:47
  annuity value, determining, 23:27

Estate and Retirement Planning Answer Book

[References are to question numbers.]

Tax-qualified retirement plan *(cont'd)*
  asset protection using, 25:1,
    25:10–25:12, 25:14, 25:17
  assets, how they are held, 16:15
  assets, sale of (business transfer),
    21:30
  bankruptcy, 25:11–25:12, 25:17
  beneficiaries
    changing, 23:56
    date for determining, 23:55
    life expectancies, 23:58
    right to designate, 23:54
    selecting, 23:50, 27:1, 27:5,
      27:20, 27:31, 27:42
    separate accounts for, 23:53
    trusts as, 27:15, 27:25–27:27,
      27:29
    who can be, 23:51, 27:34
  charitable beneficiaries, 23:63,
    27:32–27:34
  charitable remainder trust as
    beneficiary, 27:35
  creditors, 25:14
  death of participant, 23:60, 23:62,
    27:43
  design considerations, 17:7, 17:20
  disclaiming benefits, 27:27–27:28
  disqualification, 17:8–17:9
  disqualified persons, 16:27
  distribution rules
    annuities, 23:8
    consent rules, 23:85, 23:105
    on death, 23:69–23:70
    designated, explained, 23:84
    determining initial year, 8:37
    determining the number of
      payments, 23:24
    discretionary to beneficiaries,
      23:52
    elections by beneficiaries, 23:57,
      27:43
    employer securities, 23:79
    lump-sum options, 23:10–23:12
    maximum number of installment
      payments, 23:59
    maximum number of years,
      8:36–8:37
    maximum payout period,
      27:37–27:38
    minimum, 23:78
    to a non-spouse beneficiary, 23:62
    recomputing life expectancy,
      27:39–27:40
    required, 23:46–23:49
    separation from service, 8:72
    spouse's right to choose form of,
      23:98
    start date, 23:61
    trust as beneficiary, 27:41
  divorce, 23:77, 27:10
  early withdrawal, 8:71, 23:2–23:3
  eligibility requirements, 17:11–17:12
  employer contributions to an
    annuity, 23:28
  escheat laws, 25:18
  estate planning considerations,
    27:1, 27:5
  excess accumulations, 27:23–27:24
  exclusion ratio, 23:5–23:7
  exercise-of-control requirements,
    16:19, 16:21
  fiduciaries, scope and liability of,
    16:17–16:18, 16:23
  five-year rule, 23:62–23:63
  funding through insurance,
    17:3–17:4
  general consent and spousal rights,
    23:102–23:106, 27:16–27:17
  health insurance, 17:19
  incidental benefit requirement,
    23:71, 27:42
  informed-decision-making rules,
    16:20
  investment, calculation of, 23:29
  investment alternatives, 16:22
  investment management of, 20:30
  life expectancy
    designated beneficiary's, 23:68
    recalculation, reasons for, 23:66
    recalculation rules, 23:65, 23:67

Index

[References are to question numbers.]

loans to participants, 17:17, 23:81–23:83
lump sums, interest rates used to calculate, 23:34–23:35
marital deduction, 27:21
marital trust as beneficiary, 27:25
master and prototype distinguished, 17:5
Medicaid eligibility, 26:44
minimum distribution individual benefit (MDIB), 23:71, 23:73–23:77
nondiscrimination rules, 17:14–17:15, 17:18
nonretirement benefits, 17:16, 17:19, 23:71
overview, 16:2, 17:1
parties in interest, 16:27
plan year, changing, 17:72
prenuptial planning, 27:19
preretirement incidental benefit rules, 23:71–23:72
profit sharing plan. *See* Profit sharing plan
prohibited transactions, 16:24–16:27, 18:16
qualified domestic relations order, 23:29, 25:19, 25:23–25:36, 27:10
reporting and disclosure rules, 16:28
rollovers, 23:38–23:45, 23:105–23:106, 25:29
sale of stock by, 17:21
separate lines of business, 17:18
service credit, 17:13
simplified safe harbor exclusion, 23:13–23:21, 23:23
survivor annuity requirements, 23:90–23:97, 23:99–23:101, 23:106, 27:5–27:8, 27:10–27:14, 27:19
taxation
  annuity payments, 8:46–8:47, 23:30, 23:32
  at death, 2:55, 23:80, 27:2, 27:44
  deferring, 23:37
  distribution options and, 23:10–23:12
  distributions, 17:2, 23:1, 23:4–23:5
  distributions received before the annuity starting date, 23:30
  of employer contribution, 23:9
  exclusions, 23:12–23:22, 23:25–23:26
  non-annuity payments, 23:31
  vesting rules, 17:10
  veterans, 16:32
  withholding and notice rules, 23:84, 23:86–23:89
Tax-qualified retirement plans multiemployer plans, 16:36–16:38
Tax Reform Act of 1986 (TRA '86), 17:65, 23:36
Tax returns
  final, 15:6–15:7
  liability for joint tax returns, 14:43–14:45
  required after death, 15:2–15:3
Technical and Miscellaneous Revenue Act of 1988, 4:5
TEFRA (Tax Equity and Fiscal Responsibility Act of 1982), 23:113
Tenancy by the entirety, 2:24–2:25
Tenancy in common
  converting to from joint tenancy, 2:37
  explained, 2:25
  gross estate, 3:12
Terminal interest rule
  estate trust, using to avoid, 4:26
  explained, 4:6
  marital deduction, 4:9, 27:21
  tax-qualified retirement plans, 27:21
Term insurance, 7:2
Testamentary trust
  compared to unfunded revocable living trust, 2:64
  defined, 2:64
  Medicaid eligibility, 26:45
Testate estate, explained, 2:3
Thrift plan, 17:28

[References are to question numbers.]

Throwback rule, 2:54
Top-hat plans, 19:34
Totten trust(s), 2:44
Transfer for value rule, 7:18, 7:28, 7:53–7:54
Treasury bills, notes and bonds, 20:24
Trust(s). *See also* specific type; Trustee(s)
 administrative requirements, 2:54
 advantages of, 12:2–12:3
 asset protection through use of, 25:6
 beneficiaries, conflict among, 3:60
 as beneficiary of a tax-qualified retirement plan, 23:51, 27:15
 for children, 3:52–3:53
 cost of, 12:5
 design considerations, 3:61, 12:1
  generation skipping transfer concerns, 5:29, 5:31–5:33, 5:37
  IRS ruling letter, 12:8
 explained, 4:16, 12:3
 factors to consider in creating, 4:17, 6:30, 12:9
 forfeiture clause, 13:12
 fraudulent conveyance, 13:18–13:19, 13:21
 gift tax exclusion and, 6:31, 7:15
 income tax rates of, 3:32, 6:39
 as IRA beneficiaries, 22:19
 IRS ruling letter, 12:8
 life insurance and, 7:11, 7:15, 7:42, 7:56, 11:6
 living, 26:14
 lookback rule, 26:33
 Medicaid eligibility and, 26:40–26:42
 for pets, 12:4
 protector, role of, 13:26
 retaining income in, 6:39
 start date, 12:6
 types of, 12:10
 using, to avoid probate, 2:24
 using for distribution income planning, 15:25

Trust assets
 gifts from, 2:53
 growth in, 3:51
 located outside the U.S., 2:51
 probate and tax treatment of, 2:46, 2:50–2:51. *See also* Taxable estate
Trustee(s)
 children as their own, 3:57
 duties of, 2:13
 irrevocable insurance trust, 7:38
 removing, 3:58, 6:47
 selecting, 3:54–3:57, 6:45–6:46, 26:20–26:21
 siblings, 3:56, 6:45
 successor, provisions for, 3:59, 6:48
 who can be a, 20:51
Trust income
 attribution of, 4:28
 tax treatment of, 2:50–2:51, 6:49, 19:30
 throwback rule, 2:54
Trust principal
 removing, tax considerations, 6:44
 surviving spouse, access to, 3:50, 4:29, 5:2, 5:4–5:6, 5:10–5:11
Tuition
 generation skipping transfer tax, 5:35
 gift tax exclusion, 3:33, 6:12
 to private or parochial schools, 10:8
209(b) states, definition, 26:32

U

UFTA (Uniform Fraudulent Transfer Act), 13:18–13:19
Unbundling, 20:28, 20:52
Undue influence, 2:21
Unfunded revocable living trust(s), 2:63–2:64
Unified credit, 3:25, 3:35, 4:10, 6:5, 6:16
Unified transfer tax, 3:25

Index

[References are to question numbers.]

Uniform Anatomical Gifts Act (UAGA), 6:52–6:53, 6:55–6:56
Uniformed Service Employment and Retirement Act (USERA), 16:32
Uniform Fraudulent Transfer Act (UFTA), 13:18–13:19
Uniform Limited Partnership Act, 31:19
Uniform Marital Property Act, 3:9
Uniform Transfers to Minors Act (UTMA), 6:2, 6:29, 6:38
Union retirement plans, 16:34–16:35, 16:39, 16:41
Unit benefit plan, 17:37
Unity of ownership, IRS approach, 9:28
Universal life insurance, 7:2
USERA. *See* Uniformed Service Employment and Retirement Act

V

Valuation of assets. *See also* Basis
  buy/sell agreement(s), 9:35
  closely held securities and businesses, 9:8, 9:10–9:15
  family limited partnership, 31:5
  methods of
    book value approach, 9:11
    cost approach, 9:6
    earnings approach, 9:12
    income approach, 9:5
    market approach, 9:4, 9:13
  mortgages and notes, 9:7
  overview, 9:1–9:3
  penalty for excess, 15:17
  special elections, 15:18, 15:20–15:21
  valuation date, 9:9, 15:16
Variable annuity, 8:2–8:3
VCR program, 17:9
Vesting rules, ERISA, 19:35
Veterans, 16:32
Voluntary Compliance Resolution (VCR) program, 17:9

W

WARN (Worker Readjustment and Retraining Act), 16:5, 16:33
Whole life insurance, 7:2
Will(s)
  anatomical gift(s), 6:52–6:53, 6:56
  consequences of failing to leave, 2:3
  durable power of attorney, 26:10
  living, 26:4–26:5
  pour-over provision, 26:19
  property not subject to probate, 2:8
Will contest, 2:21
Worker Readjustment and Retraining Act (WARN), 16:5, 16:33
Wrap-around annuity, 8:21–8:22
Wrap fee, 20:29, 20:43